EIGHTH EDITION

WORK, INDUSTRY,

AND CANADIAN

SOCIETY

EIGHTH EDITION

WORK, INDUSTRY, AND CANADIAN SOCIETY

HARVEY J. KRAHN
University of Alberta

KAREN D. HUGHES
University of Alberta

GRAHAM S. LOWE
The Graham Lowe Group Inc.
and University of Alberta

NELSON

NELSON

Work, Industry, and Canadian Society, Eighth Edition

by Harvey J. Krahn, Karen D. Hughes, and Graham S. Lowe

VP, Product Solutions, K–20:
Claudine O'Donnell

Director, Qualitative Publishing:
Jackie Wood

Senior Publisher, Digital and Print Content:
Leanna MacLean

Product Marketing Manager:
Sydney Pope

Content Developer:
Laura McReynolds

Photo and Permissions Researcher:
Jessica Freedman

Senior Production Project Manager:
Imoinda Romain

Production Service:
SPi-Global

Copy Editor:
SPi-Global

Proofreader:
SPi-Global

Indexer:
SPi-Global

Design Director:
Ken Phipps

Post-secondary Design PM:
Pamela Johnston

Interior Design:
deboraH brock

Cover Design:
deboraH brock

Cover Image:
©Drazen_/iStockphoto.com

Compositor:
SPi-Global

Library and Archives Canada Cataloguing in Publication

Title: Work, industry, and Canadian society /
Harvey J. Krahn, University of Alberta, Karen D.

Hughes, University of Alberta, Graham S. Lowe,
the Graham Lowe Group Inc. and University
of Alberta.

Names: Krahn, Harvey, author. | Hughes, Karen
D., author. | Lowe, Graham S., author.

Description: Eighth edition. | Includes
bibliographical references and index.

Identifiers: Canadiana (print) 20190235454
| Canadiana (ebook) 20190235462 | ISBN
9780176724436

(softcover) | ISBN 9780176892784 (PDF)

Subjects: LCSH: Work—Social aspects—
Canada—Textbooks. | LCSH: Industrial
sociology—Canada—

Textbooks. | LCGFT: Textbooks.

Classification: LCC HD6957.C3 K72 2020 | DDC
306.3/60971—dc23

ISBN-13: 978-0-17-672443-6
ISBN-10: 0-17-672443-5

BRIEF TABLE OF CONTENTS

CONTENTS

In this eighth edition of *Work, Industry, and Canadian Society*, we have again drawn on the growing literature on work and employment, organizations, and management approaches to incorporate recent empirical findings, review new and ongoing theoretical and policy debates, and provide a more international perspective. In revisions of previous editions, the author team worked as equal partners. As individual careers unfold, however, changes in work collaborations are inevitable. Hence, this revision was largely completed by the first two authors, who continue to work at the University of Alberta. The third author, who now is a workplace consultant, provided editorial advice and resource material. Despite major revisions to this new edition, there continue to be substantial sections originally written by the third author; after several decades, however, it is difficult to remember where or how specific ideas originated and took shape.

NEW TO THIS EDITION

Reflecting the changing contours of scholarship and public debate about work, we significantly changed the book's structure for the seventh edition in 2015. For this new eighth edition, we have retained the same 14-chapter framework. In the Introduction, we outline the content of each of these chapters, highlighting some of the new topics we cover. For example, we have expanded or added new coverage of some of the biggest work challenges we face now and in the future. These topics include the following:

- Canada's increasingly diverse and aging workforce demographics
- The work experiences and opportunities of Indigenous peoples in Canada
- The actions being taken to eliminate sexual harassment from workplaces in the wake of the #MeToo movement
- The relentless push of globalization and the counter pressures from populist politicians (notably U.S. President Donald Trump) to dismantle the global economic system

- The expanded focus of workforce diversity initiatives to include members of the LGBTQ+ community
- The rise of the app-based "gig economy," and current speculation about the impact of robots and artificial intelligence on future jobs and work organization

Virtually all of the tables and figures have been updated, using the most current data available. We have incorporated well over 400 new references (and deleted almost as many old ones). We have also updated many of the opening vignettes that personalize the topic of each chapter. And just as in the seventh edition, each chapter ends with Discussion Questions, lists of songs and other forms of audio, and movies about work. While bringing media into the classroom was once a laborious exercise, today's "smart classrooms" let us easily stream films, music, and news clips in ways that can greatly enrich student learning. To that end, we offer illustrative lists of resources that we have used in our own teaching, that colleagues have recommended, or that we have identified through research.

We enjoyed compiling these lists but recognize that our selections of songs and movies may not suit all tastes. Valuing a broad historical understanding of work as we do (and being of a certain demographic), our choices cover a broad span of time. We note that not all the content of these songs and movies focuses exclusively on work, though work typically forms a strong theme. Nor is the content necessarily in line with our personal beliefs or values. In choosing material, we have been struck by how many songs and films depict work traditionally done by men or, if they feature women, place them in traditional roles. It quickly becomes apparent that the movie and music industries remain highly gendered, just like many of the workplaces described in this book. Where possible, we have tried to identify both mainstream and independent productions, balancing this with the goal of ensuring that material can be easily accessed.

Developing these lists has brought far more material to our attention than we can include in this text. Recognizing that instructors and students may want to explore further, we note several valuable resources here. For movies and films, Tom Zaniello's compilations—*Working Stiffs, Union Maids, Reds, and Riffraff: An Expanded Guide to Films about Labor* (2003), and *The Cinema of Globalization: A Guide to Films about the New Economic Order* (2007)—

offer synopses of more than 500 films. Likewise, websites for the National Film Board (NFB), CBC's Doc Zone, and Participant Media list a number of interesting short and long films on work-related topics. For music, several recent books examine the fascinating relationship between music and work—in particular, Marek Korczynski, Michael Pickering, and Emma Robertson's (2013) *Rhythms of Labour*, Ted Gioia's (2006) *Work Songs*, and Archie Green's (1993) *Songs about Work*. Together, these volumes illustrate the rich history of what folklorists call "work songs," sung by farmers, seafarers, weavers, miners, and others to lighten loads, lift spirits, coordinate tasks, and forge bonds of collective identity. Industrialization silenced these work soundscapes (Korczynski et al. 2013), with employers disciplining and fining workers for singing in an effort to "modernize production." Others experimented with music, piping loud tunes into factories in attempts to boost productivity or developing company songs to inculcate corporate identity. Of course, music played a central role in organizing labour and social protest, as discussed in Ronald Cohen's (2010) *Work and Sing: The History of Occupational and Labor Songs in the United States*, and as illustrated in Utah Phillip and Ani DiFranco's album *Fellow Workers*. For those interested, these materials offer rich histories of songs at work and raise intriguing questions about the role of music in workplaces today.

Along with Nelson, we would like to thank the following reviewers for their help in developing this eighth edition of *Work, Industry, and Canadian Society*: Fiona Angus, MacEwan University; Chris Hurl, Concordia University; and Melissa Godbout, University of Toronto. We also acknowledge and thank Susan Cake (doctoral candidate in sociology) and Harleen Padda (law student) at the University of Alberta, who were superb research assistants. They spent many hours locating new scholarly sources and checking references, preparing tables and charts, and helping compile resources for instructors.

We also thank Statistics Canada for continuing to make available data that we have mined extensively in all eight editions of the text. EKOS Research Associates also has shared some of its extensive survey data on work issues. At Nelson, Senior Publisher Leanna MacLean encouraged us to take on yet another revision, and kept the process running smoothly. We would also like to thank Imoinda Romain, the production project manager; Laura McReynolds, content developer; our copy editor, Dawn Hunter, for helpful editing suggestions that have improved the text; and Praveen Kumar RS, for expertly handling the production process. Any errors and omissions are, of course, our own responsibility.

Professor Harvey J. Krahn, Department of Sociology, *University of Alberta*

Professor Karen D. Hughes, Department of Sociology and Department of Strategic Management and Organization, *University of Alberta*

Professor Emeritus Graham S. Lowe, Department of Sociology, *University of Alberta and The Graham Lowe Group Inc.*

Edmonton and Kelowna, August 2019

Harvey Krahn

Harvey Krahn is a professor of sociology at the University of Alberta. He received his Ph.D. from the University of Alberta and his earlier degrees from Western University. Before that, he spent one year as a waiter/bartender and four years employed as a childcare worker. Along with the sociology of work, Dr. Krahn's research interests include the sociology of education, political sociology, immigration studies, environmental sociology, and life course studies. His most significant research accomplishment is a 32-year longitudinal study (1985–2017) that tracked hundreds of Edmonton high-school graduates through their transitions from school to work, from youth to adulthood, and into midlife (Dr. Graham Lowe was the co-investigator on this study from 1985 to 1999). In 2009, Dr. Krahn received the Outstanding Contributions Award from the Canadian Sociological Association, and in 2015 he was awarded the University Cup, the University of Alberta's highest honour for academic staff.

Karen Hughes

Karen Hughes is a professor of sociology, and strategic management and organization, at the University of Alberta, where she teaches courses in the sociology of work, entrepreneurship, and organizations. She holds a Ph.D. from the University of Cambridge and has published widely on work-related issues, focusing on women's entrepreneurship, gender and work, paid and family caregiving, and work–family balance. Dr. Hughes is the author of *Female Enterprise in the New Economy* and co-editor of *Global Women's Entrepreneurship*. She is a past recipient of the Social Science and Humanities Research Council's Thérèse Casgrain Fellowship for leading research on women and social change, and an editorial board member of the journals *Gender in Management* and *International Small Business Journal*. Before becoming an academic, she held many "good" and "bad" jobs in Canada's economy, the best leading trail rides in the beautiful Rocky Mountains as a university student, and the worst involving mercifully short stints in retail and accounting.

Graham Lowe

Graham Lowe is president of The Graham Lowe Group Inc., a workplace consulting and research firm. He also is a professor emeritus at the University of Alberta, where he was a member of the Sociology Department from 1979 to 2003, and holds a Ph.D. in sociology from the University of Toronto. He has over three decades of organizational, labour market, and employment policy consulting experience across Canada and internationally. His books include *Creating Healthy Organizations: How Vibrant Workplaces Inspire Employees to Achieve Sustainable Success* and (with Frank Graves) *Redesigning Work: A Blueprint for Canada's Future Well-Being and Prosperity*. He has contributed many articles to publications such as *The Globe & Mail*, *Policy Options*, *HR Professional*, *Health & Productivity Management*, and *Healthcare Quarterly*. Dr. Lowe has given hundreds of conference talks and workshops across Canada and internationally. He is a recipient of the Canadian Workplace Wellness Pioneer Award.

Work is an essential human activity, the basis for the economic survival of individuals and society. Beyond this, an individual's work activity structures much of her or his time and, one hopes, provides a source of personal fulfillment. An occupation also shapes a person's identity and, in the eyes of others, largely determines that person's status in society. Stepping back to gain a wider historical perspective, one sees that Canadian society and the quality of life we have come to enjoy are products of the collective work efforts of millions of women and men. Thus, while the *sociology of work and industry* may, at first glance, seem as potentially boring as the part-time job you just quit at the shopping mall, there is no doubting the subject's social relevance. We also believe that, once you begin reading, you will not find the subject matter boring!

Let's start with a few basic definitions. First, *work* refers to activity that provides a socially valued product or service. In other words, through our work we transform raw materials as diverse as information, iron ore, and wheat into something that is needed or desired by all or part of society. The emphasis in this definition is on activity; action verbs such as *cook, hammer, clean, drive, type, teach, sculpt, serve,* or *care* are typically used to describe work. Such a broad definition covers both paid and unpaid work, and activities ranging from the legal to the illegal, from the highly esteemed to the undesirable and despised. Most of our focus in this book is on paid work, recognizing the centrality of the employment relationship in modern capitalist societies; however, we also devote Chapter 7 to household, caring, and community work, both because of its central importance in society and the economy and because of the many hours most Canadians spend in this unpaid but highly valued activity.

In previous editions of this book, going back to the late 1990s, we began each Introduction by commenting on the increasing pace and scope of change in Canadian workplaces, labour markets, and the global economy. Yet despite some remarkable developments in the local, national, and global employment contexts over the past decades, the overall pattern of change is still best called "evolutionary" rather than "revolutionary." You'll understand why when you read in Chapter 1 about the massive social, economic, and political changes unleashed by the Industrial Revolution.

Nevertheless, looking at the national economy, we have seen substantial change since the beginning of the 21st century. A decade of unprecedented economic prosperity in Canada came to a sudden halt in 2008 when the global financial system nearly collapsed, economies were pitched into one of the deepest recessions since the 1930s, and unemployment rates suddenly rose. By 2010, recovery had taken root, unemployment rates began to decline, and dire predictions of the collapse of capitalism and the need to "reset" the world economy had faded into the background. Still, the 2008–9 recession caused many individuals, families, and organizations to rethink their plans and goals—a mood of caution, uncertainty, and economic insecurity that still lingers. Today, we are still watching all of this unfold.

Prominent trends documented in earlier editions have continued, most notably increasing social inequality and labour market polarization in Canada and in many other countries. Global economic integration also has surged forward. However, it is now under threat from not only grassroots opponents on the political left seeking social justice, but from U.S. President Donald Trump, Britain's pro-Brexit Prime Minister Boris Johnson, and other populist politicians on the political right seeking to dismantle the global rules-based economic system that evolved after World War II. This populist backlash against globalization—which is closely linked to rising economic inequality in advanced industrial countries—could have significant impact on people's work lives and surely is important to monitor.

New information and communication technologies continue to push the frontiers of work, both in how it is done and where, as many high-tech jobs have been outsourced to developing countries where labour costs are lower. In the manufacturing sector, China has become the new global economic powerhouse, overtaking some other Asian countries—Japan and South Korea, for example—that were reshaping the world economy in earlier decades. Today, China is flooding world markets with inexpensive but increasingly high-quality goods and showing an insatiable appetite for natural resources. India is also quickly establishing a global economic presence, in both traditional manufacturing and high-tech industries.

Unemployment was a leading public concern in Canada in the 1980s and 1990s. However, the unemployment rate began dropping in the 21st century. By the end of 2018, it was at its lowest level since 1976 and much lower than in some European economies such as Greece and Spain. Still, joblessness remains a concern in Canada, affecting some groups far more than others. Yet employers and policymakers are voicing concerns about labour shortages caused by the combination of a strong economy, an aging workforce, and baby-boomer retirements. Canadian immigration policies have been adjusted to emphasize labour market needs compared to humanitarian concerns. While the trend toward more nonstandard (part-time and temporary) employment has levelled off, "precarious work" is now being fuelled by the rise of the app-based gig economy. Consequently, labour market polarization continues, and social inequality has increased. With this come signs of growing public and political concern, as in the federal Liberal Party's focus on the "shrinking middle class," the push for a $15 per hour minimum wage in many U.S. and Canadian cities, and the rising frustration—even anger—that Donald Trump and other populist politicians have tapped into as segments of the population feel they are falling behind.

In this eighth edition, we revisit these and other trends that continue to influence the work opportunities and experiences of Canadians. We highlight the consequences of different types of work arrangements for both the individual and society. Diversity and flexibility in jobs and work organizations remain prominent issues. As the book's title suggests, a sociological analysis of work must be grounded in its industrial context—hence our emphasis on the underlying economic forces that have shaped and continue to shape work opportunities.

But a comprehensive understanding of the world of work also requires us to consider other features of society. For example, there are basic connections between a person's paid work and her or his family responsibilities. Social values influence the work expectations of employees, as well as the behaviour of employers. Recent examples are the strong public reaction to charges of sexual harassment made against powerful men, resulting in the #MeToo movement, and more-accepting attitudes toward same-sex marriage and protecting the rights of the LGBTQ+ community. As well, the state plays a pivotal role in determining the nature and rewards of work through its employment standards, occupational health and safety, and labour legislation, various labour market programs, and the education system. Consequently, our discussion of work also requires a close look at many other aspects of Canadian society.

The sociology of work and industry is not a neatly defined area of scholarship, which in our opinion is a good thing. More than for most sociological specialties, we must incorporate the insights of related disciplines. Classic sociological theory, political economy, organization and management studies, industrial relations, labour history, labour economics, macroeconomics, health and safety, gender studies and feminist theory, stratification, race and ethnic relations, and social policy are some of the diverse literatures upon which we draw. Given this wide scope, our coverage of the literature is far from exhaustive. Instead, we selectively examine theoretical discussions and research findings from all these areas in an effort to highlight key themes and debates in the sociology of work and industry.

The relationship between employers and those who work for them is the cornerstone of the sociological study of work. By centring our analysis on workplace relations and the organizational and institutional structures in which these are embedded, we encounter many core themes in classical sociological theory, including *inequality* and the distribution of scarce resources, *power* and how it takes shape in authority relations, and the shaky balance between the ever-present potential for *conflict* and the need for *cooperation* and *consensus*. A basic problem in all societies involves the distribution of wealth, power, and prestige. Paid work is central to this dilemma of distribution. Put more concretely, who gets the well-paying, interesting, and high-status jobs? Who is most vulnerable to unemployment? How does cooperation among employees and between management and employees occur? Are there inherent conflicts of interest between employers and workers?

Another central theoretical concern in research on the sociology of work and industry is the interplay between the actions of individuals and the constraints exerted on them by social structures. For us, this *agency–structure debate* translates into some basic and practical questions: How limiting and restrictive are today's work organizations for individuals? How much can workers' action, individually or collectively, reshape these structures? In addressing the obvious tensions between individual action and social structures, it is helpful to distinguish between *macro* (social structure) and *micro* (individual) *levels of analysis*. At the macro level, we focus on the changing global economy, labour markets, industries and occupations, bureaucracies, unions and professional associations, and a variety of institutions that *structure* regular and predictable patterns of work activity in society. We must be careful, however, not to place too much emphasis on social structures, because in doing so, we risk losing sight of the individuals who are engaged in performing the work and, sometimes, reshaping these very structures.

Counterbalancing this macro view is an individual-level, or micro, perspective on work in Canadian society. We provide this by asking questions such as these: What types of work values are held by Canadians, and what kinds of jobs do they want? How do individuals experience their work situation? What are the ingredients of job satisfaction? Or, looking at the negative side, what causes job dissatisfaction, alienation, and work-related stress? Overall, what factors contribute most to overall quality of working life as well as life away from work? In short, a micro-level analysis investigates how people experience their jobs, how they adapt to less than ideal working conditions, and how, in some instances, they try to improve these conditions (that is, exert *agency*) within the confines of what is possible given existing work institutions.

To elaborate this point, while an individual's work options may be limited by social structures, there is nothing inevitable about the daily work routines, employment relationships, and legislative frameworks found in capitalist societies. Thus, we will argue throughout the book that work can be demeaning or rewarding and fulfilling, depending, in large part, on how it is organized and who has authority. Further, we highlight some of the possibilities offered by more egalitarian and humanized forms of work. However, we stop short of advocating a utopian vision of work. Instead, we approach the subject of work from a *reformist perspective*, arguing that even within post-industrial capitalism, there is solid evidence showing that the quality of working life can be improved. We believe that through careful theoretical reasoning and rigorous empirical research, sociologists can further the development of enlightened employment practices and public policy and help individuals create better workplaces for themselves.

It will quickly become clear that we are not presenting a strictly Marxist analysis of work. Similarly, we go beyond a simplistic Weberian approach that gives undue emphasis to employees' understandings of their work situations. And we certainly do not advocate a functionalist or Durkheimian model of the work world, one that over-emphasizes the need for social integration and stability. To varying degrees we and many other sociologists have been influenced by these classical theoretical orientations but, as our discussion in

Chapter 2 indicates, a number of influential 20th-century social theorists also assist us in understanding the changing world of work. More than anything, our starting point is a *conflict perspective* on society. Thus, a Marxist or materialist perspective has informed the book's emphases on inequality, power, conflict, and control. The Weberian approach sensitizes us to the centrality of individual actors, and their beliefs and behaviours, in sociological analysis. The Durkheimian tradition reminds us that social integration, consensus, and stability within work organizations are the motivation for much management theory and practice.

We have kept the same chapter structure as in the seventh edition, thoroughly updating each chapter by adding the latest research, data, and current examples. **Chapter 1** begins with an overview of the industrialization process and the rise of capitalism in Europe. This provides a backdrop for understanding the somewhat later Canadian industrialization experience, including its impact on Indigenous peoples. We also introduce some aspects of the theoretical ideas of Karl Marx, Adam Smith, Max Weber, and Émile Durkheim. These influential thinkers developed their assessments of the problems and prospects of work in industrial capitalist societies from their observations of how Europe was transformed during the Industrial Revolution.

But the global economy, the industrial systems of advanced capitalist societies, employment opportunities, and work rewards have changed dramatically since the mid-20th century, as we explain in **Chapter 2**. Economic globalization, the impact of new technologies, and social polarization have become prominent issues in public debates and scholarly research today. Rapidly developing economies, primarily in Asia, are reshaping the international balance of power. Sophisticated supply chains and information technology give goods production and service provision an increasingly global reach. It is easier than ever to shift the locations where work is completed. One result, which we examine, has been the growth of new kinds of work at the top and bottom of the labour market, exemplified by the well-educated and generously rewarded knowledge worker, and the precarious life of the gig economy worker who relies on a phone app for their next piece of work.

In **Chapter 3**, our focus shifts to a detailed empirical overview of the major industrial, labour market, and labour force trends in Canada. We begin by examining changes that have altered the composition of the labour force: the workforce has become older and more educated, while immigration and a growing Indigenous population have added to its diversity. We then turn our attention to changing labour force participation patterns, highlighting differences based on gender, disability, Indigenous status, age, and region. We then outline the emergence of a service-based economy with a very different mix of industries and occupations than existed a century ago.

Chapter 4 builds on this statistical overview of the labour market, assessing the varying quality of jobs in terms of income, other employment benefits, and the risk of unemployment. We highlight the rise of nonstandard or precarious work (such as temporary or part-time jobs) and how this trend is eroding economic security for growing numbers of Canadians. We explore the surge of solo self-employment and the rise of a 21st-century gig economy, in which apps hand out little pieces of work to freelancers on an as-needed basis. In this chapter we also examine a topic that is bound to receive much attention in the future: the impact of robots and artificial intelligence on work.

Labour markets basically determine who gets the good jobs and who ends up in the less desirable ones. In **Chapter 5**, we explore how the Canadian labour market operates via the lenses of human capital and labour market segmentation theory, two competing approaches to explaining the distribution of job opportunities and work rewards in the labour market. This leads us into discussions of how labour market outcomes are unequally distributed based on personal characteristics, such as race, ethnicity, immigrant status, Indigenous status, gender, age, disability, sexual orientation, and gender identity. Prominent themes in this chapter are growing labour market polarization and increasing social inequality.

The increasing labour force participation of women is one of the most significant social changes of the last half century. Picking up on our discussion of this trend in Chapters 3 through 5, **Chapter 6** provides a more in-depth analysis of gendered jobs, workplaces, and labour markets. After outlining the transformation of women's economic roles over time, we explain how gender has become a source of entrenched divisions and inequality within the labour market and within work organizations. We also address sexual harassment in workplaces, an issue that is receiving increased public scrutiny.

Chapter 7 focuses on household, caring, and community work, much of which is typically unpaid. We discuss recent research on the household division of labour, on mothering, fathering, eldercare, volunteer work, and work–family balance. By examining different theoretical approaches to caring work, we link this discussion to the paid work themes in other chapters. We also consider the important role of the early childcare system, and the "outsourcing" of household work (e.g., house cleaning and meal delivery), in supporting working parents, but also as a site of low-paid work that is done primarily by women.

The organization and management of paid work, and how they have changed over time, are the core topics in Chapters 8 and 9. **Chapter 8** describes the emergence of large bureaucracies and assembly-line factories in the early 20th century, along with the management problems they created. We show how the early solutions—"scientific management" and "human relations"—generated their own problems. **Chapter 9** critically reviews a variety of more recent managerial approaches for overcoming the problems of bureaucracy by decentralizing authority and improving working conditions, while at the same time increasing productivity and profits for owners.

Chapter 10 is best viewed as a sociological debate with the mainstream management approaches. Our starting point is the labour process perspective, a more critical assessment of employer–employee relationships in capitalist society. Consistent with the prominent sociological themes of power and control we introduced in earlier chapters, we examine different methods managers have used to control and gain compliance from workers. We also ask whether workers today are using fewer or more skills in their jobs than a half century ago. In addition, we consider the potential impact of new technologies, including robots and artificial intelligence, on workers' skills and decision making, as well as on patterns of social inequality.

While we touch on unions in earlier discussions, we take an in-depth look in **Chapter 11**. We discuss various theories about the origins and functions of unions, document the development of the organized labour movement in Canada and the United States, and compare key Canadian labour relations trends with those in other advanced industrial nations. We also describe the legal framework—the industrial relations system—that has emerged for regulating union–management relations and collective bargaining. After profiling the characteristics of union members in Canada, with particular emphasis on gender and age, we conclude by examining strike patterns to see how they are linked to the changes in industrial structures, labour market processes, and management approaches outlined in earlier chapters.

Chapter 12 invites readers to step back from the current pattern of labour–management relations and institutionalized conflict described in previous chapters and look for alternatives. We begin by describing current approaches to addressing health and safety concerns in the workplace since they require workers and managers to cooperate. We also consider different forms of industrial democracy as well as examples of worker ownership, arguing that these approaches to organizing and managing work do have something to offer.

In the last two chapters, we shift our attention from the largely macro-level analysis in the previous chapters to a micro-level examination of how individuals experience work. In **Chapter 13**, we discuss society-wide work values and how they vary across time and culture. We then examine work orientations, asking what individuals want from their work. Are a person's work preferences shaped by the work opportunities available to them or by other factors? Equally important, are there signs of new work orientations emerging in response to growing employment insecurity and income inequality? In **Chapter 14**, we summarize the diverse research literatures on three related topics: job satisfaction, alienation from work, and work-related stress. A major theme we explore in this chapter is that negative work experiences can have serious and lasting effects on individuals.

Finally, in our **Conclusions**, we raise important questions about the future of work in Canada. As the 21st century advances, a number of trends are worthy of close monitoring. Corporate and public-sector downsizing, the outsourcing of jobs, and continued growth of precarious work and the gig economy mean that, for a growing number of Canadians, their economic and social well-being is at risk. Some sub-groups of the Canadian population are much more likely than others to be unemployed, underemployed, or inadequately rewarded for their work. In short, social inequality is slowly increasing, as is polarization in the quality of working life. New human resource management strategies and workplace technologies such as artificial intelligence have the potential to create better jobs and fairer workplaces. But they could just as easily have negative effects on the quantity and quality of work. We do believe, however, that Canadians can exercise more control over their destiny. In our opinion, what Canada needs is informed public debate among employers, governments, unions, and other labour market organizations to determine how best to balance the interests of workers, who want both a decent standard of living and an improved quality of working life, with the economic growth sought by employers and government. Yet public debate is only the first step. We also need political leaders and policy makers to put in place effective policies and legislation to ensure that these goals are balanced. It is our job, as citizens, to challenge them to do so.

HISTORICAL PERSPECTIVES ON WORK

"Canada was a settler society, in which the native population was pushed back and European social patterns were transplanted. There was also a colonized population of Europeans—the French Canadians centred in the future province of Quebec—which kept alive its distinct culture, despite English hostility and assimilationist efforts. Throughout the British North American colonies, the landed aristocracy, once a distinct social class, quickly disappeared in the nineteenth century, and an ambitious, powerful capitalist class of merchants, manufacturers, bankers, and sundry financiers took shape, initially regionally based and competitive, but increasingly cohesive by the turn of the century."

Source: Craig Heron. (2012). *The Canadian Labour Movement: A Short History*. 3rd ed. Toronto: James Lorimer and Company, pp. xiii.

"Canada was a country that depended on workers. . . . How did our work-ancestors live a hundred years ago? It is very hard to generalize across a century in which remarkable stability in the value of money concealed enormous changes in every other economic and social factor. An unskilled day-labourer in 1867 might earn a dollar a day for a ten-hour day, six days a week. A highly skilled craftsman might earn three times as much. A woman's wage would be half that of a man—as little as thirty-five to sixty cents a day. A child earned as little as twenty-five cents. Employers offered no paid holidays, and they rarely felt obliged to make provision for sickness, injury, or old age except to dismiss or reduce the wages of workers who were past their prime. Until 1877, masters and servants acts allowed the courts to send disobedient or absentee workers to jail at an employer's request."

Source: Desmond Morton. (2007). *Working People: An Illustrated History of the Canadian Labour Movement*, 5/e. McGill-Queen's University Press.

INTRODUCTION

In the mid- to late 1800s in Montreal, it was common to find young children working in the textile, cigar, and other factories springing up along the Lachine Canal. The canal powered the factories and provided a route to transport goods to the Old Port of Montreal. Once the centre of the fur trade, Montreal was now an industrializing city, with a rapidly growing population, as rural and immigrant families arrived in search of work. French Canadian workers held the most skilled jobs, leaving poor paying menial jobs for Irish and other immigrants. Though men had the pick of jobs as family breadwinners, seasonal downturns and poor pay meant that all family members had to pitch in.

In the working class districts of Sainte Anne and Sainte Jacques, young children not only worked in the factories but could also be found scrounging for coal and wood to keep home fires burning, or helping with the gardens, pigs, and chickens kept by urban households to make sure there was food on the table. Mothers took in work from nearby factories, stitching garments between laundering, cleaning, and cooking for their large families. They also cooked and cleaned for boarders in already cramped family spaces, with income from room and board generating essential household funds.[1]

Reflecting on these working patterns, it is hard not to be struck by the huge change that has occurred in just a few generations. Large families, boarders, and working children are no longer the norm. Factory work has been replaced by white-collar, retail, and knowledge-based jobs. Canada still relies on immigrants to fuel its economy, but not primarily those from Europe as was once the case. Although people still migrate for work, work itself is increasingly mobile, with production being spread across the globe.

This book examines these changes and the types of paid work now done by Canadians. Today, most people work for wages or a salary in bureaucratic organizations. In most two-adult households, both partners are employed outside the home. In a labour force of nearly 20 million individuals, three in four workers are in the service sector. Children stay in formal schooling for much longer, with university education being increasingly common. Compared to a few decades ago, fewer workers are full-time employees. More than one in four is working in either a temporary or a part-time job, and growing numbers are self-employed. For every 15 employed Canadians, roughly one is unemployed, though rates vary widely across the country.

These labour market realities become more interesting when we realize that just a few generations ago, some of these trends had just begun to emerge. And going back over a century and a half, as we have seen, the differences in work patterns are huge. What social and economic forces led to the shifts from agriculture to manufacturing, then to services? Why did bureaucracies develop? Why has education become more important? Why are Indigenous peoples, women, and visible minorities underrepresented in better-paying jobs—and what are the social consequences? To answer these and many related questions, we look back in history and at other societies to examine the complex process of industrialization. This historical and comparative approach will help us to understand present patterns and trends, assess their significance for individuals and society, and respond to the future challenges they pose.

Industrialization refers to the technical aspects of the *accumulation* and processing of a society's resources. *Capitalism* is a term used to describe key aspects of the economic and social organization of the productive enterprise. In an *industrial society*, inanimate sources of energy, such as coal or electricity, fuel a production system that uses technology to process raw materials. But labelling a society "industrial" tells us little about the relationships among the individuals involved in the productive process. In a *capitalist system of production*, a relatively small number of individuals own and control the means for creating goods and services, while the majority have no direct ownership stake in the economy and are paid a wage to work by those who do.

Studying the rise of capitalism requires us to make sense of large, complex processes spanning generations and leaving no aspect of daily life unaffected. The theoretical writings of Adam Smith, Karl Marx, Émile Durkheim, and Max Weber help us to explain, rather than simply describe, the causes and consequences of capitalist development. As we will see, the sociological concepts of *power, control, inequality,* and *conflict* that these early social scientists used to analyze changes in their times continue to be central to today's debates about the nature of 21st-century post-industrial society. Therefore, this chapter provides vital history that we can build on in subsequent chapters to address questions such as these: Has the rise of knowledge-based, high-tech economies benefited some groups more than others? How are new digital technologies and gig platforms such as Uber transforming the content and organization of work? Is economic globalization increasing the power of transnational corporations at the expense of national governments? And with global economic changes, such as the rise of China and India and other market-based economies, do we need to rethink long-accepted explanations of capitalist development?

THE ORIGINS OF INDUSTRIAL CAPITALISM

Capitalism and industrialization dramatically reshaped the structure of European society economically, socially, and spatially. As Jeremy Black explains in *Why the Industrial Revolution Happened Here* (see Work at the Movies at the end of the chapter), these changes occurred over centuries, with a different pace and pattern in each country. While the details of these changes differed internationally, and regionally within countries, the result was profound change in how, where, for whom, and under what conditions individuals worked.

The emergence of capitalism in Europe consisted of two basic periods: *mercantile* or *commercial capitalism*, which began in the 1500s, and *industrial capitalism*, which evolved somewhat later.[2] In the mercantile period, merchants and royalty in Spain, Holland, England, and France accumulated huge fortunes by trading internationally in a variety of goods, including spices, precious stones and metals, sugar, cotton, and slaves. An elaborate trading network evolved, linking Africa, Asia, and the North and South American colonies with Europe. This global trade and pillage of cultures (slaves from Africa, for example, and vast amounts of gold and silver from Central and South America) provided wealth that would subsequently fuel the growth of industrial capitalism in Europe (Beaud 1983). Colonization, aimed at the control of other people's land, resources, and autonomy was thus central to these early processes, with disastrous consequences for Indigenous peoples in many parts of the world (Dubinsky et al. 2016; Truth and Reconciliation Commission of Canada [TRCC] 2015).

These early signs of capitalist commercial activity emerged out of a *feudal society*—the *Industrial Revolution* had not yet begun. Most people still lived in the countryside. The class structure of these agrarian societies consisted of a relatively small aristocracy and merchant class, most of whom lived in the cities; a rural landowning class; and a large rural peasantry. Work typically involved peasants farming small plots of land they did not own. Landowners received rent, usually in the form of agricultural produce, little of which was sold for cash. Generations of peasant families lived and died on the same feudal estates.

Thus, feudal Europe was predominantly a *pre-market* economy in which the producer was also the consumer. It was also a *pre-capitalist* economy because wage labour was rare and a business class had not yet become dominant. Feudal lords accepted rent and expected services in the form of manual labour required for the upkeep of the estate. In return, they allowed historical tenancy relationships to continue and provided some protection, if necessary, for their tenants. Feudalism was thus built upon a system of mutual rights and obligations, reinforced by tradition. One's social position was inherited. The society was relatively stable, but it stifled economic progress.[3]

Did the decline of feudalism lead to the rise of capitalism, or was it the other way around? Scholars are divided on this question. Some argue that factors internal to feudal society, such as growing rural populations, deterioration of land, and landlords demanding more rent, forced people off the land and into the cities where they could form an urban working class. Others counter that as mercantile capitalism developed in urban areas and as the market economy slowly began to make an impact on rural life, cities began to attract landless serfs. This debate is difficult to resolve, since the two processes influenced each other (Hilton 1976). What is undisputed is that capitalism brought with it an entirely new social order.

Early Capitalism

Industrial capitalism began to emerge in the early 1700s, taking hold first in Britain. A potent mix of new technologies, innovative ideas, and abundant energy (in the form of coal and steam power) spurred this change (Black 2015). Over time, the production of goods by artisans, or by the home-based *putting out system* in which merchants distributed work to peasant households, led to larger workshops (manufactories) that made metal, cloth, glass, and other finished goods (Beaud 1983). By the late 1700s, various inventions were revolutionizing production techniques. James Hargreaves's spinning jenny transformed work in textile industries. Growth in trade and transportation, the construction of railways, and military demand for improved weapons encouraged new techniques for processing iron and other metals. Inventors also were devising ways of harnessing water and steam, as exemplified in James Watt's steam engine (Black 2015).

These early inventions facilitated a new form of work organization: the *industrial mill*. A technical breakthrough that involved harnessing many machines to a single inanimate energy source, the mill also had immense social implications, centralizing production and consolidating many workers under one roof and the control of managers (Beaud 1983: 66–67; Burawoy 1984).

A growing class of impoverished urban wage-labourers endured horrific working conditions in early industrial mills. Some workers resisted this trend, particularly artisans, such as bootmakers and tailors, who previously had controlled their own labour. Episodes of destroying textile machinery occurred between 1811 and 1816 in a number of British communities. The unemployed craftworkers involved (called Luddites) were not unthinking opponents of technological innovations, but skilled workers frustrated by changes that were deskilling their work and bringing it under the control of managers and industrialists. These uprisings were quashed by the state; some participants were jailed or deported, while others were hanged (Beaud 1983: 65; Grint and Nixon 2015).

The emergence of industrial capitalism in Britain also changed the *gender-based division of labour*. While women, men, and children had done different types of work in feudal times, much of it at home, they were often engaged in parallel work activities (Middleton 1988). The putting out system, particularly in the textile industries, brought many women into the paid labour force along with men, since they could work out of their home and still carry out domestic work and childcare. Early textile factories also employed men, women, and children (Berg 1988). But as manufacturing developed and expanded, it became the preserve of men. While a gendered division of labour had long existed, it became more pronounced with the rise of industrial capitalism (Grint and Nixon 2015).[4]

The Great Transformation

In only a matter of decades, factory production dominated capitalist societies. The urban landscape also changed as manufacturing cities in Britain, such as London, Manchester, and Birmingham, grew to accommodate the new wage-labour force. Mechanization and the movement to factory-based production proceeded even faster in the 1800s than it had in the previous century. Manufacturing surpassed agriculture in the value of its annual output. Industrial production in Britain, for example, increased by 300 percent between 1820 and 1860. The portion of the labour force employed in agriculture in Britain, France, Germany, the United States, and other industrializing countries declined, while employment in manufacturing and services rose rapidly. By the end of the 19th century, industrial capitalism was clearly the dominant system of production in Western nations.

According to Karl Polanyi, the *great transformation* that swept Europe with the growth and integration of capital, commodity, and labour markets—the foundation of capitalism—left no aspect of social life untouched (Polanyi 1957).[5] The struggle for democratic forms of government, the emergence of the modern nation-state, and the rapid growth of cities are all directly linked to these economic changes.

Along with new technologies, the replacement of human and animal sources of energy with inanimate sources, and the emergence of an integrated market system for finance, commodities, and labour, this era also saw dramatic changes in how work was organized. Over time, the relatively stable landlord–serf relationships of feudalism were replaced by wage-labour relationships between capitalists and labourers. Employers paid for a set amount of work but also determined exactly how, and under what conditions, work would be done. Previously independent artisans lost out to the factory system. In the end, the result was a higher standard of living for many citizens of industrialized countries. But the interrelated processes of change that created a market economy also led to new problems of *controlling, coordinating,* and *managing* work—central themes in this book.

Equally crucial, the rise of capitalism was intertwined with processes of *colonialization,* as Britain and European countries sought control of other people's lands, resources, and autonomy (Loomba 2007). Such forces had profound negative outcomes for Indigenous people, which persist to the present day (TRCC 2015: 16).

CANADA'S INDUSTRIALIZATION

The process of industrialization in Canada lagged behind that in Britain, Europe, and the United States, and can be traced back to the mid-1800s.[6] As a British colony, Canada had been expected to provide raw materials, rather than to produce finished goods that would compete on world markets with those of the mother country. Canadian economic elites focused on traditional activities, such as exporting *staple products*, including timber and fur, to sell on world markets, and developing transportation networks (particularly railways) that could link the resource-producing regions of the country with the port cities involved in export trade.

Chapter 1: Historical Perspectives on Work

Work in Preindustrial Canada

The first half of the 19th century, then, was a pre-industrial economic era in Canada. Canada still had a pre-market economy, since most production and consumption took place in households. In fact, given the peculiarities of a colonial economy dependent on Britain, land was not a marketable commodity. By the mid-1830s, less than one-tenth of the vast tracts of land that had been given by the French, and later British, monarchy to favoured individuals and companies had been developed for agriculture.

Land settlement was strongly intertwined with industrialization processes, with the Canadian state negotiating 11 numbered treaties with Indigenous peoples between the late 1880s and early 1900s. These treaties would have profound consequences for Indigenous peoples. As the Truth and Reconciliation Commission of Canada (2015: 17) observes:

> The mere presence of Indigenous people in newly colonized lands blocked settler access to the land. . . . To gain control of the land of Indigenous people, colonists negotiated Treaties, waged wars of extinction, eliminated traditional landholding practices, disrupted families, and imposed a political and spiritual order that came complete with new values and cultural practices.

Immigration played a critical role in pre-industrial Canada, with significant numbers of people from Europe arriving. Shortages of land for small farmers, potato famines in Ireland, and dreadful working conditions in many British factories fuelled immigration to the New World. Large numbers of immigrants landed in Canada, only to find shortages in urban factory jobs and little available agricultural land. As a result, most of these immigrants sought employment in the United States, where factory jobs and land were more plentiful (Teeple 1972).

Some of the immigrants who stayed in Canada were employed in building the Welland and Rideau canals—the first of many transportation megaprojects—in the first half of the 19th century. The influx of unskilled workers created a great demand for such seasonal jobs, which often involved 14 to 16 hours a day of hard and poorly paid work. Consequently, poverty was widespread. In the winter of 1844, the *St. Catharines Journal* (Bleasdale 1981: 13) reported that the greatest distress imaginable has been, and still is, existing throughout the entire line of the Welland Canal, in consequence of the vast accumulation of unemployed labourers. There are, at this moment, many hundreds of men, women, and children, apparently in the last stages of starvation, and instead . . . of any relief for them . . . in the spring . . . more than one half of those who are now employed must be discharged.[7]

The Industrial Era

By the 1840s, Canada's economy was still largely agrarian, even though the two key ingredients for industrialization—an available labour force and a transportation infrastructure—were in place. Before Confederation in 1867, some of Canada's first factories were set up not in Ontario or Quebec, as we might expect, but in Nova Scotia. Shipbuilding, glass, and clothing enterprises were operating profitably in this region before the Maritime provinces entered Confederation (Veltmeyer 1983: 103). After 1867, manufacturing became centralized in Ontario and Quebec, resulting in the *deindustrialization* of the Maritimes. A larger population base, easy access to U.S. markets, and railway links to both Eastern and Western Canada ensured that the regions around Montreal and Toronto would remain the industrial heartland of the country.

At the time of Confederation, half the Canadian labour force was in agriculture. This changed rapidly with the advance of industrialization. By 1900, Canada ranked seventh in production output among the manufacturing countries of the world (Laxer 1989). The large factories that had begun to appear decades earlier in the United States were now springing up in Montreal, Toronto, Hamilton, and other central Canadian cities. American firms built many of these factories to avoid Canadian tariffs on goods imported from the United States. This initiative began a pattern of direct U.S. foreign investment in Canada that continues today.

These economic changes brought rapid urban growth and accompanying social problems. Worker exploitation was widespread, as labour laws and unions were still largely absent. Low pay, long hours, and unsafe and unhealthy conditions were typical. Workers lived in crowded and unsanitary housing.

Health care and social services were largely nonexistent. In short, despite economic development in the decades following Confederation, poverty remained the norm for much of the working class in major manufacturing centres such as Montreal and Toronto (Copp 1974; Piva 1979).

Industrialization in Canada also deeply affected Indigenous populations. To aid the settlement of immigrants and the building of a national railway, the Canadian state negotiated a series of numbered treaties between 1871 and 1921, beginning with Treaty 1 between the Crown and the Anishinabek and Swampy Cree in what is now southern Manitoba. Indigenous peoples ceded vast tracts of lands and faced significant restrictions on their economic activities. For instance, under the federal *Indian Act* of 1867 those with "Indian status" were prohibited from selling crops and taking out loans (TRCC 2015). Racism and prejudice also kept Indigenous people out of many occupations, except the most dangerous and menial jobs in fishing, forestry, mining, and other resource sectors (High 1996; Knight 1996; Patrias 2016). In *Lost Harvest*, Sarah Carter (1993) shows how the efforts of the Plains Indians to farm were undermined by government policies that limited their land to one or two acres (less than one hectare), and denied access to new technologies thus necessitating seeding and harvesting by hand.

The Decline of Craftwork

One of the most important changes in the industrial era was the decline of craftworkers' control over their own labour. Traditionally, *skilled craftworkers* had the advantage of being able to determine their own working conditions, hire their own apprentices, and frequently set their pay. Some worked individually, while others arranged themselves into small groups in the manner of European craft guilds. But this craft control declined as Canada moved into the industrial era. Factory owners were conscious of the increased productivity in American factories, where new technology and "modern" systems of management were applied. Dividing craft jobs into many simple tasks allowed work to be performed by less skilled and lower-paid employees. Mechanization further cut costs while increasing productivity. These changes in work processes, known as *scientific management*, are discussed further in Chapter 8.

Such changes reduced the job autonomy of craftwork in Canada, resulting in considerable labour unrest. Between 1901 and 1914, for example, more than 400 strikes and lockouts occurred in the 10 most industrialized cities of southern Ontario (Heron 2012). Although these conflicts may look like working-class revolt, they are more accurately seen as a relatively privileged group of workers resisting efforts to reduce their occupational power. While large numbers of skilled workers experienced the "crisis of the craftsmen" (Heron 2012), there were larger numbers of unskilled manual labourers—often immigrant or Indigenous peoples—whose only alternative to arduous factory work was seasonal labour in fishing, canning, agricultural and transportation job, or unemployment (Gautor 2011; Patras 2016)

Indeed, thousands of such workers were employed in the resource extraction industries throughout Canada, and many others worked constructing essential infrastructure, such as canals and railways. In *The Bunkhouse Man*, Edmund Bradwin estimates that up to 200,000 men living in some 3,000 work camps were employed in railway construction, mining, and the lumber industry during the early 20th century. These workers were from English Canada and Quebec, as well as from Europe and China. Employers considered immigrants to be good candidates for such manual work, as they were unlikely to oppose their bosses. This hiring strategy often did ward off collective action, although immigrants sometimes were the most radical members of the working class.[8]

The creation of a transcontinental railway led to a high demand for coal. Mines were opened on Vancouver Island and in the Alberta Rockies, with immigrants quickly taking the new jobs. Mine owners tried to extract a lot of work for little pay, knowing they could rely on the military to control unruly workers. It has been estimated that, in the early 1900s, every 1 million tons of coal produced in Alberta took the lives of 10 miners, while in British Columbia, the rate was 23 dead for the same amount of coal.[9] These dangerous conditions led to strikes, union organization, and even political action. In 1909, Donald McNab, a miner and socialist, was elected to represent Lethbridge in the Alberta legislature. The same year, the Revolutionary Socialist Party of Canada elected several members to the British Columbia legislature (Marchak 1981: 106). Nonetheless, although the labour movement took root in resource industries, it never had the revolutionary spark that some of its radical leaders envisioned.

THEORETICAL PERSPECTIVES

Now that we have some historical background on industrialization and capitalism, we can examine major explanations of the causes and consequences of these changes. The next sections discuss four key thinkers, beginning with the ideas of economist Adam Smith (1723–90), followed by early sociologists and political economists Karl Marx (1818–83), Émile Durkheim (1858–1917), and Max Weber (1864–1920). In Chapter 2, we explore contemporary theories. After we have acquainted ourselves with the theorists and their analytic concepts, we can apply their insights throughout the book when considering specific work issues.

Adam Smith: Competition, Not Conflict

Adam Smith (1723–90) wrote *The Wealth of Nations* in 1776, during the early Industrial Revolution in England, extolling the wealth-producing benefits of capitalism. Thus, he is often portrayed as the economic theorist whose ideas outlasted those of Karl Marx, who, writing some time later, predicted the eventual downfall of capitalism. Even today, Adam Smith's ideas are frequently used to call for less government intervention in the economy, the argument being that what Smith famously termed "the unseen hand of the market" is best left alone.

In *The Wealth of Nations*, Smith identified the *division of labour*—how tasks are organized and distributed amongst workers—as a key to capitalism's success. Using the example of a pin factory, he described how productivity could be greatly increased by assigning workers to specific tasks such as stretching wire, cutting it, and sharpening it. Whereas individual workers might produce 20 pins a day each by doing all the operations themselves, with a well-defined division of labour, 10 people could make 48,000 pins a day. The greater productivity, Smith reasoned, came from the increased dexterity a worker could master in repeating a single task over and over again, the time saved in not having to change tasks and shift tools, and the added savings obtained from designing machines that workers could use to repeat the single task (Smith 1976; Braverman 1974: 76). The real advantage of this form of work organization would be realized only when factories made large quantities of a product—precisely the goal of industrial capitalism.

In 1832, Charles Babbage translated Smith's principles into practical cost-cutting advice for business owners. By subdividing tasks, he argued, less skill was required of any individual worker. Consequently, employers could pay less for this labour. Workers with fewer skills cannot demand as high a reward for their work (Braverman 1974: 79–83). The early history of industrialization is full of examples of this basic economic principle at work. The advent of factories with detailed divisions of labour invariably replaced skilled craftworkers with unskilled factory workers who were paid less—just the sort of outcome that Karl Marx and other early thinkers criticized.

It is important to note, however, that Adam Smith did not condone the exploitation of workers. He recognized that working conditions in the industrializing British economy were far from satisfactory and argued that higher wages would increase the productivity of workers and the economy as a whole (Weiss 1976; Saul 1995: 150). But Smith was clear about what he saw as a key underlying principle of capitalism. *Competition among individuals and enterprises*, each trying to improve their own position, led to growth and the creation of wealth. As he put it, "It is not from the benevolence of the butcher, the brewer, or the baker, that we expect our dinner, but from their regard to their own self-interest" (Smith [1776] 1976: Book 2, Chapter 2: 14).

For Adam Smith, the profit motive was a beneficial driving force of capitalism. Individuals and firms in aggressive competition with each other produced the "wealth of nations." Where Marx, some decades later, would see conflict, exploitation, and growing inequality, Smith saw competition leading to greater wealth.

Karl Marx on Worker Exploitation and Class Conflict

Karl Marx (1818–83) spent a lifetime critically examining the phenomenon of industrial capitalism. His assessment of this new type of society was presented within a very broad theoretical framework. He called the overall system of economic activity within a society a *mode of production*, and he identified its major components as the *means of production* (the technology, capital investments, and raw materials) and the *social relations of production* (the relationships between the major social groups or classes involved in production).

Marx focused on the manner in which the ruling class controlled and exploited the working class. His close colleague, Friedrich Engels, documented this exploitation in his 1845 book, *The Condition of the Working Class in England*. Engels described one of London's many slum districts, noting that other industrial cities were much the same (63):

> St. Giles is in the midst of the most populous part of the town, surrounded by broad, splendid avenues in which the gay world of London idles about . . . . The houses are occupied from cellar to garret, filthy within and without, and their appearance is such that no human being could possibly wish to live in them. But this is nothing in comparison with the dwellings in the narrow courts and alleys between the streets, entered by covered passages between the houses, in which the filth and tottering ruin surpass all description . . . . Heaps of garbage and ashes lie in all directions, and the foul liquids emptied before the doors gather in stinking pools. Here live the poorest of the poor, the worst paid workers with thieves and the victims of prostitution indiscriminately huddled together.

It was from such first-hand observations of industrializing Europe that Marx developed his critique of capitalism.

Class conflict was central to Marx's theory of social change. He argued that previous modes of production had collapsed and been replaced because of conflicts among class groups within them. Feudalism was supplanted by capitalism as a result of the growing power of the merchant class, the decline of the traditional alliance of landowners and aristocracy, and the deteriorating relationship between landowners and peasants. Marx identified two major classes in capitalism: the capitalist class, or *bourgeoisie,* which owned the means of production, and the working class, or *proletariat,* which exchanged its labour for wages. A third class—the *petite bourgeoisie*—comprising independent producers and small business owners, would eventually disappear. Marx argued that capitalism would eventually be replaced by a socialist mode of production. The catalyst would be revolutionary class conflict, in which the oppressed working class would destroy the institutions of capitalism and replace them with a *socialist society* based on collective ownership of the means of production.

Marx also focused on the negative consequences of an excessive *division of labour*. For him, capitalism itself was the source of the problem. The division of labour was simply a means to create greater profits from the labour of the working class. The development of huge *assembly-line factories* in the early 20th century epitomized this trend. Henry Ford, the inventor of the assembly line, took considerable pride in recounting how his Model T factory had 7,882 specific jobs. Ford calculated that about half the jobs required only "ordinary men" and 949 required "strong, able-bodied men"; the rest, he reasoned, could be done by women, older children, or men who were physically disabled. These observations do not reflect a concern for workers with disabilities; instead, they highlight the extreme fragmentation of the labour process, to the point that even the simplest repetitions became a job.[10]

Marx sparked ongoing debate on the nature of work and of class conflict in capitalist societies (Zeitlin 1968; Coser 1971). Ever since, social, political, and economic analysts have tried to reinterpret his predictions of a future worker-run socialist society. No capitalist society has experienced the revolutionary upheavals Marx foresaw. And the collapse of the Soviet communist system in Eastern Europe ended speculation that communism would evolve into true socialism. In fact, Marx probably would have been an outspoken critic of the Soviet communist system, given its extreme inequalities in power distribution and harsh treatment of workers. He would also have condemned the inequalities in today's capitalist Russia.

Marx's critique of capitalism has also shaped research in the sociology of work and industry, as analysts try to refine or refute his ideas. First, Marx emphasized how the capitalist profit motive is usually in conflict with workers' desires for better wages, working conditions, and standards of living. Second, Marx argued that the worker–owner relationship led to workers losing control over how they did their work and, hence, to the dehumanization of work. Third, Marx predicted that the working class would eventually organize to more actively oppose the ruling capitalist class. In short, Marx wrote about inequality, power, control, and conflict. His enduring legacy for sociology was this more general *conflict perspective*. He recognized that the relations of production in industrial capitalist society typically are exploitative, with owners (and their representatives) having more power, status, and wealth than those who are hired to do the work. Almost all the debates about better ways of organizing workplaces and managing employees, the need for unions and labour legislation, and the future of work in our society stem from this basic inequality.

Émile Durkheim: Interdependence and Social Cohesion

Émile Durkheim (1858–1917), an early French sociologist, provided an alternative, conservative assessment of capitalist employment relations, particularly the *division of labour*. Human societies have always been characterized by a basic division of labour. In primitive societies, work roles were assigned mainly according to age and gender. But with economic development, these roles became more specialized, and the arrival of industrial capitalism further intensified this process. After a certain scale of production was reached, it was much more efficient to break complex jobs into their component tasks.

Durkheim noted that industrial societies contained diverse populations in terms of race, ethnicity, religion, occupation, and education—not to mention differences in beliefs and values. He noted evidence in European industrialization of group differences creating conflict over how scarce resources should be distributed, over rights and privileges, and over which beliefs and values set the standard. Given this, Durkheim viewed the division of labour as a potential source of *social cohesion* that could operate to reduce conflict.[11] He reasoned that individuals and groups working together, and engaged in different tasks in a complex division of labour, would recognize their mutual interdependence. In turn, tolerance and social harmony would be generated.

Durkheim believed that individuals in modern society are forced to rely on one another because of the different occupational positions they fill. In simple terms, lawyers need plumbers to fix their sinks while plumbers need teachers to educate their children. By the same logic, capitalists and their employees are interdependent. Without cooperation between the two groups, the economy would grind to a halt. We will see in later chapters how Durkheim's positive assessment of the division of labour shaped management theories that assume shared interests in the workplace. While Marx has influenced conflict perspectives on work in modern society, the conservative assumptions of Durkheim's general model are the backbone of the *consensus approach*.

Max Weber on Bureaucratic Organizations

Max Weber (1864–1920), a German sociologist writing in the early 20th century, addressed yet another major change accompanying capitalist industrialization: *bureaucracy*. Weber noted that Western societies were becoming more rational, a trend most visible in the bureaucratic organization of work. Informal relationships among small groups of workers, and between workers and employers, increasingly were being replaced by more formal, impersonal work relations in large bureaucracies. Rules and regulations were now determining workers' behaviour. Although Weber was concerned about the resulting loss of personal work relationships, he believed that this development was far outweighed by greater organizational efficiency. For Weber, bureaucracy and capitalism went hand in hand. Industrial capitalism was a system of rationally organized economic activities; bureaucracies provided the most appropriate organizational framework for such activities.

What defined Weber's "ideal-type" bureaucracy were formal rules, with a precise division of labour, within a hierarchy of authority (Weber 1946: 196–98). Each job had its own duties and responsibilities, and each was part of a chain of command in which orders could be passed down and rewards and punishments used to ensure that the orders were followed. But the power of the employer could not extend beyond the bureaucracy. The *employment contract* linking employer and employee was binding only within the employment relationship. Also necessary for efficiency were extensive written records of decisions made and transactions completed.

Recruitment into and promotion within the bureaucratic work organization were based on *merit*—that is, demonstrated competence, performance skills, and qualifications such as educational credentials. Individual employees could make careers within the organization as they moved as far up the hierarchy as their skills and initiative would carry them. Employment contracts assured workers a position so long as they were needed and competently performed the functions of the office. In short, for Weber, rationality, impersonality, and formal contractual relationships defined the bureaucratic work organization.

Yet bureaucracies were not new to 19th-century capitalism. A somewhat similar form of centralized government had existed in ancient China, and European societies had been organizing their armies in this manner for centuries. What was unique, however, was the extent to which workplaces became bureaucratized under capitalism. At the beginning of the 20th century, increased competition and the development of big, complex industrial systems demanded even more rationalized production techniques and worker-control systems. Large bureaucratic work organizations would become the norm throughout the industrial capitalist world. But bureaucracy also became the norm during the 20th century in industrialized communist countries of the former Soviet bloc. So, while closely intertwined, *bureaucracy* and *capitalism* are, in fact, separate phenomena.

CONCLUSION

From feudalism to early capitalism to the rise of industrialization in Canada, we have covered a lot of ground in this chapter. We began with a historical overview of the origins and development of industrial capitalism, focusing first on Europe and then on Canada as a late industrializing nation. We also considered various theories that explain and evaluate the causes and consequences of this complex process. As economies and societies continually evolve and the nature of work is transformed, new social theories have emerged, as we will see in Chapter 2.

In this chapter, we have highlighted the most important social and economic changes unleashed by the Industrial Revolution in Europe. As feudalism gave way to capitalism, markets grew in importance. From the standpoint of work, the emergence of a *paid labour market* was key. A new class structure evolved, and a predominantly rural society became urban. Factory-based wage labour became the norm, while craftwork declined. Larger workplaces demanded new organizational forms and, in time, bureaucracies evolved to fill this need. And while industrial innovations led to substantial increases in productivity, it was some time before the standard of living of the working class began to reflect this increase. These far-reaching social and economic changes were the focus of early sociologists such as Karl Marx, Émile Durkheim, and Max Weber, as well as economists like Adam Smith. Many of the key questions they raised—especially over capitalism's capacity to generate inequality and conflict, or greater prosperity and interdependence—continue to be debated today. Although late to industrialize, compared to Britain and the United States, Canada faced many similar concerns. Having had a brief look at the changing worlds that these thinkers were observing, we are now better equipped to understand how their concerns and conclusions carry into the present day.

DISCUSSION QUESTIONS

1. What is industrial capitalism, and how did it differ from previous ways of organizing work?
2. How did industrial capitalism develop in Canada? In what ways did Canada follow the path of other countries, such as Britain? In what ways was the Canadian experience unique?
3. How did Karl Marx, Adam Smith, Émile Durkheim, and Max Weber believe industrial capitalism would affect workers? What are some of the main differences in their ideas?
4. How does the nature of work in early industrializing Canada compare to work today? Thinking broadly, what would be some of the essential similarities and differences?

ADDITIONAL RESOURCES

WORK AT THE MOVIES

- *Why the Industrial Revolution Happened Here* (produced by Charles Colville, 2013, 57:55 minutes). This BBC documentary examines the economic, social, and political conditions that sparked the Industrial Revolution in Britain and led to a massive transformation of the British economy.
- *Margaret's Museum* (directed by Mort Ransen, 1995, 114 minutes). Adapted from the book *The Glace Bay Miners' Museum* by Canadian Sheldon Currie, this film explores the impact of mining on individuals, families, and communities in 1940s Cape Breton, as seen through the eyes of Margaret MacNeil (played by Helen Bonham Carter).
- *The Grapes of Wrath* (directed by John Ford, 1940, 129 minutes). Based on John Steinbeck's novel, this film follows the Joad family who lose their Oklahoma farm during the Great Depression and become migrant workers in search of new opportunities.
- *The Voyageurs* (directed by Bernard Devlin, 1964, 19:50 minutes). This short historical film re-creates scenes of 19th-century fur-trade work in Canada. It is available through the National Film Board of Canada: http://www.nfb.ca/film/voyageurs.

SOUNDS OF WORK

- "Dust Bowl Refugee" (Woody Guthrie). Based, in part, on Guthrie's own experiences in the American Dust Bowl in the 1930s, this song tells the story of the travelling migrant workers of that era.
- "John Henry" (Traditional/Bruce Springsteen). Springsteen's rendition helps preserve the legacy of American folk hero John Henry, who perished during the construction of a railroad tunnel.
- "Peg and Awl" (Traditional). This tune conveys how the Industrial Revolution brought new technologies that caused the demise of many pre-industrial crafts.

NOTES

1. Based on Bettina Bradbury's (1993) *Working Families: Age, Gender and Daily Survival in Industrializing* Montreal. Toronto: McClelland & Stewart.
2. Beaud's (1983) history of capitalism is a major source for our brief discussion; see also Grint and Nixon (2015) on pre-industrial and early industrial work.
3. Over the centuries, however, technological innovations did lead to important changes in work patterns. See, for example, White's (1962) detailed historical analysis of the impact of draught horses and the wheeled plough on agriculture, and of the effects of the invention of the stirrup on the practice of warfare.
4. Cohen (1988: 24) concludes that industrialization in Canada did not lead to a sharper gender-based division of labour since (as was not the case in England) such segmentation already existed.
5. See Boyer and Drache (1996: 8–12) for an application of Polanyi's ideas to the current era.
6. This discussion is drawn from a variety of sources, many of which are cited individually below. For a useful overview of this period in Canadian history, see Ryerson (1968), Laxer (1989), Kealey (1995: Part 1), Palmer (1992), and the Canadian labour studies journal Labour/Le Travail.
7. See also Wylie (1983) on the building of the Rideau Canal.
8. See Avery (1995), Creese (1988–89), and Guotor (2011) on strikes and radical behaviour among immigrant workers.

9. Mine accidents that took the lives of many miners at one time are mainly responsible for these high averages. For example, 189 miners died in a mine explosion in Hillcrest, Alberta, in 1914. A memorial to these miners and background on the disaster can be found at http://coalminersmemorial.tripod. com/hillcrestminedisaster.html. See McCormack (1978: 9) on British Columbia and Caragata (1979: 16–21) on Alberta coal miners during this era.

10. Toffler (1980: 50) provides the quote from Henry Ford.

11. Durkheim (1960) did allow that a "forced" division of labour, where individuals have no choice over how they participate in the productive system, would not lead to increased social solidarity. He argued, however, that this and other "abnormal" forms of the division of labour would disappear as industrial capitalism matured further.

2

CONTEMPORARY DEBATES AND ISSUES

"On April 24, 2013, the eight-story Rana Plaza building outside Dhaka, Bangladesh, collapsed, killing more than 1,100 people and injuring thousands of others. At the time, the building housed five garment factories that manufactured goods for major retail companies in Europe and North America. It is considered the deadliest disaster in the global garment industry. The causes included shoddy construction, a building with too many floors and too much heavy equipment for the structure to withstand. The incident shook Bangladesh's $28 billion garment industry, the second largest in the world behind China. It drew attention to horrific conditions for factory employees, and raised questions about transparency in the global garment industry in which they work. . . . Since the Rana Plaza collapse, Bangladeshis have become increasingly vocal about demanding better wages and working conditions. The country's minimum wage is just 32 cents an hour."

Source: Ashely Westerman. "4 Years After Rana Plaza Tragedy, What's Changed For Bangladeshi Garment Workers?" National Public Radio, April 30, 2017.

INTRODUCTION

Today's global economy offers some starkly contrasting images of work. In cities such as Toronto, Vancouver, New York, and London, we see well-dressed, mobile professionals streaming through bustling airports and gleaming office towers, working their cellphones while hailing cabs or boarding planes, en route to the next destination. Surrounding them, in restaurants, hotels, taxis, and rideshares, such as Uber, are legions of service workers—often immigrant, working class, and youths—rustling up meals, scrubbing floors, driving and delivering, all for minimum wage. Halfway around the globe, in countries such as Bangladesh, Vietnam, India, and China, young workers, typically women, stitch the latest fashions or assemble laptops, working long days in poor conditions that eerily resemble the early factories and sweatshops just discussed in Chapter 1.

Such images highlight the dramatic, and uneven, changes taking place as a result of innovative new technologies and the global flow of workers and work. In recent decades, new occupations and ways of working have sprung up, most visibly in the so-called *gig economy*. Artificial intelligence also promises to alter work in significant ways. New economic regions and new forms of globalized production have also emerged, along with political arrangements favouring freer trade, globalization, and the deregulation of labour markets. Alongside the flow of jobs and opportunities to new regions are also risks, as illustrated by the tragic collapse of Rana Plaza in Bangladesh which we discussed above.

Together, these developments raise important questions. How is the nature of work and inequality changing, both within Canada and other nations, and between the Global North and South? Are we witnessing fundamental, epochal changes in the world of work? Or are recent developments more incremental, mixing elements of continuity and change? Building on our historical discussions in Chapter 1, this chapter examines contemporary developments in work, including postindustrialism, globalization, economic restructuring, and the rise of new economic regions. We also discuss new forms of work, such as interactive service work and emotional work, and consider how more recent thinkers, such as Ulrich Beck, Pierre Bourdieu, and Michel Foucault, may help us understand contemporary workplace and economic change.

CHANGING ECONOMIES IN THE 20TH AND 21ST CENTURIES

In recent decades, the Canadian economy and workplace have undergone significant transformation. Here we discuss four key changes: the managerial revolution, postindustrialism, industrial restructuring, and globalization.

The Managerial Revolution

Despite being a late industrializer, Canada had a strong resource- and manufacturing-based economy by the early 20th century. Large corporations had also begun to dominate business affairs. Formerly, most manufacturing enterprises had been owned and controlled by individuals or families. But the creation of joint-stock companies marked a pivotal change, with hundreds, sometimes thousands, of investors sharing ownership and profits. Such a diverse group of owners could not directly control the giant corporation in which they had invested. Consequently, a class of managers who could run the enterprise became essential.

As this pattern spread, sociologists began to question the Marxist view of industrial capitalism as a simple two-class system: capitalists who owned and controlled the means of production versus workers who had little choice but to exchange their labour for a wage. An alternative view—the *managerial revolution* theory—became popular, predicting a new era of reduced conflict and greater harmony in the workplace (Burnham 1941). This theory held that *managers*, who were salaried workers and not owners, would look beyond profits when making decisions: the good of both the company and the workers would be equally important. Since ownership of the firm was now diffused among many individuals, power and control of the enterprise had essentially shifted to a new class of professional managers (an occupational group that has grown dramatically in size, as we discuss in Chapters 3 and 4).

Many decades later, it is generally agreed that this perspective was overly optimistic and exaggerated the degree of change (Zeitlin 1974). First, family ownership patterns may be less common, but they have not disappeared. In Canada, the prominence of names such as Molson, McCain, Bronfman, and Weston (as in Galen Weston Jr. in the Superstore commercials) demonstrate the continuing role of powerful families in the corporate sector. Furthermore, while ownership of corporations involves more individuals, many corporations are still controlled by small groups of minority shareholders. Individuals who serve as directors of major corporations are linked in a tight network of overlapping relationships, with many sitting on the boards of several major corporations simultaneously. Another postwar trend has been the corporate ownership of shares. Concentration of ownership increased as a few large holding companies replaced individual shareholders. Thus, the belief that the relatively small and powerful capitalist class described by Marx has virtually disappeared is not supported by current evidence.[1]

Advocates of the managerial revolution theory must also demonstrate that, compared with earlier capitalists, the new breed of managers is less influenced by the bottom line of profit. But research shows that senior managers and corporate executives think and act in much the same way as capitalist owners. They share similar worldviews and social backgrounds as owners, and hold large blocks of shares in the corporation, where they frequently serve as directors, as well. In addition, globalization, which we discuss below, appears to have spurred the growth of a transnational managerial class that supports the interests of wealthy elites, coordinating their business activities within the global economy (Kaya and Martin 2016).

Postindustrialism

Postindustrial Society

A second critical change in Canada and other countries in the last decades of the 20th century, is the shift away from an *industrial era* into a *postindustrial society*. Daniel Bell (1973), writing in the early 1970s, was the first to note these transformations in the U.S. occupational structure.[2] The Industrial Revolution had seen jobs in the manufacturing and processing sectors replace agricultural jobs. After World War II, jobs in the service sector became much more prominent. The number of factory workers was decreasing, while employment in the areas of education, health, social welfare, entertainment, government, trade, finance, and a variety of other business sectors was rising. White-collar workers were beginning to outnumber blue-collar workers.

Bell argued that postindustrial societies would engage most workers in the production and dissemination of knowledge, rather than in goods production as in industrial capitalism. While industrialization had brought increased productivity and higher living standards, a postindustrial society would usher in an era of reduced concentration of power (Bell 1973: 358–67). Power would no longer merely reside in the ownership of property but in access to knowledge and the ability to think and to solve problems. *Knowledge workers*—technicians, professionals, and scientists—would become a large and important class. Their presence would begin to reduce the polarization of classes that had typified the industrial age. In contrast to the managerial revolution thesis, which envisioned a new dominant class of managers, Bell felt that knowledge workers would become the elites of the postindustrial age.

Creative Economies

In the early 2000s, Richard Florida (2002) added to this line of thinking in *The Rise of the Creative Class*. Like Bell, Florida argued that the shift from goods to knowledge production marked a crucial change. But for Florida, knowledge and information were simply the tools and materials for what would drive growth in a postindustrial age—*creativity*. Mapping the U.S. economy, Florida argued there was an emerging *creative class* that accounts for roughly one-third of workers. At the top is a *super creative core* of scientists and engineers, writers, professors, entertainers, and artists. A second layer includes *creative professionals*, who possess high levels of human capital and formal education, and work in a range of fields, such as business, finance, and law. According to Florida, the *creative class* was transforming the economy through a new work ethic that placed high priority on interesting work, flexible forms of organization, and creative and diverse places in which to live.

But what about those left out of this elite group? In *The Flight of the Creative Class*, Florida (2005) acknowledges a growing divide between creative workers and a *service class* who provide cleaning, childcare, and other services for them. Other writers such as Robert Reich (2000, 2015) concur that the knowledge economy offers great opportunities for well-educated, creative workers. But at the other end of the economic spectrum, job quality has eroded sharply through declining pay and job security and increased demands for continual effort. Reflecting on this economic divide, Reich (2002) remarks, "Not for a century has America endured, or tolerated, this degree of inequality" (107). Examining long-term trends, Reich (2015) argues that inequality is increasingly driven by the "working poor" rather than the "idle poor." In the United States, average hourly wages (adjusted for inflation) are lower than 40 years ago (162). One-quarter of U.S. workers are now earning wages below the poverty line (134).

Why the optimism in the early theories of postindustrial society? These explanations of social and economic change were developed in the decades following World War II, a time of significant economic growth in North America.[3] White-collar occupational opportunities were increasing, educational institutions were expanding, and the overall standard of living was rising: hence, the optimistic tone of the social theories being developed. Yet, as we discuss at various points in this book, other commentators paint a negative picture of the rise of service industries and an expanding white-collar workforce. These critical perspectives point to job deskilling, reduced economic security, the dehumanizing impact of computers, and widening labour market polarization—trends that have become more pronounced since the early 1980s (Beck 1992, 2000).

Industrial Restructuring and Precarious Work

Technological change continues to accelerate at a time when the global economy is also undergoing dramatic change. With growing economic interdependence, it is becoming more difficult to think in terms of discrete national economies. Think of the complex global supply chains that link factories in Bangladesh with the clothing stores in your local shopping mall. This *globalization* of economic activity has sparked, and continues to bring about, fundamental readjustments in the Canadian economy and labour market, including plant shutdowns, job loss through downsizing, corporate reorganization and mergers, and the relocation or expansion of company operations outside Canada.[4]

Writing in the early 20th century, economist Joseph Schumpeter considered *industrial restructuring* to be a basic feature of capitalism. According to Schumpeter, this process of "creative destruction" involves breaking down old ways of running industry and building up more competitive, efficient, and high-technology alternatives.[5] But while necessary for the economy as a whole, industrial restructuring can also diminish the quality and quantity of work for individuals. Job losses may be part of the process for some, while others may experience reduced job security and job quality.

Industrial restructuring involves interrelated social, economic, and technological trends. Crucial is the shift from manufacturing to services. In recent decades, Canada's service industries have rapidly grown, as we have already discussed, compared with declining employment in agriculture, resource, and manufacturing industries. Both Canada and the United States have experienced *deindustrialization*. This concept refers to declining employment caused by factory closures or relocation, typically in once-prominent manufacturing industries: steel, automotive, textiles, clothing, chemicals, and plastics. Once mainstays of the Canadian and U.S. economies, these industries are now called *sunset industries*. Factories have been shut down or relocated to Mexico, China, or other developing nations, where labour is cheap and employment rights and environmental standards are lax.

Canada has been vulnerable to processes of deindustrialization for some time. In the 1990s, dozens of large multinationals, encouraged by the Canada–U.S. Free Trade Agreement (FTA), announced plant closures in central Canada, seeking cheaper labour and fewer regulations. For example, after purchasing the Bauer hockey equipment company, Nike announced in

1997 that it was closing the Ontario factory.[6] Canadian corporate giants, like Bombardier, have also shifted jobs to lower-wage countries. Today Canada's once-strong manufacturing sector is increasingly vulnerable, with many workers facing layoffs and unemployment (Bernard 2009; Vrankulj 2012). For instance, General Motors is closing its Oshawa, Ontario, factory, once one of the largest auto assembly plants in the world.

Industrial restructuring is thus often tied to the rise of *precarious work*— that is, work that is insecure and unstable (Kalleberg 2018). As once secure, well-paying, often unionized, manufacturing jobs move elsewhere, long-time employees can find themselves unemployed or forced to take lower paying jobs to support their families and themselves. Retraining for more highly skilled knowledge jobs is often not an option, especially for older workers and those with families to support. At the same time, the rapid growth of retail, hospitality, and other service industries has generated larger numbers of low-quality jobs. Thus, in a postindustrial economy, job quality is not uniformly high. In addition to many low-paying service jobs with traditional employers, digital platforms such as Uber, Freelancers, and Mechanical Turk are spurring the growth of the gig economy—another source of precarious work (Anani 2018; Hansen 2018; Hill 2015; Kalleberg 2018; Stanford 2017). We discuss this in greater detail in Chapter 4.

Global Transformations

Globalization

The term *globalization* has become part of everyday language, but what does it really mean, and can evidence document such a trend? The basic idea is not new; in Canada's colonial past, the masters of the British empire no doubt envisioned their reach as global. Yet searching for a definition of *globalization*, you may be struck by the great many meanings it conveys. Advocates of globalization echo ideas discussed later in this chapter: notably, the "logic of industrialism" view, which sees the spread of capitalist markets and national convergence as inevitable. As Gordon Laxer (1995, 287–88) explains, globalization typically refers to four interrelated changes:

> *Economic changes* include the internationalization of production, the harmonization of tastes and standards and the greatly increased

mobility of capital and of transnational corporations. *Ideological changes* emphasize investment and trade liberalization, deregulation and private enterprise. *New information and communications technologies* that shrink the globe signal a shift from goods to services. Finally, *cultural changes* involve trends toward a universal world culture and the erosion of the nation-state.

Corporations and some governments promote globalization as a means by which expanding free markets will generate economic growth and elevate living standards. Signs of an increasingly global economy are visible in multinational trade agreements, financial markets, and economic treaties. Examples include the United States-Mexico-Canada Agreement (USMCA)—previously known as the North American Free Trade Agreement, or NAFTA—the European Union (EU), and the Trans-Pacific Partnership (TPP), along with international regulatory frameworks such as the World Trade Organization (WTO), and the integration of financial markets through information technology. Critics—and there are many—detect more sinister aspects in globalization. For example, in recent years, activists have voiced concerns that globalization threatens workers' rights, national cultures, and the environment—and ultimately, democracy. Even mainstream commentators such as Nobel Prize–winning economist Joseph Stiglitz recognize basic challenges (Stiglitz 2002, 2017). As Friedman (2000: 42) observed in his early book on globalization, *The Lexus and the Olive Tree*:

> Any society that wants to thrive economically today must constantly be trying to build a better Lexus and driving it out into the world. But no one should have any illusions that merely participating in this global economy will make a society healthy. If that participation comes at the price of a country's identity, if individuals feel their olive tree roots crushed, or washed out, by this global system, those olive tree roots will rebel.

Community-based opposition is only one reason why a globally integrated economic system remains largely an ideal. In a truly global economy, corporations would operate in a completely transnational way, not rooted in a specific national economy. But research suggests that there are few such corporations (Hirst et al. 2009). While McDonald's, IBM, and General Motors may do business in many countries, operating vast networks of subcontractors and suppliers, they remain U.S. based. The United States and the EU still account for a significant part of world trade (both goods and services) through corporations located mainly in those countries, though China now plays a leading role (WTO 2018). While multinational corporations (MNCs) account for roughly one-third of global production, they employ only 2 percent of the world's labour force (OECD 2018; *Economist* 2019). Even so, computers, software, clothes, shoes, cars, and a vast range of other goods are produced by global business networks that span several continents. Yet globalization has not spurred the growth of genuinely global firms, as many believed it would. In fact, recent evidence suggests that MNCs are actually in decline, with poor growth and performance dramatically reducing investor enthusiasm for this mode of organizing (*Economist* 2017).

Indeed, it is much easier to imagine production systems spanning several continents than it is to envision a large global labour force. Despite expanding international markets for some goods and services, labour is still a local resource. According to Hirst et al. (2009), except for highly skilled, globally mobile professionals, and desperate migrants and refugees fleeing intolerable conditions, most of the world's population cannot easily move. In fact, Canada plays an important role in this regard, being one of the few nations to accept relatively large numbers of immigrants annually.

Taking up this theme, Saskia Sassen (2002) argues that mainstream accounts of globalization have tended to focus on the export of low-wage jobs to developing nations, while ignoring the growing role of migrant workers in the Global North. As Sassen points out, the managerial, professional, and technical elite who live in global cities are increasingly dependent on low-paid service workers to maintain the infrastructure that allows them to do their work. Office buildings need to be cleaned; young children and elderly parents need to be cared for. Groceries must be purchased, meals made, and dishes done. Much of this work, as well as other vital services, is done by migrant women, many of whom have moved in search of work to support their own families back home (see also Zimmerman, Litt, and Bose 2006).

Although labour might not become part of a truly global market, globalization may still have an impact on labour practices, notably through the public's growing concern about the labour practices of nationally based firms operating in developing countries (one could say the same about environmental practices). Global media coverage has helped to raise North Americans' awareness. In the past, multinational corporations such as Nike and Gildan Activewear have been the targets of public campaigns because of their global labour practices. More recently, in response to devastating tragedies involving garment workers—for example, the 2012 fire in the Tazreen Fashion Factory and the 2013 collapse of the Rana Plaza in Bangladesh, which, together, claimed over 1,200 lives—there is growing public and political pressure for compensation, improved working conditions, and stronger legal protection of workers. Canadian brands, such as Joe Fresh (owned by Loblaws), that subcontracted work to Rana Plaza, have faced class action lawsuits as a result of the tragedy. The Senate of Canada has held hearings into the global garment sector to better understand how to address labour, safety, and human rights concerns (Canada 2015).

Following the Rana Plaza tragedy, organizations such as the International Labour Organization (ILO), Clean Clothes Campaign, and Maquila Solidarity Network (MSN) have sought to improve conditions for workers and set up compensation for families.[7] Nearly 250 companies have signed *The Accord on Fire and Building Safety in Bangladesh*. Still, conditions in Bangladesh garment factories remain hazardous, with over 100 more incidents of fire or building collapse since the Rana tragedy (Lowe 2019).

Canada and Free Trade

Since the late 1980s, Canada's economy has been increasingly shaped by free trade agreements. This has been part of a broader trend towards *neo-liberalism* in many countries, which has promoted free markets, deregulation, and a minimal role for the state in economic affairs (Saul 1995). In Canada, this trend played out in 1989 with the Free Trade Agreement (FTA) with the United States, and in 1994 with North American Free Trade Agreement (NAFTA), which included Canada, the United States, and Mexico. Both agreements sought a continental free trade zone, aimed at more open, less regulated markets and greater integration in key industries, such as auto and garment manufacturing. In 2018, the awkwardly named United States–Mexico–Canada Agreement (USMCA) was negotiated, replacing NAFTA. It was ratified in 2020. While promising some important changes (e.g., labour and environmental standards), many analysts do not view the USMCA as significantly different, referring to it as "NAFTA 2.0" (Lemieux 2018; Wolf 2018). Despite this, a backlash against free trade, not only in parts of the United States but in Britain and some EU countries, has led to the rise of populist or anti-globalization politicians, such as Donald Trump.

To put the USMCA (and NAFTA before it) into perspective, the three participating countries have a combined labour force of approximately 244.2 million in 2018, with about 68 percent of workers in the United States (164.9 million), 24 percent in Mexico (59 million), and 8 percent in Canada (20.3 million) (World Bank Indicators 2019). In the early 2000s, all three countries had roughly similar levels of growth in gross domestic product (GDP), ranging from 2.3 to 2.6 percent. Since the 2008 financial crisis, however, Mexico has seen higher rates of GDP growth than Canada and the United States in all years except for just two. Reflecting this positive economic performance, Mexico also has an expanding middle class. These patterns have sparked concern about the ongoing loss of jobs in the United States and Canada, to Mexico and other countries where labour costs are lower. Indeed, this was the key issue that Donald Trump ran on in the 2016 US presidential election, with his populist anti-trade message. Since his election, NAFTA has come under increasing fire as part of a broader war on trade. But NAFTA has been a concern as far back as 2008, when U.S. Democratic Party candidates Hillary Clinton and Barack Obama both promised to reopen core provisions of the treaty, including existing side agreements on labour and environmental issues (Alexandroff, Hufbauer, and Lucenti 2008). It has also been a concern in Canada, especially in the auto and garment manufacturing sectors, which have been significantly altered by these agreements.

What has been the impact of free trade between Canada, Mexico, and the United States thus far? At the outset of the FTA and NAFTA, the migration of jobs from Canada or the United States to Mexico was a major concern. While claims of massive job losses directly from these agreements have not been borne out, permanent factory closures and job losses in central Canada in the early 1990s were partly linked to free trade. For instance, between 1990 and 1991, Canada lost 273,000 manufacturing jobs, or 13 percent of the industry as a whole. Nevertheless, new job creation and growth in Canada and the United States offset these losses, reflecting the process of creative destruction we discussed earlier. At the same time, in Mexico, the *maquiladora* factories along the northern border were booming; indeed, from 1990 to 2000, the number of *maquila* plants and employees saw dramatic growth, effectively doubling in numbers, though levels then tailed off (Commission for Labor Cooperation 2003: 81; Scott, Salas, and Campbell 2006: 44). Were these "new" jobs or jobs relocated from high-wage countries, such as Canada and the United States? From available evidence, it seems that fewer jobs than expected have migrated south.[8] And much of the new foreign investment in Mexico is due not just to NAFTA but to the proliferation of global trade and production, with firms based in Japan, East Asia, and Europe seeking a Mexican base from which to supply the North American consumer market. Over time, the manufacturing sector in Mexico has become more diverse, as auto and pharmaceutical manufacturers such as Volkswagen, Honda, Eli Lilly, and Mercedes Benz have set up operations.

Thus, jobs may be migrating south, but only in some manufacturing industries, and if firms seek low wages, they are as likely to relocate to China, Bangladesh, Vietnam, and other low-cost countries, not just Mexico. There is just as much concern that competitive pressures from NAFTA in auto and auto parts manufacturing have accelerated the trend toward *nonstandard or contingent* work in the United States and Canada. As quickly as manufacturing employment has declined, there has been a steady increase in higher-quality, knowledge-intensive jobs in financial and business services—jobs that are filled by members of Florida's (2002) creative class, not by displaced autoworkers. Others argue that the group most negatively affected by free trade are Mexican workers. While their low pay, lack of rights, and working conditions may be deplorable by Canadian standards, they are part of an emerging middle class in Mexico and relatively advantaged compared to the majority of Mexicans, the rural poor. Though Mexican workers face an uphill battle, they have had some success organizing for better pay and labour protection. The MSN in Canada and the United Students Against Sweatshops (USAS) are just two examples of global solidarity networks that help monitor and challenge working conditions.

Looking ahead, the USMCA (if ratified) may bring improvements in working conditions and wages for Mexican workers. Canada made a concerted push for a more progressive agreement, gaining the inclusion of a labour chapter requiring that all three countries commit to the ILO labour rights. The USMCA also addresses issues of Indigenous rights, with Chapter 32 specifying that legal obligations to Indigenous peoples take priority over the USMCA (Wolfe 2018; Lemeiux 2019). Finally, with respect to concerns over job loss in Canada and the United States, stronger rules of origin require a greater proportion of auto manufacturing (40 percent, up from 30 percent) to be carried out by workers earning $16/hour or more, attempting to ensure more work is done in Canada and the United States. Having said this, following the USMCA announcement, General Motors announced it was closing several auto plants in the United States and one in Canada, in Oshawa, the latter employing 2,500 unionized workers (Fife and Atkins 2018; Frazier and Kaufman 2019).

RETHINKING INDUSTRIALIZATION

Contemporary changes, such as globalization, have prompted rethinking of traditional ideas about industrialization. Although countries differ in the timing, pace, and form of industrialization, there appear to be some similar underlying dynamics and processes. Industrialized countries tend to be highly urbanized; production typically takes place on a big scale using complex technologies; workplaces tend to be organized bureaucratically; and white-collar workers make up much of the workforce. Citizens are reasonably well educated, and generally an individual's level of education and training is related to her or his occupation. Many decades ago these similarities led American social scientists (Kerr, Dunlop, Harbison, and Myers 1973: 29) to claim,

> The world is entering a new age—the age of total industrialism. Some countries are far along the road, many more are just beginning the journey. But everywhere, at a faster pace or a slower pace, the peoples of the world are on the march towards industrialism.

This is the *logic of industrialism thesis*, a deterministic and linear argument about the sweeping inevitability of industrial technology. It contends that industrialism is such a powerful force that any country, whatever its original characteristics, will eventually come to resemble other industrialized countries. In current debates about globalization, the same argument has been restated as a *thesis of economic, political, and cultural convergence.* Yet, as we will see in later chapters, comparisons of work patterns in various industrialized countries do not support this prediction. For example, pronounced cross-national variations exist in unemployment rates, innovative forms of work organization, unionization and industrial relations systems, and education and training. And as noted below, globalization is not a standardized process, but rather is playing out quite differently at national, regional, and community levels.

Our historical overview in Chapter 1 illustrates that Canada's industrialization occurred later and was shaped by its colonial status, that immigration was a major factor in creating a workforce, and that resource industries played a central role. Other countries such as Sweden and Japan also industrialized later, but their experiences differed from Canada's. In recent decades, many nations have undergone rapid industrialization. For example, countries such as Mexico, Bangladesh, Malaysia, and Indonesia have seen rapid industrialization as well as rising inequality (Piketty 2014; World Economic Forum 2017). In each case, however, the process has varied. Likewise, the experiences of the East Asian Tigers—Singapore, Hong Kong, Taiwan, and South Korea—at the end of the 20th century, and more recent expansion in countries such as China, India, and Russia, highlight great diversity in how change unfolds. Other than at the broadest level of analysis, there does not appear to be an inherent *logic of industrialism* (Rodrik 2007; Whyte 2009).

This observation becomes clear when we compare the countries presented in Table 2.1. Keep in mind that comparing nations in different phases of development presents challenges because perfectly comparable data are lacking. However, the World Bank has comparative measures that we can use in Table 2.1. Canada is listed first to provide a benchmark for interpreting the relative socioeconomic conditions in other countries. After noting which countries are included in Table 2.1, scan each column to get a sense of the huge differences in population, urbanization, per capita income, annual economic growth, education, female labour force participation, and inequality (the last item is measured by the GINI coefficient, where 0 is perfect equality and 100 is maximum inequality). Keep in mind that, in many developing nations, significant economic activity still occurs in informal sectors of the economy, so it may not be captured in the official statistics in Table 2.1 (Jütting and de Laiglesia 2009). Still, these basic indicators raise a host of questions about the underlying historical, cultural, and political contexts in which countries industrialize.

TABLE 2.1 Social and Economic Indicators for Selected Countries

Country	Population (millions) 2017–18	GNI (PPP) per Capita in $U.S.^[a] 2014–17	Average Annual GDP % Growth^[b] 2018		% of Labour Force with Advanced Education^[c] 2014–18	Ratio of Female to Male Labour Force Participation 2018	GINI Coefficient^[d] 2010	Unemployment Rate	
			2010	2017				2010	2018
Canada	36.7	42,383	3.08	3.04	75.0	87.1	33.6	8.1	5.9
United States	325.7	52,751	2.53	2.27	73.2	81.6	40.4	9.6	4.0
Mexico	129.2	16,928	5.1	2.0	77.5	56.1	45.8	5.3	3.4
United Kingdom	66.0	37,597	1.69	1.79	83.8	83.5	34.4	7.8	4.0
Germany	82.7	44,429	4.0	2.2	73.5	83.4	30.2	7.0	3.7
France	67.1	38,085	1.9	1.8	76.6	84.3	33.7	8.9	8.8
Japan	126.8	38,674	4.2	1.7	—	71.8	32.92	5.1	2.4
Italy	60.5	33,946	1.7	1.5	74.8	68.0	34.7	8.4	10.6
Sweden	10.1	45,149	5.9	2.3	83.6	90.4	27.7	8.57	6.31
China	1,386.4	15,269.3	10.6	6.9	—	80.4	43.7	4.2	4.71
India	1,339.1	6,359.1	10.3	6.7	62.7^[e]	34.2	—	3.5	3.5
Brazil	209.3	13,852	7.5	0.9	81.1	71.2	53.3	7.3	12.0
Russian Federation	142.8	24,232	4.5	1.5	66.6	78.9	39.9	7.4	5.06
Indonesia	264.0	10,846	6.2	5.1	85.2	62.1	36.4	5.6	4.3
South Korea	51.5	35,944	6.5	3.1	77.9	71.9	32.0	3.7	3.8
Turkey	80.7	24,808	8.5	7.4	80.1	46.2	41.9	10.7	10.9

Iran	81.1	19,011	5.8	3.8	67.7	23.6	40.0	13.5	12.0
Egypt	97.5	10,351	5.1	4.2	—	75.9	30.2	11.8	11.8
Nigeria	191.0	5,202	8.0	0.8	—	84.6	—	3.9	7.0
Philippines	104.9	9,156	7.6	6.9	63.3	61.7	40.1	3.6	2.5
Pakistan	197.0	5,311	1.6	5.7	61.2	30.4	29.8	—	4.2
Bangladesh	164.7	3,677	5.6	7.3	79.6	41.6	32.1	4.4	4.3
Vietnam	95.5	5,857	6.4	6.8	87.6	88.1	35.3	—	1.9
Thailand	69.0	15,510	7.5	3.9	85.7	78.2	39.4	0.6	1.3
Malaysia	31.6	26,119	7.4	5.9	68.2	65.8	—	3.3	3.4
Ethiopia	105.0	1,719	12.5	10.2	—	88.1	33.2	4.9	5.3

Source: World Bank Data Bank. World Development Indicators. Available online at https://databank.worldbank.org/data/reports.aspx?source=2&series=SP.POP.TOTL&country=#advancedDownloadOptions.

a Gross national income (GNI) per capita based on purchasing power parity (PPP). PPP GNI is gross national income (GNI) converted to international dollars using purchasing power parity rates. An international dollar has the same purchasing power over GNI as a U.S. dollar has in the United States.

b Annual percentage growth rate of gross national product (GDP) at market prices based on constant local currency. GDP is the sum of gross value added by all resident producers in the economy plus any product taxes and minus any subsidies included in the value of the products.

c Advanced education includes short-cycle tertiary education, bachelor's or equivalent degree, master's degree or equivalent, or doctoral degree or equivalent according to the International Standard Classification of Education 2011 (ISCED 2011).

d The GINI coefficient measures how the distribution of income among individuals or households within an economy deviates from a perfectly equal distribution. A GINI coefficient of 0 indicates perfect equality; 100 indicates perfect inequality.

e 2010

We should also be attuned to matters of timing and the changing fortunes of national economies. For example, after World War II, Japan attracted great attention due to its rapid growth—the "Japanese miracle"—and unique management practices (see also Chapter 9). In the 1980s, the East Asian Tigers (Singapore, Hong Kong, Taiwan, and South Korea) attracted great interest. At the start of the 21st century, attention shifted to the so-called BRIC countries (Brazil, Russia, India, and China). More recently, we see interest in the Next Eleven or N-11 (Mexico, Indonesia, South Korea, Turkey, and others), and in subsets of this group, such as the MINTs (Mexico, Indonesia, Nigeria, and Turkey). Despite the often gimmicky nature of these labels, and the fact that groupings are based on shared economic indicators (e.g., high GDP growth), rather than deep historical connections or national political developments, they do help us identify where significant changes are taking place (Frankopan 2019). We discuss these countries briefly to highlight similarities and differences as globalization continues to unfold, and to put work and economic change in Canada into a comparative context.

The East Asian Tigers

In the final decades of the 20th century, the four East Asian Tigers—Singapore, Hong Kong, Taiwan, and South Korea—attracted significant attention. In a short time, they underwent rapid industrialization, either surpassing or fast approaching per capita incomes in the major Western industrial nations. While it took Britain 58 years (1780 to 1838) and the United States 47 years (1839 to 1886) for per capita GDP (the total output of the economy) to double, it took South Korea only 11 years (1966 to 1977) (World Bank 1991). In the same region, another set of *newly industrializing countries* (NICs)—Thailand, Indonesia, and Malaysia—were following just behind. But a major financial crisis that hit Asia in 1997–98 shook the foundations of many of these economies, and subsequent recovery and economic growth was tempered by events such as the 2001 dot-com crash, the devastating 2004 tsunami that affected Indonesia and Thailand, and the 2008 global financial crisis and subsequent recession (World Bank 2005b).

Signal features of the "East Asian miracle" were spectacular growth rates and greater reductions in income inequality than in other developing nations (World Bank 1993: 277). But other factors were important, too; these included rising output and productivity in agriculture at the same time that a manufacturing export sector was developing, steep declines in birthrates so that population growth was constrained, heavy investment in educational systems, and a bureaucratic state run by a career civil service.

But this summary overstates similarities, disregarding the fact that capitalism took distinctive forms in each country.[9] In South Korea, for instance, a few giant diversified corporations, called *chaebol,* dominated the economy, with close ties to the state. In Taiwan, a dynamic export sector was sustained by a network of highly flexible small- and medium-sized manufacturing firms with extensive *subcontracting systems* that extended into the informal sector of the economy. In Hong Kong (and also Taiwan), the main organizing unit of business is the Chinese *family enterprise,* where long-term prosperity and the reputation of the family is key—in stark contrast to the rugged individualism of North American capitalism. Singapore is set apart by the prominent role of the state in directing industrialization and greater reliance on foreign MNCs.

The Rise of Capitalism in the BRIC Economies (Brazil, Russia, India, and China)

In the early 2000s, attention turned to the most populous countries in the world—China and India—as they underwent unprecedented economic and social change. Media stories of rich "peasants" in China buying German luxury cars, India's thriving "Silicon Valley," and the garishly lavish lifestyles of Russia's new entrepreneurs highlighted the complex changes occurring in what social scientists call "transitional economies." Dubbed the BRIC economies (or BRICS, with some including South Africa), these countries illustrate that globalization is not just an economic process. Factors such as a society's culture, norms, and customs, as well as political trends and government policies and work organization, all influence how markets take shape and how individuals pursue new opportunities within them (Basu 2004; Jha 2002; Rodrik 2007; Whyte 2009; Winters and Yusuf 2007). The BRIC economies illustrate the uncertainties of globalization. Today, China and India continue to experience rapid growth, while Russia has struggled because of volatile oil prices (upon which it heavily depends for government revenue), and Brazil has floundered amid economic and political crises.

China offers a fascinating case study. Since introducing market reforms in the late 1970s, the Chinese economy has grown at an astonishing rate, though this has slowed in recent years with a shift from high-speed to high-quality

Chapter 2: Contemporary Debates and Issues   **39**

growth (*Economist* 2009; Frankopan 2019: 73). Even after the financial crash of 2008, China continued to grow rapidly with an average GDP growth of 10.6 percent in 2010. Though average GDP growth slowed to 6.9 percent in 2017, China's expansion continues to outstrip all industrialized nations, and most other countries in Table 2.1. As the world's most populous nation, with nearly 1.39 billion inhabitants, China is seen by corporations as a huge market to conquer. Its workers are now increasingly integrated into the global economy, especially in special economic zones, which have attracted foreign firms such as Apple, Wal-Mart, and The Gap. China is a leading recipient of foreign direct investment by multinational corporations, with more than half of its trade now controlled by foreign firms (UN 2018; Whyte 2009).[10] It has also made huge investments in resource-rich countries, including in Canada's oil sector. Based on their revenues and profits, Chinese firms are now among the largest in the world.

Has communist China been overtaken by capitalist free enterprise? The short answer is no, and the democratic reforms many hoped would flow from economic change have not taken root. But remarkable social and economic transformations are occurring. And looking ahead, China's Belt and Road Initiative (BRI), designed to increase economic trade through new land and sea routes—building on the ancient Silk Roads—will continue to fuel growth into the next century (Brakman et al. 2019; Frankopan 2019; Zhang et al. 2018).

Unlike the former Soviet Union, where privatization is now widespread, state ownership of property remains dominant in mainland China — though some changes are occurring. Farming has shifted from collective farms to households, giving farmers full return on anything they produce over a set quota. And while state-owned enterprises are still prominent, at the local level, hybrid corporations straddling the state and private sector are permitted. China's largest private company is information and communication technology giant Huawei (it sells more smart phones than Apple); while ostensibly privately owned it still has close connections with the Chinese government—a reason that some Western countries are leery of its 5G technology (Wente 2019). Although the Communist Party and state institutions still strongly influence individuals' occupational rewards, housing, and personal freedom, it is clear that market reforms have brought rising inequality—across occupational, urban–rural, and regional lines (Wu and Xie 2002; Feng 2008).

India is another country that has received enormous attention. Like China, it has a huge population: more than 1.34 billion (see Table 2.1). With its higher birthrate and growing life expectancy, India is projected to surpass China's population within the decade (*Economist* 2009). Despite high levels of poverty and illiteracy, India has invested heavily in computer engineering and science, creating a two-tiered economy where highly skilled, cutting-edge knowledge services sit alongside a subsistence agriculture sector that employs most of the country's poor. India's technological savvy helped to fuel rapid economic growth of over 7 percent for much of the 2000s, with a peak of 10.3 percent in 2010, and slightly lower growth of 6.7 percent in 2017 (see Table 2.1).

White-collar outsourcing has been central to India's growth, whereas manufacturing has played a minor role compared to China. In recent years numerous jobs have moved to India from North American and European firms—from call-centre work to software engineering, income tax preparation, and the reading of CAT scans. Though some of this work—notably, call-centre jobs— has since moved on to other countries, such as the Philippines, India's continued attraction is not simply lower labour costs and time differences that facilitate 24/7 production. A deep pool of highly skilled technology workers and fluency in English as a legacy of British colonialism are added attractions.

As in China, India's economic growth has come through conscious state planning, especially in the mid-1980s under then Prime Minister Rajiv Gandhi, who pushed India into the high-tech sector. But because India is a democratic society, with an increasingly fragmentary political system, there has been difficulty furthering reform, especially at the local level (Jha 2002; Basu 2004; Parthasarathy 2004). Thus, companies such as Dell, Microsoft, and IBM employ an elite group of knowledge workers in specially created campuses or software technology parks. For example, at InfoSys campus, the jewel of India's IT sector, employees enjoy a resort-size swimming pool, putting greens, restaurants, and a health club (Friedman 2005: 4). Outside the gates of InfoSys, however, other parts of the economy remain untouched. Today a significant portion of the population continues to live in poverty, and rates of adult literacy and life expectancy remain low.

Compared to China and India, the former Soviet Union has taken a much different course. As Robert Brym observes, a "strange hybrid of organized crime, communism and capitalism grew with enormous speed in the post-Soviet era" (1996: 396). Private enterprise, or market liberalization—introduced in the mid-1980s—was a relatively chaotic process, ensuring that competitive capitalism as we know it failed to emerge. The reason, in Brym's view, is that the old Communist Party elite, along with organized criminal gangs that had prospered in the corruption of the Soviet economy, were well placed to take advantage of any new opportunities. The result is a predatory form of capitalism, described in Bill Browder's (2015) *Red Notice*, that has enriched a small elite, or oligarchy, while breeding corruption and making life worse for ordinary Russians.

Despite an emerging private sector and successive state policies aimed at reform, Russia has not seen the development of a vibrant, diversified, entrepreneurial sector or reductions in social inequality. This reality is contrary to *market transition theory*, which was developed to explain recent social and economic changes in China and the former Soviet Union. Strong growth of 6.8 percent from 2002 to 2008 slowed notably to average growth of 4.5% in 2010 and just 1.5% in 2017 (see Table 2.1). Russia's economy relies heavily on volatile oil and gas sectors. Income inequality is a significant issue, as are demographic pressures sparked by plummeting male life expectancy and an aging population (*Economist* 2009; Gerber and Hout 1998).

A broadly similar pattern is typical of other Eastern bloc nations. Former Communist Party elites, who still control state resources and have good business networks, continue to benefit in the post-Soviet era, while living standards for the majority have declined (Rónas-Tas 1994; Szelényi and Kostello 1996). Unlike earlier transitions to capitalism in Western Europe and North America, what is occurring in the former Soviet bloc does not involve the rise of a new economic elite or the creation of a working class—both of which existed in different forms under communism. Thus, Polanyi's "great transformation" from feudalism to a market economy in 19th-century Europe represented a unique experience of social and economic change. Subsequent transformations to market-based capitalism have taken some unexpected twists and turns.

The Next Eleven (N-11)

Looking forward, a group of countries named the N-11 have been identified as high potential economies: Mexico, Bangladesh, South Korea, Indonesia, Turkey, Iran, Egypt, Nigeria, the Philippines, Pakistan, and Vietnam. Together these countries represent nearly 1.5 billion people, accounting for GDP of around $6.5 trillion (O'Neill 2018). Most of the N-11 (with a few exceptions) have experienced steady and often high rates of growth over the past two decades. As we can see from Table 2.1, Indonesia, the Philippines, Turkey, and Bangladesh had annual GDP growth ranging from 5.1 to 7.4 percent on average in 2017. Other countries, such as Nigeria and Pakistan, have more volatile growth patterns but are still viewed as having enormous potential (O'Neill 2018).

NEO-LIBERALISM AND THE ROLE OF THE STATE IN TODAY'S ECONOMY

Clearly, economic globalization, technological advances, and industrial and labour market restructuring have proceeded in a political context dominated by laissez-faire beliefs that advocate free markets with little or no government interference.[11] In a sense, this political environment is also a key determinant of Canadians' future employment prospects. These trends have the potential to either improve employment opportunities for Canadians or lead to further labour market disruptions. It is difficult to predict just what their ultimate impact might be, but it is important to consider how these forces could be shaped to our collective advantage. Public policy in other industrial countries in Europe and Asia has been more proactive in trying to influence the course of technological, labour market, and economic change.

The FTA, NAFTA, and USMCA were negotiated by governments and have been hotly contested political issues in all three countries affected. These trade agreements underscore the evolving role of the state (or government) in the economy and the labour market. The history of industrial capitalism is replete with instances of different forms of state intervention. For example, in the early Industrial Revolution, the French government forced unemployed workers into factories in an effort to give manufacturing a boost. We noted in Chapter 1 that in the early 19th century the British government dealt harshly with the Luddite protests against new technologies. And the Canadian government adopted its National Policy in 1879 to promote a transcontinental railway and settlement of the West.

In fact, as Canada industrialized, the government heavily subsidized the construction of railways to promote economic development. It also actively encouraged immigration to increase skilled labour for factory-based production and unskilled labour for railway construction. At times, it provided military assistance to employers combating trade unionists and introduced laws discriminating against Chinese and other non-white workers. But the Canadian government also passed legislation that provided greater rights, unemployment insurance, pensions, and compensation for workplace injuries. Although some might argue that these initiatives were designed mainly to ensure industrial harmony and to create an environment conducive to business, it remains true that these labour market interventions benefited workers.

A consensus, or compromise, was reached between employers and workers (mainly organized labour) in the prosperous post–World War II period. Acting on *Keynesian economic principles* that advocated an active economic role for the state, the Canadian government sought to promote economic development, regulate the labour market, keep unemployment low, and assist disadvantaged groups—in short, to develop a "welfare state." While the Canadian state was never as actively involved in the economy and the labour market as some European governments, it still played an important role.

But industrial restructuring has been accompanied (some would say facilitated) by conservative political doctrines based on free-market economics (Saul 1995; Kapstein 1996). In the 1980s, Ronald Reagan in the United States, Margaret Thatcher in Britain, and Brian Mulroney in Canada argued that economies would become more productive and competitive with less state regulation and intervention. Public policy was guided by the assumption that free markets can best determine who benefits and who loses from economic restructuring. The ideas of Adam Smith were used to justify the inevitable increases in inequality. High unemployment came to be viewed as normal. In some jurisdictions, labour rights were diluted, social programs of the welfare state came to be seen as a hindrance to balanced budgets and economic competitiveness, and government-run services were privatized, changes that directly or indirectly affected employment.[12] As John Ralston Saul (1995) argues, these free-market ideologies erode democratic freedoms, threatening to bring about what he calls "the great leap backward." Similarly, with many rapidly developing economies, governments routinely use economic imperatives to restrict individual and collective rights.

Thus, in today's economic climate of globalization and restructuring, proponents of free-market economics seem to have a strong influence. But as we noted when discussing the ideas of Adam Smith, an unchecked marketplace generally leads to greater inequality. So, what kind of society do we want? When answering this question, we will have to determine the role of the state in achieving the desired society. Looking back, we can see that differing government policies have interacted with economic globalization to produce different effects at the local level. Looking forward, globalization has no fixed trajectory. Political choices by citizens and their governments undoubtedly will continue to shape the process in diverse ways. Canadians are concerned about labour market inequalities, employment, workers' rights, and employers' responsibilities to communities. The extent to which governments are held accountable for these issues will determine the impact of global economic forces on our daily economic lives. Increasingly, albeit slowly, some large corporations are beginning to take responsibility. This comes out in their corporate social responsibility reporting (Lowe 2019).

GREAT TRANSFORMATIONS REVISITED

To this point our discussion has focused largely on economic and political change. But equally important since the 1950s have been dramatic shifts in gender, family, and household life. While we examine these changes in greater depth in Chapters 6 and 7, a key point for our discussion here is that postindustrialism and globalization have unfolded alongside dramatic shifts in women's paid work activity, as well as the growing "marketization" of household work (e.g., cooking, cleaning, caring). Speaking to this, U.S. sociologist Arlie Hochschild (2009) argues that contemporary households offer another example of Polanyi's "great transformation," with family relationships coming under the sway of market forces and new forms of paid work emerging as a result (see also McDowell 2009; Reich 2000; Lair and Ritzer 2009; Anderson and Hughes 2010). Here we highlight some key consequences, returning to these issues in later chapters.

Interactive Service Work, Caring Work, and Emotional Labour

Perhaps one of the most notable outcomes of this shift is the rise of *interactive service work*, which involves significant contact with clients or customers (McDowell 2009). Some work may be tightly routinized, requiring workers to follow scripts; in other cases, workers may have far more autonomy and discretion (Leidner 1993). Many such jobs (though certainly not all) also involve *caring work*—activities necessary for the sustenance of human life. Serving meals, providing paid childcare, driving elderly seniors to appointments, and cleaning homes are all examples of such work (Hochschild 2009; Lair and Ritzer 2009). A unique feature of these jobs is that many also involve *emotional labour*—the management of our emotions to conform to employer-defined rules (e.g., "service with a smile"). To the extent that emotional control (often thought of as a private matter) becomes a requirement of the job, it becomes work: hence the term *emotional labour*.[13]

One of the most influential early studies on emotional labour—Arlie Hochschild's (1983) *The Managed Heart*—found that workers (in this case, flight attendants) used "feeling rules" to determine appropriate emotions on the job, engaging in "surface acting" (simply projecting required emotions, such as a smile) or "deep acting" (where they actively tried to change what they were feeling). Of concern to writers such as Hochschild was whether harnessing emotions for market purposes created emotional dissonance, with workers developing a sense of distress or self-estrangement because of the emotional demands of their job. Since then, many studies have examined the concept of emotional labour (now often called "emotion management") to understand the extent to which service work and emotional labour can be scripted or regulated; how different types of workers experience such work; and how the nature of service, caring, or emotional work might vary across diverse sectors and work settings. For instance, some studies suggest distinctions between an "emotional proletariat" (low-skilled jobs with high emotional demands and little control) and "privileged emotional managers" (high-skilled jobs offering autonomy); see Bolton (2005) and Wharton (2009) for reviews of such work.

The rise of interactive service work also raises important questions about the growing role of customers in controlling worker behaviour, through instruments such as customer feedback forms. It has also raised awareness about safe and civil work environments where workers are protected from harassment and abuse. Some writers contend that the traditional dyad of employer–employee control has been replaced by a "triangle of power" comprising customer, employer, and employee (for discussions, see Korczynski and Macdonald 2009).[14] Our purpose here is not to settle these debates—we return to them in later chapters—but simply to highlight the growing complexity of work in contemporary economies.

Mobile Workers and Mobile Work

Earlier we noted how globalized production practices have meant the outsourcing of work to other countries. But this outsourcing is just one dimension of increasing work-related mobility. Globally, we also see growing mobility of workers, both between and within countries, although we would emphasize that mobility remains the exception, not the norm. In Canada, the United States, and European countries, however, we do see a growing reliance on "transnational caregiving," where workers—typically women, but also men—migrate temporarily or permanently from the Global South to work as nannies, personal care attendants, caregivers, or housekeepers in private homes, childcare centres, or long-term care centres (Zimmerman et al. 2006; Ehrenreich and Hochschild 2002). Temporary foreign workers have also become more common in fast-food service, cooking, cleaning, health care, and agricultural work, prompting heated public debate (D. Thomas 2010). Professional workers are also increasingly global, although this remains a tiny elite (Elliott and Urry 2010).[15] Despite moving to countries where employment standards and human rights legislation provide reasonable protections for citizens, mobile temporary workers often fall through the regulatory cracks.

Mobility is not simply global, however. Nationally, in Canada, we have strong interprovincial mobility—for example, between Newfoundland and Labrador and Fort McMurray—where workers travel between a permanent home (where their family resides) and work sites (where they work 14 days and then have 7 days off). Capturing this trend, a CBC *Ideas* program profiled *mobile workers* in the oil sands. An ongoing project, *On the Move*, documents the growing range of employment-related mobility in the country.[16] Within local settings, some workers are highly mobile, either because of their occupation (e.g., couriers) or the need to travel to different employers to secure a full week's work (Vosko 2005). Of note, recent changes to *Employment Insurance* require workers to become increasingly mobile by accepting jobs within a one-hour commute from home, which is more than twice the average commuting time in Canada (Statistics Canada 2013g).

Beyond mobile people, mobile technologies are also altering how work is done, allowing more "knowledge work" to be carried out, coordinated, and monitored across geographical space. Some workers, for instance, no longer go into the office but instead *telecommute* (working partly from home), *hot-desk* (using desks at clients, suppliers, or employers), or work in *virtual teams* (where

Chapter 2: Contemporary Debates and Issues **47**

members are spread across different cities, regions, or countries). Spurring this trend are increasingly affordable, powerful laptops, iPads, and cellphones, as well as a plethora of apps, that allow workers, managers, and customers to connect with their data and with one another. As these technologies become more common, some routine rituals of the workplace, such as face-to-face meetings and water-cooler conversations, are replaced by Skype, FaceTime, and Google Chat. That said, such change also appears to be more selective and slower to catch on than predicted (Noonan and Glass 2012).

We return to these issues in later chapters, but what is germane to our discussion here is the way that virtual work extends both the temporal and spatial boundaries of the workplace. Whereas the office tools of the mid- to late-20th century—for instance, typewriters or large mainframe computers—stayed put at the end of the day, today's mobile technologies allow work to be accessed *anywhere, anytime*. With this come demands for 24/7 availability, as well as greater potential for work–family conflict (Perlow 2012), drawing our attention again to the shifting boundaries between home and work. Highlighting the benefits and downsides of virtual work, a study of 30,000 Canadian office workers found that while virtual work boosted productivity and generated more interesting work, it also increased stress and workloads. Work–life balance proved to be harder to maintain, with it being easier and too easy to work from home (Towers et al. 2006). This is despite the fact that some workers seek virtual work because of the flexibility and reduced commuting time it offers. Of note, some technologies, such as e-mail, may be more stressful for workers (compared to face-to-face meetings or hallway conversations), since communications accumulate regardless of time or place, making workers feel mentally taxed and less in control (Barley, Meyerson, and Grodal 2011). In light of these pressures, countries such as France have a "right to disconnect" law which allows workers to turn off electronic devices outside of regular working hours— something the Canadian government is now considering (Press 2018).

CONTEMPORARY THEORETICAL PERSPECTIVES

Just as the rise of capitalism and industrialization sparked theoretical analyses from early sociologists, such as Marx, Weber, and Durkheim (as discussed in Chapter 1), ongoing economic change has captured the attention of more recent thinkers. Casting an eye over a diverse range of theorists—for example, Jürgen Habermas, Michel Foucault, Pierre Bourdieu, Ulrich Beck, Zygmunt Bauman, and Anthony Giddens—we see that many have engaged with central work-related themes, such as *power, control, inequality, consensus,* and *conflict*—albeit in new ways (Korczynski, Hodson, and Edwards 2006; Hancock 2009). Thus, despite suggestions that sociology's attention has shifted largely to questions of identity, culture, and consumption, it appears that sociological thinking about work and economic issues remains alive and well. Below, we offer a brief and selective sampling of contemporary ideas; those interested in reading further can consult a number of valuable books and discussions.[17] In later chapters, we examine additional theories on specific topics, for instance, feminist theory as it addresses gender and work (see Chapters 6 and 7).

Michel Foucault on Surveillance and Self-Discipline at Work

One writer who has influenced contemporary thinking about work and organizations is Michel Foucault (1926–84), a French theorist often associated with postmodernist thought (though Foucault himself did not claim that label) (Burrell 2006). While Foucault's primary interests were not explicitly on work and economic matters—but rather, psychiatry, medicine, the penal system, sexuality, and knowledge—a unifying interest was in understanding how power operates. Foucault's ideas on power are distinct; rather than viewing power as a resource wielded by individuals or social groups, he argued that power was diffused, operating through discourse and knowledge to "produce" the reality of everyday life. His interest, then, was not in the "organization of production," but in the "production of organization" (Burrell 2006: 168). Not surprisingly, some scholars have found his concepts of *power, discipline,* and *surveillance* highly relevant, using them to study issues of team work, electronic surveillance, and human resource management practices (Burrell 2006; Townley 1994).[18]

One of Foucault's most important contributions comes from *Discipline and Punish* (1975), a historical examination of penal systems. Using the metaphor of the Panopticon, a prison design conceived by Jeremy Bentham (1748–1832), an English philosopher and social reformer, Foucault develops his ideas about how power operates in society. Physically, the Panopticon is circular in design, with a central watchtower, surrounded by concentric circles of cells (with windows facing outward only). Because all prisoners fall under the *gaze* of a single guard, the Panopticon thus maximizes external *surveillance*. Moreover, because prisoners cannot see the watchtower or one another, they do not know if or when they are being observed. They thus control their own behaviour, becoming (to use Foucault's language) *self-disciplining*.

Applying these ideas to contemporary organizations, writers such as Sewell and Wilkinson (1992) examine teamwork (discussed in Chapter 9), showing how worker control is maintained through peer surveillance and self-discipline. Other writers use Foucault's ideas on *discourse* and the *body*. For instance, Townley (1993) shows how human resource management (HRM) can be seen as a discourse of what is acceptable and unacceptable at work, thus producing workers who can be measured, analyzed, and compared against an ideal. HRM practices such as job descriptions and performance appraisals operate to rank, discipline, and sequester workers. Studies of specific types of work, such as secretaries (Pringle 1989), show how HRM systems emphasizing "service with a smile" bring the body into the service of the corporation (Burrell 2006).

Pierre Bourdieu: Work, Practice, and Social Reproduction

Another influential thinker in discussions of work and social inequality is Pierre Bourdieu (1930–2002), a French anthropologist and sociologist, and contemporary of Foucault's. Bourdieu's work is equally wide-ranging, but focuses more explicitly on work-related themes. Early in his career, Bourdieu carried out fieldwork in Algeria, leading him to move away from a purely philosophical approach to embrace sociological and anthropological methods. This, and subsequent work on education and social reproduction, as well as capital, class, and cultural distinctions, have led to many of his ideas being used to examine issues of workplace practices, organizational culture, and economic and social inequality (Everett 2002; Lizardo 2012).

Like Foucault, Bourdieu was interested in how power operates in society. But he came to his own distinct point of view. His most important concepts are *field*, *habitus*, and *capital*, which developed over the course of his career. *Fields* are sites of structured social relationships where struggles occur for position and access to resources (Everett 2002). *Habitus* is best described as the dispositions, lifestyles, and values of social groups that are acquired as part of belonging to that collectivity. Applying these ideas, we can think of workplaces and organizations as fields, where individuals earn a living and build relationships, reputations, and careers. Likewise, we can see habitus as the common sense idea of how things are done in a particular work setting. For instance, studies show how workers as diverse as servers at McDonalds and litigators in law firms come to understand expected workplace behaviours (Leidner 1993; Pierce 1995). Finally, *capital* is central for determining a person's position in the field and for establishing habitus (or what can be thought as the rules of order).

For Bourdieu, there are several types of capital. *Economic capital* (material wealth such as cash, land, and other assets) is the most fundamental; however, it can be converted into other forms of capital—specifically, *social capital*, *cultural capital*, and *symbolic capital* (Bourdieu 1986; Everett 2002). *Social capital* involves relationships and networks between individuals that generate resources. Here we can think of senior executives who work and golf together, exchanging information about business opportunities. *Cultural capital* involves cultural facility and knowledge, and ranges from formal credentials and degrees (institutionalized cultural capital) to possessions such as books, paintings, and music (objectified cultural capital) to ways of speaking, dressing, and presenting the self (embodied cultural capital). In some professions, such knowledge can be critical for fitting in and moving ahead. Finally, *symbolic capital* comes through honours or recognition, such as winning an Oscar or a Grammy. Together, these forms of capital operate to position individuals within a society and within the workplace.

Scholars have taken Bourdieu's ideas in many directions. For instance, Bauder (2003) shows how the *cultural capital* of immigrant workers coming to Canada is devalued, leading them into lower-tier work. Likewise, Ross-Smith and Huppatz (2010) show how female managers use *gendered capital* to build their careers. In later chapters we return to Bourdieu, discussing some of his ideas further.

Ulrich Beck: The Risk Society

A final thinker who is important for understanding contemporary economic trends is Ulrich Beck (1944–2015), a German social theorist born towards the end of World War II. Along with other prominent social theorists, including

Anthony Giddens, Zygmunt Bauman, and Scott Lash, Beck has argued that recent decades have seen a transition from a modern society to a risk society, where individuals increasingly navigate more complex and risky work and life trajectories.[19] Central to these changes, as outlined in his book *Risk Society: Towards a New Modernity* (1992), Beck sees two interrelated processes. The first involves the shifting relationship between capital and labour that dramatically alters labour markets and economies. The second is greater *reflexivity* and *individualization*, creating more varied paths through the once predictable life course from childhood to career, marriage, parenthood, and retirement.

With respect to the economic changes, Beck highlights—as have other writers—a shift away from full-time, secure, career opportunities toward more flexible labour markets, offering part-time, temporary jobs, with poorer pay, career prospects, and security. Equally important is growing global competition for jobs, heightened skill and credential requirements, and the erosion of traditional social safety nets (e.g., unemployment insurance), along with a decline of state- and employer-sponsored training (as evidenced by rising tuition and decreased workplace training). Bundled together, these changes operate both to heighten economic risk and to download it onto workers—thus individualizing risk. In Western economies, Beck argues, the result is to dramatically erode the quality of work, bringing it in line with poorer countries. Describing this in *The Brave New World of Work*, Beck (2000: 1) states:

> Equally remarkable is the new similarity in how paid work itself is shaping up in the so-called first world and the so-called third world; the spread of temporary and insecure employment, discontinuity, and loose informality into Western societies that have hitherto been the bastion of full employment. The social structure in the heartlands of the West is thus coming to resemble the patchwork quilt of the South, characterized by diversity, unclarity and insecurity in people's work and life.

Building on Beck's work, studies have explored questions about growing risk and insecurity in a variety of settings, from youth labour markets to freelance and manual workers (Mythen 2005; Fevre 2007). While some see great merit in Beck's ideas, others suggest they overstate the degree of change. In Chapters 3 and 4, we will have some opportunity to consider their merit in the Canadian context.

CONCLUSION

From the managerial revolution to postindustrialism, globalization, and the rise of new economic regions such as China and India, we have covered many significant developments in this chapter. Our discussion has focused on trends from the 1950s to the present, exploring how new technologies, trade agreements, globalized production, and changing modes of work and family organization have reshaped economies and the nature of daily work. We have also considered how some contemporary theorists, specifically Foucault, Bourdieu, and Beck, add to our understanding of economic and workplace change.

Our overview highlights some key changes over the past half century or more. Much larger workplaces, new technologies, a more complex division of labour, growth in white-collar occupations, and a new class of managers were among the changes observed as industrial capitalism matured in 20th-century Canada. Once again, these changes generated new ideas and concerns about the impact of technology, social inequality, skills, knowledge, and labour–management cooperation and control. But the optimistic predictions of reduced inequality and conflict in a postindustrial era have not been well supported by the data. Instead, as we will see in Chapters 3 and 4, contemporary employment trends raise questions about a growing gap between more and less advantaged workers—with risk and insecurity being distributed unequally, both on a national and a global scale.

We have also highlighted a number of global economic and technological forces now re-shaping employment patterns. Like other advanced capitalist societies, Canada has become a service-dominated economy. New technologies are having a major impact on both the quantity and the quality of work in the Canadian labour market, as are processes of industrial and labour market restructuring. The eventual outcomes of these trends are still unclear. We will also have to confront the limits to growth, as environmental sustainability becomes a pressing global problem (World Commission on Environment and Development 1987; Gomez and Foot 2013). We may see a general improvement in the standard of living and the quality of working life, or the benefits may go primarily to those who already have better jobs, thus contributing to increased polarization in the labour market and in society as a whole. In subsequent chapters, we will return frequently to these fundamental questions.

DISCUSSION QUESTIONS

1. What is meant by the logic of industrialism thesis? Using three countries discussed in the text, how would you evaluate the merits of this idea?
2. What is a postindustrial society? Based on material you have read in this chapter, would you characterize Canada as postindustrial? Why? Why not?
3. Drawing on your reading in this chapter, discuss how free trade, globalization, and industrial restructuring are reshaping the Canadian economy. What do you see as the most important changes taking place?
4. What are some new types of work that have emerged in Canada? What has led to their development?
5. In your opinion, how do the contemporary theories of Beck, Foucault, and Bourdieu explain current workplace trends in Canada and other countries?

ADDITIONAL RESOURCES

WORK AT THE MOVIES

- *El Contrato* (directed by Min Sook Lee, 2003, 51:11 minutes). This National Film Board documentary outlines the experiences and working conditions of people from Central Mexico who migrate each year to tend Ontario's tomato farms. It is available through the National Film Board of Canada: http://www.nfb.ca/film/el_contrato.
- *The Best Exotic Marigold Hotel* (directed by John Madden, 2011, 124 minutes). This British comedy about retirees in India explores a wide range of themes, including the globalization of call-centre work, retirement, and health care.
- *For Man Must Work or the End of Work* (directed by Jean-Claude Burger, 2000, 52:01 minutes). Debates over the potential impact of globalization, economic restructuring, and technological change are explored in this NFB film, available through the National Film Board of Canada: http://www.nfb.ca/film/for_man_must_work.
- *Bombay Calling* (directed by Ben Addelman and Samir Mallal, 2006, 70:14 minutes). This NFB documentary explores globalization in India, focusing on the call-centre industry. It is available through the National Film Board of Canada: https://www.nfb.ca/film/bombay_calling/.

- *The End of the Line* (*New York Times* Magazine). This photo essay documents the recent closing of the GM plant in the Lordstown, Ohio, and the workers and families impacted by this change. Available at https://www.nytimes.com/interactive/2019/05/01/magazine/lordstown-general-motors-plant.html [retrieved May 4, 2019].

SOUNDS OF WORK

- "Elf's Lament" (Barenaked Ladies). A lively take on globalization and working conditions in the run-up to Christmas consumption.
- "My Home Town" (Bruce Springsteen). Springsteen's song laments the impacts of economic downturn for small-town America.
- "Six Days on the Road" (Dave Dudley). Dudley sings about the realities of mobile (trucking) work and the difficulties it creates for balancing work and family.
- "On the Move to Fort McMurray" (*Ideas with Paul Kennedy*, CBC podcast, November 22, 2013). The episode looks into employment-related geographical mobility in Fort McMurray, Alberta. Available at https://www.cbc.ca/radio/ideas/on-the-move-to-fort-mcmurray-1.2913681.

NOTES

1. See Carroll (2004), Grabb (2009), Kaya and Martin (2016), and Reich (2015).
2. Additional perspectives on the postindustrial society are reviewed by Krishnan Kumar (1995), Clement and Myles (1994), and Nelson (1995).
3. The managerial revolution perspective (Burnham 1941; Berle and Means 1968) was developed earlier, during an era when corporate concentration in North America was proceeding rapidly and when concerns about the excessive power of the corporate elite were being publicly debated (Reich 1991: 38).
4. See Lowe (2000: Chapter 4) for a discussion of industrial restructuring and the rise of the new economy in Canada. See also Pupo and Thomas (2010) for critical perspectives on restructuring, globalization, and the new economy.
5. Schumpeter's views are discussed in Bluestone and Harrison (1982: 9) in their highly influential book on deindustrialization in the United States.
6. Drache and Gertler (1991: 12–13). See Heinzl (1997) on Nike's closure of the Bauer factory. See also Mahon's (1984) analysis of restructuring in the Canadian textile industry.

7. For information and reports on globalization and labour rights, see the Maquila Solidarity Network (http://en.maquilasolidarity.org), Clean Clothes Campaign (http://www.cleanclothes.org), and the International Labor Organization (ILO) at http://www.ilo.org.

8. See Orme (1996: 13). Evaluations of NAFTA continue to offer widely divergent views. For earlier assessments, see Arsen, Wilson, and Zoninsein (1996) and Bognanno and Ready (1993). For more recent assessments, see Scott, Salas, and Campbell (2006), Alexandroff, Hufbauer, and Lucenti (2008), Schott and Huffbauer (2007), and Kay (2011).

9. See World Bank (2001), Holzer (2000), and Hsiung (1996) for accounts of economic development in the region. The argument about the critical role of a Weberian form of government bureaucracy is presented by Evans and Rauch (1999).

10. Central to China's development has been a high level of foreign direct investment within manufacturing in the special economic zones. For example, in 2007, foreign investment accounted for 57 percent of all Chinese exports (*Economist* 2009; Whyte 2009). For valuable accounts of China's economic development, see Guthrie (2006), Sharman (2009), Whyte (2009), and Winters and Yusuf (2007).

11. See Saul (1995) for a critique of this ideology.

12. See MacDonald (2014) for a discussion of the impact of neo-liberalism on labour–management relations in Canada and the United States. See Bamber, Lansbury, and Wailes (2011) for a comparative analysis.

13. For valuable discussions and reviews of interactive service work, or frontline service work, see McDowell (2009), Korczynski and Macdonald (2009), and Bélanger and Edwards (2013), among others. On caring work, see Ehrenreich and Hochschild (2002), Zimmerman et al. (2006), Yeates (2009), and Anderson and Hughes (2010). For helpful reviews and discussions of emotional labour, see Leidner (1993), Bolton (2005, 2009), Bolton and Boyd (2003), Brook (2009), Cranford and Miller (2013), Grandey, Diefendorff, and Rupp (2013), Lopez (2006), Payne (2009), and Wharton (1993).

14. For early examples of work on this topic, see Fuller and Smith (1991) and Leidner (1993). For more recent discussions, see Lopez (2010), Bolton and Houlihan (2010), and others in a special issue of *Work and Occupations*; Bélanger and Edwards (2013); and a special issue of *Work, Employment and Society*, edited by Korczynski (2013).

15. On transnational caregiving, see, for example, Ehrenreich and Hochschild (2002); Spitzer et al. (2003); Parreñas (2001); Torres et al. (2012); Yeates (2009); Zimmerman et al. (2006). For discussions on temporary foreign workers in Canada, see Thomas (2010); Fuller (2011); Taylor, Foster, and Cambre (2012);

and Foster and Barnetson (2012). Elliott and Urry's (2010) *Mobile Lives* offers interesting discussions of professional work, among other topics.

16. A feature on mobile workers and the oil sands can be found on the CBC Radio program *Ideas with Paul Kennedy*, at https://www.cbc.ca/radio/ideas/on-the-move-to-fort-mcmurray-1.2913681. The episode highlights one of many projects on mobile workers in Canada undertaken through the *On the Move Project*: see http://www.onthemovepartnership.ca. For a personal account of mobile work, see Wood (2013).

17. For students who want to know more about contemporary social theory, as well as work, organization, and economic life, we suggest reading the collection of articles in *Social Theory at Work*, edited by Marek Korczynski, Randy Hodson, and Paul Edwards (2006). Additional insightful discussions of work-related theorizing are provided by Hancock (2009), who discusses critical theory traditions, and by Burrell (2006), who discusses Foucault's reception by sociologists of work and impact on the sociology of work, labour process theory, and organizational studies.

18. Despite Foucault's relevance to work and organizations, Burrell (2006) argues that his ideas, as well as general currents in postmodern theory, have been taken up only selectively, with some sociologists of work remaining resistant, uninterested, or highly critical of the ideas.

19. In addition to Beck, other theorists have developed compatible ideas. For instance, see Zygmunt Bauman, who develops the idea of "liquid modernity" (Bauman 2000; Clegg and Baumeler 2010), and Scott Lash and John Urry, who theorize about "the end of organized capitalism" (Lash and Urry 1987, 2013).

3

CANADIAN EMPLOYMENT TRENDS

"I think one of the new things that is part of this new economy is . . . the rise of part-time work, and as far as a pool of part-time workers, I mean students are sort of the epitome of that."

Source: Queen's University student. Steven Tufts and John Holmes. (2010). "Student Workers and the 'New Economy' of Mid-Sized Cities: The Cases of Peterborough and Kingston, Ontario." In Norene J. Pupo and Mark P. Thomas, eds., *Interrogating the New Economy: Restructuring Work in the 21st Century.* Toronto: University of Toronto Press, p. 139.

"I'm in a decent job now . . . a good paying job with benefits. I like what I do and I'm not worried about getting laid off every 6 months. I'm glad to get out of the auto industry."

Source: Former autoworker. Sam Vrankulj. (2012). *Finding Their Way: Second Round Report on the CAW Worker Adjustment Tracking Project,* p. 30. http://www.caw.ca/assets/images/phase-Two-Tracking-study.pdf.

"I call it a 'factory of voices.' That's all it is. Instead of assembling parts for the cars, you're just processing people or processing calls—a 'factory of voices.' Everybody is sitting there in their little stalls talking and producing customer service."

Source: Call centre worker. Norene J. Pupo and Andrea Noack. (2010). "Dialling for Service: Transforming the Public-Sector Workplace in Canada." In Norene J. Pupo and Mark P. Thomas, eds., *Interrogating the New Economy: Restructuring Work in the 21st Century.* Toronto: University of Toronto Press, p. 124.

"I wouldn't recommend the driving industry to anyone anymore. It used to be very good. Now you kill yourself. You have to work thirteen, fourteen hours. Usually if you have family you cannot work that long. It used to be very good hours. . . . Now you have to work six or seven days, twelve to fourteen hours. . . . Uber, Lyft, the others, they take too much."

Source: New York Uber driver. Alex Rosenblat. (2018). *Uberland: How Algorithms are Rewriting the Rules of Work.* Oakland, CA: University of California Press, p. 169.

INTRODUCTION

Scan through any story on work-related topics in Canada on social media, in your local newspaper, or in the *Globe and Mail*. You'll likely come across articles based on labour force statistics collected by Statistics Canada or by some other public- or private-sector data collection agency. Most common are the unemployment rates, updated monthly. But you will also find stories on a wide array of themes, such as youth employment, minimum wages, gender pay gaps, retirement patterns, and artificial intelligence and the future of work.

Understanding these labour force statistics is important both for learning more about the Canadian labour market and for developing statistical literacy. In a society in which we are regularly bombarded with the latest figures on one social trend or another, and in which false claims are increasingly common, it is important to have a solid understanding of the definition and source of these numbers, and even more important, to be able to interpret them critically. Hence, we will discuss these trends with reference to some of the broad theories of social and economic change discussed in Chapters 1 and 2. At the same time, this statistical overview will provide us with the background needed to evaluate the ideas discussed in later chapters about competing theories of labour markets.

We begin by outlining key demographic factors shaping the workforce, such as aging, immigration, and rising education levels. We then discuss labour force participation trends and Canada's occupational and industrial structures, emphasizing the rise of the service economy and the emergence of new occupations. As we will see, Canada has a dynamic, ever-changing labour market, shaped by the rise and fall of key industries, as well as specific regional forces. In Chapter 4, we delve into related issues of job quality, working hours, and unemployment.

DATA SOURCES

A major data source is the Canadian Census, conducted every five years by Statistics Canada. Because it is an enumeration of the entire population, the Census provides the most complete and reliable picture of the Canadian labour market. In this chapter we examine data from the most recent 2016 Census, as well as earlier census data to focus on historical trends.[1]

A second useful source is the monthly Labour Force Survey, also conducted by Statistics Canada. Unlike the Census, which attempts to cover a range of topics, this random sample survey is designed to collect only work-related information and so provides much more detail. Because the survey is done every month, information is always updated. To obtain precise estimates of the labour market activities of Canadians ages 15 and older, a large sample is needed. Approximately 54,000 households (most providing information on more than one adult living in that household) are included in the sample.[2] Households remain part of the sample for six months before being replaced.

The Labour Force Survey provides, for example, monthly estimates of unemployment and labour force participation rates, and descriptions of industries and occupations experiencing job growth or decline.[3] Periodically, more detailed surveys, designed to study specific work-related topics or current concerns, are added to the Labour Force Survey. Examples include student summer employment, self-employment, involuntary part-time work, and job search behaviour. Many of the statistics cited in this chapter are obtained from this useful source.[4]

THE DEMOGRAPHIC CONTEXT OF LABOUR MARKET CHANGE

Whether our focus is on the labour market today or 10 to 20 years in the future, *demographic shifts* (population changes) under way in Canadian society undeniably set some basic parameters. Of all the employment trends we will consider in this chapter, those related to the demographic composition of the labour force are perhaps the only ones we can confidently project into the future. While economists debate whether the unemployment rate may rise or decline next year, demographers (who specialize in studying the structure and dynamics of the population) can quite accurately predict birthrates, life expectancy, population growth, and related trends. Three trends in particular deserve our attention: workforce aging, cultural diversity, and educational attainment.

Workforce Aging

In their best-selling book, *Boom, Bust and Echo*, David Foot and Daniel Stoffman claimed that "demographics explain about two-thirds of everything." Although we might dispute that claim, we do agree that Canada's demographic trends influence many economic and social changes.[5] Foremost among these demographic factors is *population aging*, which has significant implications for job opportunities, pensions, work values, organizational structures, and economic growth (Gomez and Foot 2013; Foot et al. 2015).

The *baby-boom generation*, born between 1946 and 1965, is the largest generation in Canadian history. Writing about them in *Born at the Right Time*, historian Doug Owram observes, "Economics, politics, education, and family life would all have been considerably different without the vast demographic upsurge of births after the Second World War" (1996: xiv). As baby boomers have moved through the life course, they have left few institutions unchanged—from a revolution in popular music in the 1960s, to the rapid expansion of postsecondary institutions in the 1970s, to debates over mandatory retirement in the 2000s.

Sharply declining birth rates over the past decades, however, have resulted in smaller birth cohorts (e.g., Gen-X, Millennials, Gen-Z) following in the wake of the baby boom. The huge and slowly aging baby boom cohort has significantly affected their career opportunities. The baby boomers entered the workforce when the economy was still expanding, and many obtained good jobs. Smaller cohorts following them have been less fortunate, since higher unemployment and global economic uncertainties in the 1990s and 2000s have frequently led to layoffs, not hiring.

At the same time, many baby boomers hit *career plateaus*. Because many work organizations are built on a career pyramid, success is defined in terms of climbing a ladder that has room for fewer people on each higher rung. But with growing numbers of older workers, the competition for the few top jobs has intensified. For younger workers experiencing difficulty finding satisfactory entry-level jobs, this may not seem a serious problem. But for older, long-term employees who have come to view personal success as upward movement, career blockages, as well as growing risk and insecurity, can be unsettling (Lippmann 2008; Smith 2002).

Figure 3.1 documents the workforce aging process by profiling the *age distribution* of labour force participants in 1976 and 2018. Note the decline in the relative proportion of teenagers (15 to 19 years) and young adults (20 to 24 years) over the three decades. Compare this with the increased size over time of the cohorts who are 35 to 44 years old, 45 to 54 years old, 55 to 64 years old, and 65 years and older. While we saw a marked trend toward *early retirement* in the 1980s and 1990s, because of labour market restructuring and downsizing,

FIGURE 3.1   Age Distribution of the Labour Force by Gender, Canada, 1976 and 2018

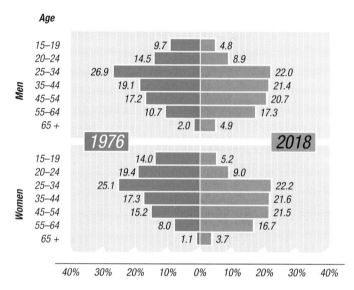

Source: Statistics Canada, Labour Force Characteristics by Sex and Detailed Age Group, Annual, Table 14-10-0327-01. https://www150.statcan.gc.ca/t1/tbl1/en/tv.action?pid=1410032701

this trend began to reverse in the 2000s (Belanger et al. 2016). The proportion of 55- to 64-year-olds and those 65 and older in the workforce has increased, as growing numbers of boomers reach their late 50s or early 60s (Fields et al. 2017; Belanger et al. 2016). According to the 2016 Census, over 4.2 million people ages 55 and older were in the workforce, representing 21.3 percent of total employment and up from 11.3 percent in the 1976 Census. Statistics Canada predicts that by 2026, 40 percent of workers will be 55 years and older (Fields et al. 2017). Basically, the late-20th-century idea of retirement as an abrupt exit from the workforce is being redefined as more boomers seek opportunities to remain in the workforce.

Looking back over history, in 1921 only 5 percent of Canadians were 65 years of age and older. Over the next 50 years, this figure grew slowly to 8 percent. Then the aging of the Canadian population began to accelerate, and by 2000, almost 13 percent of Canadians were senior citizens. Today's seniors are healthier and have a much longer life expectancy than previous cohorts of seniors. Looking ahead, by 2036, about one person in four will be 65 years of age or older.[6] The relative size of the working-age population that funds government old-age security programs through payroll contributions will shrink considerably. The earliest baby boomers, now in their early 70s, have entered their retirement years. While some may delay retirement—or "unretire" by returning to paid work (McDaniel et al. 2015)—the long-term effects of boomer aging on the labour market will continue to be profound.

Pensions have been a prominent public concern in many industrialized countries, including Canada, as have issues of mandatory retirement and expected skill shortages (Belanger et al. 2016). Will the Canada/Quebec Pension Plan (CPP/QPP), one of Canada's main *social safety nets*, be able to support all current and future retirees? Will today's youth have to pay more to cover the costs? Or, as an alternative solution, will Canadians have to wait until they are a few years older than 65 to begin collecting CPP/QPP or Old Age Security (OAS)? This is a difficult political issue. For example, the plans of Stephen Harper's Conservative government to extend the age of eligibility for CPP and OAS were over-turned in 2015 by the Trudeau Liberal government (Taylor 2019)

Will employer-sponsored pension plans make up the difference? The answer is probably not. As we show in Chapter 4, access to such plans has never been widespread and now is in decline. As for personal savings for retirement, according to Statistics Canada, just 37.1 percent of Canadians were covered by a registered retirement plan (RRP) in 2018, down from 42.8 percent in 1995.[7] How to balance the needs of retiring baby boomers against the needs of people still in or joining the Canadian workforce remains a big policy challenge. One way that growing numbers of older Canadians are responding to these uncertainties is by waiting longer to retire (Belanger et al. 2016).

What about the impact for younger workers? It is reasonable to expect workforce aging to open up some opportunities for young workers (Easterlin 1980). Indeed, a number of occupations in Canada have a high presence of older workers (age 55 plus), sparking concerns over future labour shortages in these areas. Examples of occupations with one-third or more workers aged 55 years and up include senior managers in health and construction, bus drivers and taxi drivers, farm managers, fishers, accounting technicians, and realtors.[8] Who will fill these jobs, especially in blue-collar areas, when there is growing emphasis on gaining postsecondary education? Consider, as well, the relatively small size of the 15-to-19-year-old and 20-to-24-year-old cohorts in today's labour force (Figure 3.1). As more and more baby boomers retire, labour shortages in some sectors and regions may be a concern. While some argue that skill shortages will not be pressing until the 2030s (McDaniel et al. 2015), population aging will undoubtedly be a steady driver of change.

Immigration and Greater Workforce Diversity

For centuries, Canada has been a country of immigrants, with successive governments tailoring immigration policy to labour market needs. Indeed, immigration has been central to the processes of colonization and nation building we discussed in Chapter 2. Historically, when economic expansion required more workers, immigration was strongly encouraged. There have been times when immigration levels were considerably higher than they are today. For example, following a decade of rapid settlement in the western provinces, 22.3 percent of Canadians were immigrants in 1920 (Statistics Canada 2017b). Alternatively, during times of economic distress such as the Great Depression, immigration was sharply curtailed. Along with economic factors, immigration policies have been shaped by other demographic trends. In recent decades, as Canadian birthrates have fallen below *replacement level* (the number of births required to maintain a steady population), immigration has been used to compensate.

Canada today has one of the highest proportion of immigrants among G7 nations, with 21.9 percent of the population having been born outside the country (Statistics Canada 2017b). The federal government's quotas continue to notch up, from 240,000 to 265,000 immigrants per year (less than 1% of the total population) in the 2010s, to a goal of 340,000 in 2020.[9] In 2017, Canada took in 286,000 permanent residents (IRCC 2018). Despite concerns by some that immigrants take jobs away from those born in Canada, research shows that this is rarely the case. Immigrants frequently create their own jobs or take jobs that others do not want, as we discuss in Chapter 5. Or they are selected to match shortages of workers in specific occupational categories. With anticipated labour shortages because of population aging in coming years, there is much interest by federal and provincial governments in ensuring that immigrants' skills are recognized and properly used.

Until quite recently, there was far less *visible* diversity among immigrants to Canada. In 1971, over 61.6 percent of recent immigrants came from Europe. Today, the source countries have dramatically changed. Between 1991 and 2001, over half of immigrants came from Asia, with top countries including China,

India, Pakistan, and the Philippines. Just 20 percent of immigrants came from Europe (Statistics Canada 2003). In the 2000s and 2010s, this trend continued. The 2016 census shows that Asia is now the birth country for approximately 70 percent of recent immigrants. Just 11.6 percent came from European countries. The top 10 countries for recent immigrants are the Philippines, India, China—which together account for over one-third of the total—followed by Iran, Pakistan, the United States, Syria, the United Kingdom, France, and South Korea (Statistics Canada 2017b: 5; IRCC 2018). Why the shift? Canadian immigration policies no longer favour European immigrants but, more important, the demand to immigrate to Canada has declined in Europe while it has increased dramatically elsewhere. Consequently, more immigrants are members of visible minority groups with distinctive cultural backgrounds.

According to the 2016 Census, 22.3 percent of the Canadian population identified themselves as a member of a *visible minority* group (excluding Indigenous peoples). Of this number, only 30 percent were born in Canada (Statistics Canada 2017b: 6). In large urban centres, such as Toronto and Vancouver, visible minorities now comprise just over half of the population (51.5 percent and 51.6 percent, respectively).[10] Together, three main groups account for nearly two-thirds of all visible minorities in Canada: South Asian Canadians make up 25.1 percent of all visible minorities, Chinese Canadians compose about 21 percent, and 15.6 percent identify as Black (Statistics Canada 2017b). Recent estimates suggest that, with current immigration patterns, the proportion of visible minorities in the Canadian population will increase to approximately 30 percent by 2036 (Statistics Canada 2017b).

Equally important for the diverse nature of the Canadian labour market are the nearly 1.7 million Indigenous peoples (First Nations, Métis, and Inuit) who make up nearly 5 percent of Canada's population (Statistics Canada 2017c). First Nations people, who comprise 57 percent of this group, are the first inhabitants of what is now known as Canada. Highly diverse, they represent over 600 unique communities, from the Salish and Haida on the West Coast, to the Mi'kmaq on the East Coast, and the Blackfoot, Plains Cree, and Algonquin in between, to name only a few. The Métis, who are of mixed First Nation and European ancestry, and comprise nearly 600,000 people, reside primarily in Western Canada and Ontario. Inuit, original inhabitants of the Northern Artic, are smaller in number (65,000 people). Finally, another 40,000 people claim multiple or other Indigenous identities (Statistics Canada 2017c).[11]

The Indigenous population is growing rapidly, at about four times the rate of the non-Indigenous population in Canada. This figure will increase in the decades ahead, given the younger age profile of Indigenous Canadians—a median age of 32 years compared to 41 years for the non-Indigenous population (Statistics Canada 2017c). Immigrants are also younger, on average, so both Indigenous peoples and immigrants will make up a growing share of the workforce as older Canadians retire.[12] As with the immigrant population, the Indigenous population is not spread evenly across the country. Over half of the First Nations are located in Western Canada, compared to just 30% of the non-Indigenous population. Over 80 percent of the Métis live in Ontario and the Western provinces, with the majority (two-thirds) living in metropolitan areas. Most of the Inuit population (roughly three-quarters) resides in Inuit Nunangat, which spans the westernmost Arctic to Newfoundland and Labrador's eastern shores (Statistics Canada 2017c).

A Better-Educated Workforce

Canadians are also becoming increasingly well educated, a trend that has fundamentally changed the character of the labour force. Figure 3.2 shows the dramatic change in *educational attainment* of the labour force between 1975 and 2018. In 1975, 66 percent of females and 68 percent of males in the labour force had only a high-school education or less. Very few (only 7 percent and 10 percent, respectively) had a university degree. In the more than 40 years since, large numbers of both women and men obtained postsecondary credentials. In 2018, roughly 30 percent of labour force participants had a university degree (33.7 percent for women and 27.6 percent for men).

Rising educational attainment has been the backdrop for a debate on the role of education in a rapidly changing and increasingly global and technological environment. In fact, many analysts argue that a well-educated workforce is a nation's key resource in today's global marketplace (Munro 2019). Business and government have argued that additional education and training, and an overhaul of the education system to make it more job-relevant, will help Canada become more competitive internationally.[13] The latest variant of this perspective is found in the concepts of *learning organizations* and or *lifelong or continuing learning* (see Chapter 9).[14] Essentially, these refer to ongoing education, both formal and informal, throughout one's life that takes place

FIGURE 3.2 Educational Attainment of the Labour Force by Gender, Canada, 1975 and 2018

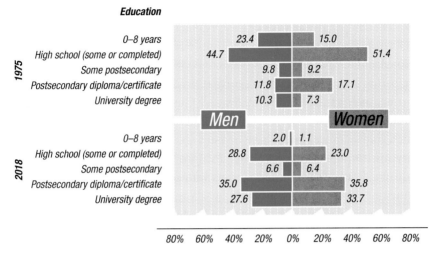

Education

	Men	Women
1975		
0–8 years	23.4	15.0
High school (some or completed)	44.7	51.4
Some postsecondary	9.8	9.2
Postsecondary diploma/certificate	11.8	17.1
University degree	10.3	7.3
2018		
0–8 years	2.0	1.1
High school (some or completed)	28.8	23.0
Some postsecondary	6.6	6.4
Postsecondary diploma/certificate	35.0	35.8
University degree	27.6	33.7

80% 60% 40% 20% 0% 20% 40% 60% 80%

Source: Statistics Canada, Labour Force Indicators by Educational Attainment, Table 14-10-0118-01. https://www150.statcan .gc.ca/t1/tbl1/en/tv.action?pid=141001180

in educational institutions and at work and home. Educators, parents, and students have responded by raising concerns over the rising costs of education and whether closer links between education and the economy mean too much business influence over what is taught at all levels of the education system.

By international standards, Canadians are well educated in terms of post-secondary credentials and enrollment levels.[15] Nonetheless, there is more to developing a nation's human resources than the acquisition of formal education. Currently educational systems aim to develop more skilled, flexible, and enterprising labour force participants. Basic literacy and numeracy, along with other essential skills, are lacking in small pockets of the workforce.[16] But work-related training is not the responsibility of the education system alone. Canada has a mediocre record of employer-sponsored workplace training (Munro 2019). According to the 2016 General Social Survey (GSS),[17] 41.7 percent of Canadians had access to formal training at work in the past 12 months that was paid for by their employer. Access to training is higher for employees who are university educated (46.9 percent), union members (51.0 percent), and in large firms with 500+ employees (50.9 percent). Large gaps in training exist between young workers ages 15 to 24 (45.6 percent) and workers ages 65 years and up (23.0 percent). Much smaller gaps are found between full-time and part-time employees (42.2 percent versus 38.7 percent) and men and women (43.3 percent versus 39.9 percent).

Recent comparative analysis by the Organisation for Economic Co-operation and Development (OECD 2019) on adult training (which includes employer-sponsored and self-funded learning) also finds about 4 in 10 working Canadians participating in some kind of training (OECD 2019). Compared to other countries, such as the United States and Germany, Canada's participation levels are average at best (OECD 2019; Munro et al. 2014). Over the past two decades, Canadian employers have invested less in training, expecting postsecondary institutions to fulfill this role (Munro 2019: 17–18). In addition, as already noted, it is well educated workers who access the most training, further accentuating labour market inequalities. Illustrating this, the OECD (2019) finds *participation rates* in adult learning for high-skilled workers to be about 40 percent higher than for low-skilled workers. Yet there is only a 20 percent gap in their "willingness to train". In short, low-skilled workers are interested in training but face significant barriers, most notably a lack of time (work-related and personal) and costs for self-directed learning (OECD 2019: 251, 254).[18]

The assumption underlying the education and training solution to economic growth is that our workforce is not sufficiently educated and trained; yet the above discussion suggests that there is more to the problem. For one thing, while unemployment is higher among the less educated, a considerable number of Canada's unemployed are well educated. In addition, many Canadians are in jobs that require little education or training. For example, when asked in the 2016 General Social Survey (GSS), nearly one in five (18 percent) Canadian workers indicated they felt *overqualified* for their current job. Feelings of over-qualification were considerably higher for university educated (23.7 percent), part-time (23.7 percent), and temporary workers (26.0 percent).[19] This mismatch between education and job requirements is often referred to as *underemployment*. Young Canadians are more likely to be underemployed, as are well-educated new immigrants.[20] Beyond subjective assessments of under-employment, another approach compares the education attainment of workers to the educational requirements of their job. Statistics Canada finds roughly 18 percent of university-educated women and men in jobs requiring high school or less (Uppal and LaRochelle-Cote 2014). Not surprisingly, research also shows those with an education–job mismatch earn lower wages (Yuen 2010).

Underemployment highlights the need to go beyond the supply side of the education–job equation to examine how job content and skill requirements could be upgraded—in short, asking how *skill utilization* and the demand for educated labour can be improved (Livingstone 2017). Clearly, there are deeper problems in the structure of our economy, and concerted efforts by government, the private sector, organized labour, and professional associations are needed to address them. As two American sociologists concluded about the United States: "The problem is a shortage of good jobs to a greater extent than it is inadequate training and development" (Bellin and Miller 1990: 187).[21] With new technologies set to transform many more jobs in coming years, the issue of job quality will only become more important (Autor 2015).

LABOUR FORCE PARTICIPATION TRENDS

With a better demographic understanding of the workforce, we can now discuss where, how, and for whom Canadians work. *Labour force participation* (LFP) is the main indicator of a population's economic activity, at least from the perspective of paid employment. Calculations of labour force size and participation rates are based on the number of individuals 15 years of age or older who are working for pay (including self-employed individuals working on their own or employing others) and those who are looking for work. Hence, the *unemployed* (those out of work but who have actively looked for work in the past four weeks) are counted as part of the labour force. Individuals performing unpaid household and child-care work in their home, however, are not included in official labour force calculations, even though their labour makes essential economic and social contributions. We explore such work in Chapter 7.

Using this official LFP definition, in 1901 only 53 percent of Canadians (15 years of age and older) were participating in the labour force. LFP increased to 57 percent by 1911 but did not go much higher for many decades, By the mid-1970s, however, more than 60 percent of the eligible population was in a paid job or seeking one (Figure 3.3). Participation rates rose to 67 percent in 1989 and then fell slightly during the recession of the early 1990s. Since then they have hovered somewhere between 65 and 67 percent. The 2018 LFP rate was 65.4 percent, representing 19,812,800 labour force participants.

FIGURE 3.3 Labour Force Participation Rates by Gender, Canada, 1976–2018

Participation rate (%)

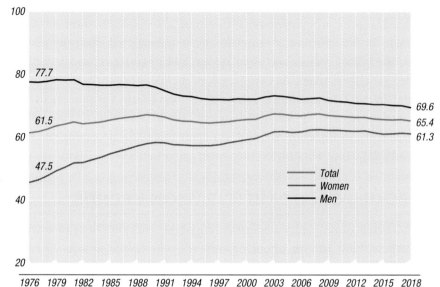

Source: Statistics Canada, Labour Force Participation Rates by Gender, 1976–2018, Table 14-10-0327-01. https://www150.statcan.gc.ca/t1/tbl1/en/tv.action?pid=1410032702

Gender Differences in Labour Force Participation

Breaking down the LFP rate by gender, we find striking differences. In 1901, only 16 percent of females 15 years of age or older were in the paid labour force. However, this rate increased with each 10-year census. After World War II, the size of these increases was substantial. Between 1960 and 1976, female LFP jumped from 28 to 45 percent, and the following decade also saw a steady rise. The landmark year was 1980, the first in which a majority of Canadian women were part of the labour force (which, as officially defined, leaves out unpaid family and household work).

By 1990 and 1991, female LFP had risen to almost 59 percent; it then dropped slightly for a number of years before rising to a high of 62.7 percent in 2008 and then falling again slightly to 61.3 percent in 2018. Thus, over the course of a century, female labour force participation in Canada almost quadrupled, from 16 percent to over 61 percent. As we will see in Chapter 6, the impact of this long-term trend on workplaces, families, and society as a whole has been immense.

During the 1960s and 1970s, much of the growth in female labour force participation was due to larger numbers of women returning to paid employment after their children were in school or had left home. In contrast, most of the female employment growth in the 1980s and 1990s occurred among mothers who were working for pay and raising young children at the same time. By 2016, roughly 70 percent of mothers with children under six years of age worked for pay, compared to just one-third of mothers in the mid-1970s (Moyser 2018: 12).

While female participation rates were climbing, male rates declined over most of the past century, although not as steeply. Between 1901 and 1931, male LFP remained close to 90 percent, but it dropped to the mid-80s in the decades before and after World War II. In the 1970s and 1980s, male LFP fluctuated between 76 and 78 percent, but it then declined quickly from 77 percent in 1989 to 72 percent in 1996. It stayed at this level until 2009 and then steadily declined to 69.6 percent in 2018. Glancing back over the past two decades, we see a 3 to 4 percent increase in female labour force participation, compared to a 3 to 4 percent drop for men. Since the economic downturn of 2008, LFP rates have declined for both sexes, but more notably for men.

Thus, the long-term growth in total LFP rates in Canada has been the product of substantial increases for women and less dramatic declines for men. The latter reflects two trends: men are living longer (with more men living past the conventional retirement age, the proportion of all men out of the labour force is increasing), and more men are retiring earlier (that is, before age 65) than they did many decades ago—though there has been an upswing in the average age of retirement for men in recent years, a point we return to later.[22] The more complex causes of growing female LFP are discussed in Chapter 6. A similar convergence of female and male LFP rates has occurred in other industrialized countries (e.g., the United States, Britain, Germany, France, Italy, and Japan). But in recent decades, Canada has experienced one of the largest jumps in female labour force participation.

It is important to note that these LFP rates are annual averages. Given the seasonal nature of some types of work in Canada (jobs in agriculture, fishing, forestry, construction, and tourism, for example), higher levels of labour force participation are typically recorded in the spring, summer, and autumn months. Furthermore, taking a full 12-month period, we observe higher proportions of Canadians reporting labour force participation at some point during the year. Thus, annual averages do not reveal the extent to which Canadians move in and out of different labour market statuses—for example, by changing employers or becoming unemployed.

In recent years, concerns over *job stability* (average length of time in a job) in industrialized countries have increased (Hollister 2011; Gallie and Green 2017). In Canada, however, job stability does not appear to have eroded (average job tenure in 2018 was 102 months, compared to 97 months in 1998).[23] However, average job tenure statistics mask great variation by job status (e.g., full time versus part-time, temporary versus permanent), educational attainment, and socio-demographic characteristics. During the recession of 2008–9, for example, better-educated workers had the most stable employment, while immigrants, Indigenous peoples, less-educated workers, and youth experienced the greatest labour market instability. Industries such as manufacturing have also seen sharp declines in job stability.

Other Differences in Labour Force Participation

Several groups, however, have experienced lower-than-average LFP rates for a much longer time. In particular, many Indigenous peoples continue to be economically marginalized, facing huge barriers to paid employment. Labour Force Survey data for 2007–15, for example, confirm much higher unemployment for Indigenous workers than non-Indigenous workers, and a more severe, sustained impact from the 2008 downturn (Statistics Canada 2017d). According to the 2016 Census, Indigenous peoples had an unemployment rate of 8.4 percent, compared to 4.8 percent for non-Indigenous workers. Likewise, median employment earnings were $23,345 for First Nations, $31,423 for Métis, and $20,984 for Inuit populations, compared to $34,013 for the non-Indigenous population.[24]

Similarly, research shows that Canadians with disabilities are much less likely to be in the paid labour force. According to the 2017 Canadian Survey on Disability (CSD), approximately one in five Canadians (ages 15 years or older) report having one or more disabilities that limits their daily activities. Disability increases with age, with 1 in 10 Canadians aged 15 to 24 years reporting a disability (typically mental illness or a learning disability) compared to 4 in 10 seniors (65 years plus; most often involving pain, mobility, or flexibility). While employment rates for people with disabilities have risen in recent decades in Canada, people with disabilities are still less likely to be employed, and more likely to work fewer hours. According to the 2017 CSD, only 59 percent of those with a disability were employed, compared to 80 percent of those without a disability. Only 30 percent of those reporting a severe disability were employed.

It is not surprising, then, to learn that roughly one-third of Canadians with a disability live in poverty (Statistics Canada 2018; Morris et al. 2018). But poverty is not simply a function of lower employment rates. Even after taking into account other demographic factors, Canadians with disabilities earn up to 20 percent less than those without disabilities (Galarneau and Radulescu 2009). This suggest problems of direct or systemic discrimination, similar to those we see for gender, race, and ethnicity (discussed in Chapter 5). Indeed, about 12 percent of those with disabilities believe they have been refused a job because of their condition, with much higher rates (around 30 percent) for those with severe disabilities (Turcotte 2014).[25]

Age and Labour Force Participation

Younger Canadians

How does age shape labour force participation? With the exception of a small decline coinciding with the recession of the early 1980s, the labour force participation of Canadian youth (ages 15 to 24, females and males combined) rose more or less steadily from an annual average of 64 percent in 1976 to 71 percent in 1989. Figure 3.4 shows that the youth LFP rate then declined rapidly in the 1990s, dropping to 61 percent by 1997. Rebounding, it rose again to 67.3 percent in 2003, then wavered back and forth, falling post-2008. Notably, in this period of time, female and male youth LFP rates have converged sharply, with identical rates for males and females by 2018. Over the past two or three decades, LFP rates for teenagers (ages 15 to 19) have always been considerably lower than LFP rates for young adults (ages 20 to 24), since a larger proportion of the latter group have left the education system.

Why did youth LFP rates decline so notably in the 1990s? The recession that lasted until mid-decade sharply reduced the number of "good" entry-level jobs for youth. In fact, during this period, youth wages declined more than for any other age group in the labour force. In turn, a larger proportion of youth decided to continue their education to improve their employment prospects. For example, between 1989 and 1998, the percentage of Canadian youth (ages 15 to 24) who were in school and not working rose from 29 to 40 percent. Furthermore, the size of the 20-to-24-year-old cohort declined, compared to the 15-to-19-year-old cohort. Since young adults have historically had higher LFP rates than teenagers, the overall youth LFP rate declined.[26]

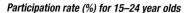

FIGURE 3.4   Youth Labour Force Participation Rates by Gender, Canada, 1976–2018

Participation rate (%) for 15–24 year olds

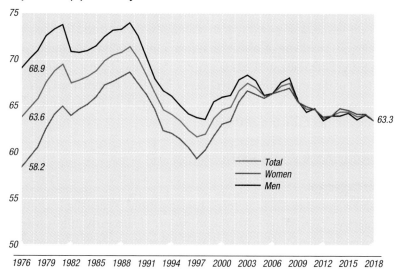

Source: Statistics Canada, Labour Force Participation Rates by Gender, 1976–2018, Table 14-10-0327-01. https://www150.statcan.gc.ca/t1/tbl1/en/tv.action?pid=1410032702

What about trends since then? Certainly the stronger economy in the early 2000s, as well as more rapidly rising postsecondary tuition costs, have led some Canadian youth to choose work over school. Since 2008, however, youth LFP rates have again declined, likely reflecting narrowing job prospects as many older Canadians seek paid work and pressures increase on youth to gain post-secondary credentials in a highly competitive labour market.

Labour Force Participation among Older Canadians

In recent decades, labour force participation of older Canadian men has taken an interesting turn. From 1976 to 2002, the LFP rate for men ages 60 to 64 fell dramatically, from 66.5 to 50.0 percent. After that, it rose steadily to 62.4 percent in 2018. A similar pattern of declining, and then increasing, labour force participation for older men is also evident in the United States (Hazel 2018).

Declining labour force participation for older men in the 1980s and 1990s was no doubt due to better public pension and other benefits provided to the elderly by government, and larger numbers of older men having employer-sponsored pensions and other savings (RRPs, for example). All of this bolstered economic security. Consequently, men's average retirement age fell from 65 years in 1976 to a low of 61 years in 2002. But the average age of retirement has slowly increased, returning to 65 years in 2018.[27] Such changes reflect growing economic insecurity, related to declining pension coverage, as well as concerns over the adequacy of retirement savings in the post-2008 climate. They may also result from more positive developments, such as enhanced work opportunities for older workers in key sectors where labour shortages exist (Hazel 2018; McDaniel et al. 2015).

Many factors influence plans to retire or continue working, including health and financial and family situation, as well as job demands and opportunities (Hazel 2018). Research suggests that while the majority of workers retire because of health reasons or the desire to have more leisure time, about one-third of retirees would keep working under different circumstances—for example, if they could work fewer days or hours, take more vacation time, or work part time. Those who retire "involuntarily" are far more likely to retire because of poor health or downsizing, and to report low income and low life satisfaction (Morissette, Schellenberg, and Silver 2004; Schellenberg and Silver 2004). The odds of working well into one's senior years increase with higher education and professional status (Hazel 2018). By age 70, the majority of those still working (about two-thirds) are doing so by choice, rather than necessity. These patterns challenge the traditional three-stage model of the work life— education, employment, then retirement. Many researchers now use a *life-course perspective* that views individuals' roles as more fluid and examines the choices and constraints underlying transitions across roles.[28]

Despite a small trend toward re-employment (or un-retirement) among retired men the fact remains that older men who lose their jobs have more difficulty finding work, since many employers are reluctant to hire and retrain older workers. In addition, older men are more likely to be employed in industries where employment is declining (manufacturing and the resource-based industries, for example). As a rule then, most unemployed older men decide to retire. Some are offered early retirement packages by employers trying to downsize their workforce, while others decide that "retired" would be an easier label to live with than "unemployed." Thus, while a shortage of jobs may push some men over the age of 55 out of the labour force, an adequate pension encourages others to retire voluntarily.

Among older women, we see different work and retirement patterns. Typically, women have retired at an earlier age than men. That is still the case, with women having an average retirement age of 63 years in 2018. But LFP rates for older women have still increased because of their historically lower levels of participation. In 2018, for example, the LFP rate for women ages 55 to 59 was 71.5 percent, up dramatically from 38.2 percent in 1976. For women ages 60 to 64, LFP increased from 24.4 percent in 1976 to 50.7 percent in 2018. In fact, roughly one in five women ages 65 to 69 were still in the labour force in 2018. Financial reasons may be a key motivator for women. Typically, they earn less than men and receive fewer benefits, including government and employer pensions (Moyser 2018), as discussed in Chapter 6. Compared with men of the same age, then, fewer older employed women have the financial resources needed to retire.

INDUSTRIAL CHANGES: THE EMERGENCE OF THE SERVICE ECONOMY

The work done by labour force participants can be classified in several ways. We begin by discussing industrial shifts and then examine occupational changes in the following section. *Industry* refers to the major type of economic activity occurring within a workplace. In the broadest sense, we can distinguish the *primary sector*, including agriculture, mining, forestry, and other resource extraction industries, from the *secondary sector* (manufacturing and construction), where goods are produced from the raw materials supplied by the primary sector, and the *tertiary sector*, where services rather than products are provided. A *service*, simply defined, is the exchange of a commodity that has no tangible form. These general categories can be further subdivided into more specific industries. The service sector, for example, includes, among others, the finance, education, retail trade, government (public administration), and health service industries.

Service-Sector Growth

In 1891, the primary industries accounted for 49 percent of the Canadian labour force; the secondary sector, for 20 percent; and the service sector, for the remaining 31 percent (Matthews 1985: 36). In the following half-century, the primary sector lost its dominance, while the manufacturing industries expanded. At the same time, the service industries were increasing in size. By 1951, almost half (47 percent) of all employed Canadians were working in the service industries, while the secondary sector accounted for almost one-third

(31 percent) of employment (Picot 1987: 11). The relative size of both the primary and secondary sectors has been declining steadily ever since. By 2018, 78.9 percent of employed Canadians held service-sector jobs, and 21.1 percent were working in the goods-producing sector. Agriculture and natural resources, once dominant industries more than a century ago, now account for just 1.5 percent and 1.8 percent of all employment in Canada. In contrast, the portion of workers in the service sector has more than doubled over this long span of time. It has also come to represent a much larger share of the total value of goods and services produced in the Canadian economy.[29]

These statistics clearly demonstrate that we are now living in a service-dominated economy. A similar transition from a preindustrial to an industrial to a service economy has occurred in other capitalist countries such as the United States, the United Kingdom, Japan, Sweden, and Germany, although manufacturing continues to play a larger role in some of these countries. In 2018, Hong Kong and Singapore were leading services economies, with 88 percent of workers in that sector. Following closely were the United Kingdom, the Netherlands, Sweden, and Israel, with 81 percent of all workers in that sector, and then Canada and the United States, with service employment accounting for 79 percent of the labour force. But even Japan and Germany, two leading exporters of manufactured goods, have service sectors accounting for about 72 percent of all employment (World Bank 2018).

The rise of the service sector can be attributed to a combination of factors. Productivity gains because of new technologies and organizational forms in manufacturing, but also in the resource industries, have meant that fewer people can produce much more. In primary industries, the growing size and declining number of farms in Canada is perhaps the best indicator. As for manufacturing, factory mechanization toward the end of the 19th and into the early 20th century greatly enhanced workers' productivity, despite a reduction in hours worked. In more recent decades, automated production systems (robotics and information technology) have once again accelerated this trend.

Industrial expansion and productivity gains over the years have also led to higher incomes and increased leisure time. These factors, in turn, have fuelled the demand for a wider range of services, particularly in the last few decades when the recreation, accommodation, and food service industries have been growing rapidly. In addition, the expansion of the role of the state as a provider of educational and social services and as a funder of health services contributed significantly to service sector growth. In the 1990s, governments' pursuit of deficit reduction resulted in reduced program funding, organizational downsizing, and privatization, thus slowing public-sector employment. In the early 2000s, however, governments at all levels and public services, particularly education and health care, increased their hiring—in part to replace the growing number of retiring baby boomers. With massive stimulus spending by governments in response to the 2008–9 recession, the hiring trend continued. But government deficits are a constant public concern, so the pressure to reduce public-sector hiring and wages continues, as we see currently in provinces like Ontario and Alberta.

Employment Diversity within the Service Sector

The many specific industries within the broad service sector can be usefully categorized into six major groups: (1) distributive services (transportation, communication, and wholesale trade); (2) business services (finance, insurance, real estate, and other services to business); (3) the education, health, and welfare sector; (4) public administration; (5) retail trade; and (6) other consumer services. Distributive services differ from the others by being the final link in the process whereby raw materials are extracted, transformed, and then delivered to the ultimate consumer. Business services also provide support to the primary and secondary industries (the goods-producing sector), but in a less tangible way. Like public administration, the education, health, and welfare sector contains primarily non-commercial services provided by the state, while retail trade and other consumer services (e.g., food and beverage, accommodation, and the tourism industries) are commercial services aimed directly at consumers.[30]

It is useful to further combine the six service categories into an *upper tier* (distributive, business, education, health and welfare, and public administration) and a *lower tier* (retail trade and other consumer services) since, as we will demonstrate later, many more good jobs are located in the former. Table 3.1 uses these concepts to profile the industrial distribution of Canada's employed (other tables in this chapter also include only employed members of the labour force). As already noted, in 2018 just over one-fifth (21.1 percent) of employed Canadians were working in the goods-producing sector while 78.9 percent were employed in the service industries. Just over half (56.6 percent) were working in the upper-tier services, while almost one-quarter (22.4 percent) had jobs in the lower-tier service industries.[31]

TABLE 3.1 Industry by Gender, Employed Population, Canada, 2018

Industry	% of Total	% of Women	% of Men
Goods-producing sector	21.1	9.4	31.7
Agriculture	1.5	0.9	2.0
Natural resource–based	1.8	0.7	2.9
Manufacturing	9.3	5.3	12.9
Utilities	0.8	0.4	1.1
Construction	7.7	2.1	12.8
Services-producing sector	78.9	90.6	68.3
Upper-tier services (total)	56.6	65.2	48.7
Wholesale trade	3.5	2.3	4.6
Transportation and warehousing	5.3	2.7	7.7
Finance, insurance, real estate, rental and leasing	6.3	7.1	5.5
Professional, scientific, and technical services	7.9	7.1	8.6
Business, building, and other support services	4.2	3.9	4.4
Educational services	7.1	10.2	4.3
Health care and social assistance	12.9	22.1	4.5
Information, culture, and recreation	4.2	4.2	4.3
Public administration	5.2	5.6	4.8
Lower-tier services (total)	22.4	25.4	19.6
Retail trade	11.5	12.6	10.4
Accommodation and food services	6.6	7.9	5.5
Other services	4.3	4.9	3.8
Total percent	100.0	100.0	100.0
Total number of employees (in 000s)	18,658	8,320	9,188

Source: Statistics Canada, Labour Force Characteristics by Industry, Annual (x 1,000), Table 14-10-0023-01

We have already observed that similar proportions of workers are employed in the service and goods-producing sectors in Canada and the United States. However, we find a very different industrial distribution in Mexico, the other major North American economy. Compared to Canada and the United States— where about four-fifths of workers hold service jobs—Mexico has a smaller service sector, employing just 61 percent of workers there. In contrast, Mexico's agricultural sector employs 13 percent of workers, compared to just 1 percent in the United States and 1.5 percent in Canada. Likewise, the industrial sector is larger in Mexico (26 percent) than in the United States (19 percent) and Canada (19 percent), although the difference is not as marked.[32]

Gender and Age Differences in Service-Sector Employment

Table 3.1 also reveals distinct gender differences in industrial locations. In 2018, almost 31.7 percent of employed Canadian men were working in the goods-producing sector, compared with 9.4 percent of employed women. Women were more likely to be employed in the lower-tier services (25.4 percent, compared with 19.6 percent of men—though this gap has narrowed in recent years). Within the upper-tier services, women were much more heavily concentrated in the health, education, and social services industries than were men. Men were considerably more likely to be employed in transportation and warehousing industries.

Age plays an important part in further stratifying the employed labour force across these industrial categories. Young workers (ages 15 to 24) are much less likely to be employed in the upper-tier services, and more likely to hold jobs in the lower-tier retail trade and consumer service industries. Many of these young workers are students in part-time jobs. Thus, the expansion of the lower-tier service industries (for instance, shopping malls, fast-food restaurants, and tourism) since the 1970s has relied heavily on the recruitment of student workers, creating a distinct student-worker segment of the labour force. However, older female workers are also much more likely than older male workers to be employed in the retail trade and other consumer service industries.

OCCUPATIONAL CHANGES

While the industrial classification system is based on what is being produced, we also can categorize workers according to their *occupation*. Occupational distinctions are determined by the work an individual typically performs: the actual tasks that she or he completes. Thus, secretaries, managers, office cleaners, and accountants (which are *occupational titles*) work in mining companies, automobile factories, and government bureaucracies—that is, in the primary, secondary, and tertiary (or service) sectors of the economy. In contrast, teachers, nurses, and retail clerks are occupational groups largely unique to the service sector. So the two classification systems parallel each other to an extent but also overlap considerably.

As we noted earlier in our discussion of education and training, developing human resources—the skills of the Canadian workforce—has been a public policy priority for several decades now. In the 1990s, Statistics Canada developed an occupational typology that focuses on *skills*. The National

Occupational Classification (NOC) provides information on nine different *skill types* (e.g., business, natural sciences, arts, trades) and four basic *skill levels* (tied directly to the education and training required) for each of the 40,000 detailed occupations in the Canadian labour market. For example, occupations in skill level A include managers and the professions, and require a university education, while occupations in skill level D require no formal education and only short demonstrations or some on-the-job training. Generally, the highest-skill groups are concentrated mainly in what we earlier referred to as "upper-tier services," while skill-level-D occupations are in lower-tier services and goods production. The NOC is revised and updated every five years by Statistics Canada and Employment and Social Development Canada to ensure that it reflects the changing nature of the labour market (Statistics Canada 2018b).

Blue-Collar, White-Collar, and Pink-Collar Occupations

The term *blue-collar* has traditionally been used to distinguish occupations with physically demanding and potentially hazardous working conditions (e.g., farming, mining, truck driving, construction work, and factory work) from *white-collar* occupations (clerical, sales, managerial, and professional). The explanation, of course, is that for the former jobs, wearing a white collar would be inappropriate, since it would not stay clean. In the past, white-collar occupations were viewed as having higher status. But with the expansion of the service sector, especially lower-tier services where low-paying jobs are quite common, the white-collar occupational category has come to include the majority of the labour force, including many people in less desirable jobs.

As primary-sector industries became less important over the last century, the size of some occupational groups decreased immensely and others increased proportionally. A few examples can make this point. The 1911 Census reported that 34 percent of the labour force worked in agricultural occupations, compared with only 4 percent in clerical occupations and a similarly small proportion in professional occupations. By 1951, agricultural occupations had declined to 16 percent of the labour force, compared with 11 percent in clerical occupations and 7 percent in professions (O'Neill 1991: 10). The 1996 Census revealed less than 5 percent of the labour force in occupations unique to primary industry;

9 percent in management; 19 percent in business, finance, and administrative occupations; and almost 20 percent in natural science, social science, government, and other white-collar occupations (Statistics Canada 1998).[33] Thus, over the course of the past century, white-collar jobs have come to dominate the Canadian labour market.

Of note, many of the new white-collar positions have been filled by women, while the remaining blue-collar jobs in the primary and secondary sectors are still typically held by men. In fact, given the heavy concentration of women in clerical, sales, and service occupations, the term *pink collar* has been used to describe these occupational categories. Recently, we also see the terms *green collar*, to describe jobs in the emerging clean energy sector, and *no collar* jobs, to describe creative professionals.

Using a revised occupational classification to ensure comparability with earlier data, Table 3.2 presents a gender breakdown of Canadian occupational distributions for 1987 and 2018.[34] Note that the total employed labour force increased from 12.3 million to 18.7 million workers. Hence, even though some occupational categories may have declined slightly in relative (percentage) size, they might still have increased in absolute size between 1987 and 2018.

TABLE 3.2   Occupation by Gender, Employed Population, Canada, 1987 and 2018

	1987			2018		
	Women	Men	Total	Women	Men	Total
	%	%	%	%	%	%
Management occupations	6.9	13.8	10.8	6.7	11.4	9.2
Business, finance, and administration						
Professionals	2.1	2.5	2.4	5.0	3.6	4.2
Administrative and clerical	27.4	7.6	16.1	18.4	5.8	11.8
Natural and applied sciences	2.3	7.0	5.0	4.0	11.6	7.9
Health occupations	9.2	1.8	5.0	12.6	2.9	7.5
Education, law, social, community, government	11.9	6.4	8.7	16.2	6.4	11.1
Art, culture, recreation, and sport	2.5	2.0	2.2	3.5	2.5	3.0
Sales and service occupations	28.9	17.2	22.2	28.2	20.5	24.2
Trades, transportation, equipment, and related	1.7	28.1	16.8	2.0	25.7	14.4
Natural resources, agriculture, and related	1.5	3.9	2.9	0.8	3.2	2.0
Manufacturing and utilities occupations	5.8	9.6	7.9	2.7	6.4	4.6
Total percent	100.0	100.0	100.0	100.0	100.0	100.0
Total number of employees (in 000s)	5,308	7,025	12,333	8,899	9,758	18,658

Source: Statistics Canada. Labour Force Participation Rates by Gender, 1976–2018, Table 14-10-0327-01. https://www150 .statcan.gc.ca/t1/tbl1/en/tv.action?pid=1410032702

Considering first the total distributions (female and male combined), we note stability, as well as small changes. Managerial occupations account for roughly 10 percent of occupations across this period. In contrast, professional occupations in business, finance, and administration have expanded to 4.2 percent of all employed, while the other administrative and clerical category occupations (office jobs without major planning and supervisory roles) shrunk notably, from 16.1 to 11.8 percent. An increase is seen in natural and applied science, health occupations, and social sciences, education, and government-related occupations (many of these would be professional positions). The remaining white-collar occupational categories in sales and service have seen slight changes, with an overall upward trend.

However, in the blue-collar occupations, we see relative declines in natural resource, agriculture and related occupations and especially in manufacturing occupations (from 7.9 percent to 4.6 percent), continuing a long-term trend in job losses in these sectors as a result of restructuring and technological change. The changes in clerical occupations reflect a complex set of related changes, from advancing information technology to downsizing to the upgrading of some of these jobs to administrative roles.

Chapter 6 focuses on the unequal employment experiences and rewards of women and men, so we will comment only briefly at this point on the gender differences in Table 3.2. The 2018 data show a more even distribution of men than women across the occupational structure, though not in blue-collar jobs. Overall, women are more heavily concentrated than men in pink-collar occupations, with one in five (18.4 percent) employed in administrative and clerical occupations in business, finance, and administration; 16.2 percent in education, law, social, community, and government services; and 28.2 in sales and service occupations, totalling 62.8 percent. In contrast, just 32.7 percent of men are employed in these three occupational groups. Women are also relatively overrepresented in health-related occupations (12.6 percent), which includes nurses, physiotherapists, and related jobs.

Nonetheless, it is important to note some change over time in the gender composition of the occupational structure, albeit at a slow pace. In 1987, for instance, only 9.0 percent of employed women were in managerial or professional administrative occupations. In 2018, nearly 12 percent of women worked in these higher-status white-collar occupations. Table 3.2 also shows a small increase over time in the proportion of women in the natural sciences, and a notable decline in the percentage of women in administrative and clerical jobs in business, finance, and administration.

To conclude, some significant shifts have occurred in the Canadian occupational structure, especially between white-collar, blue-collar, and pink-collar jobs. Although female–male differences have not disappeared, we must keep in mind that Table 3.2 shows very broad occupational categories. Health occupations, for example, include doctors, nurses, orderlies, nursing assistants, and other support workers. Women are still more likely to be in the lower-status occupations within these broad categories and are still typically supervised by men. Hence, it is necessary to look in more detail at the specific occupations within which women and men typically are employed, as we do in Chapter 6.

THE CANADIAN LABOUR MARKET: REGIONAL VARIATIONS

So far, we have treated Canada as a single economic entity, putting aside important regional differences. Yet anyone who has travelled across Canada will have a strong sense of its regional diversity. The fishing boats and lumber mills of the West Coast are left behind as one begins to head east toward the Prairies, where there are oil wells, windmills, potash mines, and a few remaining wooden grain elevators. The flat landscape disappears soon after leaving Winnipeg, and one is faced by the rocks, forests, and water of the Canadian Shield. The smokestacks (some functioning and some abandoned) of Sudbury and other mining communities are reminders of the natural resource base of that region, but they eventually give way to the old grey barns of Ontario, symbols of an agricultural economy older than the one observed on the Prairies.

But the barns are unlikely to be the only memory of the trip through Ontario and into Quebec. Heading east, away from the gleaming office towers of Toronto, the huge Highway 401 pushing its way past kilometres of warehouses and suburban factories will also leave a strong impression of the industrial heartland of the country. Then, repeating the pattern observed in the West (but in reverse, without the mountains, and on a smaller scale), the farming economies of Quebec and the Atlantic provinces begin to merge with a forest-based economy. Eventually, one returns to a region where fisheries are once again important. In short, regional diversity means economic diversity.

This description obviously overgeneralizes. There are high-technology firms in Vancouver, the Fraser Valley, and the Toronto-Waterloo corridor; large factories in Calgary; and oil wells off the East Coast. And in northern parts of Canada, energy development and mining compete uneasily with Indigenous traditions of hunting, fishing, and trapping. Some regions are much more economically advantaged than others, as we point out below in our discussion of unemployment trends. Labour force participation rates also vary significantly across provinces and territories. For example, in 2018, Alberta's LFP rate of 71.9 percent was much higher than the 58.9 percent rate in Newfoundland and Labrador.

Table 3.3 highlights these regional variations. For example, in 2018, 7.2 percent of the employed labour force in Manitoba and Saskatchewan had jobs in agriculture, compared with less than 2 percent in nearly every other region save Alberta (2.1 percent). Larger-than-average concentrations

TABLE 3.3   Industry by Region, Employed Population, Canada, 2018

Industry	Total	Atlantic Provinces	Quebec	Ontario	Manitoba/ Saskatchewan	Alberta	British Columbia
	%	%	%	%	%	%	%
Goods-producing sector							
Agriculture	1.5	1.5	1.3	1.0	7.2	2.1	0.9
Natural resource–based	1.8	3.0	0.9	0.5	4.8	6.6	2.0
Manufacturing	9.3	7.1	11.5	10.6	5.1	5.6	7.0
Utilities	0.8	0.9	0.6	0.8	1.1	1.0	0.6
Construction	7.7	7.4	5.9	7.3	8.3	10.5	9.6
Service sector							
Upper-tier services							
Wholesale trade	3.5	2.6	3.7	3.6	3.7	3.7	3.3
Business services	18.3	13.4	17.8	21.0	12.7	16.0	18.4
Education/health/ welfare	20.0	23.8	20.9	19.0	21.1	18.7	19.7
Public administration	5.2	6.9	5.8	5.0	5.8	4.7	4.2
Lower-tier services							
Retail trade	11.5	13.7	11.8	11.2	11.3	10.6	11.5
Other consumer services	20.5	19.7	19.8	20.1	19.0	20.5	22.8
Total percent	100.0	100.0	100.0	100.0	100.0	100.0	100.0
Total (in 000s)	18,658	1,111	4,262	7,242	537	2,331	2,494

Source: Statistics Canada, Employment by Industry, Annual, Table 14-10-0092-01. https://www150.statcan.gc.ca/t1/tbl1/en /tv.action?pid=1410009201

of workers in the resource-based industries reflect the presence of the fishing industry on the East Coast and in British Columbia; forest-based industries in the Atlantic provinces, Alberta, and British Columbia; and the oil and gas industry in Alberta and Saskatchewan. Meanwhile, approximately 11 percent of workers in both Quebec and Ontario had jobs in manufacturing, compared with less than 7 percent in other regions. Of note, Alberta, Ontario, and BC had the lowest employment in publicly funded industries (education, health and welfare, and public administration).

Canada is not unique in having some regions in which primary industries are most important and others in which manufacturing is concentrated. But its economic history is marked by a reliance on exports of raw materials such as furs, fish, timber, wheat, coal, natural gas, and oil. Indeed, exporting raw materials was Canada's colonial role in the British Empire, and even as an independent industrialized nation, Canada has continued to provide natural resources to the global economy. The *staple theory of economic growth*, developed by Harold Innis and others, documents the economic, political, and social consequences of this dependence on the export of unprocessed staple products. The theory argues that overreliance on the extraction and export of a single or few resources makes a nation or region vulnerable in world markets. The relative absence of manufacturing industries means that large portions of the workforce remain employed in lower-skill primary- and tertiary-sector jobs. In addition, a weak manufacturing sector does not encourage significant quantities of research and development and does not generate spin-off industrial activity. These factors create a "staples trap" in which there are few economic development alternatives (Watkins 1991).

Indicative of Canada's natural resource base is the number of single-industry communities scattered across the country. These towns and cities, often situated in relatively isolated areas, exist only because the extraction of some natural resource requires a resident labour force. While some of these communities have attempted to diversify their economies, few have been successful. Instead, their economic activity remains dominated by the primary resource extraction industry (oil in Fort McMurray, Alberta, for example, or nickel in Sudbury, Ontario). If the market for the staple declines or the resource is depleted, the economic base of the community will crumble. Examples over the past several decades include mine shutdowns in Saskatchewan, Quebec, and Ontario; the struggle for Newfoundland and Labrador fishing communities to survive; mill closures in forestry-dependent towns in British Columbia; and recent auto and auto-parts plant closures in Ontario.[35] In *One Job Town*, Steven High (2018) conveys the profound sense of loss felt by workers and families in the community of Sturgeon Falls in Ontario, where the closure of paper mills decimated not only their economic livelihood, but a way of life.

Over the decades, the prospects of better jobs and higher incomes have led many thousands of people to move to the industrial cities of central Canada. But many have also been attracted to the resource towns of the hinterland for the same reasons. Such communities have historically provided work for unemployed or underemployed migrants from other regions of the country. However, work opportunities for residents and migrants in resource towns, which move through fairly predictable stages of development, do not remain constant. Moreover, since mining, forestry, the railway, and other blue-collar industries traditionally have been male occupational preserves, women have had trouble finding satisfactory employment. Many single-industry towns are located in areas with sizable Indigenous populations, yet these groups seldom benefit from the employment opportunities generated by the towns. But this may be changing with recent developments such as Project Reconciliation, an Indigenous-led organization that in 2019 was seeking to buy a majority share (51 percent) of the Trans Mountain pipeline. The goal is to exercise more control over sensitive environmental development, provide employment opportunities in Indigenous communities, and retain a portion of annual revenues for investment into an Indigenous sovereign wealth fund (Nickel and Williams, 2019).

CONCLUSION

Over the past century or more, profound changes have occurred in how, where, and for whom Canadians work. The late 19th and early 20th centuries were times of rapid industrialization and workplace rationalization. Years that followed brought further growth in white-collar occupations, expansion of the service sector, and a decline in self-employment. By the 1960s, the Canadian work world had been largely transformed. But as our examination of more recent trends has shown, the Canadian labour market has once again gone through a significant restructuring in the final decades of the 20th century and the early decades of the 21st.

The service sector has expanded enormously, producing both good and bad jobs, with many more of the latter in the lower-tier service industries. Meanwhile, manufacturing industries have continued to contribute less to employment growth in Canada. As we will discuss in the next chapter, we have also seen a substantial increase in part-time employment, while other forms of nonstandard work (temporary or contract work, for example) have become more prevalent. The recent rise of online platform based work—or gigs—is also an important development. Finally, unemployment rates, as we discuss in Chapter 4, remain an ongoing concern for certain groups in the labour market—especially in the aftermath of the 2008 Great Recession, one of the most notable economic collapses in recent memory.

With respect to the trends discussed here, what lies ahead? We can be fairly certain that several trends will continue. Demographic changes are a given, especially workforce aging and the increasing diversity of the labour force. We can also expect continued expansion of service-sector employment, and the ongoing decline of manufacturing work. The impact of new and emerging technologies remains a wild card but will no doubt strongly shape job outcomes in the future.

Currently, some of the most debated questions pertain to the quality and types of jobs the economy is producing, as well as employment levels and the likely trajectories of growth in the Canadian and global economies. In particular, the following questions will have to be addressed: Given concerns over the environment and sustainability, what levels of economic growth are sustainable? And what new green jobs and industries will emerge to mitigate the impact of climate change? What are the limits posed by population aging and a shrinking workforce in many industrialized countries? What types of jobs will be generated in an increasingly service-oriented context? And how will new technologies such as artificial intelligence transform jobs, and needed skills, in the future? We continue to explore these questions in the next chapter where we discuss trends such as job quality, unemployment, working hours, and the rise of nonstandard work.

DISCUSSION QUESTIONS

1. What are three of the most important demographic changes occurring in Canada? Explain what is involved in these trends and how they will affect employers and workers in the next 10 to 15 years.

2. In your view, what, if anything, could federal or provincial and territorial governments do to respond to demographic changes occurring in the next 10 to 15 years?

3. How and why does labour force participation vary by region, age, and gender?

4. What are the most important occupations and industries in the Canadian economy? How has the occupational and industrial structure changed over time, and why?

5. Work in Canada is strongly shaped by regional location. Discuss how region influences key aspects of the work experience, such as unemployment, labour force participation, and industry location.

ADDITIONAL RESOURCES

WORK AT THE MOVIES

- *Boomer Revolution* (directed by Sue Ridout, 2013, 45 minutes). This film explores the impact of an aging population in Canada on trends in work, retirement, and consumption. It is available through Curio at https://curio.ca/en/video/the-boomer-revolution-2557/.
- *About Schmidt* (directed by Alexander Payne, 2002, 125 minutes). After retiring from his long-held office job, Schmidt (Jack Nicholson) embarks on a road trip and experiences a journey of self-discovery and an awakening to life outside work.
- *A Better Life* (directed by Chris Weitz, 2011, 98 minutes). After illegally immigrating to the United States from Mexico and finding work as a gardener, a father struggles to provide better economic and social opportunities for his son.
- *Park Avenue: Money, Power and the American Dream* (directed by Alex Gibney, 2012, 59 minutes). This documentary film offers an analysis of growing income inequality in the United States and the difficulty of achieving upward mobility for the working poor.

SOUNDS OF WORK

- "Shiftwork" (Kenny Chesney). This country song describes the perils of nonstandard working arrangements. Chesney notes the presence of shiftwork in diverse workplaces.
- "Make and Break Harbour" (Stan Rogers). In this song, Rogers comments on the downslide of Atlantic Canada's fisheries and considers its effect on community and out-migration.

- "The Idiot" (Stan Rogers). Rogers addresses migrant work and regional employment opportunities in this song about an East Coaster working in Western Canada's oil industry.
- "Trouble in the Fields" (Nanci Griffith). Griffith sings about the challenges involved with rural work, particularly as they relate to shifts in the economy and changing expectations of family.

NOTES

1. In 2011, the Conservative government of Stephen Harper replaced the mandatory long-form census with the non-mandatory National Household Survey (NHS). Numerous concerns were raised about the NHS, including higher costs and lower response rates among marginalized groups, which led to less reliable counts of income and other labour market measures (Chase and Grant 2013; Sheikh 2013). In 2016, the mandatory census was reinstated by the Trudeau Liberal government (Jackson 2016). Because of the NHS's reliability problems, we rely on earlier census data (e.g., 2001 or 2006) for historical comparisons to the 2016 census whenever possible.

2. Excluded are those residing on reserves or in other Indigenous settlements, those living in institutions such as prisons or nursing homes, full-time members of the Canadian Armed Forces, and those in very remote areas (these groups represent less than 2 percent of the Canadian population overall). While both provinces and territories are included in the survey's coverage, data on the latter are not included in national estimates but published separately. For further details, see Statistics Canada (2018a) and https://www.statcan.gc.ca/eng/survey/household/3701#a2

3. For an overview of changes made to the Labour Force Survey (LFS) see: http://www23.statcan.gc.ca/imdb/p2SV.pl?Function=getMainChange&Id=1250547

4. Unless otherwise noted, the data (1976–2018) in this chapter come from annual averages compiled by Statistics Canada and made available through its online data portal: https://www150.statcan.gc.ca/n1/en/type/data?MM=1. Because estimates from the Labour Force Survey are regularly adjusted, the figures presented here are not comparable to data in earlier editions of this text.

5. In this best-selling book, Foot and Stoffman (2001) offer a fascinating account of how demographic trends influence all aspects of society. While we agree that demographic trends are critical for understanding the labour market, in our view Foot and Stoffman underestimate the effects of other economic, political, ideological, and organizational changes. For additional discussion on demography, labour markets, and economic growth in Canada, see Gomez and Foot (2013), Foot et al. (2015), McDaniel et al. (2015), Belanger et al. (2016), and Fields et al. (2017).

6. For historical trends, see Statistics Canada (2010). For future projections, see Statistics Canada (2015). Population projections take into account trends in fertility, mortality, international migration (immigration and emigration), non-permanent residents (NPR), and internal migration.

7. See Statistics Canada (2019a). For a valuable discussion of the policy and politics of pensions and other social programs in Canada and the United States, see the special issue of *Journal of International and Comparative Policy*, edited by Béland, Daniel, and Alex Waddan (2019).

8. Calculations by the authors from 2016 Census Data Tables, Occupation—National Occupational Classification (NOC), Class of Worker, Labour Force Status, Age, and Sex, Aged 15 Years and Over, Canada.

9. See Immigration, Refugees and Citizenship Canada (2018) and Statistics Canada (2017). See also Boyd and Vickers (2000) on historical Canadian immigration trends and Hou and Picot (2016) on economic outcomes in recent decades.

10. Statistics Canada Census 2016 Profile Tables can be searched by major cities at: https://www12.statcan.gc.ca/census-recensement/2016/dp-pd/prof/index.cfm?Lang=E

11. For an interactive map of First Nations communities, see https://geo.aandc-aadnc.gc.ca/geoviewer-geovisualiseur/index-eng.html

12. Indigenous statistics are based on Statistics Canada (2017c), which presents findings from the 2016 Census. For a valuable infographic, see: https://www150.statcan.gc.ca/n1/pub/11-627-m/11-627-m2017027-eng.htm

13. See Reich (2000), Florida (2002), OECD and Statistics Canada (2011), Livingstone and Guile (2011), and Slowey and Schuetze (2012) on the role of education in a global knowledge economy.

14. On lifelong learning trends in Canada, see Statistics Canada (2009b). For a more global perspective, see Slowey and Schuetze (2012).

15. For a profile of educational attainment in Canada, see Statistics Canada (2008d) and Schuetze (2012). See also Clark (2000), who provides a long-term overview of the growth of the formal education system in Canada.

16. See Grenier et al. (2008). See also OECD and Statistics Canada (2011) and Krahn and Lowe (1999) on workplace literacy concerns.

17. Calculations by authors based on Statistics Canada's 2016 General Social Survey.

18. For valuable comparative discussions of adult training, see Chapter 5 of the OECD (2019) *Future of Work, Employment Outlook*, as well as specific country level reports available at https://www.oecd.org/employment/outlook/. On Canada, see Munro et al. (2014) and Munro (2019).

19. Calculations by authors based on Statistics Canada's 2016 General Social Survey.

20. For discussions of skills and underemployment in Canada, see Livingstone (2009), Galarneau and Morisssette (2009), and Yuen (2010). For valuable overviews of underemployment and skill underutilization, see Livingstone (2017) and the edited volume by Warhurst et al. (2019).

21. For past discussions on presumed skill shortages, see Green and Ashton (1992) on the United Kingdom and Krahn and Lowe (1999) on Canada. For more recent discussions, see Burleton et al. (2013) and McDaniel et al. (2015).

22. Calculations from Statistics Canada, Table 14-10-0060-01, Retirement Age by Class of Worker, Annual: https://www150.statcan.gc.ca/t1/tbl1/en/cv.action?pid=1410006001#timeframe

23. Calculations from Statistics Canada, Table 14-10-0051-01, Job Tenure by Type of Work, Annual: https://www150.statcan.gc.ca/t1/tbl1/en/tv.action?pid=1410005101 For past trends in job stability, see Heisz (2005). On the 2008–9 downturn, see LaRochelle-Côté and Gilmore (2009). For youth trends, see LaRochelle-Côté (2013).

24. Unemployment data are from Statistics Canada, Table 14-10-0359-01 Labour Force Characteristics by Aboriginal Group. Median employment earnings are from the 2016 Census Data Tables, Aboriginal Identity, Income Statistics Catalogue 98-400-X2016170. For an overview of labour market patterns for Indigenous peoples, see Statistics Canada (2017d).

25. See Morris et al. (2018) for an overview of results from Statistics Canada's 2017 Canadian Disability Survey. Turcotte (2014) and Galarneau and Radulescu (2009) offer useful analysis based on other Statistics Canada data.

26. See Morissette (1997), Marquardt (1998), and Clark (1999) on labour market difficulties faced by Canadian youth in the 1990s; Picot (1998) on declining youth wages; and Bowlby (2000) on school-to-work transition trends, including information on the number of youth attending school and not working.

27. Labour force participation rates come from Statistics Canada, Table 14-10-0327-01, Labour Force Characteristics by Sex and Age. Retirement rates come from Statistics Canada, Table 14-10-0060-01, Retirement Age by Class of Worker. For discussions of aging, retirement and labour force participation, see Belanger et al. (2016), Fields et al. (2017), and Taylor (2019).

28. Marshall and Mueller (2002) use a life-course perspective to discuss the aging workforce and social policy. Myles and Quadagno (2005) address population aging and retirement issues in a variety of countries.

29. Historical data are from Crompton and Vickers's (2000) century-long overview of labour force trends in Canada. The 2018 data on industry come from Statistics Canada Table 14-10-0023-01.

30. Also see the Economic Council of Canada (1990), which distinguishes between *dynamic services* (distributive and business services), *non-market services* (education, health and welfare, public administration), and *traditional services* (retail trade and personal services).

31. Please note that comparisons of the percentages in Table 3.1 to similar industry distributions in earlier editions of this textbook are inappropriate, because of changes to Statistics Canada's industry classification system in 1999.

32. Data come from World Bank Indicators, Social Protection and Labour https://data .worldbank.org/indicator/ [retrieved 19 July 2019].

33. As some occupations (e.g., agricultural) have declined in size, Statistics Canada has combined them with related occupations. Alternatively, as other occupations have grown in size, they have been subdivided and renamed.

34. As of 1999, Statistics Canada began to use a revised Standard Occupational Classification System (SOC91), rather than the SOC80, for presentations of Labour Force Survey and census data. The biggest impact of the change was on the management category, with some occupations formerly coded in this category now being placed in other categories. Statistics Canada revised its databases only back to 1987, so Table 3.2 begins with that year.

35. See Lucas (1971), Angus and Griffin (1996), and Palmer and Sinclair (1997) on single-industry communities, and Dorow and O'Shaughnessy's (2013) special issue of the *Canadian Journal of Sociology* for a contemporary examination of the resource town of Fort McMurray.

4

GOOD JOBS, BAD JOBS, NO JOBS

"Last year, during his best three-month stretch, Jordan Golson sold about $750,000 worth of computers and gadgets at the Apple Store in Salem, N.H. It was a performance that might have called for a bottle of Champagne—if that were a luxury Mr. Golson could have afforded. 'I was earning $11.25 an hour,' he said. 'Part of me was thinking "This is great. I'm an Apple fan, the store is doing really well." But when you look at the amount of money the company is making and then you look at your paycheck, it's kind of tough.' . . . Last year, the company's 327 global stores . . . sold $16 billion in merchandise. But most of Apple's employees enjoyed little of that wealth. . . ."

Source: David Segal. "Apple's Retail Army, Long on Loyalty but Short on Pay." *New York Times*, June 23, 2012. http://www.nytimes.com/2012/06/24/business/apple-store-workers-loyal-but-short-on-pay.html?_r=0.

"'I'll say I'm grateful for it,' Jake says about working for Uber. 'Our business took a hit, and I had to scramble, and it's been paying my mortgage so, you know, it's great for what it is.'"

Source: Alex Rosenblat. (2018). *Uberland: How Algorithms are Rewriting the Rules of Work*. University of California Press, p. 56–57.

"Driving full-time is a nice little fantasy, but reality soon slaps you in the face when you end up living in your car to make ends meet . . ."

Source: Alex Rosenblat. (2018). *Uberland: How Algorithms are Rewriting the Rules of Work*. University of California Press, pp. 64–65.

"Retiring early if you call it that has not been good for me. I'm ok financially but I wasn't ready to retire. My wife goes to work every day and I've run out of projects around the house. Having me home all day while she works causes tension. I've got too much time on my hands. . . . I've looked for a job, but no luck. I planned to work another five or six years before I retired. Being 56 and unemployed passes for early retirement these days. Not exactly how I saw it playing out."

Source: Former autoworker. Sam Vrankulj. (2012). *Finding Their Way: Second Round Report on the CAW Worker Adjustment Tracking Project,* p. 23. http://www.caw.ca/assets/images/phase-Two-Tracking-study.pdf.

INTRODUCTION

Three decades ago, the Economic Council of Canada's *Good Jobs, Bad Jobs* (1990) posed important questions about the future of job quality in Canada's emerging "new economy." Highlighting the rise of the service sector, shifts in new technologies and trade, and the growing role of knowledge and education, the Council asked whether Canada might see growing polarization between those with "good jobs" and "bad jobs," and those with and without employment. Fast-forward to the present day: public attention is again fixed firmly on such questions. While some regions and industries in Canada boom, others are in decline. Artificial intelligence and "digital platform capitalism" have raised fears for many. Of note, the Economic Council of Canada itself no longer exists—a victim of government cuts and restructuring in the 1990s.

Amid this landscape, there is growing debate over the need for inclusive growth, where economic value is more fairly distributed. In Canada and the United States, campaigns for a $15 minimum wage (Fight for $15) have drawn public attention to the struggles of low-paid workers. The Trudeau government campaigned on a promise to strengthen middle-class jobs. In the United States, the Green New Deal has tied together issues of climate change and the need for fair and sustainable growth. Books such as *Capital in the Twenty-First Century* by Thomas Piketty (2014), *The Value of Everything* by Mariana Mazzucato (2018), and *Saving Capitalism* by former U.S. labour secretary Robert Reich (2016) have been surprise bestsellers. Even YouTube has seen the dryly titled video *Wealth Inequality in America* go viral, attracting over 22 million views to date. Clearly, economic inequality and labour market polarization are growing concerns for many.

In this chapter, we examine empirical evidence on this issue, exploring current trends in job quality, income, benefits, and occupational status. We also explore the emergence of *nonstandard* (also called *precarious* or *contingent*) jobs, such as part-time, temporary, and self-employment, as well as trends in work hours. Moving beyond questions of "good jobs" versus "bad jobs," we also consider the question of "no jobs", examining how access to employment has changed over time in Canada and how unemployment varies across regions, occupations, and socio-demographic characteristics. As will become clear, an important question concerns the trade-offs we are seeing between the quantity and quality of jobs.

WHAT IS JOB QUALITY?

For many Canadians, the ideal job is full time, full year, and permanent, providing steady income and security. Sociologists refer to this as the "standard employment relationship" (SER), a cornerstone of the labour market that developed in the 20th century with the rise of a breadwinner wage (Fudge 2017). While some individuals prefer part-time or temporary jobs, for educational, personal, or family reasons, such nonstandard jobs are less likely to be "good jobs." Certainly, some types of nonstandard work—for example, business consulting or computer programming on a contract basis—pay very well. But as we will see, well-paying nonstandard work is the exception, not the rule.

Yet, the criteria for deciding whether a job is good or bad are not universal.[1] Individuals compare the rewards a job provides against their own needs, preferences, ambitions, and past work histories (see Chapter 13). Personal decisions are also shaped and constrained by the quality and quantity of jobs available in one's community. Since most workers are concerned about maintaining or improving their standard of living and quality of life, material or *extrinsic job rewards* are important. For instance, how much does the job pay? Does it provide medical or pension benefits? Is it part time or full time, seasonal or secure? In the following section, we examine some of the most important differences in job quality. We also look at *occupational status*, which refers to the prestige ranking of a particular job. Other factors, such as *intrinsic work rewards*, are discussed in Chapter 14.

Income Differences

Income is one of the most commonly considered job features for anyone seeking employment. Statistics Canada collects information about income through the Census and the monthly Labour Force Survey (Chapter 3). Using the latter source, which provides data for 2018, we can examine earnings by industry and occupation. Considering only *paid employees* (that is, excluding the self-employed, discussed later in this chapter), we can see that incomes in the service industries are typically lower than in the goods-producing industries. For example, in 2018, average (median) weekly earnings for full-time workers in the goods-producing sector were $1,057, compared to $961 for services. Looking more closely at the goods sector, we see further differences, with weekly median earnings ranging from $1,549 in resource extraction (e.g., forestry, mining, and oil and gas) to $1,125 in construction to $945 in manufacturing. In contrast, weekly median earnings in the service sector were just $576 in accommodation and food services, and $769 in retail and whole-sale trade. But the large and growing service sector contains both lower-tier and upper-tier services, with many better-paying jobs in the latter. Hence, we also see higher weekly earnings in public administration ($1,330), educational services ($1,249), and professional, technical, and scientific services ($1,200).[2]

Moving from industry to occupation comparisons, again drawing on 2018 Labour Force Survey data for individuals working full time, we see notable differences when we examine broad occupational groupings. For instance, average (median) weekly earnings are highest among senior managers ($2,211); professionals in natural and applied sciences ($1,500); professionals in health care, excluding nursing ($1,463); and educational jobs, such as teachers and professors ($1,442). But middle managers in trades, transportation production, and utilities also earn relatively high weekly incomes ($1,600). In contrast, the lowest weekly earnings are found in service-related occupations, notably sales representatives ($656) and sales support occupations ($530).[3]

Higher earnings in some goods-producing and upper-tier services, and in managerial and professional occupations, are due partly to the presence of unions and professional associations that have bargained for higher incomes and full-time jobs (more on this in Chapters 5 and 11). It is also apparent that workers with specific professional skills (e.g., teachers, doctors, and engineers) and more years of formal education are paid more than those with less training. Thus, some of the industrial and occupational differences in earnings are due to supply and demand factors in a labour market that rewards educational investments.

These occupational earning patterns also hide large gender differences. According to the 2018 Labour Force Survey, among Canadians working full time, women received 81 percent of men's median weekly earnings. Looking more closely, we learn that the female–male earnings gap varies considerably by occupation. For instance, the gap is much narrower in senior manager occupations (92 percent), finance, insurance and business-related occupations (94 percent), and para-professional occupations in legal, social, community, and educational services (98 percent). In some cases, such as professional nurses, women out-earn their male peers (104 percent). In other occupations, such as in natural resources and agriculture jobs (67 percent) and middle manager occupations in retail and wholesale trade (64 percent), the female–male earnings gap is much larger. It is important to remember that these figures reflect median weekly earnings for full-time workers. Since women are more likely to work part time, as discussed in Chapter 3, the female–male earnings gap for all employed Canadians (full time and part time) is even wider than what we observe above.[4]

By restricting our discussion to these broad occupational categories, we also overlook the extreme ends of the *income distribution* in the Canadian labour market. At the top of the earnings hierarchy, chief executive officers (CEOs) of Canada's largest firms typically earn huge incomes (based on salaries, performance bonuses, and options to purchase stocks in their company at below-market value). In 2016, for instance, the CEOs of the top 100 companies listed on the Toronto Stock Exchange received an average compensation package of $10.4 million—209 times the average Canadian employment income in the same year (Macdonald 2018: 4). Looked at another way, by about mid-day on January 2, the average CEO had taken home as much pay as the average Canadian workers earns in a year (Macdonald 2018: 4). Equally telling, the earnings of the average Canadian worker in 2016 failed to keep up with inflation (they rose by just 0.5 percent), while the average pay of CEOs increased by 8 percent.

Although business executives have always been generously compensated, current ratios are far higher than in the past. In 1995, for instance, the top 50 CEOs made 85 times as much as the average income (Mackenzie 2016: 11). Analyzing 2016 executive compensation for the 100 highest earners in Canada, Macdonald (2018: 10–11) notes several key trends: rising levels of compensation, the growing use of shares and stock options (which have tax advantages), and generous "golden parachute" retirement packages of $80.1 million in total shared by six retiring CEOs in 2016. There is also a wide range of compensation. For instance, the top earning CEO, from Valeant Pharmaceuticals (now Bausch Health Companies Inc.), received total compensation (base salary plus options) of approximately $83.1 million, with the bulk coming from shares and stock options (approximately $68 million). This compares to compensation of $5.2 million at the bottom of the list. Certain industries figure prominently; for instance, five of the top 40 earners head Canada's largest banks—Royal Bank of

Canada, Toronto-Dominion Bank, Scotiabank, Bank of Montreal, and CIBC. Mining, communications, transportation, and resource firms are also strongly represented. Only three women appear in the top 100 list: Linda Hasenfratz (Linamar, $14.6 million); Dawn Farrell (Transalta Corp, $7.4 million); and Nancy Southern (ATCO Ltd. and Canadian Utilities, $5.3 million). And two of them (Hasenfratz and Southern) are the daughters of the founding CEOs of family firms. Similar family ties are also evident among male CEOs, such as Galen Weston (chair and CEO of George Weston Ltd. and Loblaws, $7.5 million).[5]

At the other end of the scale are numerous workers with very low incomes. Legislated minimum wages in Canada have always been low, and in the past several decades, they have not kept up with inflation. Thus, in 2018, if a worker earning a minimum wage worked 40 hours a week for 52 weeks, she or he would earn anywhere from $23,004 annually in Saskatchewan (the province with the lowest minimum wage of $11.32 per hour) to $31,200 in Alberta (with the highest provincial minimum wage of $15.00 hour, for employees over 18 years of age).[6] However, few, if any, minimum wage workers would be employed year-round for 40 hours a week, so these estimates of annual income are likely too high for this group of workers.

In recent years there has been growing concern over low pay and "living wages" in Canada, the United States, and other countries. Campaigns such as Fight for $15 have advocated for fairer treatment of low-paid workers in the food and service sector, organizing walkouts to support an hourly minimum wage of $15 (vanden Heuvel 2019; Bricker and Dalton 2019; Franco 2019).[7] In Canada, the Liberal Ontario government's 2013 Minimum Wage Advisory Panel recommended regular reviews of minimum wages to ensure their adequacy (Ontario 2014). More recently, the federal Liberal Government's *Federal Minimal Wage: Issue Paper* examined research on whether increases to the minimum wages negatively impact job levels, concluding that, on balance, employment impacts are minimal (Canada 2019). Both reports highlight growing concerns over whether current wage levels provide sufficient income to cover basic needs and allow workers to escape poverty. More recently, in the United States, the House of Representatives passed the Raise the Wage Act in July 2019, in response to growing support for Fight for $15. Unfortunately, it is unlikely to gain support as long as the U.S. Senate is controlled by business-friendly Republicans (vanden Heuvel 2019).

Many, but certainly not all, of these lowest-paid workers in the lower-tier services (retail trade and consumer services) are students, frequently working part time. Women, immigrants, and Indigenous workers are also more likely to hold low-paid jobs. Some older, full-time workers also have minimum wage jobs, but many more are hired at pay rates only a few dollars above the minimum wage. As a second income in a household, such salesclerk, server, cashier, and service-station attendant jobs might help pay some bills. However, if a household relied only on this income, especially if it contained children, it would likely be living well below the official *low-income cutoff*, more commonly called the "poverty line."[8]

Hourly wage rates in blue-collar occupations, such as construction or manufacturing, are typically at least twice as high as the minimum wage. Yet even with a $20-per-hour wage and working full time and year-round, these earnings would still make it extremely difficult to raise a family in most major Canadian urban centres. Furthermore, many of these blue-collar jobs are seasonal and are subject to frequent layoffs. Service jobs are also prone to erratic and insufficient hours. Consequently, when we look closely at the characteristics of Canadian families living below the poverty line, we find that low wages, insufficient work (part time or part year), and periodic unemployment combined are usually the problem. Some of the *working poor* lack education or marketable skills, but many simply cannot find well-paid and secure employment.[9]

Other Employment Benefits

Additional *employment benefits*—a form of indirect pay and increased income security—are another important dimension of the quality of jobs. Canadian employers are legally required to contribute to Employment Insurance (EI), the Canada/Quebec Pension Plan, and Workers' Compensation. Many employers, particularly large firms and public-sector organizations, also spend large amounts on additional benefits, including: paid vacation; sick leave; medical, dental, disability, and life insurance; private pension plans; and maternity/paternity leave. Over the second half of the last century (mid-1950s to late 1990s), the costs of non-wage benefits doubled in Canada, from about 15 percent of total labour costs to more than one-third. Given how much employers spend on such non-wage forms of compensation, it is probably inappropriate to call them "fringe benefits" any longer, as has been the custom (Budd 2004: 597).[10]

According to Statistics Canada's 2016 General Social Survey, nearly half of Canadian workers (46 percent) have access to an employer-sponsored medical or dental benefit plan, and just over one-third of workers (38.5 percent) will receive a pension from their employer. Much like income, access to benefits varies widely across socio-demographic characteristics, work status, and occupation. As shown in Figure 4.1, men are more likely than women to have medical/dental and pension benefits, though the gap for pensions is narrower. Younger workers are also less likely to receive either medical/dental or pension benefits; just one in five do. Work status also makes a significant difference. Full-time and regular/permanent workers are at least twice as likely as part-time and temporary workers to receive medical/dental or pension benefits. Of all groups, those belonging to a union have the best access to medical /dental benefits (56.8 percent) and pensions (60 percent). Those in high-status professional occupations also have far greater access to most non-wage benefits than those working in more routine work, such as service and sales. The higher rates for manufacturing workers no doubt reflect their higher rate of unionization compared to other workers. In short, the distribution of benefits, like income, is highly polarized within the Canadian labour force.

Occupational Status

We seldom find doctors, lawyers, scientists, or professors avoiding the question: "What do you do?" But for retail sales clerks, janitors, parking-lot attendants, and many others, the same question might elicit an apologetic "I'm just a . . ." In short, there is wide consensus in our society about which jobs have higher status. Although less important than income and benefits (which directly determine someone's standard of living) and job security (which ensures continuity of that standard), *occupational status* (or prestige) is something we must also consider when comparing different jobs. To a great extent, our self-image and the respect we receive from others are determined by our occupational status, although there is probably also a tendency for individuals situated higher within a stratification system to take

FIGURE 4.1   Non-wage Benefits by Socio-demographic and Work
Characteristics, Canada, 2016

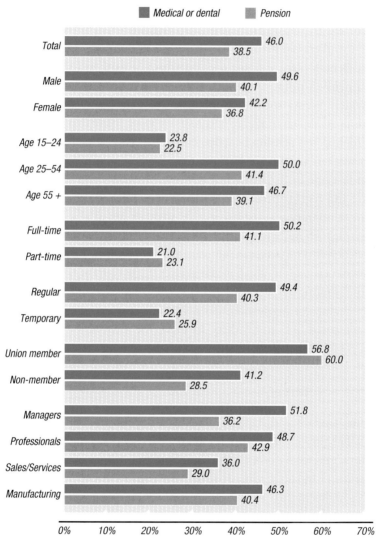

Source: Statistics Canada, 2016 General Social Survey, Public Use Data file (*N* = 8,820; person-weighted data).

occupational status more seriously (Ollivier 2000). Status also plays a key role
in solidifying inequalities. As Cecilia Ridgeway (2014) notes, status reflects
shared cultural beliefs about which groups are "better," shaping evaluations

of competence and value, and the subsequent allocation of resources and power in organizations.

On average, individuals in higher-status occupations have higher incomes. It may seem that both higher pay and higher status are a direct result of the greater skill and responsibility required by certain jobs. Generally, higher-status jobs do require more education, cognitive ability, and skill (Boyd 2008). But it is also possible that some occupations have come to be seen as more prestigious because, over time, incomes in this line of work have risen. Higher incomes, in turn, might be the result of skill increases, but they may also reflect the ability of a powerful occupational group to limit entry into its field or to raise the prices for the services it provides. It is also clear that some occupations have traditionally had higher social status because they were viewed as men's work rather than as women's work (see Chapter 6). Thus, for a variety of reasons, jobs defined as "better" in terms of extrinsic rewards (e.g., pay, benefits) typically also have higher status in society.

Researchers have developed two different basic types of occupational status scales to rank occupations—one focusing on *occupational prestige*, and the other on *socioeconomic status*. In Canada, we now have updated scales of both types. Using the first approach, Goyder and Frank (2007) used a national survey to ask Canadians to rank the 26 major occupational categories in the National Occupational Classification (NOC) system (discussed in Chapter 3) on their *occupational prestige*. This scale (ranging from 0 to 100) provides prestige scores as low as 52 for unskilled labourers in primary industries, as well as unskilled sales and service occupations, rising to, for example, 57 for clerical occupations, 67 for skilled occupations in primary industries, 72 for professional occupations in business and finance, and 81 for professional occupations in health (2007: 69).

Boyd (2008) used a different approach, ranking occupations by the average income and education of Canadians in these occupations according to Canadian Census data. This produced a *socioeconomic status* (SES) scale ranging from a possible low of 0 to a possible high of 100 that ranked more than 500 detailed NOC categories. Examples of SES at the detailed occupational level range from 9 for nannies, 29 for hairstylists, 38 for receptionists, 53 for radio announcers, and 75 for dental hygienists, up to 92 for psychologists and 100 for doctors. While the SES scale has a much wider actual range than does the prestige scale, both scales help us to compare shared perceptions of "good jobs" and "bad jobs" and the many in between.

NONSTANDARD WORK ARRANGEMENTS

Varieties of Nonstandard Work

While most employed Canadians have a full-time, year-round, permanent paid job, alternatives to this standard type of employment arrangement—referred to as either *nonstandard*, *precarious*, or *contingent* work—have been slowly increasing, not just in Canada, but in all industrialized societies.[11] *Part-time work* is the most common type of nonstandard work, but the number of *multiple-job holders* has also been expanding. The *self-employed* category, especially *own-account* (who work alone), has likewise grown. And there are also indications that *temporary* (or contract) work has become more widespread.

Why these changes? Nonstandard work may be mandated by employers or initiated by individual workers. Many employers, in both the private and public sectors, have responded to economic difficulties in recent decades by replacing full-time with part-time workers (and sometimes part-year workers) and by eliminating permanent positions. The latter have sometimes been replaced with temporary (limited-term contract) positions or workers hired from a temporary help agency (Fuller 2011; Fuller et al. 2014). These employment strategies allow employers greater flexibility to respond to uneven demands for goods and services, and they clearly reduce labour costs (probably a more important factor, in many cases). This "flexible firm" model (see Pollert 1988) is discussed in Chapter 9. At the same time, a growing number of Canadians have chosen to set up their own business (the own-account self-employed) or to take on a second job (Hughes 2005; Doody et al. 2016). Finally, the rise of the service sector has driven some of these trends to the extent that workers may be needed only for a few hours at a time to cover peak periods, such as lunch- or dinner-time in restaurants and cafés.

Some workers choose alternative forms of employment (part-time work or self-employment, for example) because of personal preference. But for many others, such choices are a response to a difficult labour market. Workers may create their own jobs because few paid jobs are available to them; accept temporary or part-time work only when permanent, full-time jobs are scarce; or take on a second job because their first job pays poorly. Nonstandard jobs typically pay less, provide fewer benefits, are less likely to be covered by labour legislation, and have less employment security (Vosko 2005; Law Commission of Ontario 2012; Kalleberg 2018; Kalleberg and Vallas 2018), so an increase in nonstandard employment means an increase in the precariousness of employment and income for many Canadian workers. Furthermore, there is evidence that a job history of nonstandard work carries a long-term cost or *cumulative disadvantage.* Such workers have reduced access to workplace training and education, making it difficult to move into better-paying, more stable, jobs.

We mentioned the increase in *own-account self-employment* in the past decades. This refers to people who are self-employed, but without employees, working only for themselves. In 2018, approximately 10.6 percent of working Canadians were in this category, which includes farmers, doctors, lawyers, and business consultants, as well as the small entrepreneurs we typically associate with self-employment. This is up from 6.4 percent four decades earlier.[12] *Multiple-job holding* increased from 2 percent in 1977 to roughly 5 percent in 1993 and held steady there until the mid-2000s, inching up to 5.6 percent in 2018.[13] People take on a second job for a variety of reasons, including topping up an inadequate income, paying off debts, and saving for the future. However, since most are supplementing a full-time job, and a notable group have professional or managerial jobs, we should be cautious about assuming that all Canadians with more than one job are in a precarious financial or employment situation (Patterson 2018).

Nonstandard jobs are much more common in some industries. Agriculture has the highest rate of nonstandard work. A large proportion of these nonstandard workers are the own-account self-employed. Construction also has a high rate of nonstandard work, reflecting extensive self-employment and temporary contract work. But given their relative size in the economy, the lower-tier service industries—retail and other consumer services—are the main source of nonstandard employment. A worker's demographic characteristics also influence her or his likelihood of being employed in a nonstandard job. Women are more likely to be in nonstandard jobs than are men. Nonstandard forms of employment also are concentrated among the youngest and oldest members of the workforce.

Part-Time Work

Half a century ago, less than 4 percent of employed Canadians held part-time jobs, but that is far from the case now. During the 1960s and 1970s, part-time work became more common, and today it is the most prevalent type of nonstandard work. Until recently, *full-time work* was defined by Statistics Canada as working 30 or more hours per week in total. But the rise in multiple-job holding forced a rethinking of this definition, since some people holding several part-time jobs (totalling more than 30 hours) were being counted as full-time workers. Since 1996, *part-time workers* have been defined as those who work fewer than 30 hours per week in their *main* job.

Figure 4.2 displays part-time rates for the past several decades, calculated using the new definition. Back in 1976, the national part-time rate for all employed Canadians (ages 15 and older) was roughly 13 percent. The recession in the early 1980s pushed the part-time rate much higher, to 17 percent by 1983. The recession at the beginning of the 1990s led to another increase in part-time employment rates to 19 percent in 1993. Since that time, the part-time rate has hovered between 18 and 19 percent. In 2018, 18.7 percent of all employed Canadians (nearly 3.5 million) were working part time.

Part-time rates for adult women and men (ages 25 and older) are also plotted in Figure 4.2. It is apparent that few employed men 25 years of age and older are working part time, although the rate for this group climbed from 2 percent in the mid-1970s to 8.1 percent in 2018. As for adult women, their much higher part-time rates have fluctuated in the low to mid-20 percent range over the same period. In 2018, 21.1 percent of women 25 years of age and older worked part time. Overall, three-quarters of all part-time workers are women (Moyser 2017: 16).

The most prominent trend observed in Figure 4.2 is the increase in part-time employment among young people (ages 15 to 24). In 1976, the youth part-time employment rate was 21 percent. By 1983, the rate had jumped to over 30 percent, then climbed further to 41 percent by 1991. By 1995, the youth part-time rate hit 45 percent, before dropping slightly to 43.5 percent in 2001, and then rising to nearly 48 percent in 2018. Thus, in the first decade of the 21st century, nearly half of all employed 15- to 24-year-olds in Canada were working part time. As with older workers, youth part-time rates vary by gender, with a male rate of 40.3 percent and a female rate of 55.2 percent in 2018.

Some people choose part-time work because it allows them to balance work and family responsibilities, to continue their education while still holding a job, or simply to have more leisure time. Others, *involuntary part-time workers*, are forced to accept part-time jobs because they cannot find one that is full time (Patterson 2018). The monthly Labour Force Survey asks part-time

FIGURE 4.2   Part-Time Employment by Age and Gender, Canada, 1976–2018

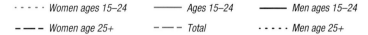

· · · · · Women ages 15–24   ——— Ages 15–24   ——— Men ages 15–24

– —– Women age 25+   – – – Total   · · · · · Men age 25+

Part-time employment rate (%)

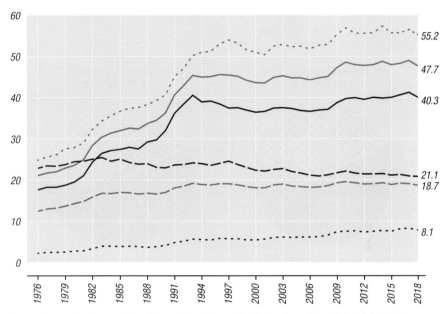

Source: Statistics Canada, Labour Force Characteristics by Sex and Detailed Age Group, Annual, Table 14-10-0327-01.

workers why they are working part time, providing a range of answers. Figure 4.3 displays the reasons given by Canadian part-time workers in 1975 and 2018. The 1975 and 2018 data are not strictly comparable because of changes in how "reasons for part-time work" have been measured (Statistics Canada 2011: 15). Still, they offer the best available information on changing patterns over time.

In 1975, 37 percent of less than one million part-time workers stated that they did not want a full-time job; they had a personal preference for working part time. Another 35 percent chose part-time work because they were attending school. For a majority of youth, such jobs fit well alongside high school, college, or university. Eleven percent of part-time workers indicated they were working part time "involuntarily"—that is, they were "only able to find part-time work," suggesting a lack of suitable alternatives. Finally, 12 percent of

FIGURE 4.3 Reasons for Part-Time Work, Canada, 1975 and 2018

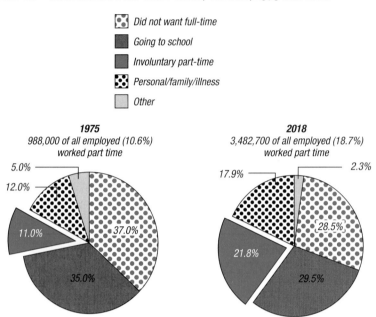

Legend:
- ☒ Did not want full-time
- ■ Going to school
- ■ Involuntary part-time
- ☒ Personal/family/illness
- ☐ Other

1975
988,000 of all employed (10.6%)
worked part time

5.0%
12.0%
11.0%
37.0%
35.0%

2018
3,482,700 of all employed (18.7%)
worked part time

17.9%
2.3%
28.5%
21.8%
29.5%

Source: Adapted from Statistics Canada. 1975 data from Labour Force Historical Review 2001, Cat. No. 71F0004XCb. 2018 data from Statistics Canada, Part-Time Employment by Reason, Table 14-10-0029-01. https://www150.statcan.gc.ca/t1/tbl1/en/tv.action?pid=1410002901.

part-time workers indicated personal reasons, such as illness or family matters, and 5 percent provided "other" unspecified reasons.

Adult women working part time, especially those with children, are most likely to cite personal or family reasons, or simply state that they do not want full-time work. But had such workers been asked whether they would still prefer a part-time job if they had access to adequate and affordable childcare, it is likely that at least some would have expressed interest in full-time work. In other words, traditional assumptions about caregiving responsibilities, together with a shortage of affordable, quality childcare, may lead us to underestimate the real level of involuntary part-time work among adult women (Duffy and Pupo 1992; McRae 2003; Lewis and Simpson 2017).

Looking at the 2018 data, we see both continuity and change—though again, we note that "reasons for part-time work" have been measured somewhat differently. A fairly sizable group (28.5 percent) did not want full-time work; for some Canadians, part-time work remains a preference. Similar to 1975, another sizable group (29.5 percent) were working part time while also attending school. Personal, family illness, and other reasons together accounted for about 18 percent of workers in 2018. What is most notable, however, is the larger size of the "involuntary" part-time group, which accounted for 21.8 percent of part-time workers (twice as high as in 1975). These individuals indicated they were working part time because of "business conditions" or being "unable to find full-time work" (whether or not they had looked for full-time work in the last month). While part of the rise in involuntary part-time work may reflect measurement issues, some part is also a result of employer practices as they seek to increase the flexibility of their staffing and hours, and to reduce payroll and benefit costs.

Part-time rates vary considerably across industries and occupations. In 2018, the part-time rate in the goods-producing sector was still low (only 6.1 percent). Thus, most of the part-time jobs are in the service industries, in both the lower- and upper-tier services. For example, in 2018, 33.4 percent of workers in retail trade were employed part time. High rates are also found in accommodation and food services (41.0 percent), culture and recreation (28.9 percent), education (25.1 percent), and health care and social assistance (22.5 percent). However, many of the part-time jobs in the upper-tier services (nurses and teachers, for example) are better-paid than the part-time jobs (often held by students) in the retail trade and other consumer services.[14]

Temporary Employment

Some forms of temporary employment, like seasonal employment in the tourism or construction industry, have been part of the Canadian labour market for many decades (Vosko 2000; Smith and Neuwirth 2008; Stanford 2017). However, both private- and public-sector employers now hire more employees on a limited-term contract basis (perhaps six months or a year), rather than offering permanent positions as was the custom in past decades. In addition, temporary help agencies have been hiring more workers to be sent out on assignment to employers seeking to fill a temporary need. Such trends are also evident in industrialized economies around the world (Fudge and Strauss 2014; Fuller et al. 2015; Pedulla 2016).

In terms of detailed statistical trends, though, we know less about the growth in *temporary employment*, since Statistics Canada has monitored this phenomenon on a regular basis only since the late 1990s. Defining temporary jobs as those with a specific end date, the Labour Force Survey shows 13.3 percent of Canadians (2,103,500 workers) were in such positions in 2018, up from just over 11 percent in 1997 when Statistics Canada began tracking this trend. One-fifth (20 percent) of all temporary workers were in seasonal jobs, and one-quarter (25.9 percent) were in casual jobs (very short-term, with no specific contract). Most others (53 percent) held positions with a specific, contracted term. Of note, temporary jobs grew by 63 percent between 1997 and 2008, compared to a 35 percent growth rate for permanent jobs.[15]

Gender differences in temporary work are minimal, with roughly 12 percent of men and 14 percent of women holding such jobs. As with part-time work, however, young workers are heavily overrepresented. In 2018, approximately 32 percent of 15- to 24-year-old employed Canadians were in a job with a specific end date, compared to just 10 percent for those 25 years and older. Young student workers are more likely to be employed in the lower-tier consumer services, where low-paying temporary jobs are common. In the upper-tier services (education, health, social services, and public administration, for example), it has become common to offer new (younger) employees a contract position rather than a permanent job (Stecy-Hildebrandt et al. 2019).

Quite often, contract employees work alongside permanent employees, performing similar tasks and for comparable pay, but without the guarantee of long-term employment. While some people, often those with highly marketable skills, find such arrangements satisfactory, others feel frustrated and worried by their insecurity and future prospects. Studies show that temporary workers experience a wage gap relative to permanent workers (Galarneau 2010; Fuller 2011; Fuller et al. 2014), with potential for negative career effects (or *scarring*) over the long term. While the majority of temporary workers do move into permanent jobs or see some income gains in time, this depends on the type of temporary work involved (Fuller et al. 2015).[16]

Finally, as noted in Chapter 2, another form of temporary work that has become increasingly common, and controversial, in Canada involves temporary foreign workers (TFWs) who migrate to fill jobs in a variety of low-paid sectors. In recent years, the number of individuals admitted to Canada to work temporarily has grown rapidly (Foster 2012; Lenard and Straehle 2012). Typically,

TFWs are restricted to specific occupations and locations, and to prescribed employers—for instance, working as live-in caregivers to young children or the elderly (Torres 2012), or working as seasonal agricultural workers (Vosko 2018). This raises concerns about the potential for the exploitation of TFWs as they are unable to leave unacceptable working conditions or to seek jobs that can improve their income, benefits, or opportunities. While we discuss this trend in greater detail in Chapter 5, we note here that, in recent years, fewer TFWs have been employed in higher-skilled jobs, raising questions about whether TFWs are being used not to fill labour supply gaps but instead to increase labour supply and keep wages low. Beyond live-in jobs (e.g., nannies/babysitters), the most common TFW jobs have been food counter attendants and kitchen helpers, cooks, construction trades helpers and labourers, light duty cleaners, musicians and singers, and food and beverage servers (Foster 2012: 29).

SELF-EMPLOYMENT, GIGS, AND ENTERPRISE CULTURE

Like many other industrialized capitalist economies, Canada has seen a resurgence of self-employment in recent decades. Often seen as part of the "new economy," this trend is, in some ways, also a return to historical patterns. In the middle of the 20th century, one-third of Canadians were self-employed, working as farmers, shopkeepers, tradespeople, or in small family businesses. But by the early 1980s, just 10 percent of Canadians were self-employed (Riddell 1985: 9). In the last few decades, however, this decline has reversed. In 2018, nearly 2.9 million working Canadians (15.3 percent of the total) were self-employed.[17] Self-employment has risen in other industrialized countries as well, such as the United States, Australia, and the United Kingdom. But the trend in Canada has been especially pronounced (Hughes 2017).

At the same time, we have seen a growing emphasis on "enterprise culture," with federal and provincial and territorial governments promoting business start-up programs in hopes of boosting "high-growth entrepreneurship" (Aldrich and Reuf, 2018). But most self-employment is far removed from this Silicon Valley ideal and, instead, reflects *everyday entrepreneurship* (Welter et al. 2017), that is, self-employed caregivers, tradespeople, and professionals; small home-based or main-street businesses; and increasingly "gig workers," such as Uber drivers, TaskRabbits, and the like (Doody et al. 2016; Hughes 2005,

2017; Grekour and Liu 2018). Complicating things, some of these workers may be "disguised employees'" rather than truly independent, self-employed workers. For instance, many contend that Uber drivers are really disguised employees, as the company sets the prices drivers charge, monitors their performance, and can end their access to the platform at any time (Tucker 2018).

In Canada, the number of self-employed *employers* (those who hire others to work for them) has always been much smaller than the number of *own-account self-employed*, also called "solo self-employed" (Hughes 2005). But in recent decades, this latter group has grown rapidly. Compared to the 1980s when there were just 1.2 solo workers for every small-business employer, in 2018 there were 2.3. solo workers for every small-business employer. Thus, roughly 70 percent of Canada's self-employed work on their own account.[18]

Self-employment is still more prevalent among men than among women, but women are making up an increasing proportion of the self-employed. Some women seek greater challenge and opportunity, and others better work–family balance (Hughes 2017). Interestingly, although younger people are often believed to be more entrepreneurial, self-employment is higher among older workers, declining only after aged 65. This makes sense, as older workers have had more time to accrue the key resources (e.g., human capital, finances, social networks) needed for self-employment success. They have also had more time to identify and refine their business ideas, while working for others.

When asked about their reasons for choosing self-employment, about one-third of Canadian self-employed workers cite "independence, freedom, and being one's own boss" as their top reason, about 15 percent say the "nature of the job," and a combined total of 17 percent cite "work–balance" or "more flexible hours." Just under 7 percent report being unable to find suitable employment (Yassad and Ferrao 2019). Though economic recessions in the 1980s and 1990s in Canada were accompanied by a rise in self-employment—especially own-account—the relationship between economic downturns and self-employment growth is weak (Arai 1997; Hughes 2005; Manser and Picot 1999: 43). In Canada, self-employment gains have been strongest among well-educated workers and those in professional, science, and technical occupations. This suggests self-employment is more opportunity-driven than necessity based. But for some, self-employment is clearly a job of last resort.

Employment careers vary widely for the self-employed. Solo workers are less likely to remain self-employed long term, with just one-third continuing after five years, compared to more than half who employ others (Grekour and Liu 2018). This may be partly explained by greater earnings polarization among the self-employed (than paid employees). While well-educated professionals and high-growth entrepreneurs generally report high incomes, less educated self-employed workers typically struggle (Barley and Kunda 2006; Hughes 2005; Wall 2015).

Even among similarly situated self-employed workers, however, assessment of job quality can vary, reflecting a complex trade-off workers make between different benefits and risks. Illustrating this, with respect to the "gig economy," Rosenblat (2018) found very mixed opinions amongst Uber drivers about their jobs, noting that assessments were relative to available options. For one former child-care provider, there were clear gains:

> I try it and I love it . . . Because the money, amazing schedule, you can have your own schedule, you meet many different people . . . My life changed one thousand percent, not one hundred percent . . . I miss the kids, but not the money and the job. (Rosenblat 2018: 73)

For others, like this less enamoured driver, this is clearly not the case: "Yeah, all the free time you're supposed to have, well that's bullshit, you work your ass off, drive your car into the ground for nothing. If you have a job, I recommend you keep it" (Rosenblat 2018: 64).

HOURS OF WORK AND ALTERNATIVE WORK ARRANGEMENTS

Canadians spend far less time at work than they did over a century ago. In 1870, the standard number of hours in a workweek (the number beyond which overtime would typically be paid to full-time workers) in the manufacturing sector was 64, dropping to 59 by 1901. Through the 20th century, working hours further declined as a result of trade union pressure and the introduction of new technologies that produced goods more efficiently. By 1976, average working time (for all workers, manufacturing and service) was 39 hours per week.

Since then, working hours have continued to decline to an average of 36 weekly hours in 2018.[19]

A closer look, however, reveals another important change. In particular, we have witnessed a polarization in hours worked—with some people working long hours and other people working part time (Usalcas 2008).[20] In 2018, over 61 percent of all employed Canadians 15 years and older worked between 35 and 40 hours per week in their main job, down from 66 percent in 1976. Just over one-quarter worked fewer than 35 hours. The remainder worked over 40 hours, with 5 percent working between 41 and 49 hours, and 7 percent working 50 hours or more each week. Thus, while the average number of hours worked has declined slightly since the mid-1970s, the much bigger story concerns the proportion of Canadians working long hours, as well as the long-term rise of part-time work.

We have already discussed part-time work. But a few observations about longer hours are necessary. For some workers, particularly the self-employed and professionals, long hours are expected and generate higher incomes. For others, the added work may simply be an attempt to avoid a decline in standard of living when real incomes stagnate. But longer hours cut into leisure and family time, and have been shown to have detrimental effects on health and work–life balance (Sullivan 2016). In countries such as Japan, a culture of extreme hours and resulting law suits against employers have led to social and legal recognition of *karoshi,* death by overwork (Sullivan 2016). Overwork is also seen as a growing problem in other countries, due to *greedy organizations* (Coser 1967) that push their workers harder than they should and *work extension* (the spread of work time into personal and family time) facilitated by mobile communication technologies and round-the-clock expectations by employers (Wajcman 2015).

Overtime work is excluded from Statistics Canada's reporting of regular workweeks, but the Labour Force Survey does ask respondents whether they have worked any paid or unpaid overtime in the week before the survey. Over the past decade, more than one in five workers reported putting in some overtime. What is particularly interesting is that about half of total overtime worked is unpaid. So, in 2019, for example, 10 percent of all workers worked unpaid overtime in a typical month, usually giving about eight hours, on average, to their employer without receiving any compensation in return. Unpaid overtime violates employment standards legislation and is increasingly regarded as a form of *wage theft* (Vosko et al. 2017). Because of this, class-action lawsuits have been filed by employees at several Canadian banks, seeking compensation for their unpaid overtime hours.[21]

Shift work has long been common, but not always welcome, in some industries (e.g., health, consumer services), but there does seem to be some interest among both workers and employers in alternative work schedules. *Flextime* (choosing the time to start and stop work) and *job sharing* (where two individuals share a full-time job) have received more attention in recent decades, as have *teleworking* and *mobile work* (working at home or in a remote site, often using computer technology), as noted in Chapter 2. These options can help workers achieve better work–life balance, though they may also at times hinder collaboration and reduce satisfying interactions with coworkers.[22] Yet one of the most rigorous studies to date in the United States found that providing workers with greater control over their schedule, and the specific timing of their work, had a number of positive effects, reducing burnout, perceived stress, and psychological distress while also improving job satisfaction (Moen et al. 2016).

UNEMPLOYMENT TRENDS

Counting the Unemployed

Labour Force Survey estimates indicate that, during 2018, there were 19.8 million Canadians ages 15 and older in the labour force, with 18.7 million of them employed or self-employed. The unemployed, numbering just over 1.1 million, made up the difference. To put this in perspective, the number of unemployed people in 2018 was equivalent to the total population (children included) of Nova Scotia (959,942) and Prince Edward Island (155,324) combined. The official *unemployment rate* is calculated by dividing the number of individuals out of work and actively looking for work (the unemployed) by the total number of labour force participants (including the unemployed). In 2018, the national unemployment rate was 5.8 percent—down significantly from 8.3 percent in 2009, following the 2008 financial crash, which had ripple effects throughout the Canadian and global economy. Unemployment is now at a 43-year low, a significant change from the dramatically high levels of unemployment (which peaked around 11 percent) of the recessions of the early 1980s and 1990s.

Such calculations reveal the percentage of labour force participants who are unemployed at a particular point (an annual average provides the average of 12 monthly estimates). But over a year, many people find jobs while many others quit or lose them. Consequently, if we were to count the number of people who had been unemployed at some point during a year, this alternative unemployment rate would be higher. For example, in 1997, when the annual average unemployment rate was high (9.1 percent), over the entire year, 17 percent of individuals and 28 percent of all families had experienced unemployment (Sussman 2000: 11).

The official definition of unemployment, whether we calculate rates for a single point in time or over the full year, identifies a state of being without paid work (including self-employment). It excludes students who do not want to work while studying, individuals performing unpaid work in the home, people with disabilities who are not seeking work, and the retired, all of whom are considered to be outside the labour force. It also excludes potential labour force participants who have given up the search for work, believing no work is available. Historically, economic downturns create a surge in these *discouraged* workers. For example, we saw a significant pool of discouraged workers in Canada during the 1981–82 recession, numbering nearly 200,000. In the early 1990s recession, we saw roughly half that many (Akyeampong 1992). Lower numbers of discouraged workers in the 1990s reflected some of the labour market changes already discussed: declining youth labour force participation, rising educational enrollments, and earlier retirement. In other words, rather than waiting for new jobs to materialize, a larger proportion of jobless Canadians may have stayed in or returned to school, or retired early, during the 1992–93 recession.

Canadian Unemployment Rates over Time

Canadian unemployment rates reached their highest point in the last century (around 20 percent) during the Depression of the 1930s (Brown 1987). But these hard times were quickly replaced by labour shortages during World War II and in the immediate postwar years. The average national unemployment rate was only 2 percent during the 1940s. Since the end of

World War II, unemployment has slowly climbed higher, responding to successive business cycles of recession and expansion.

Figure 4.4 outlines unemployment rates from the mid-1970s to 2018, the period for which the Labour Force Survey provides comparable data. As we can see from the "total unemployment rate," unemployment rates peaked during two recessions, one at the beginning of the 1980s (11.9 percent in 1983) and another in the 1990s (11.4 percent in 1993). Since 2000, the national jobless rate has fallen sharply, though with ups and down. This marked the reversal of a long-term upward trend in unemployment that had taken place in the 1980s and 1990s. Looking at the first two decades of the 21st century, we see a boom–bust picture of the economy and, therefore, unemployment. After dipping below 7 percent in 2000, unemployment rates increased slightly in the early 2000s and then fell steadily, hitting a 33-year low in 2008. The Great Recession in late 2008, however, caused a spike in unemployment. Yet rates did not reach 9 percent in 2009. Thus, despite periods of high unemployment in the late 2000s, recent decades resemble the 1970s more than the 1980s or 1990s, when high and persistent unemployment was a significant problem.[23]

Long-term unemployment (defined as 52 weeks or more) can have a *scarring effect* on workers, leaving gaps in their resumé and careers that make it much

FIGURE 4.4   Unemployment Rates by Age and Gender, Canada, 1976–2018

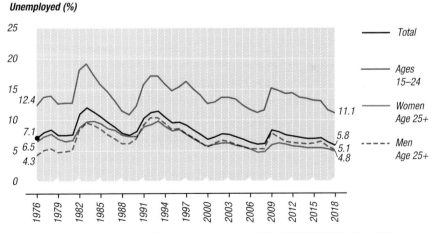

Source: Statistics Canada. Employment and Unemployment Rate, Annual. Table 14-10-0106-01. https://www150.statcan. gc.ca/t1/tbl1/en/tv.action?pid=141001060.

harder to return to work. In the late 1980s and 1990s, as unemployment rates climbed, the duration of unemployment increased. In 1976, the average spell of unemployment was about 14 weeks. By 1983, average duration was 21 weeks, falling and then rising again to 26 weeks in 1994. Many older workers laid off during the recessions of the early 1980s and 1990s experienced prolonged periods of unemployment, creating a significant group of discouraged workers. A similar situation emerged several decades later, following the Great Recession of 2008. In 2009, nearly 8 percent of the unemployed had not worked in at least a year. In 2018, the average duration of unemployment was down to 16 weeks, close to mid-1970s levels. But nearly 10 percent of workers were long-term unemployed, suggesting some deeper structural changes still at work in key sectors or affecting specific demographic groups.[24]

Regional Variations in Unemployment

National rates of unemployment conceal considerable variation across regions of the country. In 2018, Newfoundland and Labrador's unemployment rate averaged 13.8 percent, compared with 8.0 percent in New Brunswick, 7.5 percent in Nova Scotia, and 9.4 percent in Prince Edward Island. Ontario and Quebec at 5.6 and 5.5 percent, respectively, were just below the national average of 5.8 percent. Moving through the Prairies, the rate rose to 6.0 percent in Manitoba, 6.1 percent in Saskatchewan, and 6.6 percent in Alberta, before shifting down to 4.7 percent in British Columbia.[25] The Atlantic provinces, particularly Newfoundland and Labrador, have had higher-than-average rates of unemployment for decades, while Ontario and Quebec have typically had lower rates—despite recent shocks in the manufacturing sector. Manitoba and Saskatchewan are just above the national average, while Alberta has higher unemployment given its ongoing reliance on the more volatile energy sector.

Unemployment also tends to be concentrated within specific occupational groups and industrial sectors. Seasonal work such as fishing, logging, and construction carries a high risk of unemployment and helps account for some of the higher levels of unemployment in the natural resource–dependent regions of the country. Manufacturing jobs are also prone to unemployment because economic downturns often lead to layoffs and plant shutdowns. In the downturn of the late 2000s, the manufacturing sector in Canada was particularly hard hit. Globalization continues to contribute to job loss and insecurity in manufacturing, as the recent closure of the General Motors plant in Oshawa, Ontario, attests (Fife and Atkins 2018). In contrast, professional and technical services have been somewhat more protected, though this is also changing.

In 2018, the unemployment rate for Indigenous workers ages 15 and older was 10.1 percent, compared to only 5.7 percent for the non-Indigenous population. Combined with lower-than-average rates of labour force participation, it is clear this group faces serious labour market disadvantages. Indigenous unemployment rates have decreased over the long term, but higher unemployment rates for Indigenous workers persist, especially for those living on-reserve (HSRDC 2013). Isolated Indigenous communities in regions such as northern Manitoba, Saskatchewan, Alberta, and the territories offer few employment opportunities. In contrast, in urban census metropolitan areas, unemployment rates are lower but still high relative to the rest of the Canadian population. For instance, according to the 2006 Census, in the six Canadian cities with the largest Indigenous populations—Winnipeg, Vancouver, Edmonton, Calgary, Toronto, and Saskatoon—unemployment rates were two to four times as high for Indigenous people.[26]

Higher Indigenous unemployment is the result of direct and indirect discrimination by employers, lower levels of education among Indigenous workers, and gaps in their work experience resulting from employment in short-term, low-skilled jobs (Lamb 2015, 2018). These dynamics emerge from ongoing processes of colonization, as discussed in Chapter 1, which have led to limited employment prospects for Indigenous people and marginalized them in precarious work (Camfield 2019). Reflecting this, Lamb (2015) finds that Indigenous workers were more severely affected by the 2008 financial crash than were non-Indigenous workers, experiencing a higher increase, and longer duration, of unemployment in the two years following. Not surprisingly, they were also more likely to become discouraged workers—that is, no longer actively seeking employment.[27] We return to these issues in Chapter 5.

Gender and Unemployment

A comparison of female and male unemployment rates since the end of World War II reveals some interesting shifts in relative position. Looking at adult workers (25 years and older), during the 1950s and early 1960s, male unemployment rates were generally about twice as high as those for females. The two rates converged in the mid-1960s, and by the 1970s, female rates were typically about 2 percent higher than male rates. This trend continued until the recession of the early 1980s when, for a second time, the two rates came together. For the rest of that decade, female rates of joblessness were again higher than male rates, but the difference was always less than 1 to 2 percent. During the 1990–92 recession and its aftermath, men were slightly more likely to be unemployed. Since the mid-1990s, however, there has been a third convergence, and in the past few years, women's unemployment has fallen slightly below that of men. In 2018, as Figure 4.4 shows, unemployment rates for women and men (ages 25 and older) were 4.8 and 5.1 percent, respectively.

We would need a much more detailed analysis than is possible here to explain these shifts in female and male unemployment rates. Nevertheless, a large part of the explanation would focus on women's locations in the labour market. Female labour force participation was much lower in the 1950s and 1960s, and women were employed in a limited number of traditionally female occupations. Unemployment then, as now, was considerably higher in the blue-collar occupations, in which few women were found. Since that time, women have made their way into the rapidly expanding service sector alongside men. But many women continue to be employed in lower-level, less secure positions and thus have become more vulnerable to unemployment in recent decades. For men, however, the recessions at the beginning of the 1980s and 1990s, as well as the downturn of 2008–9, have meant widespread layoffs in blue-collar industries (manufacturing, for example), thus leading to higher male rates when the economy weakens. In short, more men are located in vulnerable sectors.

Youth Unemployment

Young Canadians (ages 15 to 24), particularly those with the least education (high-school dropouts, for example), have also experienced high rates of unemployment (Lowe and Krahn 1999). In the 1970s, youth unemployment fluctuated between 9 and 14 percent. As Figure 4.4 shows, the 1981–82 recession pushed the rate to about 20 percent, before it dropped back to around 11 percent by 1989. Following the recession that began in 1990, youth unemployment rates rose again to the 15 to 17 percent range in 1993–94. By 2000, as the economy strengthened and unemployment dropped, the youth unemployment rate fell to a low of 11.2 percent in 2007, before spiking to 15.2 percent in 2009. By 2018, it had again declined slightly to 11.1 percent.

Even though youth unemployment is affected by the same economic forces that determine joblessness for adults, young workers have fared worse for several decades in the Canadian labour market—in fact, the youth unemployment rate has not been below 10 percent since the early 1970s. Moreover, even though young people typically have shorter spells of unemployment, because more of their previous employment is part time or part year they are less likely to have accrued sufficient hours to be eligible for EI.

Throughout the past several decades, unemployment rates for teenagers (ages 15 to 19) have been higher than jobless rates among young adults (ages 20 to 24). Compared with teenagers, young adults are typically better educated and have more work experience. In 2018, for example, the unemployment rate for 15- to 19-year-olds was 15.3 percent, compared with 8.8 percent for 20- to 24-year-olds. While female and male adult (25 and older) unemployment rates have again converged (see Figure 4.4), we still see a gender difference in joblessness among youth. For teenagers, the female unemployment rate in 2018 was 13.8 percent, compared to 16.8 percent for males. Among young adults, the female unemployment rate (7.2 percent) was also lower than the male rate (10.2 percent). These differences reflect, in part, the higher proportion of young males who seek employment in blue-collar industries where unemployment rates remain higher than in service industries (where a larger proportion of young women look for work).[28]

Causes of Unemployment

We have already hinted at some of the causes of rising unemployment over the past several decades. Obviously, there are demographic factors to consider. The sizable increase in the birthrate in the years following World War II led to rapid growth in the labour force several decades later. In addition, the increased proportion of women entering the labour force generated greater demand for jobs. But people working for pay are also people with money to spend, so the growth in labour force participation led to substantial job creation. Thus, past economic analyses conclude that these demographic shifts have had little impact on the overall increase in unemployment (Gera 1991).

Another basic explanation focuses on the characteristics of the jobless. Such arguments are typically supported by anecdotal evidence and little else. One version suggests that many of the unemployed could be working if only they would accept the less attractive jobs available. In many communities, however, the number of jobless far exceeds the total number of available jobs (Hironimus-Wendt 2008). Furthermore, many of the jobs that may be available (and perhaps are even hard to fill) are part-time positions in the lower-tier services with pay rates so low that it would be impossible to support one person, let alone a family. For many of the unemployed, accepting such work would be economically irrational because it would force them to try to survive on very little income and discontinue actively searching for a better job.

A different version of the "blame-the-unemployed" explanation argues that they have insufficient skills and so are unable to compete for the jobs available in the new knowledge-based economy. However, studies have concluded that there is little evidence of a *skills gap* in Canada that might explain high rates of unemployment (Burleton et al. 2013; Livingstone 2017). In fact, there is at least as much evidence of widespread underemployment in Canada as there is evidence of a skills shortage, as we discussed in Chapter 3 (Warhurst et al. 2017).

Yet another version of this type of explanation of high unemployment is the presumed laziness of the unemployed, in combination with the generosity of the government (Swanson 2001). But it is hard to believe that more than a few Canadians would prefer the low level of government social assistance to a higher earned income. Indeed, research on work values (discussed in Chapter 13) suggests that few Canadians would choose the economic hardship and the stigma of unemployment over a regular job. Furthermore, since the mid-1990s, EI has become much more difficult to access. For instance, in 1996, the old Unemployment Insurance program was replaced by the current Employment Insurance (EI) program. Eligibility requirements were increased as part of this process. By the late 1990s, only 36 percent of unemployed individuals received EI support, down from 74 percent in 1989 (Jackson et al. 2000: 153). More recent changes to EI now require job seekers to accept work at lower rates of pay (anywhere between 70 to 90 percent of previous earnings), depending on their eligibility and weeks of EI received. Thus, after six weeks of benefits, unemployed workers could be expected to accept a job paying $11.25 per hour, even if they had earned $16 per hour in their prior job. This is deemed "suitable employment," matching the type of work previously done but not the pay (Grundy and Rudman 2018).

Economists make important distinctions between different types of unemployment. *Cyclical unemployment* rises during recessions and then declines as the economy recovers, while *frictional unemployment* results from the ongoing movement of workers in and out of jobs as they seek to match their skills and interests with the jobs offered by employers. Some unemployment, therefore, is normal, even in the strongest economy, since a perfect match between all jobs and workers is never possible. In the 1980s and 1990s, researchers were concerned that periods of high cyclical unemployment had increased the natural rate of unemployment to such a degree that it might be unlikely to go back down. Accordingly, some believed Canada had developed a serious problem of *structural unemployment*, one that would require new policy approaches because it was more deeply rooted and permanent than cyclical or frictional unemployment. Through the early 2000s, however, record low unemployment levels and increased baby-boom retirements shifted the focus to addressing labour shortages within a highly competitive—and, in some industries, global—job market. While the 2008–09 recession put such discussion on hold, now there is renewed debate over whether labour shortages may emerge as a result of population aging (McDaniel et al. 2015).

Certainly some of the industrial and employment trends discussed in Chapter 3 have contributed to unemployment. With industrial restructuring, many corporations have shifted their activities to countries and regions where labour costs are lower, and where government legislation regarding labour relations, worker safety, and environmental protection is less developed. In private and public firms, employers have responded to financial problems by downsizing, cutting full-time jobs, and relying increasingly on nonstandard forms of work. Canada's staple- and manufacturing-based economy has been hit hard by global economic shifts. Automation and information technologies have replaced workers in some sectors and appear poised to have greater impact in the future.

Robots and Artificial Intelligence: Need Humans Apply?

Predicting future employment and unemployment patterns is difficult, given new technologies that promise to significantly transform work in the future (a topic we also explore in Chapter 11).[29] Robots, autonomous vehicles, and other forms of artificial intelligence are just some of the technologies enabling work to be done more efficiently, safely, and at a lower cost than that done by humans (West 2015; Frey 2019). Illustrating this, in the United States, an estimated 200 robots are being used in manufacturing per 10,000 workers, with the hourly cost of a robot at roughly one-tenth of the average hourly manufacturing wage (Wike and Stokes 2018). Understandably these new innovations raise fears of *technological displacement*, or what Autor (2015: 28) calls "automation anxiety." A recent PEW Research Center survey of nearly 10,000 people in 10 countries (including Canada) found that one-third of Canadians believe that, within 50 years, robots and computers will be doing much of the work that is now done by humans. Four in five Canadians believe it will be harder to find a job and that economic inequality will worsen. Less than one-half agree that technological change will result in new, better-paying jobs. Younger Canadians (18–29 years old) have far more negative expectations, as do those who currently view the economic climate as poor (Wike and Stokes 2018).

Some high-profile commentators share this concern, writing books with titles like *The Second Machine Age* (Brynjolfsson and McAffee 2016) or *What Happens When Robots Take All the Jobs?* (West 2015). However, others argue that while technological change may displace workers, historical patterns suggest that routine and more hazardous forms of work are the most likely to disappear, being replaced by more challenging, high-skilled work. In an influential article titled "Why are there still so many jobs?," David Autor (2015) at MIT argues that new technologies are more likely to *complement*, than *replace*, workers, leading to new configurations and bundling of skills. Discussing what he terms "Polyani's paradox" (11), he argues that most jobs involve many hidden (or tacit) skills that cannot be easily done by inflexible, non-human production systems. In his view, jobs requiring adaptability, common sense, and intuition will persist.

Making similar points, Frey and Osborne (2013) analyze jobs by their task content, estimating that, in the United States, 47 percent of jobs are at high risk of displacement, 19 percent are at medium risk, and 33 percent are at low risk. Lamb (2016: 10–14) has replicated their approach in Canada. Using 2011 Statistics Canada data, he finds roughly similar patterns, with 42 percent of jobs deemed high risk, 22 percent medium risk, and 36 percent low risk. The top five high-risk occupations are retail sales, administrative assistants, food counter attendants and kitchen helpers, cashiers, and transport truck drivers. Low-risk occupations generally involve non-routine, knowledge intensive, interactive forms of work and include a range of jobs in the broad categories of education, law, social, and community services; management; health care; natural and applied sciences; business; and occupations in arts, recreation, and sport. But it must be emphasized that just because a job is deemed to be at risk does not mean that this necessarily will happen. There have been a litany of "automation scares" and incorrect predictions in the past (Autor 2015). But current worries about the end of work are likely overstated and, worse, ignore the potential for technological impacts to be mitigated through effective labour market policies (Jackson 2018).

International Comparisons

It is useful to consider how Canada compares to other countries with respect to job creation and unemployment. In 2009, the global economy experienced the worst recession since the 1930s. Even so, unemployment rates did not rise as much as during previous recessions. This change was partly due to massive government stimulus spending, which preserved jobs in some sectors, and the cushion provided by record high employment levels and low unemployment rates in most industrial nations heading into the recession. Today, in 2018, Canada's unemployment rate of 5.8 percent seems high when compared to that of Japan (2.4 percent), South Korea (3.8 percent), Germany (3.4 percent), Norway (3.8 percent), the Netherlands (3.8 percent), and the United States (3.9 percent). Jobless rates during 2018 were slightly higher, however, across the 28-nation European Union (6.8 percent) and even higher within specific countries. For instance, Greece's unemployment rate reached 19.3 percent; Spain's, 15.3 percent; Italy's, 10.3 percent; and France's, 9.1 percent (OECD 2018).[30]

Given that these countries have struggled with economic challenges similar to those of Canada, why do some have high unemployment while others have nearly full employment? In terms of labour market policies, Canada lies between the laissez-faire, or free-market, approach of the United States and the more interventionist European approach. In countries such as the Netherlands and Japan, employers, organized labour, and governments frequently work together toward a common goal of full employment. If not for proactive labour market programs, such as subsidized work sharing, in other European countries, the unemployment rates likely would have been higher in the recent recession.

Interesting differences in unemployment trends are also evident in North America. Mexico's unemployment rate was just 3.3 percent in 2018 and has been below that of Canada for decades (OECD 2018). Low rates in Mexico are, in large part, a function of the much larger informal economy and self-employment sector. Individuals seeking work are more likely to find jobs, albeit low-paying and insecure jobs, in the informal sector, or to support themselves with small-scale entrepreneurial activities (Martin 2000). Comparing Canada and the United States, unemployment rates were similar in the 1950s to 1970s; however, with the early-1980s recession, Canada's jobless rate began to outstrip that of the United States, with the gap increasing in the 1990s. It was only during the 2008–9 recession that this trend finally reversed, with the U.S. rate surging ahead of Canada.[31] But this reversal was short-lived and, in 2018, the U.S. rate (3.9 percent) was again well below that of Canada.

Canada has typically relied on the marketplace to reduce unemployment, while instituting EI and social assistance programs to help deal with the problems created by persistently high levels of unemployment. Changes to EI in recent years have curtailed support to unemployed workers, however, making it a policy challenge to improve support and opportunities for unemployed job seekers (Grundy et al. 2018). Some argue that while Canada once treated unemployment as a "national problem," working to provide a collective safety net, it now views it as more of an "individual problem" with fewer workers deserving support. For example, during the Great Recession of 2008–9, when unemployment soared, less than half of unemployed workers were eligible to receive benefits, compared to 76 percent in the 1990-91 recession (Grundy et al. 2018). Increased precarious work poses a particularly challenging problem, making it difficult for Canadian workers to accumulate the necessary hours for EI eligibility. Paradoxically, then, it is the workers most in need of support who are increasingly the least likely to receive it.

CONCLUSION

As our examination of recent trends has shown, the Canadian labour market underwent significant change in the final decades of the 20th century, and the trend continued into the early decades of the 21st. The service sector has expanded enormously, producing both "good" and "bad" jobs, with many more of the latter in the lower-tier service industries. Meanwhile, manufacturing industries contribute much less to employment growth in Canada than once was the case. We have also seen a substantial increase in part-time employment, while other forms of nonstandard or precarious work (temporary or contract work, for example) are now much more prevalent. Though unemployment rates declined in the late 1990s and into the early to mid-2000s, they are still high enough in certain sectors and among certain socio-demographic groups to cause concern—especially in the aftermath of the Great Recession. While general public concern about high unemployment abated in the strong economic climate of the early to mid-2000s, today it remains a pressing concern in certain regions and sectors. Most important, with respect to inequality and polarization, certain populations—especially youth, Indigenous peoples, immigrants, and people with disabilities—have not experienced the same economic opportunities as others have. As a result, there are grounds for concern both with the quantity and quality of jobs, and the rising incidence of low-paying, vulnerable work.

What lies ahead? By posing this question, we enter the debates and controversies surrounding the future of work, which often set out a bewildering range of contradictory scenarios and need to be assessed critically. Reflecting on the trends presented in Chapters 3 and 4, it is clear that most evidence does not support a view of radical or extreme transformation, even in the face of what might seem like revolutionary technologies. Still, changes are occurring, and we can be fairly certain that several of the trends we have documented will continue. Demographic factors (discussed in Chapter 3) are a given, especially workforce aging and the increasing diversity of the labour force. So, too, we can expect continued expansion of service-sector employment. Nonstandard work, as discussed in this chapter, is now a central feature of the labour market, but equally a growing source of concern given the precariousness experienced by many workers. In 2018, the future of work in Canada and other global economies is uncertain. What level of economic growth is reasonable to expect? And what is sustainable, given growing concerns over the environment, the limits posed by population aging, and a shrinking workforce in many industrialized countries? Finally, to what extent might current public interest and debate over precarious work, economic disparities, and inequality spark meaningful efforts to reduce labour market polarization? To our mind, this latter question is a central one as we move into the future.

DISCUSSION QUESTIONS

1. Discuss the concept of job quality. How would you define a "good job" and a "bad job"? How does job quality vary by industry and occupation? Thinking about the jobs you have had so far, where would they fit in the discussion of good jobs and bad jobs?

2. What is nonstandard employment, and how has it grown in Canada in recent years? Are all nonstandard jobs also precarious? What are some implications of these trends for workers, employers, and society in general?

3. Unemployment has been a significant worry for many Canadian workers and their families. What are recent trends in unemployment, within Canada and across countries? How do they compare to longer-term trends?

4. Based on your reading in Chapters 3 and 4, outline what you see as the most important challenges facing Canadian workers in the next 10 years.

ADDITIONAL RESOURCES

WORK AT THE MOVIES

- *Roger & Me* (directed by Michael Moore, 1989, 91 minutes). American filmmaker Michael Moore explores the economic and social impact of the demise of General Motors in Flint, Michigan.
- *The Full Monty* (directed by Petter Cattaneo, 1997, 91 minutes). In this British comedy set in Sheffield, England, six unemployed men decide to form a male striptease act. The film explores issues of unemployment, job retraining, working-class culture, restructuring, economic depression, and alienation.
- *Generation Jobless* (directed by Sharon Bartlett and Maria LeRose, 2013, 45:13 minutes). *Generation Jobless* explores the challenges facing Canadian youth in finding meaningful employment. It is available through CBC Doc Zone: https://curio.ca/en/video/generation-jobless-2594/.
- *Inequality for All* (directed by Jacob Kornbluth, 2013, 89 minutes). This award-winning documentary examines growing economic disparities and inequality, weaving together analysis from economist and former U.S. Labor Secretary Robert Reich, with personal stories from the lives of workers and families.

- A discussion panel on "Precarious Work and the Changing Nature of Employment" by *Policy Options* is available at https://policyoptions .irpp.org/magazines/february-2018/precarious-work-and-the-changing-nature-of-employment/.

SOUNDS OF WORK

- "Little Man" (Alan Jackson). This country song considers how small independent businesses will struggle for survival when big-box stores and chains come to town.
- "Telephone Road" (Steve Earle). In this song, Earle writes of families being split up when members are forced to migrate to find work.
- "Atlantic City" (Bruce Springsteen). Springsteen highlights how individuals struggle for survival when well-paying work is hard to find.
- "Hallelujah, I'm a Bum" (Traditional). This song describes an individual who cannot find work and so lives as a hobo.

NOTES

1. In 2007, Statistics Canada and European government agencies set up a Task Force on Measurement of the Quality of Employment to try to reach agreement on how best to measure "employment quality" (Jin 2008: 7). For early discussions of job quality, see the Economic Council of Canada's (1990) *Good Jobs, Bad Jobs: Employment in the Service Economy.* For more recent discussions, see Chen and Medhi (2018) and Lewchuk (2017).
2. Earnings figures by industry are from Statistics Canada's Labour Force Survey, Table 14-10-0064-01, Employee Wages by Industry, Annual, https://www150 .statcan.gc.ca/t1/tbl1/en/tv.action?pid=1410006401.
3. Earnings figures by occupation are from Statistics Canada's Labour Force Survey, Table 14-10-0340-01, Employee Wages by Occupation, Annual, https://www150 .statcan.gc.ca/t1/tbl1/en/tv.action?pid=1410034001. For an interesting data visualization of earnings by occupation using data from the 2016 Census, see https:// www12.statcan.gc.ca/census-recensement/2016/dp-pd/dv-vd/occ-pro/index-eng.cfm.
4. Calculations for the female–male earnings gap are based on Statistics Canada's Labour Force Survey, Table14-10-0340-01, Employee Wages by Occupation, Annual.

5. Data on executive pay come from the *Globe and Mail's* (2018) annual report on executive compensation for 2017 and analysis by Macdonald (2018) and Mackenzie (2016) for the Canadian Centre for Policy Alternatives.

6. Data for minimum wages is current as of October 2019 and comes from two sources: the Canadian Payroll Association at https://www.payroll.ca/Compliance /Legislative/Minimum-Wage-Updates and the Retail Council of Canada at https:// www.retailcouncil.org/resources/quick-facts/minimum-wage-by-province/. Please check these sources for updated rates.

7. These and other articles appear in a special issue of *Critical Sociology* on precarious work and worker resistance, edited by Chan et al. (2019).

8. Statistics Canada's low-income cutoff (LICO) is the measure most often used to index poverty in Canada. A family (of a given size) is considered to be in the low-income category if, compared to the average Canadian family of that size, it spends at least 20 percent more of its total income on food, clothing, and shelter. LICOs are calculated separately for communities of different sizes since the cost of living varies. For current LICOs, see Statistics Canada, Table 11-10-0241-01, Low-Income Cutoffs at https://www150.statcan.gc.ca/t1 /tbl1/en/tv.action?pid=1110024101.

9. See Winson and Leach (2002) and Fleury (2008) on Canada's working poor; Ehrenreich (2001), Duncan, Huston, and Weisner (2007), and Thiede et al. (2015) on the working poor in the United States; and LaRochelle-Côté and Dionne (2009) on international differences in low-paid work.

10. Marshall (2003) outlines the growing costs to Canadian employers of non-wage benefit packages. Waldie (2005) notes that in the mid-2000s General Motors spent more on health care for its employees than it spent on steel for automobile production.

11. For discussions of nonstandard work, also referred to as *contingent* or *precarious work*, see Krahn (1995); Vosko, Zukewich, and Cranford (2003); Lowe and Schellenberg (2001); and Law Commission of Ontario (2012). Regarding such work in the United States, see Kalleberg (2018) and Kalleberg and Vallas (2018).

12. Calculations for own-account self-employment are from Statistics Canada, Table 14-10-0027-01, Employment by Class of Worker, Annual.

13. For historical data, see Sussman (1998). Recent calculations are based on Statistics Canada, Table 14-10-0044-01, Multiple Jobholders by Industry, Annual.

14. 2018 calculations for part-time work are from Statistics Canada, Table 14-10-0023-01.

15. Statistics for temporary and permanent employment come from Statistics Canada's Labour Force Survey, Table 14-10-0072-01, Job Permanency (Permanent and Temporary) by Industry, Annual. Lowe and Schellenberg (2001: 12) suggest that

because some individuals working for temporary help agencies report themselves to be in permanent jobs, LFS estimates of temporary employment may be too low.

16. For excellent analysis and discussions of temporary employment in Canada, see Fuller (2011), Fuller et al. (2014, 2015) and Stecy-Hildebrandt et al. (2019). Fuller et al. (2015) trace the complex pathways through temporary employment. For discussions of temporary and nonstandard employment in the United States, see Pedulla (2013, 2016).

17. Statistics for self-employment come from Statistics Canada's Labour Force Survey, Table 14-10-0027-01, Employment by Class of Worker, Annual.

18. Calculations based on Statistics Canada's Labour Force Survey, Table 14-10-0027-01, Employment by Class of Worker, Annual.

19. Current data are from Statistics Canada Table 14-10-0043-01, Average Usual And Actual Hours by Type of Work, Annual.

20. Data on usual hours come from Statistics Canada, Table 14-10-0031-01, Usual Hours by Job Type (Main or All Jobs), Annual. For discussions of changes in working time in Canada, see Usalcas (2008). For the United States see Jacobs and Gerson (2004) and Sullivan (2016).

21. Calculations are based on data from Statistics Canada, Table 14-10-0076-01, Employees Working Overtime (Weekly) by Industry, Annual. For discussions of long work hours, see Bunting (2004), Moen et al. (2013), and Shields (2000). On class-action lawsuits in Canada, see updates from McCarthy and Tetrault at https://www.mccarthy.ca/en/insights/blogs/canadian-employer-advisor /update-overtime-class-actions-canada-0.

22. See Turcotte (2010) and Hilbrecht et al. (2013) on the benefits and costs of teleworking; Akyeampong (1993) on flextime work arrangements; and Marshall (1997) on job sharing. Teasdale (2013) discusses their impact on working relationships.

23. For historical discussions of unemployment trends in previous decades, see Riddell (2018) and MacLean and Osberg (1996). More recent trends are discussed in Riddell (2005) and Jones and Riddell (2019).

24. All calculations for unemployment are from Statistics Canada Labour Force Survey, Table 14-10-0057-01, Duration of Unemployment, Annual.

25. Regional unemployment data are from Statistics Canada Labour Force Survey, Table 14-10-0090-0, Labour Force Characteristics by Province, Annual.

26. Unemployment rates are from Statistics Canada Labour Force Survey, Table 14-10-0359-01, Labour Force Characteristics by Aboriginal Group and Educational Attainment. At the time of writing, 2016 Census data were not available for unemployment rates in specific Canadian cities; thus we rely on 2006 data. In discussing statistical trends, we do so with an awareness of the issues raised by Walter and Andersen (2013) concerning the tendency for official statistics to highlight, by

Chapter 4: Good Jobs, Bad Jobs, No Jobs

virtue of chosen indicators, the "shortcomings" of Indigenous peoples rather than their contributions and strengths.

27. See Heslin et al. (2012) for a valuable discussion of the links between discrimination and discouraged workers.

28. Calculations are from Statistics Canada, Labour Force Survey, Table 14-10-0327-01, Labour Force Characteristics by Sex and Detailed Age Group, Annual.

29. For a provocative thought piece on the potential impact of new technologies, see CPG Grey's video *Humans Need Not Apply*, which has been viewed over 11 million times. https://www.youtube.com/watch?v=7Pq-S557XQU.

30. International unemployment figures are 2018 annual averages from the OECD Data Portal at https://data.oecd.org/unemp/unemployment-rate.htm.

31. For discussions of Canada–U.S. unemployment trends, see Riddell (2005), Jones and Riddell (2019), and the special issue of *Journal of Labor Economics* edited by Card and Oreopoulos (2019).

LABOUR MARKETS: OPPORTUNITIES AND INEQUALITY

5

"Increasingly, private security is a preferred option among newcomers, who haven't been able to find work in their own field. . . . I have first-hand experience—for the last six months, I have been working as a security officer myself [in Toronto]. After two months of futile attempts to get a job in the media (my profession for two decades prior to immigrating to Canada from India in July 2008), I had little choice but to take up a job as a security officer. . . . Facing barriers to finding employment in their area of expertise because of a lack of Canadian experience and credentials, newcomers turn to survival jobs out of desperation. Some work as telemarketers at call centres, others as maintenance workers, still others as security officers. But working in security is often considered a better choice than doing pressure sales over the phone or cleaning toilets. . . . It seemed the better choice for me. Although wages are low (around $9–12 an hour in the first year), it's enough for survival and paying bills. . . . Every night when I leave for my site to begin my shift I ponder, 'Is this what I came to Canada for?' Every morning when I return home and see my son's face, I stay determined that I'll do what it takes to survive and succeed here—even if it means patrolling a damp and bitterly cold parking lot in the dead of night."

Source: *Canadian Immigrant. (May 29, 2011).* http://canadianimmigrant.ca/immigrant-stories/nightshift-as-security-officer-a-survival-job-for-many-immigrants. Courtesy of Mayank Bhatt.

INTRODUCTION

As we saw in Chapter 4, there are large differences in income and other employment benefits, as well as varying risks of unemployment, across occupations. Why do high-school teachers earn more than retail salesclerks, or engineers more than construction workers? Presumably it's because teachers and engineers have invested in extra years of education that, in turn, lead to more skilled and responsible jobs. Why do electricians make more money than child-care workers? Although wiring a house requires considerable skill and we don't want electricians to make mistakes, caring for and teaching young children is also a highly complex task, with its own risks and responsibilities. Why are the children of middle-class parents much more likely to go to university compared with the children of less affluent Canadians? Why are Indigenous peoples, immigrants, and members of visible minority groups overrepresented in less rewarding jobs, and why are younger workers and Canadians living in different regions more likely to be unemployed?

Such questions about variations in educational outcomes, job rewards, and career patterns are central to the sociological study of labour markets. We can define a *labour market* as the arena in which employers want to purchase labour from potential workers who are seeking jobs suitable to their education, experience, and preferences. In the labour market, workers exchange their skills, knowledge, and loyalty for pay, status, career opportunities, and other job rewards.

A number of other institutions and organizations support or interact with the operation of the labour market. Among their other functions, schools and families prepare individuals for entry (or re-entry) into the labour market. Government legislation affects how labour markets operate—minimum wages, occupational health and safety regulations, and legislation aimed at trade unions are examples. The government may also assist the unemployed with financial support or job-training programs. Unions and professional associations are active in the labour market, protecting the interests of their members by bargaining for additional job rewards and, sometimes, by limiting access of non-members to good jobs. Organizations representing employers also try to influence labour market operations, sometimes lobbying governments to change laws regarding unions or to maintain a low minimum wage, or encouraging schools to include more employment-related content in their teaching.

Labour economists and sociologists study many of these institutions and how they influence labour market operations.[1] Of particular interest to sociologists are the distributive aspects of the labour market; that is, how the profits generated by workers are shared. In other words, does the labour market provide opportunities for hardworking individuals to improve their social position and quality of life, does it reinforce long-standing patterns of inequality in Canadian society, or does it do both?

In this chapter, we address questions about who gets better jobs and why, and how patterns of social inequality are reinforced, by comparing two alternative theoretical perspectives and relevant data that claim to support them.

According to *human capital theory*, jobs requiring more effort, training, and skill typically receive greater rewards. This theory assumes that labour market participants compete openly for the best jobs and that the most qualified people end up in the jobs requiring their particular skills. The outcome should be an efficient and productive economy and a fair allocation of job rewards. But in reviewing research on how the labour market really operates, we find considerable evidence that the open competition assumptions of human capital theory have been seriously challenged. As *labour market segmentation theory* explains, many substantial barriers keep disadvantaged groups from gaining access to better jobs. Thus, the study of labour markets is not only about who gets better and worse jobs. It also addresses the much broader questions raised in Chapters 1 and 2 about how social inequality is created, reinforced, intensified, and sometimes reduced.[2]

THE HUMAN CAPITAL MODEL OF LABOUR MARKET PROCESSES

Chapter 3 explained that many jobs today require specific skills and extensive training, while Chapter 4 showed how some jobs are clearly better than others. Ideally, jobs with specific requirements would be filled by individuals most suited for these positions. If that means having an advanced education, then it would only be reasonable that workers with more education should obtain the better jobs. Stripped to its essentials, these are the basic premises of *human capital theory*, a prominent explanation of how today's labour market operates favoured by economists.

This theoretical perspective assumes that a job's rewards are determined by its economic contribution to society. It also predicts that more dangerous and unhealthy jobs should be paid more, since workers should be compensated for taking on greater risks. The model rests on four basic assumptions: (1) labour market participants are all competing for jobs in a single, open labour market; (2) information about available jobs is assumed to be widely circulated; (3) all potential employees with the necessary qualifications have equal access to job openings; and (4) when it comes to choosing whom to hire, employers make rational decisions, based on an assessment of an individual's ability.

To get ahead in the work world, people may decide to obtain more education and training. Doing so means delaying entry into the labour market and forgoing immediate earnings. Yet this loss is not permanent because by obtaining more education, one is "investing" in *human capital*, which can later be "cashed in" for a better job. In short, the human capital model emphasizes the *supply side* of labour markets and largely overlooks the behaviour and characteristics of employers and work organizations (the *demand side*). It also ignores unequal power relationships within the labour market. The human capital perspective on labour markets is premised on a *consensus* view of society, in contrast to the assumptions of *conflict* underlying class-based and labour market segmentation approaches.[3]

The basic logic of human capital theory is compelling, given the evidence that better-educated individuals generally are less likely to be unemployed and more likely to hold well-paying, high-status jobs (Davies and Guppy 2018).[4] But it is also difficult to ignore the contrary evidence. There are many examples of well-trained and highly motivated people working in poorly paid, low-skill jobs—such as the individual we quoted at the start of the chapter. For example, although most recent university graduates manage to find reasonable jobs, compared to graduates a decade or two ago, a larger minority have difficulty finding full-time, permanent work that matches their training.[5] Clearly, the problem is not one of insufficient education or effort. Instead, much of this youth underemployment can be traced directly to organizational downsizing and large-scale cutbacks in the hiring of entry-level workers by employers in both the public and private sectors (see Chapters 2 and 4).

To make the same point, while many of the wealthiest members of our society are no more educated than the rest of us, they frequently appear to have had a head start in the career race. We continue to see the powerful influence of huge family firms largely controlled by individuals who inherited their money. For example, in 2019, David Thomson and his family were estimated to be worth $32.5 billion as a result of their control of Thomson Reuters Corporation, a media and publishing conglomerate (*Forbes Magazine* 2019). Thomson took over control of the company in 2002 from his father, who, in turn, had inherited it from his father, who started it in 1934. In short, the social standing of one's parents and grandparents strongly influence life outcomes. Other examples of inherited wealth and power include Galen Weston, Linda Hasenfratz, and Nancy Southern, all children of founding CEOs, as discussed in Chapter 4.

Thus, the relationships among initiative and effort, education and training, on the one hand, and occupational attainment and income, on the other, are not nearly as consistent as the human capital model would suggest. In fact, research shows that some groups are systematically less likely than others to have benefited from their investments in human capital and that good returns on education and training are obtained only in certain industrial sectors or from some types of employers. Furthermore, much evidence shows that some groups in society are more likely to have access to higher education. Thus, to really understand who gets the good jobs, we must look beyond the labour market to families, schools, colleges and universities, and other institutions that shape labour market outcomes.

Social Structure and Occupational Choice

The human capital model attempts to explain how people are sorted into different occupational positions by focusing on the characteristics of individual workers. People whose skills and abilities are more valued by society, and who have invested more in education and training, will be leading candidates for the better jobs, according to this model. Another assumption is that individuals choose among work options, eventually settling in the job that best suits them. But to what extent do individuals have a choice from among the wide range of occupations? Does everyone start the "career race" from the same position, or are some groups disadvantaged at the outset? Does chance play a role in matching individuals and jobs? We probably all know a few people who accidentally ended up in their present job with little planning, or who landed a great position by being in the right place at the right time or having the right personal contacts. We probably also know people who, as children, decided they wanted to be a doctor or lawyer and then carefully pursued the educational route to achieve this goal. Such behaviour and outcomes are consistent with human capital predictions, although the theory does not ask why these individuals had such high occupational goals.

We can easily imagine how socioeconomic origins might influence career patterns. It would be hard to picture a member of the wealthy Thomson family aspiring to be a bus driver. In contrast, many people who make their living as farmers would probably cite growing up on a farm as a major career influence, while growing up in a working-class family in a single-industry community would likely channel a young person into one of the local mills or mines (High 2018). It is also clear that many women in today's labour force were constrained in their career choices by society's attitudes about appropriate gender roles. As Chapter 6 will show, until only a few decades ago it was typically assumed that women could work as teachers and nurses—the stereotypical female-dominated professions—but not in traditionally male occupations. Thus, while aptitudes and investments in education do play an important role, for many working Canadians, *family socioeconomic status* (SES) and community of origin, along with personal attributes such as gender, race, and ethnicity, are important determinants of educational and occupational choices and outcomes.

Equality of Educational Opportunity

One core value underlying our education system is that of *equality of opportunity*. According to this belief, gender, ethnicity, family background, region of residence, or other individual characteristics should not be an impediment to obtaining a good education and, through this, access to good jobs and a decent standard of living. As we have already seen (Chapter 3), basic gender differences in educational attainment have disappeared (although, as Chapter 6 discusses, there are substantial gender differences in educational choices). But research continues to show large differences in educational attainment depending on one's family background (SES).

For instance, analysis by Statistics Canada of postsecondary enrolments among 19-year-olds from 2001 to 2014 shows that, in 2014, roughly four in five (78.7 percent) of Canadian youth from high-income families (the top 20 percent) were attending university. This compares to just under half (47.1 percent) of those from low-income families (the bottom 20 percent) (Frenette 2017). While postsecondary attendance rates increased for both groups from 2001 to 2014, gains were largest for those in the lower-income groups, rising from one-third (37.7 percent) in 2001. Still, striking gaps in access remain.

Studies that focus on parents' education, rather than their income, show even larger differences. For instance, Chatoor and colleagues (2019) compare postsecondary education (PSE) for "first-generation" students (those whose parents did not attend university) and "second-generation" students (those whose parents had PSE). Coming from a family with a "university tradition" substantially increases the odds of personally acquiring postsecondary credentials. Just over half of first-generation students (56 percent) earned a postsecondary degree, but this number rises steadily with parents' PSE attainment—from 74 percent (mother only having PSE), to 79 percent (father only having PSE), to 89 percent (both parents having PSE credentials).[6]

How do such patterns of *intergenerational transfer of advantage* develop? Over the past several decades, a number of different studies have highlighted how middle- and upper-class parents have higher expectations of their children, serve as role models for postsecondary educational participation and successful careers, and raise them in neighbourhoods and send them to schools where others also have high postsecondary expectations. These parents are also more able to financially support their children's postsecondary activities. For example, an Ontario study tracked high-school graduates from the "class of 1973" for several decades conclusively demonstrating that a more advantaged background led to higher *educational and occupational aspirations*, greater educational attainment, and, in time, higher-status occupations and higher incomes (Anisef et al. 2000). Rural youth were less likely to aspire to and participate in higher education. The researchers speculated that the more "limited horizons" of rural youth might be due to less exposure to beliefs in the value of higher education (143). Rural youth may also have to leave their home communities to go to college or university, making the transition costlier. Other studies reinforce the challenges faced by rural youth wishing to continue their education (Looker 2010; Finnie et al. 2015). This is a particular challenge for Indigenous youth, who are more likely to live in remote areas (Barnetson 2018; Simon et al. 2014).

But the world of postsecondary education has changed dramatically since the 1970s. The proportion of Canadian youth going on to college or university has risen sharply with the opening of new postsecondary educational institutions, continued demand by employers for people with higher qualifications, and the introduction of new student finance systems (Davies and Guppy 2018). So, has inequality in access to higher education declined? Yes, to some extent. Historical gender-based differences in postsecondary educational aspirations and participation have all but disappeared. In fact, young women today are more likely than young men to complete university (Finnie et al. 2015; Frenette 2013)—although women still enroll in many traditional "female" areas such as education, nursing, and the humanities (see Chapter 6). Online learning and the construction of community colleges in smaller urban centres in some provinces has also reduced rural–urban differences in postsecondary educational participation (Krahn and Hudson 2006; Finnie et al. 2015).

In addition, improved access to higher education has somewhat reduced the impact of family SES on university participation. For example, in 1986, among Canadians between 25 and 39 years old, 12 percent of those from families where neither parent had a degree had completed university, compared to 45 percent of those with at least one parent with a degree. But, as noted earlier, from 2001 to 2014, those in lower-income families saw the biggest gains in university attendance (Frenette 2013). So the SES gap in access to higher education has narrowed. But even so, children from more affluent and better-educated families still are significantly overrepresented among university students. How does family status boost the odds of pursuing higher education? Do higher family incomes help pay for tuition and living costs, allowing students to forgo part-time jobs and, instead, study harder? Or is it more about cultural factors, such as valuing and aspiring to higher education (Finnie et al. 2015)?

School-to-work transition studies, which track individuals over long periods, confirm the importance of higher educational aspirations for postsecondary participation and completion. For example, in 1985, we began a longitudinal study of high-school graduates in Edmonton. Much like the 1970s Ontario studies, noted earlier, we found much higher educational aspirations among young people from higher-SES families. For instance, nearly two-thirds of high-school graduates from families where at least one parent had a supervisory, managerial, or professional occupation planned to obtain a university degree, compared to just over one-third of those from lower-SES families. Four years later in 1989, we found that university participation rates for students from higher-SES families were double that of those from lower-SES families. Over the next two decades, study participants were interviewed several more times. By 2010, 25 years after this cohort had left high school, SES differences in postsecondary educational attainment were highly pronounced. Sixty percent of those from families where at least one parent had completed university had themselves acquired a university degree, compared to only 28 percent of those from families without a university tradition (Krahn 2017).[7]

Economic Advantage and Cultural Capital

The fact that children of university-educated parents are more likely to graduate from university is not simply a function of their higher educational and occupational aspirations. More highly educated parents also have higher incomes, on average, and more money means access to more and better post-secondary education (Davies and Guppy 2018; Chatoor et al. 2019). The rapid expansion of Canada's postsecondary system in the 1970s increased access to higher education, and the introduction of new student finance systems (student loans) allowed more children from lower-SES families to take advantage of the new universities, community colleges, and technical schools. However, some of these gains have been lost as postsecondary tuition fees have increased in recent years (Luong 2010; Shaker and Macdonald 2015).[8] Furthermore, higher tuition fees may affect postsecondary dropout and completion, creating additional stresses for low-income families juggling other financial responsibilities.[9]

So parents' money continues to matter. But the process whereby advantaged backgrounds translate into educational success and better jobs begins long before high-school students begin to consider postsecondary education. Children in Canada's poorest families frequently go to school hungry. Parents with low incomes may have to work long hours to cover basic living costs and will have less time and money to invest in their children's education and in extra-curricular activities. Schools in poorer neighbourhoods tend to have fewer resources. Not surprisingly, children in Canada's poorest families are three times more likely than children of the wealthy to be in remedial education classes at school. In contrast, economically advantaged children are far more likely to be in classes for "gifted" students (Domina et al. 2017). Though the high-school completion rate has steadily increased in recent decades, teenagers from less affluent families are still much more likely to leave school without a diploma.[10]

These are among the more obvious explanations of the relationship between economic disadvantage and less successful educational outcomes. In his analysis of social stratification in contemporary society (see Chapter 2), Pierre Bourdieu (1986) introduced the concept of *cultural capital* to further explain why middle-class youth perform better in the education system. Schools encourage and reward the language, beliefs, behaviour, and competencies of the more powerful groups in society. Middle-class youth bring more of this cultural capital to school with them, and so have a distinct advantage. They are more likely to speak like their teachers, to be comfortable in a verbal and symbolic environment, to know something about the subjects being taught, to have additional skills (music training, for example), and to have access to learning resources at home.[11]

Thus, schools are not neutral institutions; rather, they contribute to reproducing structural inequalities and power differences within society because the culture of the more powerful classes is embedded within them. In fact, this process continues within universities as well. A study of the experiences of working-class youth in an Ontario university showed how their ambitions for, and chances of entry into, high-paying and high-status occupations were reduced over the course of their studies (Lehmann 2012). *Extra-credential experiences*, such as spending a year studying abroad or interning in a prestigious law firm during the summer, can increase an undergraduate's chances of being admitted into law or medical school. Such experiences can be interpreted by selection committees as indicators of motivation and the willingness to take on challenges. Working-class youth, however, are unlikely to have the money for foreign travel or study abroad experiences (Lehmann and Trower 2018). Nor can they afford to take on unpaid internships, even if they had the social connections required to obtain them. Indeed, the use of unpaid internships has attracted growing concern as another source of unequal educational outcomes in Canada and the United States (Levitt 2014).

LABOUR MARKET SEGMENTATION

While the human capital model assumes a single, open labour market in which everyone competes equally, *labour market segmentation* researchers question this assumption, arguing instead that "good" and "bad" jobs tend to be found in very different settings and are usually obtained in distinctly different ways. Certain types of labour force participants (women, visible minorities, immigrants, and youth, for example) are concentrated in the poorer jobs.

Segmentation theories also highlight the slim chances of moving out of poorer jobs in the *secondary labour market* into better jobs in the *primary labour market*. This is a key proposition, since the human capital model does not deny that some jobs are better than others; it simply maintains that the system is meritocratic and that those individuals who have the most ability and initiative, and who have made the largest investment in education and training, are more likely to obtain highly skilled and rewarding jobs. The segmentation perspective emphasizes the barriers that limit access to the primary labour market for many qualified individuals, as well as the ability of primary labour market participants to maintain their more advantaged position.[12]

The three varieties of labour market segmentation research are each outlined below. All share these basic propositions, but they differ in their explanations of the origins of segmentation and in their breadth of analysis.

Dual Economies

The *dual economy* perspective describes how capitalist economies changed in the 20th century, with a few large and powerful firms coming to dominate key industries such as automobile manufacturing, mining, oil and gas, railways and airlines (Edwards 1979; Hodson and Kaufman 1982). Similarly, the finance sector came to be controlled by a handful of large banks, investment firms, and insurance companies. These dominant firms can exert considerable control over suppliers and markets, and are also able to manipulate their political environment. For example, at various times automobile manufacturers have been able to limit foreign imports, and mining and oil companies have influenced government environmental policies.

These *core-sector* firms operate in an economic environment very different from the *periphery sector*, where we find many much smaller companies. Because they are smaller and generally face more intense competition, these smaller businesses have a much greater chance of failure. Many lower-tier service-sector firms (e.g., small retail shops and restaurants) are found here, as are some smaller firms in the upper-tier services (e.g., small office-supply firms in the business services) and in the goods-producing sector (e.g., small manufacturing companies). Such enterprises are typically less profitable, have lower capital investments, are less technologically advanced, and are generally more labour intensive.

The dual economy perspective proposes that the core sector contains a *primary labour market* with better jobs, while the periphery sector contains a *secondary labour market*. Capital-intensive core enterprises, by definition, require fewer workers to equal or exceed the productivity of more labour-intensive firms, although they frequently require workers who are more highly trained and better educated than those hired in the periphery sector.

In fact, replaceable unskilled or semiskilled workers are often preferred by employers in the secondary labour market. The large and bureaucratic nature of core-sector enterprises means that there are reasonably good opportunities for career mobility. The workers in these firms tend to be well paid and to have good benefit packages; they are also more likely to receive training and may have greater job security.[13]

Why would core-sector employers be willing to pay more than the going rates in the secondary labour market? Higher profit margins make it easier to do so, of course, but equally important are the strong labour unions and professional associations that have been much more active in the primary sector, demanding higher pay and better benefits (see Chapter 11), or the unique qualifications required of workers (think of Apple or Google). Further, it would be too costly for core-sector firms not to pay well. Such enterprises have sizable capital investments so would try to avoid costly shutdowns due to labour disputes. In addition, high labour turnover resulting from low wages would lead to the expense of training many new employees. It is simply good business practice to offer job security (negotiated with a union, if necessary), provide generous wage and benefit packages, and endeavour to improve working conditions.

In contrast, in the secondary labour market, smaller profit margins, more intense competition, difficulties in passing along increased labour costs to customers, and greater vulnerability to economic cycles keep wage levels down. In addition, labour turnover is less of a problem for many periphery-sector employers: lower skill requirements and little on-the-job training make workers easily replaceable. Consequently, labour turnover is high, making union organizing more difficult (and some employers may value steady turnover for this reason). The term *job ghettos* has been used to describe work in such labour markets.

In a classic study of job ghettos, Ehrenreich (2001) describes how difficult it is to make a living in the secondary labour market. In researching her book *Nickel and Dimed: On (Not) Getting By in America*, she worked as a waitress, an assistant in a nursing home, an employee of a "cleaning maid" company, and a salesperson at Wal-Mart. Her coworkers, who impressed her with how hard they worked, were often women, immigrants, members of visible minority groups, and students. The jobs they held were characterized by low pay, absent benefits, limited training, physically demanding work, limited authority, lack of respect (both from employers and members of the public), and lack of protection from exploitation and harassment. These difficult working conditions were matched by the equally difficult experiences her coworkers faced finding affordable housing and adequate transportation to get to work. Although the hard work and stress often led to health problems, her coworkers could not afford to be sick: they had no health benefits and a week without a paycheque could mean a missed rent payment.[14]

Internal Labour Markets

There are typically fewer chances for career mobility within firms in the periphery sector. A carwash attendant, a cleaner, or a mechanic in an automobile repair shop would have few promotion prospects simply because the workplace would not have a bureaucratic hierarchy with well-defined career ladders. Conversely, many employees of Ford Canada, the Royal Bank, and other large private-sector firms do have such mobility opportunities, as do government employees and many health care workers. In contrast to the often dead-end jobs within the secondary labour market, most large corporations and public institutions have a well-developed internal training and promotion system, or what may be called an *internal labour market* (Althauser 1989). From the perspective of the work organization, such internal labour markets help retain skilled and valuable employees by providing career incentives. They also transmit important skills and knowledge among employees. From the perspective of employees, internal labour markets mean additional job security and career opportunities.

Researchers who study internal labour markets have usually sidestepped larger questions about the changing nature of capitalism, concentrating instead on specific features of these self-contained labour markets. Focus has been on *ports of entry*, specifically, the limited number of entry-level jobs that are typically the only way into such an internal labour market; *mobility chains*, or career ladders, through which employees make their way during their career within the organization; and training systems and seniority rules, which govern movement through the ranks.[15] Essentially, these concepts elaborate and update Max Weber's theory of bureaucracy (see Chapter 1).

Early segmentation researchers tended to assume that all core-sector firms contain well-developed internal labour markets open to all employees. However, while many major corporations have long career ladders, these are open to only some of their employees. Support and administrative workers (usually women and younger workers) have often been restricted from moving into higher ranks. Some large corporations, particularly in the fast-food industry, are built around small local franchises. These workplaces typically have all the characteristics of a secondary labour market. In addition, corporate and government downsizing and the increased use of temporary and other nonstandard workers, often by contracting non-core functions to third party providers, mean that the number of advantaged workers in internal labour markets has declined dramatically.[16]

Labour Market Shelters: Unions and Professions

Internal labour markets are created by employers. In contrast, unions and professional associations have tried to improve job and income security for their members by setting up *labour market shelters*, sometimes within specific work organizations but more often spanning a large number of similar workplaces. Some occupational groups have restricted access to certain types of work since government legislation requires that such tasks be completed only by certified trades (e.g., electricians). Public safety is the rationale for this legislation, but it also serves to protect the jobs and (relatively high) incomes of members of these often-unionized trades.

Industrial unions bargain collectively with employers to determine the seniority rules, promotion procedures, and pay rates within manufacturing establishments (see Chapter 11). Such contracts shelter these workers from the risk of job loss or pay cuts for a specified time. Negotiated staffing restrictions also restrict non-members from access to the better jobs by giving laid-off members priority if new jobs open up.

Professional associations also provide labour market shelters for their members, using tactics different from those of unions. *Professions* have been distinguished from occupations in a variety of ways, but certain key features appear in most definitions. Professionals such as doctors, lawyers, engineers, and psychologists work with specialized knowledge acquired through extensive formal education in professional schools. They enjoy a high level of work autonomy and are frequently self-regulating, controlling admission and regulating themselves through their own professional associations (Adams 2010, 2018). Professionals also exercise considerable power over their clients and other lower-status occupational groups, emphasizing the altruistic nature of their work.[17]

For example, doctors spend many years training in medical schools, where they acquire knowledge specific to their profession, and then have to pass rigorous licensing exams before being able to practise. They go on to determine their own working conditions, whether they are employed in large health care institutions or work as self-employed professionals. In the past few decades, many doctors have increased their work autonomy by setting up professional corporations. Through their own professional associations, doctors can censure colleagues who have acted unprofessionally in the course of their work. Doctors have much power over their patients and those in helping occupations, such as nurses and medical laboratory technicians. Finally, members of this profession emphasize their code of ethics, by which they are committed to preserving human life above all other objectives.

In short, professions are much more powerful than occupations.[18] The concept of *market closure* (Collins 1990) describes the ability of professionals to shape the labour market to their advantage, rather than simply responding to it as do most occupational groups. Like the craft guilds of the preindustrial era (Chapter 1), professional groups in contemporary Western society can restrict others from doing their type of work by controlling entry into their profession. Professional associations have close relationships with their (typically university-based) professional schools and can strongly influence both course content and entrance quotas. Many professional groups have actively lobbied for and obtained legislation that both requires practitioners of their profession to be officially licensed and prohibits anyone else from performing certain tasks.

BARRIERS TO PRIMARY LABOUR MARKET ENTRY

We can now see how internal labour markets and labour market shelters not only provide better work rewards to some groups but also help them maintain labour market closure. There are a limited number of positions within the primary labour market, and entry is often restricted to those with the proper credentials—a degree, union membership, or professional certification (Kim 2013). A more advantaged family background also gives one a substantial head start on obtaining such credentials. Despite the increase in job postings and recruitment online, through sites such as GlassDoor, LinkedIn, and ZipRecruiter, information about job vacancies, especially the most desirable jobs, is not always widely available. Often, it is only passed through informal, exclusive networks (Marin 2012). Without contacts within the primary labour market, gained through family and friends—that is, without sufficient social capital—qualified applicants may never be aware of job openings (Rivera 2016; Petersen, Saporta, and Seidel 2000).

For some individuals, a history of employment in marginal jobs may act as a barrier—such as the "scarring" effects of nonstandard jobs (Chapter 4). Another example can be found in Atlantic Canada where the collapse of the fishing industry, and the prevalence of seasonal work in resource industries in general, have forced many people into an annual cycle where income is obtained from part-year jobs, supplemented by Employment Insurance and welfare assistance.[19] Thus, a work record of frequent layoffs or job changes may simply reflect the nature of the local labour market. But employers may interpret it as a sign of unstable work habits. Similarly, a string of temporary and part-time jobs, a common career path for many well-educated and highly motivated young Canadians across Canada, can be a disadvantage, if employers assume the problem originates with the job applicant, rather than with the labour market.[20]

Historical Patterns of Racial and Ethnic Discrimination

Employer *discrimination* in hiring and promotion can also block movement into better jobs, leading to overrepresentation of disadvantaged groups in secondary labour markets. Before we discuss this, it would be useful to look back in Canadian history at examples of officially sanctioned racial and ethnic discrimination (Backhouse 1999). After Canada was colonized, members of various Indigenous nations were frequent participants in the preindustrial labour market, acting as guides, fighting for the French against the English (and vice versa), and providing the furs sought by the trading companies for their European markets.[21] But as central Canada began to industrialize, and later as Western Canada was opened for settlement, the traditional economies of the Indigenous nations in these regions were largely destroyed. As discussed in Chapter 1, the presence of Indigenous groups was often seen as an impediment to economic development. The most common solution was to place them on reserves, far out of sight (Truth and Reconciliation Commission of Canada 2015; Camfield 2019).

Nevertheless, some Indigenous workers were employed in the resource industries (forestry, mining, and commercial fishing and canning, for example), in railway construction, and in agriculture (High 1996; Denis 2015). Indigenous workers were often given the most menial and difficult work (Patrias 2016). Not all of this paid employment was voluntary, however. For example, in the 1950s and 1960s, by cutting off social assistance benefits, the provincial and federal governments forced many Indigenous people to migrate to southern Alberta to work in the sugar-beet industry (Laliberte and Satzewich 1999). The decline in demand for large numbers of unskilled and semiskilled workers in Canada's resource and transportation industries meant declining wage-labour opportunities for Indigenous people. Even when jobs were available, racist attitudes and labour market discrimination were rampant (Knight 1978). In a society that viewed Indigenous people as second-class citizens, these problems should not be surprising—for instance, Indigenous people were not even allowed to vote until 1960. Even in communities with long histories of daily contact and family ties between Indigenous and non-Indigenous peoples, what Denis (2015) calls "laissez-faire racism" nonetheless persists.

During the 1880s, many Chinese men were recruited to work on railway construction in Western Canada and in resource-based industries. They were generally paid much less than what others received for the same job and encountered much hostility from the white population (Anderson 1991: 35). Labour unions lobbied for legislation restricting Chinese workers from entering specific (better-paid) trades. Chinese workers were forced into marginal jobs in a racially split B.C. labour market. In addition, the B.C. government passed legislation that severely restricted the civil rights of Chinese residents of the province. For its part, the federal government required Chinese immigrants to pay a head tax on entering Canada, while other immigrants were not required to do so; later, it passed the Chinese Immigration Act, which, for several decades, virtually stopped all potential Chinese immigrants from entering the country.[22]

Perhaps the discrimination faced by Chinese workers was simply the result of white workers' fears that they would lose their jobs to non-whites who were willing to work for lower wages. However, studies of this era suggest that racist attitudes—fears about the impact of too many Asian immigrants on a white, anglophone society—were frequently the underlying source of publicly expressed concerns about job loss and wage cuts. White workers seldom tried to bring Chinese workers into their unions (a tactic that would have enhanced their bargaining power and reduced employers' ability to pay lower wages to non-whites), even though the Chinese workers frequently showed interest in collectively opposing the actions of employers.[23]

Peter Li (1982) has described how, early in the 20th century (1910–47), Chinese Canadians living in the Prairie provinces encountered similar forms of racial discrimination. Barred from entry into many trades and professions, Chinese workers were mostly restricted to employment in *ethnic business enclaves* where, by supporting one another and working extremely hard, they could make a living. Chinese restaurants and laundries, for example, provided employment for many members of the Prairie Chinese community. Looking at earlier periods, Chan (2014) outlines how the Chinese were legally excluded from many jobs in B.C. in the 1870s but then hired en masse to build the trans-Canada railway from 1881 to 1884. Nearly 17,000 Chinese workers carried out the most dangerous jobs, such as blasting, earning $1 per day (less food and board), half the wage of white workers, who also were not required to pay for living costs or equipment.

Similar experiences of racial discrimination were encountered by Black Canadians in preindustrial and early industrial Canada. Some members of the Canadian Black community were descendants of slaves brought to Nova Scotia by Loyalists leaving the United States (Milan and Tran 2004). Others were former American slaves who had left the United States, often via the Underground Railroad (a network of sympathetic individuals and groups in the United States and Canada who assisted slaves fleeing north), and had settled in the area west of Toronto to the Detroit River. During the mid-19th century, white Canadians frequently lobbied to have Blacks sent back to their former owners in the United States (Pentland 1981: 1–6).

By the 1860s, officially sanctioned discrimination against Blacks had largely disappeared, but labour market discrimination continued. For example, many Blacks worked for railway companies but were restricted to a limited number of lower-paying jobs, such as sleeping-car porter. White workers had the better-paying, less menial jobs such as sleeping-car conductor or dining-car steward. Such patterns were embedded in the contracts between railway companies and their unions. The system was supported by societal values that took for granted that Blacks should work in menial jobs. Not until 1964 were the arrangements that legitimized this *racially split labour market* abolished (Calliste 1987).

Today, labour laws and human rights legislation make it more difficult for employers to explicitly discriminate against specific groups of labour market participants. Nevertheless, some groups are still severely disadvantaged in the contemporary Canadian labour market for various reasons. The following three sections of this chapter focus on some of the most important of these groups. Chapter 6 is devoted to a discussion of the experiences of women in the paid labour market.

Immigrants and Visible Minorities

As discussed in Chapter 3, visible minorities (not including Indigenous peoples) made up 22.3 percent of the Canadian population (approximately 7.7 million people) in 2016, a dramatic increase from just 4.7 percent (1.1 million people) in 1981. If current trends continue, roughly one-third of the Canadian population will be a visible minority by 2036 (Statistics Canada 2017b).

Immigration has helped boost education levels and innovation in Canada since, compared to the rest of the adult population, recent immigrants are more highly educated and more likely to be trained in science, technology, engineering, and math (STEM) specializations that are in high demand (Picot and Hou 2018). Recent immigrants are also more likely to be in the labour force because of their higher level of education and their somewhat younger age profile. Since Canadian immigration policies favour better-educated immigrants, these higher education and labour force participation patterns are not surprising (Immigrant, Refugees and Citizenship Canada 2018).

That said, research also confirms that university-educated immigrants, particularly recent ones, are much more likely than native-born Canadians with university degrees to be underemployed—that is, working in jobs in sales and services with low education requirements (Reitz 2007b; Reitz and Banerjee 2017). According to the most recent analysis by Statistics Canada, about 10 percent of Canadian-born workers with university degrees were employed in such low-skill jobs, compared to 44 percent of recently immigrated women with degrees and 28 percent of recently immigrated men with degrees (Galarneau and Morissette 2009: 15).

It is not surprising, then, that immigrants earn far less than their native-born counterparts with equivalent education. For example, in 2016, recent immigrants (in Canada for five years or less), who held a university degree and were 25 and 54 years of age, earned just 68 percent of their Canadian-born counterparts. For established immigrants (in Canada 10 years or more), however, the earnings ratio was 93 percent. These statistics suggest a "catch-up" process, whereby immigrants close the earnings gap with Canadian-born workers as they settle in Canada and learn to navigate the labour market (Yssaad and Fields 2018).

This "catch-up" process has been observed for some time, but long-term trends (though not strictly comparable) suggest it is shifting over time. In the early 1980s, the earnings ratio for male immigrants in Canada for one year was 72 percent, while male immigrants in Canada for 10 years had completely caught up to Canadian-born coworkers. In the early 1990s and 2000s, however, not only was the earnings ratio for recent (one-year) male immigrants lower (63 percent in both years), but the catch-up process appeared to stall, with an earnings ratio of 90 percent for 10-year immigrants in 1991, and 80 percent in 2001.[24] Data from 2016 (a 93 percent earnings ratio for 10-year immigrants) thus suggest some improvement—though the persistence of an earnings gap of any kind remains a significant concern.

Indeed, chronic and unexplained gaps in employment outcomes—whether for income, hiring, or promotions—are a serious social and economic problem, not only for immigrant workers and their families but for Canadian society as a whole. It confirms that immigrants face barriers in receiving the returns they should expect from their investments in human capital—that is, both the educational credentials and prior work experience that they bring to Canada. Immigrants report that finding an adequate job is the biggest problem they experience after arriving in Canada (Schellenberg and Maheux 2007: 7). For society as a whole, the underutilization of recent immigrants' skills and training comes at a significant cost to the larger economy. It may also have a deleterious effect on economic growth, discouraging such workers from pursuing further education in the belief that will not be fairly rewarded (Green et al. 2016).

A substantial part of the problem lies in the non-recognition or undervaluing of non-Canadian educational credentials (Reitz 2007a; Banerjee et al. 2018). Canadian employers and professional licensing organizations (e.g., medical or engineering associations) often assume that university degrees or technical diplomas acquired outside Canada are inferior and use such assumptions to avoid hiring (or licensing) well-educated immigrants who came to Canada with hopes of finding good jobs in their areas of training. Along with the undervaluing of their non-Canadian credentials, some recent immigrants may be held back by language barriers (Fuller and Martin 2012), or by having few personal or professional contacts in the primary labour market.[25]

In addition, racial discrimination continues to handicap visible minority immigrants, as well as some Canadian-born visible minority groups, seeking to improve their employment situation. According to Statistics Canada's Ethnic Diversity Survey, 20 percent of visible minority labour force participants report experiencing discrimination or unfair treatment in the previous five years based on their ethnicity, language, accent, or religion. This compares to just 5 percent of Canadians who are not members of visible minorities (Palameta 2004: 37).[26] In some cases, discrimination may be *overt*—that is, it is obvious and blatant. In other cases, it may involve *implicit bias*, based on negative stereotypes, or systemic *discrimination*, where bureaucratic rules or procedures screen out qualified visible minority candidates when making hiring or promotion decisions (Beck, Reitz, and Weiner 2002).

A Toronto study of Filipino and West Indian women recruited to work in Canada as nannies and nurses offers telling examples. The owner of a nanny agency explained her hiring and referral practices as follows: "If you're from Jamaica, I won't even interview you. I know this is discrimination but I don't have any time for this . . . Jamaican girls are just dumb. They are not qualified to be childcare workers." Black nurses told the researchers how their ward assignments typically required much heavier physical labour, involved considerably less skilled work, and offered few supervisory opportunities. The long-term impact for them is less upward career mobility (Stasiulis and Bakan 2003: 78, 128–36).[27]

Likewise, a large-scale study of Canadian employers by Banerjee et al. (2018) found significant evidence of discrimination against Asian job candidates (Chinese, Indian, or Pakistani). This study sent out 12,910 resumés for 3,225 job postings, recording whether a call back for an interview was received. Overall, resumés with Asian names had a 28 percent lower call-back rate than those with anglo names. Of relevance to labour market segmentation theory, call-back rates were far lower in small firms than in firms with 500 or more employees. And although call backs did not vary by skill level, when an Asian candidate's resumé for "high-skilled" jobs showed foreign credentials or training, the call-back rate dropped sharply. Having "extra" credentials (for example, a Canadian master's degree for a job requiring only a bachelor's degree) helped boost call backs for Asian candidates, but not enough to overcome the original disadvantage.

Given such results, it is not surprising that many members of visible minority groups engage in "resumé whitening"—that is, downplaying or concealing racial clues on their job applications (Kang et al. 2016). Yet, while job applicants are less likely to do so when applying to companies with stated commitments to diversity, it appears that such companies are not any less likely to engage in discriminatory practices. For this reason, some experts suggest that more employers should move toward anonymizing resumés in the first round of drawing up a short list, as a way to end such discriminatory practices (Banerjee et al. 2018).

Related to these issues, it is important to note the "changing colour of poverty" in Canada (Das Gupta et al. 2018; Kazemipur and Halli 2001). As noted earlier, the majority of recent immigrants are visible minorities, primarily newcomers from South and East Asia, the Middle East, and, to a smaller extent, Africa, Central America, and South America. Compared to the significant difficulties they face in the labour market, evidence suggests Canadian-born visible minority group members earn as much as their white counterparts with similar amounts of education and training.[28] In other words, it is not visible minority status per se that is associated with labour market disadvantage, but the combination of visible minority and recent immigrant status. Currently, such workers have much higher odds of underemployment in the secondary labour market: taxi drivers, janitors, domestic workers, parking-lot attendants, security guards, and workers in ethnic restaurants are obvious examples.

Indigenous Peoples

As we discussed in Chapter 3, about 1.7 million Indigenous peoples (roughly 5 percent of the total population) lived in Canada in 2016, including about 970,000 self-identifying as members of a First Nation, 600,000 as Métis, and 65,000 as Inuit. This population is very diverse and is spread unevenly across the country. First Nations peoples are more likely to reside in western Canada, with about half of that population there. Inuit are largely concentrated in Canada's north. Roughly 80 percent of Métis reside in Ontario, with about two-thirds living in metropolitan areas (Statistics Canada 2017c). We also noted that the Indigenous population is much younger than the non-Indigenous population and growing at a faster rate. Indigenous peoples have a median age of 32 years, compared to 41 years for the non-Indigenous population (Statistics Canada 2017c). Hence, a much higher proportion of Indigenous people are of working age (25 to 64 years old) or will soon move into this age category, potentially making up an increasingly larger share of Canada's workforce.[29]

Indigenous peoples have lower employment rates and higher unemployment rates, and are much more likely to be living in low-income households (Statistics Canada 2017d; OECD 2018). In 2015, the employment rate for Indigenous workers ages 25 to 54 years who were living off-reserve was 75.8 percent, compared to 86.5 percent for non-Indigenous workers in the same age range. The 2015 Indigenous unemployment rate was 11.0 percent, nearly twice the rate of 5.9 percent for non-Indigenous Canadians.[30] Further differences are evident within the Indigenous population. For instance, in 2015, Métis had a much higher employment rate of 73.1 percent, compared to 62.4 percent for First Nations. The unemployment rate was 8.8 percent for the Métis population, much lower than the rate of 13.2 percent for First Nations (Moyser 2017).

We also see a significant earnings gap when comparing the Indigenous and non-Indigenous populations. In 2016, non-Indigenous workers earned, on average, $2.50 more per hour than Indigenous workers, with this average varying across industries and occupations. It is noteworthy that this earnings gap has changed little over the last decade (OECD, 2018). Not surprisingly, then, Indigenous peoples are far more likely to experience low income; in 2016, 23 percent of the Indigenous population, compared to 14 percent of the non-Indigenous population, reported low incomes (OECD 2018: 31).

What produces these very large differences? On average, Indigenous peoples are less likely than non-Indigenous Canadians to have acquired the educational credentials that translate into better jobs (Davies and Guppy 2018; Uppal 2017). In 2016, more than four in ten Indigenous people ages 25 to 64 years had completed some form of postsecondary education, but just one in ten had a university degree. And it is university degrees that matter in labour market success.[31] Comparing earnings by education level, for instance, we see that the hourly wage gap, noted above, almost disappears for Indigenous and non-Indigenous workers who hold a university degree (Moyser 2017). More finely grained analysis, controlling for education, as well as for literacy, numeracy, technical skills, and socio-demographic characteristics, also finds comparable earnings for Indigenous and non-Indigenous workers. But once again we must emphasize the substantial barriers Indigenous people face in accessing comparable levels of education and training in the first place (Hu et al. 2019).

Clearly, access to education has been a serious problem for Indigenous peoples for generations, as has racism and discrimination within the education system (Schissel and Wotherspoon 2003; Truth and Reconciliation Commission of Canada 2015). The brutal legacy of residential schools, established in the 1870s, not only deprived Indigenous people of their culture, language, identity, and family histories, but also contributed to deep intergenerational mistrust of formal education systems (Milne 2016; Wotherspoon 2015). Addressing this, Senator Murray Sinclair, chief commissioner of the Truth and Reconciliation Commission, points out that while the residential school system played a central role in the oppression and marginalization of Indigenous peoples, education also holds the "key to reconciliation." But it must be a two-way street, he notes—aiding the skill development of Indigenous peoples, and educating non-Indigenous peoples about the damage done by colonization and the persistence of racism. In his words:

> I would like to see an education system that teaches Canadians that this country had a long, rich history before contact; that Canada was created using European and Indigenous legal and social systems. We would learn about treaties, inherent rights, forced relocations and residential schools. With a full history, we wouldn't be surprised by the social, economic, political and cultural despair that currently impacts Indigenous peoples. (*Globe and Mail*, 2019)

Compounding educational inequalities, the labour market position of some Indigenous peoples is also tied to their geographical location. In 2016, roughly 44 percent of First Nations Canadians with Registered Indian status (about 330,000 people) were living on reserves (Statistics Canada 2017c) where their great-grandparents were forced to settle when white settlers took over their ancestral lands, destroying their livelihood, and making them dependent on a far-from-charitable government (Shewell 2004; Camfield 2019; Truth and Reconciliation Commission of Canada 2015). Employment opportunities are severely limited in many of these frequently isolated communities, as they also are in many of the smaller communities inhabited by Métis and Inuit in Canada. Large industrial megaprojects in northern Canada (e.g., mines, mills, pipelines, and dams) have typically offered only limited employment to residents of local Indigenous communities. At the same time, these projects have often damaged traditional hunting, trapping, and fishing economies, further undermining traditional culture, and caused environmental damage.[32]

In urban centres, the employment situation of the Indigenous population is slowly improving but there is still a huge gap separating them from non-Indigenous residents (Luffman and Sussman 2007; Moyser 2017). The former may have a patchy employment record, which can seriously restrict entry into the primary labour market. They may also often encounter prejudice among employers, which, along with a lack of contacts and limited job-search resources (such as transportation), can further handicap them in their search for satisfactory employment. Thus, an explanation for the disadvantaged labour market position of Indigenous peoples must examine the many other factors beyond the acquisition of human capital that contribute to the segmenting of the Canadian labour market and to the generation of urban poverty.

Disability and Age

Canadians with disabilities are another group characterized by low labour force participation and high unemployment rates, fewer hours of work, and lower incomes. As with the Indigenous population, people with disabilities who obtain employment are frequently found working in low-skill, poorly paid jobs in the secondary labour market. As we noted in Chapter 3, roughly one in five Canadians (ages 15 years or older) have one or more disabilities, according to the 2017 Canadian Survey on Disability (Statistics Canada 2018c). *Disability* is a fluid and often invisible category, which individuals may move in and out of over their life (Maroto et al. 2019). Typically, it is more prevalent with age, with four in ten seniors reporting a disability in Canada. But one in ten youth also report a learning, mental health, physical, or other disability.[33]

Canadians with disabilities have very low employment rates. In 2017, just 59 percent of adults with a disability were employed, compared to 80 percent of those without a disability. Only 30 percent of those with very serious disabilities were employed (Statistics Canada 2018c). Huge barriers keep people with disabilities from obtaining satisfactory employment. Many employers assume that those with visual, hearing, cognitive, and movement disabilities are unable to contribute to the workplace, though many of these individuals would do well in a variety of jobs, with limited assistance (Lindsay et al. 2014). Some employers may be uncomfortable with or fearful of people who have disabilities—or simply not know how to relate to them. People with disabilities often also face serious problems with transportation or are held back by buildings designed without their needs in mind. The emphasis on having stylish employees with a certain "look" in some service jobs—what researchers call "aesthetic capital"—may create further barriers (Anderson et al. 2010).[34]

In Canada, provincial/territorial and federal human rights legislation such as the 1985 Canadian Human Rights Act prohibits discrimination on the basis of disabilities. The 1986 Employment Equity Act, which we discuss further in Chapter 6, also encourages "reasonable accommodation" of those with disabilities in the workplace. While some believe that the current legislative and policy framework offers an adequate basis for promoting labour market inclusion of people with disabilities, studies continue to find significant levels of discrimination in hiring processes (Schur et al. 2016). Canadians with disabilities are thus significantly overrepresented in the secondary labour market. Many find work only in special institutional settings where pay is low and career opportunities are nonexistent.

While employers may make assumptions about the "shortcomings" of people with disabilities (Lindsay et al. 2014), those who do make the effort to accommodate them report positive outcomes (Schur et al. 2009). While some jobs may not be adaptable, in other cases very small changes are all that is needed. As one employer explains:

> We, for example, have this employee he's severely autistic and has no communication skills . . . We talked about what he likes and repetition was one of the things. So we had him folding laundry twice a week for three hours and loved it and then we added in shredding. Then we added washing down the windows outside of our building and then we added sweeping up around the building and before you knew it he was really, truly contributing meaningfully to our environment. (Lindsay et al. 2014: 963)

Finally, *age discrimination* occurs when older workers, laid off in factory shutdown or a company or government department downsizing, for example, apply for another core-sector job and are rejected in favour of younger applicants because of the belief that older workers are harder to retrain and will have difficulty adapting to new technologies. It may also occur when qualified and hardworking older workers are passed over for promotions within companies in favour of younger workers or when older workers are actively encouraged to retire to reduce payroll costs.[35] With an aging population, we are seeing growing evidence of age discrimination in some sectors (Neumark et al. 2016; Colella and King 2018), along with discrimination lawsuits by older workers (Cohen 2019). But in other sectors, employers are working to retain older workers and build more "age-inclusive" workplaces (Lowe and Graves 2016).

Youth seeking their first permanent job also face age discrimination. Even if they have the educational qualifications, they find it far easier to gain employment in the part-time student labour market within the lower-tier services than to get an interview for a full-time career position in a major corporation or a government department. "Lack of experience" is a term heard all too frequently by unsuccessful young job applicants. Discrimination not only occurs in hiring, but in legislated wage rates as well. For instance, in Alberta, the $15 hourly minimum wage, instituted by the former NDP government in October 2018, was amended in June 2019 by Jason Kenney's United Conservative government. It now excludes students under 18 years of age, for whom the minimum wage has been dropped to $13 an hour (Keller 2019).

Sexual Orientation and Gender Identity

In recent years, sociologists and economists have paid growing attention to work-related discrimination on the basis of sexual orientation and gender identity.[36] *Sexual orientation* is multifaceted, including sexual identity, sexual attraction, and sexual behaviour (Waite and Denier 2019). *Gender identity* refers to one's sense of self, as male, female, or non-binary (Pichler and Ruggs 2018). To date, studies have primarily focused on sexual orientation, gathering data through survey questions. For instance, the Canadian General Social Survey asks: "Do you consider yourself to be: heterosexual, homosexual, bisexual, don't know/no answer, refused" (Waite and Denier 2019). A challenge facing researchers is that not all surveys and official statistics include the questions, though this is beginning to change (Waite and Denier 2019; Ng and Rumens 2017). While early research focused primarily on lesbians and gays, studies now address a diverse range of sexual orientations and gender identities. We use LGBTQ+ to be as inclusive as possible, recognizing that language varies and continues to change.[37]

A central question researchers have examined is whether, and how, labour market outcomes (e.g., wages, benefits, hiring, and promotion) vary between heterosexual and non-heterosexual workers. Beyond the outcomes for individual workers, organizational scholars also consider how workplaces are shaped by *hetero-normativity* and *cis-normativity*—that is, assumptions that people are heterosexual, with a gender identity that corresponds to their birth sex (Ng and Rumens 2017). These types of assumptions shape organizations in significant ways—for instance, through workplace policies (e.g., who gets spousal benefits or work–family support), organizational rituals (e.g., what are acceptable jokes, who attends family events), and organizational climate and coworker support (e.g., who feels valued and included) (Guiffre and Williams 2011; Hearn et al. 1989).

Of these issues, income and wages have been the most widely studied. Evidence confirms gaps between heterosexual and non-heterosexual workers, but also complex dynamics. Gay and bisexual men typically earn less than heterosexual men, but estimates vary, with some studies finding up to a 30 percent gap (Pichler and Ruggs 2018). Some hypothesize that gay men may trade higher pay for "gay-friendly" workplaces (termed "gay ghettos") where they do not have to conceal their sexual orientation (Williams and Guiffre 2011). For women, wage patterns are mixed, with some studies finding that lesbian women earn a *wage premium* over heterosexual women, and other studies finding no gap at all (Waite and Denier 2015; Picher and Ruggs 2018). As much past research is U.S.-based, a recent study in Canada by Waite and Denier (2015) on this topic offers valuable insights. They find a pattern where heterosexual men have the highest earnings, followed by gay men, lesbians, and then heterosexual women. We discuss their research further in Chapter 6.

Discrimination in hiring and promotion processes is also a critical issue for LGBTQ+ workers, as for other groups we discuss in this chapter (DeSouza et al. 2017; Ng and Rumens 2017). For instance, the Pew Research Center Survey on LGBT Americans reports that that one in five (21 percent) have experienced some form of unfair treatment by an employer due to their sexual orientation or gender identity (Pew Research Center 2013). Over one-third of workers report concealing their identities for fear of unfair treatment. Bullying and microaggressions are also a frequent concern (Ng and Rumens 2017). Currently, we have far fewer studies of transsexual and transgender workers, but available evidence suggests they experience some of the highest rates of discrimination, with over half (56 percent) reporting perceived discrimination from an employer or coworker (Pichler and Ruggs 2018).

This highlights how prejudice and stigma may vary across the LGBTQ+ population. Indeed, Williams and Guiffre (2011) argue that despite a shift from "closeted" to "gay-friendly" organizations, and greater acceptance of gays and lesbians in particular, we have not yet seen a shift to "queer organizations," which are inclusive of all sexualities and genders. While more studies are needed, especially of understudied workers who are transsexual and transgender (Pichler and Rugg 2018), valuable insights can be gleaned elsewhere. One such example—*The Autobiography of a Transgender Scientist*—by the late Ben Barres (2018), illustrates both the harmful effects of discrimination and the positive force of supportive coworkers and inclusive organizations. Barres was a highly successful neurobiologist at Stanford University School of Medicine, admired not only for his path-breaking scientific accomplishments but also for his passionate advocacy for workplace inclusion (Freeman 2018; Barres 2006).

In Canada, discrimination on the basis of sexual orientation is illegal in provincial and territorial human rights codes and the Charter of Rights and Freedoms (Ng and Rumens 2017). Employers in some sectors are also making efforts to develop LGBTQ+ inclusive environments, as are schools, colleges, and universities. There is strong evidence of the value and importance of such efforts. Organizations that actively work toward inclusion—through initiatives on workplace climate and inclusion, policies and benefits, or employee resource groups and alliances —see higher job satisfaction and organizational commitment amongst LGBTQ+ workers (Ely and Feldberg 2018). There is still far to go in many workplaces. But the potential benefits for workers, organizations, and Canadian society are clear.

CHANGING PATTERNS OF SOCIAL INEQUALITY

Questions about how labour markets work, about why some people get better jobs than others do, are really questions about social inequality. As we saw in Chapter 1, Karl Marx used the concept of social class to analyze inequality, focusing on economic and social relationships between capitalists and the proletariat and on what he believed to be a declining middle class (the petite bourgeoisie). He predicted growing class conflict that would eventually lead to the emergence of a new type of egalitarian society. While Marx's theories have been useful for explaining conflict within industrial capitalist societies and for helping us understand how people feel about work (see Chapter 10), they are unable to accurately map the complexities of employment structures (see Chapters 3 and 4) and patterns of social inequality in contemporary Western societies. Social scientists have taken two different approaches to going beyond Marx: the first involving descriptions of the class structures of post-industrial societies and the second focusing on how labour market segmentation has evolved over the past two centuries.

Post-industrial Class Structure

Sociologists have developed many competing classification systems to capture the changing occupational and class structure in industrialized economies (Savage 2015; Skeggs 2015). One of the most influential, the Goldthorpe scale, developed in Britain in the late 20th century, differentiated between employers and employees, with the latter group separated into those in a labour contract (e.g., routine, semi-routine, technical employees), or those in a more autonomous relationship with an employer (managers and professionals).

In the United States, another influential approach, developed by Erik Olin Wright (Wright et al. 1982) built directly on the ideas of Marx, taking several factors into account: ownership of the means of production, the employment of others, the supervision of others, and control over one's own work. Wright's classification distinguished between large business owners and small employers, and the petite bourgeoisie, who own their businesses (or farms) but have no employees (we refer to them in Chapter 4 as *own-account self-employed*). It also separated paid employees into four main groups: managers, who are involved in decision making with business owners; supervisors, who exercise authority over others; semi-autonomous workers (e.g., lawyers) who retain control over their work; and workers who generally have no ownership rights, decision-making power, or authority over others.[38]

More recently, evidence of growing inequality in the distribution of income has sparked a renewed interest in class analysis. In Britain, Savage et al.'s (2013)

Great British Class Survey builds on the ideas of Pierre Bourdieu (see Chapter 2). Rather than relying solely on occupation, it captures *economic capital* (income, occupation, wealth), *cultural capital* (tastes, interests, activities) and *social capital* (friends, networks, associations), identifying seven major groups. At the top are "the elite" (CEOs, judges, senior managers, with high incomes and highbrow tastes), followed by the "established middle class" (engineers, police officers, urban planners), "technical middle class" (pharmacists, scientists, teachers), and "new affluent workers" (electricians, postal workers, retail workers). Three final classes include the "traditional working class" (drivers, secretaries), "emergent service workers" (bartenders, chefs, care workers), and "the precariat" (cleaners, retail sales) (Savage et al. 2013; Savage 2015). While occupations are used to illustrate each group above, the full analysis shows how each class varies in their occupational diversity (or lack thereof), their social networks, their cultural preferences (e.g., music, travel, food, hobbies), and the way the classes are spatially distributed across the country.[39]

Evolving Labour Market Segmentation in North America

In contrast to class analysis, another approach to understanding contemporary patterns of inequality focuses on labour market segmentation. In the United States, Gordon, Edwards, and Reich (1982) examined long-term changes, arguing that three major epochs have shaped inequality. In the period of *initial proletarianization* (roughly 1820 to 1890), a large, relatively homogeneous industrial working class emerged. Because capitalist management techniques were still in their infancy, craftworkers initially retained control over their labour process. But this changed during the second phase, the era of *homogenization of labour* (1890 to 1940), which saw extensive mechanization, the deskilling of labour (see Chapter 10), the growth of very large workplaces, and the rise of a new managerial class. A third phase (from the end of World War II to the early 1980s), marked the *segmentation of labour*—where distinct primary and secondary labour markets emerged.

As discussed in Chapter 1, Canada began to industrialize later and has always remained a heavily resource-based economy. Thus, the same three stages do not precisely describe our economic history—though some similarities exist. However, the emphasis on change in this historical overview encourages us to ask whether further changes in labour market segmentation have been occurring as we have moved into the 21st century? The answer is yes. Accumulating evidence suggests fundamental realignments in the industrial and occupational structures, and in the nature of employment relationships, not only in Canada, but also in the United States and other Western industrialized countries.

Labour Market Polarization

Manufacturing and other goods-producing industries have declined significantly over the past several decades. From the 1980s to the present, as noted in Chapters 2 and 4, factory closures have been common, with the movement of factories to low-wage countries such as Mexico in the 1990s and, more recently, China, India, and other rapidly industrializing countries. New robotic technologies have allowed other manufacturers to maintain production levels with fewer employees. A similar situation has developed in Canada's resource industries, where unstable world markets, in combination with technological innovations, have reduced the need for labour.[40]

During the 1990s, downsizing and hiring cutbacks were extensive in many large corporations in the business and distributive service industries, and by the turn of the century, many white-collar jobs were also being outsourced to other countries. As for the public sector, downsizing became the norm in the 1990s as governments (both federal and provincial) cut deficits by laying off employees or privatizing some of the services they had previously provided directly to the public. Thus, while the economic expansion that took place in the first part of the 21st century slowed down some of these trends, the global recession that began in 2008 intensified them once again.[41]

Despite these transformations, there has still been employment growth over the past three decades. But as we've already emphasized, much of it has been in the service sector, although new high-skill, well-paying jobs have been created, leading some observers to proclaim the emergence of a "knowledge economy" (Drucker 1993; Florida 2002). However, the proportion of jobs in the secondary labour market has grown steadily, leading to parallel concerns about a "risk society" (Beck 1992, 2000). Many of these new jobs are part-time or temporary, paying less and offering fewer benefits and career opportunities than the full-time, permanent jobs that have disappeared (Fudge 2017). In addition, employers in some industries have come to rely on *temporary foreign workers* whose labour force situation is even more precarious because they do not have Canadian citizenship and are not as protected by labour legislation (Foster 2012; Lenard and Straehle 2012). Thus, nonstandard jobs with less security have been increasing, leading to new forms of labour market segmentation (Hudson 2007).[42]

Industrial restructuring and the growth in nonstandard work have led to *labour market polarization.* Compared to the 1970s and 1980s, the 1990s saw more Canadians unemployed and relatively fewer people employed in the well-paying, full-time, permanent jobs that were once taken for granted. Put another way, the primary labour market shrank during the 1990s, leaving fewer workers with access to its good jobs, as defined by income, benefits, and job security. The economic recovery at the end of the last century and the beginning of the 21st century slowed, but did not reverse, this polarization trend as relatively fewer of the new jobs were "good jobs." And polarization became even more apparent in the aftermath of the 2008–9 global financial crisis and subsequent recession it triggered.

Within the broadly defined secondary labour market, three relatively distinct new segments have emerged. The first is a *student labour market,* consisting mainly of part-time jobs, most of them in the lower-tier consumer services and retail trade industries (Lowe and Krahn 1999; Tufts and Holmes 2010). Many young Canadians participate voluntarily in this labour market, using their low-wage, part-time jobs to earn discretionary income or to pay for their education. But this part-time workforce also contains non-students, women who cannot work full time because of their family responsibilities, and others who simply cannot find a full-time job (see Chapter 4).

The *temporary/contract labour market* exists in both the upper- and lower-tier service industries (Vosko, Zukewich, and Cranford 2003; Fuller 2008). As employers in both the private and public sectors have come to rely more heavily on temporary workers for both low- and high-skill jobs (Stinson 2010), a larger proportion of well-educated young adults are spending some years in such jobs before they are able to obtain more secure employment. Women, immigrants, and members of visible minority groups are also over-represented in this labour market segment (Hudson 2007; Fuller and Vosko 2008). While some of these temporary and contract jobs require higher levels of skill and training, they nevertheless offer less job security, fewer benefits, fewer training and career opportunities (Davis 2010), and less income (Galarneau 2005).

Temporary foreign workers, or TFWs, recruited to fill specific jobs in Canada (often with specific employers, such as Tim Hortons) for specified periods of time inhabit a third, somewhat different labour market segment that has emerged in the 21st century. According to Statistics Canada, TFWs have increased from 52,000 in 1996 to 310,000 in 2015. While most are truly temporary, staying for two years on average, some stay longer and this trend is rising. In the 1990s, about 15 percent of TFWs remained in the country after five years. From 2005 to 2009, this was the case for over one-third of TFWs (Prokopenko and Hou 2018).[43]

Most TFWs fill low-paid jobs in the secondary labour market, working as janitors, short-order cooks, or hotel cleaners. Others work on tomato farms and wineries, through the Seasonal Agricultural Workers Program, returning each year on an eight-month contract, or as nannies, through the Live-In Caregiver Program, where they reside in their employer's home (Brickner and Straehle 2010; Hennebry and McLaughlin 2012). Less commonly, TFWs are recruited to work in higher-paying occupations like nursing (Taylor, Foster, and Cambre 2012). Because TFWs are in Canada on a time-limited basis, whether they are employed in high- or lower-skill jobs, they work in a precarious environment with limited job security, less legal protection than Canadian citizens have, and fewer opportunities for developing a rewarding and long-term career.

Rising Income Inequality

Real earnings (taking inflation into account) rose systematically in Canada in the three or four decades following World War II, but this trend stopped in the 1980s, for the reasons discussed above. For many workers, more often men, real incomes have declined since then. At the same time, incomes have risen dramatically for the highest-paid groups in society. Thus, labour market polarization has contributed to a substantial increase in *income inequality* in Canada over the past several decades (Green et al. 2016).[44] Looking at employment earnings before taxes for families, from the mid-1970s to the early 2010s, inequality (as measured by the Gini coefficient) rose by roughly 22 percent. Focusing on after-tax earnings, and taking into account government transfer payments (e.g., family allowances, old age pensions), income inequality still rose by 10 percent (Green et al. 2016). Put another way, in 2012 (the last year for which we have data), the average income of the top quintile (20 percent) of families was roughly 13 times that of the bottom quintile (Uppal and LaRochelle-Cote 2015).

Canada is not alone. Income inequality has been increasing in many other Western industrialized countries (Piketty 2014; Reich 2015). While income inequality today is somewhat lower in Canada than in the United States or the United Kingdom, it is higher than in Sweden, Norway, and Switzerland, for example (Green et al. 2016). It is an increasingly troubling trend. In the United States, former president Barack Obama identified inequality as one of the "defining issues of our time." In Canada, Prime Minister Justin Trudeau came to office on a promise to "strengthen the middle class." And based on polling by EKOS Research Associates, a majority of Canadians surveyed agree that we are becoming a more divided society of haves and have-nots, with the prospect that the next generation will have a lower quality of life (Lowe and Graves 2016: 34, 134).

Many factors explain rising inequality. One of the most comprehensive studies in Canada to date by Green et al. (2016)—*Income Inequality: The Canadian Story*—highlights three key concerns: new technologies, globalization, and institutional factors. We have discussed the first two already and their potential to displace or deskill workers or to relocate work to lower-wage countries. The third item, *institutional factors*, highlights a mix of employment legislation, including laws determining minimum wages, and the strength of unions, which, together, create a minimum floor for how workers are treated and paid. Weakening institutional factors are central to the "new inequality" in Canada—disproportionately affecting young workers, immigrants, and Indigenous people; those with little education; and those in specific regions of the country (e.g., Atlantic provinces, rural areas). In fact, some warn that a "clear generational divide has emerged in the Canadian labour market.[45]

It is apparent that new forms of labour market segmentation pose a significant problem. For some commentators, a key concern is the rise of the *working poor*, as poverty increasingly touches the *gainfully employed*, rather than only the unemployed or retired seniors, as was once the case (Fleury 2008; Murphy, Zhang, and Dionne 2012). For others, the central issue is a *declining middle class* (Reich 2015). For yet others, it is the rise of elites and the "1 percent." In short, many different concepts are used to frame the inequality debate, without being well defined (Banting and Myles 2016). We prefer to use the term *labour market polarization* to refer to the interrelated trends involved—industrial and occupational realignment, rising levels of nonstandard work, weakening institutional standards, and growing individual income and wealth inequality as a result. But whatever the term used, it is clear that inequality is a pressing concern.

POLICY RESPONSES TO LABOUR MARKET BARRIERS AND GROWING INEQUALITY

What might be done to create better jobs and to counter the trend toward greater labour market polarization? Responses based on a human capital perspective would primarily emphasize access to education as the most important public policy goal. In fact, access was a central concern of Canadian governments throughout the second half of the last century, particularly during the 1960s and 1970s when many new postsecondary educational institutions were opened and student loan systems were introduced. In the late 1990s and the start of this century, provincial governments once more undertook to improve access to postsecondary education.

These policy efforts did have an effect. Over time, the average educational attainment of the Canadian population rose dramatically, and some of the *systemic barriers* to equal access to education were reduced. Even so, as we have seen in this chapter, not all groups in Canadian society have equal educational opportunities. Consequently, continued policy responses targeting this goal are needed. Rising postsecondary tuition costs, and provincial governments struggling with deficits (leading them to reduce funding for postsecondary education) raise concerns that we may see a reversal of the slow trend toward greater equality of educational opportunity that characterized the last part of the 20th century.

Over the past several decades, government education policies also began focusing on encouraging young Canadians to stay in school (thereby reducing high-school dropout rates) and promoting skill upgrading among older labour force participants, particularly the unemployed. At the same time, more emphasis was placed on policies promoting formal training and skill upgrading in the workplace.[46] Concerns about reducing labour market inequalities, however, were not the reason. Governments were becoming anxious about Canada's competitive position in the global economy. Without a heavier investment in human capital, along with more advantage taken of it, it was argued, Canada would fall behind in the global economy.

Clearly, greater investments in education and training are important but they cannot resolve all problems. Some groups of Canadian labour force participants are still educationally disadvantaged, and some could benefit from improvements in their literacy skills. If global competitiveness is our goal, greater investments in human capital are part of the longer-term solution. However, if reducing labour market inequalities is equally important, then human capital investments are only a partial solution. Certainly education and training can assist many workers. But cost barriers exist for many, and cultural barriers are equally significant for first-generation students (Lehmann 2012; Green et al. 2016). Furthermore, some Canadians with university degrees feel they are overqualified for their jobs. Thus, we need greater recognition that *underemployment* is a problem in the Canadian economy (Barnetson 2018).[47]

While human capital explanations focus our attention on education as the key policy variable, the labour market segmentation perspective encourages us to identify the barriers, and process of social closure, that keep large numbers of qualified individuals out of better jobs. Obviously, a shortage of "good jobs" is part of the problem. So, too, is labour legislation that overlooks the rights and needs of the working poor, of nonstandard workers, a majority of whom are women, and of temporary foreign workers. Legislation that increases the minimum wage in all provinces and territories would also make a difference, particularly for the working poor.

Based on the evidence we have reviewed, stronger legislation and improved human resources policies and practices by employers that eliminate discrimination against disadvantaged groups are needed. Equity programs that help disadvantaged groups catch up with mainstream labour market participants are also important. Improved school-to-work transition programs, language training, and credential upgrading programs would also assist youth, Indigenous, and immigrant workers in their search for rewarding jobs and careers. If more Canadian workers were covered by union contracts, some of the inequality within the labour market could also be reduced. And if unions were involved on a more equal basis in decisions about national, regional, and firm-level industrial strategies, we might also move further toward the goal of global competitiveness. Indeed, many argue that strong, inclusive economic growth is the key to reducing inequality. Without it, they warn, we will see growing social resentment and conflict, protectionism, populism, and political unrest (Green et al. 2016; Reich 2015).

CONCLUSION

After examining the varying quality of jobs and the problems of unemployment and underemployment in Chapter 4, in this chapter we discussed the human capital and labour market segmentation explanations of labour market processes in order to answer the critical question of why some people tend to get better jobs. While the human capital model highlights the central role of education in determining occupational outcomes, it fails to account for the many examples of qualified and highly motivated individuals working in unrewarding jobs; it also ignores intergenerational transfers of advantage. In contrast, the segmentation approach recognizes inequalities in labour market outcomes and provides a better account of how such power differences are created and maintained. Our analysis of the segmented nature of the Canadian labour market led us to conclude that it has become more polarized and that income inequality has increased over the past several decades. The following two chapters, on gender in the paid workplace and on household, caring, and community work, focus in detail on another critically important source of differentiation—between women and men—in work opportunities, experiences, and rewards.

DISCUSSION QUESTIONS

1. Many people would argue that, in Canadian society today, everyone has more or less the same chance to get ahead in life. Do you agree or disagree? Why?
2. Compared to several decades ago, does education play a larger or smaller role in determining labour market outcomes? Why?
3. Based on what you read in Chapters 3 and 4, and in this chapter, in your opinion, how effectively do human capital and labour market segmentation theories explain present and past patterns of social inequality in Canada?
4. In your opinion, which groups of Canadian workers are most disadvantaged? Have these patterns of labour market inequality changed over time?
5. Should the state—that is, the provincial, territorial, and federal governments—get involved in trying to reduce labour market inequalities? If no, why not? If yes, what would be some of the most effective approaches?

ADDITIONAL RESOURCES

WORK AT THE MOVIES

- *The Road Taken* (directed by Selwyn Jacob, 1996, 52:00 minutes). This NFB documentary explores racism and the fight against discrimination by sleeping-car porters working on Canada's railways during the first six decades of the 20th century. It is available through the National Film Board of Canada: http://www.nfb.ca/film/road_taken.
- *High Steel* (directed by Don Owen, 1965, 13:47 minutes). This NFB documentary provides an interesting historical perspective on the experiences of Kahnawake Mohawks who migrated to do steelwork on Manhattan skyscrapers. It is available through the National Film Board of Canada: http://www.nfb.ca/film/high_steel.
- *Farmingville* (directed by Carlos Sandoval and Catherine Tambini, 2004, 79 minutes). In this documentary film on migrant and illegal workers in the United States, the story of the attempted murder of two Mexican labourers in Farmingville, New York, is told.
- *Chinese Cafés in Rural Saskatchewan* (directed by Tony Chan, 1985, 26:25 minutes). This documentary profiles the lives of four Chinese café owners and their families in Saskatchewan, examining the contemporary and historical, social, and economic issues they faced.

SOUNDS OF WORK

- "Jack of All Trades" (Bruce Springsteen). Springsteen's song explores labour market inequality and the experiences of workers forced to take any jobs available in the context of the 2008 global downturn.
- "Allentown" (Billy Joel). Joel examines the impact of socioeconomic change during the 1970s and 1980s on the opportunities for blue-collar workers.
- "Tramp Miner" (The Rankin Family). These Cape Bretoners sing about migrant miners who find jobs in unhealthy work environments and dream about returning home.

- "Jobs" (Chris Tse). This spoken word piece addresses the intersections of work, race, and immigration by highlighting the work and education experiences of the Canadian poet's father.
- "Income Inequality in Canada" (Policy Options Podcast with David Green and France St-Hilaire, 16:03 minutes). An interesting discussion with the editors of the 2016 book *Income Inequality: The Canadian Story*, which showcases research from nearly 30 Canadian experts on labour markets and inequality. https://policyoptions.irpp.org/2016/02/23/po-podcast-5-inequality/

NOTES

1. See Rubery (1996), Jones (1996), and van den Berg and Smucker (1997) on how economists and sociologists analyze labour markets.
2. See Clement and Myles (1994), Spilerman (2000), and Browne and Misra (2005) on labour markets and social inequality.
3. Becker (1975), with his book first published in 1964, is credited for developing human capital theory, although its basic premises originate in neoclassical economics. As we describe it here, the model is closely linked to the functionalist theory of stratification (Davis and Moore 1945).
4. See also Conference Board of Canada (2013) and Boudarbat, Lemieux, and Riddell (2010).
5. See Livingstone (1999), Lowe (2000), Mills (2004), Côté and Bynner (2008), and Krahn, Howard, and Galambos (2012) on problems of underemployment among Canadian youth.
6. See Alon (2009), Faas, Benson, and Kaestle (2013), and Rivera (2012, 2016) for discussions of the links between socioeconomic status, postsecondary education, and career outcomes in the United States. See Savage (2015) and Laurison and Friedman (2016) on the British context.
7. In Canada, see also Finnie et al. (2015), Chatoor et al. (2019), and Davies and Guppy (2018). Andres and Wyn (2010) also show strong SES effects on postsecondary educational outcomes, but important cultural and institutional differences, using longitudinal data from similar studies in British Columbia and Victoria, Australia.
8. Shaker and Macdonald (2015) report that average Canadian undergraduate tuition fees have roughly tripled from 1993–94 to 2015–16. Their "cost of learning index" ranks provinces by the affordability of education.

9. For a valuable comparison of the effects of tuition levels and student loan availability on university participation in Canada and the United States, see Belley et al. (2014). In the United States, Goldrick-Rab (2006) find that young people from lower-SES backgrounds are more likely to interrupt their postsecondary studies rather than moving straight through as do most middle-class youth. In Italy, Bernardi (2012) shows that, among students who drop out of postsecondary studies, those from higher-SES families are more likely to have a "second chance" at earning a postsecondary degree.

10. Uppal (2017) discusses Canadian high-school completion and dropout rates.

11. See Frenette (2007a), Davies, Maldonado, and Cyr (2017), and Lehmann and Tower (2018) for valuable discussions of the impacts of cultural capital on educational outcomes.

12. See Rubery (1996), Leontaridi (1998), Bauder (2001a), and Lehmann and Adams (2017) on labour market segmentation theory.

13. See Lowe and Schellenberg (2001) for Canadian data on better jobs in large, capital-intensive firms, and Kalleberg and Van Buren (1996) for U.S. data. Park (2012: 34) reports higher levels of training in the public sector and in white-collar occupations.

14. Aguiar (2001) describes low-paid, low-skill work in the contract building-cleaning industry in Toronto; see Backett-Milburn et al. (2008) on British women working in the low-paid food-retailing sector.

15. Smith (1997), Camuffo (2002), and Osterman and Burton (2005) discuss research on internal labour markets. See also Barnett, Baron, and Stuart (2000) and Petersen, Saporta, and Seidel (2000).

16. See Vosko (2000, 2005), Vosko, Zukewich, and Cranford (2003), and Fuller and Vosko (2008) on precarious work in Canada; Kalleberg (2009) and Young (2010) discuss the same trends in the United States.

17. Macdonald (1995), Leicht and Fennell (2001), and Evetts (2003) discuss the sociology of professions; see Witz (1992) for an early feminist critique of research on professionals. Adams (2010) offers a valuable discussion on the concept of professions, and also an overview of recent scholarship in Canada, the United States, the United Kingdom, and western Europe (Adams 2015).

18. Over time some occupational groups have gained more autonomy and power, while others have experienced *de-professionalization*. See Drudy (2008), Randle (1996), Adams (2000, 2018), and Cant and Sharma (1995) for how these processes have affected a wide variety of professions (e.g., scientists, dentists and dental hygienists, and practitioners of nontraditional medicine).

19. See Osberg, Wein, and Grude (1995) and Palmer and Sinclair (1997).

20. See Mills (2004), Worth (2005), Fuller (2008), and Krahn, Howard, and Galambos (2012) on career liabilities of irregular work histories.

21. See Jenness (1977: 250–51) and Patterson (1972); Pentland (1981: 1–3) reports that some Indigenous people were kept as slaves in Quebec, but this practice had largely disappeared by the early 1800s.

22. See Li (1982), Anderson (1991), and Chui, Tran, and Flanders (2005).

23. See Baureiss (1987), Creese (1988–89), Muszynski (1996), and Anderson (1991).

24. Statistics Canada, *The Daily* (March 11, 2003). See Reitz (2007a, 2007b) and Morissette and Sultan (2013) on changing patterns of immigrant employment success in Canada.

25. See also Thomas (2009) and Creese and Kambere (2003) on immigrants' language disadvantages, and Lamba (2003) on how refugees with more extensive social networks tend to find better jobs.

26. See also Gupta (1996), Satzewich (1998), and Creese (2007).

27. See also Milan and Tran (2004) on the disadvantaged labour market situation of Blacks in Canada.

28. See Bauder (2001b), Tran (2004), Palameta (2004), and Maximova and Krahn (2005).

29. See Statistics Canada (2013d) for 2011 National Household Survey data on Indigenous Canadians.

30. Data are from Moyser (2017) who analyzes Labour Force Survey trends from 2007 to 2015 for those living off-reserve.

31. Data are from the 2016 Census as reported in Statistics Canada (2017c).

32. For historical examples, see Stabler and Howe (1990) and Niezen (1993). Armitage (2005) and O'Faircheallaigh and Corbett (2005) discuss the involvement of Indigenous groups in environmental assessment and management in Canada and Australia, respectively.

33. See Shuey et al. (2017) for a discussion of disability and social inequality in Canada. In the United States, Maroto et al. (2019) examine economic insecurity at the intersection of disabilities, gender, and race. Jones and Wass (2013) discuss the situation in the United Kingdom.

34. Prince (2009) examines Canadian public policy as it relates to people with disabilities; Burkhauser, Schmeiser, and Weathers (2012) discuss the impact of anti-discrimination laws on employment opportunities for Americans who have disabilities.

35. See Roscigno et al. (2007), Mendenhall et al. (2008), and Kunze, Boehm, and Bruch (2011) on age discrimination.

36. For valuable discussions of existing scholarship, see Waite and Denier (2019) and the special issue of *Canadian Journal of Administrative Science* (Vol. 34, No. 2) edited by Ng and Rumens (2017).

37. For a useful discussion on terminology, see Gold (2018). Of note, many of the studies discussed in this section use the acronym LGBT and often focus on specific subsets of this population (e.g., lesbians and gays only). We have tried to indicate where possible who is included in specific studies. Having said this, Waite and Denier (2019) also note some of the difficulties that arise with survey questions, which do not always perfectly measure what they purport to (e.g., sexual orientation).

38. We use Wright's typology to describe the contemporary Canadian class structure, since the Statistics Canada data sources we used in Chapters 3 and 4 do not contain information on planning, decision making, and control over others. Livingstone (1999: 158) describes Ontario's workforce in the mid-1990s using Wright's classification system. Wright (2009: 14) offers a concise description of the class structure of the United States at the beginning of the 21st century.

39. For further details of the Great British Class Survey, see Savage et al. (2013) and Savage (2015). For discussions and critiques of this classification, see the 2015 special issue of *Sociological Review* (Volume 62, No 2) and the 2014 special issue of *Sociology* (Volume 48, No 3).

40. Clement's (1981) study of technological change at INCO documented the beginning of this trend. Osberg, Wein, and Grude (1995) and Russell (1999) discussed the continuing trend.

41. Zuberi (2013) shows how the contracting-out of hospital support staff jobs in Canada, the United States, and Europe has led to reductions in pay for workers and greater health risks for patients. Winson and Leach (2002) and Ehrenreich (2001) discuss the effects of industrial restructuring and downsizing during the 1990s on Canadian and U.S. families, respectively. See Harrison (2005), Shalla and Clement (2007), and Camfield (2011) for more studies of downsizing and layoffs in the Canadian private and public sectors.

42. See Vosko (2000), Vosko, Zukewich, and Cranford (2003), Galarneau (2005), Young (2010), and Fuller (2011) on trends in nonstandard work.

43. Changes have been made to the temporary foreign worker program in recent years, because of concerns over wages, working conditions, and treatment of workers, as well as questions about whether the program was being used to keep wages artificially low in some sectors. For details, see https://www.canada.ca/en/employment-social-development/services/foreign-workers/reports/overhaul.html#h2.3-3.3.

44. See also Murphy, Roberts, and Wolfson (2007) on growing income inequality and Morissette and Zhang (2007) on increases in wealth inequality. Along with labour market restructuring, changes to income tax policies that favour the very rich have also deepened income inequality (Yalnizyan 2010). Neckerman and Torche (2007) discuss similar trends in the United States.

45. Statistics Canada, *The Daily* (March 11, 2003); see also Bell and Blanchflower (2011) who show, how in both the United States and the United Kingdom, young people were most severely affected by the Great Recession of 2008–9.
46. On work-related training, see Jackson and Thomas (2017: Chapter 3), Underhill (2006), and Hurst (2008).
47. See Livingstone (2017), Lowe (2000), Frenette (2001), and Yuen (2010) on self-reported underemployment in Canada; on literacy underutilization, see Krahn (1997).

GENDER AND PAID EMPLOYMENT

6

"In October 2017, five days after the *New Yorker* published Ronan Farrow's first article on Harvey Weinstein, the actress and activist Alyssa Milano was lying in bed with her daughter when her phone buzzed; her friend . . . had sent her a screenshot. It read: 'Suggested by a friend: if all the women who have been sexually harassed or assaulted, wrote "Me too" as a status, we might give people a sense of the magnitude of the problem.' Milano added a sentence to her friend's message and posted it on Twitter: 'If you've been sexually harassed or assaulted, write 'me too' as a reply to this tweet.' . . .

"When Milano woke up the next day, #MeToo was trending number one on Twitter. It had been retweeted fifty-five thousand times. In the next six weeks, the hashtag appeared on Facebook eighty five million times. Milano didn't know it at the time but the actual #MeToo hashtag was started by African American activist Tarana Burke and had a long history online as a grassroots movement against sexual abuse of women of color. . . .

In the December 2017 issue of *Time* magazine, the impact of the stories empowering marginalized victims and humiliating the abusers was clear. *Time* named the women who came forward, including Milano and Tarana Burke, as its People of the Year. The Silence Breakers, *Time* called them."

Source: Linda Hirshman. (2019). *Reckoning: The Epic Battle Against Sexual Abuse and Harassment.* Boston and New York: Houghton Mifflin Harcourt, p. 209-212.

INTRODUCTION

In 2015, after winning the Canadian federal election, Prime Minister Justin Trudeau made headlines around the world by appointing a gender-balanced cabinet. Asked why gender equity was such an important priority, Trudeau replied simply: "Because it's 2015." Despite some criticism of the move, most Canadians seemed to agree that recognition of women's leadership ability was welcome and long overdue.[1] Among the 15 women appointed to cabinet was Jody Wilson-Raybould, a lawyer and former chief of the BC Assembly of First Nations, and the first Indigenous woman to hold the post of Minister of Justice and Attorney General. Also appointed was Chrystia Freeland, a former *Financial Times* journalist, who as Minister of International Trade would go on to negotiate the free trade agreement between Canada, the United States, and Mexico (USMCA), discussed in Chapter 2.

Yet just two years after Trudeau's historical act, the #MeToo and #TimesUp movements provided an abrupt reminder that, for many women, gender equity at work still remains far out of reach. In selecting the #MeToo movement (and the "Silence Breakers" who sparked it) as 2017 Person of the Year, *Time* magazine noted the critical role the movement had played in sparking debate and change, and renewing attention to persistent gender inequities in paid work. Despite women's increased education and career goals, today sexual harassment, gender discrimination, and unequal pay remain all too common problems. Perpetuating the situation, men continue to hold more lucrative, powerful positions, while persistent barriers to women's leadership remain. Illustrating this, Jody Wilson-Raybould later resigned after a high-profile dispute with Trudeau in which she defended the integrity of Canada's justice system in the wake of the SNC Lavalin scandal.

Tackling these issues, this chapter examines contemporary gender patterns of work in Canada. We discuss the dramatic rise of women's participation in higher education and paid work in recent decades, but also the marked gendering of work in the labour market. Central to our discussion are two seemingly contradictory trends: on the one hand, significant gains in women's employment opportunities, aspirations, and rewards, and on the other, the persistence of major work-related gender inequities. As we will see, despite gains by some women, a great deal of women's work continues to be undervalued and poorly rewarded. Consequently, gender remains a key determinant of inequality in our society.

To better grasp the causes and consequences of gender inequity in the work world, we examine historical and contemporary questions: What forces in the past created a gender divide between the home and paid labour market? What factors have either pushed or pulled women into paid employment in recent decades? Why do women remain concentrated in a limited range of jobs at the bottom of the occupational ladder? How did these jobs come to be labelled "female"? Conversely, why do men still predominate in the most rewarding jobs that have come to be defined as "male"? Finally, what barriers and practices operate to preserve gendered patterns of work, and how can gender equity and inclusivity in the workplace be achieved?

Before we proceed, a word of clarification on terms. We use a common sociological distinction between *sex* and *gender*. Basically, *sex* is the biological distinction between men and women; *gender* is socially constructed, reflecting how a particular society defines "masculine" and "feminine" roles. Thus, we can observe sex segregation in occupations—that is, men and women holding distinct jobs. But to explain this, it is necessary to look at how jobs are *gendered*— that is, how they become associated with "masculine" and "feminine" roles, practices, and identities. Following sociologists of work and organizations, we prefer the term *gender*, given that male–female differences in employment are almost solely a product of socially constructed ideas about gender. Reflecting recent insights, we also note that gender identity and expression more typically reflect a continuum, than a strict male–female dichotomy and may not always correspond to biological sex. Equally important, gender intersects with other important categories of social difference, such as ethnicity and race, sexual orientation, class, age, and generation (Messerschmidt et al. 2018).

GENDER AND WORK IN HISTORICAL CONTEXT

Although history has, for the most part, been written from the perspective of men, even a quick glance back to the past reveals that women have always performed a vital, if somewhat unacknowledged, economic role. Indigenous women, for example, were indispensable to the fur trade, the major industry during much of Canada's colonial period. Sylvia Van Kirk's (1980) important historical work *Many Tender Ties* demonstrates how male traders relied on Indigenous women to act as interpreters, prepare food, clean pelts for market, and teach them wilderness survival skills. Little wonder that fur traders sought them out as wives (see also Racette 2012; Williams 2012). When an agrarian economy began to develop in Upper Canada (now Ontario) during the 19th century, the family was the basic production unit, in which women played a key role. Men worked the fields, while women looked after all domestic work associated with child rearing, tending the livestock and garden, making clothes, and preparing food.[2] Similarly, in the Canadian West in the early 1900s, women contributed significantly to agricultural development by working on their family farms and by making the farm home "a haven of safety and healthfulness."[3]

Industrialization and Women's Work

In Chapter 1, we noted that one consequence of the rise of large-scale factory production was a growing separation between the work that men and women did. Men were drawn into the industrial wage-labour market; women were increasingly confined to the domestic sphere of the household. Marjorie Cohen's feminist analysis of economic development in 19th-century Ontario reveals that, prior to wide-scale industrialization, an integration of family and household existed within the emerging market economy (Cohen 1988). Traditional theories of industrialization, Cohen points out, tend to ignore the contribution of households to the economy. Ontario's early economy was primarily based on two staple exports, wheat and timber, which were subject to unstable international markets. Consequently, women's household labour had to fulfill two functions: generate family income by producing agricultural goods to sell in the local consumer market, and perform the domestic chores necessary for the family's survival. Cohen's research underlines the importance of examining how the public and private spheres of market and household have been intertwined in diverse ways during all phases of economic development, with women always performing pivotal roles, albeit quite different from those performed by men.

The absence of a wage-labour market and the necessity of contributing to the household economy meant that few women were formally employed outside the home before the rise of industrial capitalism. Even in late 19th-century Canada, only a fraction of women were engaged in paid employment. In 1891, for example, 11.4 percent of girls and women over the age of 10 were employed, accounting for 12.6 percent of the entire labour force (Lowe 1987: 47). But as factories sprang up in the late 19th century, they began to redefine women's economic role. Employers in some light industries, such as textiles, recruited women as cheap unskilled or semiskilled labourers who, according to prevailing stereotypes, would be less likely to unionize and more tolerant of boring tasks.

By focusing only on paid employment, we risk ignoring the work activities of most women during this era. The *unpaid domestic labour* of women—raising the future generation of workers and feeding, clothing, and caring for the present generation of workers—was an essential function within capitalism (also referred to as *social reproduction*). Out of these competing pressures on women emerged a gendered division of labour that persists today. As we discuss in more detail in Chapter 7, this now takes the form of the *double day* (or, in equally graphic terms, the *second shift*), whereby many women spend their days in paying jobs, yet still assume most of the responsibilities of childcare, elder-care, and domestic chores when they get home.

Early-20th-century attitudes about women's economic roles reflected traditional ideas about marriage and motherhood, as well as about class, race, and ethnicity (Campbell 2009; Patrias 2016). Expanding manufacturing and service industries had an almost insatiable demand for both blue- and white-collar workers. The employment of young, single women prior to marriage came to be tolerated and socially acceptable in domestic, clerical, sales, and some factory jobs. Once married, however, women were expected to retreat into the matrimonial home. Of course, some wanted to remain in the labour force, and others were forced to stay through economic necessity. In these cases, married women laboured at the margins of the economy in domestic and other menial jobs that usually had been abandoned by single women.[4]

Industrialization accentuated age, gender, and other divisions in the economy. Examining the work patterns of working-class women in Montreal, Canada's first large industrial city, Bettina Bradbury documents how age and sex determined who was drawn into wage-labour. Women made up about 35 percent of the city's industrial workforce during the 1870s. In certain industries, such as domestic work and the sewing and dressmaking trades, four out of five workers were women, and most of them were single. Given the scarcity of wage-labour for wives because of strong sanctions against their employment, such women could make a greater contribution to the family economy by being *household managers*. In this role, wives "stretched the wages" of male family members and single daughters as far as possible, occasionally supplementing this by taking in boarders or turning to neighbours or charities for help (Bradbury 1993).

The Family Wage Ideology

Powerful social values justified this division of labour. Especially influential in perpetuating women's subordinate role as unpaid family workers was the ideology of the *family wage*. As working-class men began organizing unions to achieve better wages and working conditions, one of the labour movement's demands was that wages should be high enough for a male breadwinner to support a wife and children. The labour movement's successes in this regard

Chapter 6: Gender and Paid Employment

had the effect of drastically reducing women's presence, and the cheap labour they provided, in the workplace (a policy typical of unions until a serious male labour shortage arose in World War I). Middle-class reformers also lobbied for restrictions on female industrial employment due to its presumed harmful personal and social effects. In response, employers limited their hiring mainly to single women, further reinforcing this ideology. Despite its sexist tone, the family wage ideology may have helped raise the standard of living in working-class families. The price, of course, was female dependence and the restriction of women's labour market opportunities to areas where they did not compete directly with men—hence the endurance of the term *male breadwinner*.[5]

The family wage ideology tells only part of the story of women's lives during early industrialization, however. Joy Parr's (1990) study of two Ontario industrial towns, Paris and Hanover, between 1880 and 1950, clearly shows there was variation in the broad contours of gendered work patterns. On the surface, both Paris and Hanover appeared to be typical small, thriving manufacturing communities. But the knit-goods industry based in Paris relied on a largely female workforce, while in Hanover's large furniture factory, the workers were almost exclusively male. Consequently, different gender identities, attitudes, and behaviours arose to maintain each town's labour force. In Paris, employers organized production to fit around childbearing and child rearing, and it was common for women to work for pay throughout their lives. Certainly, Paris was the exception at the time in Ontario. Nonetheless, its flow of daily life during the 80 years covered by Parr's study forces us to reconsider a model of industrialization based on one dominant mode of production in which males are the breadwinners.

This brief historical sketch has identified a number of prominent themes. First, although their widespread participation in the paid labour force is a recent development, women have always made essential economic contributions. Second, women's entry into paid employment occurred in ways that reproduced their subordinate position in society relative to that of men, although the specific forms this took varied across time and place. Women's position was also shaped by class, ethnicity, age, and other social differences. Third, the changing interconnections among households, families, and the wage-labour market are crucial to understanding women's roles in the continuing evolution of 21st-century capitalism.

GENDER AND LABOUR FORCE PARTICIPATION PATTERNS

Few changes in Canadian society since World War II have had as far-reaching consequences as women's influx into paid work. Virtually all industrialized nations have experienced rising *female labour force participation rates* since the end of World War II. This trend has been especially rapid in Canada. Figure 6.1 provides a comparison of labour force participation rates among adult women (ages 15 and older) for nine major industrial nations, over nearly four decades, from the mid-1970s to the early 2010s. Note that rising female employment is a trend in virtually all countries. Canada experienced one of

FIGURE 6.1   Labour Force Participation Rates in Nine Industrialized Countries, Women Ages 15 and Older, 1975 and 2018

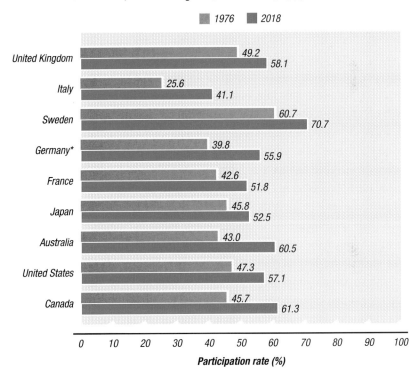

*West Germany in 1975; the unified East and West Germany in 2012.

Source: Adapted from U.S. Bureau of Labor Statistics, 2013, *International Comparisons of Labor Force Statistics*, 1970–2012. Full Series by Indicator and Underlying Levels (Tables 3-4 and 3-5). http://www.bls.gov/fls/#laborforce.

the largest changes, along with Australia, Germany, and Italy. The tremendous expansion of white-collar service-sector jobs, coupled with rising education and a declining birthrate, drew millions of Canadian women into employment at an accelerated rate. As early as the mid-1980s, Canada's female labour force participation rate had surpassed that of all countries in Figure 6.1 except for Sweden. The latter is an interesting case, as it shows far less change than nearly all other countries during this time: women's employment had been actively encouraged by Swedish state policies for decades.

Factors Influencing Women's and Men's Employment

What social and economic factors account for this remarkable increase in Canada's female labour force participation? Clearly, there was no single cause. The huge postwar baby-boom generation was completing its education and flooding into an expanding job market by the late 1960s. Young women were becoming much better educated, which raised their occupational aspirations and made them more competitive with men in the job market. Traditional stereotypes of women's work no longer fit reality. The massive expansion of white-collar service-sector jobs boosted the demand for female labour, and the growth of feminism contributed to more liberal social values regarding women's work roles. As we have seen (Chapter 4), service-sector growth also fuelled a trend to part-time jobs, which are convenient for women with family responsibilities. Shrinking family size, due to accessible and reliable birth control (Nelson 1996), enabled married women to pursue employment more readily. Rising divorce rates in the 1980s and 1990s forced a growing number of women to earn their own income. Finally, in many families, the reality (or threat) of declining living standards made a second income essential.

In short, the interaction of supply and demand factors underlie the sharp rise in female employment. How women make choices and trade-offs between paid work, family life, and child rearing has been the subject of much debate. On one side, researchers such as Catherine Hakim (2000) argue that women's "preferences" explain the growing diversity in female employment. Downplaying the role of gender segregation or discrimination, Hakim contends women choose one of three patterns: "home-centered" (where family is the priority), "career-centered" (where work is the priority), or "adaptive" (where non-career jobs are blended with family responsibilities). Similar ideas have informed public debates over the "opt out revolution" (Belkin 2003), suggesting that highly educated women are choosing motherhood over paid work.

Yet while work preferences play a role, so do many other factors, including workplace inflexibility, access to childcare, discrimination, and the availability of suitable work. For instance, Joan Williams and colleagues (2013, 2014) critique the "opt out" thesis. They show that "maternal walls" and "glass ceilings" play an equal role in shaping women's work, while noting that for many women, work is a necessity, not a choice. Likewise, Stone's (2007) study of professional women shows they are more likely to be "shut out" than to "opt out" of the workplace. Warner (2013) also highlights the challenges faced by working mothers who have "opted out" as they try to re-enter paid work. All of this suggests, as McRae (2003: 317) has argued, that an adequate analysis of women's work "depends as much on understanding the constraints that differentially affect women as it does on understanding their personal preferences (see also Lewis and Simpson 2017).

Indeed, there is no question that many factors have a bearing on the labour force participation of women and men. Figure 6.2 identifies important variations in 2018 participation rates in seven provinces and by age, marital status, family status, and educational level. Women in Alberta have the highest participation rate (66.1 percent), followed by those in Manitoba (62.3 percent). Newfoundland and Labrador has the lowest rate at 55.3 percent. Men's rates in all seven provinces are higher than women's, though the gender gap is more pronounced in some provinces than others. Local and regional job opportunities have a direct bearing on female and male participation rates, as do regional differences in age structure and educational attainment. For example, until recently, Alberta has had a relatively strong economy, with a young and well-educated workforce—hence, its high rate of labour force participation for both women and men. But Alberta also has a higher gender gap, given a population in prime childbearing years and an oil and gas dominated economy in which "male jobs" often pay considerably more than "female jobs" in other sectors. In contrast, Newfoundland and Labrador has far fewer employment opportunities for women (and men) given economic underdevelopment, the decline of the fisheries, and an older population, resulting on lower employment rates overall.

Personal characteristics, such as education and family status, also influence work patterns. For instance, women with higher levels of educational

FIGURE 6.2 Female and Male Labour Force Participation Rates by Selected Characteristics, Canada, 2018

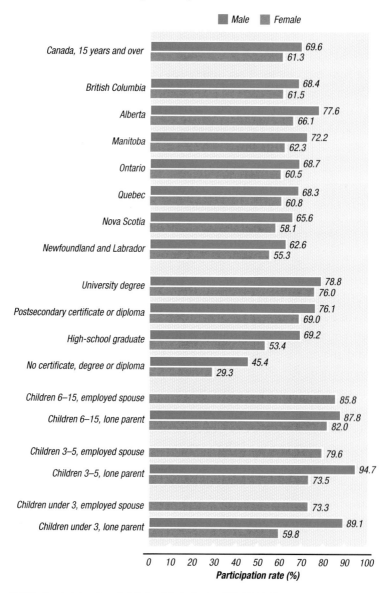

Source: Statistics Canada. Labour Force Participation Rates by Gender, 1976–2018, Table 14-10-0327-01. https://www150. statcan.gc.ca/t1/tbl1/en/tv.action?pid=1410032702; and Statistics Canada. Labour Force Characteristics by Family, Age Composition, Annual, Table: 14-10-0120-01. https://www150.statcan.gc.ca/t1/tbl1/en/tv.action?pid=1410012001

attainment are more active in the labour force—76.0 percent of women with university degrees compared with 29.3 percent who do not complete high school. For men, we see the same pattern of rising labour force participation with education, though participation rates are higher for less-educated men than they are for comparable women. Family status situation also matters; however, because a high proportion of mothers with children under the age of 15 are relatively young and well educated, their labour force participation rates are also above average. For example, well over 80 percent of mothers with school-aged children (6–15 years) and an employed spouse participate in the labour force, either part time or full time. Indeed, this rise of "working mothers" is one of the most significant changes of the past several decades in Canada. Still, rates of labour force participation for mothers are some-what lower when they have younger, preschool children, or are raising chil-dren alone. Though not shown in Figure 6.2, age is also a key consideration. Among young people 15 to 24 years old, both women and men are less likely than adults of 25 to 54 years old to work for pay, largely because more of them are full-time students.

Financial necessity is often a major factor in the decision to seek paid work. Generally, wives in low-income families or women who are lone parents may be compelled to work to meet basic expenses. As Figure 6.2 shows, the participation rate for female lone parents with school-aged children (6–15 years old) was 82.0 percent in 2018, just below that of mothers with simi-larly aged children who had an employed spouse. Rates fall for lone mothers with preschool children, especially when children are under three years of age. For many single mothers, finding or keeping a job may be difficult, depending on level of educational attainment and availability of childcare. Low-paid, unstable work is a major reason for the high incidence of poverty in this group.[6] In contrast, better-educated, urban, middle-class women who are married and whose spouse or partner is a professional or a manager have greater opportunities and the luxury of choice with regard to employment. Among families with the highest incomes in Canada, it is very likely that the female partner is a high-earning manager or professional. This reflects a recent trend in Canada, the United States, and other advanced industrial coun-tries towards "assortative mating" in opposite-sex families, whereby highly educated women and men become partners.[7]

Chapter 6: Gender and Paid Employment

GENDER SEGREGATION IN THE LABOUR MARKET

At the heart of gender inequality in the workplace is the structuring of the labour market into male and female segments. *Occupational gender segregation* refers to the concentration of men and women in different occupations.[8] Sociologists distinguish between *horizontal segregation* (segregation across distinct occupations) and *vertical segregation* (segregation at different levels within the same occupation). A potent combination of gender-role socialization, education, and labour market mechanisms continue to channel women into a limited number of occupations in which mainly other females are employed, or at lower occupational levels in more integrated occupations.

Female Job Ghettos and Gender Labelling

Female *job ghettos* typically offer little economic security and opportunities for advancement; furthermore, the work is often unpleasant, boring, and sometimes physically taxing. Women in job ghettos lack ready access to the more challenging and lucrative occupations dominated by men. These male segments of the labour market operate as *shelters*, as discussed in Chapter 5, conferring advantages on workers through entrance restrictions. The concepts of ghettos and shelters emphasize the unequal rewards and opportunities built into the job market on the basis of a worker's sex. It is especially important to recognize that job opportunities determine an individual's living standard, future prospects, and overall quality of life—in Max Weber's words, *life chances*.

One fundamental mechanism underlying segmentation is the *gender labelling* of jobs. Employers do not always make hiring decisions on strictly rational grounds, despite what economics textbooks would have us believe (Rivera 2012). If all hiring decisions were completely rational, women would have been recruited much earlier in the industrialization process and in far greater numbers, given they were routinely paid less than men. But, as discussed, men historically opposed female employment for fear of having their wages undercut. Traditional values also narrowly defined women as being naturally suited to child rearing and homemaking. Women, therefore, were relegated to the poorer jobs that men did not want. Because these occupations came to be labelled "female," future employers would likely seek only women for them, and, regardless of the skills demanded, pay and status remained low.

Dominant social values about femininity and masculinity have long been used to define job requirements. For instance, by the late 19th century, teaching, social work, nursing, and domestic work were seen as socially acceptable for women. Society could justify this on the ideological grounds that these occupations—caring for the sick, the old, and the unfortunate, transmitting culture to children, and performing domestic chores—demanded essentially "female" traits. Exclusive male rights to the better jobs and higher incomes thus went unchallenged, and the role of homemaker and wife was preserved for women. Once a job was labelled male or female, it was difficult for workers of the other sex to gain entry (Lowe 1987). These processes continue to be evident, in modified form, today.

Trends in Labour Market Gender Segregation

In Chapter 3, we noted a number of gender differences in the occupational distribution of the labour force. Figures 6.3a and 6.3b explore this further, summarizing employment distribution and concentration in 2018. Figure 6.3a identifies the percentage of female and male employees in each occupation. Here we see that health occupations, such as nursing, have high concentrations of women (nearly 80 percent). So do jobs in business, finance, and administration (69.4 percent), which include administrators, secretaries, and various professionals such as accountants and financial planners; and in education, law, social, community and government services (69.7 percent), which include teachers, civil servants, social workers, and lawyers. Sales/service occupations (e.g., jobs in restaurants, bars, hotels, hairdressing, and child-care facilities, and as domestics and building cleaners) are more mixed, with just over 55 percent women. By contrast, women form a small minority of workers in the sciences, trades, primary industries, and manufacturing. Here men predominate, accounting for over 75 percent of jobs in natural and applied sciences (e.g., engineers, computer programmers), over 93 percent in trades, transport, and equipment operation, over 80 percent in primary industries (e.g., forestry, mining, fishing, farming), and over 70 percent in processing and manufacturing.

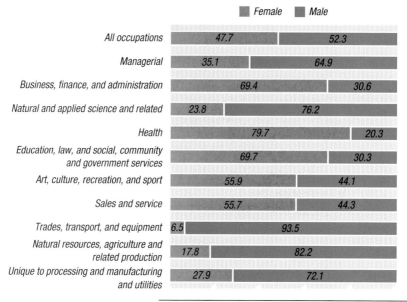

FIGURE 6.3a   Employment Concentration of Women and Men, Canada, 2018

■ Female   ■ Male

Occupation	Female	Male
All occupations	47.7	52.3
Managerial	35.1	64.9
Business, finance, and administration	69.4	30.6
Natural and applied science and related	23.8	76.2
Health	79.7	20.3
Education, law, and social, community and government services	69.7	30.3
Art, culture, recreation, and sport	55.9	44.1
Sales and service	55.7	44.3
Trades, transport, and equipment	6.5	93.5
Natural resources, agriculture and related production	17.8	82.2
Unique to processing and manufacturing and utilities	27.9	72.1

0% 10% 20% 30% 40% 50% 60% 70% 80% 90% 100%

Source: Statistics Canada, Labour Force Characteristics by Occupation, Annual, Table 14-10-0335-01. https://www150.statcan.gc.ca/t1/tbl1/en/tv.action?pid=1410033501

Figure 6.3b shows the distribution of the female and male labour force across all occupations in 2018. Of note, two broad occupational groups account for more than half of the female labour force, attesting to women's continuing concentration and overrepresentation in key sectors. Sales and services jobs employ well over one in four women workers, as do jobs in business, finance, and administration, which are largely clerical and secretarial. Health occupations (12.6 percent), and education, law, social, community, and government service jobs (16.2 percent), together employ just over another quarter of women. It is notable that among men, there is more dispersion across occupational groups, although they also cluster into distinct realms. Trade, transport, and equipment-related occupations employ over one in four men, while sales and service jobs account for one in five male workers. Three other broad groupings—management jobs; business, finance, and administration; and natural and applied science—are important, accounting for 3 in 10 male workers overall. Interestingly, these gender-based patterns have barely changed over the past several decades.

FIGURE 6.3b   Occupational Distribution of Women and Men, Canada, 2018

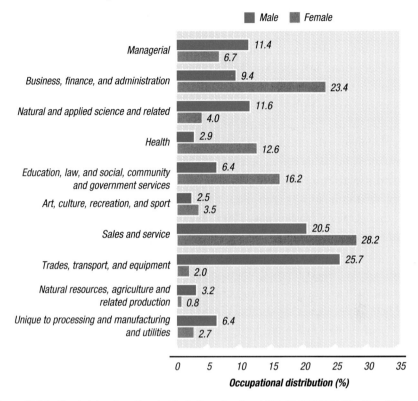

Source: Statistics Canada, Labour Force Characteristics by Occupation, Annual, Table 14-10-0335-01. https://www150. statcan.gc.ca/t1/tbl1/en/tv.action?pid=1410033501

For a more complete understanding of where men and women are located in the labour market, we must also investigate the industrial distribution of employment. Recall from Chapters 3 and 4 that Canada's service-based economy is generating polarization between good jobs and bad jobs. How then are men and women distributed within the upper and lower tiers of the service sector? Referring back to Table 3.1 (see Chapter 3) helps to answer this question. Here, we can see that nearly one-third of the male labour force are in the goods sector—a trend with potential downsides for men given dramatic restructuring and outsourcing in manufacturing areas such as the auto sector. Women's jobs are far more likely to be in services; indeed, nearly 90 percent of women worked there in 2018, with nearly 25 percent in lower-tier services such as retail and over 65 percent in upper-tier sectors. Women's greater likelihood to be in upper-tier services (65.2

Chapter 6: Gender and Paid Employment

percent of women compared to 48.7 percent of men) is a result of women's strong presence in the education, health, and social services sectors. Despite there being good jobs in these areas, however, we know from discussions in Chapters 3 and 4 that relatively more women than men are in nonstandard, precarious jobs.

Indeed, there is a growing body of research on the gendered nature of nonstandard or precarious work, such as self-employment, part-time, and temporary contract work (Rubery et al. 2018; Vosko 2010; Wall 2015). The notion of "standard job" or a "standard employment relationship" reflects a masculine norm of employment—the husband as family breadwinner, working full time and in a permanent job with the same employer throughout his working life. These standard job assumptions underlay the postwar employment contract, which has changed dramatically with the spread of nonstandard and more precarious work arrangements (Vosko 2000, 2005, 2010; Fudge and Owens 2006). A major reason some women seek self-employment, for example, is to gain the flexibility they need to balance work with family life (Thébaud 2015). But there are costs, including lower wages than employees receive and the lack of benefits and career supports, such as access to training or business networks (Hughes 2005).

Linked to gender is also a racial dimension of nonstandard work (Zeytinoglu and Muteshi 2000; Fuller and Vosko 2008; Premji et al. 2014). Visible minority women are employed in economically marginal forms of work, family-run businesses, domestic labour, or the garment industry. Perhaps the most feminized form of nonstandard work is temporary employment (Vosko 2000; Fernandez-Mateo 2009). As Leah Vosko (2000) argues, the expanding temporary-help industry is based on traditional stereotypes of "women's work," even though the flexible and impermanent employment relationships it offers are seen as a hallmark of the "new economy."

With women's rising participation in the labour force, how has the segregation of women's work changed over the long term? Table 6.1 shows that, in 1901, 71 percent of all employed women were concentrated in five occupations. Within this small number of socially acceptable women's jobs, that of domestic servant employed the greatest portion of working women at 36 percent. Next in importance were those of seamstress and school teacher, each employing roughly 13 percent of the female labour force. These three occupations fit our description of a job ghetto, given that three-quarters or more of all workers in the job were female. In the early 20th century, outright exclusion was the prominent form of gender-based labour market segregation, with professions such as law and medicine barring women, while others, such as dentistry, allowed women to enter but under conditions that ensured their marginalization (Adams 1998).

TABLE 6.1   Five Leading Female Occupations in Canada, 1901, 1951, 2011

Occupation	Number of Employed Women	Percent of Total Female Employment in Occupation	Females as Percentage of Employment in Occupation
1901			
1. Domestic servants	84,984	35.7	87
2. Seamstresses	32,145	13.5	100
3. School teachers	30,870	13.0	78
4. Office clerks	12,569	5.3	21.4
5. Farmers and stock raisers	8,495	3.6	2
All five occupations		71.1	
1951*			
1. Stenographers and typists	133,485	11.5	96.4
2. Office clerks	118,025	10.1	42.7
3. Salesclerks	95,443	8.2	55.1
4. Hotel, café, and private household workers n.e.s†	88,775	7.6	89.1
5. School teachers	74,319	6.4	72.5
All five occupations		43.8	
2011			
1. Retail salespersons	371,345	4.7	56.6
2. Administrative assistants	316,565	4.0	96.3
3. Registered nurses	270,425	3.4	92.8
4. Cashiers	260,190	3.3	84.2
5. Elementary and kindergarten teachers	227,810	2.9	84.0
All five occupations		18.3	

*1951 Census does not include the Yukon or the Northwest Territories.
†n.e.s.: Occupations not elsewhere specified.

Source: Adapted from *Occupational trends in Canada*, 1891–1931, Statistics Canada, Call Number 98-1931M-4 1939; *Occupation and Industry Trends in Canada Ninth Census of Canada*, 1951, Statistics Canada, Call Number 98-1951M-4 1954; and Statistics *Canada 2011 National Household Survey*, Data Tables—Occupation— National Occupational Classification (NOC) 2011 (691), Class of Worker (5), Age Groups (13B) and Sex (3) for the Employed Labour Force Aged 15 Years and Over, in Private Households of Canada, Provinces, Territories, Census Metropolitan Areas and Census Agglomerations, Cat. no. 99-012-X2011033.

This pattern was not the case, however, for the two other main female occupations. Clerical work at the turn of the century was still a man's job, although by the 1940s, the gender balance had shifted toward women. It is interesting to note that clerical work was one of the few traditionally male jobs to undergo this *feminization* process. Behind this change was the rapid expansion of office work accompanied by a more fragmented and routinized division of labour. As a result, a layer of new positions emerged at the bottom of office hierarchies, opening office doors to women (Lowe 1987). Finally, the fact that farmers and livestock raisers appear as

Chapter 6: Gender and Paid Employment

one of the five prominent female occupations may seem peculiar. Considering that Canada was an agricultural economy in 1901, it is understandable that women would form a small part of the paid agricultural workforce (Carter 2016).

The 20th-century march of industrialization saw a decline in some female jobs, such as those of domestic servant and seamstress, and the rise of new employment opportunities in booming service industries. By 1951, the two leading female occupations were in the clerical area. Along with salesclerks, hotel, café, and domestic workers, and teachers, stenographers and typists and office clerks made up 44 percent of the female workforce.

As we have seen, female job ghettos still exist. Office and sales jobs have topped the list since World War II. Still, while gender segregation remains a persistent problem in many countries (Charles and Bradley 2009), it is also important to note that women have entered a broader range of occupations and professions, and secretarial and support functions have diminished with the proliferation of mobile technologies and a younger generation adept at using them (Twenge et al. 2018). By 2011, the top five female-dominated jobs accounted for just over 18 percent of the entire female labour force—a dramatic decline. This change is a positive sign of occupational diversification, but how far have women moved into non-traditional (in other words, male-dominated) occupations? Karen Hughes's analysis of the 484 detailed occupations in the 1971 Census shows that 86 percent of women worked in traditionally female occupations.[9] Over the next 15 years, the proportion of women in these traditional occupations declined to 79 percent, then changed little between 1986 and 1991. This pattern raises questions about the degree to which women can move out of gender-typed occupations over their working lives— "female" jobs can be seen as a way station through which some women pass on their way to better jobs that are not gender typed (Chan 2000). Having said this, however, some women did make gains into *non-traditional jobs.* By the early 1990s, women had achieved equal representation with men in optometry and financial management, and nearly equal representation in sales management and government administration (Hughes 1995, 2001). Trends for the 2000s, in both Canada and the United States, suggest that progress toward gender equity has stalled (England 2010; Guppy and Luongo 2015; Levanon and Grusky 2016), a point we return to later in the chapter when discussing the gender wage gap.

Additional insights about gender and work can be gleaned by focusing on professional occupations. Because professions are organized around specific bodies of knowledge and expertise, usually acquired through a university degree, access to these jobs is strongly shaped by changing gender patterns in education. Figure 6.4 shows the steady rise of women in university programs over the last few decades. From the early 1970s to 1990s, women's share of undergraduate

FIGURE 6.4   Women as a Proportion of Total Full-Time University
Enrolment, by Degree and Program, Canada, 1972–73, 1992–93,
and 2006–7

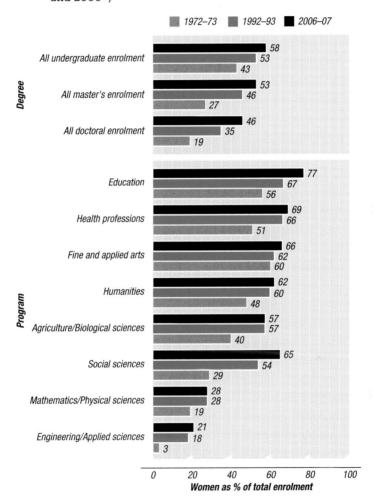

Source: Adapted from Statistics Canada (2005), *Women in Canada: A Gender-Based Statistical Report*, Cat. no. 89-503XIE 2005001; and Table 37-10-0072-01 (formerly CANSIM Table 477-0013), University Enrolments, by Registration Status, Program Level, Classification of Instructional Programs, Primary Grouping (CIP_PG) and Sex, Annual. http://www5.statcan.gc.ca/cansim/ a26?lang=eng&retrlang=eng&id=4770013&paSer=&pattern=&stByVal=1&p1=1&p2=-1&tabmode=datatable&csid=

Chapter 6: Gender and Paid Employment

registrations jumped from 43 to 53 percent, and then again to 58 percent in 2006–7. Gains are also notable at the master's and doctoral levels. Most programs saw rising female enrolments. Despite ongoing attempts to attract more women into STEM fields, math, science, and engineering are the only fields in which women did not make up more than half of all students; in fact, women are significantly underrepresented in these areas, and female enrolment has declined or stabilized in recent years. Data for 2015–16 from Statistics Canada, which uses a different classification than that in Figure 6.4, shows that women made up just 27.8 percent of students in math, computers, and information systems and 23.6 percent in architecture, engineering, and related areas (Statistics Canada 2017).

Higher education has contributed to women's growing presence in professional and managerial positions. In 2017, for instance, well over half (56.8 percent) of new graduating physicians were women (AFMC 2018). Roughly 50 percent of graduate law students are women (Kay et al. 2016). Pharmacy is also an interesting case, having become 50 percent female by the mid-1980s (Tanner et al. 1999). Compared to other professions, at least on the basis of evidence in the United States, pharmacy is also the leading profession in offering gender parity in pay (Goldin 2014).

Still, many professions present hurdles to female entry and mobility, and gender segregation by specialization is notable. For instance, despite the sharp rise in female physicians in Canada, they are concentrated in areas such as pediatrics, gerontology, and obstetrics (AFMC 2018). Similar patterns exist in the legal profession, where women predominate in areas such as family law and are less likely to become senior partners in private practice (Kay et al. 2016). Equally if not more important, there has been relatively little movement of men into female-dominated occupations. While men have entered some previously "female occupations," such as nursing, librarianship, and elementary-school teaching, their presence still remains low (Williams 1995, 2011). Thus, to the extent that occupational gender segregation is breaking down, it is largely due to women moving into male-dominated areas, not vice versa (England 2010; Hughes 1995; Statistics Canada 2000: 128).[10]

Equally important, many occupations that have seen changes are small, compared to other occupations in the labour force. Thus, when we look at the top 20 largest occupations for women and men, in Table 6.2, we still see

TABLE 6.2   Top 20 Jobs for Women and Men, Canada, 2016

Occupation	Female	Occupation	Male
Retail salespersons	56.9%	Transport truck drivers	96.5%
Cashiers	81.9%	Retail salespersons	43.1%
Registered nurses and registered psychiatric nurses	91.7%	Retail and wholesale trade managers	58.1%
Food counter attendants, kitchen helpers, and related support	62.4%	Construction trades helpers and labourers	93.2%
Elementary-school and kindergarten teachers	84.3%	Janitors, caretakers, and building superintendents	75.9%
Administrative assistants	95.6%	Carpenters	98.1%
Administrative officers	83.6%	Material handlers	86.4%
Nurse aides, orderlies, and patient service associates	86.8%	Auto service techs, truck and bus mechanics, and mechanical repairers	97.9%
General office support workers	83.9%	Food counter attendants, kitchen helpers, and related support	37.6%
Early childhood educators and assistants	96.4%	Cooks	58.8%
Food and beverage servers	78.7%	Store shelf stockers, clerks, and order fillers	65.8%
Light duty cleaners	69.7%	Information systems analysts and consultants	72.5%
Retail and wholesale trade managers	41.9%	Managers in agriculture	74.9%
Receptionists	92.9%	Landscaping and grounds maintenance labourers	83.5%
Other customer and information services representatives	63.7%	Welders and related machine operators	95.9%
Accounting and related clerks	83.4%	Electricians (except industrial and power system)	97.8%
Accounting technician and bookkeepers	86.5%	Security guards and related security service occupations	76.1%
Social and community service workers	77.6%	Heavy equipment operators (except crane)	96.1%
Financial auditors and accountants	56.1%	Computer programmers and interactive media developers	83.5%
Elementary- and secondary-school teacher assistants	90.1%	Financial auditors and accountants	43.9%
Percentage of Female Labour Force	**43.5%**	**Percentage of Male Labour Force**	**30.1%**
Number of Female Workers (millions)	**3,887,045**	**Number of Male Workers (millions)**	**2,933,015**

Source: Statistics Canada. Labour Force Characteristics by Occupation, Annual. Table 14-10-0335-01. https://www150.statcan.gc.ca/t1/tbl1/en/tv.action?pid=1410033501

Chapter 6: Gender and Paid Employment

firm boundaries between "female" and "male" jobs. Nursing, administrative support, and childcare remain strongly female dominant. Conversely, truck driving, carpentry, auto mechanics, construction, and other trades such as welding are predominantly male. This does not mean that gender change is not taking place, but that it typically occurs in elite occupations. Of note, too, in Table 6.2, the top 20 jobs account for a larger portion of the female labour force (20 percent) than is the case for the male labour force (15 percent).

Gender Stratification within Occupations

Thus far, we have traced broad historical patterns of *horizontal* occupational gender segregation—that is, segregation across different occupations. Now we will examine a related obstacle women face: *vertical* segregation, or the gendered division of status, responsibilities, and tasks within specific occupations. As a rule, men experience more upward mobility than women in organizations, and thus tend to have positions of greater authority and receive better job rewards. Consider the teaching profession. Women made up 84.3 percent of elementary and kindergarten teachers, and 78.4 percent of educational counsellors in 2016. In contrast, men composed just 15.7 percent of elementary and kindergarten teachers, and only 3.6 percent of early childhood educators. Looking at the education profession overall, men are also far more likely to be found in higher-status, better-paying jobs in universities, colleges, high schools, and educational administration. Yet women have made some inroads into leadership roles. In 2016, they held 58.1 percent of school administrative and principal positions in elementary and secondary schools (Statistics Canada 2016).

As noted earlier, this situation is similar in other professions, such as law and medicine. But it is not just that women occupy "different" areas, such as family law or pediatrics. It is that these positions are of lower-status, with fewer economic rewards.[11] Driving such patterns are gender stereotypical assumptions that women are well suited to tasks involving supposedly "natural skills" as caregivers. Such assumptions not only channel women into certain specialties but also shape ideas about their career aspirations. In a classic study of the changing legal profession in Canada, John Hagan and Fiona Kay (1995) portrayed a gender-stratified profession in which work environments were not family-friendly. Large numbers of women entered law in the 1970s and 1980s, when the profession was expanding and reorganizing into larger firms. According to Hagan and Kay (1995: 182), women were recruited into the profession during a period when they were needed to fill entry- and intermediate-level positions and were perceived to be compliant employees. . . . It is possible that . . . many partners in law firms were encouraged by the belief that as in the teaching profession of an earlier era, women would assume entry-level positions in the profession, work diligently for a number of years, and then abandon their early years of invested work to bear children and raise families, leaving partnership positions to men assumed to be more committed to their occupational careers.

While these types of gender assumptions and bias have been increasingly challenged, more recent empirical studies suggest they are still in play. For instance, law firms restrict opportunities for both men and women to attain partnerships—a financial and management stake in the firm that results in much higher earnings. However, women are still less likely to attain partnership and appear to lose out more than men, because of conflicts and compromises made in the interplay between professional demands and family responsibilities. For instance, women who continue to practise law full time after having children have high work commitment but lower earnings than men. Women are less likely than men to have children once they become lawyers and more likely to leave the profession because of work–family conflict, relatively low pay, and discrimination. Finally, women appear to face barriers with respect to mentoring and promotion, making it more difficult to keep moving up the ranks relative to their male peers (Gorman and Kmec 2009; Kay and Gorman 2012; Kay et al. 2016; Sterling and Reichman 2016).

Medicine, dentistry, and business are also areas where women have made breakthroughs. According to the 2016 Census, women made up 49.0 percent of general practitioners, 39.3 percent of specialist physicians, 38.8 percent of dentists, and 37.9 percent of all managers. However, in management, especially at the senior levels, women have lower representation and distinct patterns of segregation. For instance, the 2016 Census shows that women accounted for just 14.0 percent of senior managers in construction and 24.9 percent in finance, communications, and other business services. Likewise, few female managers are found in natural sciences and engineering or in the mining and oil sector. Instead, women are concentrated in "female" enclaves, such as health, education, community and social services (56.9 percent) or human resources (67.4 percent) where they make up the majority of managers.

Chapter 6: Gender and Paid Employment

Women still encounter a *glass ceiling*—barriers to advancement that persist despite formal policies designed to eliminate them. Looking at the 561 employers covered by the federal *Employment Equity Act* (discussed in more detail below) in 2017, women made up 40.2 percent of the 740,420 employees (8 percentage points below their representation in the labour market overall). Women's share of senior management posts is strong, just slightly above the labour force overall, but they are overrepresented in support and mid-level occupations, especially in clerical and administrative positions. Men are well-represented at senior management levels and in semiskilled and technical jobs. In short, gender segregation persists in this workforce, despite women's gains into professional and middle management jobs. Of note, women's success has occurred largely in the banking sector; in other industries, especially transportation, their presence remains low, as does their likelihood of being hired and promoted. Comparing salaries, women are less likely to be top earners—just 14.4 percent of women earn $100,000 or more, compared to 23.5 percent of the full-time male workforce.[12]

At the executive and board levels, women remain few in number. Despite select appointments of women to top corporate jobs—such as president, chief executive officer (CEO), executive vice-president, or chief operating officer—Canadian women held less than one in five (19.5 percent) senior officer positions in the *Financial Post* 500 firms in Canada in 2018 and just 24.5 percent of board seats, a trend that is in line with a many other industrialized countries (CBCD 2019: 14, 31). While women's board presence in Canada is up from 10.9 percent in 2001, we see more significant change in other countries, such as Norway and France, where legislation requires over 40 percent of board seats to be held by women (Deloitte 2017). Striking differences also exist between industries in Canada. For instance, in finance and health care sectors, one-third of board seats are held by women. This compares to just 15 to 17 percent in mining and construction (CBDC 2019: 15). Many analysts argue that much greater progress is needed with respect to gender diversity on corporate boards, as well as visible minority, Indigenous, and LGBTQ representation. Illustrating this, the Canadian Board Diversity Council which produces an annual report each year, notes that of the board seats held by women in TSX60-listed firms (top 60 firms listed on the Toronto stock exchange), just 6.3 percent of those women are visible minorities and 0 percent are Indigenous (CBDC 2018: 35).

In sum, although women now experience much wider employment horizons than was once the case, we are a long way from gender equity. Achieving change requires women and men to be more evenly distributed across occupations and industries, rather than segregated along the gender lines we now observe. We also need to see more women at senior occupational levels. More fundamentally, however, shifting the numerical representation of women and men requires significant change in workplace cultures. This immediately raises the question of how such change might be achieved.

THE WAGE GAP

One obvious consequence of labour market segmentation is the *gender wage gap* (or female–male earnings ratio). Looking back historically, Figure 6.5 outlines how the wage gap has changed over time in Canada, from 59.4 percent in 1976 to 72.0 percent in 2011 for those in full-time, full-year employment. Focusing only on full-time, full-year employees provides a more valid estimate of changes over time in the gender wage gap since the proportion of part-time workers who earn less and are disproportionately female has been increasing (Chapter 4). The changes charted in Figure 6.5 are particularly interesting

FIGURE 6.5 Average Earnings for Full-Time/Full-Year Workers, by Gender, Canada, 1976–2011 (in 2011 Constant Dollars)

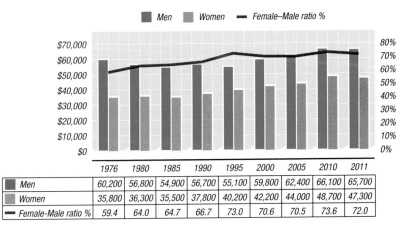

	1976	1980	1985	1990	1995	2000	2005	2010	2011
Men	60,200	56,800	54,900	56,700	55,100	59,800	62,400	66,100	65,700
Women	35,800	36,300	35,500	37,800	40,200	42,200	44,000	48,700	47,300
Female-Male ratio %	59.4	64.0	64.7	66.7	73.0	70.6	70.5	73.6	72.0

Source: Statistics Canada, Average female and male earnings, and female-to-male earnings ratio, by work activity, 2011, constant dollars, Annual, Table 11-10-0143-01 (formerly CANSIM Table 282-0102). http://www5.statcan.gc.ca/cansim/a26?lang=eng&retrlang=eng&id=2020102&paSer=&pattern=&stByVal=1&p1=1&p2=-1&tabmode=datatable&csid=

Chapter 6: Gender and Paid Employment **201**

when we remember gender changes in occupational location during this time as well. Despite women entering some of the higher-paying managerial and professional jobs, the wage gap narrowed by just 9 percentage points from 1980 to 1995. It then plateaued at the low 70 percent range for nearly two decades. This pattern reflects the way in which employment growth trends often counteract each other. During the 1970s, the number of women in the 20 highest-paying occupations swelled more than fourfold, compared with a twofold increase for men (Boulet and Lavallée 1984: 19). But this trend was offset by an expansion of female employment at the lower end of the pay scale. According to the most recent Census data, the wage gap in 2016 was 74.2 percent for full-time, full-year workers. While this is a significant narrowing of the gap, for reasons we discuss below, we remain a long way from gender parity.

Gender-Based Inequality of Earnings

Trends in earnings patterns between 1976 and 2011 deserve further comment. Figure 6.5 displays *real earnings*, which means that the effects of inflation have been eliminated by adjusting earnings. Looking at the 1976–2011 period (in 2011 constant dollars) illustrates the startling fact that male real earnings declined in the 1980s and 1990s, while women's earnings slowly nudged upwards. Quite different labour market and organizational processes underlie these divergent earnings profiles. While women were being recruited into intermediate-level professions and junior- and middle-level management, males were losing ground as traditionally well-paying (often unionized) manual occupations became less common and downsizing pushed older professionals and managers (mostly men) into early retirement. Trends discussed in Chapters 2 and 3, such as globalization, free trade, new technologies, and population aging, are relevant here. Within the labour market as a whole, some of men's losses were women's gain. Indeed, a growing group of employed women, with incomes higher on average than women a generation earlier, kept family incomes from dropping as far as they otherwise might have. Without a second income, some two-parent families in the middle or working class would likely join the ranks of the poor.

Wages are a basic indicator of overall job quality. Recall from Chapters 4 and 5 that high wages also are part of a larger package of extrinsic and intrinsic job rewards. Stated simply, in addition to paying relatively well, "good jobs" usually offer other advantages: a range of benefits, job security, advancement opportunities, and interesting and challenging work. Also recall from Figure 4.1 that access to various benefits, such as pensions and medical or dental insurance, varies by occupation, union membership, and full-time and part-time status. Access to benefits also varies by gender. Working women are less likely than men to receive a variety of non-wage benefits, such as a group RRSP, life and disability insurance, supplementary health insurance, or a dental plan (Fox and Moyser 2018: 20–21). Lack of access to benefits is especially noticeable in part-time employment, where women are highly concentrated. In short, the gender wage gap is part of a much more broadly based discrepancy between the quality of jobs performed by men and women.

Women's lower earnings also mean reduced living standards. Historically, women have been more likely than men to live in low-income households. This has been especially true for older women due to inadequate pensions. Improvements in income support programs for elderly Canadians have helped narrow this gap. Yet, some women are still at high risk of living in poverty. For example, in 2015 one-third of female lone parents with children under 18 had low income, compared to 15.7 percent of male lone-parent families. Women 65 years and older are also more likely than elderly men to have low income (16.3 percent versus 11.9 percent, respectively), notwithstanding the improvements in living standards noted above (Fox and Moyser 2018: 13–16). Looking at long-term trends, rates of low-income for these groups decreased notably from the mid-1970s to the mid-1990s but have risen steadily ever since. But current rates are still lower than they were in the mid-1970s, largely because of women's improved education and work experience, as well as government support.[13]

Shifting our focus from the bottom to the top of the income distribution, average male and female earnings in the 20 highest-paying occupations are displayed in Table 6.3. We draw on data from the 2016 Census, which provide median employment income for full-time, full-year employees. Observe that, in many of these jobs, but not all, the female–male earnings gap is narrower than in other occupations. Looking down the list, we see some jobs with very narrow gaps, such as mining engineers (99.8 percent), judges (93.9 percent), followed by others, such as dentists (86.8 percent) and lawyers (86.7 percent). Yet even in these 20 highest-paying occupations, women still receive a lower salary, although it is far higher than the average female worker earns. Moreover, with few exceptions, the highest-paid occupations are still very male dominated. Senior government

TABLE 6.3 Median Employment Income of Full-Time, Full-Year Workers in the 20 Highest-Paying Occupations, Canada, 2016

	Median Income Men ($)	Median Income Women ($)	F–M Earnings Ratio	Men as % of Total Employees	Women as % of Total Employees
Judges	287,291	269,902	93.9	60.2	39.8
Petroleum engineers	163,022	131,735	80.8	84.2	15.8
Managers in natural resources production and fishing	143,818	116,391	80.9	89.7	10.3
Supervisors, mining and quarrying	132,148	97,927	74.1	95.6	4.4
Senior managers—financial, communications and other business services	132,939	116,835	87.9	75.8	24.2
Specialist physicians	138,353	100,096	72.3	61.3	38.7
Mining engineers	125,830	125,613	99.8	86.3	13.7
Contractors and supervisors, oil and gas drilling and services	122,295	85,392	69.8	94.0	6.0
Engineering managers	122,256	95,062	77.8	86.5	13.5
Commissioned police officers	123,094	94,049	76.4	77.3	22.7
Utilities managers	120,214	103,725	86.3	81.2	18.8
University professors and lecturers	124,328	106,227	85.4	59.2	40.8
Dentists	120,253	104,372	86.8	62.1	37.9
Central control and process operators, petroleum, gas, and chemical processing	118,000	76,184	64.6	92.3	7.7
Lawyers and Quebec notaries	122,884	106,566	86.7	57.6	42.4
Railway and yard locomotive engineers	113,709	105,216	92.5	94.7	5.3
Fire chiefs and senior firefighting officers	112,679	93,019	82.6	95.2	4.8
Senior government managers and officials	119,300	97,886	82.1	54.1	45.9
Geoscientists and oceanographers	115,879	94,033	81.1	75.2	24.8
Air traffic controllers and related occupations	119,586	76,404	63.9	75.9	24.1

Source: Statistics Canada, 2016 Census, Employment Income by Gender and Detailed Occupation. https://www12.statcan. gc.ca/census-recensement/2016/dp-pd/dt-td/Rp-eng.cfm?LANG=E&APATH=3&DETAIL=0&DIM=0&FL=A&FREE=0&GC=0& GID=0&GK=0&GRP=1&PID=110698&PRID=10&PTYPE=109445&S=0&SHOWALL=0&SUB=0&Temporal=2017&THEME=1 24&VID=0&VNAMEE=&VNAMEF=

managers have the highest female presence (45.9 percent women), followed by lawyers (42.4 percent) and university professors (40.8 percent). In large part, this is due to the public-sector employers in these industries having taken steps over the past several decades to provide women with increased opportunities. In other occupations, especially in resource-based and engineering occupations, women's presence is in the single digits—for instance, supervisors in mining (4.4 percent) and fire chiefs and senior firefighting officers (4.8 percent). Similarly, if we examine patterns for the CEOs of Canada's top 250 companies in 2017, we find a pay gap that is larger than the national average, with female CEOs earning just 68 percent of their male counterparts. Here, again, women are a tiny minority, composing just 4 percent of all CEOs.[14]

When interpreting such data, we should keep in mind that because women are more recent entrants (historically speaking) in managerial and professional jobs, they may have less experience and seniority, which could account for part of the earnings gap, though not all. That said, such explanations are less convincing than was once the case, given that women's educational attainment and labour force participation has risen sharply in recent decades (Blau and Kahn 2017). Yet recent studies of women and men with comparable education, age, and work experience still find a wage gap (albeit a small one) immediately after graduation. Even among teenagers, we see a wage gap between boys and girls with comparable education (Besen-Cassino 2017). Studies also highlight gender bias in lower starting salaries for women (Moss-Racusin et al. 2012) and, at later career stages, a "motherhood penalty" in the form of lower pay for working mothers (Budig and England 2001; Budig and Hodges 2010; England et al. 2016). Importantly, even when we take into account many key factors (e.g., education, work experience, field of study, occupation, industry) that help explain the wage gap, some of the gap remains unexplained (Drolet 2011; Blau and Kahn 2017).[15]

Recent research has also explored the intersection of gender and sexual orientation in shaping the wage gap. For instance, in Canada, Waite and Denier (2015) find that heterosexual men earn most, followed by gay men, lesbians, and heterosexual women. As with other studies, education and industry, especially public-sector employment, are important factors for narrowing the observed

Chapter 6: Gender and Paid Employment

wage gap. Interestingly, while heterosexual women experience a "motherhood penalty," heterosexual men experience a "fatherhood premium," but family status and the presence of children have no effect on the earnings of gay men or lesbian women.

Accounting for Women's Lower Earnings

Two forms of discrimination affect female earnings. The first is *direct wage discrimination*, where an employer pays a woman less than a man for performing the exact same job. However, women and men typically work in different occupations as we have seen. Thus, a second form of discrimination stems from the *gender-segregated structure* of the labour market, discussed earlier. *Occupational gender segregation* results in lower female wages by channelling women into low-paying job ghettos which, in turn, provide few opportunities for mobility into more rewarding jobs. Industry segregation also has an effect as well (Blau and Kahn 2017). Historically based cultural ideas about the value of women's and men's work serve to depress wages in female-dominant occupations. A prime example of this is the low pay for early childhood educators.

To what extent does each form of discrimination contribute to the overall wage gap? To answer this question, analysts carefully compare earnings, taking into account education, training, and work experience, as well as the occupation, industry, and geographic location of employment. All of these factors may influence a worker's productivity and earnings. Historically, in Canada, Gunderson (1994) found that when productivity factors (e.g., hours of work) were taken into account (that is, statistically controlled), the gender wage gap rose from 60 percent to between 75 and 85 percent. Key determinants of the pay gap were differences in work experience and gender segregation. In short, there was little evidence of *direct* pay discrimination by employers. Instead, the division of the labour market into male and female jobs, and the historic undervaluing of female areas of work, are the primary drivers (Glauber 2012; Mandel 2013; Perales 2013; Yu and Kuo 2017).[16]

How have such patterns changed in recent years? Blau and Kahn (2017) have studied the gender wage gap extensively in the United States. They trace trends over three decades (1980–2010), finding a 91 percent wage gap, controlling for all productivity factors, such as education and work experience. Accounting for the bulk of the remaining gap are occupational and industrial segregation, as well as "penalties for career breaks and flexibility." Education, while important in earlier periods, explained less of the gap over the 1980–2010 period, given that women's and men's education levels in the United States have converged, just as in Canada.

This latter point is especially important as human capital theory emphasizes that education is the great equalizer. Ideally, people with identical educational credentials have the same amount of human capital and, therefore, are equally competitive in their earning power. But as Chapter 5 emphasized, human capital theory fails to explain why some individuals with equivalent education are much better paid. Education continues to matter, as we have seen in how postsecondary education has helped narrow the gender wage gap. Yet while some highly educated women have moved into better-paying occupations, as we saw in Table 6.3, far more women remain in traditional areas which pay less. Equally important, STEM areas of study—that is, science, technology, engineering, and math—remain heavily male dominated. The 2016 Census shows that women hold just 10.9 percent of all bachelor degrees in computing and information sciences, and 21.9 percent of all bachelor degrees in engineering (see Statistics Canada, Census 2016, Table 98-400-X2016241). Looking back at the high-paying science and engineering occupations in Table 6.3, we can easily see the impact these educational patterns have on female earning potential.

The challenge of attracting more women into these areas has received growing attention (Canadian Committee on Women in Engineering 1992: 1).[17] In Canada, organizations such as WinSETT (Canadian Centre for Women in Science, Engineering, Trades and Technology), CCWESTT (Canadian Coalition of Women in Engineering, Science, Trades and Technology), and Move the Dial have undertaken research and advocacy to improve women's presence in the technology sector (WinSETT 2016; Move the Dial Benchmark Report 2017). In the United States, Ellen Pao, CEO of Project Include, has been a strong advocate for gender equity and inclusion in the technology sector, following her high-profile lawsuit against a venture capital firm in Silicon Valley. In her book, *Reset: My Fight for Inclusion and Lasting Change,* Pao—who holds an engineering degree from Princeton, as well as a law degree and MBA from Harvard University—provides a disturbing account of the pervasive sexism, racism, and sexual harassment she experienced as a visible minority woman in the technology sector (Pao 2017).

Furthermore, women are vastly underrepresented not only in STEM jobs but also in well-paying trades, where they make up only a fraction of apprentices. In Canada in 2016, women composed just 3.0 percent of heavy equipment operators, 1.9 percent of crane operators, 1.7 percent of carpenters, and 1.5 percent of electricians (see also Skof 2010; Braundy 2011; Canada 2015). Given looming labour shortages in some trades, because of an aging male workforce, the Canadian federal government has dedicated significant funding to promoting gender equity in trades, with $76 million dollars allocated to programs in the 2018 budget and another $3.1 billion in 2019 to boost women's presence, with special attention to Indigenous women (Canada 2018).

Sexual Harassment in the Workplace

Though #MeToo has drawn enormous attention to sexual harassment recently, it is a long-standing problem (Tippett 2019). First recognized in the mid- to late 1970s (MacKinnon 1979), sexual harassment has been widely studied by sociologists and legal scholars since. In one of the most comprehensive reviews to date, McDonald (2012: 2) defines *sexual harassment* as belonging to "a range of abusive or counterproductive workplace behaviours, which have hierarchical power relations at their core." Though definitions of *sexual harassment* vary, most emphasize that it involves *unwelcome* behaviour that is *sexual in nature* and either *directly or indirectly* threatens one's employment (Williams 2018). The *Canada Labour Code* defines sexual harassment as "any conduct, comment, gesture or contact of a sexual nature that is likely to cause offence or humiliation for any employee; or that might, on reasonable grounds, be perceived by that employee as placing a condition of a sexual nature on employment or on any opportunity for training or promotion" (Canada 2019). This differentiates it from general harassment, or what is called *bullying*.

Sexual harassment can take many forms, from a one-time episode to sustained behaviour over a long time. It can range from minor incidents (e.g., an inappropriate joke) to serious behaviour involving a *quid pro quo* (e.g., threatening job security in exchange for sexual compliance) or a *toxic workplace* (e.g., where sexual harassment is allowed to thrive). Harassment, or the fear of it, may lead women to quit jobs or avoid entering non-traditional occupations (Barling, Kelloway, and Frone 2005; McLaughlin et al. 2017). Sexual harassment is not limited to employers, supervisors, or coworkers;

it may originate from customers as well (Hughes and Tadic 1998). New forms of harassment, such as "textual harassment," have also become more common, with mobile technologies being used to send inappropriate, offensive messages virtually (Mainiero and Jones 2013).

#MeToo has highlighted many glaring instances of unacceptable behaviour we immediately recognize as sexual harassment. But there are challenges in studying sexual harassment and getting reliable estimates of this behaviour because of its subjective nature. Christine Williams (2018) notes that studies typically ask about specific observable behaviours (e.g., unwanted touching, comments and jokes, staring). But such approaches have generated wildly different estimates over the years (ranging from 41 to 90 percent reporting sexual harassment). Moreover, individuals reporting specific behaviours (e.g., staring) do not always feel they have been sexually harassed. Though this might seem surprising, Williams observes that it highlights the "institutionalized" nature of harassment—that is, the way some workplace cultures normalize it as "part of the job." Williams argues that a broader approach to sexual harassment is needed, which focuses not just on individual behaviours but on workplace cultures and organizational norms.

One of the most comprehensive studies ever conducted, the 1993 national Violence Against Women Survey, found that 23 percent of Canadian women 18 years old and over had experienced some form of workplace sexual harassment, the most common being inappropriate comments about their bodies or sex lives.[18] More recently, a 2017 study by the Canadian federal government, titled *What We Heard*, found that approximately one-third of respondents had experienced sexual harassment during their working lives. The vast majority (94 percent) of those reporting harassment were women. Visible minorities and persons with disabilities reported higher than average rates of sexual harassment. Harassment was more common in workplaces with high ratios of men in positions of power and low awareness of reporting or grievance procedures.

While three-quarters of respondents in the 2017 study worked for employers that had a sexual harassment policy, only half felt their employer took preventive measures. A key message from the study was that there should be more strongly enforced obligations for employers to ensure that workplaces are free of sexual harassment. The 2018 federal Liberal budget allocated funds to boost legal aid funding support for sexual harassment complaints, and to develop a pan-Canadian strategy to combat sexual harassment, including stronger incident reporting.[19]

THEORETICAL PERSPECTIVES ON WORK AND GENDER INEQUALITY

How has gender inequality become so deeply entrenched in the workplace? And how can it be disrupted? Such questions have sparked research and advocacy over the last several decades, but have taken on renewed urgency in light of the #MeToo and #TimesUp movements that have unveiled the problems of sexual harassment and unequal pay, among many other issues. Research addressing these questions is vital for identifying pathways to change and informing public discussion, policies, and laws focused on creating equitable workplaces. But a comprehensive theory of work-related gender inequities has yet to be formulated.

Feminist research has provided a much needed corrective to the male bias inherent in early sociological research on work. Feldberg and Glenn (1979) characterized research in the 1970s in terms of *job* and *gender models* of the workplace. Whereas studies of male workers used an implicit "job model," focusing on working conditions and organizational factors to explain workplace dynamics and outcomes, studies of women's employment favoured a "gender model," emphasizing women's personal dispositions and family roles.[20] Since then, feminist analysis has probed the link between the public sphere of paid employment and the private sphere of family work, showing how the formal economy depends on unpaid caring work (largely done by women), while rewarding the "ideal worker" who is free of caregiving responsibilities. While gender remains a key consideration in the sociology of work, research is increasingly "intersectional," exploring how factors such as motherhood, ethnicity and race, family status, sexual orientation, and age work together to create differences and similarities in women's and men's economic lives.[21]

Human Capital and Labour Market Segmentation Models

Two of the main competing theories of how labour markets operate are *human capital theory* and *labour market segmentation theory*, as discussed in Chapter 5. We have already criticized the human capital model for its inability to explain the persistence of gender segregation.[22] While the human capital model is concerned with worker characteristics—the supply side of the labour market—the segmentation model examines how employers organize work to generate a demand for specific types of workers. Labour market segmentation theory distinguishes between secondary and primary labour markets. Secondary labour markets are located in competitive industries that continually shave wages and operating costs. In contrast, corporations and state bureaucracies in the primary sector offer high wages, decent benefits, job security, and pleasant working conditions. They also have well-developed internal labour markets providing employees with good career opportunities and employers with a stable, committed workforce.

For the segmentation model to accurately explain why men and women hold different kinds of jobs, women would have to be concentrated in the secondary segment of the labour market. This idea holds true in some part since relatively more women than men are employed in lower-tier service industries. However, many women are also employed in the primary sector. Thus, a segmentation perspective cannot account for gender differences within the same industry or establishment, or inequalities among women. It also does not explain how gender segregation developed in the first place.[23]

Additional factors need to be considered to explain why gender is a major source of inequality in the labour market. Some researchers, for instance, link women's labour market position to their traditional roles within the family. Women's family roles have centred on activities such as raising children and caring for dependents; cooking, cleaning, and other services essential to enabling family members to hold down jobs; and contributing a secondary income to the family budget—roughly in that order. Many employed women experience a conflict when forced to choose between work and family (Blair-Loy 2003). According to this view, women's loyalty usually goes to the latter, and employers consequently often view these women as lacking commitment to their work. Barriers to interesting and better-paying jobs therefore persist.

Gender-Role Socialization

But how are employers' stereotypes of women, women's personal expectations and restricted employment opportunities, and women's family roles linked to their employment patterns within the workplace? Are such patterns best explained by women's early socialization, including family roles and feminine qualities, or as a response to their employment conditions? It is clear that both processes may be involved.

The socialization of girls and boys into traditional gender roles creates cultural norms, expectations, and discourses that carry into the workplace. Historically this has contributed to very sharp patterns of gender segregation. Looking back to the 1980s, for instance, research on children ages 6 to 14 in Ontario, Quebec, and Saskatchewan found that despite discourses encouraging an expansion of occupational horizons for young women, at a personal level many still held traditional aspirations. Here's what the researchers concluded: "Many seem to be saying 'Yes, women can become doctors, but I expect to be a nurse'" (Labour Canada 1986: 55). When girls imagined themselves as adults, most expected to be mothers with small children, supported by a husband, reflecting traditional gender norms. In the 1990s, a survey of Grade 12 students in Alberta found that while gender attitudes were becoming more egalitarian, the top three career choices for young women were still nurse, social worker, and teacher, compared with computer programmer/analyst, engineer, and auto mechanic for males.[24]

In more recent years, studies suggest that young women's occupational aspirations have widened notably, but are still shaped by traditional messages (Ezzedeen 2015), especially with respect to combining work and motherhood—though this point is increasingly debated. For instance, while Bass (2015) found that future family plans had a stronger impact on career aspirations for young women, compared to young men, Cech (2016) found no gender differences in occupational choice or expectations of a continuous career. Race, class, and cultural background, not just gender, also shape young women's ideas about their future labour force attachment and desirable work, with some expecting to work continuously in adulthood, and others holding more traditional ideas of taking career breaks to raise a family (Massoni 2004; Damaske 2011).

Gendered Work and Organizations

Indispensable to an understanding of female work behaviour is how socialization patterns are built upon, strengthened, and reproduced within the workplace. Early pioneering work by Rosabeth Moss Kanter established that the main sources of gender inequality are located within work organizations. Her core argument was that "the job makes the person." As she explains:

Findings about typical behaviour of women in organizations that have been used to reflect either biologically based psychological attributes or characteristics developed through a long socialization to the female sex role turn out to reflect very reasonable and very universal responses to current organizational situations. (1977: 67)

In Kanter's view, men and women employed in similar jobs in an organization react in similar ways to their job conditions. (We return to this subject in Chapters 13 and 14.) A good example is Donald Roy's (1959–60) study of male machine operators. These men escaped the drudgery and isolation of their work— "kept from 'going nuts,'" in Roy's words—by engaging in idle chatter, playing games, and fooling around. Similar dynamics can be observed with women in a variety of routine jobs—domestic cleaners, sales clerks, receptionists— trying to cope with the numbing tedium of their work. In either case, management may view the coping behaviour as evidence that these workers are incapable of performing more demanding jobs. This perception creates a "double bind" for employees: the most effective ways of personally coping in jobs at the bottom of the organization are also indications to management that workers in these jobs deserve to be kept there.

Kanter does not ignore possible gender differences in socialization or non-work roles. Rather, she underlines the pervasive influence of an individual's job content and organizational position on her or his attitudes and behaviour. She also advances our understanding of gender at work by showing how management reproduces the organization through social processes that rely heavily on trust and conformity.[25] To reduce uncertainty, managers recruit and promote people like themselves—a process referred to as *homophily*. This social cloning reproduces male dominance in management, creating enormous barriers for women. While "managers" thus become equated with "men," in sharp contrast, perceptions of female occupations, such as secretary or executive assistant, draw on female stereotypes. Men who receive more opportunities take advantage of them, developing behaviours, values, and work attitudes that help them move ahead. Once young male management trainees are identified as "fast trackers," the resulting halo effect creates the impression that they do not make mistakes and that gives their careers momentum. Conversely, women in dead-end jobs quite rationally decide to give up, losing both work commitment and motivation. Their supervisors will then determine that they do not deserve promotions or raises.

Women who do succeed in entering management face the problem of *tokenism*. Kanter argues that a goldfish bowl phenomenon, resulting from being an identifiable minority, means women or members of visible minorities must work harder to demonstrate their competence—a "prove it again" pattern that reinforces the view they are different and do not belong (Williams and Dempsey 2014). Tokens also lack the support systems essential for surviving in the middle and upper ranks of organizations. According to Kanter, the problem is not sex or race per se; it is part of being a numerical minority. Other empirical research, however, suggests tokenism is specific to women in traditionally male occupations (Yoder 1991). In fact, research suggests men in non-traditional jobs may in some cases benefit from token status, depending on the context and available opportunities (Williams 1989, 2011). Yet Kanter's general point still holds: the *structure of opportunities* in an organization—basically, who has access to which positions, resources, and rewards—creates self-fulfilling prophecies that reinforce the subordinate status of women.

Acker (1990) further develops these ideas, showing how gender is firmly embedded in organizations at multiple levels, from organizational culture, to policies and procedures, to employee interactions, and worker identities (see Britton and Logan 2008 for a valuable review). Views of the "ideal worker" are built around masculine qualities, putting women at a disadvantage. Cultural stereotypes that women are more oriented toward pleasing others and putting domestic responsibilities first infuse organizational policies, job descriptions, managers' assessments of employees, and promotion opportunities. Likewise, the tendency to equate stereotypically male behaviours with leadership may rule women out as "natural leaders." Ridgeway (2011) contends that gender has a "master status" in organizations, operating through ingrained bias and assumptions to shape assessments of competency and suitability. Ely, Ibarra, and Kolk (2013) show how "second-generation bias" operates in subtle ways through stereotypes and organizational practices that position women and men unequally.

Reflecting these processes, a growing number of studies show how bias operates both in hiring and pay decisions (Moss-Racusin et al. 2012; Rivera 2012; Correll 2007). In a well-known study, Goldin and Rouse (2000) found the use of "blind auditions" by orchestras led to a significant increase in the hiring of female musicians from 1970 to 1996—a period when women were commonly thought to be "inferior" players. Having musicians audition behind blinds eliminated visual cues about gender, and ultimately boosted women's evaluations and hiring. Other studies confirm that formalized procedures are required to override bias in hiring decisions (Correll 2017; Reskin and McBrier 2000).

ACHIEVING WORKPLACE EQUALITY

We have catalogued the inequities women face in terms of work opportunities and rewards. Some of the evidence leads to optimism that barriers to equal labour market opportunities and rewards are slowly being pushed aside. But gender equity can be achieved sooner through innovative policy and workplace initiatives. We conclude this chapter with a brief overview of some policy options that have been pursued to date. Unions and collective action can also play a decisive role in achieving gender equity at work, as discussed in Chapter 11.

Employment Equity

One important set of initiatives in Canada stems from the 1984 Royal Commission on Equality in Employment (chaired by Rosalie Abella, now a Supreme Court judge). It introduced the concept of *employment equity* as a strategy to eliminate the effects of discrimination and fully open up competition for job opportunities to those who had been excluded and disadvantaged in employment historically. Four groups were identified as "equity groups": women, visible minorities, Indigenous peoples, and persons with disabilities. With respect to women, the Abella Commission asserted that equality in employment required a revised approach to ensure that all individuals, regardless of their personal characteristics, be treated fairly in recruitment, hiring, promotions, training, dismissals, and any other employment decisions.

A central contribution of the federal 1986 *Employment Equity Act* was the argument that *systemic discrimination* creates work barriers that can only be dismantled through strong legislation. Unlike *direct discrimination,* which is intentional and obvious, systemic discrimination is the unintentional consequence of employment practices and policies that have a differential effect on specific groups. This form of discrimination is built into the system of employment, rather than reflecting the conscious intent of individuals to discriminate. Good examples of systemic discrimination are minimum height and weight requirements for entry into police or fire departments, which use white males as the norm; they operate to exclude women and members of certain visible minorities, even though that was not the intent.

The 1986 *Employment Equity Act* covers federal government employees, federally regulated employers and Crown corporations, and employers that have 100 or more employees and bid on government contracts worth more than $200,000 (universities, for example). The Act has three main goals. First, it requires employers to identify and remove employment practices that act as systemic barriers to the four *designated groups* (women, visible minorities, Indigenous peoples, and persons with disabilities). Second, it establishes targets for achieving a more representative workforce that will reflect the proportion of qualified and eligible individuals from designated groups in the appropriate labour pool (not in the entire population). Third, it requires employers to file annual reports to assess progress in recruiting and promoting members of the four designated groups.[26]

Employment equity recognizes the need for positive measures to rectify historic imbalances in staff composition (e.g., targeted leadership training programs for women or Indigenous peoples) and the "reasonable accommodation" of differences (e.g. changing the RCMP dress code to permit Sikhs to wear turbans and Indigenous officers to have braids) to make workplaces more accessible and inclusive. It also encourages learning initiatives so that employees and managers become more knowledgeable about the value of diversity and techniques for building more inclusive workplaces. Through such efforts, organizations can become more representative of Canadian society, both in terms of numerical representation and workplace culture.

Overall, employment equity has had some success. However, legislation covers just a fraction of Canada's workforce and change has been uneven. On the positive side, evidence points to increased access of designated equity groups to professional, supervisory, and upper-management positions; a reduced wage gap as a result; and improved human resource practices.[27] Critics of employment equity, however, have also noted limitations of existing legislation and the need for stricter monitoring and enforcement, inclusion of more workplaces, and greater employer commitment to the equity goals, timetables, and plans. Backlash and resistance to employment equity is also a problem, especially the mistaken perceptions that such equity programs involve "quotas" and ignore issues of merit, which they do not (McGown and Ng 2016).

Stronger equity legislation could speed progress toward gender equity. However, many business organizations have also launched their own initiatives, focusing on "gender diversity and inclusion" (GDI) or "equity, diversity, and inclusion" (EDI). One of the motivations for employers is recognition that women and other equity groups will make up a larger share of the workforce as baby boomers retire. There is also growing awareness of the costs of gender inequality and potential lawsuits based on discrimination (Williams and Cuddy 2012). In the current language of employers, then, there is a "business case for diversity." GDI has thus become a human resource priority for many organizations (McKinsey & Company 2019). While some believe GDI efforts will have a positive impact, others view them as largely "symbolic" and "ceremonial" (Dobbin and Kalev 2017).

Pay Equity

Another important policy initiative is *pay equity*. Pay equity, or "comparable worth," as it is called in the United States, focuses specifically on the most glaring indicator of gender inequality in the labour market: the wage gap. Pay equity is a proactive policy, requiring employers to assess the extent of pay discrimination and then to adjust wages so that women are fairly compensated. Frequently a topic of heated public debate, pay equity recognizes that *occupational gender segregation* underlies the wage gap. It attempts to provide a gender-neutral methodology for comparing predominantly female jobs with predominantly male jobs in different occupational classifications under the same employer. For example, a secretarial job (female) would be compared with the job of maintenance technician (male) in the same organization. Using a standardized evaluation system, points are assigned to these jobs on the basis of four factors: *skill level, effort, responsibility, and working conditions.* Only after the "point value" of jobs has been determined are wages compared and (if needed) adjustments made.

Underpinning the process is the recognition that women's work is valuable but has been under-rewarded in the past. The objective is to pay employees on the basis of their contribution to the employer. Achieving this will establish *equal pay for work of equal value*, a more far-reaching concept than *equal pay for equal work* or *equal pay for similar work*, which compares women and men only in jobs that are the "same" or "substantially similar." However, developing and applying a truly gender-neutral system for evaluating jobs has proved exceedingly difficult because it challenges long-standing assumptions about the nature of skill (Steinberg 1990). Thus, we can see how historical ideas about "women's work" continue to have an imprint to the present day.

Pay equity legislation in Canada typically covers the public sector, although in Ontario and Quebec, which have the most extensive legislation, parts of the private sector are also included (Ontario Pay Equity Commission 2018).[28] Pay equity policies are explicit in their intent. As noted in the 2004 *Pay Equity Task Force Report*, one of the most comprehensive reports in Canada, pay equity begins from the premise that "differences in pay for comparable work which is based solely on differences in sex are discriminatory, and that steps should be taken to eliminate these differences" (Canada 2004: 6).

Pay equity legislation has gone some distance toward creating fairer compensation. For example, in Ontario, 100,000 women working in public-sector childcare and nursing homes received hundreds of millions of dollars in pay adjustments under provincial legislation. In Quebec, more than 300,000 women working in the public sector received substantial pay adjustments, as well as $1.5 billion in back pay, for a total settlement estimated at $4 billion.[29] While Ontario pay equity legislation was once heralded as the most comprehensive in North America, Conservative provincial governments have legislated over the years to blunt its impact (Ontario Equal Pay Coalition 2017). Thus, while pay equity has not eliminated the female–male wage gap, it has helped narrow it. Furthermore, by increasing earnings at the bottom of the female earnings distribution, the policies have benefited more than just middle-class women.[30]

Opponents of pay equity argue that the economy cannot afford wage adjustments, that businesses may be driven into bankruptcy, or that pay equity interferes with the operation of the labour market. But for millions of employed women, pay equity provides long-overdue recognition of their economic contributions to society. Speaking to this point, expert testimony to the federal 2016 Special Committee on Pay Equity indicates that costs to employers have often been lower than expected (about 1.5 percent of payroll). Yet women often have waited years for settlements (Canada 2016). In fact, one of the most protracted cases in Canadian history involves the federal government itself—it took

14 years to settle with its employees (librarians, clerks, and others). Another such case involving Bell Canada took 15 years.

Such delays have far-reaching effects according to one expert witness to the 2016 Special Committee on Pay Equity (Canada 2016: 2):

> When I speak about pay equity, I often use the phrase "justice delayed is justice denied." So I want to remember the groups of workers who had to wait decades for complaints to work their way through the courts, such as the Bell Canada workers whose case took 15 years . . . By the time the settlement was reached, almost 16% of those workers had died and many more were frail and nearing end of life. Imagine for a moment their quality of life if they hadn't had to wait. Imagine the boost to the economy if that money had been in their bank accounts the whole time.

Given this, a central recommendation of the 2016 Special Committee Report on Pay Equity was immediate drafting of proactive (rather than complaint-based) legislation, and action on outstanding recommendations from the 2004 Task Force on Pay Equity, such as extending pay equity to part-time, casual, seasonal, and temporary workers, and to Crown corporations and organizations in the Federal Contractors Program (Canada 2016: 37–43). Proactive federal legislation has now been passed (as part of Bill C-86). It will require employers not only to conduct pay equity analysis, and adjust wages but also to regularly maintain and review their plans. While it is too early to know what impact this legislation will have, based on evidence from provincial legislation in Ontario and Quebec, it should help further reduce the wage gap. In addition, other trends, such as the push toward greater "pay transparency" in Canada and other countries should help narrow the gender wage gap too (Castilla 2015; Kim 2015).

One other important instrument for achieving gender equality in employment is Section 15 of the *Canadian Charter of Rights and Freedoms*. This section of the Charter became law in April 1985. It established for the first time in our history a constitutional entitlement to full equality for women in law, as well as in the effects of law. This latter point is crucial, for regardless of the wording or intent of a law, if, in practice, it results in discrimination against women, the courts can rule it to be unconstitutional.

CONCLUSION

We began this chapter by discussing seemingly contradictory trends in gender and work—on one hand, a push toward greater gender equity, while on the other, evidence of persistent problems highlighted by recent movements such as #MeToo and #TimesUp. On the basis of a comprehensive review of past and present trends in Canada, we can conclude that while some changes have occurred for both women and men in the workplace, gender continues to be central to the organization of paid work. Certainly, we are beginning to rectify some of the most glaring problems women confront. Higher education and changing attitudes about women's capabilities and commitment as workers have played a key role, as our analysis shows. But gender segregation, inflexible workplaces, subtle forms of "second-generation" bias, and sexual harassment, all continue to create barriers for women.

Employment equity and pay equity programs now operating in Canada are reform oriented, aiming to modify existing employment institutions, values, processes, and social relationships. But how effective will these workplace reforms be? And what impact will such policies have, if any, in altering women's traditional non-work roles—especially within the family—and the supporting socialization processes and ideologies? The limitations of such reforms prompt some to argue for greater recognition of women's unpaid caregiving work and greater involvement of men in such activities—issues we take up in Chapter 7. For them, equity can be achieved only when women and men begin to share this work, and employers begin to recognize that all workers have family responsibilities. Any successful strategy must recognize that employment inequities are firmly embedded in the very structure and values of our society. So, while we look for ways of reducing the effects of traditional gender practices within families, schools, and other institutions, we also need to continue to focus directly on the organizational barriers that stand in the way of gender equality in the workplace and labour market.

DISCUSSION QUESTIONS

1. Discuss women's and men's economic contributions in the early days of Canada's industrialization. To what extent did their work differ and why?

2. Research shows that women are moving into "male" occupations more quickly than men are moving into "female" occupations. Thinking about your own career goals, why do you think this is?

3. What is gender segregation, and why is it so important for understanding inequalities in work? When you compare the jobs women and men have done historically, and those they do today, what has changed most dramatically? What has stayed the same?

4. Compare the processes and goals of employment equity and pay equity. How useful do you think these types of policies are for improving equity in the workplace? Discuss.

5. Based on your own work experience, discuss the effectiveness of sexual harassment policies and other preventive resources that employers have introduced. Include in your discussion to what extent you were made aware of these policies, and based on your observations, to what extent they actually guided employees' behaviour.

ADDITIONAL RESOURCES

WORK AT THE MOVIES

- *Time 2017 Person of the Year: "The Silence Breakers"* (5:02 minutes). This is a brief overview of the timeline, stories, and voices of the #MeToo movement.

- *Albert Nobbs* (directed by Rodrigo Garcia, 2011, 113 minutes). This mainstream film focuses on gender and the history of work, limited job opportunities, and a woman who chooses to "pass" as a man to improve her economic security.

- *Rosies of the North* (directed by Kelly Saxberg, 1999, 46:40 minutes). The NFB documentary is based on oral histories of women's contributions during World War II to aircraft manufacturing in Thunder Bay. It is available through the National Film Board of Canada: http://www.nfb.ca/film/rosies_of_the_north.

- *Norma Rae* (directed by Martin Ritt, 1979, 110 minutes). Based on real events centred on a textile factory, this dramatic film explores gender and union activism in blue-collar America.

- *North Country* (directed by Niki Caro, 2005, 126 minutes). This film explores sexual harassment in mining work and is based on the true story of Lois Jenkins.
- *The Loudest Voice.* This is a television mini-series about bully and sexual predator Roger Ailes, former CEO of Fox News.

SOUNDS OF WORK

- "Tecumseh Valley" (Townes Van Zandt). In this song, a young woman leaves her coal-mining town in search of work as a manual labourer, only to become a bartender and then a sex worker.
- "Working Man" (Rita MacNeil). Rita MacNeil sings about the lives of men who work in the coal mines on Cape Breton Island in Nova Scotia.
- "She Works Hard for the Money" (Donna Summer). Purportedly based on an experience Summer had with a female bathroom attendant, this song highlights the struggles involved in low-wage service work.
- "Bread and Roses" (James Oppenheim/Judy Collins). Collins brings Oppenheim's poem to life with this song about women and men marching for fair wages and decent living conditions.

NOTES

1. For an overview of women's gains in education, work, and the professions, see Moyer (2017).
2. See Cohen (1988). Useful sources for women's history in Canada are Bradbury (1993), Campbell (2009), Sangster (2011), and the labour studies journal *Labour/Le Travail*.
3. See Carter (2016) and Rollings-Magnusson (2000) for useful discussions of the historical contributions of women in the Canadian West.
4. For historical background on the transformation of women's work inside and outside the home during the rise of industrial capitalism, see Cohen (1988) and Bradley (1989).
5. For historical discussions of the family wage, see Land (1980) and Bradbury (1993: 80, and Chapters 3 and 5). For discussions of changing contemporary norms around breadwinning, see Livingstone and Luxton (1996), Coltrane (1996), and Marshall (2006, 2011).
6. For analyses of lone parents and income, see Morissette and Ostrovky (2007) and Williams (2010).

7. Van Bavel et al. (2018) discuss a growing body of research on "assortative mating" where partners share high levels of education, career commitment, and earnings.

8. For overviews and discussions of gender segregation in industrialized countries, see Charles and Grusky (2004), and Jarman, Blackburn, and Racko (2012). See Feuchtwang (1982: 251) for a definition of *job ghetto*.

9. Hughes (1995, 2001). Traditional occupations are those in which women constitute a greater proportion of employment than they do in the labour force as a whole.

10. On the health professions, see Armstrong, Choinière, and Day (1993), and Armstrong, Armstrong, and Scott-Dixon (2008). On men in non-traditional jobs, see Williams (1992, 1995, 2011), Synder and Green (2008), Lindsay (2007), and Lupton (2006).

11. On women in medicine, see Cassell (1998), Ku (2011), and Wallace (2014). On women's experiences in the legal profession, see Hagan and Kay (1995), Kay and Gorman (2012), and Sterling and Reichman (2016).

12. Data for 2017 are from the *2018 Annual Report, Employment Equity Act*, produced by Employment and Social Development Canada, available at https://www.canada.ca/en/employment-social-development/services/labour-standards/reports/employment-equity-2018.html#h2.02-h3.01

13. Data for lone parents and elderly families come from Fox and Moyser (2018: 15–16).

14. MacDonald (2019) analyzes gender representation and pay in 2017 among Canada's CEOs, focusing on the largest 250 companies listed on the TSX/S&P Composite Index. CEOs earned $5.1 million annually (salary plus bonuses), with a female–male earnings gap of 68 percent.

15. Drolet (2011) and Schirle (2015) discuss the wage gap in Canada, and the Canadian provinces, respectively. In the United States, Blau and Kahn (2017) review long-term trends, while Goldin (2014) analyzes how the wage gap has narrowed differently in distinct occupations in the United States.

16. For valuable discussions of the gendered wage gap in Canada, see Drolet (2011) and Cool (2010); for the United States, see Glauber (2012) and Moore (2018); for the United Kingdom, see Perales (2013).

17. For recent trends, see also Engineers Canada (2012). On the male culture of engineering, see Braundy (2011), Miller (2004), Cech (2013), and Seron et al. (2018).

18. See Johnson (1994: 11) for the 1993 survey, conducted by Statistics Canada. See Sev'er (1999) for discussions of research evidence, theoretical interpretations, and measurement issues on this topic.

19. See Leaderman (2019) for a discussion of federal government funding to support initiative by AfterMeToo and other organizations.

20. See Feldberg and Glenn (1979), Acker (1990), and Britton and Logan (2008) for classic discussions of gender bias in the sociological study of work and organizations.
21. On feminist approaches to understanding gender and work, see Reskin and Padavic (2002), Vosko (2002), Britton and Logan (2008), and Ridgeway (2011).
22. On human capital explanations of sex differences in occupations and earnings, see Blau and Winkler (2017: Chapter 8).
23. For critical discussions of occupational gender segregation, see Siltanen (1994) and Levanon and Grusky (2016). Hagan and Kay (1995) critically utilize human capital theory and a more general version of labour market segmentation theory in their study of gender inequalities in the legal profession. Problems in the measurement of occupational gender segregation and the underlying factors are discussed in Blackburn, Jarman, and Siltanen (1993).
24. Unpublished data from the 1996 Alberta High School Graduate Survey (Lowe, Krahn and Bowlby 1997). Virtually all females (97 percent) and 85 percent of males agreed or strongly agreed with the statement "a woman should have the same job opportunities as a man."
25. For a summary of related research on women and management, see Powell (2019).
26. For Employment Equity Act Annual Reports in Canada, see http://www.labour. gc.ca/eng/standards_equity/eq/pubs_eq/annual_reports/2013/index.shtml. Leck (2002) discusses a number of studies documenting a narrowing of the wage gap.
27. For critical reviews and discussions of employment equity over the years, see Leck (2002), Abu-Laban and Gabriel (2002) and Bakan and Kobayashi (2007).
28. On pay equity legislation in federal, provincial, and territorial jurisdictions, see Ontario Pay Equity Commission (2018) *An Overview of Pay Equity in Various Canadian* Jurisdictions. For discussion of federal developments, see the *Report of the Special Committee on Pay Equity* (Canada 2016). For current developments in Ontario, see the Equal Pay Coalition website: http://www.equalpaycoalition.org/. For a historical perspective on Canadian legislation, see the final report of the Pay Equity Task Force (Canada 2004).
29. For discussions of specific settlements and impacts in the Canadian context, see Cornish (2008), Canada (2016), and McDonald and Thornton (2016). For detail on the history and methodology of pay equity, see the final report of the Pay Equity Task Force (Canada 2004).
30. For critiques of pay equity, see Canada (2016), Cornish (2007), Gunderson (2002), and Forrest (2000).

HOUSEHOLD, FAMILY, AND CARING WORK

7

"When I think about what I do every day—I cook meals for my family, I make cereal for breakfast and sandwiches for lunch and meat and potatoes for supper. Nothing unusual about that. But when I think about all those thousands of other women all doing the same thing, then I realize I'm not just making porridge. I'm part of a whole army of women who are feeding the country."

Source: Stay at home mother. Meg Luxton. (2013). *More than a Labour of Love.* Women's Press, p. 13.

"There are times when I go insane. There are times when I think the demands of the home are too much, the responsibilities and the constant nagging and the whining of the kids and the diapers and the crap. . . . Sometimes I think, By God, my life would be a lot less complicated if I just had a nine-to-five job. . . . But there are other times—just being with them in the summer, being in the backyard, colouring or doing puzzles or hanging out with them, just playing squirt-gun games for an entire hour—that are just great. There is nothing that can replace that."

Source: Tom, stay at home father. Andrea Doucet. (2018). *Do Men Mother? Fathering, Care and Domestic Responsibility.* Second edition. University of Toronto Press, pp. 3–4.

"You know the first question they always ask you is, 'Well, what do you do? Where do you work?' And I say, 'Well I'm not working now. I'm staying home with my children.' And it was like this wall of invisibility. You know, I remember reading *The Invisible Man* by Ralph Ellison. . . . And that was what came to mind. It was like all of a sudden I didn't exist. If I didn't have an identity in the working world, I didn't exist."

Source: Maeve Turner, stay at home mom and lawyer. Pamela Stone. (2007). *Opting Out? Why Women Really Quit Careers and Head Home.* University of California Press, p. 145.

INTRODUCTION

Several years ago, Jessica Stilwell, a social worker and mother living in Calgary, made national and international headlines when she went on a "household strike," refusing to clean up after her 12-year-old twin daughters and their younger 10-year-old sister. Frustrated by their unwillingness to pick up after themselves and pitch in with daily household chores, Stilwell reduced her own housework to the bare minimum, cooking meals and packing school lunches. Everything else, from washing her children's dirty dishes, to picking up their toys, games, and clothes, to unpacking their school lunch bags, was left to her daughters. She did not remind or nag them about what needed to be done; in fact, she did not even tell them she was going on strike—she simply quit cleaning up after them. Six days later, her house in disarray, with dirty dishes overflowing from the dishwasher, unpacked lunch bags fermenting on the kitchen counter, and clothes, jackets, toys, and games strewn about, her children called a truce, apologizing for not doing more. The children then spent two frenzied days cleaning and returning the house to its original pristine condition, serving coffee to their mother while she watched them work.[1]

Such examples highlight the important, but often taken-for-granted and "invisible" nature of household, family, and caring work. In this chapter, we examine this work, exploring the skills and demands involved, and how participation in and responsibility for such work is distributed among family members. We also consider how families accomplish household and caring work in a context where women have increased their attachment to paid work, but where traditional ideas about gender and household responsibility persist. What is striking, for instance, about media coverage on Jessica Stilwell's strike is the sole focus on her as a mother. Her husband and the father of her daughters, who lives in the same household, merits just a passing mention, and it seems to be assumed that the work of organizing the household naturally belongs to her. What gives rise to such assumptions? And to what extent are gendered patterns of household and caring work really shifting? Moreover, how does responsibility for household and caring work underlie or contribute to the broader gender inequalities we observe in the labour market and paid work?

We examine these questions while considering how employers and governments are supporting women's and men's changing work as earners and caregivers, and their efforts to balance their work, family, and personal lives.

HOUSEHOLDS, FAMILIES, AND WORK

Conceptualizing Household and Family Work

Most early studies in the sociology of work paid scant, if any, attention to *household work*, *unpaid work*, or *caregiving*. In her classic article "Invisible Work," sociologist Arlene Kaplan Daniels (1987) suggests several reasons. First, to the extent that caring and housework are done in the private realm, they are often seen as falling outside the formal economy, thus lacking economic value. Second, the fact that household work is unpaid—that it does not receive a salary or wage—reinforces common perspectives that it lacks value, as it is not readily thought of in dollar terms. Finally, according to Daniels, women's historical and ongoing responsibility for household work further contributes to its devaluation. Rather than being seen as skilled work requiring knowledge and ability, caring and cleaning are seen as something women "naturally" do. Illustrating this, Daniels asks how many people consider the following to be work: comforting a child, cooking meals, creating warm and caring family relations. Certainly, she contends, such activities are work, but traditional ideas about family and gender impede this recognition.

Today, while some Canadians continue to hold the views described by Daniels, there is growing awareness of the importance of household and caring work. Sociologists, in particular, have increasingly focused on the household as an important site of research and study. Not only does such research help us build a more complete picture of work, it also helps us understand the fluid boundary between the labour market and household. Equally important, given that women still carry much of the responsibility for families, a sharper picture of household work is key to understanding the nature of the gender inequality that we observe in Canada and other countries. Typically, household responsibilities are far more likely to limit women's labour force participation, keeping women financially dependent on their partners (Bianchi et al. 2012).

Some sociologists argue that gender inequality is the result of two systems of domination: *capitalism* and *patriarchy*. Broadly speaking, *patriarchy* refers to male domination over women, but more specifically it describes forms of family organization in which fathers and husbands hold the power.[2] Capitalism incorporated earlier patriarchal social arrangements. Remnants of patriarchy still reinforce stereotypes of women as cheap, expendable labour. Women's traditional roles as mothers and partners also restrict their economic opportunities and, for those who are employed, create a double day of paid and unpaid work. Relations of male domination and female subordination are not universal, however, nor self-reproducing systems. They are best understood as historically varied sets of practices that intersect with other social relations (e.g., race, ethnicity, sexuality) and that can be reproduced, challenged, and/or transformed (Acker 1989; Walby 1990; Messerschmidt et al. 2018). Indeed, a central question about household work concerns the extent of change that is occurring.

Researchers have identified and shed light on a wide variety of household work, including *housework* (e.g., cooking, cleaning, laundry), *caring and emotion work* (e.g., bearing and raising children, caring for the elderly and infirm), and *kin and community work* (e.g., communicating and coordinating with larger family networks and neighbours). Taken together, such activities have often been referred to as *domestic work*, *unpaid work*, or *social reproduction* (as opposed to *production*, which occurs in the formal economy). In their influential article, Laslett and Brenner (1989: 382) define *social reproduction* as activities "involved in the maintenance of life on a daily basis, and inter-generationally." Such work is organized and accomplished through *family strategies*, decisions made by families about the nature of family life (e.g., family size) and the division of labour in the home and labour market. As we will see, the work of households is also shaped by economic realities and dominant cultural ideals about how family life should be.

Changing Family Forms

We have already outlined in previous chapters the important role of households and families in Canada's economic development. But the specific nature of that role has changed and shifted over time. Before the rise of capitalism and industrialization, the household operated as a primary site of economic production with men, women, and children working together to sustain family life (Cohen 1988). As discussed in Chapter 1, specific household patterns varied across time and space. For instance, Camfield (2019) notes that Indigenous peoples organized their subsistence production (e.g., hunting, trapping, foraging, fishing) through egalitarian-communal kinship ties that differed substantially from family formations among early British settlers. The emergence of factory production and a wage-labour economy shifted the nature of the household again, as men (primarily) were drawn into paid jobs, leaving women responsible for a wide range of work in the home—from cooking and cleaning, to caring for children, the elderly, and the infirm.

Although we tend to think of families and households as part of the private realm, standing apart from the market and economy, the household was also a site for paid work, though often at the margins of the informal economy. In early industrializing Canada, for example, working-class women often washed clothes for other families or rented rooms and served meals to boarders to earn extra money for their families (Bradbury 1993). Women also sewed at home as part of factory-based "putting out" system. At the other end of the economic spectrum, wealthier families hired servants to cook and clean, bringing employment relationships into the home. Boundaries between the *household* and *market*, and *private* and *public* realms, were fluid and not always clearly demarcated—a situation that persists today.

Traditional gender beliefs and discourses, especially the idea of "separate spheres," also played an important role, ensuring that household work remained culturally and materially associated with women. Typically, married women and mothers did not work for pay, except in cases of great economic need. Working-class, immigrant and Indigenous women were far more likely to be drawn into paid work (Chapter 1). At certain points in the 20th century, these gender norms were relaxed—for example, during World War II when women were recruited into the war effort and formal economy as a result of dire labour shortages (Pierson 1986). But such moments were fleeting. After World War II, a return to "breadwinner norms" meant that the most common pattern was for women to work briefly before having children, stay home to raise them, and then return to the labour force in middle age after the children had grown up.[3] Because most mothers in the 1950s responded to the demands of child rearing by leaving the labour force, employers tended to assume women had a weak attachment to paid work. Yet, while some women did leave voluntarily, others did not. Instead, they were forced out by *marriage* or *pregnancy bars*—formal policies and informal practices that required women to resign their jobs upon marriage or motherhood (Sangster 1995, 2010).[4]

Since the 1970s, the trend in Canada and other industrialized nations has been for mothers to continue working while raising their children. Figure 3.3 (in Chapter 3) and 6.1 (in Chapter 6) remind us how dramatic this change has been. Today, far fewer women leave the labour force when they have children, and those who "take time out" do so for much shorter periods. Growing numbers of women are now juggling paid work with family roles, and the traditional *single-earner family* has been eclipsed. In 2016, for instance, 62.1 percent of all Canadian families were *dual-earner* (Statistics Canada, Table 11-10-0028-01). In comparison, single-earner families were just over one-quarter of all families—with single female-earner and single male-earner families making up 8.5 percent and 17.6 percent of all families, respectively. *Lone-parent families* made up the remainder (11.8 percent of all families), and roughly 80 percent were headed by women (Milan et al. 2015: 16).[5] Same-sex, common-law, multi-generational, and female-breadwinner/stay-at-home-father families are also part of growing family diversity, though these families are not yet well-studied. In short, the traditional male-sole-breadwinner family is no longer the norm (Doucet 2018; Milan 2015; Pfeffer 2017).

TRENDS IN HOUSEHOLD AND CARING WORK

Given these dramatic changes, especially women's growing role as earners, how has the work of households changed? Is there now more sharing of unpaid work among family members, or do traditional patterns persist? Evidence from early studies suggested that despite change, many working women were still responsible for what U.S. sociologist Arlie Hochschild (1989) called a "second shift" in the home.[6] After working at a paid job, they come home to cook, clean, shop, and look after children—the same domestic work their mothers and grandmothers did as full-time housewives. Hochschild's findings in her influential 1989 study, *The Second Shift*, echoed those of early Canadian research on this topic: Meissner and colleagues (1975) found that a job outside the home meant a double burden for working women and a decrease of 13.5 hours per week in leisure time.

But these studies were carried out several decades ago and have been the subject of growing debate.[7] Perhaps they reflect a time when families had not yet adjusted to the new realities of working women? If so, are new generations redefining how household work is done? Media stories often give the impression that men are doing more at home, but do recent studies confirm this? These questions form a central debate over whether there is *convergence* or a *stalled revolution* in gendered patterns of unpaid work (England 2010; Bianchi 2012; Guppy et al. 2019).

Housework

To answer these questions researchers draw on *time budget data* generated from self-reported responses to survey questions or diaries, as well as qualitative information from individual- or couple-level interviews or observation. Studies of housework typically distinguish between *core/regular housework*, such as meal preparation, meal cleanup, indoor cleaning, and laundry that are done daily; and *non-core/infrequent housework*, such as outdoor cleaning, interior or exterior maintenance, and repairs (Marshall 2006: 2; Bianchi et al. 2012). Typically housework is measured separately from childcare—even though both tasks are often done at the same time, and the amount of housework is strongly shaped by the presence and age of children. An important distinction also exists between the *time* spent on activities and who holds *responsibility*—that is, planning and anticipating household work, rather than simply carrying it out (Doucet 2018).

Analyses of long-term change has been carried out in a number of countries. In the United States, Bianchi et al. (2012) find that women's housework decreased from 1965 to 2010, as their paid employment rose, challenging the idea of a stalled revolution. In a comprehensive cross-national study, Kan, Sullivan, and Gershuny (2011) compare time-use trends in housework from the 1960s to the early 2000s for 16 different countries (including Canada). They also find evidence of *convergence* in the time that women and men spend on housework, largely because of *reductions* in women's housework, but much smaller *increases* in the time contributions of men. Altintas and Sullivan (2016) examine trends for 19 countries from 1960 to 2011. They also find trends of gender convergence, but they report differences in the pace and timing of change across countries and a slowing of convergence in more recent years.

More detailed data from Statistics Canada's General Social Survey (GSS) helps us unpack these trends, since we can compare both *participation in* and *time spent on* housework in Canadian households at several points from 1986 to 2015. While early analysis in the 1990s (Marshall 1993: 12) confirmed that women in dual-earner families held primary responsibility for housework (e.g., meal preparation and cleanup, cleaning, and laundry), subsequent analysis to the mid-2000s found notable change (Marshall 2006).[8] In particular, more men were participating in housework by the mid-2000s—three-quarters (71 percent) reported they had contributed to housework in 2005, compared to just over half (54 percent) in 1986. Yet the time men spent on housework increased just slightly, from 1.1 hours in 1986 to 1.5 hours per day by 2005. In comparison, women reduced the time they spent on housework, from 3.3 hours per day in 1986 to 2.8 hours per day by 2005. Thus, gender convergence was a result of women reducing their time and men becoming more involved, but in time-limited ways.[9]

Recent studies (Moyser and Burlock 2018; Guppy et al. 2019) confirm further *gender convergence* in Canada up to 2015 but also highlight some of the challenges in studying unpaid work. For instance, Moyser and Burlock (2018) show how multitasking is important for interpreting trends (see also Bianchi et al. 2012). They distinguish between "core" and "simultaneous" unpaid work, the former being the main activity one is involved in (e.g., caring for children) and the latter involving multitasking (e.g., making dinner, doing laundry, and caring for children at the same time). Focusing on "core activities" only, women's and men's "total work burden" (i.e., total hours in paid and unpaid work) was similar in 2015, though women carry out a higher proportion of unpaid work, and men more paid work. But if one includes "simultaneous unpaid work," women's total work burden increases by 1.2 hours each day (Moyser and Burlock 2018).

Of course, these figures reflect averages, whereas contributions may vary by family type, labour force participation, age/generation, sexuality, gender attitudes, and other factors. Past studies confirm, not surprisingly, that families with younger children require more housework, and that this falls disproportionately to women. Age, education, and sexual orientation also matter, with some studies suggesting that younger, university-educated, and same-sex couples are more likely to favour less traditional patterns (Marshall 2011; Nelson 1996).[10] At a more institutional and societal level, research also shows that countries with high levels of female employment, and childhood exposure to maternal employment, have higher contributions from men to household work (Cunningham 2007; Hook 2006; Gupta 2006).

Guppy et al. (2019) provide one of the most comprehensive Canadian analyses of housework to date (as well as childcare, which we discuss in the next section). Drawing on GSS data from 1986 to 2015, they highlight several key points. First, gender convergence has occurred both in *participation in* and *time spent on* housework, with women accounting for 70.7 percent of total housework hours in 1986, but just 58.8 percent in 2015. Second, change is due both to women's reductions and to men's increases in time, with cooking accounting for a significant part of the change (see also Besen-Cassino 2019). Third, change is evident across all education groups, not just among the highly educated as some studies have suggested. In fact, less educated men account for much of the change in recent periods, "catching up" to university-educated men by 2010. Finally, age is not significant to changing patterns; convergence is evident across all age groups. Guppy et al. (2019) conclude that gender convergence is real, resulting from both "structural factors" (e.g., women's rising employment) and broad shifts in "cultural attitudes" across Canadian society.

An important caveat is that many of these studies focus on, or assume, opposite-sex households and do not explore racial or ethnic diversity. Equally important, they do not capture whether, or how, others (e.g., paid cleaners, cooking services) are involved in housework. Clearly, family income plays a critical role in how household work gets done (Moyser and Burlock 2018). As discussed in Chapter 6, trends in "assortative mating" (where people of similar class backgrounds partner) mean that households are increasingly advantaged or disadvantaged (England 2010). For working-class families, the challenge often is juggling household work alongside the demands of precarious, low-paying work, which may involve erratic schedules (Presser 2003). In contrast, professional dual-career families are often time-strapped, as are those in two-person careers (e.g., elite CEOs who are expected to have the unpaid services of a wife who can put on dinner parties, plan social events and travel, and organize household moves). Such dynamics often see well-resourced families outsourcing family work—an issue we return to shortly.

Childcare, Mothering, and Fathering

Caring for children is one of the most important and time-intensive activities in family life, involving both *instrumental care* or *caring for* (e.g., feeding, dressing, bathing) and *expressive care* or *caring about* (e.g., love, support, encouragement). Studies suggest that fathers have taken an increasingly active role as caregivers, though the extent and nature of this change continues to be debated.[11] In a fascinating study, Andrea Doucet (2018) examines a seemingly simple question posed in the title of her book—*Do Men Mother?*—showing the complexity of mothering and fathering, and the challenges for stay-at-home fathers who engage in work that has strong cultural associations with women. Traditionally, women have carried the responsibility of caring for children, leading scholars to argue that they engage in an "ethic of care," specific maternal practices, and "maternal thinking," which is attuned to the needs of children and family life (Ruddick 1995; Tronto 1993; Held 2006). Even today, when women increasingly work for pay, caring for children largely remains their responsibility. Contemporary norms around what is called *intensive mothering*, where women are expected to devote ever more of their attention, effort, and identity to their children, create sharp contradictions for working mothers who carry far more economic and workplace responsibilities than ever before (Hays 1996; Stone 2007). In her insightful study, *Competing Devotions,* Mary Blair-Loy (2003) argues that competing moral schemas—"devotion to family" versus "devotion to work"—set up cultural expectations for professional working women that are impossible to fulfill.

What does research find with respect to long-term and more recent trends in childcare? Studies typically define *childcare* as feeding, dressing, helping, reading to, talking or playing with, medical care, and related travel, such as taking children to school or sports activities (Marshall 2006: 2). Evidence from several countries suggests patterns of *gender convergence*, as mothers have increased their hours in paid employment, and fathers have taken a more active role in their children's lives (Beaujot, Liu, and Ravanera 2008; Bianchi and Milkie 2010; Marshall 2011). Yet, despite signs of change, there is still a notable gender gap, with mothers devoting more *time* to daily direct care and assuming the bulk of *responsibility* for planning and coordinating caring work. Illustrating this, the analysis by Kan and colleagues (2011) discussed in the last section, which considered 16 countries (including Canada) from the 1960s to the early 2000s, found relatively modest changes in child-care patterns, with women still assuming the bulk of *time* involved in children's care, despite an increase in father's contributions.

In Canada, several studies shed additional light on these patterns. In terms of general trends, Milan et al. (2011: 20) found that, even in 2011, mothers still spent roughly twice as much time, on average, caring for children than fathers: 2.05 hours for every hour by men (or 50.1 hours per week for mothers, compared to 24.4 hours for fathers). The gender gap in weekly hours was narrowest in dual-earner families where women worked part-time (1.47 hours for women for every one hour by men). Not surprisingly, mothers of young children (four years old or less) devoted the most time to childcare (2.23 hours for women for every hour by men). But the gender gap in hours narrowed amongst parents with school-aged children, suggesting that "involved fathering" may increase as children age (Doucet 2018; Ball and Daly 2012).

More in-depth analysis of the GSS data from 1986 to 2015 offers further insights. Focusing on the unpaid work of parents, Houle et al. (2017) find that fathers contribute more time to childcare and other traditionally "female" household tasks now than in the past. Yet the researchers also show how gender gaps in time spent and the gender segregation of tasks persist, not only in child-care but also in other household tasks, as shown in in Figure 7.1. Examining this same period, but with more sophisticated analytical techniques, Guppy et al. (2019) argue that, despite the very slow rate of change, the trend toward gender convergence in childcare is "the story" in Canada over the past 30 years. In particular, they find that the presence of children in a family increases the time spent on childcare for mothers *and* fathers alike, and that this holds regardless of other factors, such as education, age, and employment status. In their view, we are seeing an important cultural shift toward "intensive parenting," not just "intensive mothering." Moreover, evidence suggests it is a broad cultural change across education and age groups, not simply isolated to cultural forerunners (e.g., "Hipster dads").

FIGURE 7.1 Percentage of Total Hours Spent by Parents in Housework and Caring, by Specific Activity, Canada, 1986 and 2015

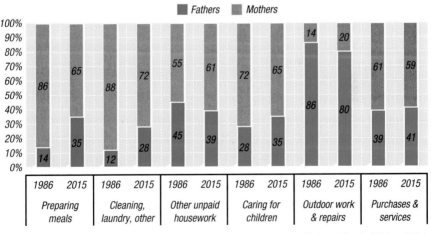

Source: Adapted from Houle et al. (2017: 5) *Changes in Parent's Participation in Domestic Tasks and Care for Children, 1986 to 2015*. Ottawa: Statistics Canada Catalogue no. 89-652-X2017001.

Such trends are encouraging from the perspective of gender equality, although the snail's pace of change is certainly highlighted by Figure 7.1. Whether trends of gender convergence persist in Canada is an important question for future research, as are questions of how changing economic opportunities and cultural attitudes are shaping trends. For example, Pedulla and Thébaud (2015) find that, in the United States, both young women and young men prefer egalitarian relationship structures (shared earning/caring), regardless of education, if that option is available. For young women, this preference is especially strong in situations where supportive work–family policies are available.

Eldercare

Caring for elderly parents and relatives is another important part of household work. Population aging (discussed in Chapter 3) has significant implications for the future, especially for women who have historically carried responsibility for eldercare. From a policy standpoint, *eldercare* is seen as a pressing issue in Canada and many other industrialized countries, and there are predictions of a "caregiving crunch" as fewer women can meet such demands because of their own jobs.[12] According to the most recent Statistics Canada data available, the 2012 GSS, roughly 8 million Canadians provided care to an aging, disabled, or chronically ill family member or friend at some point in the past year (Sinha 2012: 4). Caring for parents was the most common form of care; indeed, nearly half of caregivers (48 percent) reported that they provided care for either their own parents or parents-in-law. Typically caregivers were between the ages of 45–65 years of age. Over one-quarter of informal caregivers are part of the "sandwich generation," juggling eldercare with caring for their own children (Sinha 2013: 12; Duxbury and Higgins 2012, 2018).

What is involved in providing eldercare? According to the 2012 GSS, those helping an elderly parent or in-law spent between three and four hours, on average, each week. Of note, a small minority (about 7 percent) put in the equivalent of a full-time job with 30 hours or more of caregiving each week. Typically, the main reason for providing care to a parent, parent-in-law, or grandparent was their age and frailty, followed by specific medical conditions, such as dementia, cancer, and cardiovascular disease. The most common forms of care involved phoning and visiting (reported by 99 percent) and offering emotional support (92 percent), followed by transportation (41 percent) and meals and cleaning (37 percent). Women were slightly more likely than men to provide care to aging family members and were also at greater risk of reporting psychological distress or health impacts as a result.[13] Overall, about 60 percent of those caring for parents felt worried or distressed by their responsibilities, and about one-third had an elevated level of psychological distress (Turcotte 2013: 6–12).

Recognizing the growing demands of eldercare, the federal government introduced Compassionate Care benefits in 2004, which provided eight weeks of paid leave (through Employment Insurance) to care for a gravely ill family member. This development was important but, as with other employment-related benefits, there were barriers to these benefits because of insufficient employment-related hours and earnings or the care relationship or medical situation involved. In 2015, the federal government increased leave to 26 weeks; however, eligibility is still restricted to situations involving critically ill or dying family members, neglecting more chronic, long-lasting illnesses that are typical of aging (Stall 2019). This is a public policy concern, given that eldercare demands are expected to grow in the future, because of population aging, smaller families, and government policies emphasizing informal, family caregiving over formal, institutionalized supports (Bielski 2019; Duxbury and Higgins 2012, 2018).

Kin and Volunteer/Community Work

Two other important types of household work occur *across* and *beyond* households.

Kin work describes a wide range of work that goes into building and maintaining family ties, through communication, ritual celebrations, and the exchange of resources (di Leonardo 1987). Examples of kin work include regular or periodic phone calls, cards, and visits, as well as e-mails, texts, or Facebook posts to share family news. Special celebrations—such as birthdays, anniversaries, Thanksgiving, or other seasonal, religious, and secular holidays—are also important, creating shared family bonds, traditions, and memories. Exchanging resources is also a part of kin work—for example, sharing children's clothing, toys, tools, recipes, photos, and family history.

Kin work, like domestic work, involves not only the doing but also the mental work of conceiving, initiating, and organizing such work. It may involve pleasant tasks, such as organizing a family reunion or birthday, or difficult work, such as helping family members patch up a dispute. Studies suggest kin work is important because it fulfills deeply held cultural expectations of a satisfying family life (di Leonardo 1987). Typically, it falls to women, even when it does not involve their side of the family (e.g., in-laws or distant relatives on their partner's side). In her study of kin work, di Leonardo (1987) found it involved extensive knowledge and skill, and thus was not easily "outsourced" or passed along to others. Given this, women may often cut back on kin work during times of competing demands or stress.

Volunteer work is an equally important form of work often overlooked if we rely only on official labour force statistics. According to the 2013 GSS on Giving, Volunteering and Participation, more than four in ten (44 percent) Canadians ages 15 and over (or 12.7 million individuals) contributed time and energy to volunteer activities in 2013, down slightly from 47 percent in 2010. Canadians volunteered about 1.96 billion hours in 2013, equivalent to nearly 1 million full-time jobs. Between 2004 and 2013, the average number of hours that each volunteer contributed has declined slightly (from 168 hours to 154 hours, respectively). Younger Canadians, especially those ages 15 to19, are most likely to volunteer. This may reflect, in part, community service requirements in school programs, but many young people also volunteer to enhance their resumés and, thus, increase their chances of finding satisfactory paid work. Participation is also high for middle-aged parents, who may be helping in their children's schools and sport activities. Finally, while older Canadians are less likely to volunteer, those who do contribute many more hours, which may reflect greater time availability in retirement.[14]

Volunteer workers are found in a wide variety of clubs and associations, as well as in religious and political organizations. However, a very large number work in the publicly funded service industries, assisting in the provision of health, social, recreational, educational, environmental, and other types of services. In recent years, as governments at all levels have cut costs, volunteers have increasingly replaced paid employees—in schools, for instance, where parent-volunteers play a growing role, helping in libraries, in classrooms, and on field trips.

For individuals, volunteering provides satisfaction in helping others and contributing to one's community. It may also aid work and career interests. In her study *Opting Out?*, Pamela Stone (2007) notes that women who quit demanding professional jobs to raise young children often enjoyed volunteering as a way to maintain adult connections, overcome isolation at home, and retain a sense of their professional identity. Likewise, volunteering may offer opportunities to develop new skills and knowledge, and to expand social and professional networks (Turcotte 2015). Indeed, some employers actively support employee volunteering for these reasons, in addition to a corporate commitment to give back to the communities in which they operate.

BALANCING WORK AND FAMILY

Over three decades ago in her classic study *The Second Shift*, U.S. sociologist Arlie Hochschild observed (1989: 12):

> Work has changed. Women have changed. . . . But most workplaces have remained inflexible in the face of the family demands of their workers and at home, most men have yet to really adapt to the changes in women. This strain between the change in women and the absence of change in much else leads me to speak of a "stalled revolution."

Today, researchers continue to debate the extent of change, as noted in previous sections. While recent evidence suggests gender convergence, rather than a stalled revolution (England 2010; Guppy et al. 2019), the slow pace of change underscores that there is still a long way to go to fully reconcile work and family life (Correll et al. 2014; Pedulla and Thébaud 2015; J. Williams 2010).

Work–Family Conflict

One consequence of women's labour force participation, and the rise of dual-earner families, is work–family conflict and role overload. *Work–family conflict* involves mutually incompatible demands arising from work and family domains (Greenhaus and Beutell 1985: 77). *Role overload* involves having more role demands than one can possibly fulfill (Duxbury and Higgins 2018: 127). While some researchers use these terms interchangeably, others view them as distinct, noting that *overload* leads to *conflict* only when there are no mechanisms (e.g., resources or time flexibility) to help people meet their responsibilities. For example, as noted previously, having extra income allows families to buy household help, prepared meals, or other time-saving conveniences. Researchers also make distinctions based on the *directionality* of conflict.[15] *Work-to-family conflict* occurs when workplace demands interfere with family needs—for instance, a parent missing a family birthday because of a meeting or an evening shift. *Family-to-work conflict* occurs when family interferes with work—for example, a child's illness preventing a parent from being at work.

Distinctions can also be made by the perceived *nature* of conflict. In their classic article, Greenhaus and Buetell (1985) identified three key types of conflict. *Time-based conflict* is by far the most commonly studied type of conflict, arising when it is physically impossible to meet the time demands of different roles (e.g., official work hours prevent a parent from dropping off or picking up a child at school). *Strain-based conflict* focuses on the physical, mental, and emotional fatigue attached to meeting competing work and family demands—for example, lacking the energy to play with one's children or help with homework, when one gets home from work. Finally, *behaviour-based conflict* occurs when work and family behaviours are incompatible. For instance, managers and supervisors who act in an authoritarian, commanding manner at work may experience difficulties at home in caring for young children who need emotional warmth, connection, and flexibility. Recent research also identifies *place-based* work–family conflict caused by work-related travel and mobility demands (see Hughes and Silver 2019).

How common is work–family conflict? Empirical studies suggest it affects a significant proportion of the workforce in Canada, the United States, and other industrialized countries. Prevalence rates vary, however, depending on occupational roles, workplace demands, and family composition.[16] In Canada, three large-scale surveys conducted by Duxbury and Higgins—The National Study on Balancing Work and Caregiving in Canada—have tracked trends in 1991, 2001, and 2011.[17] Overall, these studies confirm that *role overload* and *work–family conflict* are significant issues for the working population in Canada, or at least those working in large private and public sector organizations surveyed by these researchers. In 1991, nearly one-half of respondents (47 percent) reported high levels of role overload, while over one-quarter (28 percent) reported high levels of work-to-family conflict. Rates of high family-to-work conflict were much lower, with just 5 percent of respondents reporting this (Duxbury and Higgins 2001: 14). In 2011, 40 percent of their survey respondents reported high role overload, and 30 percent reported high levels of work-to-family conflict. Of note, a larger proportion of respondents (15 percent) reported high levels of family-to-work conflict (Duxbury and Higgins 2012: 13).

What about trends in more recent years? Many commentators argue that workers are under increasing stress, due to 24/7 work cultures and mobile technologies. Rising eldercare demands, caused by population aging, also mean that more workers in Canada's aging workforce are juggling childcare and eldercare as part of the "sandwich generation" (Duxbury and Higgins 2018). Statistics Canada data sheds some light on Canadian worker's experience of work–family conflict and work–family balance in recent years, drawing on a larger and more representative sample than Duxbury and Higgins: the 2016 GSS. Concerning work–family conflict, one in five (21 percent) working Canadians in 2016 indicated that they "always" or "often" had difficulties fulfilling family responsibilities because of the amount of time they spent on the job (work-to-family conflict). Roughly 6 percent indicated that family interfered with their work (family-to-work conflict). With respect to work–family balance, 68 percent of Canadians reported being "satisfied" or "very satisfied" with their work–life balance in 2016. Yet this is lower than reported levels of satisfaction (75 percent) in 2008 (Statistics Canada 2017).

Consequences of Work–Family Conflict

Work–family conflict has many negative outcomes for individuals and their families.[18] In their 2018 book, *Something's Got to Give: Balancing Work, Childcare and Eldercare*, Duxbury and Higgins draw from their extensive research to show how work–family conflict is experienced by workers as they juggle childcare and eldercare. In their interviews with working Canadians, feelings of stress, guilt, and exhaustion were common themes, as was concern over "negative spillover" to family life:

> I felt stressed because I was worried about losing my parent . . . and I wasn't able to be there as much as I wanted to be. I felt . . . overwhelmed because I had things going on at work. I had to get back to work. I couldn't even deal full-time with the family crisis that was going on because I felt like I was needed in two places at once. I'm in a position at work where it's competitive. If you don't give 150 per cent you lose your position. (p. 135)

My spouse feels I should be at home more, and I have to balance it out so that they [my mother, my husband] don't get into an argument . . . the whole thing is having a horribly negative impact on my children. So yes, the challenge is huge, and that's on a daily basis. (p. 140)

You're tired physically; you're tired mentally thinking of what more you could do or should do to alleviate the situation . . . while at the same time trying to protect your own household and your job. It's overwhelming. (p. 125)

Such consequences are also confirmed in more comprehensive studies, using meta-analysis (in which data from many studies are pooled to identify statistically significant relationships). For example, Amstad and colleagues (2011) found that work–family conflict was significantly related to higher stress, exhaustion, and burnout, and to lower job satisfaction and organizational commitment. Reich et al. (2016) also found significant links between work–family conflict and reported levels of exhaustion and cynicism.[19]

Pressures created by work–family conflict are costly for employees, their families, and employers too. As Linda Duxbury and Chris Higgins (2018) discuss, employees who experience high work–family conflict report notably higher rates of absenteeism and turnover, as well as reduced levels of productivity and organizational commitment. Absenteeism is a significant source of lost productivity for employers. According to Statistics Canada, female rates of absenteeism have risen steadily since the late 1970s, mainly due to family or personal obligations as more mothers with preschool children entered employment. In 2018, for example, employed women lost an average of 12.3 days, compared to 8.3 for men, to illness, disability, or personal and family responsibilities (Statistics Canada, Table 14-10-0190-01).

While Canadian employers are increasingly aware of the value of family-friendly work environments, firms in the most dynamic sectors of the economy are still often defined by heavy workloads and long hours. These high-pressure workplace cultures are not sustainable, however. They may suit younger, single workers who have no dependents, but a lack of attention to work–life balance issues does cause problems (e.g., high turnover) as workers move into their 30s, find life partners, and begin raising children of their own. Recent Canadian research by Gordon (2014) confirms the lack of fit for workers with family responsibilities in IT firms, noting the challenges of "rigid" versus more "flexible" firms. Importantly, flexibility and work–life balance are a growing priority for many younger knowledge workers, including those without family responsibilities who simply want adequate time for friendships, community, and leisure (Wilkinson et al. 2017). Increasingly there is growing awareness about the costs of "greedy organizations" (Coser 1967) and "the culture of long work hours" (Burke and Cooper 2008; Correll et al. 2014). In countries such as the United Kingdom and Australia, there is now a "National Go Home On Time" day, intended to spark debate on work–family conflict and overwork (Petter 2019).

Policies Supporting Work–Family Reconciliation

What types of policies and supports help individuals reconcile their work, family, and personal responsibilities? Research suggests that flexible work hours and schedules, generous personal and family-related leave, the ability to refuse overtime, and the presence of supportive managers are all important (Butts et al. 2013; Kelly et al. 2014; Duxbury and Higgins 2018). Slowly, in part because of studies like these, heightened awareness of the costs of work–family conflict is challenging employers to reconsider long-standing workplace practices and policies. Yet many employers remain locked into a traditional 9 to 5, five-days-a-week schedule, leaving workers without flexibility in the hours or location of their work (Correll et al. 2014). Information technologies make it easy for work to intrude into employees' family lives far beyond regular work hours, though workers in France have a legal "right to disconnect" electronic devices outside regular business hours—something the Canadian government is now considering (Press 2018). Many employees also lack extended employer-sponsored coverage for paid parental or eldercare leave (beyond standard government-provisioned leaves), or may be unable to take full advantage of such policies because of insufficient earnings or hours. Ironically, it is often already privileged workers, with "good job" rewards, who have the most flexibility and control in their schedules and the resources to hire help for family and household tasks (Gordon 2014; Kossek and Lautsch 2018). Yet flexibility for these workers can also lead to blurred work–family boundaries, leading to higher stress (Schieman and Glavin 2016).

Chapter 7: Household, Family, and Caring Work **243**

Looking at Figure 7.2, we can see that many Canadian workers have quite limited flexibility in their day-to-day work. While the majority can take a paid day off work when a child is sick, or take holidays at the desired time, beyond this there is much less flexibility, especially to deal with many routine, day-to-day, family needs. For instance, a majority of Canadians find it difficult to work from home for part of the day, or to be home to meet children, or to pick them up after school. Roughly one-third of workers have little control over their work schedules, being unable to vary arrival and departure times, control the time of their specific shifts or overtime, interrupt and return to work in the case of family emergencies, or take a paid day off to help sick children or elderly relatives.

There are many barriers to creating more flexible, family-friendly, workplaces. One of the largest is the fact that society places great value, and confers rewards, on people who are successful in their careers. Sociologists note

FIGURE 7.2   Flexible Workplace Options, Canada, 2011

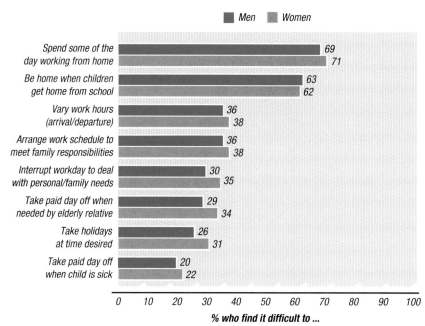

Source: Based on: Duxbury, Linda, and Christopher Higgins. (2012). *Key Findings: Revisiting Work–Life Issues in Canada—The 2011–12 National Study on Balancing Work and Caregiving in Canada*, p. 17. <http://newsroom.carleton.ca/wp-content/files/2012-National-Work-Key-Findings.pdf

how organizations are built around norms of the "ideal worker"—typically, someone who works long hours, is highly committed, and ready to put work first. Research suggest that those who deviate from these norms face difficulties. For instance, mothers (and fathers) who take advantage of flexible working arrangements (e.g., reduced hours, parental leave) may experience "flexibility stigmas" that impact their careers and future opportunities (Williams, Blair-Loy, and Berdahl 2013; Munsch 2016).

Given this, many workers may be reluctant to take advantage of such options. Yet studies confirm the benefits of greater flexibility and work–family supports. Kossek et al.'s (2011) meta-analysis shows that organizational and supervisory support, especially support that is specific to work–family challenges, is significantly related to reduced levels of work–family conflict. Likewise, Butts et al.'s (2013) meta-analysis shows that the availability and use of work–family support policies has a positive effect on job satisfaction and organizational commitment. Finally, work by Duxbury and Higgins (2012, 2018) confirms that work–family conflict is a workplace issue, not a personal one. Work–family policies and supports benefit both employees and organizations, improving job satisfaction, employee morale, and organizational commitment.

Governments are increasingly recognizing the potential benefits of stronger work–family supports—including more flexible parental leaves, better eldercare support, or enhanced early childhood care. For instance, the federal Liberal government is currently considering making it a person's right to request flexible work arrangements, as is the case Australia, New Zealand, and the United Kingdom (ESDC 2016). In their 2018 Budget, the federal government also emphasized the importance of stronger work–family supports for economic growth and gender equality, seeing these issues as closely connected. A central policy change was providing more generous and flexible maternity and parental leave, including use-them-or-lose-them "Daddy Days" designed to encourage greater take-up by fathers (these changes to the federal program emulate policies already in place in Quebec). Nevertheless, there are still significant class differences in the ability of working mothers and fathers to access benefits and take leaves, given that eligibility is tied to annual working hours and benefits range from 33 to 55 percent of earnings (McKay and Doucet 2016).

Finally, an emerging area of law on "family accommodation" in Canada and the United States suggests that employers may increasingly need to consider how work schedules, hours, and traditional practices affect working parents. In their article "Will Working Mothers Take Your Company to Court?" U.S. legal scholar Joan Williams and Amy Cuddy (2012) outline recent U.S. rulings that require companies to accommodate the needs of parents and caregivers (including elder-caregivers) where possible. Likewise, in Canada, the 2014 case of *Johnstone v. Canadian Border Services Agency (CBSA)* saw the Canadian Human Rights Tribunal rule that the CBSA had engaged in "family status" discrimination when it refused Fiona Johnstone's request for a regular schedule rather than an irregular day/night schedule that changed every six weeks, making it impossible for her to find reliable childcare.[20] Evidence presented showed the CBSA could have easily accommodated Johnstone's request, as they had done for other employees, and Johnstone was therefore awarded damages. Legal decisions such as these will hopefully help to ensure that employers take work–family issues seriously.

Early Childhood Education and Care

Of all types of support, quality childcare is perhaps the most pressing need. According to the report *Early Childhood Education and Care in Canada 2016* (Friendly et al. 2018), child-care arrangements present an ongoing problem for many parents in Canada—although preferences for different forms of child-care (e.g., family, informal, formal) vary widely (see also Statistics Canada 2019). Despite past promises by Canadian governments to improve child-care availability, the number of licensed child-care spaces by no means fills the need. In 2016, for example, there were 1,350,387 regulated child-care spaces (for children up to 12 years old) across Canada, up from 371,563 in 1992 (Friendly et al. 2018). This figure represents a nearly four-fold increase in available spaces, a positive change given the historical heel-dragging that has accompanied efforts to build a system of early childhood care in Canada (Langford et al. 2017). But even with this increase, regulated child-care spaces still only accommodate a small fraction of what is needed.

Availability, cost, and quality are all challenges to building an adequate child-care system. With respect to *availability*, in Canada the Childcare Resource and Research Unit at the University of Toronto has produced regular reports on provincial trends in childcare provision. Their most recent reports, analyzing trends to 2016, highlight ongoing shortages of child-care spots (Friendly et al. 2018). Nationally, in 2016, regulated full-time or part-time child-care spaces were available for just 28.9 percent of children five and under. Though up from 14.9 percent in 2001, this percentage still falls well short of what is needed, given that roughly three-quarters of mothers with preschool children are employed (Friendly et al. 2018: 166, 169). Care shortages also exist for older, school-age children (e.g., after-school programs), and roughly 30 percent are in the for-profit sector, with higher fees. With respect to cost, average full-time fees vary widely, from a high in Ontario of $1,758/month (for infants) and $1,354/month (for toddlers), to a low of $183 per month for infant and toddler care in Quebec's publicly subsidized system (Friendly et al. 2018: 161).

So far, Quebec is the only jurisdiction in Canada to make a concerted effort to address these issues: in 1997, it introduced a comprehensive program of universal subsidized daycare and early childhood education (Albanese 2006). Despite further change to existing programs (including an increase in cost from the original $5 per day to a sliding scale of $8 to $22 per day, depending on income), Quebec remains a leader in child-care access, offering regulated spaces to over 38 percent of children five years of age and under (Friendly et al. 2018: 170).[21] Still, even with such changes, finding high-quality, accessible childcare remains a challenge for many working parents. Given the high costs and low availability of regulated spaces, many children of working parents are looked after informally by sitters, neighbours, nannies, or relatives (Statistics Canada 2019: 2). While about two-thirds of parents report being able to find child-care in their community, over one-third experience difficulties with respect to the proximity, affordability, or quality of care, or the suitability to their work schedule. For those experiencing challenges, 10 percent had to change their work schedule, 7 percent worked fewer hours, and 6 percent postponed their return to work (Statistics Canada 2019: 4–5).

MARKETIZATION OF CARE AND THE "OUTSOURCED FAMILY"

Women's increased labour force participation has sparked a growing market for household and caring services in the formal economy, including childcare, house-cleaning, restaurant meals, and prepared deli and grocery food. Such developments respond to growing time pressures and "care deficits" within the home, yet require families to buy in services and—in the words of Robert Reich

(2000) and Arlie Hochschild (2012)—"outsource" family life. In Canada, estimates from Statistics Canada for the early 2000s found that the value of the domestic market for childcare was more than $3.5 billion (Anderson and Hughes 2010). Of note, nearly one-third of dual-earner families purchased childcare and one in 10 families purchased some type of house-cleaning service. Consumption was heavily tied to income, but even among low-income, female-headed households (typically the most financially strapped), more than one-quarter purchased childcare.

Examining this phenomenon in her study *The Outsourced Self,* Arlie Hochschild (2012) catalogues a wide array of family and household work that was once done in the home but is now being purchased in local, regional, and national markets in North America. Childcare is certainly common. But Hochschild also shows an ever-expanding range of services, much of it in the "gig economy." Beyond basic domestic assistance, such as Molly Maid, other businesses—such as BrightNest, Thumbtack, TaskRabbit, and Rent-A-Hubby—cover household repairs, outdoor work, snow shovelling, lawn mowing, and grocery delivery. Special celebrations and "kin work" can also be purchased, with children's birthdays and family gatherings falling under the purview of party planners. Other services, such as Kids in Motion and Driving Miss Daisy, Inc., help get children and elderly family members safely to school, activities, and medical and other appointments. Cooking services, such as Hello Fresh and Chefs Plate, which deliver ready to cook meals, as well as personal shoppers, who purchase gifts or run time-consuming errands, are also increasingly in demand.

Developments such as these illustrate how families are adapting to workplace demands and also highlight the fluid, ever-changing boundary between market and household work. They also illustrate how parents' search for better work–life balance is contributing to the rise of the gig economy. At the same time, the marketization of household and caring work draws sharp attention to the ways in which hierarchies based on class, race, and citizenship are reproduced. As Canadians increasingly outsource family life, they come to rely on systems of *transnational caregiving* and *stratified reproduction*—hiring working-class women and women from countries in the Global South to provide paid care as nannies or as child-care and eldercare workers, or to cook, clean, and work as housekeepers and domestic cleaners (Ehrenreich and Hochschild 2002; Duffy 2011).[22] The growing gig economy of delivery drivers draws heavily on immigrants and youth. Such arrangements may solve care deficits in one home while creating new problems, worsening inequalities and care deficits in the families of paid caregivers, both within and outside Canada.

CONCLUSION

We began this chapter by noting the often invisible nature of household and caring work, and the persistence of women's responsibility for family life. We also questioned whether gendered patterns of household caring work have shifted in recent decades as more women work as earners and breadwinners than ever before. Certainly, many people have expected to see men play a growing role in the household as women's labour force participation began to rise in the 1970s. Accumulating evidence shows small degrees of change—for example, gender convergence in household work and caring for children. Overall, however, the pace of change is slow. Reductions in the gender gap in family work stem as much, if not more, from women reducing the time they devote to certain tasks than to men dramatically expanding their contributions. But recent analysis in Canada does suggest change may be more broadly based than was previously thought.

Increasingly, one way North American families are reconciling work and family life is through outsourcing—a trend that has fuelled the growth of low paid caring work, the gig economy and the reproduction of gender-, race-, and class-based inequalities, given that such work is typically done by women, immigrants, and those with little education. Another response has been to limit family size or simply not have children—thus fuelling trends toward population aging in Canada, as we discussed in Chapter 3.

With many employers offering only limited options for effectively balancing work and family life—despite growing attention to the need for more family-friendly workplaces—these patterns are perhaps not surprising. Further, they reflect Canada's failure to develop a system of affordable, accessible, quality child-care (with Quebec being an exception). Within this context, families struggle to juggle work and household demands, with high rates of work–family conflict for a sizable group of workers Those who can afford to do so may opt out of paid work to nurture young children (typically the mother, though stay-at-home dads are a small but growing trend). Such choices, however, carry high costs for individual caregivers, reducing future earnings and job prospects, and creating risks of poverty and financial insecurity in cases of family breakdown. Sociologists, especially feminist analysts, have long noted that the costs of raising families are borne largely by individuals (mainly women), while there are many benefits that flow to the society as a whole (e.g., a new generation of health care workers, teachers, service workers, entrepreneurs who fill jobs, teach children, provide care, and so on). Shifting from a *universal breadwinner* model (which assumes that workers are endlessly available for paid work and free of caring responsibilities) to a *universal caregiver* model (which recognizes the caring responsibilities of all workers)[23] would go a long way to recognizing the economic value of care, while reducing gender and other social inequalities, and resolving persistent problems of work–family conflict.

DISCUSSION QUESTIONS

1. Discuss the changing relationship between household work and market work in the course of Canada's economic development. How has the work in each domain changed in the transition from a preindustrial, to an industrial, to a postindustrial society?
2. What is meant by the terms *household work* and *social reproduction*? What types of activities do these terms refer to?
3. Discuss key trends in women's and men's contributions to housework, childcare, and eldercare. How much change has taken place? How do we explain these patterns?
4. What is work–family conflict? What are specific types of work–family conflict and how do they affect working women and men?
5. What steps are employers and governments taking to assist in reducing work–family conflict? What other types of supports might be helpful to working Canadians?

ADDITIONAL RESOURCES

WORK AT THE MOVIES

- *Sorry We Missed You* (directed by Kenneth Loach, 2019, 100:00 minutes). This Cannes Film Festival–nominated film examines challenges faced by two British contract workers, Ricky (a delivery driver for Amazon) and

Abby (a mobile nurse who provides paid care for seniors), and their son, as they juggle work and family, zero-hour contracts, and the pressures of the gig economy.

- *Erin Brockovich* (directed by Steven Soderbergh and Susannah Grant, 2000, 132:00 minutes). This is the dramatization of a true story of a single mother of three children who fought against the giant energy corporation Pacific Gas and Electric (PG&E). In fighting against PG&E's environmental crimes, Erin faces daily challenges balancing a high stress job with parenting.

- *The Motherload* (directed by Cornelia Principe, 2014, 45:10 minutes). Focusing on working women in Canada, this documentary examines the challenges they face as they struggle to balance work and family. It is available through CBC Doc Zone: http://www.cbc.ca/doczone/episodes/motherload.

- *When Strangers Re-Unite* (directed by Florchita Bautista and Marie Boti, 1999, 52 minutes). This NFB documentary explores the challenges faced by foreign domestic workers in Canada navigating through the immigration process, dealing with being separated from their families back home, and reuniting with family as they eventually come to Canada.

- *Baby Mama* (directed by Michael McCullers, 2008, 99 minutes). A successful single businesswoman hires a working-class woman to be her surrogate child-bearer.

SOUNDS OF WORK

- "The Scaffolder's Wife" (Mark Knopfler). Knopfler's song describes the struggles of the wife of a scaffolder whose hard work, keeping company books, has helped their business stay afloat.

- "Nice Work If You Can Get It" (George Gershwin). The song champions care work, family, and human connections over paid work.

- "One's on the Way" (Loretta Lynn). Lynn describes the unpaid work that often falls to women. Her song highlights the various kinds of work women perform for the home and as caregivers.

- "Somebody's Hero" (Jamie O'Neal). Here is an ode to the women who forgo paid work to perform essential housework and care work. O'Neal's heroes work as cooks, waiters, and taxi drivers, only for no pay.

NOTES

1. News articles on the strike appeared in the *Globe and Mail*, *The Telegraph*, and *The Calgary Herald*. A personal account is provided by Stilwell at http://strikingmom. blogspot.ca/.
2. For discussions of patriarchy, see Hartmann (1976), Acker (1989), and Walby (1990).
3. This post–World War II pattern is described in a classic work by Ostry (1968). See also Canada, Department of Labour (1958). On the concept of breadwinning, see Warren (2007).
4. For a discussion of how married and pregnant women were expected to exit paid jobs, see Sangster (1995). For a personal account of a pioneering Canadian woman who transgressed cultural norms by working throughout her pregnancies, see *Rebel Daughter* by Doris Anderson (1996).
5. Calculations are from Statistics Canada, Table 11-10-0028-01, Single-Earner and Dual-Earner Census Families by Number of Children. For additional information on families, living arrangements, and unpaid work in Canada, see Milan (2015).
6. See Pupo (1997), Marshall (2006), and Beaujot and Anderson (2007) for recent trends in Canadian families. For classic studies of household divisions of labour, see Luxton (1980) and Duffy and Pupo (1992). For valuable conceptual discussions of household work, see Eichler and Albanese (2007). For poems on household work, see Treathaway (2000).
7. For surveys of trends and literature on this topic, see Altintas and Sullivan (2016), Beaujot et al. (2017), Bianchi et al. (2012), Coltrane (2000), Doucet (2018), and Kan et al. (2011). For studies of fathers' changing contributions to housework and caring, see Cunningham (2007), Gupta (2006), and Hook (2006).
8. Data are from the 1990 General Social Survey (GSS). A note of caution: There is some bias in how the survey measures housework because it is based on the perceptions of only one respondent per household.

9. See Marshall (2006: 10–13) for more details. Doucet (2018), Coltrane (2000), and McFarlane, Beaujot, and Haddad (2000) provide excellent overviews of research in this area.

10. Early research in the United Kingdom and United States finds more egalitarian patterns in time use and domestic responsibility in same-sex households (Dunne 1996; Sullivan 1996). For an alternative perspective, see Pfeffer (2017: Chapter 3).

11. On fathering, see Doucet (2018), Ball and Daly (2012), and Fox, Pascall, and Warren (2009). On mothering, see Blair-Loy (2003), Hays (1996), McMahon (2005), and Stone (2007). On parenting, see Ranson (2010), Nelson (1996), and Fox (1997).

12. For valuable discussions and overviews of recent trends in Canada, see Duxbury and Higgins (2012, 2018), Turcotte (2013), Stonebridge (2013), and Sinha (2013).

13. While Turcotte (2013) does not examine gender patterns in detail, analysis of the 2010 General Social Survey by Milan et al. (2011: 24) shows that women typically provide many more hours of care to seniors.

14. For more information about the voluntary sector, visit the websites of the Voluntary Sector Initiative (http://www.vsi-isbc.org) and Imagine Canada, which represents voluntary and nonprofit organizations (http://www.imaginecanada.ca). For a more theoretical analysis of volunteer work, based on trends in the United States, see Wilson (2000). An interesting discussion of community work is provided by Uttal (2009).

15. Concepts and measurement are discussed in Bellavia and Frone (2005), Carlson and Grzywacz (2008), and Greenhaus and Beutell (1985).

16. For valuable reviews and discussions, see Bellavia and Frone (2005), Bianchi and Milkie (2010), Byron (2005), Kelly, Murphy, and Kaskubar (2008), Korabik, Lero, and Whitehead (2008), Williams et al. (2016), and Hughes and Silver (2019).

17. See Duxbury and Higgins (2001), Duxbury (2004), and Duxbury and Higgins (2012). The 1991 study surveyed 37,000 employees across Canada, while the 2001 study surveyed close to 33,000 employees in 100 medium to large Canadian organizations: for details, see Duxbury (2004: 1–2). The third survey, conducted in 2011, surveyed more than 25,000 Canadians working in 71 public, private, and nonprofit organizations (Duxbury and Higgins 2012; 2018).

18. For excellent reviews and meta-analysis on such outcomes, see Bellavia and Frone (2005), Dorio, Bryant, and Allen (2008), Mullen, Kelley, and Kelloway (2008), and Amstad (2011).

19. In earlier meta-analyses, Allen and colleagues (2000) found strong links between high work–family conflict and reduced job satisfaction, reduced life satisfaction, and higher stress, while Kossek and Ozeki (1998) concluded there was clear evidence of a "negative relationship between all types of work–family conflict and job and life satisfaction" (p. 145).

20. For an overview and discussion of *Johnstone v. CBSA*, see the Legal Education and Action Fund (LEAF) website at https://www.leaf.ca/leaf-intervening-in-johnstone-v-canada-border-services-agency-at-the-federal-court-of-appeal/.

21. For a useful overview of childcare policy in Quebec, see Arsenault et al. (2018). For a valuable and wide ranging discussion of childcare and care-related policy in Canada, see Langford et al. (2017).

22. For additional discussions of global care deficits, see Isaksen, Devi, and Hochschild (2008), Spitzer et al. (2003), and Zimmerman, Litt, and Bose (2006).

23. These ideas have been developed in a wide body of writing by feminist scholars, and are well articulated by Nancy Fraser (1997) in her article "After the Family Wage: A Post-Industrial Thought Experiment."

ORGANIZING AND MANAGING WORK

8

"In the call centre [where I worked] workers were constantly watched. Every action was logged, from the number of sales made, to the time spent on calls and the length of breaks taken—measured precisely to the second. Because calls were recorded, errors—which were often hard to avoid under such pressurised conditions—were used to discipline and fire workers on the spot.

"Adding to the weight of surveillance were gruelling targets. These targets were displayed on whiteboards at the end of each row of desks. A large TV hung from the ceiling showing a running total of how many sales each worker made, ranked in order.

"This environment was psychologically draining for many of the workers and created a very tangible feeling of precariousness. This precariousness was used as a managerial strategy to discipline and motivate workers, creating an oppressive, stressful, and exploitative workplace. The workers had to regulate their own behaviour, knowing that at any moment they could lose their job.

"The most effective motivator the managers had at their disposal was letting workers leave early if they met their targets. Rather than paying bonuses—or offering a decent flexible working policy to fit in with the employees' lives—the option to knock off a bit earlier was dangled as a carrot, and entirely on the employer's terms. This incentive to escape the workplace perhaps helps explain why there are astonishingly high turnover rates at call centres in the UK."

Source: Jamie Wookcock, As a Call Centre Worker I Saw How Employees are Stripped of Their Rights. [Retrieved January 23, 2019]: https://www.theguardian.com/careers/2017/feb/16/as-a-call-centre-worker-i-saw-how-employees-are-stripped-of-their-rights

INTRODUCTION

The word *bureaucracy* almost always has a negative connotation when used in conversation. It is typically associated with inefficiency and with a lack of caring. While the word *management* does not elicit quite the same negative reaction, it is seldom used to make a positive statement. Cartoonists love to lampoon bureaucracies ("we need to strike a committee to study the problem of bureaucracy") and, as the popular comic strip Dilbert reveals, managers are also in their sights. Yet over a century ago when industrial capitalism was beginning to reshape Western societies, bureaucracies were seen by organizational analysts as both necessary and efficient. As for managers, the goal was, and remains as we will see in this chapter and the next, to make them more effective.

We begin by reviewing Max Weber's assessment of bureaucracy, a topic first introduced in Chapter 1. We then go beyond the theory to examine the reality of large contemporary bureaucratic work organizations, focusing on some of the key problems with this organization form, particularly when merged with assembly-line production technologies. Our attention then shifts to the role of managers within large workplace bureaucracies. The core of this chapter is a detailed discussion of two major approaches to management that emerged in the past century—scientific management and the human relations approach. We examine their assumptions about human nature, their prescriptions for how best to manage workers, and their failings. Chapter 9 will assess some of the newer managerial paradigms that emerged in response to these failings in the latter half of the 20th century.

UNDERSTANDING BUREAUCRACY

As industrialization progressed in the latter half of the 19th century, craftwork gave way to an extensive division of labour (see Chapter 1). Less skilled labourers could perform narrow tasks more cheaply. But once all the parts of a craftworker's job had been simplified and reassigned, coordinating and integrating these tasks became a problem, particularly within the large factories that were emerging. Questions about how best to integrate and coordinate the activities of large numbers of workers within a single enterprise gave rise to organizational studies and theories of management.

The organizational structure most often adopted by 19th-century businesses was the bureaucratic hierarchy. Max Weber (1946) considered *bureaucracy* to be the organizational form best able to efficiently coordinate and integrate the multitude of specialized tasks conducted in a big factory or office (see Chapter 1). He believed that capitalism could not be successful without bureaucracies. Weber's description of them has, however, become the model for a highly mechanistic type of work organization. Gareth Morgan (1997: 15–17) defines *bureaucracies* as organizations "that emphasize precision, speed, clarity, reliability, and efficiency achieved through the creation of a fixed division of tasks, hierarchical supervision, and detailed rules and regulations."[1]

Bureaucracies were clearly an improvement over the tradition-bound and frequently disorganized methods used to run most 19th-century businesses. Their predictability, and their emphasis on qualifications and merit in recruitment and promotion, rather than favouritism, greatly increased the productivity of industrial capitalism. Furthermore, a bureaucracy is a system of authority. Its hierarchical structure, formal lines of authority, and impartial rules and regulations are designed to elicit cooperation and obedience from employees. In fact, with an elaborate hierarchical division of labour, employers can gain employee commitment by offering the prospect of career advancement (the internal labour markets described in Chapter 5). It would seem that bureaucratic work organizations are ideal.

The Problems of Bureaucracy

Most sociologists, however, along with many people who work in bureaucracies, would agree that bureaucracies have some serious flaws. Organizational researchers have shown that bureaucracies are often overly complex and rule-based, and therefore difficult to manage, resistant to change, and unable to cope with uncertainties. Working conditions in large bureaucracies are frequently unsatisfying. A paradox of bureaucracy is that, far from achieving machinelike efficiency, it often unintentionally creates inefficiency, a problem Weber largely failed to see.

The notion of bureaucratic efficiency rests, in part, on the assumption that employees will readily submit to *managerial authority*. In Weber's view, workers accept the legitimacy of the existing authority structure, abide by the rules, and obey their bosses because they believe the basis for such authority is impartial and fair. In other words, underlying capitalist bureaucracies is a *rational–legal value system*. The assumption that shared goals leads to a smoothly operating organization is questionable, however, given the realities of employee–employer relations (Roscigno et al. 2018), which are frequently punctuated by conflict and resistance (see Chapter 10). People in positions of power set organizational goals. These goals are, therefore, "rational" from management's perspective but not necessarily from the perspective of workers lower down in the hierarchy. What is rational for workers is what reflects their own interests and daily work experiences, such as a secure job, higher pay, a safer and more comfortable work environment, meaningful tasks, or more scope for making work-related decisions. As we will see later in this chapter, managers have gone to great lengths to try to convince workers to accept organizational goals as their own personal goals, hoping to gain worker compliance.

Ironically, organizational efficiency may also suffer because of workers and managers following rules too closely. Decades ago, Robert Merton (1952) described how employees can acquire a *bureaucratic personality*, compulsively following procedural rules to the last detail—often to the detriment of customers or clients (Bozeman and Rainey 1998). More recently, management researchers have coined the term *managing to audit* to describe an organizational culture in some bureaucracies that discourages risk-taking and innovation because managers are fearful of being blamed for mistakes or failures (Hood 2007).

The Informal Side of Organizations

Weber's description of bureaucracies focuses on their formal structure. But all work organizations, including bureaucracies, also have an *informal* side where employees reinterpret, resist, or adapt to work structures and management directives (Thompson 2016). The organizational charts found in corporate annual reports present management's image of how things ought to operate. Employees further down the hierarchy often see things differently and act accordingly, as Scott Adams, the creator of the Dilbert comic strip, has so effectively demonstrated.[2] Thus, to get a complete picture of a work organization, we must also examine employees' informal practices and social relations (Orbach et al. 2015). Some classic sociological studies of work organizations are insightful.

Donald Roy (1952) studied *informal work groups* by working as a machinist in a Chicago factory that ran on a *piecework payment system* and carefully observed how workers responded to management. Productivity was regulated by management through bonus payments for output that was above established quotas. The machinists invented ingenious shortcuts to maximize their wages while minimizing effort. Their informal system of production involved what in shop-floor jargon was called "gold-bricking." That is, on difficult jobs for which they could not possibly earn a bonus, workers relaxed and enjoyed some free time. On easy jobs, however, they could exceed the quota and receive a bonus. Any production beyond an unofficial quota was stored up in a "kitty" to be used to boost output figures on a slow day. Management rarely challenged the workers' system because production usually fluctuated within an acceptable range.

Managers sometimes also participate in similar manipulations of informal work practices. With limited authority over workers, many middle- and lower-level managers and supervisors feel constrained in their roles. Consequently, they may not entirely follow the directives of top executives. In *Men Who Manage*, Melville Dalton (1959) described how managers bent rules to achieve their objectives. "Freewheeling," or following unofficial practices rather than formal rules, was common in the organizations Dalton studied. Employees at all organizational levels engaged in what, to the outside observer, was dishonest activity. Workers borrowed tools and equipment; managers had home improvements done at company expense. The company's resources were dispensed as personal rewards in order to keep the bureaucracy running, to acknowledge someone's special services, or to solidify social relationships to get a job done.

Going beyond the informal side of bureaucracies, we sometimes also encounter the "dark side of organizations" where things have gone seriously wrong (Vaughan 1999). Examples of such mistakes, mishaps, or misconduct include the meltdown of banks and other financial institutions that led to a global economic crisis in 2008 and British Petroleum's *Deepwater Horizon* oil spill in the Gulf of Mexico in 2010. In Canada, the Royal Canadian Mounted Police (RCMP), a traditional bureaucracy with a strong military-style culture (Hansen 2018), provides another example. A recent review of the organization, for example, concluded that "for decades, the Royal Canadian Mounted Police has struggled with the problem of workplace harassment, bullying, intimidation, and sexual harassment" without managing to solve this serious problem.[3]

Bureaucracy and Fordism

As an organizing principle, the bureaucratic hierarchy was integrated with technology to create the huge factories that formed the backbone of industrial capitalism (Chapter 1). When Henry Ford introduced the moving assembly line in 1914, launching the era of mass-production manufacturing, the machine-like logic of bureaucratic organization was intensified. By the mid-20th century, *Fordism* dominated North American manufacturing, as well as other industrial sectors. As Robert Reich (1991: 51) observes:

> It is perhaps no accident that the [WW II] war veterans who manned the core American corporations of the 1950s accommodated so naturally to the militarylike hierarchies inside them. They were described in much the same terms as military hierarchies—featuring chains of command, spans of control, job classifications, divisions and division heads, and standard operating procedures to guide every decision.... As in the military, great emphasis was placed upon the maintenance of control—upon a superior's ability to inspire loyalty, discipline, and unquestioning obedience, and upon a subordinate's capacity to be so inspired.

In *The Work of Nations*, Reich (1991) described how, by the late-20th century, the distinction between the production of goods and services had become blurred. While the key to prosperity used to be large volume production in giant factories by corporations that dominated world markets, today specialized expertise in finance and research and development, as well as marketing, human resources, and information technologies, adds considerable value to products produced, and successful corporations are more flexible, responding quickly to market demands. With rapidly changing markets in the global economy, networked forms of business organization, including franchises, joint ventures, outsourcing, and strategic alliances, have become more common (Podolny and Page 1998).[4] Thus, by the beginning of the 21st century, Fordist bureaucracies had, to a large extent, become an outmoded model of organization and management.

But bureaucracies, and the management systems used within them, have certainly not disappeared. And we continue to encounter examples of the "dark side of organizations." As organizational researchers Samuel Culbert and Scott Schroeder (2003: 105) observed, "When it comes to the conduct of hierarchical relationships and how those with organizational authority are expected to direct and account, the 20th century concluded the way it began—with a steady stream of abuses, scandals, and exposés of hierarchy gone awry." So, even though a range of new, and to some extent improved, management approaches emerged in the second half of the 20th century (Chapter 9), we have good reason to continue our analysis of bureaucratic organizations and their management systems.

THE ROLE OF MANAGERS

Managers became a prominent new social group in the early 20th century. *Cost accounting* techniques for calculating how much each factor of production, including labour, contributes to profits was one way capitalists initially tackled the problems of running increasingly large and complex enterprises. Appointing trained managers, often factory engineers, was an equally important social innovation. As business historian Alfred D. Chandler Jr. suggests, the "visible hand" of the corporate manager replaced Adam Smith's "invisible hand" of market forces (Chandler 1977). Corporate boards of directors, representing the shareholders, delegated to managers the authority to operate the business profitably (see Chapter 2), giving them a great deal of power and responsibility.

But what exactly do managers do? In the most general sense, they try to obtain employee compliance and prevent opposition to authority. In this respect, the workplace is a microcosm of the larger society. Maintaining orderly and harmonious social relations among people who are not equals has always been a problem for those in power. Managers also try to motivate workers to achieve the quantity and quality of output considered necessary by those in charge of the organization. Ideally, they would like to generate employee engagement in the enterprise by convincing employees to work hard for the good of the organization (Macey and Schneider 2008). But employers in both the private and the public sectors, and the managers who work for them, have far from complete control over the attitudes, beliefs, and effort expended by employees. Hence, conflict often erupts over different perceptions of what should be expected in return for a specific wage and work environment, a topic discussed in detail in Chapter 10.

In assessing the role of managers, it is important to distinguish between what they say they do and why, and what they may really do and for what reasons. Henry Mintzberg (1989: 9) argues that the goals that supposedly guide managers are often vaguely defined: "If you ask managers what they do they will most likely tell you that they plan, organize, coordinate, and control.

Then watch what they do. Don't be surprised if you can't relate what you see to those four words." Mintzberg's advice underscores the importance of looking closely at how management theories are applied and at the results, something we will do in this chapter and the next. All too often, descriptions of new management approaches include overly optimistic assessments of their impact (Pfeffer and Sutton 2000). On a related note, Reinhard Bendix criticizes *management ideology*, or the beliefs of managers that their higher incomes and the right to give orders to others are justified. "All economic enterprises have in common a basic social relation between the employers who exercise authority and the workers who obey, and all ideologies of management have in common the effort to interpret the exercise of authority in a favourable light" (Bendix 1974: 13).

No matter how they explain and justify their actions, managers nevertheless do try, to the extent possible, to achieve organizational goals by motivating employees, planning for and coordinating organizational change, making decisions about a variety of things, including technological change, and generally increasing productivity.[5] During the 20th century, a variety of theories of management emerged in North America. The two most influential were scientific management and the human relations approach, which we discuss below. In Chapter 9, we will examine some of the alternative managerial paradigms that later sought to take a different approach to motivating employees and increasing productivity.

SCIENTIFIC MANAGEMENT (TAYLORISM)

Charlie Chaplin's classic 1936 movie *Modern Times* humorously depicts the life of a factory worker whose job consists of nothing more than tightening a bolt every few seconds as another identical piece of equipment speeds past him on an assembly line. He gets frustrated and very agitated. Once out on the street, he continues repeating the motions on anything that fits his two wrenches. We laugh when we see the movie, but Chaplin, playing the role of the super-stressed factory worker, was criticizing a real and widespread approach to managing work organization in industrialized societies.

Scientific management began in the United States as a set of production methods, tools, and organizational systems designed to increase the efficiency of factory production. The term itself was coined over a century ago by an engineer, Frederick W. Taylor (1911). Given the extent to which he promoted his management approach and the frequency with which it was adopted in North America, as well as in Europe, the approach soon also came to be known as *Taylorism*. Taylor's theory was at the cutting edge of the "thrust for efficiency" that contributed to the rise of 20th-century industrial capitalism (Palmer 1975). Taylor and other early management consultants advocated workplace reorganization, job redesign, and tighter administrative and employee controls, all in the name of efficiency and profits.

Taylor was convinced that workers deliberately restricted production by keeping their bosses ignorant of how fast a job could be done. His solution was to determine "scientifically" the one best way of performing a job through *time and motion studies* of each step. Management consultants used stopwatches to measure how long each job took and recorded in writing exactly how workers completed each task. They then subdivided complex tasks to gain maximum efficiency and issued instructions on how each new job, now narrower in scope, was to be performed. They also sought ways of identifying potential employees who would be best able to perform each highly repetitive task and devised training strategies to ensure that new workers would follow the rules. Essentially, they removed most of the control and decision making regarding work tasks from employees and handed them over to managers. In addition, a base rate of pay was tied to a production quota. If workers exceeded the quota, they received a pay bonus. In short, scientific management was founded on the assumption that workers were motivated by economic gain alone.

Taylor's view of human nature was coloured by his preoccupation with technical efficiency. In his mind, the ideal worker was more like a machine than a human being. Taylor was also a leading spokesperson for early 20th-century management consultants, articulating their strongly expressed concerns about the "labour problem."[6] Industrial cooperation would replace class conflict, he predicted, only when both management and labour began thinking differently. As he wrote in *Industrial Canada* (Taylor 1913: 1224–25), a prominent Canadian business magazine at the time:

> The new outlook that comes to both sides under scientific management is that both sides very soon realize that if they stop pulling apart and both push together as hard as possible in the same direction, they can make that surplus [i.e., profits] so large that there is no occasion for any quarrel over its division. Labour gets an immense increase in wages, and still leaves a large share for capital.

Taylor believed his management techniques would benefit all parties involved: workers, managers, and the owners of the means of production. Yet their overriding effect was to give management tighter control over workers, allowing them to make virtually no major work decisions (Bendix 1974; Nelson 1980). As we will explain in Chapter 10, according to the *labour process perspective*, Taylorism deskilled and degraded work, minutely fragmenting tasks, reducing skill requirements, and eliminating workers' input about how their jobs should be done.[7]

The Legacy of Scientific Management

Taylor's package of managerial reforms was seldom adopted completely. Yet various aspects of scientific management, those most useful for management, were quickly introduced into Canadian factories.[8] In many ways, Taylorism represented the practical application of bureaucratic principles to a manufacturing setting. Henry Ford's moving assembly line used technology to develop the logic inherent in scientific management and bureaucracy. But the increased monotony and speed of production sparked a huge increase in employee turnover. Only by doubling wages was Ford able to induce workers to accept the new production methods (Raff 1988).

As we will see in Chapter 9, a variety of alternative management approaches have tried to move beyond Taylorism although, as we point out in Chapter 10, some have also implemented Taylor's principles of management in new ways (Crowley et al. 2010). For example, elements of Fordism can be found in *lean production*, a Japanese-inspired management system that has become widespread in vehicle production, especially by Toyota (Liker 2004). Taylorism is also still alive in other manufacturing sectors. A case study of a Welsh appliance factory described efficiency gains obtained through time and motion studies, piece-rate payments, and reduced operator discretion—practices all favoured by mid-level managers (who were work-study engineers); yet it had been the desire of senior management to change these practices (Jones 2000).

The detailed job descriptions, planned workflows, and time and motion studies of scientific management also influence job design in the service sector (Davis 2010). For instance, a Toronto study of the building cleaning industry described a shift away from a semi-autonomous and multi-skilled "zone cleaning" approach to "mono-task" assignments (Aguiar 2001: 239). The latter resulted in simplified and repetitive tasks assigned to "cleaning specialists" who did only mopping, dusting, restroom duties, or other specific tasks. Software was used to analyze building cleaning needs and design efficient ways to do more cleaning with fewer workers. While these changes were intended to improve quality and customer service, they also significantly reduced the decision making of employees. Jamie Woodcock's account (at the start of this chapter; also see Woodcock 2017) of working in a telephone call centre in the United Kingdom highlights the continuing influence of scientific management—heavy pressure to meet targets and vigorous monitoring of productivity—that shape management practices in the service sector today.

History provides many examples of workers resisting scientific management. Frustrated by managerial rationalizations in the early 20th century, skilled workers responded by striking (Heron and Palmer 1977; Kealey 1986). Autoworkers were one occupational group that experienced a barrage of scientific management, along with extensive technological change. Chapter 14 will comment further on how Fordism combined scientific management techniques with mass-production assembly-line technology to create some of the most alienating and stressful working conditions in modern industrial society.[9] In short, major human costs accompanied this drive to increase efficiency, productivity, and profits. Other schools of management have tried to counteract the harshness that resulted from Taylorism and Fordism by developing more humane working conditions. As one organizational researcher aptly concludes, scientific management principles "make superb sense for organizing production when robots rather than human beings are the main productive force, when organizations can truly become machines" (Morgan 1997: 26).

THE HUMAN RELATIONS MOVEMENT

Bureaucracy, scientific management, and mass-production technologies transformed work in the 20th century. Henry Ford, Taylor, and other efficiency experts sought to redesign production systems so that control would be firmly in the hands of management. Technical efficiency was paramount. Consequently, many jobs became routinized and monotonous, stripped of opportunities for workers to use their minds or develop their skills and abilities.

Employee dissatisfaction, in the form of high turnover and absenteeism rates or industrial unrest, threatened to undermine the machine-like efficiency of the new industrial system.

Gaining the cooperation of workers within an increasingly bureaucratized, mechanized, and regimented labour process remained difficult. Some employers responded with programs, broadly known as *corporate welfare* or *industrial betterment,* which emphasized the need to treat workers as human beings. Introduced by major North American firms in the 1920s, corporate welfare programs were intended to reduce the alienating effects of bureaucracy and Fordist technologies (Barley and Kunda 1992). The goal was a loyal and productive workforce; the means were healthier work settings and improved job benefits. Recreation facilities, cafeterias, cleaner and more pleasant work environments, coherent personnel policies, medical benefits, and pensions are major examples of corporate welfare efforts.

Taylor and other efficiency experts were quick to dismiss these ideas as a waste of money. Yet many firms committed to scientific management also used corporate welfare measures to gain greater cooperation from staff (Jacoby 1997). More than anything, the corporate welfare movement showed that the principles of bureaucracy and scientific management failed to address the key ingredient in modern industry: human beings. Not until the *human relations school of management* began to systematically examine some of the same concerns in the 1930s did the scientific management model face a serious challenge.

To operate effectively, large work organizations need employees to comply with management directives. Amitai Etzioni (1975) theorized that such *compliance* can be achieved in three different ways. *Coercive* management techniques rely on penalties and harsh discipline. *Utilitarian* methods emphasize pay and material benefits, for example, assuming that employees are motivated by economic self-interest. *Normative* approaches, however, assume that workers can and will align their own interests with organizational goals, thus becoming motivated through shared norms and values to work hard for the greater good of the company or government department.

The human relations approach that emerged several decades after Taylor first promoted his ideas employs more of a normative approach; scientific management had combined coercive and utilitarian methods, with mixed results at best. The new approach endeavoured to cultivate a community of interests throughout the work organization, trying to get workers to identify with management goals and pursue them as their own. While the management consultants from the human relations school came to be more popular than the scientific management advocates, in practice, scientific management and human relations often operated side by side.[10]

The Hawthorne Studies

The human relations school of management originated in the *Hawthorne Studies*, a series of experiments conducted by Harvard Business School researchers between 1927 and 1932 at Western Electric's Hawthorne Works on the outskirts of Chicago.[11] Western Electric management was initially concerned with the effects of fatigue and monotony on production levels. At the time, these were central concerns of industrial psychologists, who were experimenting with industrial betterment (corporate welfare) techniques. Various studies examining the effect of rest pauses, hours of work, and lighting levels on productivity led researchers to unexpected findings.

In the Relay Assembly Test Room study, workers were placed in two separate rooms. Researchers then recorded production while varying light intensity for one group but not the other. To their surprise, productivity in both groups increased, regardless of lighting level. Only when light intensity was reduced to that of bright moonlight did productivity decline. Several variations on this study came up with the same puzzling findings. Searching for possible explanations, the researchers speculated that a fundamental change had occurred in the workplace. Involving workers in the study had the unintended effect of raising their morale. They now felt that management cared about them as individuals. Productivity, concluded the researchers, increased as a result.[12] A central premise of human relations management theory was established: if workers are treated as human beings working toward a collective goal, their motivation to cooperate will improve and their productivity will increase. Because of the Hawthorne studies, workplaces came to be viewed more as social systems rather than in purely technical terms.

Later interviews with employees revealed the extent to which work groups were governed by strong informal behavioural codes (Wilensky and Wilensky 1951). The Bank Wiring Observation Room study further probed work-group behaviour. For seven months, 14 employees were observed as they wired telephone switching banks. Researchers documented how *informal group norms* replaced formal directives from management. The work team set its own production quotas, making sure that no member worked too quickly or too slowly. Infractions of the group's rules, such as reporting violations of company policy to management, were punished. This particular study was one of the first to highlight the informal side of work organizations (discussed earlier in this chapter) where workers sometimes consciously engage in practices to oppose or subvert established authority.

Assumptions Underlying Human Relations Theory

The human relations perspective on management assumes that workers want to cooperate, in contrast to the utilitarian assumptions of human nature underlying scientific management. Human relations theory emphasizes how workers' attitudes, values, emotions, psychological needs, and interpersonal relationships all shape their work behaviour. Thus, this approach to management seeks the best match between the worker, given their personal background and psychological makeup, and the job. Careful recruitment and effective training of employees, as well as good supervision and communication, are therefore essential.

Elton Mayo, a leading early proponent of the human relations approach, saw modern workplaces as a microcosm of larger society. In the same way that productive capitalist enterprises required workers to be aligned with the goals of management, he believed that the survival of society depended on cooperation. So, he advocated a new industrial order run by an administrative elite. These leaders would encourage the development of work environments that would bring out the cooperative "instincts" and productive potential of employees (Mayo 1945). In short, Mayo and other human relations advocates believed that workers needed to be trained and led by managers and corporate leaders, but in a kind and friendly fashion. Human relationships had to be taken into account by managers, and the human needs of workers had to be met within work organizations.

Critics of human relations theory point out how, in general, it assumes that industrial harmony is healthy and that conflict is abnormal and destructive. The approach advocates the close regulation of workers by management and has nothing to say about excessive inequality in power and pay within work organizations, both of which can often lead to conflict (see Chapter 10). Such inconsistency has led some to label human relations theory as an elaborate justification for management's exploitation and manipulation of workers (Rinehart 2006).

The human relations perspective dominated managerial thinking well into the middle of the 20th century. A few proponents pushed the boundaries of the theory by focusing on workers' potential for personal development and growth, in contrast to Elton Mayo's belief that workers simply needed to be treated well by managers and recognized for their contributions to the good of the organization. For example, Douglas McGregor (1960) drew on psychologist Abraham Maslow's concept of a hierarchy of human needs in his discussion of Theory X and Theory Y. He identified Taylorism as a classic example of Theory X because of its mechanistic approach to managing and motivating people, thereby stifling human potential. He contrasted it with Theory Y, which views a manager's main task as creating an environment that allows workers to develop their skills and become more fully involved in the work organization. Unfortunately, the more humanistic Theory Y did little to influence day-to-day management practice when McGregor's book was published 60 years ago.

Today, McGregor's ideas are reflected in a number of alternative managerial paradigms that we discuss in Chapter 9. Compared to the mechanistic and authoritarian approach of scientific management, and the paternalistic assumptions of the human relations perspective, these *human resource development* approaches place more emphasis on skill development and tapping into workers' creative potential. Yet the structures and cultures of most large work organizations still pose major barriers to putting these ideas into practice. In this sense, McGregor's thinking remains futuristic.

CONCLUSION

The large hierarchical work organizations that evolved with industrial capitalism were initially considered to be both necessary and efficient. The combination of mass-production factory technology with bureaucratic organizational structures (Fordism) led to huge increases in productivity. But it did not take long for organizational analysts to begin outlining the problems of bureaucracy and, in particular, Fordism. Rigid, mechanistic organizations are slow to change. They can create workplace management cultures in which rules are more important than the larger goals of the organization, as well as informal work group norms that encourage workers to act in counterproductive ways. Bureaucratic rules and excessive hierarchies can leave frontline workers feeling relatively powerless and exploited, generating widespread worker dissatisfaction and, sometimes, open conflict.

During the first half of the 20th century, several modern management approaches evolved to try to address these problems. Scientific management (Taylorism) was clearly not successful. Instead, with the excessive division of labour it encouraged, along with the belief that managers (rather than workers) should do all the decision making, it essentially provided the theoretical justification for Fordism. The human relations approach offered an alternative, encouraging managers to think about a work organization as both a social and a technological system, to improve their communication skills, and to treat workers more humanely. But neither perspective had anything to say about reducing workplace inequalities (in material rewards and in power) or about providing workers with opportunities to develop their skills and become involved in decision making.

Scientific management and the human relations approach had different assumptions about what motivates workers (money and feeling part of a group, respectively), but both approaches believed that workers and management could come to recognize their shared interests and the need to cooperate. The goal was to eliminate conflict, which was considered abnormal. Thus, both approaches can be seen as part of the consensus perspective within sociology (see Chapter 1). In the next chapter, we will examine a variety of newer managerial paradigms that gained popularity in Western industrial economies in the latter part of the 20th century. These approaches also have a consensus (versus a conflict) orientation but place additional emphasis on encouraging workers to develop their skills and to become more involved in workplace decision-making (Lawler and Mohrman 2003; Becker, Huselid, and Ulrich 2001). Key questions we will be asking include these: Are these newer management approaches effective in solving the problems of bureaucracy? And how well do they address the material and power inequalities that are part of industrial capitalist economies?

DISCUSSION QUESTIONS

1. Organizational analysts have identified many problems with bureaucratic work organizations. In your opinion, which are the most serious problems? Do bureaucracies have any value? Support your view.
2. Universities are workplaces for professors, support staff, and students. Can you point to examples of some of the problems of bureaucracy within universities?

3. Scientific management and human relations theory have been criticized for a variety of reasons. Outline these criticisms. Are there aspects of these two approaches that are nevertheless useful?
4. Think back to some of the jobs you have held. Can you remember interactions with managers or other experiences that remind you of either scientific management or the human relations approach?
5. What do you think motivates people to work hard? Assuming that people differ, at least to some extent, in their work motivations, what might account for these differences?

ADDITIONAL RESOURCES

WORK AT THE MOVIES

- *Modern Times* (directed by Charlie Chaplin, 1936, 87 minutes). In this silent comedy, Chaplin depicts his character, the Little Tramp, struggling to deal with the assembly line and routinized work in a modern factory.
- *The Informant!* (directed by Steven Soderbergh, 2009, 108 minutes). The vice-president of a large agro-business blows the whistle on the company's price-fixing tactics. This film is based on a true story.
- *The Apartment* (directed by Billy Wilder, 1960, 125 minutes). An office worker at a big insurance company is eager to climb the corporate ladder. He does a favour for four company managers in exchange for positive performance reports and the opportunity for a promotion.
- *Working Girl* (directed by Kevin Wade, 1988, 113 minutes). A secretary pretends to be her boss to get back at him for stealing one of her ideas.

SOUNDS OF WORK

- "9 to 5" (Dolly Parton). Written for the movie *9 to 5*, this song provides a commentary on women's experiences of working in corporate America, including the barriers and unfair treatment they face.
- "Boiled Frogs" (Alexisonfire). Apparently inspired by singer George Pettit's observations of his father experiencing no company loyalty in the workplace, this song speaks to the control and coercion that workers in bureaucratic organizations can experience.

- "Takin' Care of Business" (Bachman-Turner Overdrive). The song compares the routinization of white-collar office work with the flexibility that comes with self-employment.

NOTES

1. Morgan's book provides an excellent overview of the multiple images, or metaphors, of organizations found in the literature.
2. Use your preferred search engine and these three keywords: Dilbert, bureaucracy, cartoons.
3. Civilian Review and Complaints Commission for the RCMP (2017, p. 3).
4. Mahutga (2014) describes how global production networks can influence the economic development of nation-states.
5. See Crowley (2016) for an interesting study showing a positive link between management practices promoting justice and fairness in the workplace and work organization productivity and profitability.
6. Another management consultant at the time was W. L. Mackenzie King, who later (in the 1920s, 1930s, and 1940s) became Canada's longest-serving prime minister. In his book *Industry and Humanity*, King (1918) also expressed strong concerns about labour unrest. King, however, advocated a central role for government in mediating disputes between employers and unions (see Chapter 11).
7. See Locke (1982) for a systematic defence of Taylor's prescriptions for how management techniques could be improved. In contrast, Wrege and Hodgetts (2000) question Taylor's claims of efficiency gains.
8. See Palmer (1979), and Craven (1980) on Canadian employers' adoption of Taylorism. By the 1920s, Taylorism had also been used to overhaul large corporate and government offices in Canada (Lowe 1987).
9. Classic studies of auto assembly-line workers include Aronowitz (1973), Beynon (1984), and Meyer (1981). Hamper (1986) and De Santis (1999) offer more personal accounts of this type of work.
10. Barley and Kunda (1992) provide an excellent description of how managerial ideologies shifted over the 20th century.
11. The research was originally described in Whitehead (1936) and Roethlisberger and Dickson (1939), and has been vigorously debated since then (Jones 1990; Gillespie 1991).
12. This study is the source of the well-known *Hawthorne effect*, a concern of psychologists who try to ensure that results of experiments are not confounded by subjects' awareness of being part of a study.

IN SEARCH OF NEW MANAGERIAL PARADIGMS

9

"Industrial-age organizations were formal hierarchies that assigned specific roles to employees. The focus on roles put all power in the hands of managers, who governed employees by planning, organizing and controlling their work. This is essentially what made management a top-down, restricting function. . . . In modern, post-industrial organizations, all employees need to manage. Self-managing teams use complex systems to help them manage their own work, and precise performance measures are openly accessible. Knowledge workers don't need to be told what to do, and often, they know better than their managers. . . . The operating style of industrial-age managers is represented by a metaphor of the organization-as-person, where the 'head' thinks and the 'hands' do. It is no coincidence that employees were once called 'hired hands.' The implication of this metaphor is that managers do all the thinking and managing. The vision of employees as unthinking 'hands,' to be moved around at will by a remote mind, is unsustainable in an age of empowerment and employee engagement. . . . The modern manager needs to get work done through engaged, self-managing knowledge workers, who are a far cry from the 'hired hands' of the industrial age."

Source: Mitch McCrimmon (Executive Assessment and Coaching Consultant). A New Role for Management in Today's Post-industrial Organization. [Retrieved February 9, 2019]: https://iveybusinessjournal.com /publication/a-new-role-for-management-in-todays-post-industrial-organization/

INTRODUCTION

Scientific management and the human relations approach were dominant management strategies for at least the first two-thirds of the 20th century in North America and even now are still in use. Over the past four decades, however, scores of books about improving management practices have been written, many leaving the impression that large corporations and government departments are in constant upheaval. The large bureaucracies that came to dominate the economic landscape are often portrayed as dinosaurs: cumbersome, slow to respond and adapt, and, according to some critics, a dying breed. Globalization, with increased competition, rapid technological change, and heightened economic uncertainty, has prompted even the most vocal champions of bureaucracy to search for better ways to manage work.

Consultants such as the one providing advice above, practising managers, and business school academics have created a growth industry writing books and delivering workshops on changing organizations and management approaches. Together, they have been seeking a new managerial paradigm, a different approach to coordinating workplace tasks and gaining compliance from workers that will assist managers in meeting the challenges of an increasingly global, customer-focused, knowledge-based, technology-dependent economy (Pirson and Lawrence 2010). Tom Peters and Bob Waterman Jr. set the tone in their enormously influential 1982 book, *In Search of Excellence*, in which they documented how rigid, inflexible organizations are less able to survive, let alone grow and profit, in today's rapidly changing economy (Peters and Waterman 1982). Despite the fact that many of Peters and Waterman's "excellent" firms later experienced serious problems, these writers fuelled debates about the need to rethink old ways of organizing and managing derived from the legacies of Weber, Taylor, and Ford. In this respect, the *new management literature* corresponds with the sociological critique of bureaucracy, outlined in Chapter 8. While some of the many management self-help books are not very original or useful,[1] several quite different approaches to organizing workplaces and managing workers have nevertheless emerged. In this chapter, we will review them in turn, while also highlighting some of the criticisms these approaches have received.

RECONSTRUCTING BUREAUCRACY

We will see several central themes in the discussion of new managerial paradigms in this chapter. The first is *decentralization of authority*. For example, Canadian management expert Henry Mintzberg (1989: Chapter 11) is a proponent of *adhocracy*, an organizational form with a fluid and decentralized operating structure. This approach contrasts with the inflexibility of what Mintzberg calls the "machine organization," or traditional bureaucracy, and even with the "entrepreneurial organization," which is too performance oriented. The work of an adhocracy is performed by multidisciplinary teams.

Hierarchical top-down control, rigid lines of authority, and narrow job functions are replaced by a *matrix structure*, which enables experts to move between functional units for specialized administrative tasks and multidisciplinary project teams.

This description of an alternative organizational form reflects a second but related core theme, the *flattening of organizational structures*, or the removal of some of the many layers of a traditional bureaucracy. In contrast, Max Weber's ideal bureaucracy was a highly hierarchical vertical structure, which critics claim cannot easily meet today's needs for product and service quality.

Mintzberg's analysis also highlights a third core theme—*flexibility*—the ability to adapt quickly to changing economic and social environments. Peter F. Drucker, the dean of management gurus, develops the same idea by arguing that, in a knowledge- and technology-based economy, successful organizations continually change and renew themselves.

Frank Ostroff (1999) makes some of the same points but also suggests a fourth key theme: the *emphasis on customers or clients*. Ostroff is an advocate of horizontal organizations in which "the emphasis shifts from top down to focusing across at customers, from compliance with executive orders to meaningful participation in the production of customer satisfaction, quality, and team excellence"—all of which is essential in "today's radically different business world" (Ostroff 1999: 74).

In *Thriving on Chaos: Handbook for a Management Revolution*, Tom Peters (1987) refers to the same core themes but also draws attention to two more: the *empowerment of workers* (not just managers) and the *embracing* (not avoidance) *of change* by corporate leaders and managers. His model of what he calls a "winner" is based on five sets of characteristics: (1) an obsession with responsiveness to customers; (2) constant innovation in all areas; (3) the full participation and empowerment of all people connected with the organization; (4) leadership that loves change and promotes an inspiring vision; and (5) non-bureaucratic control by simple support systems.

In Chapter 8, we noted the importance of listening to what managers say they do while also watching what they really do. In the same way, while reading about new managerial paradigms in this chapter, we need to continue to ask ourselves whether bureaucracy is actually dissolving and if management practices have really changed all that much, a point clearly made by management professor Gary Hamel (2007) in *The Future of Management*.

Like some other critics, Hamel points to the persistence of bureaucracy and a preoccupation with reinventing business processes, such as logistics and customer support, rather than how things are actually managed. Hamel identifies Google, however, as an innovative organization that has gone considerably further (102):

> What makes Google unique, though, is less its Web-centric business model than its brink-of-chaos management model. Key components include a wafer-thin hierarchy, a dense network of lateral communication, a policy of giving outsized rewards to people who come up with outsized ideas, a team-focused approach to product development, and a corporate credo that challenges every employee to put the user first.

But we need to recognize that Google may be an outlier, rather than an example of a trend toward post-bureaucratic organizations.

In the remainder of this chapter, we will highlight the strengths and advantages of new approaches to organizing workplaces and managing workers, while also retaining a critical stance, asking why managers have implemented changes and if they have really made a significant difference. We will discuss the different approaches chronologically, that is, in the order that they were developed and became well known. As will become apparent, the history of new management paradigms has not necessarily been one of steady forward progress. Some of the more recent "innovations" might, in fact, be seen as steps back toward Taylorism.

JAPANESE MANAGEMENT

To better understand the social origins of the new managerial paradigms, we need to go back almost 75 years and leave North America. By the end of World War II, the Japanese military had been crushed by the Allied forces and the country's economy was a disaster. But over the next four decades, Japan grew to become a global economic powerhouse, developing a technology-driven, export-focused manufacturing industry that produced high-quality products.[2] The competition from Japan caused North American manufacturers to rethink their traditional ways of producing automobiles, appliances, and electronic goods, and the global success of Japanese corporations led many to conclude that their management systems, industrial organization, and technology were superior. Sociologists have asked whether the Japanese industrial system can be best explained by theories of social and economic organization, facilitating its adoption elsewhere, or whether the explanation lies in Japanese culture and history, in which case application outside Japan would be difficult (Jacoby 2005; Morita 2001). It is generally concluded that Japanese culture and history are less important than principles of industrial organization and management (Lincoln 1990).

The Japanese Employment System

The four basic elements of the Japanese management approach, which typically are found in the major corporations, include: (1) highly evolved internal labour markets (discussed in Chapter 5), with features such as lifetime employment (*nenko*), seniority-based wages and promotions, and extensive training; (2) a division of labour built around work groups rather than specific positions, a feature that is the basis for the well-known quality circles; (3) a consensual, participative style of decision making involving workers at all organizational levels (*ringi*); and (4) high levels of employee commitment and loyalty. As we will see later in this chapter, some but not all of these elements were adopted by management approaches that emerged at the end of the 20th century.

The core of the Japanese work organization is the *internal labour market.* Japanese employers strive to maintain a well-functioning internal labour market and to obtain a high level of employee commitment to the firm over the long term (Lincoln and McBride 1987). Teams share responsibility and accountability. When this is coupled with the consensus-building networking process used to make decisions, it is easy to see how individual workers are typically well integrated in their workplace. Japanese corporate decision-making combines centralized authority in the hands of executives who bear final responsibility for decisions with consultations that ensure everyone has some input. On the shop floor, participation commonly takes the form of *quality circles* (QCs), an approach made famous by Toyota with the objective of maintaining and improving high levels of quality. Yet elsewhere, quality circles "may be little more than collective suggestion-making exercises, imposed by management, for which workers receive little training" (Lincoln and McBride 1987: 300).

Even so, quality circles represent a potentially useful approach to worker participation. As Stephen Wood (1989a) explains, workers' *tacit skills*, or intuitive expertise about how to do their job, are being used. Workers' informal expertise is crucial for overcoming the bugs in many new technologies. Quality circles and other forms of worker participation enlarge workers' overall knowledge of the business, sharpen their analytical and trouble-shooting skills, and can keep them more engaged with company goals. What is innovative about Japanese organization, then, is how it harnesses the tacit skills and latent talents of workers.

Probably the peak performance of this Japanese model of management occurred in the 1970s. Even then, the model was subject to criticism for: stifling individual creativity through *nenko* and groupism; discrimination against non-permanent employees, particularly women; labour market rigidities that made the horizontal movement of workers among firms difficult; and long hours of work often at an intense pace (Kamata 1983). Japanese industry faced a barrage of new challenges in the 1980s and 1990s, including a prolonged recession, which weakened its established employment system (Whittaker 1990).

In the decades following, the adoption of quality-enhancing work practices was inconsistent among the dozens of suppliers that manufacture components for Japan's major exporting firms—as became evident with the massive Toyota recall of defective automobiles in 2010. Additional stimuli for change included an aging workforce, changing attitudes of young workers influenced by Western culture, and a growing female labour force. The seniority principle has given way to other means of rewarding and motivating workers. And the mobility of workers during their careers and across firms has increased. It will be interesting to see whether this restructuring signals a growing convergence of Japanese and North American approaches to organizing and managing work.

The Japanese Approach in North America

How far have these Japanese management and organizational innovations moved into North America? Some organizational design concepts, such as Toyota's *just-in-time* (JIT) system of parts delivery and focus on quality, have been extensively adopted for use outside Japan. The JIT system reduces inventory overhead costs, makes it easier to change production specifications, and forges stronger alliances between a firm and its suppliers. JIT parts delivery, however, assumes a smoothly operating transportation system, which is not always possible. For example, in 2018, the dismantling of the North American Free Trade Agreement (NAFTA) and its expected replacement by the US–Mexico–Canada Agreement (USMCA) led to many months of uncertainty among manufacturers in all three countries about the maintenance of cross-border supply chains.

QCs have become fairly popular among North American firms facing global competition. Nevertheless, they do not go as far as delegating authority to autonomous work teams, a Swedish approach to management that we discuss later in this chapter. QCs generally place responsibility for monitoring quality and troubleshooting problems on production workers without a parallel expansion of their authority or increased rewards.[3]

The obvious place to look for the successful adaptation of Japanese employment techniques is in *Japanese transplants* (local plants owned and operated by Japanese firms) or in Japanese joint ventures with North American firms. We find mixed results. The NUMMI plant in California, a unionized joint venture between Toyota and General Motors that operated from 1984 until 2010, was at one end of the continuum. Using methods imported by Toyota, employees worked in teams and contributed ideas, although the daily management style was distinctly American (Kanter 1989: 274). However, the norm in transplants or joint ventures may be much closer to what Ruth Milkman (1991) observed in Japanese transplants, also in California. These workplaces closely resembled American firms employing nonunion labour. Few had introduced QCs, and many local managers were unfamiliar with the principles of Japanese work organization or management approaches (Milkman 1991). These firms' employment strategies mainly emphasized cost reduction, leading them to take full advantage of low-wage immigrant labour.

Canada has numerous Japanese-owned plants, most notably the Honda and Toyota factories in Ontario. Managers at these plants have had to develop a hybrid system, modifying aspects of the Japanese approach in a way acceptable to Canadian workers (Walmsley 1992). The major success story among Japanese transplants is Toyota's massive plant in Cambridge, Ontario, which produced other Toyota models for three decades, until 2019, but now builds the RAV4 and the Lexus RX. The factory has won numerous quality or production awards and has frequently been named one of Canada's top 100 employers. From the workers' point of view, benefits include job flexibility, free uniforms, consensus decision-making, teamwork, good pay, and job security. However, there are drawbacks, including regular required overtime, open offices for managers, no replacement workers for absent team members, health problems, close scrutiny of absenteeism and lateness, and only selective implementation of employee suggestions. Despite efforts by the Canadian Auto Workers (now called Unifor; see Chapter 11) to organize this Toyota facility, it remains nonunion.

SWEDISH WORK REFORMS

With QCs and some input by workers into decision making about their immediate job tasks, Japanese management approaches moved beyond the human relations approach that focused primarily on treating workers humanely and providing them with good working conditions (see Chapter 8). So, too, did North American quality-of-working-life initiatives (discussed below), which focused on job enlargement, job enrichment, and autonomous work teams. However, neither Japanese management systems nor quality-of-working-life programs went as far toward redistributing power relationships and reducing bureaucratic hierarchies within factory-based work organizations as did Swedish work reforms. Decades of social democratic government, a strong organized labour movement, and legislation giving individuals the right to meaningful jobs provided fertile ground for humanistic work reforms.

The widely publicized Volvo Kalmar plant, which opened in the early 1970s and closed in 1994, was based on *sociotechnical work design*, an approach to work organization and management that attempts to optimize the fit between social and technical aspects of production (Mumford 2006). The Volvo assembly line was replaced by battery-powered robot carriers, which automatically moved car bodies to different work teams, each of which was responsible for a phase of assembly. Productivity and quality improved, but a major limitation of the Kalmar plant's sociotechnical design was that a computer (not teams) controlled the movement of the carriers and imposed short task cycles. Most jobs provided little scope for personal development or for the use of skills and initiative. Workers still complained that their jobs were boring.

Volvo's Uddevalla factory, which opened in 1989 and shut in 1993 because of a market downturn, resolved some of these problems by pushing sociotechnical design much further. Small work teams were able to build entire cars at ergonomically designed stationary work locations. By comparison with other

Volvo facilities, this plant achieved high levels of quality, productivity, and worker satisfaction.

Saab's main auto plant at Trollhattan, which has operated since 1947, although under the ownership of a number of different automobile companies, provides another example of innovative attempts to reduce the alienating monotony of assembly-line work. Back in the early 1970s, the body-assembly shop faced problems typical in mass production—a numbingly fast work pace; high turnover, absenteeism, and widespread dissatisfaction on the part of workers; and poor quality products. Reforms, in which the local union played an active role, sought to improve the work environment, make jobs intrinsically more satisfying, and boost productivity.

Some remarkable changes occurred. The assembly line was eliminated. Instead, *autonomous work teams* devoted about 45 minutes at a time to completing an integrated cycle of tasks. Robots took over arduous, repetitive welding jobs. In the welding area, groups of 12 workers controlled the entire production process, which involved programming the computers and maintaining the robots, ensuring quality control, performing related administrative work, and cleaning up their workspace. Buffer zones allowed teams to build up an inventory of completed bodies, giving them greater flexibility over how they used their time. Skill development, new learning opportunities, and a broader approach to job design provided the teams with what Saab called "control and ownership" of their contribution to the production process. Far from being victims of work degradation and deskilling through robotics, these Saab employees were the beneficiaries of upgraded job content and greater decision-making autonomy.[4] Since productivity also increased with these work reforms, both employees and employers benefited (Kochan and Osterman 1994).

NORTH AMERICAN QUALITY-OF-WORKING-LIFE PROGRAMS

Quality of working life became a popular concept among North American managers, academics, and consultants during the 1970s. *Quality of working life (QWL)* is an umbrella term covering many different strategies for humanizing work, improving employee–employer cooperation, redesigning jobs, and giving employees more opportunity to participate in decision making. The underlying goal has been to improve employee satisfaction, motivation, and commitment.

The expected payoffs are higher productivity, better quality products, and bigger profits. Proponents have argued that employers and employees alike will benefit (Levine 1995). As we will see, however, QWL programs have seldom gone as far toward sharing power within work organizations as did the Swedish work reforms.

Quality of working life has diverse intellectual roots. Its core ideas came primarily from Japanese management systems and Swedish studies on work reform. In addition, psychologist Frederick Herzberg's theory that work is satisfying only if it meets employees' psychological growth needs and Douglas McGregor's Theory Y (see Chapter 8) were influential in shaping this *human resource management* perspective that went quite far beyond human relations theory, discussed in the previous chapter (Oldham and Hackman 2010).[5]

QWL Techniques

A quick overview of core QWL techniques, some directly borrowed from Japanese and Swedish approaches, would be useful. *Job enlargement* is meant to expand a job horizontally, adding related tasks to put more variety into the work done by an individual worker. *Job enrichment* goes further by combining operations before and after a task to create a more complex and unified job. For example, in the case of a machine operator in a clothing factory, job enrichment might mean that the operator is now responsible for obtaining necessary materials, doing the administrative work associated with different production runs, and maintaining the machines. This change might not be enormous, but it would lead to a somewhat more varied, demanding, and responsible job. *Job rotation* involves workers moving through a series of work stations, usually at levels of skill and responsibility similar to their original task. This tactic is frequently used to inject variety into highly repetitive, monotonous jobs. When job rotation is combined with more fundamental redesign strategies (especially the use of work teams), an employee can develop a considerable range of new skills.

An *autonomous work team* consists of about a dozen employees who are delegated collective authority to decide on work methods, scheduling, inventory, and quality control. They might also perform what previously would have been supervisory tasks, such as administration, discipline, and even hiring. QCs, with a narrower mandate of having workers monitor and correct defects in products or services, are perhaps the best-known application of the team concept. By the late 1980s, the team concept had become quite common in some industries, and Canadian auto production plants were embracing "employee involvement" schemes to varying degrees (Robertson and Wareham 1987).

The flagship of the North American QWL movement, however, was Shell's chemical plant in Sarnia, Ontario (Rankin 1990). When the plant was built in the late 1970s, it was unique in North America because union and management had actively collaborated in its sociotechnical planning and design. Furthermore, it was a greenfield site, a completely new facility that offered greater scope for innovative work arrangements. Shell's goal was a post-bureaucratic organization that would facilitate greater employee control, learning, and participation.

Six teams of 20 workers ran the plant around the clock, 365 days a year. Along with two coordinators, a single team operated the entire plant during a shift and was even responsible for hiring new team members when vacancies occurred. Teams were supported by technical, engineering, and managerial personnel, along with a group of maintenance workers, who also taught team members craft skills. The organizational structure was flat, having only three authority levels from top to bottom. Team members had no job titles, and they rotated tasks. Pay was based on knowledge and skills obtained through job training. It took about six years of training for an operator to reach the maximum pay level.

Compared to traditional bureaucracies, this innovative organizational design empowered workers to a remarkable extent and allowed them to apply and develop their skills. We should note, however, that the continuous-process technology used in refineries involves a very high level of capital investment per worker and could lead to enormous financial losses should the system malfunction. Thus, management at the Sarnia refinery had a strong economic incentive to obtain a high level of employee commitment.

QWL Critiques

The Shell experience, however, appears to be atypical. The union's involvement came only after guarantees that it would be a full partner in the QWL process and that its ability to represent the interests of employees would not be undermined. It is noteworthy that members of the same union at an adjacent older refinery wanted nothing to do with QWL techniques. But the story of innovation at Shell's Sarnia plant is now history, because a change in management ushered in more traditional work organization and management systems. It is not unusual for work redesign initiatives to be abandoned when top management changes, especially if the new managers are mainly concerned about production goals and costs.

Overall, efforts to reform workplaces with QWL techniques generated heated debate between advocates—usually managers and consultants—and critics, who were often trade unionists. Research revealed that not all team-based production and employee participation initiatives necessarily led to improved working conditions (Milkman 1997). Frequently, changes in workers' job tasks were minimal. They did not gain the opportunity to influence decisions on larger workplace changes (the introduction of new technology, for example), and management imposed the programs rather than involving the workers in the decision (Robertson and Wareham 1987; Rinehart 2006: Chapter 6). Some critics have charged that QWL and other new management approaches are simply ways of encouraging workers to work harder and faster.[6]

In Canada, the smorgasbord of QWL programs introduced by employers has produced both successes and failures (Lowe 2000). On the negative side, some QWL experiments resulted in declining work performance, heightened union–management tensions, employee dissatisfaction, and a breakdown in communication. Alternatively, in Canada, as well as in other Western industrial democracies, positive effects have included higher employee satisfaction and commitment (Gallie 2013), higher earnings, improved labour relations, and sometimes productivity gains. As the example of Shell's Sarnia plant demonstrates, the context into which changes are introduced, the level of management commitment to fundamental reform, and the involvement (or not) of organized labour will all strongly influence outcomes.

On the whole, autonomous work teams appear to have the greatest potential for significantly reallocating decision-making power, as well as for creating more interesting, challenging, socially integrated, and skilled work. Why, then, has the Canadian labour movement often been a vocal critic of QWL techniques? The drawback for unions is that management frequently has used the QWL approach cynically, to circumvent collective agreements, rationalize work processes, and co-opt workers into solving problems of quality and productivity. The QWL approach has often been used to undermine union bargaining power and spearhead labour relations schemes intended to keep firms union-free. Thus, from organized labour's perspective, gains in the quality of working life are best achieved through collective bargaining (see Chapter 11).

TOTAL QUALITY MANAGEMENT

Total quality management (TQM) grew out of the QWL movement, adopting some of its techniques but placing a customer-focused emphasis on quality. Customers can be external consumers; citizens, in the case of public-sector organizations; or other units or individuals within the organization (internal customers). With its emphasis on continuous improvement, TQM focuses on involving employees in identifying and quickly resolving problems, or antici-pating future problems. In addition to quality control systems, typical TQM elements include performance measures, improved communications and feedback systems, problem-solving work teams, employee involvement, and a culture of trust and cooperation (Clarke and Clegg 1998: 254–65). TQM champions claim that the model reduces costs and increases productivity, cus-tomer satisfaction, job quality, and firm competitiveness.

Six Sigma, pioneered by General Electric (GE), the giant manufacturing conglomerate recently purchased by a Chinese company, is an example of a TQM-influenced production system. Since the 1980s, GE has focused on developing a workplace culture (more on this below) that looks at all business processes from the customer's perspective. This requires reducing bureaucracy and encouraging workers to bring forward ideas about what needs improving. As the GE website explains: Six Sigma "is not a secret society, a slogan or a cliché. Six Sigma is a highly disciplined process that helps us focus on devel-oping and delivering near-perfect products and services."[7] Six Sigma is GE's statistical goal of having no more than 3.4 defects per million products or services delivered: it means striving for virtual perfection. Quality is achieved, in part, by technology—extensive measurement of all work processes—but also via social processes, since it is the responsibility of all employees (Devane 2004).

TQM has also been adopted by some employers in service industries, such as retail and hospitality. For example, the luxury hotel and resort chain Four Seasons focuses on creating the highest-quality guest experience by training and enabling all employees to do whatever they can to provide exceptional service (Sharp 2009). Best Buy, a consumer electronics chain, introduced what it calls a Results Only Work Environment, or ROWE. While not described as a TQM experiment, the organizational changes implemented nevertheless fit the model. The ROWE premise is that work performance should be measured by results, not by hours and "face-time." Employees working in teams are given responsibility for delivering results and figuring out the best ways to do so. This may involve changing working hours and locations, without needing management's permission. A study conducted at Best Buy's U.S. head office showed that individuals in ROWE teams reported improved health and well-being, and increased job satisfaction (Moen, Kelly, and Chermack 2008). A second retailer, Gap Inc., implemented ROWE and documented reduced employee turnover and modest improvements in productivity and production quality, engagement, and job quality (Conlin 2009).

Assessing the TQM Approach

TQM programs have been heralded by proponents as a win-win approach to labour–management relations: workers benefit through improved working conditions, and productivity increases (Pfeffer 1994: Chapter 9). As with other management trends, however, it is sometimes difficult to sort out real change from the rhetoric. Some skeptics view TQM as just a catchy label applied to a particular set of customer service initiatives with the help of computers (Micklethwait and Wooldridge 1996: 26). Nevertheless, if a quality-improvement strategy is part of a comprehensive set of high-performance work practices (discussed below), then there is a good chance that the result will be less bureaucracy, greater customer responsiveness, organizational flexibility, and employee participation (Rosenthal, Hill, and Peccei 1997). For example, two of the winners of a national U.S. quality award, Xerox Corporation and Milliken & Company (a textile manufacturer), invest heavily in employee training and use teams extensively. However, in-depth analysis is needed to determine how specific changes contribute to measurable improvements in quality.

One example of this kind of analysis can be found in the health care sector, where, in many hospitals, patients are treated as "customers," and quality committees rethink processes and procedures in order to improve the quality of patient care and to cut costs. A study of the introduction of total quality management at an Edmonton hospital found much of the program counterproductive: it was linked in employees' minds with the downsizing of the organization, which was happening at the same time. Increased workloads, reduced competence resulting from multi-skilling, and the overall impact of doing more with less created "role ambiguity, conflicts and demoralization"—with potentially negative effects on health care costs and quality (Lam and Reshef 1999: 741).

Thus, as with other major shifts in management approaches, there is often resistance at various levels within an organization to the introduction of TQM practices, largely because they may be perceived as disrupting the existing power structure. Middle managers balk at the idea of empowering employees, knowing that it is their own power that will be redistributed downward. Employees and unions may resist, viewing TQM as yet another attempt by management to co-opt and control workers (Sewell 1998), and to avoid unions. Employees may also have trouble with such vague goals as "continuous improvement," which suggests that their best efforts today may not be good enough tomorrow. As we noted with respect to QWL initiatives, workers in organizations employing TQM approaches are seldom invited to participate in decisions about whether to introduce new technologies, or to restructure or downsize organizations. Instead of being truly empowered, critics point out, workers have been invited to find ways to work harder, often in an atmosphere of anxiety about possible job loss (Zbaracki 1998). Consequently, promises of improved working conditions have frequently translated into only superficial changes (McCabe 1999).

MANAGING VIA ORGANIZATIONAL CULTURE

During the 1980s when TQM techniques were being adopted in a range of large North American workplaces in both the private and public sectors, a parallel management literature emphasizing *organizational culture* also emerged (Martin 2002; Schein 2004). It drew heavily on one aspect of the Japanese management literature, namely, the assumption (noted earlier) that Japan's unique culture and history led to workers being more engaged with company goals. Compared to Japanese teamwork approaches, Swedish work reforms, and QWL initiatives, though, it placed relatively little emphasis on redesigning jobs to get workers more involved and on giving them more decision-making opportunities. Instead, the organizational culture approach focused primarily on finding ways to align the values of workers with the goals of management (Barley and Kunda 1992). So in many ways it closely resembled the human relations approach to management (see Chapter 8).[8]

Large workplaces can be viewed as mini-societies in which organizational culture—shared beliefs, customs, rituals, languages, and myths—serves as "social glue," binding together the diverse actors in the organization. *Culture*, then, refers to a system of shared meanings about how organizational life ought to be conducted. It can also reflect how things get done at an informal level (Morgan 1997: Chapter 5). Shaping the *dominant culture* of an organization—that is, encouraging employees to identify strongly with corporate goals and values—is central to the organizational culture approach to management. So, too, is preventing workplace *countercultures*, with dissenting norms and values, from gaining strength (the informal side of organizations discussed in Chapter 8).

Senior managers may seek to "brand" their organization by advertising their company's core values. Toyota, for example, markets itself as a corporation driven by a commitment to quality production (Liker 2004) and, as noted earlier, so does General Electric with it Six Sigma branding. Some other large companies have emphasized *corporate social responsibility* (CSR) in their public image, highlighting the extent to which their production and management practices align with environmental and social justice goals (Vogel 2005). The United Colors of Benetton's focus on cultural diversity, human rights, and environmental sustainability is a well-known example, as is the Body Shop.[9] By so doing, these companies are trying to recruit customers who presumably share these values. They are also trying to shape the values of current employees and to recruit employees with shared values.[10]

In his discussions of *learning organizations*, Peter Senge (1990) used the concept of organizational culture to promote the personal and corporate value of continued learning. He argued that to gain and keep a competitive advantage in the rapidly changing global economy, companies need to develop a learning culture that takes advantage of and enhances employees' knowledge and skills. Better-trained workers will make an organization more adaptable, innovative, and flexible. Thus, unlike organizational culture proponents who want to rally everyone in an organization around business performance goals, Senge's ideal workplace is one in which learning for its own sake becomes a valued and rewarded process that employees have the autonomy to pursue. From Senge's perspective, learning comes before earning (or productivity).

It is less clear, however, what exactly it takes for a traditional work organization to become a learning organization (Popper and Lipshitz 2000), one that is "skilled at creating, acquiring, interpreting, transferring, and retaining knowledge, and at purposefully modifying its behavior to reflect new knowledge and insights" (Garvin 2000: 11). Some firms claim to have developed a learning culture. For example, at Harley-Davidson Motorcycles, "intellectual curiosity" is a core value, "Harley University" offers extensive training programs, and the president promotes learning at every opportunity (Gephart et al. 1996: 39). Even so, it could be argued that Harley-Davidson simply has made greater investments in training, communicating this as a new value commitment. Thus, creating a learning organization remains an ideal, perhaps because the concept is overly abstract (Argote 1999).

In contrast to companies that promote quality production, continued learning, or CSR in their organizational culture pursuits, others take a short-cut, trying to reinforce corporate identity by maintaining a mythology about organizational founders and legendary past leaders. The Dave Thomas ads used by the Wendy's burger chain long after he died in 2002 are an example. Baseball hats, coffee mugs, and other items with company logos distributed to employees can be used for the same quick-fix purpose. Rituals such as award dinners, where employees' achievements are recognized, and the giving of employee of the month citations, such as McDonald's does, also seek to promote organizational culture without changing organizational structures or work tasks.

Some management experts believe that it is possible for workplaces to become "collaborative communities," grounded on a shared ethic of interdependent contributions (Adler and Heckscher 2006). However, the belief that a workplace could have a single unitary corporate culture, fashioned by management to gain employee commitment to goals they had little say in setting, greatly oversimplifies the nature of organizational life. In fact, most large organizations have a variety of cultures—dominant and alternative—depending on the degree to which particular groups or locations within them share similar work experiences and similar values. Research suggests that more successful companies will promote core values while still encouraging smaller workgroup cultures that support performance in ways that overall corporate values or codes of conduct cannot (Collins and Porras 1994).

Overall, when assessing management approaches that focus on culture alongside the other new managerial paradigms that have been promoted over recent decades, it is difficult to accept the claims by organizational culture consultants that a strong culture accounts for organizational success by providing a unique strategic advantage that competitors can't copy (Collins and Porras 1994; Stubblefield 2005). Promoting a unified core culture and incorporating smaller workgroup cultures is part of the solution to the problems of bureaucracy, as suggested earlier; however, this approach does not advance much beyond the human relations approach to management. Redesigning jobs to add rather than remove skills and involving workers in decision making at various levels within the organization are also critically important.

FLEXIBLE WORK ORGANIZATIONS

Standardized mass-production techniques were the hallmark of industrial capitalism for much of the past century. However, assembly-line mass production of standardized goods has become much less economically viable, and *flexible specialization* has become a preferred production model in some industries. Flexible production systems use computers to link all aspects of production into a coordinated whole. Much smaller product runs are possible than with assembly-line systems, and because sales trends and consumer tastes are closely monitored, changes in design or product lines can readily be made. Computers also reduce stock-control costs (zero inventory) and improve product quality (zero defects).

Describing the early success of northern Italian consumer goods firms employing this type of production system back in the 1980s, Piore and Sabel (1984) sketched out a positive view of the future of manufacturing (17):

> Flexible specialization is a strategy of permanent innovation: accommodation to ceaseless change, rather than an effort to control it. This strategy is based on flexible (multi-use) equipment; skilled workers; and the creation, through politics, of an industrial community that restricts the forms of competition to those favouring innovation.

Piore and Sabel also predicted that, as flexible specialization came to replace traditional assembly-line manufacturing, small firms would gain an advantage over huge companies. They believed that skilled workers employed in flexible specialization systems would gain more power relative to managers and employers. In a sense, they envisioned a return to craft forms of production (Chapter 1), with highly skilled, autonomous workers involved in all aspects of the production process.

There is evidence of an increase in flexible, computerized manufacturing systems, but some industries (e.g., meat processing) cannot and likely will not move quickly in this direction. Even in service industries, the shift to flexible work organizations is not as widespread as some might believe, For example, around the turn of the 21st century, high-tech firms began to spring up rapidly in Silicon Valley and elsewhere in North America and Europe, usually run by young, anti-bureaucratic entrepreneurs. These employers encouraged their creative employees to work in project-based teams, ignore conventional organizational structure, as in working regular hours, avoid workplace hierarchies, and essentially, "be their own bosses." While the term *flexible specialization* was not applied to these tech firms, their model of management reflected the same values. The limited research on the companies that stayed relatively small suggests that, in a short time, they too began to evolve into more hierarchical workplaces (Mayer-Ahuja and Wolf 2007).

Thus, Piore and Sabel's predictions of a shifting balance of power between workers and management, and between small firms and huge multinationals, appear to have been more in the realm of hope than of reality (Fox and Sugiman 1999). As Stephen Wood notes in a detailed assessment of the flexible specialization model, this part of the theory is really "an intellectual manifesto," a description of the type of workplace that Piore and Sabel believed would be preferable (Wood 1989b: 13). In a way, Piore and Sabel's optimistic predictions are reminiscent of postindustrial society theorists such as Daniel Bell, who were convinced that general skill levels would increase while inequality declined (Chapter 2).

While evidence of a significant shift toward flexible specialization in manufacturing is limited, many employers in both the manufacturing and service sectors have reorganized their workforces to gain greater flexibility and to reduce payroll costs, building what Pollert (1988) called a *flexible firm*. This more flexible type of work organization, with a core of full-time workers and a periphery of low-cost nonstandard workers whose numbers and functions vary with business conditions, gives companies a competitive advantage in an environment of quickly changing markets and technologies. This adaptability could be achieved three ways: *functional flexibility* (training workers to perform a variety of different tasks, thus making them more interchangeable); *numerical flexibility* (being able to quickly alter the size of the workforce, or the number of hours worked, through hiring of part-time, temporary, subcontracted, and other types of nonstandard workers); and *pay flexibility* (the ability to reduce pay and benefit costs by using alternative wage rates for nonstandard workers and by avoiding traditional collective agreements).

Functional flexibility (which requires employers to invest in training) and pay flexibility (which could require difficult bargaining with labour unions, see Chapter 11) have been pursued less often than numerical flexibility. In other words, flexible firm initiatives have most often relied on part-time or temporary/contract employees (see Chapter 4). In Canada, over the past decade, we have also seen a significant shift toward employment of temporary foreign workers (Gross and Schmitt 2012), as governments have sought ways of allowing private-sector firms to become more flexible (Fudge and MacPhail 2009). Thus, the economic uncertainties experienced by employers in the past several decades have also meant an increase in nonstandard jobs and a more precarious work situation for their employees (Harvey et al. 2017), more often for women than for men (Blázquez Cuesta and Carcedo 2014). All these trends are associated with greater employment insecurity and increased workplace inequality (Chapter 5).

LEAN PRODUCTION

While flexible specialization in manufacturing has not become widespread, *lean production* (LP) has certainly taken hold in North America and Europe, particularly in automobile manufacturing.[11] LP manufacturing is an evolution of earlier Japanese management innovations and also TQM, in some respects; it is well established in Japanese transplant factories in North America. LP uses a team-based approach and advanced production technology to obtain the highest amount of productivity possible. *Re-engineering*, the radical redesign of a firm's entire business process, is used to achieve maximum output and quality with the least labour input. A number of specific elements, some discussed earlier in this chapter, characterize LP: these include continuous improvement (*kaizen*), continuous innovation, flexible production, work teams, zero downtime, zero defects, JIT inventories and production, and employment security, at least when unions are involved (Drache 1994).

LP has been presented by its champions as a major improvement over mass-production manufacturing and traditional bureaucracy, as a *post-Fordist* approach to organizing work. Case studies of a GM Saturn plant in Tennessee and a GM–Toyota NUMMI factory in California (both no longer operating) have assessed these claims. Both factories were victims of GM's bankruptcy in 2009: the Saturn brand was terminated, and GM pulled out of the NUMMI joint venture before Toyota closed the factory in 2010 (it is now owned and run by Tesla). Still, the assessments of these LP examples remain relevant.

At Saturn, workers and the United Auto Workers union played an active role in all phases of designing the plant, much like what occurred with the Shell chemical plant in Sarnia, discussed earlier. A sociotechnical approach was adopted, integrating technology and the social organization of production. Work teams of 6 to 15 members were self-managed, with responsibility for deciding important issues such as workflow and quality. Teams also managed human resources, including hiring, absenteeism policies, and replacement of absent workers. Saturn employees were paid 80 percent of the industry wage in an annual salary (as opposed to hourly), but they could receive up to an additional 40 percent if production and customer satisfaction goals were met or exceeded. A unique feature was the partnership approach to strategic planning, operating, and problem-solving decisions, whereby managers were partnered with elected union representatives. In short, in the Saturn plant, LP appeared to be acceptable to both management and workers, and productivity and quality appeared to be high.

NUMMI differed from Saturn in that it was an old GM factory plagued with production problems and suffering from labour–management disputes. When it reopened as a GM–Toyota joint venture, a new approach to work organization and human resource management was applied (Pfeffer 1994). The NUMMI system included extensive employee training, promised job security, teams of multi-skilled workers, reduced status distinctions, an elaborate suggestion system, and extensive sharing of what used to be exclusively management's information. Compared with the old GM factory, this new work system resulted in impressive reductions in absenteeism and grievances, and significantly improved quality and productivity. An employee survey showed 90 percent were satisfied or very satisfied with work at NUMMI.

Assessing Lean Production

Both the Saturn and the NUMMI cases demonstrate the potential for LP to positively alter the worker–management relationship. LP goes well beyond the rigid and standardized mass production of Fordism by encouraging a flexible approach to product redesign and maintaining an emphasis on quality and continuous improvement. Like the QWL and TQM approaches, LP claims to rely on highly skilled and thinking workers, and promises a reduction in workplace conflicts through its teamwork model of decision making. With all these features, it is little wonder that LP has been portrayed by its advocates as marking the end of Taylorism and Fordism (Womack, Jones, and Roos 1990).

But the Saturn and NUMMI examples may be outliers. As with previous new management models that arrived with great promise, implementation of LP in other locations has often omitted some of the most important positive features and exacerbated some of the most problematic. Some critics have been harsh in their assessments of LP's impact on workers' lives (Rinehart, Huxley, and Robertson 1997; Russell 1999).[12] They point out that re-engineering of all the tasks involved in production is reminiscent of Taylorism and that multi-tasking (requiring one person to do several jobs) is not the same as multi-skilling (training them to complete a variety of different tasks). Instead, multitasking is one of the ways in which management has squeezed more work out of a smaller number of workers. The elimination of replacement workers, a cost-saving decision, has also had this effect, as has *kaizen*, the consensus-based approach to continuous improvement. By emphasizing how workers in a particular factory need to outperform their competition elsewhere, management essentially harnesses peer pressure to speed up production.

By way of example, James Rinehart describes a California automobile factory that, before LP, managed to keep its workers busy for 45 out of every 60 seconds they were on the job. LP brought this up to 57 out of 60 seconds. As Rinehart puts it, "to call kaizen a democratization of Taylorism is to demean the concept of democracy" (2006: 162). At least in manufacturing facilities, LP has generally not led to significant skill enhancement or to worker empowerment (Yates, Lewchuk, and Stewart 2001), to increased worker satisfaction (Vidal 2007), or to up-ending the pyramid of power (Vänje and Brännmark 2017). Rather, it has meant a faster pace of repetitive work (Schouteten and Benders 2004), higher stress for employees (Carter et al. 2013), higher injury rates (Brenner, Farris, and Ruser 2004), and increased concerns about worker health and safety (Spencer and Carlan 2008). As Rinehart (2006: 200) concludes, "lean production constitutes an evolution of rather than a transcendence of Fordism." However, if we look outside of the auto sector we can find some potentially promising applications of lean methodology, particularly in health care. Unlike in auto production, where lean principles are applied to the entire production system, in health care applications of lean methodology are typically in specific hospital units or programs, such as emergency departments (D'Andreamatteo et al. 2015).

HIGH-PERFORMANCE WORKPLACES

Another addition to the long list of alternative managerial paradigms hoping to solve the problems of bureaucracy and improve worker–management relationships is the attempt to construct *high-performance workplaces* (Godard 2004). A high-performance workplace (HPW) is characterized by employee involvement in decision making, team organization and flexible work design, extensive training and learning opportunities, open information sharing and communication, financial incentives for improved performance (including profit sharing), support for family responsibilities, and a work environment that improves health and reduces stress (Kalleberg et al. 2006). In other words, this model of an ideal organization appears to draw on most of the best features of the various other approaches described earlier in this chapter. The HPW approach goes further, however, by advocating human resource management programs that are family friendly and emphasizing the importance of a healthy, non-stressful work environment.[13]

The HPW approach emerged in the 1990s, however, when many large employers were already trying to reduce their commitments to lifetime employment for workers. Consequently, the HPW model assumes that employment security can no longer be guaranteed (Betcherman et al. 1994). Furthermore, profit sharing also means risk sharing—if the company loses money, so do the workers. In some respects, the HPW approach is an updated version of the QWL approach in an internal labour market system (see Chapter 5), but with even greater emphasis on employee participation and human resource development, including employee wellness initiatives, for the core of advantaged workers.

Unlike LP, which was most widely adopted in manufacturing, HPW practices are adaptable to a range of service industries, as one study of personal care workers suggests (Harley, Allen, and Sargent 2007). There is no single HPW model. Some employers focus more on empowerment-enhancing practices (e.g., self-directed work groups), some emphasize motivation-enhancing approaches (e.g., benefit packages and pay-for-performance), while others invest more in training or skill-enhancing practices (Chowhan, Zeytinoglu, and Cooke 2016).

Chapter 9: In Search of New Managerial Paradigms

Few combine all three. There is evidence that the use of HPW practices by employers is associated with higher job satisfaction among their employees (Zatzick and Iverson 2011). Furthermore, firms using an integrated approach to human resource management—combining training, performance-based pay incentives, and employee involvement in decision making—also tended to be more innovative in their products or services (Therrien and Léonard 2003; Mohr and Zoghi 2008).

Assessing High-Performance Workplaces

Like flexible specialization, the HPW is more a model of a desirable future than a description of current practice. Only a minority of work organizations have moved in this direction, and among those that have, a majority have adopted only some of its core features (Leckie et al. 2001; Koski and Järvensivu 2010). Furthermore, as studies evaluating the effectiveness of the HPW approach accumulate, it is becoming apparent that, in many situations, there are limited payoffs.[14] On balance, research points to potential productivity gains when "bundles" of HPW practices are introduced, especially if these changes enhance employee involvement and skill levels (Appelbaum et al. 2000). In contrast, the more that companies rely on contingent (part-time and temporary) workers, the lower their profits (Stirpe, Bonache, and Revilla 2014). As for improved quality of working life, there can be benefits for the advantaged core workers in a HPW, skill upgrading, decision-making opportunities, profit sharing, and improved working conditions among them. But there are also risks, since employment security can no longer be guaranteed, resulting in increased use of contract or temporary workers, and profit sharing is only a benefit so long as the company is making a profit. Furthermore, if HPW initiatives are introduced while companies are also downsizing or restructuring, employees "are unlikely to buy into and benefit" from these management approaches (Moen et al. 2016: 156).

Critics of the HPW approach are skeptical of the level of commitment asked of workers (Godard 2001; Danford et al. 2004), pointing to previous examples of companies using QWL, TQM, and LP approaches to speed up work and sideline unions. Nevertheless, there are some examples of unions and management working together to build high-performance organizations.

Clarke and Haiven (1999) describe how, in Saskatchewan in the 1990s, the Communications, Energy and Paperworkers Union participated in redesigning the Saskatoon Chemicals work organization, including profit sharing and payment for skills. As in other successful union–management projects, what made the difference was a strong union centrally involved in all aspects of the change process. In addition, both parties agreed to a process of *continuous bargaining*, in contrast to the traditional approach of seeking a collective agreement that would remain unchanged for several years.

There have been few efforts to introduce HPW practices in the lower-tier service industries. However, a study of large U.S. retail companies that have attempted this (e.g., Wal-Mart and Home Depot) concludes that workers have not really benefited (Bailey and Bernhard 1997). Wages did not rise appreciably, skill sets were not significantly enhanced, and only a few workers found new career opportunities. HPW organizations, while not widespread, are more likely to be found in the upper-tier services and in some of the goods-producing industries. Thus, the advent of this form of work organization may signal greater labour market segmentation. In fact, downsizing and layoffs have frequently accompanied the implementation of HPW systems (Osterman 2000; Danford et al. 2004), along with increased reliance on contingent works (Stirpe, Bonache, and Revilla 2014). Thus, to the extent that HPW become more prevalent, we may also be seeing further polarization in society, with a small, privileged elite of highly skilled, relatively autonomous workers being decently rewarded while the majority of workers face greater risk of low-skill, less rewarding, insecure work (Kashefi 2011). In short, the HPW model does not offer a solution to the larger social problem of growing labour market inequality.

CONCLUSION

We began this chapter by commenting on the decades-long search for a new managerial paradigm that will help address the problems of bureaucracy and the dilemmas of managers who are seeking to gain compliance from the workers they supervise. Japanese management approaches and Swedish work reforms provided some significant improvements over scientific management and the human relations approach, as did quality-of-working-life (QWL) programs that drew on many of the management innovations developed in Japan and Sweden. Most important, they emphasized enhancing the skills of workers and building complexity back into jobs—in contrast to scientific management (Taylorism), which took exactly the opposite approach—and recommended involving workers in decision making in a variety of different ways, something that the human relations approach felt was largely unnecessary.

However, the history of new management approaches has not been one of steady progress. Total quality management (TQM) added a focus on customer satisfaction and on continuous improvement to the recipe for effective modern organizations, and proponents of the learning organization put particular emphasis on enhancing the skills and knowledge of workers. In contrast, the organizational culture approach to gaining compliance from workers and increasing productivity seemed to be taking us back to the human relations model that was so popular in the mid-20th century. Lean production (LP) promoted the skill enhancement and worker involvement central to QWL, Japanese, and Swedish approaches to management. But it also relied on Taylorist re-engineering of job tasks in a production system to force workers to work harder and faster. The high-performance workplace (HPW) model of management added reducing workplace and work–family stress, along with profit sharing, to the checklist of criteria for effective modern workplaces, but also reminded workers that they should no longer count on job and income security. In addition, like the flexible firm model, it conceded that only a minority of workers could expect to have secure and satisfying employment and that higher social inequality might have to be accepted as the norm in contemporary Western capitalist societies.

So, a century after Taylor promoted scientific management as a solution to the dilemmas of organizing work and motivating workers in large industrial workplaces, we have made some progress but not as much as management experts have promised. To some extent, this discrepancy may be a function of what Pfeffer and Sutton (2000) call the "knowing–doing gap." Managers may believe that employees are their most valuable asset but face many barriers to acting on this understanding. Furthermore, fads launched by management consultants have a short life cycle and are difficult for senior managers to successfully implement (Carson et al. 2000). Workers faced with a succession of "new" approaches to being managed that frequently involve more talk than action might quickly become cynical and reluctant to "buy into" the latest attempt to improve productivity and service (Carter and Mueller 2002).

An alternative explanation of the relatively slow movement forward takes us back to our discussion in Chapter 1 of the *consensus* and *conflict* perspectives used by sociologists when analyzing society. All the new management approaches we have reviewed in this chapter begin with the assumption that a consensus in the workplace is possible, if we can simply find the right workplace structures and best managerial formula. In contrast, the more critical assessments of workplace social relationships presented in Chapter 10 are influenced by the conflict approach, which assumes that, in capitalist societies, there are inherent conflicts of interest between employees, on the one hand, and corporate owners and the managers who work for them, on the other. If so, we should perhaps not expect to find ultimate solutions to the problems of bureaucracy and the dilemmas of managing workers in them.

DISCUSSION QUESTIONS

1. Think back to some of the jobs you have held. Describe any interactions with managers or other job experiences that relate to managerial approaches discussed in this chapter.
2. Critically discuss the following statement: Worker participation in decision making is neither desirable from the point of view of management nor desired by workers.
3. Which of the many approaches to management discussed in this chapter would be most effective at motivating younger (age 25 and under) workers? Why?
4. Assume that, five years after graduating, you are promoted into a management position with responsibility for 50 employees. Discuss what you have learned from this chapter that could help you be an effective manager.
5. Which of the new managerial paradigms discussed in this chapter have the greatest potential to improve both productivity *and* the quality of working life?

ADDITIONAL RESOURCES

WORK AT THE MOVIES

- *The Internship* (directed by Shawn Levy, 2013, 119 minutes). Made redundant due to technological advancements, two sales people take internships with Google and cooperate and compete with other younger, tech-savvy interns for a chance at a paying job.

- *Officeland* (directed by Marcy Cuttler, 2014, 45:04 minutes). This documentary addresses the rise of open concept offices and assesses the benefits and negative aspects of this movement. It is available through CBC Doc Zone: http://www.cbc.ca/doczone/episodes/officeland.
- *The Social Network* (directed by David Fincher, 2010, 120 minutes). The film focuses on Mark Zuckerberg and the development of Facebook and its unique organizational culture.
- *Gung Ho* (directed by Ron Howard, 1986, 111 minutes). Michael Keaton plays a manager who is tasked with helping the workers at his U.S. auto plant incorporate Japanese management techniques after the car manufacturer is taken over by a Japanese corporation.

SOUNDS OF WORK

- "Factory" (Bruce Springsteen). Springsteen highlights the daily drudgery of blue-collar factory work.
- "Working Man Blues" (Merle Haggard). In Haggard's song, a hard-working family man visits a tavern and sings about his experiences to escape the daily grind.
- "Why Work Doesn't Happen at Work" (Jason Fried, 2010). In this Ted Talk, Fried discusses the challenges for collaboration and productivity in the workplace. His talk is available through Ted.com at http://www.ted.com/talks/jason_fried_why_work_doesn_t_happen_at_work.html.

NOTES

1. See Carson et al. (2000) and Miller and Hartwick (2002) on management fads, and Krause-Jensen (2010) for an anthropological analysis of the role of management consultants within large work organizations.
2. The Japanese "economic miracle" following World War II is most often attributed to the combination of extensive government intervention in the economy, resulting in manufacturers, unions, and banks working together, and large-scale foreign investment by the United States, which, during the Cold War years, was concerned about promoting Western ideas of democracy (Pyle 1996; Forsberg 2000). Gottfried and Hayashi-Kata (1998) argue, however, that non-standard employment among women also played a significant role.

3. See Knights, Willmott, and Collison (1985) and Rinehart's (1984) Canadian case study.
4. On Volvo Kalmar, see Aguren et al. (1985). On Saab's work reorganization, see Logue (1981). The specific situation in each factory could be different now. For a critical view, see Van Houten (1990).
5. See Cherns (1976) and Gardell (1977); on QWL initiatives in Canada, see Rankin (1990) and Jain (1990).
6. In the United States, some researchers have linked an increase in occupational injuries and illnesses (carpal tunnel syndrome, for example) to the increased prevalence of QCs and JIT delivery systems (Askenazy 2001; Brenner, Farris, and Ruser 2004).
7. http://www.ge.com/en/company/companyinfo/quality/whatis.htm [retrieved 17 February 17, 2019].
8. See Schneider, Ehrhart, and Macey (2013) for a useful comparison of organizational climate research, conducted by psychologists, and organizational culture research conducted by sociologists and management scholars.
9. On Benetton's and the Body Shop's corporate values, respectively, see http://www.benettongroup.com/sustainability/company-approach/ and https://www.clicksgroup.co.za/corporate-sustainability/body-shop.html [both retrieved 18 February 2019].
10. For useful, generally positive discussions of CSR, see the 2010 special issue of the *International Journal of Management Reviews* (Vol. 12, No. 1). Banerjee (2008) is much more critical, arguing that CSR and other initiatives are simply ideological rhetoric used to increase corporate power and profits. MacPhail and Bowles (2009) provide a Canadian perspective on CSR.
11. On LP in manufacturing in Canada, see Rinehart, Huxley, and Robertson (1997) and Yates, Lewchuk, and Stewart (2001). Also see Kochan, Lansbury, and MacDuffle (1997), Green and Yanarella (1996), and Vänje and Brännmark (2017). Nilsson (1996) discusses LP in a white-collar setting, and Beata, Jens, and Per-Olaf (2007) describe a health care setting.
12. Nilsson (1996) offers a somewhat more positive assessment of lean production as implemented in Sweden. So, too, do Vänje and Brännmark (2017) but they, nevertheless, disagree that lean production "turns the pyramid of power upside down."
13. It is important to distinguish HPW from the concept of *high commitment management* which has been used to describe supervisory systems in telephone call centres that combine "fun and surveillance" (Kinnie, Hutchinson, and Purcell 2000). In such settings, managers try to keep employees amused and distracted with a variety

of minor benefits, including non-traditional and trendy workplaces, while also monitoring their work closely (Baldry and Haller 2010). Research suggests that this approach seldom leads to job enlargement or employee involvement in significant decision making (Godard 2004; Fleming and Sturdy 2011; D'Cruz and Noronha 2011). Indeed, it may be resented by some workers (Baldry and Hallier 2010).

14. White et al. (2003), Leckie et al. (2001), and Kashefi (2012) assess the quality of work life in high-performance workplaces. Bowen and Ostroff (2004), Godard (2004), and Stirpe, Bonache, and Revilla (2014) examine productivity gains.

CONFLICT AND CONTROL IN THE WORKPLACE

10

"I'm finishing my maternity leave right now and am going back a week before Christmas. I was looking forward to going back, but now I'm going to go back to a really depressing thing. It's a shock and the way they did it, a month before Christmas. You can't help but feel it personally. They should be ashamed of themselves. Last Friday, I went shopping for Christmas and spent a bunch of money. I know it's not the end of the world, but I'm going to have to take it all back. I know it could always be worse, but this is what I'm feeling. This is what I'm going through. . . . "My boyfriend and I are both third-generation workers. My grandfather worked for GM, my mother worked for the cleaning company there, Robinson. My aunts, uncles, cousins, and all my siblings have all worked there at one point. It paid for my younger sister to get through nursing school. . . . My partner's dad worked there and so did his grandfather and all his siblings. . . . I'm still hopeful our union and the government can do something to prevent [the closure] from happening. But, of course, we have started to think about a plan B. . . . Going back to school is an option, but it'll be hard because to have a mortgage and a baby that we have to pay for . . . getting another job is our best option."

–Stephanie Nelles, assembly-line employee (12 years) at GM automobile factory in Oshawa, ON, after learning that, after operating in Oshawa for over a century, GM decided to close the factory, putting more than 2500 employees out of work.

Source: Flannery Dean. (2018). "'You Can't Help But Feel It Personally': 4 Women on Losing Their Jobs in the Oshawa GM Plant Closure." Chatelaine: https://www.chatelaine.com/news/oshawa-gm-plant-closing-2019/ [downloaded Jan 2 2019]. © 2019 & Used with permission of St. Joseph Communications. All rights reserved.

INTRODUCTION

Over the past century, employers sought new ways of managing workers in order to increase efficiency and productivity and to reduce workers' resistance to authority. Scientific management, with its emphasis on complete managerial control and a detailed division of labour, gave way to the softer human relations approach, which tried to motivate workers by making them feel that they were an integral part of the larger work organization. By the 1970s, North American management consultants were busy advocating changes to organizational structures and job design, drawing on principles of sociotechnical design developed in the United Kingdom, ideas about employee involvement in decision making from Sweden, and particularly, Japanese-style management (Chapter 9). The Japanese influence could be seen in quality-of-working-life (QWL) programs, total quality management (TQM) models, organizational culture initiatives, and later, lean production.

Proponents of the new managerial paradigms might argue that many of the problems of bureaucracy, as well as the dilemmas faced by managers trying to motivate workers, have been solved. Some might go so far as to propose that the outcome has been a less conflict-ridden and more egalitarian society, that we are getting closer to Émile Durkheim's vision of modern society in which employers, managers, and workers recognize that pulling together is in everyone's best interest (see Chapter 1). But if we take a more critical look at employment and managerial trends over the past decades through a conflict, rather than a consensus, lens, it can lead us to a different conclusion.

As we noted in Chapter 9, some of the new management strategies involved few real changes to employees' jobs. The organizational culture approach would be an example. In contrast, attempts to develop high-performance workplaces (HPW) put more effort into reducing the negative effects of bureaucracy, increasing job skills, enhancing worker decision making, and improving work–life balance. Even so, few work organizations have introduced the full HPW package. Furthermore, benefits to workers of this approach are counterbalanced by increased risk of job loss or pay reductions. Thus, responses to employees' desires for more autonomy and responsibility and for more family-friendly workplace benefits and policies continue to be the exception rather than the rule (Jackson 2005; Duxbury and Higgins 2017).

Furthermore, as we note later in this chapter, while some North American managers were experimenting with new approaches to organizational design and employee motivation, others were busy downsizing organizations and outsourcing jobs. There has also been a parallel trend toward replacing full-time permanent employees with part-time and temporary employees (Fuller and Vosko 2008; Kalleberg 2009) and the contracting-out of work previously done by better-paid permanent employees (Shalla 2002; Zuberi 2013). As a result, we have seen an increase in income inequality and labour market polarization (see Chapters 4 and 5). Not surprisingly, then, organized labour continues to challenge the status quo. Despite their decline in some sectors, unions still frequently oppose management policies (Collinson and Ackroyd 2005) and sometimes engage in strikes or threaten to do so (see Chapter 11).

We begin this chapter by reviewing Karl Marx's critique of work in capitalist society, since his arguments shaped the conflict perspective. We then discuss the *labour process* approach to analyzing the workplace, an effort to update Marx's ideas to explain 20th-century worker–management relationships. This alternative approach begins with the assumption that conflict is to be expected in work settings, where the interests of owners and managers are in opposition to those of workers. It focuses directly on attempts by management to control workers, and on how workers resist such efforts, trying to gain more control over their own labour. While the labour process approach has its flaws, as we will see, it provides a much more critical assessment of the new managerial paradigms. In Chapter 11, we continue the discussion by examining the origins, functions, and future of trade unions, another vehicle through which workers have tried to look after their interests.

MARX ON CAPITALIST EMPLOYMENT RELATIONSHIPS

As we observed in Chapters 1 and 5, class conflict was central to Marx's perspective on social change. Looking back in history, he argued that feudalism had been transformed into a new mode of production—capitalism, characterized by wage-labour relations of production—because of conflict between different class groupings. Looking forward, he predicted that capitalism would eventually give way to socialism because of the inherently conflictual and exploitative relationships between owners and workers.

Central to Marx's arguments was a specific economic theory of the capitalist labour market. Beginning with the premise that the value of a product was a direct function of the labour needed to produce it, Marx observed that wage-labourers produced more than the amount needed to pay their wages. *Surplus value* was being created, and employers were exploiting workers by keeping the profits from their labour. By purchasing labour, capitalists gained control over the labour process itself. Factory forms of organization and mechanization of production further increased employer control.

These relationships of production led, according to Marx, to feelings of *alienation* among workers in a capitalist economy.[1] Marx identified a number of different sources of alienation. Products did not belong to those who produced them, but rather to those who owned the enterprise and who purchased the labour of workers. Decisions about what to produce and how to sell the finished products were not made by the workers, and profits generated in the exchange remained with the owners of the enterprise. In fact, given an extensive division of labour, many of the workers involved might never see the finished product. Thus, workers were alienated from the product of their own work.

Marx also emphasized alienation from the very activity of work. Transfer of control over the labour process from individual workers to capitalists or managers meant that individual workers lost the chance to make decisions about how the work should be done. In addition, extensive fragmentation of the work process had taken away most intrinsic work rewards. Alienation also involved the separation of individual workers from others around them. Obviously, bureaucratic hierarchies could have this effect. But more important, because capitalist employment relationships involve the exchange of labour for a wage, work was transformed from a creative and collective activity to an individualistic, monetary activity. Work itself had become a commodity. As a consequence, Marx argued, workers were alienated even from themselves.[2]

Marx believed, of course, that eventually members of the working class would overcome their alienation and rise up in revolt against their exploitation. This revolt has not happened in Western industrial and postindustrial societies, in part because the extremely harsh, dangerous, and exploitative working conditions of early industrialization have been largely eliminated. Looking back, we can see that the combination of labour legislation, unions and professional associations, and more sophisticated employers has led to higher incomes and standards of living, safer working conditions, and more responsibility and autonomy for workers, at least in relative terms.

However, in earlier chapters, we documented the growing number of working poor in Canada, a polarization of work rewards, and the rise in precarious employment. Unions continue to resist management attempts to reduce wages and cut jobs (Chapter 11), while most nonunion workers have little choice but to accept what they are offered. Hundreds of workers are still killed on the job each year, and thousands suffer workplace injuries (Chapter 12). Despite the calls for new management approaches to empower workers, some employers continue to act as if control over work belongs to them and must never be shared. So, while Marx's descriptions of working conditions in early capitalist society may no longer apply, the core themes in his writings can still help us to better understand work in today's postindustrial economy. These themes—power relationships in the workplace, attempts by owners and managers to control the labour process, resistance to these attempts by workers, and conflict between class groups—are central to the labour process perspective on worker–management relationships.

THE LABOUR PROCESS PERSPECTIVE

Harry Braverman on the "Degradation of Work"

Writing almost 50 years ago in *Labor and Monopoly Capital*, Harry Braverman (1974) argued that 20th-century capitalism had changed substantially from the mode of production examined by Marx. A small number of huge, powerful corporations controlled national and international economies. The role of the state in the production process had expanded. New technologies had evolved, workplace bureaucracies had grown, and the labour process itself had become increasingly standardized.

Focusing on the transformation of office work in large bureaucracies, Braverman observed that, at the beginning of the 20th century, (male) clerks and bookkeepers had exercised considerable control over their work and had been responsible for a wide variety of tasks. But this was no longer the case. An extensive division of labour had narrowed the scope of the work done by one person. Clerks essentially processed an endless stream of paper on a white-collar assembly line, their routinized tasks devoid of much mental activity. In short, clerical work had been degraded and deskilled.

Braverman attributed these changes to management strategies designed to improve efficiency and gain more control over the office labour process, the same strategies employed in factories many decades earlier. Thus, Braverman saw Taylorist tendencies at the heart of all modern management approaches, even those used to organize the work of technicians, professionals, and middle-level managers. He believed that both lower- and higher-status white-collar workers were becoming part of the same working class. The deskilling and degradation of work in general was setting the scene for future class conflict.

Braverman's provocative book was highly influential, but it was also criticized by researchers sympathetic to its general thesis.[3] First, Braverman overgeneralized from scattered evidence in North America to assert that deskilling was a universal pattern present in all occupations within all industrial capitalist societies. Important cultural differences in the labour process were ignored, as were situations in which automation, work reorganization, and new management strategies provided more autonomy and responsibility to workers. Furthermore, while focusing on declining skills in some occupations, Braverman overlooked new skills required in industrial and postindustrial economies. For example, the management of large numbers of employees required the development of a wider range of leadership skills, office work in service industries required sophisticated people skills, and efficient use of new manufacturing and information technologies required computer skills.[4]

Second, Braverman ignored the gendered nature of workplace skills, as have many other researchers (see Chapter 6). Technical skills, frequently more central to "male" jobs, have been valued more highly than people skills, which figure more prominently in jobs typically held by women.[5] Hence, Braverman probably underrated the skill requirements of clerical work. In addition, he overlooked how race and ethnicity have played a major part in determining access to better jobs in North American labour markets (Creese 2007; see also Chapter 5).

Third, Braverman implied that workers passively accepted management assaults on their job skills and autonomy. Seldom in *Labor and Monopoly Capital* does one find mention of workers resisting management, even though power struggles have always been part of the informal side of bureaucracy (Chapter 8). Furthermore, as we will argue in Chapter 11, workers in western industrialized countries have formed unions for well over a century to collectively negotiate with their employers. The main flaw in Braverman's theory of the degradation of work, then, is its determinism, the belief that an inner logic of 20th-century capitalism compelled capitalists to devise Taylorism, Fordism, and the many managerial strategies that followed them.

Why, then, was Braverman's book so influential? The answer is that he challenged work researchers to ask new questions about changes in the labour process in contemporary capitalist societies. Braverman brought the sociology of work and organizations back to issues of class and inequality, power and control, resistance and conflict (Smith 1994). Even in his failings—overgeneralizing about deskilling, not taking account of gender, and overlooking worker resistance—he motivated other researchers to ask critical questions about shifting methods of managerial control and about trends in the deskilling of work.

Methods of Managerial Control

Richard Edwards (1979) linked labour market segmentation theory (see Chapter 5) with the labour process perspective by describing the evolution of workplace control systems in the 20th century. He distinguished between three basic types of managerial control. With *simple control*, most common in secondary labour markets, employers regulate the labour process directly with either coercive or paternalistic methods. *Technical control* is achieved by machine pacing of work and can, in part, replace the direct supervision of simple control methods. For example, Henry Ford's assembly line gave managers a powerful means of controlling the pace of work. *Bureaucratic control* has evolved in large corporations in the core sector of the economy. Good salaries, generous benefits, and pleasant work settings are the inducements provided, usually to middle- and upper-level white-collar employees and some groups of skilled manual workers. The internal labour market (see Chapter 5) and the prospects of an interesting and rewarding career are part of an employment package designed to win employees' commitment.[6]

Critics have argued that this analysis portrays workers as largely passive, without any *agency*, not recognizing how they might resist, reshape, or even actively participate in management control strategies. Andrew Friedman (1977: 82–85), for instance, describes a shifting *frontier of control*, which is influenced alternately by conflict and accommodation between employers and employees. At issue is who sets the hours, pace, and sequence of work tasks, and what constitutes fair treatment and just rewards. Sometimes, workers gain a say in these matters through union bargaining. Or, rather than using *direct control* (like the simple control described by Edwards), management may initiate some work reforms, giving workers what Friedman calls *responsible autonomy*. Examples would be the QWL programs and other participative management schemes described in Chapter 9.

A study of potash mining in Saskatchewan (Russell 1999: 193–94), for example, revealed that managers in lean production work settings were less likely to employ a "rough" style of management (*direct control* in Friedman's terms). However, it was also apparent that management could not afford to act in this manner, since doing so might jeopardize the cooperation of workers who were expected to maintain high levels of productivity in a lean-production environment. Ultimately, Russell (1999) concluded that, despite the rhetoric, workers had not really been empowered.

Turning to the service sector, a nightclub in a western Canadian city provides an interesting example of the shifting frontier of control. Mike Sosteric (1996) describes the strong informal workplace culture that had emerged in the club and the great degree of job autonomy enjoyed by workers. As a result, workers were loyal and committed, and customers received high-quality, personalized service. But new management saw some of the norms of the informal workplace culture as problematic and tried to implement what might be seen as a system of responsible autonomy. The workers were put off by the training seminars, disliked the new system of job enlargement, and found that elimination of supervisors made their work more difficult. Consequently, they actively resisted the changes. In turn, management adopted a direct and coercive control strategy that led, ultimately, to workers quitting and the quality of service in the nightclub deteriorating.

While Friedman described responsible autonomy being offered to selected groups of workers in return for their cooperation, Michael Burawoy (1979, 1984) went even further. He demonstrated that, in many work settings, employees actively choose to cooperate. In his study of machine shop workers, he described how an unspoken agreement with company goals emerged. Some employees adapted to management's control system by treating wage bonuses as a game they tried to win, thus exhibiting an individualistic adaptation to an otherwise boring job. As long as each worker had a fair chance of "winning" bonuses, management's rules went unchallenged. For these workers, coercion (Burawoy called this the *despotic organization of work*) was unnecessary since, by accepting workplace rules, they basically motivated and managed themselves.

Burawoy described the *hegemonic organization of work* in much the same way that Richard Edwards defined *bureaucratic control*. In large corporations and government departments, employees often see their own futures linked with the success of the organization. Hence, management's goals and values are dominant, or hegemonic. The presence of internal labour markets and responsible autonomy helps to maintain management control. Individual workers are subtly encouraged to adopt the value system or organizational culture of the company or department, and good job conditions foster long-term commitment to the organization (Courpasson and Clegg 2012).

A study of how the Alberta government restructured the department responsible for museums and cultural heritage sites in the 1990s is a good example (Oakes, Townley, and Cooper 1998). By requiring all government departments to develop standardized business plans, an apparently neutral strategy from which, ostensibly, everyone would benefit, senior management shifted the department's emphasis from public education and cultural preservation to the logic of business while, at the same time, gaining greater control over professionals who adopted the language and values of business planning.

Electronic Control

The rapid growth of information and communication technologies (ICT) over the past decades has given rise to yet another type of management control system: *electronic control* (Sewell 1998). This may be relatively passive, as when workplaces are monitored by security cameras, but electronic control can also be more intrusive. A 2012 Canadian survey, for example, reported 44 percent of employees saying that, during the past year, they had received work-related phone calls or e-mail messages from their employer while on vacation or during time off (Battams 2013). Electronic surveillance is even more intrusive and aggressive, with supervisors listening to telephone calls, reading e-mail messages, monitoring Internet searches, tracking work performance, and sending warning messages to workers who are not producing as much as others. It is estimated that over three-quarters of U.S. workers experience some kind of electronic surveillance (West and Bowman 2016).

Such active surveillance is particularly wide-spread within *telephone call centres* where employees using computerized systems make hundreds of outgoing calls (e.g., for telephone sales or market research) or handle equally large numbers of incoming calls from customers on every shift. The same computers can be used to monitor workers' performance, both quantitatively (How long did each call take?) and qualitatively (Was the client's problem solved?

Chapter 10: Conflict and Control in the Workplace

Did the salesperson try hard enough to make a sale?). Supervisors may or may not listen in on individual calls, but the possibility that someone is listening has the same effect. If work teams are part of the management strategy, electronic performance monitoring can be used to push teams to compete with each other against high-performance targets.[7]

In another part of the service sector, United Parcel Services (UPS) has outfitted their delivery trucks with sensors that tell management exactly where UPS drivers are at any given time, and how quickly and efficiently they are delivering packages. This "telematics" system helps improve UPS profits. As a senior UPS manager explained in 2014, "Just one minute per driver per day, over the course of a year adds up to $14.5 million." Not surprisingly, this electronic form of Taylorism can also be extremely stress-inducing for employees.[8] As a result, many workers in this and other service sectors resent the imposition of electronic control systems (Chory et al. 2016).

Some researchers have analyzed telephone call centres from the perspective of the French social theorist Michel Foucault (1977), who wrote about the all-encompassing power of surveillance in modern society (Chapter 2). Fernie and Metcalf (1998), for example, call such workplaces "electronic sweatshops" in which workers have virtually no decision-making opportunities. In fact, because they know they can be monitored at any time, workers essentially become their own taskmasters. Subsequent studies, however, have documented considerable resistance by workers to management monitoring and surveillance (Ott 2016), and have described the varying amounts of control that call-centre workers have, depending on the types of services they provide.

For example, customer service agents providing complex financial information to clients have considerably more decision-making authority and are much less likely to be working in a computer-paced environment (Batt 2000). Similarly, nurse advisers working in call centres in the United Kingdom report having some autonomy in deciding how to provide health care advice to callers, despite being expected to work from a software-driven script that is meant to ensure that only "safe advice" is provided (Mueller et al. 2008). Making a similar point, Felstead, Jewson and Walters (2003) describe how *teleworkers* (people working from their own homes) are difficult to manage via electronic control since their jobs may involve a variety of different tasks. As a result, managers keeping electronic track of their work have trouble distinguishing between productive and unproductive work.

Summing up, managers use a variety of approaches to try to control the labour process in contemporary workplaces. Direct, technical, bureaucratic, hegemonic, and electronic control, along with responsible autonomy, are all possibilities, alone or in some combination. The balance of power and control in any given workplace can range from strictly coercive, with management fully in control, to situations where workers have considerable responsibility for regulating their own work, essentially controlling themselves. As John Jermier (1998: 241) observes, regimes of control range from those "anchored in the iron fist of power [to] those that rely on the velvet glove." In turn, workers continue to find ways to resist many management control efforts (Thompson 2016). As Friedman (1997) would say, the labour process remains a shifting "frontier of control" and conflict.

The Deskilling Debate

According to Braverman, the application of Taylorist-style management, along with the adoption of new technologies, was systematically deskilling both blue-collar and white-collar work in capitalist society. In contrast, Daniel Bell and other postindustrial society theorists argued that a new economy relying heavily on highly skilled "knowledge workers" was taking shape (see Chapter 2).[9] More recently, other writers have put forward a similar *enskilling* argument about the growing number of multi-skilled workers required by flexible specialization, lean production, and other postindustrial modes of production (Chapter 9), as well as by the proliferation of information and communication technologies (ICT) and robotics in the workplace.

So have we been seeing primarily deskilling or enskilling? Researchers attempting to answer this question have generally agreed that work-related skills have two basic components, substantive complexity (the level and scope of intellectually, interpersonally, and manually challenging tasks performed) and decision-making autonomy (Ikeler 2016). Large-scale studies at the end of the 20th century reached a fairly definitive conclusion about Braverman's deskilling hypothesis. On average, the long-term trend in North America and western Europe had been in the direction of increased skill requirements in the workplace (Clement and Myles 1994: 72).

This conclusion, however, requires several important caveats. First, a broad enskilling trend can still reflect a situation where deskilling has occurred in some specific occupations and work settings. An example would be the secondary labour market jobs in the Toronto contract building-cleaning industry described by Luís Aguiar (2001). He observed how, in the traditional "zone cleaning" approach, a single individual was responsible for a range of cleaning tasks. But in order to increase efficiency (and profits), supervisors subdivided the tasks into "restroom specialists," "dusting specialists," and "mopping specialists," essentially creating a "mobile assembly line" within which workers had to work harder and faster on a more limited number of tasks. Another example is the retail sector, where Ikeler (2015) compared skill requirements of sales workers in full-line U.S. department stores with those of sales workers in a chain of large discount stores that have come to dominate the North American retail market. He observed "semi-skilled selling" in the department stores, where workers had a reasonable amount of knowledge about the products they sold and engaged in relatively complex and autonomous emotional labour in how they related to customers when making sales. In contrast, sales workers in the discount stores were involved in "deskilled selling," spending much of their time stocking shelves, checking prices, and informing customers where they could find what they were looking for.

Second, an increase in skill requirements may not be accompanied by other improvements in the quality of working life. TQM and lean production, for example, may require workers to learn additional skills, but they may also be under pressure to work faster (Russell 1999; Carter et al. 2013). Some of the critical assessments of these management strategies (see Chapter 9) distinguish between *multitasking* (simply adding more tasks to a worker's job description) and *multi-skilling* (adding to a worker's skill repertoire), arguing that the former merely makes employees work harder, not smarter (Rinehart, Huxley, and Robertson 1997).

Third, the studies showing increased skill requirements over time included data only up until the late 1980s. Until then, growth in higher-skill jobs, most in the upper-tier services and the goods-producing industries, outstripped the expansion of less skilled positions, many in the lower-tier services. But we have continued to see substantial industrial restructuring and organizational downsizing, and widespread introduction of ICT, along with robotics and artificial intelligence (AI), the sum of which might have slowed or stopped the enskilling trend (Smith 2001).

TECHNOLOGY AND THE LABOUR PROCESS

Technology figured prominently in debates about industrialization and postindustrial society, where it was typically seen as contributing to increased productivity, greater societal prosperity, and as Daniel Bell (Chapter 2) predicted, reduced social inequality. Labour process researchers, from Harry Braverman on, have focused instead on how new technologies have been used to deskill work and increase control over employees.

The new technologies of the industrial age increased productivity largely by reducing the amount of physical labour required in goods-producing industries. In contrast, today's ICT and AI technologies are significantly reshaping, and sometimes replacing, the human physical and mental requirements of work in both the goods-producing and service sectors (West 2016). Factory robots and 3-D printers in manufacturing, e-commerce and social media marketing in the retail sector, autonomous vehicles in transportation, computer-assisted design in engineering firms, computer-assisted diagnostics in health care, cloud-based information sharing and processing systems in all sectors, and smartphones, the Internet, and Skype in workers' homes are all part of a rapidly changing technological context for work (Baldry 2011; Akhtar and Moore 2016).

As with the technologies that were introduced during the industrial age, ICT innovations have clearly contributed to increased productivity. They have also eliminated some types of jobs and created new ones. In manufacturing, many dirty, dangerous, and boring jobs have disappeared with the advent of robotics. Robots are ideal for work in cramped spaces, in extreme temperatures, or in otherwise hazardous situations, and have been used to eliminate dangerous jobs in some industries (e.g., welding and painting automobiles). As for white-collar office employees, compared to a century ago, the impact of ICT has generally been more positive than negative. Many of the dreary filing and typing chores of office work have disappeared, and opportunities to acquire advanced ICT skills have produced more challenging and interesting jobs.[10]

The rapid evolution of ICT has obviously created many new types of skilled work. In Canada, for example, the number of people working in ICT industries (e.g., software development, manufacturing computer equipment, or providing computer or telecommunications services) increased rapidly from 411,000 to 546,000 between 1997 and 2001 (Beckstead and Brown 2005). Employment in the ICT sector then dropped back down to about 525,000 by 2011, as ICT industries suffered setbacks during the 2008–9 recession and some of the largest companies outsourced many of their jobs. Since then, however, ICT employment rose back to 595,000 in 2016 (3.3% of total employment).[11] Even so, as of 2011, Canada's level of employment in ICT industries was relatively lower than that of the United States and most western European countries.[12]

But have ICT innovations generally led to improvements in job quality? Chapter 9 documented how some early innovations in automobile manufacturing (e.g., in the SAAB factory in Sweden) led to skill enhancement and increased autonomy for workers. What is possible, however, is not always what happens. For example, while computer numerical control (CNC) machines, used to make metal parts and tools, can lead to enskilling, in some instances they have had the opposite effect. One skilled Canadian machinist described the impact of CNC machines on his job:

> You don't even need a man to monitor, the [CNC] machines will monitor themselves. They've got all these electronic scans that tell when the tool edge is wearing, what horsepower the machine is using. They've got all these tool change systems, so they even can change tools whenever they want, so you don't even need a man there. (Robertson and Wareham 1987: 28)

Turning to the service sector, along with the creation of thousands of highly skilled jobs, the ICT revolution has also created new frustrations and anxieties (Akhtar and Moore 2016; Chesley 2014). A recent U.S. study of "analytics workers" (people who scan websites and videos to provide data to advertisers and others) documents how, ironically, the productivity of these highly skilled and largely self-managed workers is frequently hampered because of their reliance on cloud-based "black box" analytics programs (owned by companies like Google) over which they have no control.

We have also already noted how the potential for electronic control of workers has been significantly enhanced by ICT (Trusson, Hislop, and Doherty 2018), but another example would be useful. A Swedish study of the introduction of hand-held computers for work teams providing home-care services (Hjalmarsson 2009) described how the new technology was meant to enhance the services provided and to allow caregivers to make better decisions. Instead, it was more frequently used by managers to monitor the types of services provided and how long it took workers to complete each task.

A current example of how these issues continue to play out are the concerns about intensive electronic surveillance raised by workers in Amazon's fulfilment centre warehouses, where the hourly "pick rate"" (number of customer-ordered products to be selected from shelves) is so high that workers can't even take bathroom breaks. In response, workers in some Amazon warehouses have launched unionization drives (Sainato 2019). In short, ICT may be 21st century in its complexity and design, but Frederick Taylor would still be pleased with some of the ways in which it is being used.

The evolution of ICT has created many new jobs, as already noted. But what about job loss? Has ICT created more jobs than have been eliminated? Or will the further development and spread of ICT result in the "end of work" as Jeremy Rifkin (1995) predicted more than two decades ago? At the beginning of this century, there appeared to be general agreement that, although new digital technologies had frequently led to workforce reductions within specific organizations and industries, the rise of the ICT sector had also led to a substantial number of new jobs (Frenette 2007b). Hence, on balance, ICT growth had not increased unemployment in Canada (Sargent 2000). But what has transpired since then?

Recent ICT developments may be shifting the job gain–job loss balance (West 2018). Frey and Osborne (2017) describe how, in the early era of computerization, technology-driven job loss occurred primarily in industries and occupations where production was based on "routine tasks involving explicit rule-based activity" (268). Automobile manufacturing, where robots have replaced thousands of workers is one example. More recently, however, advanced robotic technology linked with AI, including algorithmic analysis of "big data" bases, have put many more occupations in both the goods-producing and service sectors at risk of automation. Examples include truck and bus drivers in the transportation sector, retail sales clerks, administrative assistants in many offices, paralegal workers in law firms, medical diagnostics workers in the health care sector, and even computer programmers.

Frey and Osborne (2017) acknowledge that occupations involving a greater degree of creative and social intelligence will be more difficult to computerize but, nevertheless, conclude that 47 percent of *occupations* in the United States are at "high risk" of computerization in the next several decades. They do not say how many *jobs* this might involve in the United States, but a Canadian study using the same type of occupational analysis (Lamb 2016: 3) concluded that "nearly 42% of the Canadian labour force is at a high risk of being affected by automation in the next decade or two." Neither the U.S. nor the Canadian study are willing to say job loss due to computerization will either outweigh or lag behind job creation, but it is apparent to us that the debate is not settled.

Technological, Economic, or Social Determinism?

Historically, technology has been used to create jobs and to improve the quality of life. It has also been used to eliminate jobs, to destroy the natural environment, and to kill people. ICT is no different—it can have both positive and negative outcomes for society.[13] Our challenge is to find ways to use technology to provide rewarding employment for as many people as possible.

Writing in the 1960s, Canadian philosopher and media theorist Marshall McLuhan presented a highly pessimistic analysis of the impact of technology on social life. He concluded that human beings were at risk of becoming the servants of technology and suggested that, if trends continued, we might become "the sex organs of the machine world . . . enabling it to fecundate and to evolve ever new forms" (McLuhan 1964: 56, quoted in Menzies 1996: 44). Half a century later, in early 2014 at the annual meeting of the world's political and business elite in Davos, Switzerland, Eric Schmidt, the executive chairman of Google, provided another example of technology being given superhuman status when he stated, "It's a race between computers and people—and people need to win" (quoted in Young 2014: para. 6).[14]

Such statements, while likely intended as metaphors, nevertheless attribute too much independent power to technology. *Technological determinism*, the belief that technology has a life of its own, and that the developmental pattern and effects of a given technology are universal and unalterable, removes the possibility of human agency, the potential for people to shape technology for the greater social good (Edwards and Ramirez 2016). Furthermore, this position ignores the strong evidence that new technologies have been used in very different ways, with different outcomes, in different work settings and societies (Krzywdzinski 2017).

We also reject *economic determinism*, the belief that the "market knows best" how to choose and implement new technologies. It follows from such a perspective that, despite current problems with underemployment, deskilling, and loss of worker autonomy, new technologies will in time naturally lead to more positive than negative outcomes. But behind what Adam Smith called the "unseen hand of the market" are real people, making decisions about how to implement new technologies. These decisions typically have been made by only a tiny minority of citizens—owners and managers guided by the profit motive. As Charley Richardson (1996: 167) wrote, "Computers don't kill jobs, people do."

Instead, we prefer a *social determinism* perspective, advocating education, wide-ranging discussion, and open decision making about how new technologies will be used, by whom, and for whose benefit. We believe that technology should be used to serve individual, community, and societal needs, not merely the needs of a particular company or work organization. Consequently, workers must be able to participate in decisions about the choice and implementation of new workplace technologies that affect them directly, and citizens need a voice in shaping broader technology strategies.

Because the quest for increased competitiveness through technology has frequently meant job loss or job downgrading for workers, labour movements in North America and Europe have often opposed the introduction of new technology. But this does not mean that unions oppose technological change on principle. Rather, they have typically insisted that employees be consulted so that the negative effects can be minimized and opportunities for upgrading jobs, improving working conditions, and sharing the productivity gains are maximized.[15]

WHEN IN DOUBT, DOWNSIZE

The decades-long search for new managerial paradigms in North America (Chapter 9) has frequently been accompanied by large-scale organizational *downsizing*, driven by the desire to increase profits (Shin 2017) or to respond to economic downturns in the private sector, and by deficit-cutting agendas in the public sector. Large-scale job cuts, accompanied by organizational restructuring were widespread in the wake of the early-1990s recession in both Canada and the United States (McKay 1996; Lowe 2001). And extensive downsizing has continued in the 21st century (Davis-Blake and Broschak 2009; Datta et al. 2010).

Offshoring, the relocation of jobs by multinational companies to developing economies such as Mexico, India, and China where labour costs are much lower, has been frequent. Economic restructuring within an organization may also lead to sizable workforce reductions. The 2019 GM plant closure in Oshawa, Ontario, described at the beginning of this chapter may be an example, with GM stating that it was closing this factory (with 2,500 employees) and others elsewhere because it was moving towards the production of electric cars (Fife and Atkins 2018). Downsizing may also follow company mergers and subsequent large-scale reorganization of production. An example is the closing, in 2014, of the Heinz ketchup factory in Leamington, Ontario, after the Heinz company was sold to new owners. More than 700 jobs were lost. Other companies have downsized to deal with serious economic difficulties. The most prominent recent Canadian example involved BlackBerry, the Waterloo-based smartphone company, laying off 4,500 workers globally in September 2013 as it struggled to compete with Apple and Samsung products. About the same time, Canadian Pacific Railways was laying off between 4,500 and 6,000 workers in an effort to increase profits to the level of those being made by other North American railway companies.

The short-term cost savings associated with downsizing often do not translate into long-term improved profits (Baumol, Blinder, and Wolff 2003; Datta et al. 2010). Expenses may increase as managers realize they need to rehire workers or contract out work that otherwise would not be done. Large-scale staff cuts often reduce the trust and loyalty of remaining workers (Lowe and Schellenberg 2001; Feldheim 2007) and may weaken the social networks that are vital for the organization's capacity to learn and share knowledge (Fisher and White 2000). Also, departing employees may take "organizational memory" and vital skills with them (Littler and Innes 2003).

Downsizing negatively affects the health of workers who lose their jobs and become unemployed (Rege, Telle, and Votruba 2009). Medical researchers have tracked individuals who have been downsized, documenting damage to their health. For example, a study in four Finnish municipalities followed workers over 7.5 years, comparing those who experienced no downsizing, minor downsizing, and major downsizing (Vahtera et al. 2004). Those who experienced major downsizing were absent from work because of sickness at far higher rates than people in the other two groups, and they died from cardiovascular causes at higher rates.

The term *survivor syndrome* describes the negative psychological effects of downsizing on employees who remain behind (Mishra and Spreitzer 1998). Workers may experience elevated levels of stress and generally become demoralized and dissatisfied (Elmuti, Grunewald, and Abebe 2010). Motivation, loyalty, and productivity can suffer as employees avoid taking risks in their jobs and focus on protecting their own interests. This problem is exacerbated by increased workloads as the organization tries to do more with less. People may be reassigned to new duties without adequate training.[16]

Some organizations have tried to reduce the negative effects of downsizing by offering part-time or seasonal work to former full-time employees, or by covering the costs of retraining laid-off employees. Others have offered financial incentives to employees who voluntarily choose to quit or retire. Staff reductions achieved via such *employee buyouts* can create new problems for work organizations, though. If the most experienced and productive employees are among those who leave, the knowledge assets of the organization are depleted. For example, extensive downsizing through voluntary departures at NASA deprived the U.S. space program of the scientific and engineering knowledge it needed to send astronauts on another mission to the moon (DeLong 2004). A more recent and close-to-home example for the authors resulted from large-scale cuts by the provincial government to the University of Alberta budget in 2013. To reduce operating costs, the university put in place a voluntary severance package (VSP), inviting professors to resign in return for a year's salary. A significant number accepted the buyout package, and not just those close to retirement, leaving some departments struggling to offer required courses and students dealing with larger classes and fewer course options.

NEW MANAGERIAL PARADIGMS: AN IMPROVED LABOUR PROCESS?

The new managerial paradigms discussed in Chapter 9 use labels such as *participative management* and *employee empowerment*. More critical observers have described them as *neo-Fordist* or *post-Fordist*, implying that the positive changes have not been nearly as significant as their proponents claim (Vidal 2007). By offering some small concessions to workers, the new approaches have maintained the basic production framework and power structure of industrial capitalist society. Some critics go further, using a term such as *hyper-Taylorism* (Russell 1997: 28) or *neo-Taylorism* (Pruijt 2003; Crowley et al. 2010). They argue that work intensification signals a new era of "management by stress" in which workers push themselves and each other to make more profits for their employers (Kunda and Ailon-Souday 2005: 209). A good example is provided by Vivian Shalla (2004, 2007b), who documents how Air Canada required its flight attendants to work longer hours to help the company through a financial crisis and make it a more flexible and competitive global airline.

But labels are not as important as real outcomes. What do we see when we look back at four decades of new management approaches in North America? Most of them offer some potential for skill upgrading, increasing worker participation in decision making, and reducing bureaucracy. In some cases (Shell's Sarnia refinery and the Saskatoon Chemicals workplace, for example), these approaches helped to improve the quality of working life for employees. None of these new managerial paradigms, however, really provides permanent and effective avenues for workers to have ongoing input into larger organizational decisions, such as the introduction of new technologies or a decision to restructure or downsize a work organization.

Approaches that go the furthest to counter Taylorism and Fordism—HPWs, for example—have not been implemented often (Koski and Järvensivu 2010). Other approaches typically deliver less than they promise. We sometimes find that they have also been used to increase control over workers and to speed up work (Burchell, Ladipo, and Wilkinson 2002). In addition, the advent of the new management approaches has frequently been accompanied by widespread organizational restructuring and downsizing, with the result being a decline in the quality of working life for employees (Rodriquez 2017). The outcome, for society as a whole, has been a polarization of the labour force in terms of skill, income, work intensification, and job security, leading to greater social inequality (Green et al. 2011; Kristal 2013).

As we concluded about the impacts of new technologies on the labour process, the problem does not lie in the management system so much as in how it is implemented, by whom, and for what purposes. Overall, new management paradigms—we could call them *social technologies*—have almost always been introduced with productivity and profit as the main goals. For example, an in-depth study of four U.S. manufacturing plants that introduced a wide range of teamwork and other management approaches in the 1990s confirms this. Steven Vallas (2003) concluded that the overriding emphasis on increasing profit margins led managers and corporate executives to maintain or reintroduce standardized, or Taylorist, production methods, which clearly stood in the way of job enrichment and increased worker involvement in decision making. Another U.S. study concludes that one outcome of wide-scale organizational restructuring between 1984 and 2001 was an increase in managers' incomes relative to those of other workers (Goldstein 2012). In short, improvements in quality of working life and worker empowerment have been secondary motivations, while reductions in social inequality have seldom figured in the decision and have not occurred. What's more, workers have rarely been involved in the decision to implement new technologies, either directly or through their unions.

CONCLUSION

In this chapter, we have presented a more critical analysis of the new managerial approaches that have tried to solve the problems of bureaucracy, engage and motivate workers, and reduce conflict in the workplace. Our starting point was Harry Braverman's analysis of the labour process in modern societies, which was framed by a Marxist understanding of social relations of production in capitalist societies. Braverman's critique led us to focus on questions about deskilling trends, shifts in methods of controlling workers, and how technology is used in the workplace.

Our review of the evidence up until the end of the 20th century suggests that, on average, skill requirements had increased in the workplace, and job losses resulting from new technologies had not exceeded ICT-led job creation, contrary to what Braverman predicted. Since then, however, digital technologies, advanced robotics, and AI have been rapidly reshaping the labour market, leading us to conclude that debates about deskilling and technology-driven job loss are not yet over.

As for Braverman's deterministic view of owners and managers tightly controlling workers who have little or no agency, we suggested that it is an inadequate description of the contemporary labour process. Managers use a wide variety of approaches, some clearly coercive and others more participatory, to control and motivate workers. But workers also frequently resist in the shifting "frontier of control" (Friedman 1977) which characterizes the labour process today.

Even so, we concluded that the new managerial paradigms have frequently not lived up to their promises. In fact, in some cases, the rhetoric of new management models has been used to gain additional control over workers and speed up work processes. And none of the new management approaches goes so far as to directly involve workers in decisions about the choice of new hard technologies or plans to restructure or downsize organizations. Thus, with respect to both new technologies and evolving management approaches, our central point is that they are a result of human choices. We believe it is our responsibility to try to use them not simply to increase profits, but also to improve working conditions, empower workers, create jobs, and reduce social inequality.

In the next chapter, we examine the primary collective vehicle for worker resistance in North America over the past century, namely, the organized labour movement. We will explore the history of unions, how they are evolving, and the problems they are facing. In Chapter 12, we move beyond the new managerial paradigms discussed in Chapter 9 and the organized labour movement (Chapter 11), to explore some interesting alternative approaches to traditional employment relations that have potential for worker empowerment and conflict reduction.

DISCUSSION QUESTIONS

1. Some years ago, a U.S. executive told a Stanford University MBA class that "all organizations are prisons. It's just that the food is better in some than in others." What point was the executive making, and do you agree? Why or why not?
2. Some social theorists have argued that conflict is inevitable in the workplace; others believe that some kind of consensus might be possible. Critically discuss these two positions.
3. Outline the "labour process" perspective on work in industrial capitalist societies. Does this perspective have any relevance in 21st-century Canada? Explain your answer.
4. Managers use different approaches to try to control workers. In your opinion, which types of control would be most effective for workers in general? Which type of control would be most likely to make you work hard? Why?

ADDITIONAL RESOURCES

WORK AT THE MOVIES

- *Chicken Run* (directed by Peter Lord and Nick Park, 2000, 84 minutes). Having been hopelessly repressed and facing eventual certain death at the chicken farm where they are held, Rocky the rooster and Ginger the chicken decide to rebel against the evil Mr. and Mrs. Tweedy, the farm's owners.
- *Up in the Air* (directed by Jason Reitman, 2009, 109 minutes). George Clooney plays a consultant who travels around the United States firing people on behalf of his corporate clients.
- *Outsourced* (directed by John Jeffcoat, 2006, 103 minutes). This American romantic comedy is focused on the Seattle manager of a call centre who is outsourced to India and charged with motivating employees to improve call response times.
- *The Company Men* (directed by John Wells, 2010, 104 minutes). Set in the aftermath of the 2008 recession, this drama explores the impacts of corporate downsizing on the employees and CEO of a large, publicly held corporation.

SOUNDS OF WORK

- "Maggie's Farm" (Bob Dylan). A literal reading of this song suggests it is about a disgruntled worker ready to quit his or her job.
- "Take This Hammer" (Traditional/Lead Belly). This song on a work camp, prison, or forced labour theme is about defying authority and escaping work.
- "Fire in the Hole" (Hazel Dickens). Dickens sings about workers refusing to go down into a mine considered unsafe for work until the union has been consulted.
- "Will a Computer Decide Whether You Get Your Next Job?" (Planet Money podcast, NPR, January 15, 2014). This podcast examines the practice of companies preferring to use data, more than resumés, to hire new employees. It is available at http://www.npr.org/blogs/money/2014/01/15/262789258/episode-509-will-a-computer-decide-whether-you-get-your-next-job.

NOTES

1. The verb *alienate* refers to an act of separation or to the transfer of something to a new owner. Marx used the term in the latter sense and referred to the overall experience of working in a capitalist economy with the noun *alienation*.
2. See Hodson (2001: 23–25), Grabb (2002: 19–21), and Rinehart (2006: 11–20) for further discussion of Marx's writings on alienation.
3. Shalla (2007a) and Heisig (2009) discuss Braverman's contributions to the sociology of work.
4. See de Handel (2003), Carey (2007), and Krzywdzinski (2017) for contributions to the deskilling debate. Canadian studies include Russell (1999), Hughes and Lowe (2000), and Livingstone and Scholtz (2007).
5. See Hughes (1996), Brynin (2006), Kelan (2008), and Payne (2009) on the gendered nature of occupational skills.
6. Schörpf et al. (2017: 44) concludes that bureaucratic control is being used in the decidedly not-bureaucratic field of crowdsourcing, defined as "outsourcing over the Internet, of tasks, which were typically done by employees of a company, to an undefined group of potential contractors."
7. For additional call-centre research, see Wood, Holman, and Stride (2006), Schalk and van Rijckevorsel (2007), D'Cruz and Noronha (2011), Fleming and Sturdy (2011), and Nyberg and Sewell (2014).
8. On UPS, see https://www.thenation.com/article/these-workers-have-new-demand-stop-watching-us/ (retrieved 10 March 2019).
9. See Handel (2003), and Payne (2009) on the definition and measurement of skill.
10. See Zuboff (1988), Hughes (1996), and Brynin (2006).
11. Government of Canada, Canadian ICT Sector Profile 2016: https://www.ic.gc.ca/eic/site/ict-tic.nsf/eng/h_it07229.html [retrieved 22 March 2019].
12. OECD Data: ICT Employment 2011. https://data.oecd.org/ict/ict-employment.htm [retrieved 22 March 2019].
13. See Rubery and Grimshaw (2001), Mishel and Bernstein (2003), and Dolton and Pelkonen (2008).
14. Interestingly, in 2013, Spike Jonze produced and directed the movie *Her* in which the lead (Joaquin Phoenix) falls in love with his smartphone's operating system.
15. Canadian studies have demonstrated how a strong union (Clarke and Haiven 1999) and a positive labour relations climate (Smith 1999) can influence workers' willingness to accept change.
16. Gandolfi (2009) discusses the stress experienced by a third group (alongside victims and survivors), the "executioners" who must implement the layoffs.

UNIONS AND INDUSTRIAL RELATIONS

"Postal workers in Kingston walked off the job on Wednesday morning as part of a Canadian Union of Postal Workers (CUPW) strike . . . Mary Whan is the president of CUPW Local 556, which represents approximately 200 postal workers in the Kingston and Gananoque regions. 'There's an issue with forced overtime for the letter carriers. There's an issue with over-burdening of the letter carriers. Everybody deserves to go to work and come home safe.' According to Whan, more than 30,000 of Canada Post's 50,000 letter carriers have suffered an injury at work. . . . Whan said these issues stem from forced overtime, routes that are too long, and carriers being expected to haul too much weight on their routes. 'We're asking to stop the overburdening of the letter carrier,' Whan said. 'We all know that letter volumes have gone down and parcel volumes have gone up. These parcel volumes are being piled onto the letter carriers along with their mail. You're carrying a lot more stuff, and they just keep making the routes longer and longer, so the carriers are out on the street a lot longer. Some carriers work 10 to 12 hours per day.' Whan said a carrier is expected to carry up to 35 pounds in their satchels."

Source: Meghan Balogh. "Kingston postal workers walk out." Kingston Whig Standard, November 7, 2018. https://www.thewhig.com/news/local-news/kingston-postal-workers-walk-out [downloaded April 13 2019]

INTRODUCTION

After six weeks of *rotating strikes* during which members of the Canadian Union of Postal Workers in different Canadian cities took turns staying away from work, in late November 2018 the federal Liberal government passed a law forcing the union to stop the strike. The union had been using it to press for increased pay, improved job security, and workplace policies designed to reduce workplace injuries (Rieger 2018). Seven years earlier, the federal Conservative government also legislated the same union back to work to end a similar strike. In both cases, the workplace conflicts that led to the strikes were not resolved by the government's actions.

In contrast, in April 2019, after a six-month strike against the Saskatoon Co-op (part of a large prairie retail chain selling groceries, liquor, building supplies, gasoline, and other things), members of the United Food and Commercial Workers voted to accept a new seven-year contract with their employer (MacPherson 2019). At the core of this labour dispute was the employer's plan to put in place a new *two-tier pay system* that would save money by paying new employees (e.g., sales clerks) less than those who had worked longer in this retail establishment. The union was not successful in stopping this plan but felt that the final agreement they reached with the Co-op provided workers with a better deal than the original offer they had rejected. A lot of angry feelings had been expressed in the previous six months, particularly when the Co-op hired *replacement workers* to fill the jobs of unionized workers out on strike, but both sides were now speaking positively about the new agreement they had reached through collective bargaining.

At much the same time (April 2019), nurses employed by the Windsor-Essex County Health Unit in Ontario rejected the *final offer* they had received, and decided to continue their five-week strike. Barb Deter, president of the union local, explained why: "management has barely moved from their position that my colleagues and I, all women, are worth only half as much of an increase in pay as male-dominated groups of municipal workers in 2019" (Chen 2019). Meanwhile, through the lobbying efforts of the B.C. Government and Service Employees' Union (BCGEU), wildfire fighters in B.C. were given the same legislated right to compensation for workplace injuries that urban firefighters had long enjoyed (National Union of Public Employees 2019). Elsewhere in B.C., representatives of the United Steelworkers at a copper mine near Logan Lake indicated that they supported the mine owners' plan to introduce self-driving trucks to the workplace (alongside others driven by union members) even though they had concerns about long-term job losses in the mining industry. More important to union members, in the short term, was keeping this particular mine profitable so that current workers would keep their jobs ("Union at Mine" 2019).

These brief accounts highlight a number of points we will make in this chapter. First, the presence of unions in the retail industry and in the public sector (e.g., health care and the postal service) shows that the union movement is not just limited to blue-collar manufacturing and resource-extraction industries. Unions have become very active in the upper-tier services and are also trying to organize lower-tier service workers in the retail and food and accommodation sectors. The involvement of unions in all parts of the economy also reminds us that the ability to join a union is widely considered a basic human right.

These examples also show that unions are concerned not just about getting higher pay for their members but also about other issues, like pay equity and workplace health and safety. They also remind us that when labour negotiations reach an impasse and a strike or lockout occurs, we are not simply looking at a "union problem." There are two parties involved. Both employers and workers (through their unions) are trying to get a better deal for themselves, and both typically think that their own position is fair. Furthermore, when unions resort to strike action, the outcome is not always beneficial to workers. What is not evident from these examples, though, nor from media accounts of strikes and lockouts, is that the vast majority of contracts between Canadian employers and unions are settled without any work disruptions. In addition, unions remain very active between those times when contracts are negotiated, pushing for workplace policies and government legislation intended to improve the quality of workers' lives.

As we will see, a large minority of Canadian workers are already union members, but the majority are not, some because they do not have the opportunity and others because they are unaware of or ambivalent about unions' goals and methods. The Canadian public, as a whole, is similarly uncertain about its response to organized labour. For example, a 2015 EKOS Research national public opinion survey found that not quite half of Canadian adults (47 percent) agreed that "all in all, unions are a positive force in society."[1] Another survey, conducted by the Public Response Group in 2012, revealed that 61 percent of Canadians felt that unions "do a good job of protecting their members' jobs," but only 46 percent agreed that "gains made by unions for their members also improve the lives of other Canadians" ("Unions on Decline" 2012).

THEORETICAL PERSPECTIVES ON ORGANIZED LABOUR

Mainstream industrial relations theory focuses on the formal system of state-imposed rules (i.e., labour law) and institutions (e.g., labour relations boards) that govern worker–management relations in western industrialized democracies. It is assumed that these regulations inject stability into employ-ment relations by tilting the balance of power slightly away from management and towards workers. However, this perspective overplays the importance of predictable and harmonious industrial relations, and seldom questions the existing distribution of power between workers and management. As sociolo-gists, we believe it is important to recognize that work is a power relationship in which conflict is always a possibility and a contested terrain in which unions are often active players (see Chapter 10). In the following section, we highlight some central theoretical debates about the role of unions in modern society.

Unions as Democratic Organizations

Unions are democratic organizations whose constitutions allow members to elect their leaders. Thus, like politicians and the citizens who elect them, union leaders are assumed to be responsive and accountable to the members who elect them, translating their wants into collective bargaining goals. But this may not always have been the case. Robert Michels (1959) was the first to investigate the issue of *union democracy.* Based on his study of German trade unions before World War I, Michels concluded that leaders in working-class organizations always dominate members. According to Michels's *iron law of oligarchy,* union leaders develop expert knowledge, which gives them power. Once in office, they can control the organization to maintain their power. In addition, as Michels saw it, the masses tend to identify with leaders and expect them to exercise power on their behalf.

But in Canada and elsewhere, over the past half century, we have wit-nessed the emergence of strong grassroots movements challenging entrenched union leadership cliques and, in effect, opposing oligarchic rule. Most unions today espouse democratic principles, but some have been more successful in putting these into practice than others (Levi et al. 2009). Thus, what Michels (1959) thought he discovered was not a universal trait of unions, but a potential problem faced by all large bureaucratic organizations.

Unions as Managers of Discontent

Collective bargaining is the process by which a union, on behalf of its members, and an employer reach a negotiated agreement (called a *collective agreement* or a *contract*), which defines for a specific period wages, work hours and schedules, benefits, other working conditions, and procedures for resolving grievances. Collective agreements are negotiated and administered under provincial and territorial and federal labour laws and are designed to reduce conflict. Indeed, the main thrust of modern industrial relations practice is the avoidance of conflict. Thus, for the system to operate with some degree of fairness and equity for workers, who, on the whole, are in the weaker bargaining position, there must be the threat of conflict that could disrupt the employer's business. While critics often insist that the Canadian industrial relations scene is too adversarial, a federal government task force on labour relations (Canada 1969: 19) responded to these concerns decades ago, explaining that

> paradoxical as it may appear, collective bargaining is designed to resolve conflict through conflict, or at least through the threat of conflict. It is an adversary system in which two basic issues must be resolved: how available revenue is to be divided, and how the clash between management's drive for productive efficiency and the workers' quest for job, income and psychic security are to be reconciled.

As noted frequently in Chapters 8 through 10, managers of work organizations must balance the profit-seeking goals of owners (and shareholders) and the resulting need to control employees with the necessity of achieving a workable level of cooperation and commitment from them. Workers aim for higher wages, better working conditions, and more autonomy in their jobs. Employers pursue higher profits, lower costs, and increased productivity. The chronic tension between these opposing interests forces trade-offs on both sides, and may also generate open conflict.

In some respects, contemporary unions function as *managers of discontent* (Mills 1948). They channel the frustrations and complaints of workers into a carefully regulated dispute-resolution system. Unions help their members to articulate specific work problems or needs, and solutions are then sought through collective bargaining or through grievance procedures. For example, labour legislation prohibiting strikes during the term of a collective agreement puts pressure on union leaders to contain any actions by their members that could disrupt the truce with management. Thus, most unions today operate in ways that contribute to the maintenance of capitalism, seeking reforms that reduce power imbalances favouring owners and managers.

Business versus Social Unionism

Typically, the daily activities of unions focus on two types of goals: gaining more control over the labour process (Chapter 10) and increasing work rewards for members. There are frequently compromises between these two goals. Because of their immediate economic needs or because they are not all that involved in their work (Marx would have called this "alienation"), workers may want their unions to focus primarily on economic rewards. In addition, employers are sometimes willing to give up more of their profits rather than concede to workers' greater decision-making authority. This emphasis by unions on material gain rather than job control, known as *business unionism*, has long been central to the North American labour movement.

We have, however, also seen unions engaging in practices of *social unionism*. While still focusing on collective bargaining with employers over wages, benefits, and other work rewards, some public-sector unions, such as the Canadian Union of Public Employees (CUPE), along with some large private-sector unions, such as Unifor (previously the Canadian Auto Workers, CAW), have taken on a broader agenda of societal reform, entering public debates about issues such as climate change, globalization, international human rights, and health care reform. In a similar manner, some U.S. and Mexican unions have collaborated to resist the negative effects of globalization on workers in both countries (Kay 2011).

Social unionism sentiments, however, can sometimes conflict with business unionism beliefs and practices. For example, when politicians and employers were debating the pros and cons of bringing more temporary foreign workers (TFWs) into Canada a decade ago, unions were ambivalent about their stance. On one hand, they saw non-Canadian workers as a threat to their own members, since they could be hired more cheaply, but, on the other hand, they recognized that TFWs were being exploited and felt they should be better protected by labour legislation (Foster 2014).[2]

The Economic Impact of Unions

For the past half-century, research in western industrialized countries has shown that union members earn more than their nonunionized counterparts working in similar jobs in the same industry (Wilmers 2017; Finnigan and Hale 2018). At one point, the *union wage premium* in Canada was about 10 percent, but in recent years it has declined. Between 1997 and 2014, it ranged between 1 and 3 percent (Campolieti 2018).

Even so, union members are more likely than comparable nonunion workers to receive additional non-wage benefits. For example, a study of Canadian child-care workers found that unions raised wages by 15 percent, had a positive impact on benefits, and provided financial incentives for workers to improve their qualifications and skills (Cleveland, Gunderson, and Hyatt 2003). Unions also contribute to reducing overall wage inequality in a nation's labour market, although less so than in the past. The union impact on wages is greatest for workers in the lower and middle ranges of the income, education, and skill distributions. In other words, without unions, income inequality in Canada would likely be even higher (Chapter 5). Indeed, in Canada, the United States, and a number of European countries, growing income inequality has been linked, in part, to declining union membership (Lopez 2014; Bosch 2015).[3]

Access to these economic advantages of union membership obviously depends on where one works. Unionization is significantly higher in large workplaces in the core sector of the economy (Chapter 5), where employers are in a better competitive position to provide decent wages and working conditions. In turn, nonstandard or precarious jobs, with their lower wages, fewer non-wage benefits, and less job security (Chapter 4), are typically nonunionized. Barriers to unionization of part-time and temporary workers include restrictive legislation and, until recently, lack of interest among unions. However, some unions have begun to recognize the need for and importance of organizing workers in nonstandard jobs (Vosko 2000).

Several decades ago, Freeman and Medoff (1984) made a useful distinction between the two "faces" of unionism. The *monopoly* face represents unions' power to raise members' wages at the expense of employers and of nonunionized workers. The *collective voice* face shifts attention to how unions democratize authoritarian workplaces, giving workers a collective voice in dealing with management. Freeman and Medoff admitted that unions do impose some social and economic costs but felt that they are outweighed by their positive contributions, and we agree. Unions significantly advance workers' economic and political rights and freedoms. They also typically boost productivity through lower employee turnover, better management performance, reduced hiring and training costs, and greater labour–management communication and cooperation (Lee 2007; Gunderson and Hyatt 2009). But because of higher wage costs, productivity gains do not necessarily make unionized firms more profitable. Recent Canadian research, however, suggests that, when management is clear in its intentions to cooperate with unions, the positive effects of unions for the organization are greater (Pohler and Luchak 2015).

On balance, research suggests that unionization improves rather than harms social and economic systems (Walsworth and Long 2012). A recent commentary on the impact of unions in Alberta (Campanella et al. 2014) makes the same point by highlighting how higher hourly wages for union members put pressure on employers to raise wages for nonunionized workers, how unions put pressure on governments and employers to improve worker safety, and why income inequality is lower in locations where unions are stronger.

Social Movement Unionism

Some unions have gone beyond simply addressing broader social issues (social unionism) to actively collaborate with social justice organizations, and sometimes even with corporations, to implement social reforms in their communities, across the country, or even globally. David Camfield (2011) describes such involvement by unions in networks of organizations that are trying to benefit others, not just union members, as *social movement unionism*. One important example would be the Living Wage movement in the United States, which has successfully brought together coalitions of citizens and community groups, including unions, to push municipal governments to enact city bylaws that ensure that all city workers (and also workers hired by contractors working for the city) receive a wage high enough to live on (Luce 2004; Adams and Neumark 2005).

The Clean Clothes Campaign (CCC) is another example, linking trade unions and non-governmental organizations (NGOs) in Europe, North America, and Australia with a network of several hundred similar organizations in developing countries (Egels-Zandén and Hyllman 2006; Egels-Zandén 2011). Together, they have worked on educating consumers, lobbying governments, and putting pressure on retail companies in Western societies to improve the working conditions of factory workers producing clothing and sportswear in developing countries.[4]

Another remarkable example involves the Coalition of Immokalee Workers (CIW) which represents immigrant farm workers from Central America in Florida's fruit and tomato industries. Over many years, the CIW pushed for and eventually obtained solid labour standards protecting farm workers. In her book *I Am Not a Tractor*, Susan Marquis (2017) recounts how growers would refuse to pay workers a decent wage and improve working conditions, saying they could not afford it. So the CIW changed tactics. Working with student groups and religious organizations, they organized a successful national boycott of Taco Bell (and later other corporations, including McDonalds, KFC, Pizza Hut, and even Walmart). The boycotts lasted until these corporations agreed to pay growers more for their products and to ensure that the increased payments were passed on to workers and that working conditions be improved. The Fair Foods Standards Council, set up as a result of these collective actions, enforces these conditions. Growers who ignore the labour standards are not allowed to sell their products to the national buyers.

HISTORY OF THE CANADIAN LABOUR MOVEMENT

Craft Unionism

Skilled craftworkers—carpenters, bricklayers, masons, cabinetmakers, blacksmiths, shoemakers, and tailors—were the first to unionize in Canada. A strike by Toronto printers in 1872 resulted in the Trade Unions Act, which, for the first time, legalized union activity. Before that, unions had been considered a conspiracy against the normal operations of business. Other significant events that laid the foundations for trade unionism in Canada were the Nine-Hour movement in the 1870s, involving working-class agitation for shorter working hours; and the creation of the Trades and Labour Congress (TLC) in 1883 as the first central labour body.[5]

Craft pride based on the special skills acquired through a long apprenticeship, solidarity with fellow artisans, and a close integration of work and communities were the hallmarks of these early *craft unions.* They served as benevolent societies, providing members with a form of social insurance years before the rise of the welfare state. They also protected their members' position in the labour market by regulating access to the craft, thus monopolizing its unique skills. Today, this practice would be referred to as a *labour market shelter* (see Chapter 5). And as small local enterprises of the 19th century gave way to the factories and large corporations of the 20th, craft unions provided craft workers with a defence against the erosion of their way of life. Through their unions, which dominated the young Canadian labour movement well into the 20th century, artisans vigorously opposed scientific management and the mechanization and reorganization of craft production in factories.

Chapter 11: Unions and Industrial Relations

Industrial Unionism

Unlike craft unionism, with *industrial unionism* all workers in an industry are represented by the same union, regardless of their occupation. The Knights of Labour, the earliest industrial union in Canada, organized their first local assembly in Hamilton in 1875. For a brief period in the 1880s, they challenged the dominance of the craft unions. Driven by an idealistic radicalism, the Knights' immediate goal was to organize all workers into a single union, regardless of sex, skill level, craft, or industry, to eventually abolish the capitalist wage system and create a new society. Their membership peaked in 1887, with more than 200 local assemblies representing workers in 75 occupations. But rapid membership growth made it difficult to maintain an idealistic philosophy, and political rivalries both internal and external (with the craft unions) meant that the Knights had disappeared by the early years of the 20th century (Kealey 1981).

Only a handful of industrial unions emerged before World War I. They tended to be radical in ideology, and most were rooted in western Canada (McCormack 1978). The Industrial Workers of the World, for example, attracted unskilled immigrants employed in lumbering, mining, agriculture, and railways. One Big Union (OBU), a revolutionary industrial union, received widespread support in the western provinces, particularly among miners, loggers, and transportation workers. Its support for the Russian Revolution, however, brought vigorous counterattacks from employers, governments, and craft unions, and led to the OBU's demise in the 1920s.

Industrial unionism did not become firmly established in Canada until the 1940s. The breakthrough was the United Auto Workers (UAW) milestone victory in its 1937 strike against General Motors in Oshawa, Ontario. The issues were an eight-hour working day, higher wages, improved working conditions, and recognition of the union by the employer (Abella 1974). The Canadian strike followed a few weeks after a series of massive strikes by the American-based UAW against GM factories in the United States.

In 1956, Canadian craft and industrial unions united within a single central labour organization: the Canadian Labour Congress (CLC). The CLC remains Canada's "house of labour." Its affiliated unions represented 3.3 million workers in 2019, almost 70 percent of all Canadian union members. The CLC promotes the economic, political, and organizational interests of affiliated unions by providing research, education, and organizational and collective bargaining services, as well as by eliminating jurisdictional conflicts between unions. At times, the CLC has become directly involved in national politics, most recently by actively working to defeat the federal Conservative government led by Stephen Harper in 2015 (CLC n.d.). The CLC also has had strong ties to the New Democratic Party (NDP), taking a leading role in founding the party in 1961. In the last several federal elections, though, CLC leaders have been slower to encourage CLC members to vote NDP.

Quebec Labour

Quebec labour's history is a fascinating topic in its own right (Déom, Grenier, and Beaumont 2009; Frangi and Hennebert 2015) and deserves more than the brief treatment we give it here. Many of the issues central to Canada's ongoing English–French constitutional debates are amplified in the arena of labour relations. For example, industrial relations have been shaped by a different legal framework in Quebec (its laws are derived from the Civil Code of France, rather than British-based common law). A more interventionist state role has created a higher degree of centralized bargaining than in other provinces and territories, as well as resulting in some innovative legislation, such as the 1977 anti-strikebreaking law.

The development of unions in Quebec followed a different path from that of the rest of Canada. For example, in the early 20th century, the Roman Catholic Church organized conservative unions that, unlike their more radical counterparts elsewhere, emphasized the common interests of employers and employees. During the years that Premier Maurice Duplessis and the ultraconservative Union Nationale held power (from 1936 to 1960), the state took repressive actions to stifle more independent union development. Worker militancy flared up in response, the most violent manifestations being the 1949 miners' strike at Asbestos and the 1957 Murdochville copper miners' strike. Some analysts view these strikes as major catalysts in Quebec's Quiet Revolution, which ushered in sweeping social, economic, and political reforms in the 1960s.

During this period, the old Roman Catholic unions cut their ties with the church, becoming one of the main central labour organizations in the province (the CNTU, or Confederation of National Trade Unions) and adopting an increasingly radical stance. Hence, the Quebec Federation of Labour, made up of CLC-affiliated unions, differs from its counterparts in other provinces and territories; it represents only a minority of union members in the province and operates in a more independent manner.

The Role of the Canadian State in Industrial Relations

In Canada, a legislative and administrative framework that casts the state as *impartial umpire* has developed, mediating between labour and capital in an effort to establish and maintain industrial peace. The architect of this system was William Lyon Mackenzie King, the first federal minister of labour and later a Liberal prime minister. King's 1907 Industrial Disputes Investigation Act (IDIA) became the cornerstone of Canada's modern industrial relations policy that strives to *institutionalize conflict* through the control of law. The Act provided for compulsory *conciliation* (fact finding) in disputes during a "cooling off" period, a tripartite board of *arbitration*, and special treatment of public interest disputes involving public services. It also banned strikes or lockouts during the term of a collective agreement.

At first, the Act was applied to disputes in coal mines and railways. Its scope was extended during World War I, and in the 1950s its principles were incorporated into provincial and territorial legislation. In some instances, the state used the powers of the Act to legislate an end to strikes. This type of state intervention has shaped the pattern of industrial conflict in Canada—some would argue, in the interests of employers (Craven 1980; Huxley 1979).

In 1944, the National War Labour Order, regulation P.C. 1003, brought Canadian industrial relations into its modern phase. Modelled on the 1935 U.S. National Labor Relations Act (Wagner Act), P.C. 1003 granted employees in the private sector collective bargaining rights, set down union certification procedures, spelled out a code of unfair labour practices, and established a labour relations board to administer the law. These measures paved the way for a postwar labour–management pact designed to maintain industrial peace. This truce was enshrined in federal legislation in 1948 and in subsequent provincial and territorial legislation.

Another milestone in the legal entrenchment of *collective bargaining rights* came out of a 1945 strike by the UAW at the Ford Motor Company in Windsor, Ontario. The *Rand Formula*, named after Justice Ivan Rand of the Supreme Court, whose ruling helped settle the strike, provided for union security through a *union shop* and *union dues checkoff.* According to the Rand Formula, even though no one should be required to join a union, it is justifiable to automatically deduct union dues from the paycheques of all employees in a workplace because a union must act for the benefit of all employees. It does not matter whether or not the employees belong to the union.

The emergence of public-sector unions in the second half of the 20th century changed the industrial relations scene yet again. The movement toward full-fledged public-sector unionism began in Saskatchewan in 1944. The real push, however, started when Quebec public employees were granted collective bargaining rights in 1964. Another major breakthrough was the 1967 Public Service Staff Relations Act, which opened the door to unions in the federal civil service.

Some analysts argue that industrial relations entered a coercive phase during the 1980s. Leo Panitch and Donald Swartz (1993) view government imposition of wage controls, more restrictive trade union legislation, and the use of courts to end strikes as signals of the end of "free collective bargaining," as established by the industrial relations system set out in earlier federal legislation. Panitch and Swartz characterize this new era as *permanent exceptionalism*, reflecting how the suspension of labour's rights and more heavy-handed state intervention became the rule rather than the exception.[6]

Canadianizing Unions

The rise of public-sector unions has also helped to *Canadianize* the labour movement. At the beginning of the 20th century, U.S.-based international unions (such as the UAW discussed earlier) represented about 95 percent of all unionized workers in Canada. By 1969, this proportion had dropped to 65 percent. It has continued to decline steeply since then, to only 25 percent in 2015 (Employment and Social Development Canada 2016). The vulnerability of Canada's branch-plant economy, particularly during the 1980s, taught growing numbers of workers the need for greater local control of union activities. Some Canadian union locals resented seeing their union dues flowing into American union headquarters, with few services in return. Different bargaining agendas also tended to arise in the two countries, reflecting their distinctive industrial relations environments.

Chapter 11: Unions and Industrial Relations

The issue of national autonomy came to a head in the 1984 strike against General Motors by the Canadian division of the UAW. The Canadian auto-workers found themselves pitted against not only General Motors but also the UAW leadership in Detroit, which wanted Canadian workers to accept the concessions agreed to by their American counterparts. While autonomy was not the goal of the Canadian workers going into the strike, it became an inevitable result with the formation of the Canadian Auto Workers (Gindin 1995). The Communications, Energy and Paperworkers Union of Canada (CEP) also grew out of a Canada–U.S. split in an international union in the 1980s.[7]

A strong argument in support of international unions has been that they are organized labour's best defence against the global strategies of multinational corporations (Garver et al. 2007). Yet the international unions have not always been effective in dealing with the sorts of problems multinational corporations created for Canadian employees. For example, in response to the global recession in 2008, U.S.-based unions supported protectionist trade policies in an effort to preserve members' jobs within the United States, thus putting Canadian workers' jobs at risk.

UNION MEMBERSHIP TRENDS IN CANADA

Union Membership Rates

Figure 11.1 traces union membership growth in Canada since 1911, when there were only 133,000 union members in the country (5 percent of all non-agricultural paid workers). In 2018, there were approximately 4.75 million union members in the Canadian workforce (30.3 percent of non-agricultural paid workers). The exclusion of agriculture, where most workers are self-employed and are, therefore, ineligible for union membership, allows for more accurate comparisons with earlier periods when agriculture was a much larger sector in the Canadian economy.

Union membership can be measured in different ways. *Union density* refers to the proportion of actual union members to potential members. *Union coverage* is typically slightly higher than union density, since some non-members in unionized workplaces are entitled to the wages and benefits negotiated by the union in a collective agreement. Among them are supervisory employees who are excluded because of their management role, new hires on probation, and individuals who, perhaps because of their religious or other personal beliefs, opt not to join. Figure 11.1 displays union density up until 1991, and then union coverage from 1997 until 2018 (Employment and Social Development Canada 2015).[8] Canadian labour law also permits nonunion forms of collective representation, such as staff associations, which represent about 5 percent of all employees. Approximately another 9 percent of employees belong to professional associations, and some of these set wages and working conditions for members (Taras 2002).

Three major surges in Canadian union membership growth can be seen in Figure 11.1. The first two coincided with the two world wars (1914–18 and 1939–45). This pattern is not surprising because national mobilization for these wars resulted in economic growth, labour shortages, and the need for a high level of cooperation between employers and employees, all of which are key ingredients for successful union recruitment. As already noted, in the years during and immediately following World War II, Canada's contemporary industrial relations system took shape.

FIGURE 11.1 Union Membership in Canada, 1911–2018

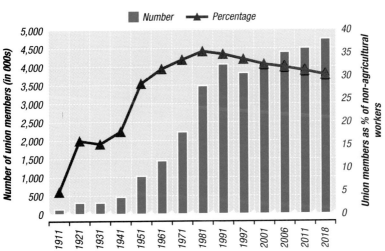

Note: Union density displayed for 1911–91 and union coverage for 1997–2018.

Source: 1911–71, Statistics Canada Archives, Table E175-177; 1976–91, Statistics Canada Archives, Table 14-10-0187-01; 1997–2018, Statistics Canada, *Union Coverage by Industry* (Table 14-10-0070001).

Chapter 11: Unions and Industrial Relations

The third growth surge, largely facilitated by supportive legislation, took place in the 1970s. This trend began in 1967 when the federal government passed the Public Service Staff Relations Act, allowing collective bargaining for federal civil servants. Provincial government employees were already moving in this direction. In Quebec, for example, public employees had received collective bargaining rights in 1965. Unionism soon spread into municipal governments, hospitals, schools, prisons, social services, and other expanding publicly funded institutions. The rise of *public-sector unions* in that decade brought many civil servants, teachers, nurses, and other public employees into the organized labour movement.

Canadian union density peaked at 37 percent in 1984. The slow decline over the next three decades can be traced to a number of recessions and to industrial restructuring, which both cut deeply into the traditional membership strength of unions in manufacturing and other blue-collar occupations. Similarly, periodic budget cuts and downsizing in the public sector, beginning in the 1990s, have led to lower union density. Employer pressures for concessions and the whittling away of collective bargaining rights by governments and the courts have contributed to a more hostile climate for labour relations, a topic to which we return below.

Canada's Largest Unions

The labour movement has also undergone organizational changes. A notable trend is consolidation, resulting from mergers and membership growth since the 1960s. In 1968, there were 14 large unions (30,000 or more members), accounting for just under half of total union membership (Chaison 2004). By 2015, 35 unions had memberships of 30,000 or more, comprising 79 percent of total union membership in the country (Employment and Social Development Canada 2015). Eight very large unions (100,000 or more members) accounted for almost half (45 percent) of all unionized workers in the country.

Canada's largest union today is the Canadian Union of Public Employees (CUPE) with 635,000 members (Employment and Social Development Canada 2015) employed in a wide spectrum of jobs in municipalities, social services, schools, libraries, colleges and universities, hospitals and nursing homes, and many other public institutions. It has clearly diversified far beyond its core membership in public administration. The National Union of Public and General Employees (NUPGE), the second-largest union in the country

(360,000 members in 2015), is also a public-sector union, as is the Public Service Alliance of Canada (PSAC), the sixth-largest Canadian union, with 181,000 members. NUPGE is an umbrella organization for various federal and provincial and territorial government unions while PSAC has members employed only in federal government departments.

Three industrial unions are in third, fourth, and fifth place on the list of Canada's six largest unions. In mid-2013, the CAW, with close to 200,000 members, merged with the CEP, which was about half this size, to form Unifor, a powerful Canadian-based industrial union. By 2015, Unifor had diversified far beyond automobile manufacturing, with 300,000 members spread across the manufacturing, transportation, utilities, and many service industries. The United Food and Commercial Workers Union (UFCW Canada), with 248,000 members in 2015, is the Canadian wing of a U.S.-based union, as is the United Steelworkers Union (190,000 members). Both the UFCW and the United Steelworkers have also gone beyond their original industrial base to organize workers in a wide range of manufacturing and service industries.

Despite the presence of a number of very large unions, a defining feature of the Canadian labour movement continues to be the large number of *locals*. In 2015, Canadian labour organizations contained over 13,000 locals, the basic self-governing unit of the labour movement and the legal entity for collective bargaining. In short, despite consolidations, Canadian labour remains fragmented and, consequently, collective bargaining is decentralized. Unlike the situation in some European nations, where industry-wide national bargaining is the norm, the Canadian pattern of single-establishment, single-union bargaining results in thousands of collective agreements in effect at any one time.

Characteristics of Canadian Union Members

Because of the large industrial and labour force changes that have occurred in Canada over the past half century (see Chapters 3 and 6), the much higher rate of union representation for men compared to women that once existed in Canada has disappeared. In fact, in 2016, 34 percent of employed Canadian women belonged to a union (or were covered by a collective agreement), compared to 30 percent of men, reflecting the large number of women employed in the public sector, which is much more highly unionized.[9] However, age remains a major source of variation in union membership rates. While 32 percent of all Canadian employees were unionized in 2016, only 19 percent of young workers (ages 15 to 24 years) belonged to unions, compared with 31 percent of 25- to 44-year-olds, 38 percent of those ages 45 to 64 years, and 24 percent of employees 65 years of age and older. Again, the explanation can be traced back to industry differences—young workers are much more likely to be employed in the retail and food and accommodation industries, which have low unionization rates (15 percent and 13 percent, respectively, in 2011).

Looking further at industry differences, education and public administration had the highest unionization rates in 2016 (75 percent and 71 percent, respectively). The rate in the utilities sector was almost as high (65 percent), since many utility companies are government owned and, hence, more highly unionized. Health care's unionization rate was somewhat lower (58 percent); although almost all nurses are unionized, doctors are not, and neither are some other health care support workers. In the transportation sector (e.g., railways, airlines, trucking), 41 percent of employees were unionized, as were 26 percent in construction, and 22 percent in manufacturing. In sharp contrast, only 9 percent of employees in finance, insurance, and real estate were union members. The unionization rate in agriculture was even lower (7 percent).

Other employment characteristics are also associated with union membership, with workplace size being one of the strongest predictors. For example, in 2016, 54 percent of employees in large workplaces were unionized, compared with 40 percent in mid-sized workplaces, and only 23 percent in small workplaces.

Provincial and territorial differences in labour legislation, and regional industrial differences, also influence union membership. Quebec (41 percent) and Newfoundland and Labrador (39 percent) had the highest rates of unionization in 2016. As already discussed, compared to the rest of Canada, Quebec's labour history is quite different. As for Newfoundland and Labrador, it has a larger than usual public sector that is highly unionized. Manitoba (37 percent) and British Columbia (33 percent) are next, for reasons that largely reflect political contexts more supportive of collective bargaining rights. In 2016, Ontario's union density was 28 percent, while Alberta's was the lowest in the country at only 26 percent. Despite the efforts of Alberta's NDP government (2015–19) to reverse the trend, over the long-term Alberta has put in place more restrictive labour legislation and American-style nonunion human resource policies (Block and Roberts 2000).

In short, the composition of the Canadian labour movement has been transformed since the 1960s. The typical unionist today is a white-collar worker employed in one of the service industries, quite likely in the public sector. Women have joined the ranks of organized labour faster than men, and some experts claim that even more women would become members if union recruitment practices were less gender-biased (Yates 2006). There also is the potential for growing union representation among immigrants and racial minorities. Wages for immigrants and visible minorities (often the same people) tend to be lower than average (Chapter 5). With the exception of Black immigrant women, immigrants and racial minorities are less likely to be union members than the white majority (Reitz and Verma 2004). This gap in unionization is somewhat reduced the longer that immigrants are in Canada.

A Comparative Perspective on Unionization

Figure 11.2 provides two key measures for 18 countries: recent rates of union membership[10] and the change in union density since 1970. In terms of current union density, Canada is higher than the United States, several European countries, the United Kingdom, Australia and New Zealand, and Japan and South Korea. But it is lower than the Scandinavian countries (Finland, Denmark, Sweden, and Norway), Austria and Italy. Union density reveals only part of the strength of unions, however; collective bargaining coverage also must be considered. In Europe, it is more common than in Canada, the United States, or Japan for workers who are not union members to have terms and conditions of employment set by collective agreements. For example, in France, the Netherlands, and Germany, where relatively few wage and salary earners are union members, between 80 and 90 percent are covered by the provisions of collective agreements that these unions negotiate (International Labour Office 1997).

What accounts for these cross-national differences? In North America, key factors are management's traditional opposition to unions, labour laws that make the certification process for new bargaining units difficult, and a decentralized industrial relations system based in local workplaces (Lipsig-Mummé 2009). In Japan, where density and coverage are similar, collective bargaining also is decentralized and firm-based. But, unlike in North America and Japan, in many western European countries there is much greater coordination within

FIGURE 11.2 Unionization Rates in 18 Countries, 2016 and Absolute Change, 1970–2016

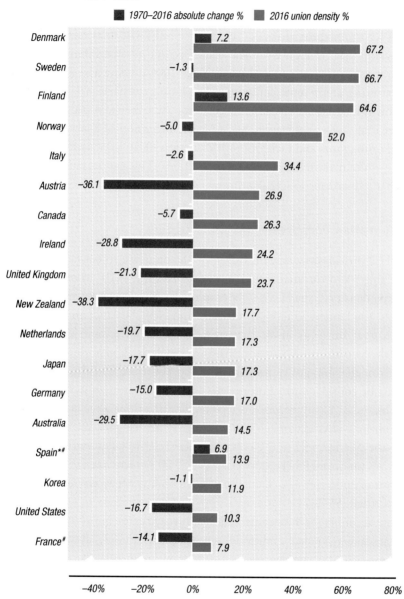

■ 1970–2016 absolute change %   ■ 2016 union density %

Country	1970–2016 absolute change %	2016 union density %
Denmark	7.2	67.2
Sweden	−1.3	66.7
Finland	13.6	64.6
Norway	−5.0	52.0
Italy	−2.6	34.4
Austria	−36.1	26.9
Canada	−5.7	26.3
Ireland	−28.8	24.2
United Kingdom	−21.3	23.7
New Zealand	−38.3	17.7
Netherlands	−19.7	17.3
Japan	−17.7	17.3
Germany	−15.0	17.0
Australia	−29.5	14.5
Spain*#	6.9	13.9
Korea	−1.1	11.9
United States	−16.7	10.3
France#	−14.1	7.9

−40%   −20%   0%   20%   40%   60%   80%

*Absolute change 1980–2010, since 1970 data are not available.
2015, since 2016 data are not available.

Sources: 1970 data from *OECD Employment Outlook,* 2004, Table 3.3, p. 145; 2016 data from OECD Statistics: https://stats.oecd.org/Index.aspx?DataSetCode=TUD

each industrial sector. This pattern is a result of highly centralized collective bargaining systems, supported by law, in which national unions negotiate with large employers' federations. Pay and other basic working conditions are set nationally or by industrial sector, greatly reducing competition among individual workplaces on these issues (unlike in Canada, where a firm may resist union pay demands because it would increase its wage costs relative to local competitors). So, in France, for example, despite a union density of less than 10 percent (Figure 11.2), employer associations are legally required to regularly negotiate broad agreements with unions, the benefits of which are extended to virtually all employers and employees.

We noted earlier that Canadian union density has been in slow decline over the last several decades. This fact is reflected in Figure 11.2, which shows an absolute change of −5.7 percent over 46 years. We also see declines in 14 of the other 17 countries listed, but they are generally much larger. Declines were larger in nations with employer-centred, decentralized industrial relations systems like the United States and Japan, but generally smaller in countries with strong sectoral or national bargaining regulated by the state to balance employers' and employees' interests.

In the field of *comparative industrial relations*, there is growing interest in the transformation of labour relations in countries with economic and political histories quite different from the countries featured in Figure 11.2 (Bamber, Lansbury, and Wailes 2011). Researchers are interested in unionization trends in Asia, the former Soviet Union, Central and South America, and Africa. At issue are how different patterns of economic development and political change affect workers' freedom to join unions and, equally important, the efficacy of unions. A recent study, for example, compared the role of unions in supporting regime change in Poland, South Africa, and Tunisia, and the dilemmas these unions faced after the new governments became more business-friendly (Hartshorn and Sil 2019).

In India, which has become much more active in globalized production networks (Chapter 2), many large employers have moved towards more Japanese-style (team-based) management approaches (Das 2010). Unions present in such enterprises, however, have continued to face significant hostility from employers (Badigannavar 2017). And in former socialist countries such as China and Russia, unions are struggling to find a new role (Clarke 2005). In China, economic reforms have reduced direct state control of production, and unions have emerged as more prominent organizations. Nevertheless, government remains much more involved in employer–union "consultations" than is the case in western democracies (Wu and Sun 2014). In foreign-owned companies, *enterprise unions* appear to function with workers' welfare in mind, but such company unions generally are dominated by, and seldom engage in direct conflict with, management (Chan et al. 2017). In Russia, former communist trade unions have pursued social partnerships to reduce industrial conflict and protect members' interests during the transition to a market economy, but these initiatives have been largely ineffective because of the history of union collaboration with government and employers during the Soviet era (Ashwin 2004).

An interesting new development, in response to the growth of *globalized production networks* that link smaller producers, manufacturers, and distribution companies in one part of the world with massive distribution and retail companies in another, is the emergence of *transnational union networks* that allow unions in different parts of the world to cooperate in pursuing common goals of safer and less exploitative working conditions and improved human rights (Helfen and Fichter 2013; Mustchin and Lucio 2017).[11] For example, unions representing seafarers and port workers (see the discussion of mobile workers in Chapter 2) have formed a global alliance through the International Transport Workers' Federation, with its Flags of Convenience campaign (Lillie 2005). Based in London, England, the federation coordinates actions to maintain minimum pay standards, negotiate collective agreements with ship owners, and oppose anti-union initiatives at ports around the world. More recently, unions in the United States and five European countries have been working together to try to organize Amazon employees who, in many countries, work for low pay in difficult working conditions for an employer that is typically hostile to unions (Birner 2015).

The Decline of U.S. Unions

While it has declined somewhat, Canadian union membership has remained relatively stable compared to that in the United States and Japan (see Figure 11.2), which also have employer-centred industrial relations. In fact, U.S. unions appear to be in a struggle for survival (Devinatz 2013). Membership has plunged from 20.1 percent of the workforce in 1983 to 10.3 percent in 2016 (Figure 11.2). Observers attribute this decline to a number of factors but, in particular, to fierce anti-union campaigns launched by private-sector employers such as Walmart (Greenhouse 2015) and labour laws that permit these sometimes coercive tactics. Ironically, the *union avoidance industry* (law firms and consulting companies that specialize in advising employers on how to resist union organizing attempts) has declined in size in the United States, in part because of its own success (Logan 2006).

In addition, management innovations offering workers some form of decision-making participation (see Chapter 9) have been used to keep unions out of many workplaces, and public-sector downsizing and the privatizing of government services have led to many fewer unionized jobs (Goldfield and Bromsen 2013). Where unions still exist, *concession bargaining* (unions agreeing to rollbacks in wages, benefits, and collective rights) has frequently weakened them. Significant, too, is the shift of employment away from the union strongholds of the northeastern industrial regions to southern states, where *right-to-work laws* undermine union security; under such laws, neither union membership nor payment of union dues may be required as a condition of employment, even if the workplace is unionized (Dixon 2008).[12]

The U.S. experience shows the decisive role of legislation and management opposition in encouraging or inhibiting free collective bargaining. Some analysts argue, pessimistically, that unions lack the resources and supportive public policies required to grow their membership. Other scholars, however, suggest ways in which organized labour must transform itself to be competitive in the 21st century (MacDonald 2014; Fine 2015) and detect some signs of union revival in the United States. Some unions, for example, have developed innovative organizing strategies that have appealed to low-wage workers, women, and racial and ethnic minorities. Others have begun to engage in "connective action," using a range of digital technologies to advance their cause, including social media for organizing workers and educating the public, and crowdsourcing to raise funds (*Economist* 2018).

The Justice for Janitors campaign in Los Angeles is an example. As in many North American cities, janitorial work in Los Angeles is done under short-term contracts by companies who employ immigrant workers. Trying to counter many years of industrial restructuring and de-unionization, in the 1990s the Service Employees International Union (SEIU) launched a successful public campaign to re-unionize the industry and improve the lot of Central American immigrants. Many of these workers were women, and many had entered the United States without documentation. The campaign focused on getting building owners to help provide health and welfare benefits to janitors and their families (Cranford 2004). Justice for Janitors shows how some U.S. unions are trying to build broad coalitions with other community groups to address social justice issues (Krinsky and Reese 2006), a strategy we earlier labelled as social movement unionism. This strategy has also been effective in some European countries (Connolly et al. 2017), as well as in Canada where, in 2010, the SEIU organized temporary foreign workers employed as janitors at the University of Alberta and helped them negotiate a better wage and overtime settlement with their private-sector employer to whom the university had outsourced its janitorial work (Foster and Barnetson 2012).

WOMEN AND UNIONS

While the unionization rate among female employees in Canada today is higher than the male rate, historically the pattern was reversed. One explanation was that women were less interested in unions because of their family responsibilities and presumed lower commitment to paid employment. Hence, work problems that might prompt unionization among men would be of secondary concern to women. Whether these assumptions were ever supported by fact is difficult to determine. But we do know that male-dominated craft unions worked with middle-class reformers to keep women out of the industrial labour force, allegedly to protect them, but also because of fears that men's wages would be undercut (Sangster 1978).

Consequently, for many women the option of joining a union simply did not exist. Only in the last three or four decades were major organizing efforts launched in the largely female retail and financial industries. Despite many efforts, in the 1970s (Lowe 1981) and since then, unions have had very little success in organizing bank workers. In contrast, unions like the United Food and Commercial Workers (UFCW) have seen somewhat more success in the retail sector. The emergence and growth of public sector unions has also meant that opportunities for women to join unions have expanded. Women are more likely to be employed in public administration and in health care than in manufacturing and transportation, two sectors in which unions have been successful for much longer (Briskin 2010). As a result, over the past half century, Canadian women have been joining unions at a much faster rate than men (Yates 2000, 2006).

In predominantly female occupations, women have a long tradition of collective action. As professionals, female teachers have been organized for many decades, although sometimes in professional associations rather than unions (Strong-Boag 1988). A history of union activism also exists among women in the garment and textile industries, particularly in unions such as the International Ladies' Garment Workers (Gannagé 1995; Frager 1992). Women also have exerted pressure on male-dominated unions to have their concerns addressed. Feminists active within the Canadian wing of the UAW during the 1960s, for example, drew on their combined experiences as autoworkers, unionists, wives, and mothers to fight for gender equality (Sugiman 1992).

Because of such pressure from feminists within the organized labour movement, *pay equity* (discussed in Chapter 6) has become a major workplace objective for many unions. Perhaps the most prominent example was the 1991 strike on this issue by PSAC, which represents federal civil servants. However, it took until the end of that decade to reach a pay equity settlement with the government for these clerical and administrative workers. Gillian Creese's (1999) case study of the white-collar workers' union at BC Hydro shows how public-sector unions' quest for pay equity in the 1990s was made more difficult by the fact that it coincided with employers downsizing, restructuring, and contracting out work.

Overall, women's demands for equality of opportunities and rewards in the workplace have had a major impact on Canadian unions. The CLC elected its first female president in 1986, and CUPE, the largest union in Canada, did the same in 1991. Women are making up a growing share of elected union officers and paid staff, especially in public-sector unions, many of which have developed policies and processes to ensure that women have equal representation in leadership positions (Parker and Foley 2010).[13] Gradually, "women's issues"—which really are issues for all workers—have come to have higher stature in labour's collective bargaining and social action (Chapter 6). Important bargaining items, at least for large unions, now include gender-neutral contract language and clauses dealing with discrimination, family-related leave, childcare, rights for part-time workers, and sexual harassment. Recently, the #MeToo and #TimesUp movements have aggressively pushed employers to deal with harassment, sexual assault, and pay inequity. These movements, no doubt, are influencing unions as well.

YOUTH AND UNIONS

Compared to other age groups, young workers are less likely to be union members. Specifically, in 2016, only 19 percent of employed Canadians ages 15 to 24 belonged to a union (or were covered by a union contract), compared to 32 percent of workers of all ages. Similar low rates of union membership are found in many other Western countries (Cha et al. 2018). A large part of the explanation is that many young people do not have the opportunity to join a union, since they are more likely to be working in the lower-tier service industries (e.g., retail sales, accommodation, and food services) where few unions are active. A smaller proportion may be interning in an upper-tier work organization within which interns are not unionized.[14]

It may also be, to some extent, that young workers are less motivated to join unions. Many are likely still students, working in part-time or temporary jobs while they prepare for anticipated careers in a different line of work. As a result, they may see less value in joining a union to improve their current working conditions. Or, perhaps, some young people perceive unions to be old-fashioned organizations with little relevance to their lives.

Looking at the research evidence, we see, first, that young workers in western countries actually hold quite positive views about unions (Simm et al. 2018; Maite and Turner 2018). In fact, a 2015 EKOS Research national survey showed younger Canadian workers (under age 35) were somewhat more likely (51 percent compared to between 43 percent and 47 percent of other age groups) to agree that "all in all, unions are a positive force in society."[15] Second, we know that young workers typically express less job satisfaction compared to older workers (see Chapter 14). One of the explanations is that many young workers are employed in poorly paid and insecure (precarious) jobs of which they can be highly critical. A recent study of comments posted by Canadian fast-food industry workers on the Rate My Employer website shows just how scathing young workers can be about both working conditions and employers (Johnston et al. 2018). Third, research shows that, in general, young people in western countries are not politically apathetic. Instead, many become actively involved in a wide range of organizations focusing on environmental, social justice, and other social concerns (Cha et al. 2018).

For unions to recruit more young workers, the problem is not so much one of changing their attitudes but of a failure to organize the industries in which young workers are typically employed. Organizing precarious workers in the lower-tier services could help unions slow their own decline and would also benefit young workers who, more than in the past, are finding it difficult to transition out of precarious work into the primary labour market (Chapter 4).

Labour researchers addressing this problem[16] have shown that a shift by unions away from traditional business unionism to social movement unionism (unions linking up with other organizations focusing on the environment and social justice issues) can attract young workers (Cha et al. 2018). But unions must also focus on the specific workplace problems faced by precarious workers, such as employers providing few or no benefits and restricting the number of hours an individual can work (Simms et al. 2018). It is also important for unions to get young people actively involved in leadership positions in the organization, rather than just passively receiving benefits (Tapia and Turner, 2018). In return, younger workers can contribute to more effective social media communication strategies and more innovative recruiting strategies. In a recent example, young unionists in Glasgow, Scotland, dressed up in scary Ronald MacDonald costumes and provided people on the street with "unhappy meal" boxes containing evidence of workers' low pay and problematic contracts (Cha et al. 2018: 461).

ORGANIZED LABOUR AND COLLECTIVE ACTION

Despite laws giving employees the right to join a union and to participate in free collective bargaining, employer opposition to unionism has historically been a major obstacle to putting these rights into practice. While disputes over *union recognition* are less common in Canada today, many employers continue to be hostile towards unions, seeing them as potentially cutting into their profits and curtailing their decision making (Ross and Russell 2018).[17] So how do workers come to join, and act collectively through, unions in a capitalist society where individualism is strongly valued and where many employers continue to actively oppose unions?

A worker must resolve two dilemmas if she or he is to consider joining a union or, if already a member, becoming an activist. The first is the *free-rider problem* (Chaison and Dileep 1992). Just like social movements concerned with environmental or social justice issues, unions provide collective goods. In other words, all potential members have access to the organization's achievements—a more sustainable environment, a world with less discrimination and inequality, or a grievance procedure and negotiated regular wage increases—whether or not they have assisted in achieving these objectives.

Albert Hirschman's (1970) comparison of *exit* and *voice* methods of expressing discontent highlights the second dilemma. According to Hirschman, a dissatisfied employee can either leave the employer or stay and push for changes. The presence of a union increases the chances that the employee will pursue the latter strategy. But in nonunion workplaces, the poor employment conditions that could spark an organizing drive also increase the chances of an individual opting to quit the job and look for another one. This kind of response is a major obstacle to unionization of workers in precarious jobs in the service industries today.

Joining and Becoming Active in a Union

The process of organizing a union within a workplace requires obtaining signed *union cards* from the majority of employees in a workplace. This effort seldom succeeds without the financial assistance and organizational expertise of an established union. Even so, it can be very difficult for many reasons.

In the lower-tier services, worker turnover is often high, making it challenging for unions to sign up employees. Union organizers must be able to convince such precarious workers that there are many others like them experiencing the same problems, and that by acting collectively they could improve their working situation (Simms and Dean 2015). A recent study of same-day messengers (workers employed by courier companies to deliver mail, on foot or by bicycle or automobile) in Toronto provides an example of a difficult-to-organize occupation (Pupo and Noack 2014). Despite their precarious work situation (no guarantee of continued work, no benefits, unsafe working conditions), the "culture of individuality" among these workers, and the "sense of freedom" and control over how they complete their delivery tasks, makes many of them unreceptive to the idea of joining a union.

In the upper-tier services, white-collar workers who have frequent contact with managers may identify more closely with them and their organization's anti-union position. In some cases, a *company union* or an employee association supported by the employer creates the appearance of democratic employee representation. New managerial strategies such as lean production and high-performance workplace models that encourage employee participation and commitment (Chapter 9) have also been used by some large companies to maintain a union-free workplace (Kumar 1995).[18] IBM is a good example of this approach in action. In Scotland in the late 1970s, the corporation's employees were balloted at the request of the government's industrial relations board to find out whether they desired union recognition. Over 90 percent voted against unionization (Dickson et al. 1988). This vote was not the result of corporate coercion or intimidation. Rather, it reflected the attention and resources that the company had devoted to employee relations.

Once organized, a union faces the problem of *mobilizing* members in support of collective bargaining goals. According to Charles Tilly's (1979) research on the causes of social protest, what is essential is a sense of shared identity with the group. Individual interests become synonymous with group interests, acting as a springboard to collective action. Strong leadership is also critical. Especially important are *organic leaders* who, by virtue of being part of the group, understand the experiences of group members and can gain their trust better than an outsider could. As in any formal organization, effective leaders will build up group solidarity, create an awareness of common interests, map out a realistic program of action, and seize opportunities to launch the plan.

The broader context also matters. A supportive community, a hostile employer, or fair labour legislation, for example, are factors that can either nurture or dampen union activity. Even if such conditions are favourable, a majority of employees may not sign union cards, or unionized workers facing a deadlock in negotiations with management over a new collective agreement may not strike.[19] Often missing is one or more precipitating factors: an arbitrary change in work practices, the denial of a long-awaited salary increase, the dismissal of coworkers, or a pent-up sense of being treated unfairly by management. Such perceived injustices could be the catalysts that mobilize workers to take collective action (Buttigieg, Deery, and Iverson 2008).

Research on the Canadian Union of Postal Workers (CUPW) shows how some of these factors contribute to *union militancy.* Julie White's (1990: 147) study quotes a postal worker in a Saint John office: "We're a militant union, and I really believe that Canada Post has made us that way." This view is typical of CUPW members, White argues, and the fact that CUPW workers were once again on strike in late 2018 (see the example at the beginning of this chapter) is further evidence. The union has developed a "culture of struggle," based on the belief that management does not have the interests of workers at heart and, further, that any past improvements have been extracted from management by militant action (Langford 1996). Against a background of unsuccessful efforts to resolve disputes through negotiation, mediation, and conciliation, this culture of struggle within CUPW has been cultivated by an openly democratic structure based on rank-and-file involvement.

Going on Strike

Strikes are high drama on the stage of industrial relations. Members of the public typically view strikes as an inconvenience or even as a major social problem. Many politicians and business leaders argue that strikes harm the economy. The participants seldom want strikes, least of all the union members, who will seldom recoup the wages lost should the dispute drag on. But if conflict has been largely *institutionalized*, as described earlier in this chapter, why do strikes occur at all? What motivates workers to strike, and what are the larger social and economic implications of their actions?

Workers go on *strike*, that is, they deliberately stop working to try to force their employer to agree to some set of demands. Since workers are selling their labour power to an employer in return for wages, their ultimate bargaining lever is to withdraw that labour. Similarly, employers may initiate a *lockout*—refusing to let workers come to work and, hence, be paid—to get workers to agree to some demand. Overall, strikes are infrequent events, as we will see in the next section, and lockouts occur even less often. So, contrary to what the news media sometimes suggest, settlement of union–management disputes without recourse to work stoppages is clearly the norm in Canada today.

But strikes are only one possible form of workplace conflict. Richard Hyman (1978) distinguishes between *unorganized* and *organized conflict*. The former typically involves individual workers responding to oppressive situations by absenteeism, quitting, or sabotage. The latter is a planned collective strategy to try to change the source of the discontent. Canadian labour legislation insists that strikes are legal only after the collective agreement has expired and specific conditions, such as a strike vote, have been met. Unauthorized strikes during the term of an agreement, often spontaneous responses by ordinary workers to an immediate problem in the workplace, are known as *wildcat strikes*. For example, in April 2013, two Edmonton jail guards were suspended for writing e-mails to management about poor working conditions. Within hours the next shift of guards was picketing the jail, and within several days, guards at 10 jails across Alberta had joined the wildcat strike.[20] In addition, many court workers, sheriffs, and parole officers, members of the Alberta Union of Public Employees, left work to take part in a *sympathy strike* (Wingrove and Walton 2013). Strikes do not necessarily entail all members of the union leaving the work site as a group. *Rotating strikes* across a number of worksites (see the CUPW example at the beginning of this chapter), *working-to-rule* (doing the minimum required or refusing overtime work), or staging work stoppages by "sitting down" on the job can also effectively communicate workers' demands to management.

Canadian Strike Trends

On an annual basis for more than the past four decades, work stoppages have typically accounted for less than one-tenth of 1 percent of all working time in Canada (Table 11.1). This pattern indicates that the seriousness of the strike "problem" often is blown far out of proportion. Historically, though, we can

TABLE 11.1   Work Stoppages (Strikes or Lockouts) Involving One or More Workers, Canada, 1976–2018, Multi-year Averages

	Work Stoppages during Year	Workers Involved	Average Number of Workers per Stoppage	Person Days Not Worked	Average Days Lost per Worker Involved	Days Lost: % of Estimated Working Time
1976–79	988	666,622	654	7,510,188	14.5	0.33
1980–84	823	293,677	445	6,401,314	18.5	0.26
1985–89	684	376,852	562	3,974,936	14.4	0.17
1990–94	338	171,986	375	2,110,056	12.8	0.09
1995–99	347	212,933	635	2,666,832	12.7	0.09
2000–04	323	153,480	538	2,349,609	14.8	0.07
2005–09	192	83,103	350	1,949,830	24.0	0.05
2010–14	184	114,493	643	1,333,457	14.2	0.03
2015–18	197	190,831	903	1,202,330	9.5	0.03

Source: 1976–2009 adapted from data provided in 2014 by Government of Canada, Labour Program via its Workplace Information and Research Division On-line Request Form: http://www24.hrsdc.gc.ca/dr-ir/default.aspx?lang=eng; 2010–14 and 2015–18 averages calculated from data provided by Government of Canada, Labour Program: https://www.canada.ca/en/employment-social-development/services/collective-bargaining-data/work-stoppages/work-stoppages-year-sector.html.

identify eras when strikes were much more common and widespread. Four particularly stormy periods of industrial conflict occurred in Canada during the 20th century, gauged by the percentage of total working time lost to strikes and lockouts.

A number of issues were at stake in early-20th-century strikes. Skilled artisans in the 19th century had been able to retain much of their craft status, pride, and economic security through their control of the production process. This privileged position was eroded by industrialization after 1900, as advancing technology and scientific management techniques undermined craft workers' autonomy. Thus, craft workers angrily resisted rationalization of their work, sparking many of the 421 strikes and lockouts that occurred between 1901 and 1914 in southwestern Ontario manufacturing cities (Heron and Palmer 1977).

Before union recognition and compulsory collective bargaining became encoded in law during World War II, many strikes were precipitated by an employer's refusal to recognize the existence of a union, much less bargain with it. The historic peak in labour militancy occurred at the end of World War I. Workers across the country were protesting against oppressive working conditions, low wages, and declining living standards that were due to soaring wartime inflation. Most of all, they wanted recognition of their unions. Western Canadian unions were far more militant and inclined toward radical politics than those in the rest of the country. Thus, a century ago, in 1919, when Winnipeg building and metal trades employers refused to recognize and negotiate with unions over wage increases, the Winnipeg Trades and Labour Council called a *general strike.*

A massive display of working-class solidarity erupted, bringing the local economy to a halt. Sympathy strikes spread to other cities across Canada and even into the United States (Finkel 2019). The battle lines of open class warfare (one of the few instances of this in Canadian history) were drawn when, fearing a revolution, Winnipeg's upper class fought back with the help of the state. For several days, strikers squared off against police and employer-sponsored armed vigilantes. The confrontation ended in violence (and two deaths) after the Royal Northwest Mounted Police, sent in by the federal government, charged a crowd of demonstrators. Strike leaders were arrested and jailed while the workers' demands were still unmet (Jolinen 2019; Naylor 2019)

Strike activity declined with rising unemployment during the Depression of the 1930s. As a rule, unions are less likely to strike in tough economic times.

Conversely, when industry is booming and there is a relative shortage of labour, reflected in low unemployment rates, a strike becomes a more potent bargaining lever. The World War II era marked the rise of industrial unionism in manufacturing industries. Organizing drives accelerated as military production demands helped to restore the ailing economy. Again, union recognition was a dominant issue, driving workers in automobile factories, steel plants, and mines onto the picket line. As mentioned earlier in the chapter, the 1945 Ford strike led to the introduction of the Rand Formula to protect union security and ensure orderly collective bargaining (Russell 1990).

Canada experienced a series of strikes in the mid-1960s. The fact that about one-third of these work stoppages involved wildcat strikes (mainly over wages) led the government to perceive a serious crisis in industrial relations. A task force, chaired by Professor H. D. Woods of McGill University, was set up to investigate the causes of industrial unrest and to recommend ways of achieving labour peace. Yet rampant inflation during the 1970s, and an increasingly militant mood among public-sector workers, escalated labour–management confrontations.

The most recent strike wave reached its apex in 1976. However, the Trudeau government's imposition of *wage and price controls* in 1975 as part of its anti-inflation program made strikes over higher wages a futile exercise (Reid 1982). In the 20 years following 1976, lost time from work stoppages dropped to post–World War II lows. The recession-plagued 1980s and 1990s dampened strike activity, a trend also evident in the recession that began in 2008.

Table 11.1 profiles the labour relations patterns of the past four decades by highlighting four ways to look at strike activity: *frequency* (number of work stoppages), *size* (number of workers involved), *duration* (days lost), and overall *volume* (days lost as a percentage of total working time). A series of multi-year averages demonstrates how strike activity has declined, according to all four indicators. For example, in the late 1970s, an average of 988 work stoppages per year involved almost 700,000 workers. Comparable figures for 2015–18 were an average of 197 work stoppages annually involving about 191,000 workers. What is most noticeable about these trends is that, even in the late 1970s, strikes and lockouts resulted in only one-third of 1 percent of estimated annual working time. By 2015–18, this figure was 10 times smaller. In short, while strikes and lockouts get a great deal of media attention, they no longer have much of a cumulative effect on Canada's total economic productivity.

Chapter 11: Unions and Industrial Relations

A Comparative Perspective on Strikes

How does Canada's strike record compare with that of other industrial nations? Even though there are some cross-national differences in how strikes are defined and measured (Ross, Bamber, and Whitehouse 1998), we can, nonetheless, get an idea of where Canada stands in this regard. Based on the annual averages of working days lost in nine industrialized countries between 1970 and 1992, Canada's rate was the second highest, with Italy first (Adams 1995: 512). But as we saw in Table 11.1, the earlier years in this period were historically high for Canada, inflating the overall average. By the mid-1990s, Canada was reporting significantly lower strike volume than Italy, France, or Australia, but considerably higher than other countries, in particular, the United States and the Netherlands (International Labour Office 1997: 249–50). It is also important to note that the strike volume in highly industrialized countries had declined in general, in large part because of difficult economic times and high unemployment through much of the 1990s.

Major institutional differences account for international variations in strikes. For instance, in Italy, disputes, while short, are frequent and involve many workers. By contrast, the Swedish system of centralized bargaining, along with the country's powerful unions and their huge strike funds, means that a work stoppage could quickly cripple the economy. This awareness imposes pressure to peacefully resolve potential disputes. In Japan, unions are closely integrated into corporations in what really amounts to a type of company unionism. Strikes are infrequent; workers voice their grievances by wearing black armbands or by making other symbolic gestures calculated to embarrass management. German union–management collective bargaining is centrally coordinated but, at the individual workplace, employee-elected works councils frequently negotiate employment conditions (see Chapter 12). German laws require these participatory councils; the same laws also make it very difficult to strike. Even though the strike rate in Canada is relatively low now, the fact that employees in this country have to confront employers when seeking collective bargaining has created a far more adversarial system than in these other countries.

Thus, legislation governing the structure of collective bargaining is vitally important. The North American system of bargaining is highly decentralized and fragmented, involving thousands of separate negotiations between a local union and a single employer, each of which could result in a strike. Low-strike nations such as Austria, Germany, the Netherlands, and Sweden avoid these problems by having national or industry-wide agreements, and by legislating many of the quality-of-working-life issues that Canadian unions must negotiate piecemeal with employers.

There are also major industrial and regional variations in strikes within Canada, which may be the result of how industries are organized. The least strike-prone industries are finance, trade, and services, which makes sense given their low unionization levels. Of the highly unionized industries, mining has historically been the most strife ridden. Similarly, Newfoundland and Labrador and British Columbia have had significantly higher-than-average strike rates because of their high concentration of primary and other strike-prone industries (Gunderson et al. 1995). With their *isolation hypothesis*, Kerr and Siegel (1954) provide one explanation of these differences, writing that isolated workers "live in their own separate communities: the coal patch, the ship, the waterfront district, the logging camp, the textile town. These communities have their own codes, myths, heroes, and social standards" (191). Canada has always had large numbers of remote, resource-based, single-employer towns, where a combination of social isolation and a limited occupational hierarchy is more likely to mould workers into a cohesive group in opposition to management.[21]

CONCLUSION

Canada's labour force has been growing steadily over the past several decades (Chapter 3). Union membership has also been growing, although not as quickly. There were about 4.75 million Canadian union members in 2018, representing about 30 percent of the non-agricultural workforce (Figure 11.1). Compared to some other Western industrialized countries, however, organized labour in Canada remains relatively strong (Figure 11.2), at least in terms of numbers. But strike activity has clearly declined in Canada over the past 35 years (Table 11.1). Does this decline signify that the Canadian industrial relations system has reached some kind of equilibrium, with all three parties involved—employers, unions, and the state—being relatively satisfied with the outcomes?

Our assessment is that it does not. As we observed in Chapter 10, the labour process can be conceptualized as a shifting *frontier of control* (Friedman 1977) in which, at different times, employers and employees gain or lose power.

The last several decades have been a time in which employers have been gaining the upper hand. As we have noted, union density has increased significantly in the public sector—CUPE and NUPGE are now the two largest unions in the country. However, for public-sector workers, their employer (typically the federal or a provincial government) is also the rule maker, and the Canadian state has not always been the "impartial umpire" that William Lyon Mackenzie King envisioned a century ago.

During the 1990s, Canadians began to see nurses, teachers, librarians, social workers, government clerks and, in some cases where they were unionized, even university professors going on strike for higher wages and improved working conditions, and to maintain the quality of public services. In response, governments frequently resorted to legislated restrictions on strike action, including declaring specific occupations (nursing or policing, for example) as *essential services*. This then meant that some members of a union would be required to continue working during a strike (Campolieti et al. 2016; Graney 2019).[22] Furthermore, the deficit-cutting strategies of both provincial/territorial and federal governments often involved imposing wage rollbacks through legislation, effectively suspending the collective bargaining rights of government employees (Reshef and Rastin 2003; Reshef and Keim 2014, Chapter 3).

This trend has continued (Canadian Foundation for Labour Rights 2018). In 2014, for example, the national Conservative government passed legislation (Bill C-525) that made it more difficult for unions to organize federal government workers. Before this, unions were automatically certified if more than half of the affected employees signed a union card. Under the new legislation, a certification vote is required, even if all the employees signed cards. At the provincial and territorial level, in 2019 the United Conservative Party government of Alberta introduced legislation rolling back labour law changes introduced by the NDP government in the previous few years, including initiatives that had made it easier for unions to organize workplaces (Simon, O'Ferrall, and Di Cesare 2018). The Progressive Conservative government of Ontario acted similarly in 2018, when it replaced the provincial Liberal government, which had also introduced legislation to remove some impediments to union organizing.

In the private sector, the Canadian labour relations environment has also generally become more restrictive (Canadian Foundation for Labour Rights 2018). *Concession bargaining*—employers trying to force unions into accepting wage rollbacks, reduced benefits packages and pensions, and greater flexibility in hiring practices—has been widespread for the past several decades. Many large employers have reduced their costs and the need to deal with unions by outsourcing much of their activity to nonunionized suppliers, in Canada or outside the country. Some employers with unionized workforces have moved quickly to lock out their workers, hoping to force them into accepting an offer. Applications for court injunctions and legislation to end strikes have been another employer strategy. In other cases, rather than trying to negotiate a settlement, employers have quickly brought in nonunionized workers, hoping to eventually force unions into accepting offers they considered to be unsatisfactory.

So, the declining strike rates in Table 11.1 clearly do not signify that organized labour in Canada is satisfied with changes in the industrial relations climate, which some analysts see as having placed severe restrictions on free collective bargaining.[23] It remains to be seen whether and where the huge unions in the public sector begin to push back more aggressively to protect the job security and economic well-being of their members.[24] As for the private sector, it will be interesting to see whether unions' current organizing efforts in the lower-tier service industries and among precarious workers are effective. In both sectors, it remains possible that a shift in tactics from business unionism to social movement unionism, and increased efforts to recruit and mobilize young workers, will have positive outcomes for organized labour.

In Chapter 12, we turn our attention to alternative approaches to economic organization that might move us beyond the adversarial nature of contemporary labour–management relations toward institutional structures that more fully recognize the rights and potential of workers and more effectively address the social problems of conflict and inequality.

DISCUSSION QUESTIONS

1. Do you think that unions have outlived their usefulness? Why or why not?
2. A century ago, in Winnipeg in 1919, workers from many different backgrounds and occupations engaged in a massive general strike because, according to Jokinen (2019: 42), they were frustrated with the "vast unfairness of everything." Do young Canadians today feel the same way about their employment prospects, and the future of democracy and the environment?

3. In the typical strike or lockout, who are most often the winners and the losers? Why?
4. Would you join a union if one existed in your workplace? Why or why not?

ADDITIONAL RESOURCES

WORK AT THE MOVIES

- *Bloody Saturday: The Winnipeg General Strike of 1919* (CBC documentary, 2013, 43:49 minutes). This video uses archival movie and print material, and commentary from historians, to describe events leading up to and following a lengthy strike involving over 30,000 workers that shut down the City of Winnipeg for many weeks: https://www.youtube.com/watch?v=V1_oKcXn8vs.
- *Matewan* (directed by John Sayles, 1987, 135 minutes). This historical film is based on the Battle of Matewan, a deadly confrontation between coal miners struggling to form a union and company operators in West Virginia.
- *24 Days in Brooks* (directed by Dana Inkster, 2007, 42:03 minutes). Set in Brooks, Alberta, this NFB documentary tracks the transformation of a socially conservative, white town. As immigrants and refugees migrate to Brooks for work in a slaughterhouse, the town experiences its first-ever strike. The documentary is available through the National Film Board of Canada: http://www.nfb.ca/film/24_days_in_brooks.
- *Bread & Roses* (directed by Ken Loach, 2000, 110 minutes). Two Latina cleaners fight for the right to unionize in this film based on the Justice for Janitors campaign of the Service Employees International Union.

Sounds of Work

- "There Is Power in a Union" (Billy Bragg). This pro-union song asserts the potential power of collective action.
- "General Strike" (D.O.A.). Canadian punk rockers put forth a straightforward message about collective action, encouraging listeners to stand up and unite.
- "Horses" (Rheostatics). After going on strike, workers watch from the outside as replacement workers are brought in. Some say this song was inspired

by the long and violent 1986 strike by the United Food and Commercial Workers against the Gainers meat-packing company in Edmonton, owned by Peter Pocklington.

- "Solidarity Forever" (Ralph Chaplin). Written in 1915 for the Industrial Workers of the World, this song carries a strong message of the power of worker solidarity. It retains relevance with many unions today.

NOTES

1. Cited with permission from EKOS Research Associates; all rights reserved.
2. See Foster, Taylor, and Khan (2015) for an analysis of the response of five Alberta unions to the temporary foreign worker issue.
3. Also see Rosenfeld (2014), Brady, Baker, and Finnigan (2013), and Card, Lemieux, and Riddell (2004).
4. https://cleanclothes.org/ [retrieved 1 May 2019]. Egels-Zandén and Hyllman (2006) discuss the conditions under which unions involved in the Clean Clothes Campaign are more likely to have an effect on corporations.
5. For historical accounts of the rise of the Canadian labour movement, see Heron (2012) and Godard (1994: Chapter 4).
6. See also Briskin (2010), Bartkiw (2008), Russell (1990), and Kettler, Struthers, and Huxley (1990). Similar concerns about collective bargaining in the United States and the United Kingdom are discussed in Freeman (1995).
7. See Roberts (1990). The Communications Workers, the Energy and Chemical Workers, and the Canadian Paperworkers Union later merged to form the Communications, Energy and Paperworkers Union of Canada.
8. Archived national data compilations on union density are our source until 1991. More recently (since 1997), Statistics Canada has been reporting union coverage rates. The 1997 and later membership rates in Figure 11.1 would be slightly lower if union density data were available.
9. Union membership (coverage) rates for all currently employed (paid and self-employed) Canadians age 15 and older are from Statistics Canada's 2016 *General Social Survey* (GSS), and were analyzed by the authors. For more information about the 2016 GSS, see: https://www150.statcan.gc.ca/n1/daily-quotidien/180613/dq180613c-eng.htm.
10. These unionization rates are based on all wage and salary earners (including agricultural workers and managers), so the Canadian rate is lower than the rate reported in Figure 11.1.

11. Dehnen (2013) refers to such networks as *global union federations*. See also Lévesque and Murray (2010) and Youngdahl (2008).

12. Bernhardt, Spiller, and Polson (2013) discuss violations of labour legislation in the United States. See Ponak and Taras (1995) on right-to-work legislation from a Canadian perspective.

13. Kirton (2015) describes how unions in the United Kingdom have moved toward gender democracy over the past several decades.

14. The Canadian Intern Association website provides useful information for young people seeking, or already employed in, an internships: http://internassociation.ca.

15. See endnote 1.

16. See the 2018 special issue (Vol. 45, No. 4) of *Work and Occupations* on "young workers and the renewal of the labor movement."

17. Campolieti, Gomez, and Gunderson (2013) report that Canadian managers are more hostile to unions, compared to managers in the United States. The researchers explain that U.S. unions are very weak and, hence, not seen as much of a threat by managers.

18. Kumar also observes that some of the more successful management innovations may have benefitted from the active involvement of unions. In most cases, however, unions have responded with passive acceptance or active rejection of new management strategies (Downie and Coates 1995).

19. See Jansen et al. (2017) whose study of Dutch workers shows that nonstandard (part-time and temporary) workers are only slightly less willing than full time workers to join a strike.

20. Another recent example of a wildcat strike involved baggage handlers at Pearson International Airport in Toronto in 2012; see: https://www.theglobeandmail.com /globe-investor/air-canada-fallout-goes-beyond-wildcat-strike/article535615/.

21. For critiques of the isolation hypothesis, see Shorter and Tilly (1974: 287–305) and Stern (1976).

22. Campolieti et al. (2015) show that the introduction of essential services legislation has led to lower wage settlements for occupation affected by it.

23. See Panitch and Swartz (1993), Russell (1990), and Godard (1997).

24. Cunningham and James (2010) discuss strategies used by public-sector unions in the United Kingdom to counter outsourcing of jobs.

ALTERNATIVE APPROACHES TO ORGANIZING WORK

"At 7:30, on a cold December morning, you might find Neil Shaw at the car wash cleaning the salt and ice off his 1994 Ford. By noon, you can usually find him in the office reviewing the financial projections. In the evening, he might be meeting with city officials to discuss rezoning or cab stands. Like most cab drivers, Neil also puts in many hours a week behind the wheel of his car. A day for Neil and others can involve these activities, which all seem quite different, but once he explains that he is president of a taxi Co-op the pieces begin to fall into place."

"First and foremost, Neil is a cab driver, sometimes working 12 hours a day. At the same time, he is an owner of the Co-op Taxi Line Ltd. which has grown from three members when it was incorporated in 1992, to the most professional cab company in Prince Edward Island's capital city with 27 cabs and 11 members. As president, Neil works more than 40 volunteer hours a month for the Co-op. 'We have no manager so therefore we are a very hands-on board,' says Neil. He also noted that the directors must look after the interests of the Co-op by lobbying government for changes in regulations when necessary and by negotiating with suppliers for discounts on bulk purchases of gasoline."

Source: Courtesy of Maureen MacLean and Brenda MacKinnon.

INTRODUCTION

In Chapter 11, we discussed the history, changing function, and future of unions, a formal and institutionalized vehicle via which workers have collectively participated in the labour process. We concluded by examining strike patterns over time in Canada, comparing them to data from other countries, and then asked about the effectiveness of this adversarial form of workers' resistance to employers' profit-driven goals. In this chapter, we discuss three alternative approaches to addressing conflict in the workplace.

We begin by examining one specific area—the critical issue of how to improve workplace health and safety—where labour and management in Canada and other Western industrial democracies have come somewhat closer to reaching a consensus. This discussion leads us into an analysis of other alternative approaches to economic organization, such as the different types of industrial democracy that have been institutionalized in Germany and Sweden, for example. The chapter concludes with a discussion of how, within capitalist industrial democracies, worker ownership of the means of production may offer the most far-reaching approach to reducing conflict and providing workers with more control over the labour process and their work organizations.

PROMOTING WORKPLACE HEALTH AND SAFETY

History proves that dangerous machinery, unsafe work sites, polluted air, and exposure to carcinogenic substances and other risks have taken their toll on the working class in terms of shorter life expectancies and higher illness and disease rates. Most of the progress made over the past century in reducing workplace health and safety risks has been the result of workers fighting for improvements, typically through their unions, and often against the strong opposition of employers. Workplace health and safety continues to be a contentious issue in union–management contract disputes today and in the larger political arena. Even so, this issue is an example, at least to some extent, of workers and their employers managing to identify and work together toward common goals. Before examining how institutionalized processes designed to further these goals have evolved, we present an overview of the risks to personal health and safety experienced by Canadian workers.

Risks to Personal Health and Safety

Every year hundreds of Canadian workers die from work-related injuries or occupational illnesses. To be precise, between 2000 and 2016, 16,216 Canadian workers—an average of almost four per working day—died as a result of their job (Bittle et al. 2018). In 2017, a total of 951 workplace and work-related deaths occurred, while over 250,000 incidents of lost time because of work-related injuries or occupational diseases were reported (Canadian Centre for

Occupational Health and Safety 2019).[1] It is important to note, however, that these statistics are based on the number of deaths and injuries that were compensated by provincial and territorial workers' compensation boards. Many other work-related deaths are not compensated, including deaths of self-employed workers or workers in agriculture, work-related suicides, and deaths of non-working victims (e.g., the 47 people who died in the Lac-Mégantic train crash in 2013). Taking such additional deaths into account, a recent study estimated that the number of annual work-related fatalities in Canada might be 10 times as high as official statistics indicate (Bittle et al. 2018).

From the mid-1980s until the mid-1990s, *industrial fatality rates* declined to 5.2 deaths per 100,000 workers in 1996, or 703 industrial fatalities (Marshall 1996). The number of fatalities then began to rise, reaching 835 in 1999, 934 in 2002, and 1,098 in 2005 when the work-related fatality rate was 6.8 deaths per 100,000 employed Canadians (Sharpe and Hardt 2006). Since then, the annual number of work-related deaths has shifted up and down between 900 and 1,000. The most recent work-related fatality count of 951 in 2017, up from 905 in 2016, (Association of Workers' Compensation Boards of Canada [AWCBC] 2017) translates into a rate of 5.1 deaths per 100,000 workers, about the same as in the mid-1990s.

Work-related fatality rates are generally much lower in the service industries than in the goods-producing sector. For example, in 2012, the fatality rates in the transportation, manufacturing, and construction industries were 11.7, 10.2, and 16.7 deaths per 100,000 workers, respectively. But these rates were still much lower than those found in the resource-extraction industries: the work-related fatality rate in mining was 23.2 deaths per 100,000 workers in 2012; in logging and forestry, it was even higher (34.3). The four leading general causes of work-related death are exposure to harmful substances and environments (41 percent of all fatalities between 1996 and 2005), accidents involving transportation vehicles (23 percent), people struck by an object or a piece of equipment (14 percent), and falls (8 percent) (Sharpe and Hardt 2006). And since high-risk jobs are typically filled by men, almost all workplace fatalities are men. In 2017, for example, 920 of the 951 people who died as a result of their work were men (AWCBC 2017).

The incidence of *work-related injury and illness* rose in Canada during the 1980s. In 1982, workers' compensation boards and commissions across the country compensated 479,558 individuals for work-related injuries and illnesses resulting in time loss or permanent disability. This number increased to 620,979 in 1989, but then began to decline steeply, to 410,464 in 1995. While the rate of decline then slowed, the number continued to drop, to 337,930 in 2005 and 251,625 in 2017 (AWCBC 2017).

As with workplace fatalities, male workers are more likely to be involved in (and compensated for) lost time claims for work-related injuries, although the gender difference is not as large. In 2017, for example, 61 percent of lost time claims for work-related injuries involved men (AWCBC 2017). Recognizing that men are more likely to be working in goods-producing industries that might be more dangerous, research suggests that gendered attitudes toward risk may also be involved. In other words, because of their adherence to norms of masculinity, men may be more likely to normalize workplace risk, resist following prescribed workplace health and safety practices, and "tough it out" when being cautious would be a safer alternative (Stergiou-Kita et al. 2015).

Very young workers (ages 15 to 19) have the lowest injury rates (AWCBC 2017), in part because many are part-time workers and, hence, at lower risk of injury, but also because few are employed in the goods-producing sector. Injury rates are also somewhat lower among workers approaching retirement (AWCBC 2017) since, by this age, fewer workers would still be in physically demanding jobs with higher risks of injury.

Summing up, over the past three decades, we have seen a steady decline in workplace injuries and illnesses. Some of this is likely due to the further shift away from goods-producing to service industries (Chapter 3), but changes in workers' compensation legislation and enforcement may also have had an effect (Breslin et al. 2006). Even so, work-related injuries and illnesses remain a serious problem, particularly since official statistics about them are likely underestimates (Bittle et al. 2018). The compensation costs for workplace injuries are huge—in 2008, for example, they totalled $7.67 billion (Gilks and Logan 2010). This figure does not include indirect costs resulting from productivity losses, damage to equipment, lower efficiency, decreased employee morale, and lost supervisory time.[2]

Evolving Politics of Workplace Health and Safety

In the early years of Canada's industrialization (Chapter 1), workers had little protection from what were often extremely unsafe working conditions. Work in resource industries, in the construction of canals and railways, and in factories was hazardous, and the risk of injury and death was extremely high. As in other industrializing countries, an *administrative model of regulation*, in which the government set standards for health and safety and tried to enforce them, slowly developed (Lewchuk, Robb, and Walters 1996). Employers frequently opposed these efforts, arguing that their profits were threatened and that the state had no right to interfere in worker–employer relationships. In turn, unions fought for change, and the public was mobilized behind some causes, including restrictions on the employment of women and children in factories. Thus, the Factory Acts of the 1880s led to improvements such as fencing around dangerous machines, ventilation standards for factories, and lunchrooms and lavatories in large workplaces. The employment of women and children was also curbed on the grounds of protecting their health.

Over the years, additional safety standards were introduced. In unionized workplaces and industries, *collective bargaining* also made a difference as unions negotiated for better working conditions and the elimination of specific health and safety hazards (Chapter 11). By the second decade of the 20th century, provincial and territorial workers' compensation boards had put in place *no-fault compensation systems*, which still exist today. Injured workers are provided with some money, the amount depending on the severity of their injury, and with partial compensation for lost wages, no matter whose fault the accident. In return, they give up their right to sue for compensation if the employer was at fault. The system is funded by contributions from employers, with the amount based, in part, on their safety record. Thus, there is a monetary incentive for employers to reduce workplace health and safety hazards and to encourage safe working practices among employees. This system has been effective in reducing the incidence of workplace injuries and in compensating injured workers. Even so, women have benefited less than have men. In the first part of the 20th century, many "female" occupations were excluded from what was then called "workmen's compensation" legislation. This exclusion is no longer the case, but women continue to be overrepresented in precarious forms of employment (see Chapter 4), where workplace hazards may be overlooked and health and safety legislation is less likely to be effective (Hopkins 2017; Kosny and MacEachen 2010). Similarly, because teenagers frequently work in precarious jobs, and because both safety enforcement institutions and organized labour tend to overlook teenage workers, they too have likely benefited less from improvements in health and safety legislation and practices (Barnetson 2015).

All these approaches to dealing with health and safety issues—standards setting and enforcement by the state, collective bargaining between unions and employers, and the no-fault compensation system—offer little room for direct involvement on the part of workers. But the introduction of the *internal responsibility system* (IRS) changed this. A core IRS principle is that workers' personal experience and knowledge of work practices and hazards are an integral part of any solution to health and safety problems. In addition, the system calls for workers to participate in identifying and eliminating workplace hazards. Furthermore, health and safety is also management's responsibility. Overall health and safety is a workplace issue—an internal responsibility—too important to be left to government alone. In the IRS, employees are directly involved with management in monitoring and inspection, and in education and health promotion in their workplaces.

Direct worker involvement in health protection and promotion in the workplace increased dramatically in Europe in the 1970s. This trend grew out of demands for greater industrial democracy (discussed later in this chapter) and government reviews of traditional and unsatisfactory approaches to occupational health and safety (Tucker 1992). In Canada, the first major IRS initiative was the 1972 Saskatchewan Occupational Health Act. It broke new ground by broadly defining occupational health as "the promotion and maintenance of the highest degree of physical, mental, and social well-being of workers" (Clark 1982: 200) and by making *joint health and safety committees* (JHSCs) mandatory. Other provinces and territories and the federal government (about 6 percent of Canadian workers are covered by federal labour legislation[3]) followed. Today, the IRS, built around JHSCs, is part of the legislated workplace health and safety system across the country, although there are significant differences in the extent to which it has been implemented and promoted by provincial governments (Tucker 2003).

JHSCs range in size from 2 to 12 members, half of whom must be non-managerial employees (either elected or appointed by a union if one exists); they are required in any workplace employing 20 or more in all provinces and territories.[4] The committees keep records of injuries, participate in safety inspections, make recommendations to management about health and safety concerns, inform employees about their rights with respect to such concerns, and develop safety enhancement and educational programs.

Along with giving JHSCs the *right to be involved* in health and safety issues, legislation also allows workers the *right to refuse unsafe work*, based on the individual employee's belief that a particular task presents a genuine risk.[5] If subsequent inspections determine otherwise, the legislation protects workers from reprisals from employers. Workers also have the *right to be informed* about potentially hazardous materials with which they might be working.

In general, the IRS appears to be effective. Research has shown that the recommendations of JHSCs to management are usually heeded (Gordon 1994). An Ontario study examining data on claims for lost time to accidents between 1976 and 1989 concluded that when both employers and unions were committed to the idea of working together in joint committees to improve workplace safety, the number of lost time accidents declined (Lewchuk, Robb, and Walters 1996: 225).

The success of JHSCs in Canada has led to recommendations that the Canadian system be copied in the United States. The more traditional U.S. system, which still relies primarily on legislation and, where unions are present, on collective bargaining, is less effective (Gordon 1994). However, as in Canada, U.S. research has shown that JHSCs can be effective (Eaton and Nocerino 2000).[6]

The Labour Process and Workplace Health and Safety

How has the IRS approach to reducing workplace health and safety risks affected the labour process, that is, the contest for power between employers/managers and employees within capitalist workplaces? Does the relative effectiveness of JHSCs indicate that workers and management are no longer in conflict over health and safety issues, that this is a win-win situation? We would argue that, in Canada, workers and management have moved further in this direction on health and safety issues than on others. In part, this movement is due to the economic incentives built into the system for employers—a better safety record means lower costs of production. More important, legislation has reduced some of the power differences between management and workers, and directly involved each in addressing health and safety issues. An example is the extent to which workplace mental health has come to be seen as a critically important issue by Canadian legislators and business leaders over the past decade.[7]

Even so, workplace health and safety remains a contested terrain, and there have been backward movements over the past decades (Tucker 2003; Foster and Barnetson 2016). An increase in nonstandard and precarious forms of employment has meant that, in some workplace settings, the IRS has become less effective (Lewchuk, Clarke, and De Wolff 2009). Political shifts have also been a factor. For example, long after farm workers were given access to workers' compensation and were covered by other labour legislation in most other provinces, Alberta lagged behind. Politicians argued that self-regulation was most appropriate, despite high injury and fatality rates in agriculture in the province (Barnetson 2013). When the New Democratic Party (NDP) took power in 2015, it moved quickly to extend health and safety and other labour legislation to farm and ranch workers, despite a great deal of resistance from farm and ranch owners (Kienlen 2018). With the election in 2019 of a United Conservative Party (UCP) government, some of that progressive legislation may be repealed (according to promises made during the UCP election campaign), based on the belief that *employer self-regulation* is more effective.[8]

Critics of the IRS have pointed out that, in many JHSCs, non-management members continue to have much less influence, particularly in non-unionized workplaces. Some employers largely ignore the joint committees, despite legislation making them mandatory (Lewchuk, Robb, and Walters 1996). Rather than seeking ways to make their workplace safer and healthier (and by so doing, reducing their costs), such employers instead focus on challenging workers' claims of injuries and pushing them to return to work sooner (Storey 2009b). Recognizing these reactions, critics have called for independent audits of how well the IRS is really working (Arntz-Gray 2016).

Research has also shown that workers are often unaware of their rights and lack the knowledge needed to address complex health hazards; further, scientific and medical experts give the appearance of impartiality to a system that continues to be dominated by employers for whom profits come first (Sass 1995). In some tragic cases, notably the Westray mine explosion in 1992 in Nova Scotia, the system failed completely (Comish 1993; McCormick 1998). Local miners had warned that the mine site was unstable, and the initial mining plan was rejected for safety reasons. But the mine still opened and remained open even after repeated problems with methane gas, coal dust, and roof falls. Eventually, 26 miners died in an explosion.

While Canadian unions have fought for safer workplaces for well over a century, they have sometimes found themselves balancing concerns about their members' health and well-being with equally strong concerns about potential job loss. Robert Storey and Wayne Lewchuk (2000) describe how, in the early 1980s, the United Auto Workers of America tried to force Bendix Automotive in Windsor, Ontario, to deal with the deadly problem of asbestos dust in its brake shoe factory. Having already closed one of its plants because of this problem, the company announced that it now planned to close the remaining factory. Some of the workers wanted their union to insist that the workplace be made safer, whatever the cost. Others, fearful that the company would close the factory and they would lose their jobs, wanted the union to back down. The factory was eventually closed anyway.[9]

Along with disputes over the rights of management and workers, the definitions and sources of work-related health problems continue to be contested. For example, there is mounting evidence that job-related stress takes a toll on employees' health. Stress-induced health problems can range from headaches to chronic depression and heart disease. But even though some new management systems (lean production, for example) are creating particularly stressful work conditions (Carter et al. 2013), stress is still frequently rejected as a legitimate concern by workers' compensation boards, which administer claims. They tend to use a narrow definition of health and illness, focusing mainly on physical injuries and fatalities. Employers and compensation boards sometimes try to place the blame for workers' health problems on their lifestyles or family situations rather than on their jobs. Such a "blaming the victim" ideology assumes that workers are careless, accident-prone, or susceptible to illness.

Rather than accepting a narrow definition of workplace health and safety issues, Robert Sass (1986: 571) has argued that we need to

> "stretch" the present legal concept of risk, which covers dust, chemicals, lighting, and other quantifiable and measurable aspects of the workplace to cover all work environment matters: how the work is organized, the design of the job, pace of work, monotony, scheduling, sexual harassment, job cycle, and similar work environment matters of concern to workers.

We have seen some progress on this front. For example, the Alberta NDP government updated the provincial Occupational Health and Safety Act in 2018 to include workplace harassment and violence as safety risks and require employers to develop and implement prevention policies and investigate incidents of harassment and violence. But more still needs to be done. In fact, Sass has argued that the "weak rights" workers now have within the IRS need to be extended. "Strong rights," as he sees it, go beyond co-management and would involve "worker control in the area of the work environment" (Sass 1995: 123). In such a democratized work environment, workers would not have to accept the constant trade-off between health risks to themselves and the efficiency and profit demanded by employers. Sass sees unions as the only vehicle for such change since they are worker controlled, even though most unions work within the current IRS and accept its basic premises and goals.

However, with some exceptions, it has not been unions that have been pushing for a broader and more inclusive definition of worker health and well-being. Corporate health promotion, or *workplace health and wellness* programs, emerged in the 1980s as yet another human resource management policy that would help to motivate workers and raise productivity (Conrad 1987). The orientation of some of these programs has been to change workers' lifestyles or health-related behaviours (exercising more and quitting smoking, for example). Others, however, have gone considerably further to promote family-friendly and less stressful employment policies and practices.[10] For example, in the United States, the National Institute for Occupational Safety and Health recently began promoting a "new framework for worker well-being" (Chari et al. 2018: 589) that puts emphasis not only on workplace safety, along with physical and mental health, but also on workplace policies and cultures that can improve worker well-being.

Workplace health and wellness programs clearly have good intentions and can benefit employees who participate in them. But they have not addressed issues of job redesign and have not had an impact on the unequal distribution of power within work organizations that contributes to health and safety problems.[11] Furthermore, because such programs are typically available only in larger work organizations, many workers are unable to participate. Thus, while offering assistance to some workers, workplace health and wellness programs do not improve working conditions for the working class as a whole.

INDUSTRIAL DEMOCRACY: RETHINKING WORKERS' RIGHTS

Our evaluation of new management paradigms (Chapter 9) concluded that none really offered workers input into decisions beyond their own jobs. Decisions about organizational restructuring, introduction of new technologies, replacement of permanent with temporary workers, or company downsizing are rarely negotiated with employees or their unions (Chapter 10). The IRS acknowledges the need to involve workers in the co-management of health and safety risks, but still does not give workers and employers equal control over the work environment. In short, within capitalism, ownership carries with it the ultimate right to control how work is organized and performed.

Industrial democracy attempts to involve workers in a much wider range of decisions within the organization, applying the principles of *representative democracy* found in the political arena to the workplace. Workers have a voice at the work-group level, as well as indirectly through elected representatives on corporate boards and other key policy-making bodies. Even so, as we will argue below, industrial democracy in its various forms has not eliminated workplace power differences. Furthermore, industrial democracy does not guarantee less bureaucracy, reduced income inequality, skill upgrading, or even more task-related autonomy for workers. Even if workers are involved extensively in decision making through elected representatives, the debates might not be around these issues. Job security, for example, or health and safety might be the major concern. Thus, in some settings, industrial democracy has led to job redesign and profit sharing. In others, the results may have been fewer layoffs or more consultation about technological change.

Industrial Democracy in North America

Attempts to involve workers in management, at least to some extent, have a long history in North America. Following World War I, *works councils*, including elected workers and management representatives, were set up in large workplaces in a number of industries in both Canada and the United States. The councils met to discuss health and safety, workers' grievances, efficiency, and sometimes even wages. In a number of settings, particularly the coal industry, the impetus for these initiatives was a series of long and violent strikes.[12]

William Lyon Mackenzie King, who later became prime minister of Canada, was a labour consultant to some of these companies at the time. He was a strong advocate of the principles of industrial democracy, believing that works councils and related initiatives would reduce industrial conflict and help usher in a new era of social harmony (King 1918). Critics argued that mechanisms to encourage more cooperation between workers and management continued to favour the latter and that works councils were just a way to deter workers from joining unions. Clearly, in many companies this was the case. With the onset of the Depression at the end of the 1920s, interest in these earlier forms of industrial democracy waned, perhaps because unemployment led to fewer strikes.

Since then, calls have periodically been made for a revival of such worker–management decision-making systems. Not coincidentally, industrial democracy has attracted more interest during periods of labour unrest—immediately after World War II, for example, and again in the 1970s. During those strike-filled eras, employers and politicians looked to Germany and other European countries where industrial democracy had been implemented more widely. North American unions have generally opposed the idea, believing that works councils and other similar forms of industrial democracy undermine collective bargaining, the more traditional means by which workers have negotiated with management for improved working conditions (Guzda 1993: 67). Thus, overall, the spread of industrial democracy in North America has been slow (Frege 2005). Most employers have been more interested in avoiding strikes than in sharing power, and unions have not been supportive.

Institutionalized Industrial Democracy in Germany

North American experiments in industrial democracy have usually been introduced by management, occasionally with some pressure from unions. In contrast, principles of industrial democracy have been institutionalized via legislation in many northern European countries. Workers are given the right to elect representatives to sit on works councils or corporate boards, the right to consultation regarding technological changes, and more grassroots control over health and safety matters.[13]

The German model of *codetermination* has a century-long history. In the 1890s, concerns about widespread labour–management conflict motivated

Chancellor Bismarck to bring in legislation giving works councils the right to advise management on workplace regulations. This legislation was broadened in the 1920s as the Weimar government sought ways to counter the threat of the Russian Revolution spreading into Germany. After World War II, concerned that labour strife would hold back the reconstruction of Germany's devastated economy, the British, American, and French administrators of occupied Germany extended the codetermination legislative framework. A number of additional changes were made in the 1970s and 1980s.

In its current form, German legislation makes works councils mandatory in any workplace with more than five employees. Elected representatives of the workforce (their number proportional to the size of the firm) share decision making with management representatives. The legislation stipulates that, in larger work organizations where unions are present, a proportion of the elected members must be from the union. But nonunionized white-collar workers must also be represented. In larger companies, there are several layers of shared decision making. The most powerful management board, a group of three or four individuals, has only one worker representative.

The codetermination legislation requires employers to advise and consult with works councils about plans to introduce new technologies, restructure work, reallocate workers to different tasks or locations, or lay off workers. Works councils can demand compensation for workers negatively affected by new technologies or organizational restructuring. Consequently, the North American strategy of downsizing has been much less common in Germany. Elected representatives are jointly involved with management in determining hours of work, pay procedures (bonus rates, for example), training systems, health and safety rules, and working conditions. However, collective bargaining between employers and unions about overall pay rates takes place outside the works councils on an industry-wide level. Consequently, the right to strike remains with the larger unions, not with the local works councils. The unions, however, have much less influence in the joint decision-making process at the local level.

The German *dual representation system* of industrial democracy—industry-wide unions and local works councils—is viewed relatively positively by both employers and workers. Research suggests that companies with works councils are more productive than those without them (Mueller 2012). There are some concerns, however, that unions may be weakened by the dual system of representation, but union members still constitute a majority of elected representatives on the works councils. Overall, joint decision making has meant better communication between workers and management, greater protection of workers' rights, improved working conditions, and a reduction in labour–management conflict. The latter was, of course, an original goal of the codetermination legislation, and it has frequently impressed North American observers concerned about strikes and reduced productivity.

Sweden: Industrial Democracy as a National Goal

In Sweden, the motivation to implement industrial democracy was somewhat different than in Germany, where concerns about strikes and social unrest led to codetermination legislation. An exceptionally strong union movement and the governing Social Democratic Party worked together to improve employment conditions and give Swedish workers more rights. During the 1970s and 1980s, industrial democracy was elevated to a national goal within a much broader policy of commitment to reduced inequality and full employment.[14]

As in Germany, Swedish law mandates employee representation on corporate boards of directors in all but the smallest firms. But the 1977 Act on Employee Participation in Decision Making extended Swedish employees' rights beyond the rights of German workers. Specifically, in addition to the obligation to inform and consult with workers on major decisions such as factory closures or introducing new technologies, Swedish employers must negotiate with unions prior to such decisions. Unions must also be given complete access to information on the economic status of the firm and its personnel policies. In 1984, Sweden went further by setting up Wage Earner Funds, which redirected corporate taxes into share purchases on behalf of employees in manufacturing and related industries (Whyman 2004).

The 1978 Work Environment Act goes beyond the goal of industrial democracy—joint decision making throughout a work organization—to address issues of worker satisfaction and personal fulfillment (see Chapter 14). The Act aims to achieve "working conditions where the individual can regard work as a meaningful and enriching part of existence." It is not enough for work to be free of physical and psychological hazards; it must also provide opportunities for satisfaction and personal growth, and for employees to assume greater responsibility. Thus, unlike recent management approaches, such as quality-of-working-life (QWL) programs, that view improved productivity and less conflict as desirable outcomes of worker satisfaction (see Chapter 9), this legislation makes worker satisfaction and individual growth the highest priority.

During the 1970s and 1980s, Sweden's impressive economic performance, low unemployment, and reduction of wage inequalities were seen as strong evidence of the success of its model of society-wide industrial democracy. But the following two decades brought changes. Some of the government's policies directed at maintaining full employment were eliminated, and unemployment was allowed to rise. Employers sought more flexibility in the allocation of labour in the production process and were able, as in Germany, to reduce the extent of nationwide centralized wage bargaining. Lean production made its appearance in Swedish factories, some of the most progressive factories (in terms of workers' autonomy and skill enhancement) closed, and employers introduced new technologies to cut jobs.[15] But the framework legislation that supports the Swedish system of industrial democracy is still in place, and the Swedish version of codetermination continues to be successful. Overall, compared to Canada and the United States, social inequality in Sweden is not as pronounced, because of its labour market policies (Olsen 2008).

WORKERS TAKING OVER OWNERSHIP

A basic capitalist principle is that ownership carries with it the right to control how work is performed and how the organization is run. By offering some degree of co-management or codetermination, the various forms of industrial democracy have given workers a few of the rights traditionally attached to ownership. However, in some settings, workers have gone much further, taking over partial or complete ownership of the means of production. How economically viable is worker ownership within a global capitalist economy? And does worker ownership provide more opportunity for control over the labour process?

Employee Share Ownership Plans

Employee share ownership plans (ESOPs) have been promoted as a way for workers to share in the profits of production and as a means of generating more consensus in the workplace. Thus, employees receive some of the company profits, in the same way as would other shareholders, although, when shares available through the plan are provided as benefits in lieu of wages, employees will also lose when the company is losing money. If workers are part-owners, the reasoning goes, they should be more likely to identify with the company, work harder, and cooperate with management (Wheeler 2008).

In some companies with ESOPs, shares in the company are purchased for employees and provided as part of a benefits package. In other workplaces, employees are allowed to purchase shares at reduced rates, or their employer pays for a portion of the cost if workers choose to buy shares (Luffman 2003). Depending on the details of the plan, employees in some categories might receive (or be allowed to buy) more shares than employees in other categories. ESOPs tend to be more common in large private-sector high-performance workplaces and, typically, higher-paid employees (e.g., managers and professionals) receive or can buy the most shares (Schwartz and Corkery 2018).

The presence of ESOPs and participation in them varies across countries. A study from a decade ago suggested that there were more than 11,400 ESOPs in the United States, with about 13.7 million employees participating (Kramer 2010). An earlier European survey of large workplaces in 10 European Union (EU) countries showed ESOPs present in about 1 in 10 private companies. ESOPs were somewhat more common in the United Kingdom than in other EU countries with histories of industrial democracy (Poutsma, Hendrickx, and Huijgen 2003). A Statistics Canada survey showed about 7 percent of all Canadian private-sector workers owned shares in their company in 2005, down from just under 10 percent in 1999 (Statistics Canada 2008f: 54–55).[16]

It is unclear whether this Canadian pattern is indicative of a similar decline in other countries, but the growth in precarious work and the shifting of manufacturing production overseas, described in earlier chapters, suggests that it might be. For example, until 2018, Amazon was giving its warehouse workers two shares per year, worth about $3500. It discontinued the practice, raising hourly wages instead and offering cash bonuses to long-time employees (Schwartz and Corkery 2018).

In North America, ESOPs have been set up primarily to provide additional benefits to workers or to allow them to purchase shares, but not to promote joint decision making. In workplaces where employees participate in an ESOP as well as in some form of joint decision making, it is usually because some other managerial model (QWL, for example) has also been implemented. However, in these types of situations, typically the predicted productivity gains associated with the plans are found. In other words, the combination of both employee ownership and worker decision making makes the difference (Pendleton and Robinson 2010).

An example of a company offering profit sharing, but going much further in terms of worker participation, is the fascinating Brazilian company SEMCO (Kruse 2016). The company has grown steadily for several decades and now has annual sales of over $210 million. The 3,000 employees in its various businesses set their own production quotas, redesign products, develop marketing plans, and determine salary ranges. Employees even choose and evaluate their own managers. For big decisions, such as buying another company or relocating a factory, every worker gets a vote.[17] Thus, SEMCO appears to have gone far beyond the basic principles of industrial democracy and also the ESOP model to give workers rights and obligations normally reserved for owners.

Workers Buying Out Their Employers

Economic restructuring and factory and mill closures over the past several decades have led to interesting examples of worker ownership of a different kind. In some settings, workers have bought out their employers in an effort to save their jobs when the company was about to close. Unlike the situation with ESOPs, the majority ownership that comes with *worker buyouts* allows them to manage their own job security (to decide whether the business closes or not). Majority ownership also allows workers to change the management system, if they want to.[18]

One prominent example of a worker buyout in Canada was the purchase of Algoma Steel in Sault Ste. Marie, Ontario, in 1992. The company had been operating in the community since 1901 and employed about 5,000 workers at the beginning of the 1990s. If the company had folded, the community would have been decimated. Through their union (the United Steel Workers of America), and with the assistance of loan guarantees from the NDP provincial government at the time, workers negotiated the purchase of a majority of shares in the company. Cost savings were obtained by a voluntary pay reduction and through a plan to eliminate several thousand jobs through attrition. A decade after the buyout, Algoma Steel ran into severe financial difficulties but, with the participation of the union, refinanced and restructured itself once more.

As a result of the public sale of shares to finance the upgrading of the steel mill, workers now owned only about one-quarter of Algoma's shares. However, they still appointed 5 of the company's 13 board members, and the participative management structure set up years earlier continued to operate effectively. More recently, in 2007, Algoma Steel was bought by a multinational steel company with its home base in India. Today, the company still has an ESOP, but the bold experiment in industrial democracy and worker ownership is over.

New worker-owners do not typically implement some form of industrial democracy (Varghese et al. 2006). For example, when forestry workers and managers bought the mills in which they had been employed for many years in Kapuskasing, Ontario (1991), and Pine Falls, Manitoba (1994), they initially experimented with forms of worker participation in decision making. But within a year or two, the traditional system of management had been reinstated at TEMBEC (Krogman and Beckley 2002). By 2010, the worker-owners had sold their shares to private investors operating a series of mills across Ontario and Quebec, and in 2017 it was sold to a very large U.S. chemical company that also has substantial newsprint and lumber holdings.

Algoma Steel and TEMBEC were successful examples of employee buyouts that eventually failed, but probably not because of the ownership structure. Instead, they were the major employer in single-industry communities, which have generally not fared well in the contemporary global economy. In contrast, most ailing companies bought by workers become successful once again. An interesting case is the Great Western Brewing Company in Saskatoon. It has operated successfully as a worker-owned business since 1989 when 16 workers bought a brewery that Carling Molson was planning to shut down because it was not profitable (Lopez-Pacheco 2014). A meta-analysis of 43 published studies (Doucouliagos 1995) showed that profit sharing, worker ownership, and institutionalized industrial democracy are all associated with higher levels of productivity, with the largest impact occurring in worker-owned firms.

The chances of a worker buyout being successful are increased when all the participants, including the union if one is present, support the buyout plan. In addition, workers typically need expert advice to assist them in deciding how to restructure the organization, since major changes (often in wage rates and staffing) are usually needed. An example is the unique working and financing arrangement developed by unionized workers and three different investor groups with various types of expertise who bought and revitalized the bankrupt Harmac pulp mill in Nanaimo in 2008 (Spalding 2010). Permanent employees each promised to invest $25,000 in the company over a three-year period. Together, they owned one-quarter of the B.C. company (Harmac Pacific 2008). Government support is also critical, particularly with respect to financing, since many banks are reluctant to gamble on worker buyouts, despite their better-than-average track record.

Producer Co-operatives

Employee-owned producer co-operatives have a long history in North America and Europe. The first appeared in Britain more than 175 years ago as workers looked for alternatives to the exploitative excesses of early capitalism (Estrin and Pérotin 1987). However, the producer co-operative movement was overshadowed by another form of collective response by workers, the formation of trade unions (Chapter 11). Even so, the co-operative alternative continues.[19]

In 2015, more than 700 employee-owned producer co-operatives were functioning in Canada (Innovation, Science and Economic Development Canada 2018). A majority of these organizations are in Quebec, in large part because the provincial government has put in place programs that provide financing for producer co-operatives. Despite being a much larger country, there are fewer producer co-operatives in the United States—a recent estimate put the number at between 300 and 400 (Chen 2016). While producer co-operatives are not a widespread phenomenon, and those that exist are typically quite small, they nonetheless offer another alternative to conventional employer–employee relationships. Examples in Canada include everything from construction companies and daycare centres to taxi firms, recycling companies, coffee roasters, and fish farms, as well as small manufacturing companies, consulting firms, restaurants, and forestry management firms.[20]

Producer co-operatives must be distinguished from other collective enterprises, including consumer co-operatives (such as co-op food stores) or housing co-ops, in which a number of individuals or families jointly own and maintain a dwelling or housing complex. They are also different from marketing co-ops (the wheat pools set up early last century by Prairie farmers are the best example) and financial services co-ops, such as credit unions. While sharing with these other organizations a general commitment to collective ownership and shared risk taking, *producer co-operatives* are distinguished by their function as collective producers of goods or services (Lindenfeld and Wynn 1997; Brown 1997).

Producer co-operatives are also different from other types of worker-owned enterprises in several important respects. First, central to the philosophy of producer co-operatives is a commitment to the democratic principle of "one person—one vote." This defining characteristic would eliminate companies with ESOPs and many examples of workers buying out their employers. Second, and related to the first point, producer co-operatives typically do not allow non-members to own shares. As a result, members cannot benefit financially from the success of the co-operative by selling their own shares. Instead, some arrangements are usually made to reimburse members for their previous contributions when they leave the organization.

Although generally quite small, producer co-operatives can nevertheless survive in a capitalist economy. A recent review of research on such workplaces in Europe, Latin America, and the United States suggested that worker-owned businesses can be more productive since they can reduce or eliminate worker–management conflict (Perotin 2016). In Canada, a study of producer co-operatives in the Atlantic provinces revealed an estimated median lifespan of 17 years for rural producer co-operatives and 25 years for those in urban settings (Staber 1993: 140). But producer co-operatives face many challenges. It is difficult to finance such enterprises, since banks are often skeptical of their ability to survive. This problem is also faced by other small businesses and by employees wanting to buy out their company. In situations where producer co-operatives are set up as a solution to high unemployment caused by economic downturns, the new worker-owned enterprises are at a disadvantage from the outset. And, as with any efforts to democratize workplaces, participants in producer co-operatives have to learn how to work collectively toward common goals, something not taught or encouraged in a competitive capitalist society. As Semuels (2015: para. 26) observes in an essay on worker co-operatives in the United States, "face-to-face democracy is a laborious, slow process."

Given their small size and collective ownership, it is not surprising that producer co-operatives tend to offer workers greater control over the labour process. Leslie Brown (1997) argues that producer co-operatives incorporate many of the democratizing and work-humanizing features of workplace reform that have been promised, but not always delivered, by the many new management approaches of the past decades (Chapter 9). She also concludes that producer co-operatives are a viable solution to problems of community economic development that have not been solved by efforts to encourage traditional forms of capitalist enterprise in underdeveloped regions of the country.[21]

Worldwide, the most successful producer co-operative is found in and around Mondragon, a city in the Basque region of Spain. There, over 80,000 worker-owners (in 2019; up from about 20,000 thirty years earlier) run over 250 diverse manufacturing and service companies and 15 technology centres with annual sales (in 2018) of almost 12 billion Euros (Mondragon Corporation 2019). Each worker has an economic stake in the enterprise where she or he works, and as a member of the firm's general assembly, helps establish policies, approves financial plans, and elects members to a supervisory board, which, in turn, appoints managers. Mondragon co-ops have replaced the private ownership of industry in this region with a system of collective ownership and control (Ridley-Duff 2010). By all accounts, these co-ops have achieved high levels of growth, productivity, and employment creation, harmonious labour relations, a satisfying and non-alienating work environment, and a close integration between workplace and community (Forcadell 2005; Flecha and Ngai 2014).

Mondragon's success is linked to, among other things, the Basque region's decades-long struggle for greater autonomy from Spain, the destruction of the area's industrial base during the Spanish Civil War in the 1930s, and support from the local Roman Catholic church and unions. This unique historical mix of political, cultural, and economic circumstances has sometimes been used as an argument that producer co-operatives could not thrive in other settings such as North America. Granted, it is never easy to transplant production systems from one cultural and political context to another. But, if we are willing to accept that Japanese management techniques or German codetermination, for example, offer alternatives to the North American approach to organizing workplaces, we should not ignore the Mondragon-style producer co-operative alternative (Macleod 1997).

CONCLUSION

In Chapter 9, we explored a range of new managerial models that, in contrast to Taylorism and the human relations approach (discussed in Chapter 8), promised to empower workers and enhance their skills. Chapter 10, with its critical assessment of the labour process in capitalist workplaces, reminded us of the power differences and inherent conflicts between owners and managers, on one hand, and employees on the other. In Chapter 11, we examined the role of unions in giving workers a voice and some organizational power in capitalist economies. In this chapter we shifted our focus to alternative ways of organizing and managing workplaces that might reduce industrial conflict and provide workers with more control over the labour process and their work organizations.

We began by reviewing statistics on workplace injuries and fatalities, and saw that workplace health and safety continues to be a contested issue in the workplace. The systems put in place to address health and safety concerns, however, provide some evidence of workers and management finding common ground. Our discussion of the different forms of industrial democracy in Germany and Sweden also revealed alternative approaches to economic organization that can empower workers and provide them with a greater collective voice while, at the same time, reducing labour–management conflict. Finally, our examination of different forms of worker ownership highlighted that there are alternatives to traditional employment relationships within capitalism that deserve serious consideration.

DISCUSSION QUESTIONS

1. Based on what you have read in Chapters 9 through 12, what do you consider to be the most effective ways to give workers a voice in their workplace today?
2. How workplace health and safety issues are handled in Canadian workplaces is an example of employers and employees working together to meet common goals. Do you agree with this proposition? Why or why not?
3. Workplaces are organized differently, workers are managed differently, and industrial relations have different rules in some European countries. What

can we learn from these societies that would lead to higher productivity and/or less conflict in North American workplaces?

4. Critically discuss the following statement: "Producer co-operatives have been successful in places such as Mondragon, Spain, and in some isolated, small Canadian communities, but they are irrelevant for modern, urban Canada."

ADDITIONAL RESOURCES

WORK AT THE MOVIES

- *Wal-Town* (directed by Sergeo Kirby, 2006, 66:09 minutes). This NFB documentary concerns the work of student activists in raising awareness about the practices of Walmart. It is available through the National Film Board of Canada: http://www.nfb.ca/film/wal_town.
- *Occupy: The Movie* (directed by Corey Ogilvie, 2013, 121 minutes). The documentary traces the rise and development of the Occupy movement following the 2008 global crash.
- *Erin Brockovich* (directed by Steven Soderbergh, 2000, 131 minutes). An unemployed single mother becomes a legal assistant and almost single-handedly brings down a California power company accused of polluting a city's water supply.
- *The Take* (directed by Avi Lewis, 2004, 87 minutes). Set in Argentina after its 2001 economic collapse, the Canadian documentary tells the story of a group of unemployed auto-parts workers who form a co-operative and strive to reopen their closed factory.

SOUNDS OF WORK

- "Join a Co-op" (Emily Erhardt). Written for the International Co-operative Alliance's Coop'Art competition in recognition of the International Year of Co-ops (2012), this song by a young Canadian rapper outlines the benefits of co-operative organizations.
- "Talkin' 'Bout a Revolution" (Tracy Chapman). Chapman sings about the need for poor people to stand up and fight for reshaping income distribution.

- "The Internationale" (Eugène Pottier). The 19th-century worker's song about the Paris Commune later became the first national anthem of the Soviet Union.
- "Chemical Worker's Song (Process Man)" (Great Big Sea). This band from Newfoundland and Labrador writes about men working in a chemical plant and suffering dire health consequences.

NOTES

1. In the United States, 4,836 workers lost their lives to work-related injuries or diseases in 2015, while close to 3.7 million were injured (AFL-CIO 2017).
2. In Canada, full-time employees in the public sector were off work because of their own illness or disability or for family or personal responsibilities for 14.6 days in 2018, while those in the private sector lost an average of 8.6 days (Statistics Canada 2019). Assuming a 250-day work year, this amounts to lost productivity equal to 5.8 percent and 3.4 percent annually in the public and private sectors, respectively. For more on absenteeism and productivity loss in Canada, see Zhang, McLeod, and Koehoorn (2016).
3. For information on federal labour legislation, see Employment and Social Development Canada: https://www.canada.ca/en/employment-social-development /programs/employment-equity/regulated-industries.html [retrieved 15 April 2019]
4. In Saskatchewan and Newfoundland and Labrador, JHSCs are required in workplaces with 10 or more employees; see the Canadian Centre for Occupational Health and Safety: https://www.ccohs.ca/oshanswers/hsprograms/hscommittees /whatisa.html [retrieved 15 April 2019]
5. In his book *Hazard or Hardship*, Hilgart (2013) presents a compelling argument for why the right to refuse unsafe work needs to be seen as a global human rights issue.
6. See Shapiro (2014) for a useful historical overview of occupational health and safety legislation in the United States. Karmel (2017) provides a contemporary assessment of the human costs of deregulation in health and safety legislation in the United States.
7. Samra (2017) discusses progress made in addressing workplace mental health issues, as well as challenges that still need to be addressed.
8. See Walters (2006) for a discussion of how the U.K. government has preferred voluntary compliance approaches over strengthening workplace health and safety legislation and promoting further employee involvement.

9. Baril-Gingras and Dubois-Ouellet (2018) discuss how unions can more effectively focus on health and safety issues in the workplace, based on their study of a large central labour organization in Quebec.

10. For information on workplace health and well-being programs, see the Canadian Centre for Occupational Health and Safety: https://www.ccohs.ca/oshanswers/psychosocial/wellness_program.html [retrieved 16 April 2019]

11. Hansen (2004: 151) is much more critical, labelling employee assistance programs as the "caring cousin" of workplace surveillance strategies, since employers can use such programs to identify workers who may potentially become less productive.

12. See Russell (1990: Chapter 3) and Rinehart (2006: 48–49) on early works councils in Canada, and Guzda (1993) on the U.S. situation. Greenwald (2005) presents a fascinating account of attempts to implement industrial democracy in early 20th-century New York.

13. See Poutsma, Hendrickx, and Huijgen (2003), Deutsch (2005), Whittal, Knudson, and Huijgen (2007), Müller-Jentsch (2008), Keller and Werner (2010), and van den Berg, Grift, and van Witteloostuijn (2011) on industrial democracy in Europe.

14. This discussion of Sweden draws on Milner (1989), Smucker et al. (1998), Levinson (2000), Whyman (2004), and Olsen (2008).

15. See Sandberg (1994), Smucker et al. (1998), and Nilsson (1996).

16. The Canadian ESOP Association provides information about employee share ownership plans in Canada: https://www.esopcanada.ca/.

17. For more on SEMCO, see Semler (2007) and Largacha-Martinez (2011).

18. This discussion of worker buyouts is based on Gunderson et al. (1995), Long (1995), and Nishman (1995).

19. See the 2014 special issue of the journal *Organization* (Vol. 21, No. 5) for a series of articles on worker co-operatives.

20. The Canadian Worker Co-op Federation provides additional information on worker co-ops in Canada: https://canadianworker.coop/about/what-is-a-worker-co-op/ [retrieved 19 April 2019]

21. See Cameron and Hanavan (2014) on problems faced by rural co-operatives in Atlantic Canada as they attempt to operate in what is becoming a more globalized economy.

13 WORK VALUES AND WORK ORIENTATIONS

"There are many people who complain that their jobs make no difference in the world. By this I mean not simply that their work has no profound effect on transforming society, which, after all, very few jobs actually do, but rather that they make no difference of any kind of all–if their position, or even the division or branch of the company where they work were to vanish, no one would notice. Their jobs literally do nothing. . . . Take Dan, who worked for a large insurance firm based in Toronto. He technically provided graphics for an online data depository no one ever consulted, but most days, he did nothing at all. "It's honestly hard," he told me, "to describe how mad and useless I felt. There were easily twice as many managers as actual employees in the building. How ridiculous is that?". . . Humans want to contribute to society. If some resist paid employment, it's largely because they are trapped between a job that doesn't contribute to society . . . and a useful job whose conditions are so extraordinarily awful that they'd literally do anything else. For proof, one need only look at prisons. Prisons house some of society's least altruistic members, but, even here, when given a choice between watching TV and playing cards all day or pressing shirts in the prison laundry, prisoners almost invariably choose the latter. Indeed, refusing prisoners the right to work is typically a form of punishment."

Source: Daniel Graeber. What's the Point of Pointless Jobs? *Globe and Mail*, May 18, 2018. Retrieved November 29, 2018: https://www.theglobeandmail.com/opinion/article-whats-the-point-of-pointless-jobs/.

INTRODUCTION

In previous chapters, we presented a structural analysis of work in Canada, discussing, among other topics, labour markets, the occupational structure, work organizations, management systems, labour unions, and gender, racial, and other forms of stratification. Some of this material addressed individual reactions to work—workers' problems in balancing work and family responsibilities, and resistance and conflict in the workplace, for example. But in this chapter and the next, we get to the very core of the individual–job relationship by examining the meaning of work in our society and workers' subjective response to their work.

We begin with a broad overview of work values. What does "work" really mean in our society today? Have work values changed over time, and are there cultural differences in work values? We then focus our analysis on the work orientations, or preferences, held by individual Canadians. How are these preferences shaped? Are alternative work orientations emerging in response to changing employment relationships and demographic shifts in Canadian society? Then, in Chapter 14, we turn our attention to job satisfaction and work-related stress. Overall, how satisfied are Canadian workers with their employment situation? Is this changing? What factors influence job satisfaction and dissatisfaction, and what are the underlying causes of work-related stress? Does satisfaction with or stress resulting from one's job have further consequences?

DEFINING *WORK VALUES* AND *WORK ORIENTATIONS*

Values, as sociologists use the term, are the benchmarks or standards by which members of a society assess their own and others' behaviour. We could talk about how personal attributes such as honesty and industriousness are valued in our society, about how we value freedom of speech, or about the value placed on getting a good education. We might also ask how work is valued, or, in other words, what the meaning of work is in a particular society.

Having identified *work values* as societal standards, we can define *work orientations* more narrowly as the meaning attached to work by particular individuals within a society. Blackburn and Mann (1979: 141) define an *orientation* as "a central organizing principle which underlies people's attempts to make sense of their lives." Thus, studying work orientations involves determining what people consider important in their lives. Does someone continue to work primarily for material reasons (either a desire to become wealthy or because of economic necessity), for income that will allow him or her to enjoy life away from work, or for the enjoyment and personal fulfillment that can come from work? Even more specifically, what types of work and work arrangements do individuals prefer?

Chapter 13: Work Values and Work Orientations

The distinction between work values and work orientations is not always clear, since it hinges on the extent to which the latter are broadly shared within a society. As we will argue below, several different sets of work values can coexist within a society, influencing the work orientations of individuals within that society in different ways. In fact, as our earlier discussion of managerial ideologies and practices showed (see Chapter 9), particular work values have often been promoted by employers to gain compliance from workers.

An individual's work orientations are also shaped by specific experiences on the job. Indeed, a worker whose job or career is dissatisfying may begin to challenge dominant work values. Thus, over the long term, shifting work orientations on the part of many workers might also influence societal work values. *Job satisfaction* (or dissatisfaction), discussed in Chapter 14, is the most individualized and subjective response of a person to the material and psychological rewards offered by a job.

WORK VALUES ACROSS TIME AND SPACE

The meaning attached to work has changed dramatically over the centuries.[1] The ancient Greeks and Romans viewed most forms of work negatively, considering it brutalizing and uncivilized. In fact, the Greek word for "work," *ponos*, comes from the root word for "sorrow." According to Greek mythology, the gods had cursed the human race by giving them the need to work. Given these dominant work values, the ruling classes turned their attention to politics, warfare, the arts, and philosophy, leaving the physical work to slaves.

Early Hebrew religious values placed a different but no more positive emphasis on work. Hard work was seen as divine punishment for the "original sin" of the first humans who ate from the "tree of the knowledge of good and evil." According to Hebrew and Christian scriptures, God banished Eve and Adam from the Garden of Eden, where all of creation was at their easy disposal, to a life of hard labour, telling them that "in the sweat of thy face shalt thou eat bread, till thou return unto the ground."[2] This perspective on work remained part of the early Christian worldview for many centuries.

A more positive view of work within Christianity was promoted by Saint Thomas Aquinas in the 13th century. In ranking occupations according to their value to society, Aquinas rejected the notion that all work is a curse or a necessary evil. Instead, he argued that some forms of work were better than others. Priests were assigned the highest ranks, followed by those working in agriculture, and then craftworkers. Because they produced food or products useful to society, these groups were ranked higher than merchants and shopkeepers. A comparison of this scheme to contemporary occupational status scales (see Chapter 4) reveals some interesting reversals. The status of those involved in commercial activity—bankers, corporate owners, and managers, for example—has increased, while farmers and craftworkers have experienced substantial declines in occupational status, in tandem with their diminishing numbers in the labour force.

During the 16th-century Protestant Reformation in Europe, Martin Luther's ideas marked a significant change in dominant work values. Luther argued that work was a central component of human life. Although he still had a negative opinion of work for profit, he went beyond the belief that hard work was atonement for original sin. When he wrote, "There is just one best way to serve God—to do most perfectly the work of one's profession" (Burstein et al. 1975: 10), he was articulating the idea of a "calling," that is, industriousness and hard work within one's station in life, however lowly that might be, as the fulfillment of God's will. Whether or not peasants or the urban working class shared these values is difficult to determine. However, to the extent that the ruling classes could convince their subordinates that hard work was a moral obligation, power and privilege could be more easily maintained.

The Protestant Work Ethic

The Industrial Revolution transformed the social and economic landscape of Europe and also generated a new set of work values. In his famous book, *The Protestant Ethic and the Spirit of Capitalism*, Max Weber (1958) emphasized how Calvinists, one of the early Protestant groups that had broken away from the Roman Catholic Church, embraced hard work, rejected worldly pleasures, and extolled the virtues of frugality. Weber argued that such religious beliefs encouraged people to make and reinvest profits and, in turn, gave rise to work values conducive to the growth of capitalism. Other scholars have questioned whether these early Protestant entrepreneurs really acted solely on religious beliefs and whether other groups not sharing these beliefs might have been equally successful (Dickson and McLachlan 1989).[3] Nonetheless, Weber did draw our attention to the role of work values in capitalist societies. He also recognized that such an *ideology of work*, while justifying the profit-seeking behaviour of capitalists, might also help control their employees who, for religious reasons, would be motivated to work hard.

Freedom and equality are additional secular values that fit into the belief system of capitalist democracies. A central assumption is that workers are participants in a labour market where they can freely choose a job. If this is so, the fact that some people are wealthier and more powerful than others must be because of their hard work and smart choices, most specifically, investments in higher education. Hence, within this ideology of work, *equality* does not refer to the distribution of wealth and power, but to access to the same opportunities for upward mobility in a competitive labour market. But, as explained in Chapter 5, some workers are advantaged by birth, and some occupational groups are more protected in the labour market. Consequently, for many workers, the daily realities of the labour market often contradict the dominant set of work values.

Work as Self-Fulfillment: The Humanist Tradition

The importance of hard work and wealth accumulation are only one perspective on work in a capitalist society. The belief that work is virtuous in itself gave rise to another set of values in western Europe in the 17th and 18th centuries. The *humanist tradition* grew out of Renaissance philosophies that distinguished humans from other species on the basis of our ability to consciously direct our labour. A view of human beings as creators led to the belief that work should be a fulfilling and liberating activity, and that it constituted the very essence of humanity.

Karl Marx fashioned these ideas into a radical critique of capitalism and a formula for social revolution (Chapter 1). He agreed that the essence of humanity was expressed through work, but argued that this potential was stifled by capitalist relations of production. Because they had little control over their labour and its products, workers were engaged in alienating work. For Marx, capitalist economic relations limited human independence and creativity. Only when capitalism was replaced by socialism, he argued, would work be truly liberating.

Marx's theory of alienation has had a major impact on the sociology of work (Chapter 10); ironically, a similar set of beliefs about the centrality of work to an individual's sense of personal well-being underlies a number of contemporary management approaches, which are decidedly non-Marxist in their assumptions (see Chapter 9). It is frequently argued, for example, that workers would be more satisfied if they were allowed to use more of their skills and make more decisions in their jobs. But these management perspectives do not see capitalism as the problem. Rather, they advocate improved organizational and job design within capitalism. Humanistic beliefs about the essential importance of work in people's lives are also espoused by many contemporary sociologists of work as well as some organizational psychologists.[4] Indeed, they underlie our own perspective (Lowe 2000). Such work values have also been promoted by various 20th- and 21st-century theologians, including the Roman Catholic priest who founded the system of Mondragon producer co-operatives in the 1950s (Chapter 12), as well as the current pope, who spoke about the dignity of work in his 2013 May Day sermon in St. Peter's Square in Rome (Francis 2013). The pope also expressed his concern for unemployed workers around the world, noting that this social problem was often the result of greater emphasis in society on profit-seeking rather than social justice.

Manifest and Latent Functions of Work

An immense amount of sociological and psychological research tells us that unemployment is extremely traumatic for jobless individuals and their families. Lost income leads to a lower standard of living, personal and family stress, and health problems (Brand 2015; Mousteri, Daly and Delaney 2018).[5] And, as the humanist perspective on work reminds us, the centrality of work to people's self-worth and identity means that unemployment has even deeper personal and social costs.

Based on her research among the unemployed during the Depression of the 1930s, Marie Jahoda (1982) identified some of the *latent functions* of work that people miss if they lose their jobs. While the *manifest function* of work is, primarily, maintaining or improving one's standard of living, the latent (less obvious) functions contribute to an individual's personal well-being. Work can provide experiences of creativity and mastery, and can foster a sense of purpose. It can be self-fulfilling, although clearly, some jobs offer much less fulfillment than others. When hit by unemployment, an individual loses these personal rewards, as illustrated by the following comments by a nutritionist about her 14 months of unemployment (Burman 1988: 161):

> I feel like I'm wasting time. I feel like I'm not accomplishing anything. I don't really feel like I'm contributing to the marriage, to society, or anything like that.

Work also provides regularly shared experiences and often enjoyable interactions with coworkers (Hodson 2004). When the job is gone, so are such personally satisfying routines. An unemployed person quickly comes to miss these social rewards and may also find that relationships away from work are no longer the same. Such feelings are expressed in the following way by an unemployed teacher (Burman 1988: 113):

> The whole feeling that I had . . . [was] that nobody really understood where I was, what I was going through, what I cared about, what was important to me. Because I was no longer talking about my job as a teacher, in fact I wasn't talking about my job as anything. I had a strong sense of not fitting in.

In addition, work structures time. Individuals who have lost their job frequently find that their days seem not only empty, but disorienting. A divorced mother of a four-year-old, living with her own mother to make ends meet, explains (Burman 1988: 144):

> If you went to work, at least you're coming home in the evening. When I'm home all day . . . I get confused. My whole metabolism's gone crazy, because it's, like, I'm coming back from . . . where I have been. Or I've gone and I'm still waiting to come home.

Being unemployed often requires that one seek financial assistance, sometimes from family members, but more often through government agencies. Dealing with the bureaucracy can be frustrating. Even more problematic, receiving social assistance carries a great deal of *stigma*. As a former factory worker, the mother of two small children, explains (Burman 1988: 86):

> When I went down there, I felt that I just stuck right out. I thought, "Oh, my God, people think I'm on welfare. . . ." You used to think "It's those people who are on welfare," and now you discover you're one of those people.

The same value system that rewards individuals for their personal success also leads to what Jean Swanson (2001) calls "poor-bashing," the perpetuation in the media, in our legislation and social programs, and in our everyday discourse, of myths and stereotypes about the poor and the unemployed being lazy, unmotivated, and undeserving of assistance. These myths and stereotypes, in turn, can lead unemployed people to blame themselves for their own problems, even if they recognize the structural barriers they are facing. Swanson (2001: 10) quotes an unemployed former bank employee who exemplifies such contradictory feelings:

> I never chose to be poor. I'm ashamed of what I am now, but it's beyond my ability to change things. I'm still alive. I haven't committed suicide. I'm living with hope. Although I know with all my heart that it's not my fault, the system makes you feel guilty. Society makes you feel guilty.

These glimpses into the lives of unemployed Canadians reflect the value placed on work in our society as a potential source of self-fulfillment and social integration. Studies of recently retired workers similarly reveal the frequent loss of personal identity tied to an occupation or profession, the loss of status in families and communities, and the loss of fulfilling workplace relationships (Barnes and Parry 2004; Radl 2012).[6] At the same time, a set of more materialistic work values is highlighted through the stigma and self-blame that can result from joblessness, seen by some unemployed people as a mark of their own labour market failure. Thus, while career success and wealth accumulation are central to the value systems in capitalist society, the humanist perspective on work as a source of self-identity and personal satisfaction reflects an equally important alternative set of work values.

Cultural Variations in Work Values?

More than a century ago, Max Weber argued that the Protestant work ethic provided a set of work values that ushered in a new capitalist mode of production in northern Europe. Over the past several decades, the remarkable economic performance of a number of emerging countries in the global economy has led some observers to make similar "cultural differences" arguments. Did Japan in the 1980s and the Southeast Asian tiger economies in the 1990s really owe some of their success to a different set of work values? What about China, India, and Brazil today?

Chapter 13: Work Values and Work Orientations

Japan's economy clearly outperformed the rest of the world in the 1980s. A common explanation was that Japanese workers had a much stronger work ethic and a higher level of commitment to their employers. Underlying such explanations was an assumption of powerful cultural differences. The Japanese, it was argued, had always exhibited strong patterns of conformity and social integration. In modern times, the corporation had come to assume the once-central roles of the family and the community. From the vantage point of North America, the presumably stronger work ethic of Japanese employees appeared to be a key ingredient in the Japanese "economic miracle."

As the economies of Singapore, South Korea, Taiwan, and Hong Kong expanded rapidly in the 1990s, similar cultural explanations about different underlying work values were proposed. Like descriptions of the presumably more motivated Japanese workers, this "Confucian work ethic" argument attributed the economic success of these economies to traditional habits of hard work, greater willingness to work toward a common social goal, and employees' ready compliance with authority.[7] While this argument might also be used to explain China's remarkable economic growth in the 21st century, it would not account for the case of India, another recent rapid-growth economy, since the dominant religion in India is Hinduism.

Undoubtedly, there are cross-national differences in the way people respond to work in general, to new technologies, and to employers' demands for compliance. North American workers, for example, may be somewhat less accepting of Japanese-style management approaches that expect workers to show unwavering loyalty to company goals (Graham 1995). Workers in some Asian countries may think of their work organization in less individualistic and more family-like terms (Jiang et al. 1995), and managers' understandings of corporate social responsibility may be somewhat different in Japan compared to Western industrialized countries (Todeschini 2011). That said, it is overstating such differences to argue that a Confucian work ethic explains the rapid growth of the East Asian economies. If it does, why did the economic growth in these countries not begin decades earlier? As for China, after more than six decades of Communist dictatorship, it is unlikely that Confucianism is still the psychological fuel for its economy (*Economist* 1996).

Conceding that there are some cultural differences in work values (Super and Šverko 1995), we argue that they are not central to explanations of national differences in economic growth in today's global economy. Far more crucial are the production decisions of firms regarding technology, employment practices, and research and development, and the extent to which governments actively participate in economic development strategies.

Japan is a good example. Its labour market is highly segmented, even more so than in Canada. Only a minority of Japanese workers are employed in the country's huge, profitable, high-technology corporations. Most people work in smaller businesses that subcontract to make parts or provide services for the giant firms. The major advantages of this arrangement for the large corporations are the flexibility of being able to expand and contract their labour force without hiring permanent employees and the reduction in inventory costs through just-in-time delivery of component parts from the subcontracting businesses.

Until the 1990s, major Japanese firms generated worker loyalty by offering lifetime employment guarantees and opportunities for upward advancement within the corporation, along with higher wages and good benefits packages (Hill 1988). Critics argued that company loyalty was built on fears of job loss and that the economic benefits provided to workers in major firms simply made it easier for their employers to demand compliance and hard work (Kamata 1983). However, job security and access to internal labour markets were severely eroded in the 1990s as major Japanese corporations struggled to adapt to a changing global economy. By contrast, in small firms and family businesses, low pay, little job security, and long working hours had been the norm. In short, precarious work has become much more common in Japan (Piotrowski et al. 2015) as it has in other Western industrialized countries (Chapter 4). Thus, for both core- and periphery-sector Japanese employees, the "willingness" to work long and hard may always have had much more to do with organizational and economic factors than with unique cultural values (Lincoln and Kalleberg 1990).

A Declining Work Ethic in North America?

While commentators have speculated about a stronger work ethic in countries like Japan or China, others have worried about a declining work ethic in North America, particularly among the poor. During the 1970s, growing awareness of extensive poverty, particularly among Black Americans, prompted fears that fewer people were willing to work. By way of example, in 1972, U.S. President Richard Nixon stated that American society was threatened by the "new welfare ethic that could cause the American character to weaken." Interestingly, a recent best-selling book (Vance 2016) makes a similar argument about poor white Americans living in de-industrialized regions of the United States.[8]

In both Canada and the United States, however, national surveys conducted in the 1970s failed to reveal a declining work ethic. Few Canadian respondents agreed that they would rather collect Unemployment Insurance than hold a job. Most stated that, given the choice, they would prefer working to not having a job, and that work was a central aspect of their lives (Burstein et al. 1975). A national survey of Canadian workers conducted almost two decades later (in 2000) led to the same conclusion: a large majority of Canadians have a strong work ethic (Lowe and Schellenberg 2001: 40). Most recently, Statistics Canada's 2016 General Social Survey revealed 90 percent of employed Canadians agreeing (to varying degrees) that "I am happiest when I work hard." Even more (96 percent) agreed that "I take pride in the work that I do."[9]

Although the work ethic of Canadians has likely not weakened, social assistance programs have been substantially altered (Weaver, Habibov, and Fan 2010) to reduce government spending but also because of long-standing beliefs that the poor are reluctant to work. For example, during the 1990s, the Unemployment Insurance program (now called Employment Insurance) was restructured, making it more difficult for seasonal workers to obtain benefits. Since then, social assistance benefits were cut back for "able-bodied" recipients, including single mothers (Gazso 2007) in several provinces, and *workfare* programs that require recipients to work in public projects were introduced.[10]

The same concern about a weak work ethic among poor people has led to opposition to a *guaranteed annual income* (GAI), which could replace a patchwork of different forms of social assistance with direct income supplements for individuals or families earning less than a set amount annually. Along with being a more efficient social assistance system for governments to deliver, a GAI would also eliminate many of the bureaucratic and complicated rules that govern when and how people living in poverty receive social assistance. Canadian legislators have begun to consider a GAI at various times over the past four decades (most recently in 2016), and even implemented an experimental test of the system in a small Manitoba town in the late 1970s (Forget 2011; Calnitsky 2016). But continued fears that Canadians receiving a GAI would have little incentive to seek paid work have led to discussions about a GAI being abandoned, despite limited evidence supporting this belief and other solid evidence demonstrating improved health outcomes for individuals and families receiving a GAI (McIntyre et al. 2016).

In Canada and elsewhere (Shildrick et al. 2013), research has shown that a weak work ethic and a lack of effort are seldom the primary source of poverty. Much more often, the problem is one of not enough good jobs and inadequate social and labour market policies.[11] In fact, a large minority of Canada's poor are not welfare dependent but "working poor," seeking to maintain their standard of living on low-paying and often precarious jobs. In 2011, for example, 44 percent of all low-income Canadians were being primarily supported by someone holding a job (HRSDC 2012). There is considerable movement in and out of poverty as individuals lose jobs, move from social assistance to a low-paying job, become divorced, or enter retirement without an adequate pension (Morissette and Zhang 2005). In short, poverty in Canada is not a result of a declining work ethic among the poor and unemployed.

Time for New Work Values?

During the 1980s and 1990s, unemployment rates rose steeply. They declined again for about a decade, then rose again sharply at the end of the first decade of the 21st century, before coming down again. In contrast, the growth in non-standard jobs that began several decades ago has continued steadily, placing more workers in precarious employment and financial situations. At the same time, a growing minority of workers have chosen or been required to work longer hours per week (Chapter 4). Given this polarization of employment experiences—not enough work for some and too much for others—perhaps we need to promote a new set of work values? If more citizens would "get a life" beyond the workplace, perhaps our society could get back on track toward a better future.

This idea is not new. Almost four decades ago, in his book *Farewell to the Working Class*, Andre Gorz (1982) argued that higher levels of unemployment at the time as well as new technologies that reduce the time it takes to make a decent standard of living have meant more free time for individuals to participate in non-paid work and leisure activities. Gorz called for a new set of values that would replace hard work, labour market competition, and consumption of material goods with more emphasis on the personal fulfillment that comes from non-paid work activities and leisure pursuits.

Jeremy Rifkin (1995) was more apocalyptic, arguing that new technologies and global production patterns would essentially mean the "end of work" as we know it for many people. Rifkin also advocated the promotion of new work values that would encourage more people to participate in the voluntary sector of the economy where they could find personal fulfillment in caring for others, improving the environment, and making other contributions to society.

Jamie Swift's (1995) concerns were less about the "end of work" than about growing labour market inequality in Canada. He observed that, along with a growing number of working poor, many well-paid labour force participants were also overworked and stressed from the long hours they put into their jobs. Swift reflected on "the lunacy of lives driven by the compulsions of work, speed, and consumption" and called for more attention to "the good life" rather than "the goods life" (Swift 1995: 221, 224). Like Gorz and Rifkin, Swift also recommended a new set of work values that emphasize working less, consuming less, and seeking self-fulfillment not only in paid work but also in healthy leisure pursuits and in (non-paid) caring for others.

The "end of work" predicted by Rifkin has not occurred (Smith 2006), but recent advances in artificial intelligence and robotics (Chapters 4 and 10) are once again turning our attention to potentially massive job loss in some sectors and possible growth in others (Brynjolfsson and McAfee 2016; West 2018).[12] Furthermore, in Canada and elsewhere, labour market polarization and growing social inequality are serious social problems that need to be addressed (Chapter 5). Emphasizing the value of non-paid work and reducing inequities in access to paid work are part of the solution. So, too, are stressing the importance of caring for others and the environment and emphasizing that there is more to a good life than merely acquiring and consuming material goods. But writers such as Gorz, Swift, and Rifkin did not explain how such a transformation of social values could be achieved, nor how high levels of inequality between those with paid jobs and those without could be avoided. In a society where women have traditionally been expected to do most of the "caring work" (see Chapter 7), would non-paid voluntary work continue to be seen as "women's work"? Furthermore, since older workers are often more economically secure, is it fair to tell young Canadians to change their values, reduce their career aspirations, and accept less paid work?

In her description of "how the overwork culture is ruling our lives" (which is also the subtitle to her book) Madeline Bunting (2004) continues the debate about the need for new work values. Like other observers of contemporary labour market trends, Bunting recognizes how industrial restructuring and organization re-engineering have deprived some people of jobs and forced others to work longer and harder to make a living. But she also documents how managers, professionals, and other advantaged workers are willingly taking part in the new culture of overwork. While leisure used to be a sign of status for the middle and upper classes, today overwork has become a status symbol as many professionals take pride in the long hours they work, how they "multitask" while on the job, and how they even continue to work while on vacation.[13]

Bunting argues that a consumer-focused culture and economy (work hard to spend more) and new managerial ideologies (work hard to show how committed you are to the company) make many of us into "willing slaves" in an era where "narcissism and capitalism are mutually reinforcing" (Bunting 2004: xxiv). What is required, she concludes, is a return to a traditional work ethic that respects human dignity and autonomy, the promotion of a "care ethic" that places high value on looking after the needs of others and that adequately compensates the women and men in "caring" occupations, and the emergence of a new "wisdom ethic" that recognizes that building a better society is more important than heating up the economy by working harder and spending more (Bunting 2004: 312–24). Thus, while reinforcing many of the points made by the other writers discussed above, Bunting places more emphasis on the need to retool our work values, in contrast to replacing them with non-work values.

WORK ORIENTATIONS

Having discussed how societal work values have changed over time, might vary across cultures, and perhaps need to be re-examined in light of today's economic realities, we now shift our analysis to individuals' job expectations—the types of work orientations they bring to their jobs. Are most Canadians motivated primarily by a desire to be successful and become wealthy? Do they seek to work as hard as possible, whatever the costs? Or is their work a source of personal satisfaction and fulfillment? Do women and men have similar orientations to work? Are today's youth different than youth from earlier generations with respect to work orientations?

Instrumental Work Orientations

In an insightful essay written back in 1966, David Lockwood discussed different ways in which British working-class men perceived social inequality. *Proletarian workers*, argued Lockwood, saw the world in much the way Marx had predicted, feeling they were in an "us against them" conflict with their employers. Lockwood noted that this worldview was more pronounced in industries such as shipbuilding and mining where large and long-standing differences between management and workers in terms of income, power, and opportunities for upward mobility had heightened class consciousness. *Deferential workers* also recognized class differences, but accepted the status quo, believing that wealth and power inequities were justified. Provided they were treated decently, deferential workers were unlikely to engage in militant actions against their employers who typically treated them paternalistically in the traditional service industries and family firms where they were employed.

Both of these traditional orientations to work were found primarily in declining industries. The third type, *instrumental work orientations*, was more typical of the work attitudes of the contemporary (1960s) working class, according to Lockwood; he labelled them *privatized workers*. Rather than expressing opposition or attachment to their employers, the dominant feeling of these workers was one of indifference. Work, whether it was interesting or boring and repetitive, was simply a way to obtain a better standard of living, an "instrument" used to achieve other non-work goals.

In contrast, based on their study of the male labour market in another British city, Blackburn and Mann (1979) found that most workers reported a variety of work orientations. In addition, there was often little congruence between an individual's expressed work preferences and the characteristics of the job. The major flaw in an *orientations model* of labour market processes, according to Blackburn and Mann (1979), was that many people have few job choices, taking whatever work they can get, even if it is not what they would prefer.

Individuals' work preferences can also be modified in the workplace. If a job offers few chances to make decisions or develop skills, workers may adjust their priorities accordingly. This idea might explain why studies have shown instrumental work orientations to be more common among workers in monotonous, assembly-line jobs (Rinehart 1978) or low-skill, low-pay service-sector jobs

(Berg and Frost 2005). Richard Sennett and Jonathan Cobb (1972) examined this theme in their book, *The Hidden Injuries of Class*. Their discussions with American blue-collar workers revealed a tendency to downplay *intrinsic work rewards*, few of which were available to them, while emphasizing *extrinsic work rewards*, such as pay and job security. Workers interviewed by Sennett and Cobb also redefined the meaning of personal success, frequently talking about how hard they were working in order to provide their children with the chance to go to college.[14] Thus, we should not be surprised if some workers do have instrumental work orientations, given the strong emphasis on material success in our society and widespread fears about job security.

But most employed Canadians today are not motivated only or primarily by work orientations that are instrumental, or extrinsic, as they are typically called in the North American research literature.[15] Instead, along with a desire for good pay, extensive benefits, opportunities for advancement, and job security, workers also want intrinsically satisfying work (Lowe and Graves 2016), as the humanistic perspective on work as self-fulfillment suggests. For example, in a 2012 EKOS Research Associates survey of more than 1,800 Canadian workers, about 60 percent of labour force participants (employed and unemployed) stated that having a sense of pride and accomplishment in their work, and having challenging and interesting work was "very important" to them (Figure 13.1).[16] Almost as many stated that job security, a healthy and safe workplace, good balance between work and personal/family life, and good pay were "very important." Given the increase in precarious work (Chapter 4), it is not that surprising that job security was seen as more important than other extrinsic rewards. These survey results also reflect a high level of concern among workers about balancing their work and family responsibilities, a theme discussed in Chapter 7. In short, Canadian workers are strongly motivated by both intrinsic and extrinsic work rewards.[17]

Gender and Work Orientations

The early British studies of work orientations focused only on men. When the work orientations of women were mentioned, it was often assumed that their interests were directed primarily toward the home. The argument that *gender-role socialization* might encourage women to place less value on intrinsic and extrinsic job rewards and more on social relationships in the family, in the

FIGURE 13.1 Extrinsic and Intrinsic Work Orientations, Canadian Labour Force, 2012*

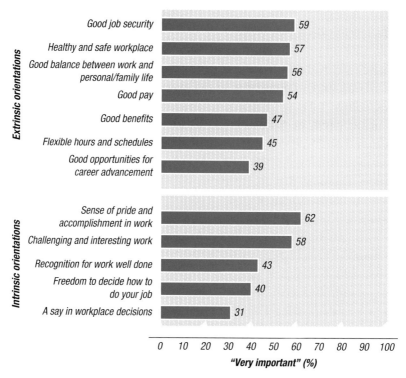

*Respondents were asked how important each of these factors would be if they were looking for a new job. They answered on a 5-point scale (very unimportant (1)–(5) very important). Sample sizes for each question ranged from 1853 to 1861.

Source: Used with permission of EKOS Research Associates, Inc. Copyright © 2013. all rights reserved.

community, and on the job seemed plausible in the 1960s and early 1970s when many of these studies were completed. However, there is another more compelling structural explanation. Women and men work in very different labour market locations, and women typically receive fewer job rewards. Hence, observed gender differences in work orientations might have reflected women's adaptations to their subordinate employment situation (Rowe and Snizek 1995: 226).

The rapid increase in female postsecondary education and labour force participation in recent decades (Chapter 3), along with movement, albeit more slowly, of more women into higher-status occupations and professions (see Chapter 6) has altered gendered patterns of work orientations. For example, recent studies of both Canadian (Krahn and Galambos 2014) and U.S. youth (Johnson and Mortimer 2011) have shown somewhat higher intrinsic work orientations among women, but negligible differences in extrinsic work orientations.

As for adults, further analysis of the 2012 EKOS survey results highlighted in Figure 13.1 showed no difference between women and men with respect to how important they felt it was to have challenging and interesting work and freedom to decide how to do their job, and also in having a say in workplace decisions. Women, however, were significantly more likely to place importance on having a sense of pride and accomplishment in their work, and in receiving recognition for work well done. Turning to extrinsic orientations, with the exception of good pay for which gender differences were non-significant, women were more likely to place value on all of the extrinsic rewards displayed in Figure 13.1. It would appear that in today's society, rather than focusing primarily on social relationships at work and at home, if in fact that was ever the case, women in the labour force today generally place more emphasis than do men on most extrinsic and some intrinsic work rewards.

Two of the gender differences in the 2012 EKOS survey deserve closer scrutiny. Sixty-two percent of the women in the survey stated that having a good balance between work and personal/family life was very important to them, compared to 51 percent of men. Similarly, 49 percent of women, compared to 42 percent of men, responded that having flexible hours and schedules was very important. Despite these strong preferences, the domestic and child-care responsibilities that many women continue to carry, even if they hold higher-status jobs, force some to readjust their work and career goals. As a part-time Canadian nurse explained (Duffy and Pupo 1992: 116):

> My career is important to me. I don't want to give that up. But my main concern is the children. . . . So I give about 100 percent to the children and maintain a career at the same time.

Similarly, in her study of young university-educated women living in Alberta, Ranson (1998) observed that, particularly for those who had chosen non-traditional careers in science and engineering, the pressures of balancing family and job demands required a reassessment of either their parenthood or career aspirations, or both. As one young woman explained when asked about her parenthood plans (Ranson 1998: 529):

> Actually I've thought, would I work or would I stay home?... I've spent a lot of time going to school. I've worked my way up. Like, do I want to give all that up? [Because] if you come back to the work force in five years you're not going to work where you left off. Then the other part of me thinks, well, you have to make that choice, it's one or the other.

Once again, these examples point to structural determinants—the gendered household division of labour and the frequent absence of family-friendly employment policies—rather than to female personality characteristics as the source of gender differences in work orientations.

The Work Orientations of Youth

Socrates is reputed to have said that "children today are tyrants. They contradict their parents, gobble their food, and terrorize their teachers." If he had lived today, he might also have added that "they don't want to work hard" since such concerns about deficient work orientations have frequently been part of the public stereotype of youth. In the 1960s and 1970s, for example, the counterculture activities of some North American youth led to fears that the work ethic of a generation of "hippies" and "peaceniks" was declining. Most members of that cohort (now remembered as "baby boomers") are now ending successful careers, however, demonstrating that these fears were largely unfounded.

Similar concerns about the weak work ethic of Generation X, Generation Y, Millennials (young people who became adults in the 21st century), and the even-younger Generation Z have been raised frequently. For example, in a best-selling book, Jean Twenge (2006) labelled Millennials as *Generation Me*, a cohort of youth who feel entitled to good jobs but have a weaker work ethic compared to previous generations. A 2015 article in the *Financial Post* described "A worrisome trend for Canada's workforce as work ethic, quality of new hires deteriorates" (Toneguzzi 2015). It was based on a survey of small-business owners and showed that three out of four believed new hires had a weaker work ethic compared to the past, and one in two felt that they expected to be paid too much.

Twenge (2016), however, relies heavily on comparisons of American high-school seniors' responses to surveys over the past four decades to make her argument. But the transition from school to work takes much longer today than it did in the 1970s (Andres and Wynn 2010; Krahn et al. 2018). Over-time comparisons of 18-year-olds' work orientations tell us little about the work ethic of entrants into today's adult labour market. In the 1970s, many were still in their teens while today most are in their mid- to late 20s. As for the survey of small-business owners, it did not examine the work ethic of young adults (only the opinions of employers), nor did it note that, on average, small businesses pay about 90 percent of the average weekly wage (Industry Canada 2012).

For young adult Canadians seeking employment today, a majority with post-secondary credentials (Statistics Canada 2017) for which they worked long and hard, and almost half with sizable student loan debt (Statistics Canada 2014), reluctance to accept a low-paying job after graduation is less a reflection of a weak work ethic than of rational decision making. The willingness of many young people to take on low-paying or unpaid internships (Chapter 4), in return for potentially acquiring useful career experience, is another indicator of a strong, not a weak, work ethic. In fact, our own analysis of the 2016 General Social Survey showed young Canadians (ages 15 to 24, and 25 to 34) being virtually no different from the Canadian (all ages) average in their level of agreement with the statements (I am happiest when I work hard," and "I take pride in the work that I do."[18]

So, are today's youth really less willing to work hard—do they really have a weaker work ethic? It seems to us that each generation, when observing the next generation, sees lifestyle experimentation, forgets its own similar experiences and how the labour market has changed, and concludes that work values are slipping. The employment difficulties faced by Canadian youth are real, as we have demonstrated in Chapters 3 through 5. Corporate and public-sector downsizing, along with an increase in precarious work, has made it much more difficult for young people to cash in their educational investments for good jobs (Tomlinson 2007). It has also led to a prolonged entry into adult roles, such as living on one's own, marriage or cohabitation, parenthood, and home ownership (Krahn et al. 2018).

Recognizing these trends early on, Douglas Coupland (1993) published a fictional account of the experiences of youth moving between jobs and relationships. *Generation X: Tales for an Accelerated Culture* was a bestseller. Its portrayal of the post-baby-boom generation as cynical and alienated, with few career goals and largely instrumental work orientations, became part of popular culture. The Generation X view of changing work orientations focused on older, more educated youth rather than on recent high-school graduates. It highlighted a devaluing of careers and intrinsic work rewards, rather than simply a reluctance to work hard, and it pointed to structural changes in the labour market—a lack of satisfactory employment opportunities—as the source of the problem.

So, again, is there good evidence of the emergence of unique Generation X (or Y or Z) work orientations? The behaviour of recent cohorts of young Canadians suggests otherwise. A large majority continue to invest in higher education, despite rising tuition fees, hoping to get good jobs (see Chapters 3 and 5). Many continue to pursue additional work-related training after obtaining formal qualifications (Jackson 2005: 47). And as we have already seen, young Canadians report a very strong desire to work. But they likely experience more anxiety about future employment prospects because of labour market restructuring and the growing prevalence of precarious jobs.

More recent cohorts of Canadian youth may also have a somewhat stronger sense of job entitlement, the belief that if a person has invested in a higher education, that person should be able to get a good job (Krahn and Galambos 2014). A generation or two ago, an expanding economy allowed a larger proportion of youth, some with limited postsecondary education, to launch satisfying careers. Today, career entry is more difficult for Canadian youth, who are even more educated on average than their counterparts several decades ago. Hence, they maintain a strong belief in the labour market value of higher education (Pullman and Andres 2018). Fortunately, there is solid evidence that, on average, investments in higher education in Canada still continue to pay off for those who have made them (Finnie 2016).

At the same time, reduced loyalty and commitment by many employers to their workers, as reflected in greater reliance on part-time and temporary workers, may also translate into less trust, commitment, and loyalty to their work organization and to their employers, by employees, both young and old. By way of example, a 2015 EKOS national survey asked Canadian employees "to what extent do you trust the senior managers in your organization to take employees' interests into account when planning changes?" Almost half (44 percent) answered "not at all" (Lowe and Graves 2016). A similar question asked in a similar survey in 2004 showed less than one-third (31 percent) answering this way.[19] This indicates a problem that employers need to address. How do you motivate workers without offering them some degree of employment security?[20]

CONCLUSION

In this chapter, we shifted from the largely structural analysis of work organizations, labour markets, and management systems presented in earlier chapters to a more individually focused discussion of work values and work orientations. We commented on how work values in Western societies have changed over the centuries and speculated about the extent to which cultural differences in work values might explain different patterns of economic growth. Focusing further on North America today, we described how individuals are exposed to at least two competing work value systems, the first suggesting that monetary rewards are paramount and the second emphasizing how work can be personally fulfilling. An examination of what unemployed people find lacking in their lives highlighted the extent to which work provides us with much more than a way of paying our bills.

Turning our attention to work orientations (or preferences), we argued that even though some workers are primarily instrumentally oriented—that is, motivated by the material rewards that work provides—most Canadians also desire work that is intrinsically satisfying as the humanist perspective on work as self-fulfillment would predict. We also observed that instrumental work orientations may be an adaptation on the part of some workers to low-skill or routinized work that has little but a paycheque to offer. We concluded our discussion of work orientations by critically examining arguments that young people today are less motivated to work than were previous generations. We essentially reversed the causal argument, suggesting, instead, that labour markets and social policies have changed, making it more difficult for young people to get good jobs.

In Chapter 14, we continue our examination of the personal experience of work, focusing specifically on job satisfaction and work-related stress. Work orientations will be part of that discussion since, to an extent, they affect how an individual feels about a job. Once again, however, we will argue that the nature of the work is likely to have a stronger impact, both on an individual's feelings of satisfaction and stress, and on his or her work orientations.

DISCUSSION QUESTIONS

1. Discuss the differences between work values, work orientations, and job satisfaction.
2. Do you think that, compared to their parents and grandparents, young people today have a weaker work ethic? How good is the evidence used to support this argument?
3. Critically discuss the following statement: "The majority of Canadians go to work just to earn money. If they won a lottery, most would quit their jobs."
4. "Most poor people are not really all that motivated to work hard." Do you agree or disagree with this statement? What is your evidence?
5. Do cultural differences in work values explain why some countries have much higher economic growth rates than other countries? Justify your opinion.

ADDITIONAL RESOURCES

WORK AT THE MOVIES

- *Clerks* (directed by Kevin Smith, 1994, 92 minutes). This film presents a day in the lives of two convenience-store clerks as they annoy customers, discuss movies, and play hockey on the store roof.
- *Waiting* (directed by Rob McKittrick, 2005, 94 minutes). In this comedy, the young employees of an American chain restaurant find creative ways to stave off boredom in the workplace.
- *Empire Records* (directed by Allan Moyle, 1995, 90 minutes). A group of workers at an independent record store come together to help the store avoid being taken over by a massive chain.
- *Apollo 13* (directed by Ron Howard, 1995, 140 minutes). Based on the 1970 Apollo 13 mission, Howard's film chronicles how flight controllers at NASA (National Aeronautics and Space Administration) and the mission's astronauts worked together to bring the astronauts home safely after they experienced technical difficulties.

SOUNDS OF WORK

- "Rich Man's War" (Steve Earle). This song highlights the variety of reasons that prompt individuals from both sides of a conflict to go to war, financial reasons, national pride, boredom, tradition, and family among them.
- "Working Class Hero" (John Lennon). The song notes the loss of individuality and how people undergo processes to conform and accept control as they enter the workforce.
- "Working Man" (Rush). This Canadian band sings about the lack of ambition that develops after working a dead-end 9 to 5 job.

NOTES

1. This short summary draws on Bernstein (1997); see also Byrne (1990: Chapter 3).
2. Genesis 2:17, 3:19 (text as it appears in the King James Version of the Bible).
3. In a contemporary U.S. study, Keister (2007) argues that Catholic work values lead to upward wealth mobility.
4. Sociologists include Hodson (2001), Rayman (2001), and Bunting (2004). From psychology, see Quinn (2015) on "positive organizational studies" and Seligman (2013) on "positive psychology."
5. See Latif (2010) and Krahn and Chow (2016) for recent Canadian studies of the negative career and psychological consequences of unemployment, Gabriel, Gray, and Goregaokar (2013) and Buffel, Missinne and Bracke (2017) for similar European research, and Weller (2012) on Australia.
6. See Fineman (2009) for a fascinating account of how the "retirement industry" tries to reshape the personal identities of retired workers while marketing services and products to them.
7. Lin, Ho, and Lin (2013) go further, distinguishing between Confucian and Taoist work values. A parallel literature on Islamic, Arab, and Egyptian work values has emerged, although the distinction between religious (Mohamed, Karim, and Hussein 2010), cultural (Sidani and Thornberry 2009), and national (Sidani and Jamali 2010) work values is unclear.
8. Nixon's comment was quoted in *Time* (September 7, 1987: 42). Unlike Nixon who was not particularly sympathetic with the poor, in *Hillbilly Elegy*, J. P. Vance (2016) does try to explain the structural changes that have led to widespread poverty and, as he sees it, a weakened work ethic in rustbelt America.

9. Data from Statistics Canada's 2016 General Social Survey (GSS) were analyzed by the authors. Responses for these two questions could range from 0 (completely disagree) to 10 (completely agree); responses of 6 through 10 were taken to signify agreement. For more information about the 2016 GSS, see https://www150.statcan.gc.ca/n1/daily-quotidien/180613/dq180613c-eng.htm

10. See Black and Stanford (2005) and Gazso and Krahn (2008) on "welfare reform" in Alberta, and Gazso (2012) on "welfare-to-work" programs in Ontario.

11. In a British study, Dunn (2010) reported that more educated individuals, who could afford to wait for a better job, were more likely to say they would not mind being on the "dole" (accepting Unemployment Insurance), compared to less educated (and poorer) people who were more concerned about finding a job, no matter what it was.

12. See Frey and Osborne (2017) for an analysis of jobs at risk of computerization in the United States and Lamb (2016) for similar data on Canada.

13. Schor (1991, 1998), Hochschild (1997), and Rayman (2001) criticize overwork and over-consumption in the United States. Green (2001) documents the extent of overwork in Britain. A 1995 Statistics Canada study revealed that 31 percent of employed Canadians considered themselves to be "workaholics" (*The Daily*, May 15, 2007).

14. Visible minority Canadian immigrants, faced with having to work in lower-tier, service-sector jobs, despite being well educated (see Chapter 5), also frequently put their efforts into ensuring that their children will get a good education and a rewarding middle-class career (Taylor and Krahn 2013).

15. Many North American researchers (e.g., Johnson, Sage, and Mortimer 2012; Wray-Lake et al. 2011) use the concept "work values" to describe what we call "work orientations" in this chapter. We prefer to use *values* to describe societal standards and *orientations* to describe individual preferences, even though when engaging with the North American research literature, we also use their terminology (Krahn, Howard, and Galambos 2012; Chow, Krahn, and Galambos 2013).

16. Data from this 2012 national survey of a random sample of Canadian workers conducted by EKOS Research Associates Inc. and the Graham Lowe Group Inc. were analyzed by the authors.

17. A recent study reports that, between 1992 and 2006, intrinsic work orientations increased among British workers (Gallie, Felstead, and Green 2012).

18. See endnote 9.

19. Data from the 2004 and 2015 national surveys conducted by EKOS Research Associates Inc. and the Graham Lowe Group Inc. were analyzed by the authors.

20. See de Gilder (2003), Coverdill and Oulevey (2007), and Stirpe, Bonache and Revilla (2014) on managing contingent workers.

JOB SATISFACTION, ALIENATION, AND WORK-RELATED STRESS

14

"Truly an inspiring and motivating place to work. Each staff member goes out of their way to help each patient . . . The most amazing and heart-warming part of the job is seeing a smile on the children's face as you're able to give them the help they need and want."

—Clinic administrative coordinator, The Hospital for Sick Children, Toronto

"They help you unlock your potential in not just the company, but also your potential in your everyday life! Everyone is there to build you up. . . . You meet so many great people that push you to be the best you can be! It never feels like work, but more like a way of life."

—Sales representative, Ledcor Construction, Vancouver

"Job security, advancements, pay, benefits and pension are attractive. It's a seniority system for when it comes to bidding on jobs so, starting here in your 20s is [a] guarantee [of] a spot in upper management by the time you're in your 40s. Everything here is by the books and nothing gets pushed under the table as the union for TTC is very strong."

—Signal technician employed by Toronto Transit Commission

"If you want a place that values your input and allows you to earn a decent salary while providing a fun atmosphere, Shaw is for you. Hours can vary, but compensation reflects that. Management always has time for you and genuinely care. This company gives back to the community in ways I have never seen. The hardest part of the job was leaving."

—Former human resources facilitator, Shaw Communications, Calgary

Source: Selected extracts from *"Top-Rated Workplaces: Best in Canada"* https://ca.indeed.com /Top-Rated-Workplaces/2017-Canada-Companies [retrieved November 27 2018]

INTRODUCTION

With its discussion of work values and work orientations, Chapter 13 shifted our attention from the structural perspective presented in earlier chapters to a more individually focused analysis of the meanings attached to work. In this chapter we continue by examining how work is personally experienced. We begin by discussing *job satisfaction* and *dissatisfaction*, defined as the subjective reactions of individual workers to the particular set of rewards, intrinsic or extrinsic, provided by their job (Blackburn and Mann 1979: 167). We then comment on a parallel line of research that uses the concept of *alienation* in a social–psychological framework, in contrast to the more structural Marxist analysis of alienation presented in Chapter 10. The third section of this chapter reviews the research literature on *work-related stress*, a complex phenomenon—with job dissatisfaction as one component—that can lead to serious health problems.

JOB SATISFACTION AND DISSATISFACTION

What do Canadians find most and least satisfying about their jobs? Are most of them satisfied? Which subgroups of workers are most or least satisfied, and why? Do people's work orientations influence what they find satisfying in a job? Can job satisfaction or dissatisfaction affect workers off the job? Some researchers assume that productivity is a function of job satisfaction. Their goal has been to discover how to organize work and manage employees in a way that leads to increased satisfaction and, hence, higher productivity and profits. Others, adopting the humanistic view that work is an essential part of being human, view satisfying and self-fulfilling work for as many people as possible as a desirable societal goal in itself.

The Prevalence of Job Satisfaction

The standard measure of job satisfaction in North American survey research is some variation of "In general, how satisfied are you with your job?" In response, a very large majority of workers typically report some degree of satisfaction. For example, Statistics Canada's 2016 General Social Survey (GSS) showed 85 percent of paid employees (i.e., excluding the self-employed) saying they were satisfied with their job (35 percent reported being "very satisfied"). Another 9 percent said they were neither satisfied nor dissatisfied, and only 6 percent admitted to being dissatisfied or very dissatisfied (see Figure 14.1).[1] The GSS asked self-employed survey respondents a different question ("In general, do you enjoy being your own boss?"). Sixty percent answered "yes," 29 percent said "often," and only 11 percent said "sometimes," but none of the self-employed answered that they "rarely" or "never" enjoyed being their own boss. These results, and many similar findings over the past several decades (Firebaugh and Harley 1995), imply that job dissatisfaction is not a serious social problem. However, there are several good reasons why we could question such a conclusion.

First, as James Rinehart (1978) observed some decades ago, workers' behaviours—strikes, absenteeism, and quitting—all indicate considerably

FIGURE 14.1 Job Satisfaction by Age, Gender, and Education, Canada, 2016*

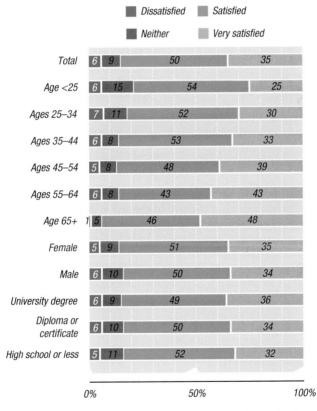

*Employees only (self-employed excluded); responses of "very dissatisfied" and "dissatisfied" combined.

Source: Statistics Canada 2016 *General Social Survey* Public Use Data file (*N* = 8,820; person-weighted data).

more dissatisfaction with working conditions than do attitude surveys. Rinehart (1978: 7) proposed that answers to general questions about job satisfaction are "pragmatic judgements of one's position vis-à-vis the narrow range of available jobs." Most workers look at their limited alternatives and conclude, from this frame of reference, they are relatively satisfied with their work. Just how limited are those alternatives? Employed participants in the 2016 GSS were asked how much they agreed or disagreed with the following statement: "If you were to quit your current job, it would be easy for you to find another job of similar salary." Less than half (46 percent) agreed, almost as many disagreed (38 percent), and 16 percent were unsure. In short, survey questions about job satisfaction tell us how people feel, given their options, but are not necessarily good measures of job quality (Brown, Charlwood and Spencer 2012).

Second, responses to general job satisfaction questions may be similar to replies to a question you might be asked daily, "How are you today?" Most of us would say "fine," whether or not we are feeling ill, worried about an assignment due in two days, or upset about a personal relationship. Hence, more probing questions may be needed to uncover specific feelings of job dissatisfaction. We should also recognize that, in a society with highly individualistic work values (see Chapter 13), people may be unwilling to express dissatisfaction with their jobs because it could reflect negatively on their own ability and efforts.

These reasons point to why more indirect measures of job satisfaction are also useful. For example, the 2016 GSS asked employed Canadians (paid workers and the self-employed) how much they agreed or disagreed that "I cannot wait to leave work at the end of the day." Almost one-half (49 percent) agreed. Another national survey some years earlier (in 2000) revealed that 73 percent of paid employees felt little loyalty to their work organization (Lowe and Schellenberg 2001). Whether measured by direct or indirect questions, job satisfaction varies substantially across some population groups but not others. Below we focus on three possible demographic predictors of job satisfaction (age, gender, and education) that have been studied extensively.

Age and Job Satisfaction

A consistent finding in job satisfaction research is that older workers generally report greater satisfaction (Firebaugh and Harley 1995; Brisbois 2003: 58). Figure 14.1 documents this pattern clearly, with the proportion answering "very satisfied" increasing from 25 percent for the youngest respondents in this 2016 study to 48 percent for the oldest survey participants. Typical of the research on differences in job satisfaction, explanations for this age-related pattern take two basic forms. Some are individualistic, focusing on motivations and work orientations, while others are more structural, pointing to characteristics of the job and the workplace (Ospina 1996: 181).

The following five hypotheses cover the range of explanations. Perhaps older workers have reduced their expectations, becoming more accepting of relatively unrewarding work—an *aging* effect. Alternatively, a *cohort* explanation emphasizes lower expectations (and consequently higher satisfaction) on the part of a generation of older workers: it assumes that older workers grew up in an era when it was enough to have a secure job and when little self-fulfillment at work was expected. Third, a *lifecycle* effect argues that older workers are more likely to have family and community interests that might compensate for dissatisfying work. A fourth explanation emphasizes the nature of the work performed (a *job* effect), suggesting that, on average, older people have been promoted into more rewarding and satisfying jobs, or have changed jobs until they found one they liked. A final explanation points to *self-selection*, arguing that less satisfied workers will drop out of the labour force as they get older, leaving behind those more satisfied.

Which is the best explanation? No clear answer emerges from the many studies on this topic, indicating that all these processes may be involved. Regardless, we know that older workers are more likely to report satisfaction with their work and that this evaluation is due mainly to the better jobs they have obtained over time and to their cumulative social experiences and adaptations in the workplace and society.[2]

Gender and Job Satisfaction

Given that women are more likely to work part time and in the secondary labour market, are they less satisfied with their jobs? The research evidence offers a clear answer. Despite large differences in work rewards, there is typically little difference between men and women in self-reported job satisfaction (Clark 1997; Brisbois 2003: 58). In fact, some studies show women reporting higher satisfaction (Zou 2015). Focusing on Canada, Figure 14.1 shows that job satisfaction rates for women and men were virtually identical in 2016. Again, as with age differences in job satisfaction, an explanation of this non-difference brings us back to the subject of work orientations. Some researchers have suggested that women have been socialized to expect fewer intrinsic and extrinsic work rewards. Hence, the argument goes, women are more likely to be satisfied with lower-quality jobs, focusing instead perhaps on satisfying social relationships within the workplace (Phelan 1994).

However, we should not explain the job satisfaction of women with a *gender model* (differences caused by prior socialization) while employing a *job model* (differences due to the nature of the job) to account for the satisfaction of men (de Vaus and McAllister 1991; Hodson 2004). It makes more theoretical sense to explain the satisfaction of both women and men with reference to the types of jobs they hold and their roles outside the workplace. While, on average, men might report high satisfaction with their relatively good jobs, women might be equally satisfied with less rewarding jobs, having modified their expectations because of the time spent in these same jobs. And as Chapter 7 demonstrated, the involvement of men and women in family and caring roles differs greatly. This reality also needs to be taken into account when explaining the non-difference in job satisfaction between women and men.

Educational Attainment and Job Satisfaction

Educational attainment and job satisfaction might be linked in several different ways. Following human capital theory (see Chapter 5), we might hypothesize that higher education should lead to a better job and, in turn, more job satisfaction. A second, more complex hypothesis begins with the assumption that better-educated workers have higher expectations regarding their careers but recognizes that not all well-educated workers will have good jobs. Hence, well-educated workers in less rewarding jobs would be expected to report low job satisfaction. As one commentator wrote several decades ago, "the placing of intelligent and highly qualified workers in dull and unchallenging jobs is a prescription for pathology—for the worker, the employer, the society" (O'Toole 1977: 60).

Job satisfaction studies completed in the 1970s and 1980s (Martin and Shehan 1989) typically found that education had little effect on job satisfaction, perhaps because the two hypothesized effects cancelled each other out. Even when comparing well-educated and less educated workers in the same blue-collar jobs, few differences in job satisfaction were observed. Perhaps the more educated workers anticipated future upward mobility and so were willing to tolerate less rewarding work for a time. The 2016 GSS data (Figure 14.1) show that the percentage of "very satisfied" is somewhat higher among more highly educated Canadian workers—36 percent of those with university degrees compared to 32 percent of those with high school only or less education. This small difference may signal a shift in the education–job satisfaction pattern, but more research is needed to confirm this.

In previous chapters, we speculated that, as education levels have been rising, the mismatch between workers' skills, credentials, and aspirations, on one hand, and their job content, on the other, may be worsening. Our single-point-in-time analysis (of 2016 survey data) cannot answer this question about change over time, but we can examine self-reported feelings of over-qualification among Canadian workers today. The 2016 GSS asked employed respondents whether: "considering your education, training and experience, do you feel that you are over-qualified, adequately qualified or under-qualified for your job?" Four out of five (80 percent) said they were adequately qualified, 18 percent felt over-qualified, and only 2 percent felt under-qualified. Not surprisingly, 38 percent of those who felt adequately qualified said they were "very satisfied" with their job, compared to 22 percent of those feeling over-qualified, and 23 percent of those feeling under-qualified. Given this and other evidence that under-employment is associated with lower levels of job satisfaction (Vaisey 2006; Green and Zhu 2010) and also reduced subjective well-being (Heyes et al. 2017), we might still hypothesize that overall levels of job satisfaction may slowly decrease in the future if larger numbers of well-educated young workers discover they cannot find jobs that meet their aspirations.[3]

In addition, job insecurity has been increasing in recent decades (Gallie et al. 2016), and several recent studies have linked perceptions of job insecurity to reduced job satisfaction.[4] The 2016 GSS allows us to compare the job satisfaction of temporary (seasonal, term, casual, or on-call) workers (19 percent of all employed) with regular employees (81 percent). A higher proportion (35 percent) of the latter, compared to 29 percent of the former, said they were "very satisfied" with their job.

Given the extent to which young people, including well-educated young workers, have been negatively affected by increased labour market polarization and reduced employment security (Chapter 5), the relationship between job security and job satisfaction is another trend to be monitored.

Work Rewards, Work Orientations, and Job Satisfaction

Our review of the effects of age, gender, and education on job satisfaction indicates that work orientations are frequently part of the explanation. Nevertheless, as we have also argued, differences in job characteristics and rewards are typically more directly linked to job satisfaction and dissatisfaction. In fact, hundreds of studies have sought to identify the specific job conditions that workers are most likely to find satisfying. Such studies have focused on pay, benefits, promotion opportunities, job security, and other *extrinsic work rewards*; autonomy, challenge, skill-use, and a range of additional *intrinsic work rewards*; satisfying (or not) *social relationships* in the workplace; *work organization features* (e.g., bureaucracy, health and safety programs, and the presence of a union); and *job task design* characteristics, including the use of new technologies.

A popular theory developed decades ago by Frederick Herzberg drew on all of these traditions, emphasizing both the extrinsic and intrinsic rewards of work. *Hygiene factors*, such as pay, supervisory style, and physical surroundings in the workplace, could reduce job dissatisfaction, Herzberg argued. But only *motivators*, such as opportunities to develop one's skills and to make decisions about one's own work, could increase job satisfaction (Herzberg 1966). Herzberg also insisted that the presence of such motivators would lead, by way of increased job satisfaction, to greater productivity on the part of workers (we will return to that issue below).

Influenced by Herzberg's *two-factor theory,* most job satisfaction researchers now use multidimensional explanatory frameworks incorporating both intrinsic and extrinsic work rewards, as well as organizational and task characteristics. Although researchers categorize the specific features of work in somewhat different ways, there is considerable consensus at a broader level. Arne Kalleberg (1977), for example, identified six major dimensions of work. The first, an intrinsic reward dimension, emphasizes interesting, challenging, and self-directed work that allows personal growth and development. Career opportunities form a second dimension, and financial rewards (pay, job security, and fringe benefits) a third. Relationships with coworkers, convenience (the comfort and ease of work), and resource adequacy (availability of information, tools, and materials necessary to do a job) complete Kalleberg's list.

It is also clear from the research we have reviewed that work orientations, or preferences, must remain part of the job satisfaction equation. Indeed,

Kalleberg argues that it is the specific fit or mismatch between work rewards (characteristics of the job) and work orientations that determines one's degree of job satisfaction. This equation would apply, he suggests, to both extrinsic and intrinsic dimensions of work. In his classic study, Kalleberg (1977) found that job rewards had positive effects on expressions of job satisfaction in the U.S. labour force, as predicted. But he also observed that, other things being equal, work preferences (orientations) had negative effects on satisfaction. In other words, the more one values some particular feature of work (the chance to make decisions, for example), the less likely it is that one's desires can be satisfied. However, job rewards had substantially greater effects on satisfaction than did work preferences. In addition, Kalleberg concluded that intrinsic job rewards were more important determinants of job satisfaction than were extrinsic rewards.[5]

The Work Orientation–Work Reward Gap

What does Canadian research tell us about intrinsic and extrinsic work rewards and their fit or mismatch with the work orientations of workers? In Chapter 13, we saw that Canadians place considerable value on both intrinsic and extrinsic job rewards (Figure 13.1). A sizable majority of respondents in the 2012 EKOS survey emphasized the importance of having a sense of pride and accomplishment in their work and having challenging and interesting work, and almost as many stated that good job security, a healthy and safe workplace, a good balance between work and personal/family life, and good pay were "very important" to them.

In 2015, in a similar EKOS survey, Canadian labour force participants were asked to choose from a list of intrinsic and extrinsic work rewards the single job characteristic that would be "<u>most</u> important in deciding which job to choose?" They were then asked "to what extent would you say you have this (most important) characteristic in your job (or previous job, for the unemployed)?" Figure 14.2 displays the five most common choices and the percentage of workers who reported that their job had this "most important" job characteristic "to a great extent."

One in four (25 percent) stated that having challenging work that gave them a sense of accomplishment was most important, while one in five (19 percent) said good pay and benefits were most important. But there is a

FIGURE 14.2 Availability of Most Important Job Characteristic, Canadian Labour Force, 2015*

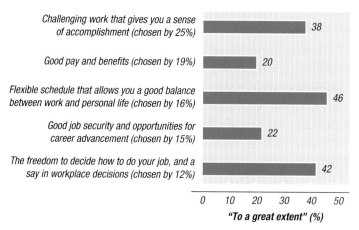

*Respondents (*N* = 6,813) were asked to identify the "most important" job characteristic when looking for a new job and whether they had this in their current/previous job ["not at all" (1) to (5) "to a great extent"].

Source: Used with permission of EKOS Research Associates, Inc.

sizable gap between what Canadian workers feel is most important and what they get from their job. Only 38 percent of those who most valued challenging work said their job provided this to "a great extent," while even fewer (20 percent) of those more focused on extrinsic rewards (good pay and benefits) felt they definitely were receiving them. We see similar gaps for the other three work orientation–work reward pairings in Figure 14.2. These discrepancies between what Canadians want from their jobs and what many of them get are, in a sense, the ingredients for the contemporary patterns of job satisfaction and dissatisfaction that we have described above.

With the exception of flexible work schedules that can improve work–family balance, the work orientation–work reward gap for the extrinsic dimensions considered in this analysis (pay, benefits, job security, career opportunities) is larger than the gap for the intrinsic dimensions (challenging work, sense of accomplishment, freedom to decide how work will be done, having a say in workplace decision making). Perhaps what we are seeing here reflects the growth in precarious employment and, more generally, the labour market restructuring and polarization that have occurred over the past several decades in Canada.

In general, however, jobs that provide considerable autonomy, complexity, and variety are more personally fulfilling for most workers. Opportunities to make decisions about how a job should be done, develop and use a wide range of skills, and do interesting work can also increase a worker's satisfaction with a job. This helps explain why self-employed workers often report higher satisfaction (Hughes 2005). For example, the 2016 GSS asked self-employed Canadians, "In general, do you enjoy being your own boss?" Sixty percent answered "always," 29 percent said "often," and 11 percent answered "sometimes," but none of the self-employed chose the "rarely" or "never" responses to this question.

In contrast, repetitive jobs with little variety often have the opposite effect. Compare the variety and challenge that are so satisfying for the male oil-field service company manager and the sense of accomplishment reported by the male professional engineer (the first two quotations below) with the comments on repetitive, low-skill work by a female food-processing factory worker and by a male assembly-line worker.[6]

> Every morning even now, I'm happy to come to work; I look forward to it. I think it's because this business is, well, you never know when you come in here in the morning what's going to be asked of you. It could be different every day; generally it is. (House 1980: 335)

***

> I love it. I think I have one of the best jobs I know of. . . . I enjoy working on projects from start to finish as opposed to just having a small piece of them. . . . I have found over the years that I am very easily bored and in this field and this environment you don't get bored very often. (Bailyn and Lynch 1983: 281)

***

> Basically, I stand there all day and slash the necks of the chickens. . . . The chickens go in front of you on the line and you do every other chicken or whatever. And you stand there for eight hours on one spot and do it. (Armstrong and Armstrong 1983: 129)

***

> Your brain gets slow. It doesn't function the way it should. You do the same thing day in and day out and your brain goes. I'm like a robot.

I walk straight to my job and do what I have to do. (Robertson and Wareham 1987: 29)

Fortunately, the jobs held by the majority of Canadians appear to be more challenging than those described in these last two quotations. A 2000 survey conducted by Canadian Policy Research Networks (CPRN) revealed, for example, about three-quarters or more of Canadian workers reporting that their jobs were interesting, required high skill levels, provided them with a sense of accomplishment, and offered some decision-making opportunities as well as chances to enhance skills and abilities. Nevertheless, when asked to agree or disagree that "your job requires that you do the same tasks over and over," 59 percent agreed or agreed strongly.[7] These findings suggest that repetitious work (a lack of variety) is more common than non-challenging, low-skill work, or work with little autonomy.

Consequences of Job Satisfaction and Dissatisfaction

"If the job's so bad, why don't you quit?" Many of us may have thought this about an unsatisfying job, but fewer have acted on the idea. There may be some features of the job—pay, hours, location, friendly coworkers—that make it palatable, despite the absence of other work rewards. In addition, unless other jobs are available, most employees cannot afford to quit. As we reported earlier, Statistics Canada's 2016 GSS showed 38 percent of employed Canadians saying it would be difficult to find another job that paid as well as their current job. Thus, job dissatisfaction will not necessarily translate into quitting behaviour (Hammer and Avgar 2005), although it may be more strongly associated with intentions of quitting (Singh and Loncar 2010).

A recent U.S. study that tracked survey respondents over a 14-year period showed that those who had consistently worked in dissatisfying jobs reported poorer mental and physical health (Dirlam and Zheng 2017). Feelings of job dissatisfaction may also allow workers to rationalize coming in late, calling in sick, or generally not working as hard as they could (Hausknecht, Hiller, and Vance 2008; Wood, Niven and Braeken 2016). Studies have also shown a relationship between job dissatisfaction and overt acts of employee deviance, such as theft of company property, or the use of drugs and alcohol on the job and away from work (Martin and Roman 1996). Dissatisfaction with work is also correlated with the number of complaints and grievances filed in unionized work settings. As for nonunion workers, surveys have shown that those dissatisfied with their work are more likely to view unions positively and are more likely to join a union, if given the chance.[8]

From an employer's perspective, however, the critical issue is whether increases in job satisfaction will boost productivity. If dissatisfaction can lead to tardiness, absenteeism, deviance, and, in some situations, quitting, surely improvements in the quality of working life will lead to a more satisfied and, hence, more productive workforce. This relationship would seem to be obvious (Fisher 2003). But although one can find studies showing such a pattern, there are also many studies that reject this hypothesis. Overviews of research on the topic typically show that the relationship between satisfaction and productivity is weak, or is present only in some work settings.

There are several possible explanations. One is that productivity is more often a function of technology and workers' skills than of their attitudes. Thus, even if high levels of satisfaction are evident, low skill levels, inadequate on-the-job training, or obsolete technology will limit opportunities for productivity increases. Another explanation is that work-group norms and expectations must be taken into consideration. Managers and consultants who have introduced job enrichment programs or high-performance work practices (see Chapter 9), and have perhaps even found higher levels of satisfaction as a consequence (Berg 1999), have frequently been disappointed when productivity increases did not follow. They may have failed to realize that workers might view an improved quality of working life as their just reward, or that informal work norms and long-standing patterns of behaviour are difficult to alter.

It may be that productivity can be influenced by job satisfaction, but only under certain conditions (Iaffaldano and Muchinsky 1985). For example, our earlier discussion suggested that workers in low-level jobs might report job satisfaction because they were assessing their work with a limited set of alternatives in mind. Workers in higher-status jobs might, on the other hand, report satisfaction because of tangible work rewards. If so, perhaps productivity increases due to job satisfaction might be expected only in the latter group. In fact, the most extensive overview of research on this topic—a meta-analysis of findings from 254 previous studies—concludes that the relationship is much stronger in high-complexity jobs (Judge et al. 2001: 388).

WORK AND ALIENATION

William Faulkner once wrote: "You can't eat for eight hours a day nor drink for eight hours a day nor make love for eight hours a day—all you can do for eight hours is work. Which is the reason why man makes himself and everybody else so miserable and unhappy."[9] Faulkner didn't use the term *alienation*, but he might have since his cynical observation about the misery of work captures some of the meaning of the term as used by social philosophers. Referring back to our discussion of the meaning of work (Chapter 13), we can define *alienation* as the human condition resulting from an absence of fulfilling work.

In his critique of capitalism, Karl Marx presented a structural analysis of how capitalist relations of production led to workers being separated—alienated—from the products they produced, from others involved in the labour process, from the very activity of work, and ultimately, from themselves as creative human beings (Chapter 10). Marx's argument rests on several key assumptions. First, alienation occurs because workers have little or no control over the conditions of their work, and few chances to develop to their fullest potential as creative human beings. Second, the source of alienation can be traced to the organization of work under capitalism. Third, given that alienation is characteristic of capitalism, it exists even if workers do not consciously recognize it.

Alienation, according to Marx, is a "condition of objective powerlessness" (Rinehart 2006: 11–20). Whether individual workers become aware of the cause of their discontent with work depends on a variety of factors. In the absence of a well-defined and legitimate alternative to the capitalist economic system, we would not expect most North American workers to be able to clearly articulate their alienation, or to act on it.

Writing more than a century after Marx, Melvin Seeman (1975) outlined his theory of alienation that emphasized workers' feelings of powerlessness, meaninglessness, social isolation, self-estrangement, and normlessness. He focused primarily on the consequences for workers' self-identity and mental health of the absence of intrinsic job rewards. Nevertheless, his more psychological perspective on alienation, which continues to influence some present-day researchers,[10] shares with Marx's structural perspective an emphasis on the powerlessness of workers and the conclusion that many jobs offer limited opportunities for personal growth and self-fulfillment. But this perspective does not lay the blame on the workplace social relations of capitalism. Instead, workplace technologies, bureaucracy, and, more recently, precarious work (e.g., DiPietro and Pizam 2008; Clark et al. 2010), along with modern mass society in general, are identified as the sources of alienation.

Richard Sennett's analysis of the negative impact of 21st-century work organizations and relationships on the minds and souls of American workers draws on both the structural and psychological perspectives. Sennett (1998) describes how today's labour market is characterized by the constant restructuring of work organizations, an emphasis on flexibility in production and the delivery of services, a greater reliance on nonstandard workers, and a glorification of risk taking. Together, these new values and practices have combined to get rid of the order and routine that traditionally defined the lives of workers and have led to a "corrosion of character." Why is this a problem? Because, Sennett argues, order, routine, and stability lead to the formation of personal and occupational identities which give meaning to our lives. In a working world where constant change is glorified and the positive aspects of structure and routine are lost, individual identities are also lost or fail to take shape. Sennett recognizes that these fleeting personal identities and the resulting concerns about "who in society needs me?" (1998: 146) are shaped in a capitalist economy. But he does not blame the capitalist relations of production that separate workers from owners and that leave control of the labour process with the latter. Instead, the postmodern alienation that he describes is attributed to the forms of work organization and the much less stable divisions of labour that characterize today's workplace.

Drawing on discussions of emotional labour (Chapter 2), the acting out of emotional scripts required of workers in various service-sector occupations, and referring back to Marx's observations about alienation in a capitalist economy, Costos and Fleming (2009) describe another form of postmodern alienation—"self-alienation." Workers in the large management consulting firm (Y-International) they studied are pushed to work long hours, presenting themselves as completely client-focused and able to successfully complete whatever projects clients want. The outcome, for many, is a strong feeling that they cannot be themselves at work. As one of the young managers (Helen) comments (Costos and Fleming 2009: 365):

> I don't feel there is much room for me to express myself here and it seems like the culture stifles you. . . . It is like you are at a masquerade party and you come to the party every day and choose a mask. And you wear that mask every day and you return it at the end of the day.

"Dis-identification" is the process whereby workers try to separate their own more authentic selves away from work from the roles they are required to perform at work. Over time, this can become very difficult, and some workers come to be unsure of who they really are. Their dis-identification is unsuccessful and they become self-alienated: "the boundary between the narrated imaginary of authenticity and corporate defined identity is difficult to sustain" (Costos and Fleming 2009: 360). Jason, another young manager describes his self-alienation (Costos and Fleming 2009: 366):

> I realize that I am not the person that I have to be at work and I am not enjoying it. I would definitely say that Y-International has separated me from my personality. May be not changing it but certainly forcing me to be two people at an expense of my happiness if you like.

WORK AND STRESS

If we take a broader *work and well-being* approach to the subject of how workers experience and react to their jobs, both physical and psychological reactions to work become part of our subject matter. This approach also encourages us to consider how paid work might affect an individual's life in their family and the community. Consequently, workplace health and safety issues, discussed in Chapter 12, are also relevant to discussions of work and well-being, as are concerns about balancing work and family responsibilities (Chapter 7). Here, we look more specifically at work and stress.

Defining *work-related stress* independent of job dissatisfaction is not easy. In fact, some researchers studying stress and its consequences rely on measures that might, in a different context, be considered indicators of job dissatisfaction. But there are important distinctions to be made between job dissatisfaction, anxiety and tension about work, job stress, and job burnout (Humphrey 1998: 4–9). It is possible to feel dissatisfied with work, perhaps even a little anxious about some aspects of a job, without experiencing a great deal of stress. But work-related stress, with its physical and mental symptoms, can also accumulate to the point of *burnout*, where an individual is unable to cope in the job (Hakanen, Schaufeli, and Ahola 2008).

It is important to distinguish stressors, or strains, from an individual worker's reactions to them. *Stressors* are objective situations (e.g., noisy work environments or competing job demands) or events (a dispute with a supervisor or news that some workers are about to be laid off) that have the potential to produce a negative subjective or physical response. Thus, work-related stress is an individually experienced negative reaction to a job or work environment. Obviously, the absence of stress does not imply the presence of job satisfaction. What distinguishes stress reactions are the wide range of ill health symptoms, both physical and psychological.

So how pervasive is work-related stress? Statistics Canada's 2010 GSS showed 27 percent of working adults (ages 20 to 64) stating that, on most days, their lives were "quite stressful" or "extremely stressful." Sixty-two percent of these highly stressed adults said that work was their main source of stress. In other words, 17 percent of working adults (about 2.3 million people) typically felt highly stressed because of their job on an almost daily basis (Crompton 2011).

More recently, in a 2015 national survey conducted by EKOS Research Associates, 15 percent of working Canadians answered "always" when asked "in the past twelve months, how often did you experience stress in your job?" Another 37 percent answered "often."[11] Although the two surveys asked about work-related stress in different ways (the first about intensity; the second about frequency), both show a sizable minority feeling seriously stressed by their work. It is clear that work-related stress is not an isolated phenomenon.

Causes and Consequences of Work-Related Stress

In their study of workers who had lost well-paying manufacturing and resource-sector jobs in five rural Ontario communities, and who were now struggling with unemployment or low-paying, part-time service-sector jobs, Anthony Winson and Belinda Leach (2002: 127–30) provided graphic examples of work-related stress. These workers and their families worried constantly about paying bills, making do with less, losing the family home, having to rely on food banks, and dealing with medical expenses that used to be covered by benefits packages.

Work-related stress, however, is not experienced only by low-income earners. The 2010 GSS discussed earlier revealed that more than half of the working Canadians feeling highly stressed because of their work on an almost daily basis were in management, professional, or technical occupations, and almost three-quarters were college or university educated (Crompton 2011). Ironically, workers in knowledge-intensive jobs where continued learning is required report higher job satisfaction while at the same time feel more stressed because of the pressure to keep learning and the time spent on the task (Valdés and Barley 2016).

A vast amount of research has drawn our attention to the many different kinds of stressors in the work environment (Barling, Kelloway, and Frone 2005; Davis et al. 2008). We have already mentioned stress resulting from concerns about job insecurity. In addition, continual exposure to health and safety hazards, working in a physically uncomfortable setting, shift work, or long hours can all be stressors. Similarly, fast-paced work, especially when the pace is set by a machine (e.g., assembly-line work) or work requiring multitasking, as many information and communication technology jobs do (Chesley 2014), can be highly stressful. The same applies to performance-based pay systems that link output to the amount earned (Ganster et al. 2011) and lean production management approaches that continually push workers to increase output (Carter et al. 2013). In a study of Ontario nurses, for example, perceptions of work intensification resulting from organizational restructuring led to significantly increased stress and, in turn, reduced job satisfaction (Zeytinoglu et al. 2007).[12]

Working at tasks that underuse one's skills and abilities, that do not meet one's expectations for the job, or that allow little latitude for decision making are also stressful for many workers. An unreasonable and overly demanding supervisor can create a great deal of stress, as can bullying by coworkers or a supervisor (Wood, Niven, and Braeken 2016).[13] Finally, workers might experience stress as a result of sexual harassment or from discrimination in the workplace based on gender, race, sexual orientation, religion, or disability (Buchanan and Fitzgerald 2008).

As Chapter 7 documented, equally stressful for some workers, especially women, but also increasingly so for men, are the pressures of meeting family responsibilities while trying to devote oneself to a job or career (Ergeneli, Ilsev, and Karapinar 2010).[14] As one of the young, university-educated western Canadian women interviewed by Gillian Ranson (1998: 527) lamented:

> In this job, in this particular job, I don't think I could do justice to the child and I've made the decision that . . . either after maternity leave or in the near future, I'm quitting, because it's not fair. I come home, I can't even talk to my husband because I'm so wound up, stressed out.

Research in many different settings has shown that physical reactions to stress can include fatigue, insomnia, muscular aches and pains, ulcers, high blood pressure, and even heart disease (Nixon et al. 2011; Steptoe, A. & Kivimäki 2013). Depression, anxiety, irritation, low self-esteem, and other mental health problems are among the documented psychological reactions to stressful work. The health effects of work-related stress can also be exacerbated by other factors. For example, a 2005 Toronto study showed strong negative health outcomes among temporary employees who were working hard to try to keep their current jobs while also looking for new jobs in case their contracts were not renewed (Lewchuk, Clarke, and de Wolff 2008). Given these widespread and serious physical and mental health consequences, work-related stress is also costly for employers and the economy, since it is associated with reduced productivity, absenteeism, and disability claims (Crompton 2011).

The "Person–Environment Fit" Model

A well-established theoretical model of work-related stress emphasizes the *person–environment fit*. According to this model, stress results when there is a significant gap between an individual's needs and abilities and what the job offers, allows, or demands (Edwards and Shipp 2007). To take a specific example, reports of stress and burnout among social workers, teachers, and nurses are common (Kim and Stoner 2008). Individuals in these helping professions have work orientations and expectations (the desire to solve problems and help people) and useful skills (training in their profession) that are frequently thwarted by the need to deal with an excessive number of clients, limited resources, and administrative policies that make it difficult to be effective.

We might also use this perspective to help us understand the stress many workers feel when they try to juggle their work and family roles. A paid job requires one to be present and involved; at the same time, family responsibilities demand time and attention. Because women continue to carry a large share of domestic and child-care responsibilities, they are more likely to experience role conflict and stress, as this individual interviewed by Duffy and Pupo (1992: 134) reported:

> When I worked full-time, I felt very guilty about the children. If they were sick and I went to work, I felt guilty. If I stayed home with them, I felt guilty about work. Part-time work could offer the flexibility that full-time work cannot.

This woman chose part-time work to try to handle her problem, but gave up additional income and career options (which are limited in most part-time jobs). From a person–environment fit perspective, she was attempting to improve the fit between demands of her family and her job (or the financial need to work). But that fit could also have been improved if structural and societal, rather than just individual, changes were implemented. If more men accepted an equal share of the responsibilities in their homes, if more employers offered flexible work schedules to their workers, and if affordable, quality childcare was more accessible, would the woman quoted above have been forced to make these choices? With respect to professional burnout, how could organizational structures and administrative policies be changed to allow social workers and nurses to be more effective?

The "Demand–Control" Model

A more useful theoretical perspective for understanding workplace stress is the *demand–control model*, which redefines *stressors* as *job demands* but also introduces the concept of *worker control* (Karasek 1979). It distinguishes between active jobs, where individual decision-making potential is high, and passive jobs, where it is largely absent. If psychological demands on a worker are high, but a worker can do something about them, stress is less likely to result. If demands are high and control is low, stress, along with the health problems that can follow, is far more often the outcome. For example, workers in jobs with high emotional labour requirements but with limited control over their work—we earlier referred to people in such jobs as an "emotional proletariat" (Chapter 2)—can experience high levels of work-related stress (Singh and Glavin 2017). A very large number of studies in many different workplace settings, employing both cross-sectional and longitudinal (de Lange et al. 2003; Bakker and Demerouti 2007) as well as experimental (Moen et al. 2016) research designs, have provided strong support for the demand–control model of workplace stress.

From this perspective, we can understand why researchers have repeatedly demonstrated that highly routinized, machine-paced work is extremely stressful. Assembly-line jobs are often considered to be among the most stressful. Demand is never-ending, the physical work can be extremely taxing, and worker control is virtually absent (Landsbergis, Cahill, and Schnall 1999). Earlier, we suggested that instrumental work attitudes may be a coping mechanism—the paycheque becomes the only relevant work reward. Some assembly-line workers rely on alcohol or drugs to get through a shift (De Santis 1999: 111–14). Others adapt to assembly-line work by "tuning out" the boredom and waiting for the chance to get away from the job. Ben Hamper (1986: 88), better known as "Rivethead," describes how he was introduced to his new job on a truck assembly line in Flint, Michigan:

"Until you get it down, your hands will ache, your feet will throb and your back will feel like it's been steamrolled . . ."

"Are there any advantages to working down here?" I asked pitifully.

The guy scratched at his beard. "Well, the exit to the time clocks and the parking lot is just down these stairs. Come lunchtime or quittin' time, you can usually get a good jump on the rest of the pack."

The widespread adoption of electronic communications systems in the contemporary workplace has created some highly rewarding and complex jobs, but also some new types of work that can be extremely routinized and, hence, very stressful. Most prominent here are jobs in call centres that require workers to repeatedly try to contact members of the public, either to sell products or services or to solicit their opinions on various topics (Chapter 10). The same technologies have also increased the scope for electronic surveillance, yet another new source of stress. This practice might involve monitoring the conversations of teleworkers and others who deal with the public by telephone, keeping track of Internet searches made by employees, recording output in settings where workers use computers or electronic communications systems, and even delivering electronic warnings to those performing below certain levels.[15]

Frederick Taylor would have applauded such high levels of work routinization and technological control, but employees do not. A Canadian call-centre employee describes her stress-inducing workplace (Buchanan and Koch-Schulte 2000: 24):

They count on a high turnover because of the way this business is run, there is a very high burnout level. People burnout quickly because of the stress, because of the pressure, because of the way people are treated, because of the degrading nature of the work.

It is not difficult to see how such working conditions—high demands and virtually no worker control—can be stressful, and can lead to physical and psychological ill health.

CONCLUSION: THE "LONG ARM OF THE JOB"

In Chapter 13, we described how North Americans today are exposed to competing work-value systems: one that views work as merely a means to an end and another that insists work can be personally fulfilling. As a result, because of different socialization experiences, some workers may be primarily instrumentally oriented while others are more motivated by the intrinsic rewards of a job. In short, it could be argued that work orientations, or preferences, are typically shaped in society and brought to the job where they influence feelings of satisfaction or alienation and experiences of stress.

But a lot of research supports an alternative explanation, namely, that participation in low-skill or routinized work can produce instrumental work attitudes. For many workers, such attitudes may be a means of adapting to employment that has little but a paycheque to offer. Although it is important to recognize that work orientations affect how an individual feels about his or her job, the nature of the work itself is likely to have a stronger impact, both on an individual's feelings of satisfaction, alienation, and stress and on that person's work orientations.

We have suggested that work-related stress does not get left behind at the end of the workday. Chronic work pressures, as well as anxiety about potential job or income loss, can undermine an individual's overall quality of life. At the same time, it is apparent that satisfaction with work translates into a broader sense of well-being (Dirlam and Zheng 2017). But are there any other more long-term, perhaps even permanent, psychological effects a job can have on an individual? The answer appears to be yes—continued exposure to some kinds of work can have long-lasting effects on non-work behaviours and on one's personality.

In a study conducted some decades ago, Martin Meissner argued that the "long arm of the job"[16] has an impact on life away from work. He studied male sawmill workers in British Columbia to test rival hypotheses about how the nature of work might affect after-work behaviours. The *compensatory leisure* hypothesis proposes that people will look for activities away from work that will compensate for what is absent in their jobs. Thus, workers who have little opportunity to develop their skills and abilities on the job might seek these opportunities away from work. The *spillover* hypothesis suggests that the effects of work will influence the choice of after-work activities. Meissner concluded that there is more of a spillover effect. Workers who had little chance to make decisions about how their work should be done were considerably less likely to engage in free-time activities that required or allowed this kind of individual discretion. Similarly, those who had few opportunities for social interactions at work were more inclined toward solitary leisure-time activities (Meissner 1971: 260).

One could still argue that the subjects in Meissner's study had chosen their jobs in order to satisfy their personal preferences. We would need longitudinal data to address this "chicken and egg" question, which is what Melvin Kohn and his associates (1983) have done, focusing on the concept of *occupational self-direction*. Kohn argues that work that is free from close supervision, that involves considerable complexity and independent judgment, and that is non-routine will have a lasting positive effect on personality and psychological functioning. To be specific, individuals whose work allows self-direction are more likely to develop a personality that values such opportunities and an approach to life that is more self-confident, less fatalistic, and less conformist. They also will exhibit greater flexibility in dealing with ideas. Alternatively, jobs allowing little self-direction are more likely to lead to psychological distress, a finding we have already documented from stress research.

By comparing the jobs and personalities of workers at two points in time (up to 10 years apart), Kohn clearly demonstrated the hypothesized personality changes in those who had and those who did not have the opportunity to work in jobs allowing self-direction. He was also able to demonstrate that "both ideational flexibility and a self-directed orientation lead, in time, to more responsible jobs that allow greater latitude for occupational self-direction."[17] The overall conclusion of Kohn's research and a number of more recent studies[18] is that intrinsically rewarding work, particularly work that allows self-direction, can have important positive long-term consequences for the personalities and careers of those fortunate enough to participate in it.

But the "long arm of the job" extends even further, beyond feelings of satisfaction, dissatisfaction, and alienation; experiences of stress; difficulties balancing work and family; and actual personality change. A growing number of population health studies have documented that poor jobs and problematic working conditions are bad for your health. We have already seen how frequently workers are injured or killed on the job, or become ill because of hazardous working conditions (Chapter 12). But strong evidence linking heart and other diseases, as well as mental illness, to work settings is also accumulating. In fact, several excellent longitudinal studies have demonstrated that, other things being equal, workers in low-skill and poor-paying jobs don't live as long.[19] That, surely, must be a sufficiently convincing argument for increasing our efforts to improve the quality of working life for as many Canadians as possible.

DISCUSSION QUESTIONS

1. When asked, a large majority of workers say they are satisfied with their jobs. So, is there any need to change working conditions, management approaches, or organizational structures? Why or why not?
2. Older workers tend to be more satisfied with their jobs. What might explain this phenomenon? Do you think this long-standing research finding will continue to be observed in the future? Explain your opinion.
3. What kinds of jobs generate the most stress for workers? Why? What might be done to reduce the stress created by such jobs?
4. What is meant by the phrase "the long arm of the job"? Are you convinced by the argument presented? Why or why not?

ADDITIONAL RESOURCES

WORK AT THE MOVIES

- *The Devil Wears Prada* (directed by David Frankel, 2006, 109 minutes). A naïve young woman comes to New York and obtains a job as the assistant to one of the city's biggest magazine editors, the ruthless and cynical Miranda Priestly.
- *Nine to Five* (directed by Colin Higgins, 1980, 110 minutes). Three female employees find a way to deal with their sexist, egotistical, lying, hypocritical bigot of a boss.
- *The Big Short* (directed by Adam McKay, 2015, 130 minutes). This film about the 2007–9 financial crisis resulting from the collapse of housing prices in the United States contains dramatic scenes showing high workplace stress and job dissatisfaction.
- *Office Space* (directed by Mike Judge, 1999, 89 minutes). In this comedic tale, company workers who hate their jobs decide to rebel against their greedy boss.

SOUNDS OF WORK

- "Stressed Out" (Twenty One Pilots) Life was much better when the band was young. Now they are stressed out by the responsibilities of adult life when "you need to make money."
- "Cleaning Windows" (Van Morrison). When he was a part-time musician, singer-songwriter Van Morrison spent his days cleaning windows. This song is purportedly autobiographical.
- "Bud the Spud" (Stompin' Tom Connors). A trucker from Prince Edward Island proudly hauls potatoes across the country.
- "Take This Job and Shove It" (David Allan Coe). This classic country song is about worker disillusionment and the fantasy of quitting a dead-end job.

NOTES

1. Job satisfaction data (including data in Figure 14.1) from Statistics Canada's 2016 General Social Survey (GSS) were analyzed by the authors. For more information about the 2016 GSS, see: https://www150.statcan.gc.ca/n1/daily-quotidien/180613/dq180613c-eng.htm
2. Kalleberg and Loscocco (1983) conclude that all of the explanations have some relevance, while Firebaugh and Harley (1995: 97) believe that "aging" and "life cycle" explanations fit the data best.
3. See also Gjerustad and von Soest (2012) who report an association between unmet occupational aspirations and negative mental health outcomes.
4. See Zeytinoglu et al. (2007) on work intensification and job satisfaction; and De Witte and Näswall (2003) on employment insecurity and job dissatisfaction.
5. See Gallie (2013) and Warr and Inceoglu (2018) for more recent studies of the impacts of both work rewards and work preferences on job satisfaction.
6. For additional graphic "tales from the assembly line," see Hamper (1986) and De Santis (1999). Hodson (2001) provides an excellent content analysis of workers' reactions to their jobs as reported in 149 published workplace ethnographies.
7. The 2000 survey data are cited with permission from Carleton University on behalf of Canadian Policy Research Networks (CPRN).
8. See Bender and Sloane (1998) on job dissatisfaction and filing grievances. Charlwood (2002) links dissatisfaction to willingness to join a union. Hammer and Avgar (2005) reverse the question by asking about the effects of union membership on job satisfaction.
9. Faulkner is quoted by Studs Terkel (1971: xi).

10. See O'Donahue and Nelson (2014), Shantz et al. (2015), and Yuill (2011) for recent discussions of the continued relevance of alienation research.

11. Data from the Rethinking Work 2015 Survey ($N = 6{,}987$ employed Canadians) used with permission of EKOS Research Associates Inc.

12. Johnston and Lee (2013) show that even being promoted can generate stress, despite the increased extrinsic rewards and greater job satisfaction than can accompany a promotion. Similarly, Valdés and Barley (2016) report that workers who need to keep learning on the job report more job satisfaction but, at the same time, experience greater work–family conflict because of longer hours and greater work-related stress.

13. Also see Agervold and Mikkelsen (2004), Tehrani (2004), and Bowling and Beehr 2006 on workplace harassment and bullying.

14. Bass and Grzywacz (2011) look at the work–family balance relationship from the opposite direction, showing how individuals with better jobs (based on both extrinsic and intrinsic rewards) are better able to handle work–family conflict.

15. See also Sewell (1998) and Felstead, Jewson, and Walters (2003) on workplace electronic surveillance. Mann and Holdsworth (2003) describe the stress generated among teleworkers, as well as the negative physical health symptoms they report as a result of their working conditions.

16. The term "the long arm of the job" was first used almost a century ago, to describe the effects of men's work on the life of their family, in the classic study of American culture in Middletown (Lynd and Lynd 1929), a fictitious name for a small U.S. city.

17. Kohn and Schooler (1983: 152); see also Miller, Kohn, and Schooler (1985). Schooler (1984) develops a more general theory of "psychological effects of complex environments," which has applicability beyond the workplace.

18. Chen et al. (2019) show how holding an intrinsically rewarding job can positively affect one's feeling of generativity–the desire to leave a legacy through establishing and guiding the next generation in midlife. Ilies, Wilson, and Wagner (2009) show how job satisfaction can "spillover" to affect marital satisfaction, while Inanc (2018) demonstrates that a person's unemployment can negatively affect the psychological well-being of their spouse.

19. See Mustard, Lavis, and Ostry (2005) for a useful summary of the linkages between work and health outcomes, and Stansfeld and Candy (2006) for a multi-study assessment.

Our discussion of work, industry, and Canadian society has ranged widely over many different topics. We have reviewed and dissected key theoretical debates and have documented emerging industrial, labour market, and workplace trends. Instead of summarizing the many issues we have covered, we conclude by highlighting some of the major themes in current debates about changing labour markets and workplaces.

Debates about how workplaces and employment opportunities are being reshaped in a changing postindustrial society and global economy have been part of sociological discourse for many decades and will continue to be in the future. Like all major industrialized nations, Canada has become a service-based society with a globally linked economy. Yet natural resource, construction, and manufacturing industries continue to play an important role in the Canadian economy, although they employ proportionately fewer people. The service sector, and the wide range of jobs it provides, now dominates. Almost four out of five employed Canadians depend on the service sector for their livelihood.

Many service industry jobs are highly skilled, well paying, and intrinsically rewarding, yet a substantial number require limited skills and offer little in the way of financial security or meaningful work. One of the most clearly defined characteristics of our postindustrial economy is this distinction between "good jobs" and "bad jobs." In particular, while most working Canadians are still employed in permanent, full-time jobs that have a Monday-to-Friday daytime schedule, a growing proportion of the almost 19 million jobs in the Canadian labour market no longer fit this post–World War II definition of a "standard" job. Employment relationships and work arrangements have diversified, and nonstandard jobs, many of them precarious in terms of income and job security, have become more common. And the recent proliferation of Internet-based platforms for buying and selling labour have given rise to the "gig economy," basically solo self-employment gone digital.

Equally important demographic trends have been systematically transforming the Canadian workforce. The population is slowly aging, because of declining birthrates over the past half century and because people are living longer. Consequently, over the last several decades, immigration has accounted for most of the growth in Canada's labour force. As a result, some of Canada's urban centres—Toronto and Vancouver, for example—are among the most ethnically diverse in the world, and members of visible minority groups now compose a much larger proportion of Canada's workforce. At the same time, the Indigenous population in Canada, which faces significant disadvantages as a historical legacy of colonization, is growing rapidly and will account for an increasingly larger share of the workforce in coming years.

The oldest members of the baby-boom generation have transitioned into retirement, many quite comfortably, since they were the beneficiaries of economic expansion, rising incomes, and a growing welfare state in the mid- to late 20th century. But the turbulent labour market restructuring of the 1990s, and the uncertain first decades of the 21st century have left those now nearing retirement less confident that their pensions and savings will be sufficient, particularly since both governments and private-sector employers are thinking about ways to reduce pension liabilities. A growing number of boomers are remaining in the workforce well into their 60s or even 70s. Some seek out personally satisfying work for its social and psychological benefits, but for others it is a matter of economic necessity, especially if they have been working in jobs with no pension or economic security. Taken together, these trends illustrate how boomers have been redefining the meaning of retirement so that it no longer means exiting the workforce at age 65 (Lowe and Graves 2016).

At the other end of the age distribution, for the past three or four decades, successive cohorts of younger workers have faced challenges finding good jobs, despite their increased investments in higher education. As we have seen, the number of well-paying, full-time, secure jobs awaiting university- and college-educated youth has not kept pace with the number of postsecondary graduates in some fields. What are the long-term implications of this kind of intergenerational inequality for Canadian society, for worker–employer relationships, and for individual feelings of job satisfaction? And will today's cohorts of younger workers be able to achieve the same living standard as their parents have?

This question highlights the issue of growing social inequality in Canadian society and in many other countries as well, clearly the most disturbing trend we have observed. While unemployment rates today are much lower than they were during the recessions of the 1980s and 1990s, we still have more than 1.1 million people seeking jobs in our society. Precarious nonstandard jobs have become much more common, and the ranks of the working poor have been growing. The causes of this increase in social inequality are complex, involving the transformation of the global economy, including the outsourcing of jobs, the desire by employers for greater workforce flexibility, continued downsizing in both the private and public sectors, the use of new technologies as labour replacements, shrinking employment in the goods-producing sector, polarization within the growing service sector, a decline in labour union membership, and governments backing away from their traditional role of labour market regulators. Together, these forces are creating wider divisions within the labour market in terms of income, benefits, job security, skill requirements, and the overall quality of work.

There are clear patterns to the inequalities within this more polarized labour market. Some regions of the country, largely bypassed by the economic growth experienced by others, continue to have higher-than-average unemployment rates. Compared to the generations following them into the labour market, baby boomers have enjoyed more labour market advantages. The lack of opportunities for and employment barriers faced by women, people with disabilities, Indigenous peoples, members of racial and ethnic minority groups, and recent immigrants are very evident in Canadian society.

When we look back at the long and difficult battles fought by organized labour to obtain employment rights and benefits and a decent standard of living, we are reminded that social inequities are not easily eliminated. As we have argued throughout this book, a strong case can be made for further focused action by governments to improve employment standards (e.g., minimum wages, working hours, health and safety issues) and to revamp Employment Insurance, pension, childcare, and other work-related policies and programs so that more Canadian workers benefit, and perhaps even to implement a guaranteed annual income. The Canadian economy would benefit as well, since workers who are healthy and secure in decent jobs are likely to be more engaged and productive. Equally important, there is a continued need for a strong organized labour movement and for socially and environmentally responsible corporate leaders. Much the same argument has been made about the U.S. economy (Osterman and Shulman 2011; Kochan 2013; Findlay et al. 2017).

There are a few signs of positive change. Some employers are taking their social and environmental responsibilities more seriously. For example, a larger number of employers have begun to address their employees' work–life balance needs and to support workplace health and wellness initiatives. Even so, we need to remember the segmented nature of the Canadian labour market and acknowledge that some workers are much more likely than others to enjoy these improvements.

Canadian unions have continued to play a strong role in promoting workers' rights and in seeking ways to improve the quality of jobs. In addition, some have shifted their emphasis from business unionism to social movement unionism by becoming more involved in broader social justice issues in Canada and other countries. And a few more politicians are beginning to recognize the vital role of caregiving in our society, and the negative consequences, for the economy and society as a whole, of growing social inequality.

Over the past few decades, we have made progress in the struggle for gender equality in the labour market and in work organizations. There is also greater awareness of the barriers faced by LGBTQ+ workers and the need to create more inclusive workplaces. While we acknowledge the present flaws of employment equity, pay equity, sexual harassment, and work–family policies, their very existence has begun a slow process of institutional change that has benefited some, but not all, women. Although members of visible minority groups continue to encounter labour market barriers, there are signs that discrimination against them is becoming less acceptable. Unfortunately, there is also evidence that recent immigrants to Canada, most of whom are non-white, are not faring as well in the labour market as did earlier waves of immigrants. Even more troubling are the persistent disadvantages faced by Indigenous peoples in Canada. The levels of unemployment and underemployment in their communities are unacceptably high. Despite these concerns, Canada still remains a relatively diverse and open society when compared with the inequalities, racial tensions, and anti-immigrant sentiments that have come to define the United States, Britain, and some other European countries.

Our examination of shifts in management strategies within North American work organizations also identifies colliding trends. On one hand, we have seen how downsizing, outsourcing, and increasing reliance on nonstandard workers have frequently been the substitute for innovative approaches to increasing productivity. Similarly, despite their promise for humanizing work and empowering workers, new management schemes have frequently been used to push workers harder with no compensation in terms of autonomy, skill enhancement, or improved incomes. And with the application of artificial intelligence and other advanced technologies to a growing array of jobs, we can only speculate at this point as to who will be the winners and losers.

Yet, on the other hand, some of the management literature advocates significant workplace reforms, and there are some positive examples of their implementation. Furthermore, important alternatives, including legislated industrial democracy and incentives to encourage worker ownership, could lead to more worker autonomy, increased job security, and reduced social inequality. The challenge will be to convince employers of the business benefits of real workplace reform, to assist workers in their efforts to obtain reform, and to encourage governments to remove legislative and other barriers to improvements. Recognizing that unions have been responsible for many of the gains made by working Canadians over the past century, it is crucial to maintain and strengthen the labour legislation that has allowed this to happen, rather than to weaken it. As we have argued, unions remain a highly effective way for employees to have a voice in the workplace.

The issues we have been raising here are ultimately about the kind of society that Canadians want. Is economic competitiveness at any social and environmental cost our objective? Or would we prefer that the primary goal be a better quality of life, achieved through a reasonable standard of living, improved employment security, and more opportunities for personally rewarding work for as many Canadians as possible within an environmentally sustainable economy? If it is the latter, and we strongly believe it should be, then a political response is also needed. Governments, at various levels, need to consider raising minimum wages, improving labour legislation in a way that benefits workers and not just employers, and implementing tax and other policies that might encourage employers to create more and better jobs (Warhurst et al. 2012; Kochan 2013; Findlay et al. 2017).

As we have noted throughout this book, a "let the market decide" approach (the position taken by most provincial, territorial, and federal governments during the past several decades) is unlikely to help us reach these social and environmental goals. We need to remind ourselves that ideally, the market is a mechanism for improving society (Levitt 2013). Robert Reich, commenting on American society three decades ago, but with observations equally relevant to Canada today, alerted us to the connection between economic globalization and polarization within national economies. In his view, left as things are, we will see further inequality between nations and within industrialized capitalist nations. In his words (1991: 313):

> The choice is ours to make. We are no more slaves to present trends than to vestiges of the past. We can, if we choose, assert that our mutual obligations as citizens extend beyond our economic usefulness to one another, and act accordingly.

We agree.

REFERENCES

Abella, Irving 1974 "Oshawa 1937." In Irving Abella, ed., *On Strike: Six Key Labour Struggles in Canada, 1919–1949*. Toronto: James Lewis and Samuel.

Aboriginal Affairs and Northern Development Canada 2013 *Fact Sheet— 2011 National Household Survey Aboriginal Demographics, Educational Attainment and Labour Market Outcomes*. Ottawa: Aboriginal Affairs and Northern Development Canada. http://www.aadnc-aandc.gc.ca/eng/13763292 05785/1376329233875.

Abu-Laban, Yasmeen, and Christina Gabriel 2002 *Selling Diversity: Immigration, Multiculturalism, Employment Equity, and Globalization*. Peterborough, ON: Broadview Press.

Acker, Joan 1989 "The Problem with Patriarchy." *Sociology* 23(2): 235–40.

——— **1990** "Hierarchies, Jobs, Bodies: A Theory of Gendered Organizations." *Gender & Society* 4(2): 139–58.

Akhtar, Pav, and Phoebe Moore 2016 "The Psychosocial Impacts of Technological Change in Contemporary Workplaces, and Trade Union Responses." *International Journal of Labour Research* 8(1–2): 101–31.

Adams, Roy J. 1995 "Canadian Industrial Relations in Comparative Perspective." In Morley Gunderson and Allen Ponak, eds., *Union–Management Relations in Canada*. 3rd ed. Don Mills, ON: Addison-Wesley Publishers.

——— **2006** "The Campaign to Organize Wal-Mart in Canada." *Social Policy* 36(3): 12–15.

Adams, Roy J., and Parbudyal Singh 1997 "Worker Rights under NAFTA: Experience with the North American Agreement on Labor Cooperation." In Rick Chaykowski, Paul-André Lapointe, Guylaine Vallée, and Anil Verma, eds., *Worker Representation in the Era of Trade and Deregulation*. Selected Papers from the 33rd Annual Canadian Industrial Relations Association Conference, Brock University, St. Catharines, ON. CIRA.

Adams, Scott, and David Neumark 2005 "The Effects of Living Wage Laws: Evidence from Failed and Derailed Living Wage Campaigns." *Journal of Urban Economics* 58: 177–202.

Adams, Tracy L. 1998 "Gender and Women's Employment in the Male-Dominated Profession of Dentistry: 1867–1917." *Canadian Review of Sociology and Anthropology* 35(1): 21–42.

——— **2000** *A Dentist and a Gentleman: Gender and the Rise of Dentistry in Ontario*. Toronto: University of Toronto Press.

——— **2010** "Profession: A Useful Concept for Sociological Analysis?" *Canadian Review of Sociology* 47(1): 49–70.

——— **2015** "Sociology of Professions: International Divergences and Research Directions." *Work, Employment and Society* 29(1): 154–65.

——— **2018** *Regulating Professions: The Emergence of Self-Regulation in Four Canadian Provinces*. Toronto: University of Toronto Press.

Adler, Paul S. 2007 "The Future of Critical Management Studies: A Paleo-Marxist Critique of Labour Process Theory." *Organization Studies* 28(9): 1313–45.

Adler, Paul S., and Charles Heckscher 2006 "Towards Collaborative Community." In Charles Heckscher and Paul S. Adler, eds., *The Firm as a Collaborative Community*. Oxford: Oxford University Press.

AFL-CIO (American Federation of Labor and Congress of Industrial Organizations) 2017 "Death On the Job: The Toll of Neglect, 2017." https://aflcio.org/reports/ death-job-toll-neglect-2017 [retrieved 29 March 2019].

AFMC (2018) 2017 *Canadian Medical Education Statistics*. https://afmc.ca/ publications/canadian-medical-education-statistics-cmes/archives [retrieved May 19, 2019].

Agervold, Mogens, and Eva Gemzoe Mikkelsen 2004 "Relationships between Bullying, Psychosocial Work Environment and Individual Stress Reactions." *Work & Stress: An International Journal of Work, Health & Organisations* 18(4): 336–51.

Aguiar, Luís L. M. 2001 "Doing Cleaning Work 'Scientifically': The Reorganization of Work in the Contract Building Cleaning Industry." *Economic and Industrial Democracy* 22(2): 239–69.

Aguren, Stefan, Christer Bredbacka, Reine Hansson, Kurt Ihregren, and K. G. Karlson 1985 *Volvo Kalmar Revisited: Ten Years of Experience.* Stockholm: Efficiency and Participation Development Council.

Akyeampong, Ernest B. 1992 "Discouraged Workers—Where Have They Gone?" *Perspectives on Labour and Income* (Winter): 38–44.

———— **1993** "Flextime Work Arrangements." *Perspectives on Labour and Income* (Autumn): 17–30.

Albanese, Patrizia 2006 "Small Town, Big Benefits: The Ripple Effect of $7/day Childcare." *Canadian Review of Sociology and Anthropology* 43(2): 125–40.

Aldrich, Howard, and Martin Reuf 2018 "Unicorns, Gazelles, and Other Distractions on the Way to Understanding Real Entrepreneurship in the United States." *Academy of Management Perspectives* 32(4): 458–72.

Alexandroff, Alan S., Gary Clyde Hufbauer, and Krista Lucenti 2008 *Still Amigos: A Fresh Canada–U.S. Approach to Reviving NAFTA.* Toronto: C.D. Howe Institute.

Allen, Tammy D., David E. L. Herst, Carly S. Bruck, and Martha Sutton 2000 "Consequences Associated with Work-to-Family Conflict: A Review and Agenda for Future Research." *Journal of Occupational Health Psychology* 5(2): 278–308.

Alon, Sigal 2009 "The Evolution of Class Inequality in Higher Education: Competition, Exclusion, and Adaptation." *American Sociological Review* 74(5): 731–55.

Althauser, Robert P. 1989 "Internal Labor Markets." *Annual Review of Sociology* 15: 143–61.

Altintas, Evrim, and Oriel Sullivan 2016 "Fifty Years of Change Updated: Cross-national Gender Convergence in Housework." *Demographic Research* 35: 455–69.

Amstad, Fabienne T., Laurenz L. Meier, Ursula Fasel, Achim Elfering, and Norbert K. Semmer 2011 "A Meta-analysis of Work–Family Conflict and Various Outcomes with a Special Emphasis on Cross-Domain versus Matching Domain Relations." *Journal of Occupational Health Psychology* 16(2): 151–69.

Anani, Namir 2018 "Paving the Way for the Future of Work." *Canadian Public Policy* (November): S167–S176.

Anderson, Doris 1996 *Rebel Daughter.* Toronto: Key Porter Books.

Anderson, Kay J. 1991 *Vancouver's Chinatown: Racial Discourse in Canada, 1875–1980.* Montreal: McGill–Queen's University Press.

Anderson, Nickela, and Karen D. Hughes 2010 "The Business of Caring: Women's Self-Employment and the Marketization of Care." *Gender, Work & Organization* 17(4): 381–405.

Anderson, Tammy L., Catherine Grunert, Arielle Katz, and Samantha Lovascio 2010 "Aesthetic Capital: A Research Review on Beauty Perks and Penalties." *Sociology Compass* 4(8): 564–75.

Andres, Lesley, and Johanna Wyn 2010 *The Making of a Generation: The Children of the 1970s in Adulthood.* Toronto: University of Toronto Press.

Angus, Charlie, and Brit Griffin 1996 *We Lived a Life and Then Some: The Life, Death, and Life of a Mining Town.* Toronto: Between the Lines.

Anisef, Paul, Paul Axelrod, Etta Baichman-Anisef, Carl James, and Anton Turrittin 2000 *Opportunity and Uncertainty: Life Course Experiences of the Class of '73.* Toronto: University of Toronto Press.

Appelbaum, Eileen, Thomas Bailey, Peter Berg, and Arne L. Kalleberg 2000 *Manufacturing Advantage: Why High-Performance Work Systems Pay Off.* Ithaca, NY: ILR Press.

Arai, Bruce A. 1997 "The Road Not Taken: The Transition from Unemployment to Self-Employment in Canada, 1961–1994." *Canadian Journal of Sociology* 22(3): 365–82.

Argote, Linda 1999 *Organizational Learning: Creating, Retaining, and Transferring Knowledge.* Boston: Kluwer Academic.

Armitage, Derek R. 2005 "Collaborative Environmental Assessment in the Northwest Territories, Canada." *Environmental Impact Assessment Review* 25(3): 239–58.

Armstrong, Pat, and Hugh Armstrong 1983 *A Working Majority: What Women Must Do for Pay.* Ottawa: Canadian Advisory Council on the Status of Women.

———— **1990** *Theorizing Women's Work.* Toronto: Garamond Press.

Armstrong, Pat, Hugh Armstrong, and Krista Scott-Dixon 2008 *Critical to Care: The Invisible Women of Health Services.* Toronto: University of Toronto Press.

Armstrong, Pat, Jacqueline Choinière, and Elaine Day 1993 *Vital Signs: Nursing in Transition.* Toronto: Garamond Press.

Arntz-Gray, Jules 2016 "Plan, Do, Check, Act: The Need for Independent Audit of the Internal Responsibility System in Occupational Health and Safety." *Safety Science* 84: 12–23.

Aronowitz, S. 1973 *False Promises: The Shaping of American Working Class Consciousness.* New York: McGraw-Hill.

Arsen, David D., Mark I. Wilson, and Jonas Zoninsein 1996 "Trends in Manufacturing Employment in the NAFTA Region: Evidence of a Giant Sucking Sound?" In Karen Roberts and Mark I. Wilson, eds., *Policy Choices: Free Trade among NAFTA Nations.* East Lansing, MI: Michigan State University Press.

Arsenault, Gabriel, Olivier Jacques, and Antonia Maioni 2018 "What Makes Quebec Such An Outlier on Child Care." *Policy Options.* April 24. https://policyoptions. irpp.org/magazines/april-2018/what-makes-quebec-such-an-outlier-on-child-care/ [retrieved June 30 2019].

Ashwin, Sarah 2004 "Social Partnership or a Complete Sellout? Russian Trade Unions' Responses to Conflict." *British Journal of Industrial Relations* 42(1): 23–46.

Askenazy, Philippe 2001 "Innovative Workplace Practices and Occupational Injuries and Illnesses in the United States." *Economic and Industrial Democracy* 22(4): 485–516.

Autor, David 2015 "Why Are There Still So Many Jobs? The History and Future of Workplace Automation." *Journal of Economic Perspectives* 29(3): 3–30.

Avery, Donald H. 1995 *Reluctant Host: Canada's Response to Immigrant Workers, 1896–1994.* Toronto: McClelland & Stewart.

AWCBC (Association of Workers' Compensation Boards of Canada) 2017 "Statistics." http://awcbc.org/ [retrieved 29 March 2019].

Backhouse, Constance 1999 *Colour-Coded: A Legal History of Racism in Canada, Montreal, 1900-1950.* Toronto: University of Toronto Press.

Backett-Milburn, Kathryn, Laura Airey, Linda McKie, and Gillian Hogg 2008 "Family Comes First or Open All Hours? How Low Paid Women Working in Food Retailing Manage Webs of Obligation at Home and Work." *The Sociological Review* 56(3): 474–96.

Badigannavar, Vidu 2017 "Is Social Partnership the Way Forward for Indian Trade Unions? Evidence from Public Services." *International Labour Review* 156(3–4): 367–94.

Bailey, Thomas, and Annette D. Bernhard 1997 "In Search of the High Road in a Low-Wage Industry." *Politics and Society* 25(2): 179–201.

Bailyn, Lotte, and John T. Lynch 1983 "Engineering as a Life-Long Career: Its Meaning, Its Satisfactions, Its Difficulties." *Journal of Occupational Behaviour* 4: 263–83.

Bain, George S. 1978 *Union Growth and Public Policy in Canada.* Ottawa: Labour Canada.

Bakan, Abigail, and Audrey Kobayashi 2007 "Affirmative Action and Employment Equity: Policy, Ideology, and Backlash in Canadian Context." *Studies in Political Economy* 79(1): 145–66.

Bakker, Arnold B., and Evangelia Demerouti 2007 "The Job Demands-Resources Model: State of the Art." *Journal of Managerial Psychology* 22(3): 309–28.

Baldry, Chris 2011 "Editorial: Chronicling the Information Revolution." *New Technology, Work and Employment* 26(3): 175–82.

Baldry, Chris, and Jerry Hallier 2010 "Welcome to the House of Fun: Work Space and Social Identity." *Economic and Industrial Democracy* 31(1): 150–72.

Ball, Jessica, and Kerry Daly 2012 *Father Involvement in Canada: Diversity, Renewal and Transformation.* Vancouver, BC: University of British Columbia Press.

Bamber, Greg J., Russell D. Lansbury, and Nick Wailes, eds. 2011 *International and Comparative Employment Relations: Globalisation and Change.* 5th ed. London: Sage.

Banerjee, Rupa, Jeffrey G. Reitz, and Phil Oreopoulos 2018 "Do Large Employers Treat Racial Minorities More Fairly? An Analysis of Canadian Field Experiment Data." *Canadian Public Policy* 44(1): 1–12.

Banerjee, Subhabrata Bobby 2008 "Corporate Social Responsibility: The Good, the Bad and the Ugly." *Critical Sociology* 34(1): 51–79.

Baril-Gingras, Genevieve, and Sarah Pier Dubois-Ouellet 2018 "Framing, Resources, and Repertoire of Local Trade Union Action for Health and Safety: A Study Conducted with a Quebec Central Labour Body." *Relations Industrielles/Industrial Relations* 73(3): 429–60.

Barley, Stephen, Debra Meyerson, and Stine Grodal 2011 "Email as a Source and Symbol of Stress." *Organization Science* 22(4): 887–906.

Barley, Stephen R., and Gideon Kunda 1992 "Design and Devotion: Surges of Rational and Normative Ideologies of Control in Managerial Discourse." *Administrative Science Quarterly* 37: 363–99.

——— 2006 *Gurus, Hired Guns, and Warm Bodies: Itinerant Experts in a Knowledge Economy.* Princeton, NJ: Princeton University Press.

Barling, Julian, Clive Fullagar, and E. K. Kelloway 1992 *The Union and Its Members: A Psychological Approach.* New York: Oxford University Press.

Barling, Julian, E. Kevin Kelloway, and Michael Frone, eds. 2005 *Handbook of Work Stress.* Thousand Oaks, CA: Sage.

Barnes, Helen, and Jane Parry 2004 "Renegotiating Identity and Relationships: Men and Women's Adjustments to Retirement." *Ageing & Society* 24: 213–33.

Barnetson, Bob 2013 "Alberta's Most Vulnerable Workplace." *Alberta Views* 16(4): 28–32.

——— 2015 "The Prospects for Greater Enforcement of Teen Employment Laws in Alberta, Canada: 'Politically, How Do You Make It Relevant? […] Kill More Young People!'" *Relations Industrielles/Industrial Relations* 70(3): 558–83.

——— 2018 *Canada's Labour Market Training System.* Edmonton, AB: Athabasca University Press.

Barnett, William P., James N. Baron, and Toby E. Stuart 2000 "Avenues of Attainment: Occupational Demography and Organizational Careers in the California Civil Service." *American Journal of Sociology* 106: 88–144.

Barres, Ben 2006 "Does Gender Matter?" *Nature* 442: 133–36.

——— 2018 *The Autobiography of a Transgender Scientist.* Boston: MIT Press.

Bartkiw, Timothy J. 2008 "Manufacturing Descent? Labour Law and Union Organizing in the Province of Ontario." *Canadian Public Policy* 34(1): 111–32.

Bass, Brenda L., and Joseph G. Grzywacz 2011 "Job Adequacy and Work–Family Balance: Looking at Jobs as a Whole." *Journal of Family Issues* 32(3): 317–45.

Bass, Brooke Conroy 2015 "Preparing For Parenthood? Gender, Aspirations, and the Reproduction of Labor Market Inequality." *Gender & Society* 29(3): 362–85.

Basu, Kaushik, ed. 2004 *India's Emerging Economy: Performance and Prospects in the 1990s and Beyond.* Cambridge, MA: MIT Press.

Batt, Rosemary 2000 "Strategic Segmentation in Front-Line Services: Matching Customers, Employees and Human Resource Systems." *International Journal of Human Resource Management* 11(3): 540–61.

Battams, Nathan 2013 "Out of the Office: Workshifting and Remote Work in Canada." *Fascinating Families* [A Vanier Institute of the Family Publication], Issue 56 (August): 1–2.

Bauder, Harold 2001a "Culture in the Labor Market: Segmentation Theory and Perspectives of Place." *Human Geography* 25(1): 37–52.

——— 2001b "Employment, Ethnicity and Metropolitan Context: The Case of Young Canadian Immigrants." *Journal of International Migration and Integration* 2(3): 315–41.

Bauder, Harald 2003 "Brain Abuse, or the Devaluation of Immigrant Labour in Canada." *Antipode* 35(4): 699–717.

Bauman, Zygmunt 2000 *Liquid Modernity.* Cambridge: Polity Press.

Baumol, William J., Alan S. Blinder, and Edward N. Wolff 2003 *Downsizing in America: Reality, Causes, and Consequences.* New York: Russell Sage Foundation.

Baureiss, Gunter 1987 "Chinese Immigration, Chinese Stereotypes, and Chinese Labour." *Canadian Ethnic Studies* 19: 15–34.

Beata, K., J. D. Jens, and B. Per-Olaf 2007 "Measuring Lean Initiatives in Health Care Services: Issues and Findings." *International Journal of Productivity and Performance Management* 56: 7–24.

Beaud, Michel 1983 *A History of Capitalism 1500–1980.* New York: Monthly Review.

Beaujot, Roderic, and Robert Anderson 2007
"Time-Crunch: Impact of Time Spent in
Paid and Unpaid Work, and Its Division in
Families." *Canadian Journal of Sociology* 32(3):
295–315.

**Beaujot, Roderic, Jianye Liu, and Zenaida
Ravanera 2008** "Models of Earning and
Caring: Trends in Time-Use." *PSC Discussion
Papers Series* 22(2). http://ir.lib.uwo.ca/
pscpapers/vol22/iss2/1.

———— **2017** "Gender Inequality in the Family
Setting." *Canadian Studies in Population*
44(1): 1–15.

**Beck, J. Helen, Jeffrey G. Reitz, and Nan
Weiner 2002** "Addressing Systemic Racial
Discrimination in Employment: The Health
Canada Case and Implications of Legislative
Change." *Canadian Public Policy* 28(3):
373–94.

Beck, Ulrich 1992 *Risk Society: Towards a New
Modernity*. London: Sage Publications.

———— **2000** *The Brave New World of Work*.
Cambridge: Polity Press.

**Becker, Brian E., Mark A. Huselid, and Dave
Ulrich 2001** *The HR Scorecard: Linking
People, Strategy, and Performance*. Boston:
Harvard Business School Press.

Becker, Gary S. 1975 *Human Capital: A
Theoretical and Empirical Analysis with Special
Reference to Education*. 2nd ed. Chicago:
University of Chicago Press.

**Beckstead, Desmond, and W. Mark Brown
2005** *An Anatomy of Growth and Decline:
High-Tech Industries through the Boom and
Bust Years, 1997–2003*. Ottawa: Statistics
Canada. Cat. no. 11-624-MIE-No. 010.

Béland, Daniel, and Alex Waddan 2019
"Unidentical Twins: Recent Social Policy
Developments in Canada and the United
States." *Journal of International and
Comparative Public Policy* 35: 1–4.

**Bélanger, Alain, Yves Carrière, and Patrick
Sabourin 2016** "Understanding Employment
Participation of Older Workers: The Canadian
Perspective." *Canadian Public Policy* 42(1):
94–109.

Bélanger, Jacques, and Paul Edwards 2013
"The Nature of Front-Line Service Work:
Distinctive Features and Continuity in
the Employment Relationship." *Work,
Employment and Society* 27(3): 433–50.

Belkin, Lisa 2003 "The Opt-Out Revolution."
New York Times, October 26.

Bell, Daniel 1973 *The Coming of Post-industrial
Society*. New York: Basic Books.

**Bell, David N. F., and David G. Blanchflower
2011** "Young People and the Great
Recession." *Oxford Review of Economics* 27(2):
241–67.

**Bellavia, Gina M., and Michael R. Frone
2005** "Work–Family Conflict." In Julian
Barling, E. Kevin Kelloway, and Michael R.
Frone, eds., *Handbook of Work Stress* (Chapter
6). Thousand Oaks, CA: Sage Publications.

**Belley, Phillipe, Marc Frenette, and Lance
Lochner 2014** "Post-secondary Attendance
by Parental Income in the U.S. and Canada:
Do Financial Aid Policies Explain the
Difference?" *Canadian Journal of Economics*
47(2): 664–96.

Bellin, Seymour S., and S. M. Miller 1990
"The Split Society." In Kai Erikson and
Steven Peter Vallas, eds., *The Nature of Work:
Sociological Perspectives*. New Haven, CT:
American Sociological Association and Yale
University Press.

Bender, Keith A., and Peter J. Sloane 1998
"Job Satisfaction, Trade Unions, and Exit-
Voice Revisited." *Industrial and Labor
Relations Review* 51(2): 222–40.

Bendix, Reinhard 1974 *Work and Authority
in Industry*. Berkeley, CA: University of
California Press.

Berg, Maxine 1988 "Women's Work,
Mechanization and the Early Phases of
Industrialization in England." In R. E. Pahl,
ed., *On Work: Historical, Comparative and
Theoretical Approaches*. Oxford, England: Basil
Blackwell.

Berg, Peter 1999 "The Effects of High
Performance Work Practices on Job
Satisfaction in the United States Steel
Industry." *Relations Industrielles/Industrial
Relations* 54(1): 111–34.

Berg, Peter, and Ann C. Frost 2005 "Dignity
at Work for Low Wage, Low Skill Service
Workers." *Relations Industrielles/Industrial
Relations* 60(4): 657–82.

Berle, Adolf A., and Gardiner C. Means 1968
The Modern Corporation and Private Property.
Rev. ed. New York: Harcourt, Brace and
World. (Orig. pub. 1932.)

Bernard, Andre 2009 "Job Stability and
Employment Duration in Manufacturing."
Perspectives on Labour and Income
(November): 5–14.

Bernardi, Fabrizio 2012 "Unequal Transitions: Selection Bias and the Compensatory Effect of Social Background in Educational Careers." *Research in Social Stratification and Mobility* 30: 159–74.

Bernhardt, Annette, Michael W. Spiller, and Diana Polson 2013 "All Work and No Pay: Violations of Employment and Labor Laws in Chicago, Los Angeles and New York City." *Social Forces* 91(3): 725–46.

Bernstein, Paul 1997 *American Work Values: Their Origin and Development*. Albany: State University of New York Press.

Besen-Cassino, Y. 2019 "Gender Threat and Men in the Post-Trump World: The Effects of a Changing Economy on Men's Housework." *Men and Masculinities* 22(1): 44–52.

Betcherman, Gordon, Kathryn McMullen, Norm Leckie, and Christina Caron 1994 *The Canadian Workplace in Transition*. Kingston, ON: IRC Press.

Beynon, H. 1984 *Working for Ford*. 2nd ed. Harmondsworth, England: Penguin.

Bianchi, Suzanne M., and Melissa A. Milkie 2010 "Work and Family Research in the First Decade of the 21st Century." *Journal of Marriage & Family* 72(3): 705–25.

Bianchi, Suzanne M., Liana C. Sayer, Melissa A. Milkie, and John P. Robinson 2012 "Housework: Who Did, Does or Will Do It, and How Much Does It Matter?" *Social Forces* 91(1): 55–63.

Bielski, Zosia 2019 "With a Looming Aging Crisis, Who Is Helping the Caregivers?" *Globe and Mail*, April 13. https://www .theglobeandmail.com/canada/article-with -a-looming-aging-crisis-who-is-helping-the -caregivers/ [retrieved June 29 2019].

Birner, Kathrin 2015 "One Click to Empowerment? Opportunities and Challenges for Labour in the Global Value Chain of E-commerce." *International Journal of Labor Research* 7(1–2): 55–73.

Bittle, Steven, Ashley Chen, and Jasmine Hébert 2018 "Work-related Deaths in Canada." *Labour/Le Travail* 82(Fall): 159–87.

Black, Jeremy 2015 *A Short History of Britain*. London: Bloomsbury Academic.

Black, Julie, and Yvonne Stanford 2005 "When Martha and Henry Are Poor: The Poverty of Alberta's Social Assistance Programs." In Trevor Harrison, ed., *The Return of the Trojan Horse: Alberta and the New World (Dis)Order*. Montreal: Black Rose Books.

Blackburn, Robert M., Jennifer Jarman, and Janet Siltanen 1993 "The Analysis of Occupational Gender Segregation over Time and Place: Considerations of Measurement and Some New Evidence." *Work, Employment and Society* 7: 335–62.

Blackburn, R. M., and Michael Mann 1979 *The Working Class in the Labour Market*. London: Macmillan.

Blair-Loy, Mary 2003 *Competing Devotions: Career and Family among Women Executives*. Cambridge, MA: Harvard University Press.

Blau, Francine D., and Lawrence M. Kahn 2007 "The Gender Pay Gap: Have Women Gone as Far as They Can?" *Academy of Management Perspectives* 21(1): 7–23.

——— 2017 "The Gender Wage Gap: Extent, Trends, and Explanations." *Journal of Economic Literature* 55(3): 789–865.

Blau, Francine D., and Anne E. Winkler 2017 *The Economics of Women, Men and Work*. 8th ed. Oxford: Oxford University Press.

Blázquez Cuesta, Maite, and Julián Moral Carcedo 2014 "Women's Part-Time Jobs: 'Flexirisky' Employment in Five European Countries." *International Labour Review* 153(2): 269–92.

Bleasdale, Ruth 1981 "Class Conflict on the Canals of Upper Canada in the 1840s." *Labour/Le Travail* 7: 9–39.

Block, Richard N., and Karen Roberts 2000 "A Comparison of Labour Standards in the United States and Canada." *Relations Industrielles/ Industrial Relations* 55(2): 273–306.

Bluestone, Barry, and Bennett Harrison 1982 *The Deindustrialization of America*. New York: Basic Books.

Bognanno, Mario F., and Kathryn J. Ready, eds. 1993 *The North American Free Trade Agreement: Labor, Industry, and Government Perspectives*. Westport, CT: Praeger.

Bolton, Sharon 2005 *Emotional Management in the Workplace*. London: Palgrave.

——— 2009 "Getting to the Heart of the Emotional Labor Process: A Reply to Brook." *Work Employment and Society* 23(3): 549–60.

Bolton, Sharon, and Carol Boyd 2003 "Trolley Dolly or Skilled Emotion Manager? Moving on from Hochschild's Managed Heart." *Work, Employment and Society* 17(2): 289–308.

Bolton, Sharon, and Maeve Houlihan 2010
"Bermuda Revisited: Management Power
and Powerlessness in the Worker-Manager-
Customer Triangle." *Work and Occupations*
37: 378–403.

Bosch, Gerhard 2015 "Shrinking Collective
Bargaining Coverage, Increased Income
Inequality: A Comparison of Five EU
Countries." *International Labour Review*
154(1): 57–66.

**Boudarbat, Brahim, Thomas Lemieux, and
W. Craig Riddell 2010** *The Evolution of
the Returns to Human Capital in Canada,
1980–2005.* Working Paper No. 53.
Vancouver: Canadian Labour Market and
Skills Researcher Network (CLSRN). http://
www.clsrn.econ.ubc.ca/home.php.

Boulet, Jac-André, and Laval Lavallée 1984
The Changing Economic Status of Women.
Ottawa: Supply and Services Canada
(Economic Council of Canada).

Bourdieu, Pierre 1986 "The Forms of Capital."
In J. C. Richardson, ed., *Handbook of Theory
and Research for the Sociology of Education.*
New York: Greenwood Press.

Bowlby, Geoff 2000 "The School-to-Work
Transition." *Perspectives on Labour and Income*
12(Spring): 43–48.

———— **2002** "Farmers Leaving the Field."
Perspectives on Labour and Income 14(Spring):
23–8.

Bowling, Nathan A., and Terry A. Beehr 2006
"Workplace Harassment From the Victim's
Perspective." *Journal of Applied Psychology*
91(5): 998–1012.

Boyd, Monica 2008 "A Socioeconomic Scale
for Canada: Measuring Occupational Status
from the Census." *Canadian Review of
Sociology* 45(1): 51–91.

Boyd, Monica, and Michael Vickers 2000
"100 Years of Immigration in Canada."
Canadian Social Trends (Autumn): 2–12.

**Boyer, Robert, and Daniel Drache, eds.
1996** *States against Markets: The Limits of
Globalization.* London: Routledge.

Bozeman, Barry, and Hal G. Rainey 1998
"Organizational Rules and the 'Bureaucratic
Personality.'" *American Journal of Political
Science* 42(1): 163–89.

Bradbury, Bettina 1993 *Working Families:
Age, Gender, and Daily Survival in
Industrializing Montreal.* Toronto:
McClelland & Stewart.

Bradley, Harriet 1989 *Men's Work, Women's
Work: A Sociological History of the Sexual
Division of Labour in Employment.* Cambridge:
Polity Press.

Bradwin, Edmund 1972 *The Bunkhouse Man:
A Study of Work and Pay in the Camps of
Canada.* Toronto: University of Toronto Press.
(Orig. pub. 1928.)

**Brady, David, Regina S. Baker, and Ryan
Finnigan 2013** "When Unionization
Disappears: State-Level Unionization and
Working Poverty in the United States."
American Sociological Review 78(5): 872–96.

**Brakman, S., P. Frankopan, H. Garretsen,
and C. van Marrewijk 2019** "The New Silk
Roads: An Introduction to China's Belt and
Road Initiative." *Cambridge Journal of Regions,
Economy and Society* 12: 3–16.

Brand, Jennie E. 2015 "The Far-Reaching
Impact of Job Loss and Unemployment."
Annual Review of Sociology 41: 359–75.

Braundy, Marcia 2011 *Men and Women and
Tools: Bridging the Divide.* Halifax: Fernwood
Books.

Braverman, Harry 1974 *Labor and Monopoly
Capital: The Degradation of Work in the
Twentieth Century.* New York: Monthly
Review Press.

Breitkreuz, Rhonda, and Kerryn Colen 2018
"Who Cares? Motivations for Unregulated
Child Care Use." *Journal of Family
Issues* 39(17): 4066–88.

**Brenner, Mark D., David Farris, and John
Ruser 2004** "'Flexible' Work Practices and
Occupational Safety and Health: Exploring
the Relationship between Cumulative Trauma
Disorders and Workplace Transformation."
Industrial Relations 43(1): 232–66.

**Breslin, F. Curtis, Peter Smith, Mieke
Koeboorn, and Hyunmi Lee 2006** "Is the
Workplace Becoming Safer?" *Perspectives on
Labour and Income* 20(Autumn): 36–41.

**Brickner, Rachel K., and Christine
Straehle 2010** "The Missing Link: Gender,
Immigration Policy and the Live-in Caregiver
Program in Canada." *Policy and Society*
(2010): 309–20.

**Brickner, Rachel K., and Meaghan Dalton
2019** "Organizing Baristas in Halifax
Cafes: Precarious Work and Gender
and Class Identities in the Millennial
Generation." *Critical Sociology* 45(4–5):
485–500.

Brisbois, Richard 2003 *How Canada Stacks Up: The Quality of Work—An International Perspective.* Research Paper No. W/23. Ottawa: Canadian Policy Research Networks.

Briskin, Linda 2010 "Militancy and Resistance in the New Economy." In Norene J. Pupo and Mark P. Thomas, eds., *Interrogating the New Economy: Restructuring Work in the 21st Century* Toronto: University of Toronto Press.

Britton, Dana M., and Laura Logan 2008 "Gendered Organizations: Progress and Prospects." *Sociology Compass* 2(1): 107–21.

Brohawn, Dawn K., ed. 1997 *Journey to an Ownership Culture: Insights from the ESOP Community.* Washington, DC: The ESOP Association and Scarecrow Press.

Brook, Paul 2009 "In Critical Defense of 'Emotional Labour': Refuting Bolton's Critique of Hochschild's Concept." *Work Employment and Society* 23(3): 531–48.

Browder, Bill 2015 *Red Notice: How I Became Putin's Number One Enemy.* Random House.

Brown, Andrew, Andy Charlwood, and David A. Spencer 2012 "Not All That It Might Seem: Why Job Satisfaction Is Worth Studying Despite It Being a Poor Summary Measure of Job Quality." *Work, Employment and Society* 26(6): 1007–18.

Brown, Leslie H. 1997 "Organizations for the 21st Century? Co-operatives and 'New' Forms of Organization." *Canadian Journal of Sociology* 22: 65–93.

Brown, Lorne 1987 *When Freedom Was Lost: The Unemployed, the Agitator, and the State.* Montreal: Black Rose Books.

Brown, Jennifer S. 1980 *Strangers in Blood: Fur Trade Company Families in Indian Country.* Vancouver: UBC Press.

Browne, Irene, and Joya Misra 2005 "Labor-Market Inequality: Intersections of Gender, Race, and Class." In Mary Romero and Eric Margolis, eds., *The Blackwell Companion to Social Inequalities.* Malden, MA: Blackwell.

Brym, Robert 1996 "The Third Rome and the End of History: Notes on Russia's Second Communist Revolution." *Canadian Review of Sociology and Anthropology* 33: 391–406.

Brynjolfsson, Erik, and Andrew McAffee 2016 *The Second Machine Age: Work, Progress and Prosperity in a Time of Brilliant Technologies.* New York: WW Norton.

Brynin, Malcolm 2006 "Gender, Technology and Jobs." *British Journal of Sociology* 57(3): 437–53.

Buchanan, Nicole T., and Louise F. Fitzgerald 2008 "Effects of Racial and Sexual Harassment on Work and the Psychological Well-Being of African American Women." *Journal of Occupational Health Psychology* 13(2): 137–51.

Buchanan, Ruth, and Sarah Koch-Schulte 2000 *Gender on the Line: Technology, Restructuring and the Reorganization of Work in the Call-Centre Industry.* Ottawa: Status of Women Canada. Cat. no. SW21-44/2000E. http://www.swc-cfc.gc.ca.

Buckingham, Alan 1999 "Is There an Underclass in Britain?" *British Journal of Sociology* 50(1): 49–75.

Budd, John W. 2004 "Non-wage Forms of Compensation." *Journal of Labor Research* 25(4): 597–622.

Budig, Michelle, and Paula England 2001 "The Wage Penalty for Motherhood." *American Sociological Review* 66(April): 204–25.

Budig, Michelle, and Melissa Hodges 2010 "Differences in Disadvantage: Variation in the Motherhood Penalty across White Women's Earnings Distributions." *American Sociological Review* 75(5): 705–28.

Buffel, Veerle, Sarah Missinne, and Piet Bracke 2017 "The Social Norm of Unemployment in Relation to Mental Health and Medical Care Use: The Role of Regional Unemployment Levels and of Displaced Workers." *Work, Employment and Society* 31(3): 501–21.

Bunting, Madeline 2004 *Willing Slaves: How the Overwork Culture Is Ruling Our Lives.* London: HarperCollins.

Burawoy, Michael 1979 *Manufacturing Consent: Changes in the Labor Process under Monopoly Capitalism.* Chicago: University of Chicago Press.

——— **1984** "Karl Marx and the Satanic Mills: Factory Politics under Early Capitalism in England, the United States, and Russia." *American Journal of Sociology* 90: 247–82.

Burchell, Brendan, David Ladipo, and Frank Wilkinson, eds. 2002 *Job Insecurity and Work Intensification.* London and New York: Routledge.

Burke, Ronald, and Cary L. Cooper 2008 *The Long Work Hours Culture: Causes, Consequences, and Choices.* Bingley, England: Emerald Group Publishing.

Burkhauser, Richard V., Maximillian D. Schmeiser, and Robert R. Weathers II 2012 "The Importance of Anti-discrimination and Workers' Compensation Laws on the Provision of Workplace Accommodations Following the Onset of a Disability." *Industrial and Labor Relations Review* 65(1): 161–80.

Burleton, Derek, Sonya Gulati, Connor McDonald, and Sonny Scarfone 2013 *Jobs in Canada: Where, What, and for Whom?* Toronto: TD Economics. http://www. td.com/document/PDF/economics/special/ JobsInCanada.pdf.

Burman, Patrick 1988 *Killing Time, Losing Ground: Experiences of Unemployment.* Toronto: Wall & Thompson.

———— **1996** *Poverty's Bonds: Power and Agency in the Social Relations of Welfare.* Toronto: Thompson Educational Publishing.

Burnham, J. 1941 *The Managerial Revolution.* Harmondsworth, England: Penguin.

Burrell, Gibson 2006 "Foucaldian and Postmodern Thought and the Analysis of Work." In Marek Korczynski, Randy Hodson, and Paul Edwards, eds., *Social Theory at Work.* Oxford, England: Oxford University Press.

Burstein, M., N. Tienharra, P. Hewson, and B. Warrander 1975 *Canadian Work Values: Findings of a Work Ethic Survey and a Job Satisfaction Survey.* Ottawa: Information Canada.

Buttigieg, Donna M., Stephen J. Deery, and Roderick D. Iverson 2008 "Union Mobilization: A Consideration of the Factors Affecting the Willingness of Union Members to Take Industrial Action." *British Journal of Industrial Relations* 46(2): 248–67.

Butts, Marcus M., Wendy J. Casper, and Tae Seok Yang 2013 "How Important Are Work–Family Support Policies? A Meta-Analytic Investigation of their Effects on Employee Outcomes." *Journal of Applied Psychology* 98(1): 1–25.

Byrne, Edmund F. 1990 *Work, Inc.: A Philosophical Inquiry.* Philadelphia: Temple University Press.

Byron, Kristin 2005 "A Meta-analytic Review of Work–Family Conflict and Its Antecedents." *Journal of Vocational Behavior* 67: 169–98.

Calliste, Agnes 1987 "Sleeping Car Porters in Canada: An Ethnically Submerged Split Labour Market." *Canadian Ethnic Studies* 19: 1–20.

Calnitsky, David 2016 "'More Normal Than Welfare': The Mincome Experiment, Stigma, and Community Experience." *Canadian Review of Sociology* 53(1): 26–71.

Cameron, Greg, and Louise Hanavan 2014 "Re-imagining Rural Cooperation in Atlantic Canada." *Journal of Agriculture, Food Systems, and Community Development* 4(3): 29–45.

Camfield, David 2011 "The 'Great Recession,' the Employers' Offensive and Canadian Public Sector Unions." *Socialist Studies* 7(1/2): 95–115.

———— **2019** "Settler Colonialism and Labour Studies in Canada." *Labour/Le Travail, 83,* 147–72.

Campanella, David, Bob Barnetson, and Angella MacEwan 2014 *On the Job: Why Unions Matter in Alberta.* Edmonton: Parkland Institute. https://s3-us-west-2.amazonaws.com/parkland-research-pdfs/onthejob. pdf [retrieved 25 June 2019].

Campbell, Lara 2009 *Respectable Citizens: Gender, Family and Unemployment in Ontario's Great Depression.* Toronto: University of Toronto Press.

Campolieti, Michele 2018 "Matching and Inverse Propensity Weighting Estimates of the Union Wage Premium: Evidence from Canada, 1997–2014." *Industrial Relations* 57(1): 101–30.

Campolieti, Michele, Rafael Gomez, and Morley Gunderson 2013 "Managerial Hostility and Attitudes towards Unions: A Canada–U.S. Comparison." *Journal of Labor Research* 34: 99–119.

Campolieti, Michele, Robert Hebdon, and Benjamin Dachis 2016 "Collective Bargaining in the Canadian Public Sector, 1978–2008: The Consequences of Restraint and Structural Change." *British Journal of Industrial Relations* 54(1): 192–213.

Camuffo, Arnaldo 2002 "The Changing Nature of Internal Labor Markets." *Journal of Management and Governance* 6(4): 281–94.

Canada 1969 *Canadian Industrial Relations: The Report of the Task Force on Labour Relations.* Ottawa: Queen's Printer.

———— **1984** *Report of the Commission on Equality in Employment* [The Abella Report]. Ottawa: Supply and Services.

———— 1985 *Employment Equity Act.* Chapter 23, 2nd Supplement, Revised Statutes of Canada.

———— 2004 *Pay Equity: A New Approach to a Fundamental Right. Final Report, Pay Equity Task Force.* Ottawa: Department of Justice.

———— 2015 *Fast Fashion: Working Conditions in the Garment Industry.* Ottawa.

———— 2018 *Federal Budget.* https://www.budget.gc.ca/2018/docs/plan/toc-tdm-en [retrieved June 21, 2019].

Canada, Department of Labour 1958 *Survey of Married Women Working for Pay in Eight Canadian Cities.* Ottawa: Queen's Printer.

Canadian Business 2013 "Canada's Top 50 Jobs 2013." April 12. http://www.canadianbusiness.com/companies-and-industries/canadas-top-50-jobs-2013-edition/.

Canadian Committee on Women in Engineering 1992 *More Than Just Numbers: Report of the Canadian Committee on Women in Engineering.* Fredericton: Faculty of Engineering, University of New Brunswick.

Canadian Foundation for Labour Rights (CFLR) 2018 "Restrictive Labour Laws in Canada." https://labourrights.ca/issues/restrictive-labour-laws-canada [retrieved 5 June 2019].

Canadian Immigrant 2011 "Night Shift as Security Officer, a Survival Job for Many Immigrants." May 29. http://canadianimmigrant.ca/immigrant-stories/night-shift-as-security-officer-a-survival-job-for-many-immigrants.

Canadian Labour Congress n.d. "President Hassan Yussuff." https://canadianlabour.ca/who-we-are/officers/hassan-yussuff/ [retrieved 2 May 2019].

Cant, Sarah, and Ursala Sharma 1995 "The Reluctant Profession: Homeopathy and the Search for Legitimacy." *Work, Employment and Society* 9: 743–62.

Caragata, Warren 1979 *Alberta Labour: A Heritage Untold.* Toronto: James Lorimer.

Card, David, and Philip Oreopoulos 2019 "Introduction: Labor Markets and Public Policies in the United States and Canada." *Journal of Labor Economics* 37, S2: S243–S252.

Card, David, Thomas Lemieux, and W. Craig Riddell 2004 "Unions and Wage Inequality." *Journal of Labor Research* 25(4): 519–62.

Carey, Malcolm 2007 "White-Collar Proletariat: Braverman, the Deskilling/Upskilling of Social Work and the Paradoxical Life of the Agency Care Manager." *Journal of Social Work* 7(1): 93–114.

Carlson, Dawn S., and Joseph G. Grzywacz 2008 "Reflection and Future Directions on Measurement in Work–Family Research." In Karen Korabik, Donna S. Lero, and Denise L. Whitehead, eds., *Handbook of Work–Family Integration.* London: Elsevier.

Carroll, William K. 2004 *Corporate Power in a Globalizing World: A Study of Elite Social Organizations.* Toronto: Oxford University Press.

———— 2013 *The Making of a Transnational Capitalist Class: Corporate Power in the 21st Century.* London: ZED Books.

Carson, Paula P., Patricia A. Lanier, Kerry D. Carson, and Brandi N. Guidry 2000 "Clearing a Path through the Management Fashion Jungle: Some Preliminary Trailblazing." *Academy of Management Journal* 43(6): 1143–58.

Carter, Bob, Andy Dunford, Debra Howcroft, Helen Richardson, Andrew Smith, and Phil Taylor 2013 "'Stressed out of My Box': Employee Experience of Lean Working and Occupational Ill-Health in Clerical Work in the U.K. Public Sector." *Work, Employment and Society* 27(5): 747–67.

Carter, Chris, and Frank Mueller 2002 "The 'Long March' of the Management Modernizers." *Human Relations* 55(11): 1325–54.

Carter, Sarah 1993 *Lost Harvests: Prairie Indian Reserve Farmers and Government Policy.* McGill-Queen's Press.

———— 2016 *Imperial Plots: Women, Land, and the Spadework of British Colonialism on the Canadian Prairies.* Winnipeg: University of Manitoba Press.

Cascio, Wayne F. 2002 *Responsible Restructuring: Creative and Profitable Alternatives to Layoffs.* San Francisco: Berrett-Koehler Publishers.

Cassell, Joan 1998 *The Woman in the Surgeon's Body.* Cambridge, MA: Harvard University Press.

Catalyst Canada 2012 *Financial Post 500 Senior Officers and Top Earners.* Toronto: Catalyst Canada.

CBC News 2013 "Bangladesh Probes Garment Factory Fire That Killed 10." *CBC News World*, October 9.

CCOHS (Canadian Centre for Occupational Health and Safety) 2019 "April 28 Day of Mourning." https://www.ccohs.ca/events/mourning/ [retrieved 29 March 2019].

Cech, Erin A. 2013 "Ideological Wage Inequalities? The Technical/Social Dualism and the Gender Wage Gap in Engineering." *Social Forces* 91(4): 1147–82.

——— **2016** "Mechanism or Myth? Family Plans and the Reproduction of Occupational Gender Segregation." *Gender & Society* 30(2): 265–88.

Cha, J. Mijin, Jane Holgate, and Karel You 2018 "Emergent Cultures of Activism: Young People and the Building of Alliances Between Unions and Other Social Movements." *Work and Occupations* 45(4): 451–74.

Chaison, Gary 2004 "Union Mergers in the U.S. and Abroad." *Journal of Labor Research* 25(1): 97–115.

Chaison, Gary N., and Dileep G. Dhavale 1992 "The Choice Between Union Membership and Free-Rider Status." *Journal of Labor Research* 13(4): 355–69.

Chan, Andy W., Ed Snape, Michelle S. Luo, and Yujuan Zhai 2017 "The Developing Role of Unions in China's Foreign-Invested Enterprises." *British Journal of Industrial Relations* 55(3): 602–25.

Chan, Arlene 2014 *Righting Canada's Wrongs: The Chinese Head Tax and Anti-Chinese Immigrant Policies in the Twentieth Century.* Toronto: James Lorimer and Company.

Chan, Jenny, Manjusha Nair, and Chris Rhomberg 2019 "Precarization and Labor Resistance: Canada, the USA, India and China." *Critical Sociology* 45(4–5): 468–83.

Chan, Tak Wing 2000 "Revolving Doors Reexamined: Occupational Sex Segregation over the Life Course." *American Sociological Review* 64: 86–96.

Chandler, Alfred D. Jr. 1977 *The Visible Hand: The Managerial Revolution in American Business.* Cambridge, MA: Harvard University Press.

Charles, Maria 2011 "A World of Difference: International Trends in Women's Economic Status." *Annual Review of Sociology* 37: 355–71.

Chari, Ramya, Chia-Chia Chang, Steven L. Sauter, Elizabeth L. Petrun Sayers, Jennifer L. Cerully, Paul Schulte, Anita L. Schill, and Lori Uscher-Pines 2018 "Expanding the Paradigm of Occupational Safety and Health." *Journal of Occupational and Environmental Medicine* 60(7): 589–93.

Charles, Maria, and David B. Grusky 2004. *Occupational Ghettos: The Worldwide Segregation of Women and Men.* Stanford, CA: Stanford University Press.

Charles, Maria, and Karen Bradley 2009 "Indulging Our Gendered Selves? Sex Segregation by Field of Study in 44 Countries." *American Journal of Sociology* 114(4): 924–76.

Charlwood, Andy 2002 "Why Do Non-union Employees Want to Unionize? Evidence from Britain." *British Journal of Industrial Relations* 40(3): 463–91.

Chase, Steven, and Tavia Grant 2013 "Experts Debate How Much National Household Survey Statistics Count." *Globe and Mail,* May 6.

Chatoor, Ken, Emily MacKay, and Lauren Hudak 2019 *Parental Education and Postsecondary Attainment: Does the Apple Fall Far from the Tree?* Toronto: Higher Education Quality Council of Ontario.

Chen, Dalson 2019 "Nurses Reject Offer from Windsor-Essex Health Unit, Return to Picket Lines." *Windsor Star,* April 11. https://windsorstar.com/news/local-news/nurses-return-to-picket-lines-as-dispute-with-windsor-essex-health-unit-continues [retrieved 29 April 2019].

Chen, Jiawen, Harvey J. Krahn, Nancy L. Galambos, and Matthew D. Johnson 2019 "Wanting to Be Remembered: Intrinsically Rewarding Work and Generativity in Early Midlife." *Canadian Review of Sociology* 56(1): 30–48.

Chen, Michelle 2019 "Worker Cooperatives Are More Productive than Normal Companies." *The Nation.* March 28. https://www.thenation.com/article/worker-cooperatives-are-more-productive-than-normal-companies/ [retrieved 19 April 2019].

Chen, Wen-Hao, and Tahsin Mehdi 2019 "Assessing Job Quality in Canada: A Multidimensional Approach." *Canadian Public Policy* 45(2): 173–91.

Cherns, A. 1976 "The Principles of Socio-Technical Design." *Human Relations* 29: 783–92.

Chesley, Noelle 2014 "Information and Communication Technology Use, Work Intensification, and Employee Strain and

Distress." *Work, Employment and Society* 28(4): 589–610.

Chory, Rebecca M., Lori E. Webb, and Theodore A. Avtgis 2016 "Organizational Surveillance of Computer-mediated Workplace Communications: Employee Privacy Concerns and Responses." *Employee Responsibilities and Rights Journal* 28(1): 23–43.

Chow, Angela, Harvey Krahn, and Nancy Galambos 2013 "Developmental Trajectories of Work Values and Job Entitlement Beliefs in the Transition to Adulthood." *Developmental Psychology* 50(4): 1102-1115.

Chowhan, James, Isik U. Zeytinoglu, and Gordon B. Cooke 2016 "Immigrants and Job Satisfaction: Do High Performance Work Systems Play a Role?" *Economic and Industrial Democracy* 37(4): 690–715.

Chui, Tina, Kelly Tran, and John Flanders 2005 "Chinese Canadians: Enriching the Cultural Mosaic." *Canadian Social Trends* (Spring): 24–32.

Citizenship and Immigration Canada 2009 *Annual Report to Parliament on Immigration.* Ottawa: Citizenship and Immigration Canada. http://www.cic.gc.ca/english/pdf/pub/immigration2009_e.pdf.

Citizenship and Immigration Canada 2012 *Annual Report to Parliament on Immigration, 2012.* http://www.cic.gc.ca/ENGLISH/RESOURCES/publications/annual-report-2012/index.asp.

Civilian Review and Complaints Commission for the RCMP 2017 *Report Into Workplace Harassment in the RCMP.* https://www.crcc-ccetp.gc.ca/pdf/harassmentFinR-eng.pdf [retrieved 27 January 2019].

Clark, Andrew E. 1997 "Job Satisfaction and Gender: Why Are Women So Happy at Work?" *Labour Economics* 4(4): 341–72.

Clark, R. D. 1982 "Worker Participation in Health and Safety in Canada." *International Labour Review* 121: 199–206.

Clark, Sara K., Jonathon R. B. Halbesleben, Scott W. Lester, and Robert Heintz 2010 "Temporary Worker Alienation and Job Performance: The Impact of Rating Source." *Journal of Leadership and Organizational Studies* 17(3): 287–97.

Clark, Warren 1999 "Search for Success: Finding Work after Graduation." *Canadian Social Trends* (Summer): 10–15.

——— **2000** "100 Years of Education." *Canadian Social Trends* (Winter): 3–7.

Clarke, Louise, and Larry Haiven 1999 "Workplace Change and Continuous Bargaining: Saskatoon Chemicals Then and Now." *Relations Industrielles/Industrial Relations* 54(1): 168–91.

Clarke, Simon 2005 "Post-socialist Trade Unions: China and Russia." *Industrial Relations Journal* 36(1): 2–18.

Clarke, Thomas, and Stewart Clegg 1998 *Changing Paradigms: The Transformation of Management Knowledge for the 21st Century.* London: HarperCollins Business.

Clegg, Stewart, and Carmen Baumeler 2010 "Essai: From Iron Cages to Liquid Modernity." *Organization Studies* 31(12): 1713–33.

Clement, Wallace 1981 *Hardrock Mining: Industrial Relations and Technological Changes at Inco.* Toronto: McClelland & Stewart.

Clement, Wallace, and John Myles 1994 *Relations of Ruling: Class and Gender in Postindustrial Societies.* Montreal: McGill–Queen's University Press.

Cleveland, Gordon, Morley Gunderson, and Douglas Hyatt 2003 "Union Effects in Low-Wage Services: Evidence from Canadian Childcare." *Industrial and Labor Relations Review* 56(2): 295–305.

Cobb, Clifford, Ted Halstead, and Jonathan Rowe 1995 "If the GDP Is Up, Why Is America Down?" *Atlantic Monthly* (October): 60–74.

Cockburn, Cynthia 1991 *In the Way of Women: Men's Resistance to Sex Equality in Organizations.* Ithaca, NY: ILR Press.

Cohen, Marjorie Griffen 1988 *Women's Work, Markets and Economic Development in Nineteenth-Century Ontario.* Toronto: University of Toronto Press.

Cohen, Patricia 2019 "New Evidence of Age Bias in Hiring, and a Push to Fight It." *New York Times*, June 7.

Cohen, Ronald 2010 *Work and Sing: The History of Occupational and Labor Songs in the United States.* Champaign IL: University of Illinois Press.

Colella, Adrienne J., and Eden B. King, eds. 2018 *The Oxford Handbook of Workplace Discrimination.* Oxford University Press.

Colen, Kerryn, and Rhonda Breitkreuz 2019 "Paying The Price: Constrained Choice and the Consumption of Unregulated Child Care in Alberta." *Community, Work & Family.* doi:10.1080/13668803.2019.1584088.

Collins, J. C., and J. I. Porras 1994 *Built to Last: Successful Habits of Visionary Companies.* New York: HarperCollins.

Collins, Randall 1990 "Market Closure and the Conflict Theory of Professions." In Michael Burrage and Rolf Torstendahl, eds., *Professions in Theory and History: Rethinking the Study of the Professions.* London, England: Sage.

Collinson, David, and Stephen Ackroyd 2005 "Resistance, Misbehaviour, and Dissent." In Stephen Ackroyd, R. Batt, P. Thompson, and P. S. Tolbert, eds., *The Oxford Handbook of Work and Organization.* Oxford, England: Oxford University Press.

Coltrane, Scott 1996 *Family Man: Fatherhood, Housework, and Gender Equity.* New York: Oxford University Press.

——— 2000 "Research on Household Labor: Modeling and Measuring the Social Embeddedness of Routine Family Work." *Journal of Marriage and Family* 62(4): 1208–33.

Comish, Shaun 1993 *The Westray Tragedy: A Miner's Story.* Halifax: Fernwood Publishing.

Commission for Labor Cooperation 2003 *North American Labor Markets: Main Changes since NAFTA.* Washington, DC: Secretariat of the Commission for Labor Cooperation.

Conference Board of Canada 2013 *Return on Investment in Tertiary Education.* Ottawa: Conference Board. http://www.conference-board.ca/hcp/details/education/tertiary.aspx.

Conlin, M. 2009 "Gap to Employees: Work Wherever, Whenever You Want." *BusinessWeek.com,* September 17. http://www.businessweek.com/careers/managementiq/archives/2009/09/gap_to_employee.html.

Connolly, Heather, Stefania Marino, and Miguel Martinez Lucio 2017 "'Justice For Janitors' Goes Dutch: The Limits and Possibilities of Unions' Adoption of Organizing in a Context of Regulated Social Partnership." *Work, Employment and Society* 31(2): 319–35.

Conrad, Peter 1987 "Wellness in the Workplace: Potentials and Pitfalls of Work-Site Health Promotion." *Milbank Quarterly* 65: 255–75.

Connell, Robert W., and James W. Messerschmidt 2005 "Hegemonic Masculinity: Rethinking the Concept." *Gender & Society* 19(6): 829–59.

Cool, Julie 2010 *Wage Gap between Women and Men.* Ottawa: Library of Parliament Research Paper.

Copp, Terry 1974 *The Anatomy of Poverty: The Condition of the Working Class in Montreal, 1897–1929.* Toronto: McClelland & Stewart.

Cornish, Mary 2007 "Closing the Global Gender Pay Gap: Securing Justice for Women's Work." *Comparative Labor Law and Policy Journal* 28(2): 219–49.

Correll, Shelley J. 2007 "Getting a Job: Is There a Motherhood Penalty?" *American Journal of Sociology* 112(5): 1297–338.

——— 2017 "SWS 2016 Feminist Lecture: Reducing Gender Biases in Modern Workplaces: A Small Wins Approach to Organizational Change." *Gender & Society* 31(6): 725–50.

Correll, Shelley J., Erin L. Kelly, Lindsey Trimble O'Connor, and Joan C. Williams 2014 "Redesigning, Redefining Work." *Work and Occupations* 41(1): 3–17.

Coser, Lewis A. 1967 "Greedy Organisations." *European Journal of Sociology* 8(2).

——— 1971 *Masters of Sociological Thought: Ideas in Historical and Social Context.* New York: Harcourt Brace Jovanovich.

Costas, Jana, and Peter Fleming 2009 "Beyond Dis-identification: A Discursive Approach to Self-Alienation in Contemporary Organizations." *Human Relations* 62(3): 353–78.

Côté, James, and John M. Bynner 2008 "Changes in the Transition to Adulthood in the U.K. and Canada: The Role of Structure and Agency in Emerging Adulthood." *Journal of Youth Studies* 11(3): 251–68.

Coupland, Douglas 1993 *Generation X: Tales for an Accelerated Culture.* New York: St. Martin's Press.

Courpasson, David, and Stewart Clegg 2012 "The Polyarchic Bureaucracy: Cooperative Resistance in the Workplace and the Construction of a New Political Structure of Organizations." *Research in the Sociology of Organizations* 34: 55–79.

**Coverdill, James E., and Pierre Oulevey
2007** "Getting Contingent Work: Insights into On-Call Work, Matching Processes, and Staffing Technology from a Study of Substitute Teachers." *The Sociological Quarterly* 48(3): 533–57.

Cranford, Cynthia J. 2004 "Gendered Resistance: Organizing Justice for Janitors in Los Angeles." In Jim Stanford and Leah F. Vosko, eds., *Challenging the Market: Struggles to Regulate Work and Income.* Montreal: McGill–Queen's University Press.

Cranford, Cynthia, and Dianna Miller 2013 "Emotion Management from the Client's Perspective: The Case of Personal Home Care." *Work Employment and Society* 27(5): 785–801.

Craven, Paul 1980 *An Impartial Umpire: Industrial Relations and the Canadian State, 1900–1911.* Toronto: University of Toronto Press.

Creese, Gillian 1988–89 "Exclusion or Solidarity? Vancouver Workers Confront the Oriental Problem." *B.C. Studies* 80: 24–51.

——— **1999** *Contracting Masculinity: Gender, Class, and Race in a White-Collar Union, 1944–1994.* Don Mills, ON: Oxford University Press.

——— **2007** "Racializing Work/ Reproducing White Privilege." In Vivian Shalla and Wallace Clement, eds., *Work in Tumultuous Times: Critical Perspectives.* Montreal: McGill–Queen's University Press.

**Creese, Gillian, and Edith Ngene Kambere
2003** "What Colour Is Your English?" *Canadian Review of Sociology and Anthropology* 40(5): 565–73.

Crompton, Susan 2011 "What's Stressing the Stressed? Main Sources of Stress among Workers." *Canadian Social Trends* (Winter): 46–53.

**Crompton, Susan, and Michael Vickers
2000** "One Hundred Years of Labour Force." *Canadian Social Trends* (Summer): 2–14.

Crowley, Martha 2016 "Neoliberalism, Managerial Citizenship Behaviors, and Firm Fiscal Performance." *Research in the Sociology of Work* 28: 213–32.

**Crowley, Martha, Daniel Tope, Lindsey Joyce Chamberlain, and Randy Hodson
2010** "Neo-Taylorism at Work: Occupational

Change in the Post-Fordist Era." *Social Problems* 57(3): 421–47.

**Culbert, Samuel A., and Scott J. Schroeder
2003** "Getting Hierarchy to Work." In Subir Chowdhury, ed., *Organization 21C: Someday All Organizations Will Lead This Way.* Upper Saddle River, NJ: Financial Times Prentice Hall.

Cunningham, Ian, and Philip James 2010 "Strategies for Union Renewal in the Context of Public Sector Outsourcing." *Economic and Industrial Democracy* 31(1): 34–61.

Cunningham, Mick 2007 "Influences of Women's Employment on the Gendered Division of Household Labor over the Life Course: Evidence from a 31-Year Panel Study." *Journal of Family Issues* 28(3): 422–44.

Dalton, Melville 1959 *Men Who Manage: Fusions of Feeling and Theory in Administration.* New York: John Wiley & Sons.

Damaske, Sarah 2011 "A 'Major Career Woman'? How Women Develop Early Expectations about Work." *Gender & Society* 25(4): 409–30.

**D'Andreamatteo, Antonio, Luca Ianni, Frederico Lega, and Massimo Sargiacomo
2015** "Lean in Healthcare: A Comprehensive Review." *Health Policy* 119(9): 1197–209.

Danford, Andy, M. Richardson, P. Stewart, S. Tailby, and M. Upchurch 2004 "High Performance Work Systems and Workplace Partnership: A Case Study of Aerospace Workers." *New Technology, Work and Employment* 19(3): 14–29.

Daniels, Arlene Kaplan 1987 "Invisible Work." *Social Problems* 34(5): 403–15.

Das, Subesh 2010 *Managing People at Work: Employment Relations in Globalizing India.* New Delhi: Sage Publications India.

Das Gupta, Tania 1996 *Racism and Paid Work.* Toronto: Garamond Press.

Datta, Deepak K., James P. Guthrie, Dynah Basuil, and Alankrita Pandey 2010 "Causes and Effects of Employee Downsizing: A Review and Synthesis." *Journal of Management* 36(1): 281–348.

Davies, Lorraine, and Patricia J. Carrier 1999 "The Importance of Power Relations for the Division of Household Labour." *Canadian Journal of Sociology* 24(1): 35–51.

Davies, Scott, and Neil Guppy 1998 "Race and Canadian Education." In Vic Satzewich, ed., *Racism and Social Inequality in Canada: Concepts, Controversies and Strategies of Resistance*. Toronto: Thompson Educational Publishing.
———— **2018** *The Schooled Society: An Introduction to the Sociology of Education*. 4th ed. Don Mills, Ontario: Oxford University Press.

Davies, Scott, and Vicky Maldonado 2009 "Changing Times, Stubborn Disparities: Explaining Socio-economic Stratification in Canadian Schooling." In Edward Grabb and Neil Guppy, eds., *Social Inequality in Canada: Patterns, Problems, and Policies*. 5th ed. Toronto: Pearson/Prentice Hall.

Davies, Scott, Vicky Maldonado, and Darren Cyr 2017 "Changing Times, Stubborn Inequalities: Explaining Socioeconomic Stratification in Canadian Schooling" in Edward Grabb, Jeffrey G. Reitz, and Monica Hwang, eds., *Social Inequality in Canada: Dimensions of Disadvantage*. 6th ed. Don Mills, Ontario: Oxford University Press.

Davis, Gerald F. 2010 "Job Design Meets Organizational Sociology." *Journal of Organizational Behavior* 31: 302–8.

Davis, Kelly D., W. Benjamin Goodman, Amy E. Pirretti, and David M. Almeida 2008 "Nonstandard Work Schedules, Perceived Family Well-Being, and Daily Stressors." *Journal of Marriage and Family* 70(4): 991–1003.

Davis, Kingsley, and Wilbert E. Moore 1945 "Some Principles of Stratification." *American Sociological Review* 10: 242–49.

Davis-Blake, Alison, and Joseph P. Broschak 2009 "Outsourcing and the Changing Nature of Work." *The Annual Review of Sociology* 35: 321–40.

D'Cruz, Premilla, and Ernesto Noronha 2011 "High Commitment Management Practices Re-examined: The Case of Indian Call Centres." *Economic and Industrial Democracy* 33(2): 185–205.

de Gilder, Dick 2003 "Commitment, Trust and Work Behaviour: The Case of Contingent Workers." *Personnel Review* 32(5): 588–604.

Dehnen, Veronika 2013 "Transnational Alliances for Negotiating International Framework Agreements: Power Relations and Bargaining Processes between Global Union Federations and European Works Councils." *British Journal of Industrial Relations* 51(3): 577–600.

de Lange, Annet H., Toon W. Taris, Michael A.J. Kompier, Irene L.D. Houtman, and Paulien M. Bongers 2003 "'The *Very* Best of the Millennium': Longitudinal Research and the Demand-Control-(Support) Model." *Journal of Occupational Health Psychology* 8(4): 282–305.

DeLong, David W. 2004 *Lost Knowledge: Confronting the Threat of an Aging Workforce*. New York: Oxford University Press.

Denier, Nicole, and Sean Waite 2017 "Data and Discrimination: A Research Note On Sexual Orientation in the Canadian Labour Market." *Canadian Studies in Population* 43(3–4): 264–71.

Denis, Jeffrey S. 2015 "Contact Theory in a Small Town Settler-Colonial Context: The Reproduction of Laissez-Faire Racism in Indigenous-White Canadian Relations." *American Sociological Review* 80(1): 218–42.

Déom, Esther, Jean-Noël Grenier, and Marie-Pierre Beaumont 2009 "Union–Management Relations in Quebec." In Morley Gunderson and Daphne Taras, eds. *Canadian Labour and Employment Relations*. 6th ed. Toronto: Pearson Addison Wesley.

De Santis, Solange 1999 *Life on the Line: One Woman's Tale of Work, Sweat, and Survival*. New York: Doubleday.

DeSouza, Eros R., Eric D. Wesselmann, and Dan Ispas 2017 "Workplace Discrimination against Sexual Minorities: Subtle and Not-so-subtle." *Canadian Journal of Administrative Sciences* 34(2): 121–32.

Deutsch, Steven 2005 "A Researcher's Guide to Worker Participation, Labor and Economic and Industrial Democracy." *Economic and Industrial Democracy* 26(4): 645–56.

Devane, Tom 2004 *Integrating Lean Six Sigma and High-Performance Organizations: Leading the Charge toward Dramatic, Rapid and Sustainable Improvement*. San Francisco: Pfeiffer.

de Vaus, David, and Ian McAllister 1991 "Gender and Work Orientation: Values and Satisfaction in Western Europe." *Work and Occupations* 18: 72–93.

Devinatz, Victor G. 2013 "The Crisis of U.S. Trade Unionism and What Needs to Be Done." *Labor Law Journal* 64(1): 5–19.

De Witte, Hans, and Katharina Näswall 2003 "'Objective' vs 'Subjective' Job Insecurity: Consequences of Temporary Work for Job Satisfaction and Organizational Commitment in Four European Countries." *Economic and Industrial Democracy* 24(2): 149–88.

Dickson, Tony, and Hugh V. McLachlan 1989 "In Search of the Spirit of Capitalism: Weber's Misinterpretation of Franklin." *Sociology* 23: 81–89.

Dickson, Tony, Hugh V. McLachlan, Phil Prior, and Kim Swales 1988 "Big Blue and the Unions: IBM, Individualism and Trade Union Strategy." *Work, Employment and Society* 2: 506–20.

di Leonardo, Micaela 1987 "The Female World of Cards and Holidays: Women, Families, and the Work of Kinship." *Signs* 12(3): 440–53.

DiPietro, Robin B., and Abraham Pizam 2008 "Employee Alienation in the Quick Service Restaurant Industry." *Journal of Hospitality and Tourism Research* 32(1): 22–39.

Dirlam, Jonathan, and Hui Zheng 2017 "Job Satisfaction Developmental Trajectories and Health: A Life Course Perspective." *Social Science and Medicine* 178: 95–103.

Dixon, Marc 2008 "Movements, Countermovements and Policy Adoption: The Case of Right-to-Work Activism." *Social Forces* 87(1): 473–500.

Dobbin, Frank, and Alexandra Kalev 2017 "Are Diversity Programs Merely Ceremonial? Evidence-Free Institutionalization." In Royston Greenwood, Christine Oliver, Thomas Lawrence, and Renate Meyer, eds., *The SAGE Handbook of Organizational Institutionalism*. 2nd ed. London: Sage Publications.

Dolton, Peter, and Panu Pelkonen 2008 "The Wage Effects of Computer Use: Evidence from WERS 2004." *British Journal of Industrial Relations* 46(4): 587–630.

Domina, Thurston, Andrew Penner, and Emily Penner 2017 "Categorical Inequality: Schools as Sorting Machines." *Annual Review of Sociology* 43: 311–30.

Dorow, Sara, and Sara O'Shaughnessy 2013 "Fort McMurray, Wood Buffalo and the Oil/Tar Sands: Revising the Sociology of Community. Introduction to the Special Issue." *Canadian Journal of Sociology* 38(2): 121–40.

Doucet, Andrea 2001 "You See the Need Perhaps More Clearly Than I Have: Exploring Gendered Processes of Domestic Responsibility." *Journal of Family Issues* 22(3): 328–57.

———— **2018** *Do Men Mother? Fathering, Care and Domestic Responsibility.* 2nd ed. Toronto: University of Toronto Press.

Doucouliagos, Chris 1995 "Worker Participation and Productivity in Labor-Managed and Participatory Capitalist Firms: A Meta-analysis." *Industrial and Labor Relations Review* 49(1): 58–77.

Downie, Bryan, and Mary L. Coates 1995 "Barriers, Challenges, and Future Directions." In Bryan Downie and Mary L. Coates, eds., *Managing Human Resources in the 1990s and Beyond: Is the Workplace Being Transformed?* Kingston, ON: IRC Press.

Drache, Daniel 1994 "Lean Production in Japanese Auto Transplants in Canada." *Canadian Business Economics* (Spring): 45–59.

Drache, Daniel, and Meric S. Gertler 1991 "The World Economy and the Nation-State: The New International Order." In D. Drache and M. S. Gertler, eds., *The New Era of Global Competition: State Policy and Market Power*. Montreal: McGill–Queen's University Press.

Drolet, Marie 2011 "Why Has the Gender Wage Gap Narrowed?" *Perspectives on Labour and Income* (Spring): 3–13.

Drucker, Peter F. 1993 *Post-capitalist Society.* New York: HarperBusiness.

Drudy, Sheelagh 2008 "Gender Balance/Gender Bias: The Teaching Profession and the Impact of Feminization." *Gender and Education* 20(4): 309–23.

Dubinsky, K., A. Perry, and H. Yu, eds., 2016 *Within and Without the Nation: Canadian History as Transnational History.* Toronto: University of Toronto Press.

Duffy, Ann, and Norene Pupo 1992 *Part-Time Paradox: Connecting Gender, Work and Family.* Toronto: McClelland & Stewart.

Duffy, Mignon 2011 *Making Care Count: A Century of Gender, Race and Paid Care Work.* New Brunswick, NJ: Rutgers University Press.

duGay, Paul 1996 *Consumption and Identity at Work.* London: Sage Publications

Duncan, Greg J., Aletha C. Huston, and Thomas S. Weisner 2007 *Higher Ground: New Hope for the Working Poor and Their Children.* New York: Russell Sage.

Duncan, Greg J., W. Jean Yeung, Jeanne Brooks-Gunn, and Judith R. Smith 1998 "How Much Does Childhood Poverty Affect the Life Chances of Children?" *American Sociological Review* 63: 406–23.

Dunn, Andrew 2010 "The 'Dole or Drudgery' Dilemma: Education, the Work Ethic and Unemployment." *Social Policy & Administration* 44(1): 1–19.

Dunne, Gillian 1996 *Lesbian Lifestyles: Women's Work and the Politics of Sexuality.* Toronto: University of Toronto Press.

Durkheim, Émile 1960 *The Division of Labour in Society.* New York: Free Press. (Orig. pub. 1897.)

Duxbury, Linda 2004 *Dealing with Work-Life Issues in the Workplace: Standing Still is Not an Option.* Don Wood Lecture in Industrial Relations, Queen's University. http://irc. queensu.ca/gallery/1/dwls-linda-duxbury -on-work-life-conflict.pdf.

Duxbury, Linda, and Christopher Higgins 2001 *Work–Life Balance in the New Millennium.* Ottawa: Canadian Policy Research Networks.

——— **2012** *Key Findings: Revisiting Work–Life Issues in Canada—The 2011–12 National Study on Balancing Work and Caregiving in Canada.* http://newsroom.carleton.ca/ wp-content/files/2012-National-Work-Key-Findings.pdf.

——— **2018** *Something's Got to Give: Balancing Work, Childcare and Eldercare.* Toronto: University of Toronto Press.

Easterlin, Richard 1980 *Birth and Fortune: The Impact of Numbers on Personal Welfare.* New York: Basic Books.

Eaton, Adrienne E., and Thomas Nocerino 2000 "The Effectiveness of Health and Safety Committees: Results of a Survey of Public-Sector Workplaces." *Industrial Relations: A Journal of Economy and Society* 39: 265–90.

Economic Council of Canada 1990 *Good Jobs, Bad Jobs: Employment in the Service Economy.* Ottawa: Supply and Services Canada.

——— **1992** *Pulling Together: Productivity, Innovation, and Trade.* Ottawa: Supply and Services Canada.

Economist 2005 "The Tiger in Front—India." March 3, 3–5.

——— **2009** *Country Profiles—China, India, Russia.* Economist Intelligence Unit. http:// www.eiu.com.

——— **2017** "The Retreat of the Global Company." January 28.

——— **2018** "Technology May Help to Revive Organised Labour." *The Economist* (15 November 2018). https://www.economist. com/briefing/2018/11/15/technology-may-help-to-revive-organised-labour?frsc=dg%7Ce [retrieved 4 June 2019].

Edwards, Jeffrey R., and Abbie J. Shipp 2007 "The Relationship between Person-Environment Fit and Outcomes: An Integrative Theoretical Framework." In Cheri Ostrof and Timothy A. Judge, eds., *Perspectives on Organizational Fit.* Milton Park, England: Taylor and Francis.

Edwards, Paul, and Paulina Ramirez 2016 "When Should Workers Embrace or Resist New Technology." *New Technology, Work and Employment* 31(2): 99–113.

Edwards, Richard C. 1979 *Contested Terrain: The Transformation of the Workplace in the Twentieth Century.* New York: Basic Books.

Egels-Zandén, Niklas 2011 "Clean Clothes Campaign." In Thomas Hale and David Held, eds., *Handbook of Transnational Governance: Institutions and Innovations.* Cambridge: Polity Press.

Egels-Zandén, Niklas, and Peter Hyllman 2006 "Exploring the Effects of Union-NGO Relationships on Corporate Responsibility: The Case of the Swedish Clean Clothes Campaign." *Journal of Business Ethics* 64: 303–16.

Ehrenreich, Barbara 2001 *Nickel and Dimed: On (Not) Getting By in America.* New York: Henry Holt and Company.

Ehrenreich, Barbara, and Arlie Russell Hochschild, eds. 2002 *Global Woman:*

Nannies, Maids, and Sex Workers in the New Economy. New York: Metropolitan Books.

Eichler, Margrit, and Patricia Albanese 2007 "What Is Household Work? A Critique of Assumptions Underlying Empirical Studies of Housework and an Alternative Approach." *Canadian Journal of Sociology* 32(2): 227–58.

Elliott, Anthony, and John Urry 2010 *Mobile Lives.* New York: Routledge.

Elmuti, Dean, Julian Grunewald, and Dereje Abebe 2010 "Consequences of Outsourcing Strategies on Employee Quality of Work Life, Attitudes, and Performance." *Journal of Business Strategies* 27(2): 177–203.

Ely, Robin, and Alexandra Feldberg 2018 "Organizational Remedies for Discrimination." In Adrienne J. Colella and Eden B. King, eds., *The Oxford Handbook of Workplace Discrimination.* Oxford: Oxford University Press.

Ely, Robin, Hermina Ibarra, and Deborah Kolk 2013 "Women Rising: The Unseen Barriers." *Harvard Business Review* (September): 61–66.

Employment and Social Development Canada (ESDC) 2015 *Labour Organizations in Canada 2015.* https://www.canada.ca/en/employment-social-development/services/collective-bargaining-data/labour-organizations.html [retrieved 10 May 2019].

Employment and Social Development Canada (ESDC) 2016 *Flexible Work Arrangements: A Discussion Paper.* http://www12.esdc.gc.ca/sgpe-pmps/servlet/sgpp-pmps-pub?lang=eng&curjsp=p.5bd.2t.1.3ls@-eng.jsp&curactn=dwnld&pid=49878&did=4771.

Engels, Friedrich 1971 *The Condition of the Working Class in England.* Oxford: Basil Blackwell. (Orig. pub. 1845.)

Engineers Canada 2012 *Canadian Engineers for Tomorrow: Trends in Engineering Enrollment and Degrees Awarded, 2007–11.* Ottawa: Engineers Canada.

England, Paula 2010 "The Gender Revolution: Uneven and Stalled." *Gender & Society* 24(2): 149–66.

England, Paula, Jonathon Bearak, Michelle J. Budig, and Melissa Hodges 2016 "Do Highly Paid, Highly Skilled Women Experience the Largest Motherhood Penalty?" *American Sociological Review* 81(6): 1161–89.

Equal Pay Coalition 2008 *A Framework for Action on Pay Equity in Ontario: A Special 20th Anniversary Report Contributing to Ontario's Future.* Toronto: Equal Pay Coalition.

Ergeneli, Azize, Arzu Ilsev, and Pinar Bayhan Karapinar 2010 "Work–Family Conflict and Job Satisfaction Relationship: The Roles of Gender and Interpretive Habits." *Gender, Work and Organization* 17(6): 679–95.

Estrin, Saul, and Virginie Pérotin 1987 "Producer Cooperatives: The British Experience." *International Review of Applied Economics* 1(2): 152–75.

Etzioni, Amitai 1975 *A Comparative Analysis of Complex Organizations.* 2nd ed. New York: Free Press.

Evans, Peter, and James E. Rauch 1999 "Bureaucracy and Growth: A Cross-National Analysis of the Efforts of 'Weberian' State Structures on Economic Growth." *American Sociological Review* 64: 748–65.

Everett, Jeffery 2002 "Organizational Research and the Praxeology of Pierre Bourdieu." *Organizational Research Methods* 5: 56–80.

Evetts, Julia 2003 "The Sociological Analysis of Professionalism: Occupational Change in the Modern World." *International Sociology* 18(2): 395–415.

Ezzedeen, Souha R. 2015 "Portrayals of Career Women in Hollywood Films: Implications for the Glass Ceiling's Persistence." *Gender in Management: An International Journal* 30(3): 239–64.

Faas, Caitlin, Mark J. Benson, and Christine E. Kaestle 2013 "Parent Resources during Adolescence: Effects on Education and Careers in Young Adulthood." *Journal of Youth Studies* 16(2): 151–71.

Feldberg, Roslyn, and Evelyn Nakano Glenn 1979 "Male and Female: Job versus Gender Models in the Sociology of Work." *Social Problems* 26: 524–38.

Feldheim, Mary Ann 2007 "Public Sector Downsizing and Employee Trust." *International Journal of Public Administration* 30(3): 249–70.

Felstead, Alan, Nick Jewson, and Sally Walters 2003 "Managerial Control of Employees Working at Home." *British Journal of Industrial Relations* 41(2): 241–64.

Feng, Wang 2008 *Boundaries and Categories: Rising Inequality in Post-socialist Urban China.* Redwood City, CA: Stanford University Press.

Fernandez-Mateo, Isabel 2009 "Cumulative Gender Disadvantage in Contract Employment." *American Journal of Sociology* 114(1): 871–923.

Fernie, Sue, and David Metcalf 1998 *(Not) Hanging on the Telephone: Payment Systems in the New Sweatshop.* London, England: Centre for Economic Performance, London School of Economics.

Ferus-Comelo, Anibel 2008 "Mission Impossible? Raising Labor Standards in the ICT Sector." *Labor Studies Journal* 33(2): 141–62.

Feuchtwang, Stephen 1982 "Occupational Ghettos." *Economy and Society* 11: 251–91.

Fevre, Ralph 2007 "Employment Insecurity and Social Theory: The Power of Nightmares." *Work, Employment and Society* 21(3): 517–35.

Fields, A., Uppal, S., and LaRochelle-Côté, S. 2017 "The Impact of Aging on Labour Market Participation Rates." Insights on Canadian Society. Ottawa: Statistics Canada. Cat. no. 75-006-X.

Fife, Robert, and Eric Atkins 2018 "General Motors to Shut Down Oshawa Plant in Global Restructuring." *Globe and Mail Report on Business.* November 26. https://www.theglobeandmail.com/business/article-general-motors-to-shut-down-oshawa-plant-sources-say/ [retrieved 25 March 2019].

Findlay, Patricia, Chris Warhurst, Ewart Keep, and Caroline Lloyd 2017 "Opportunity Knocks? The Possibilities and Levers for Improving Job Quality." *Work and Occupations* 44(1): 3–22.

Fine, Janice 2015 "Alternative Labour Protection Movements in the United States: Reshaping Industrial Relations?" *International Labour Review* 154(1): 15–26.

Fineman, Stephen 2009 "'When I'm Sixty Five': The Shaping and Shapers of Retirement Identity and Experience." In Philip Hancock and Melissa Tyler, eds., *The Management of Everyday Life.* New York: Palgrave Macmillan.

Finkel, Alvin 2019 "Our Almost-Revolution: The Centennial of Alberta's Workers' Uprising." *Alberta Views* 22(5): 30–33.

Finnie, Ross 2016 "Barista or Better? Where Post-secondary Education Will Take You."

Policy Magazine September/October: 47–50. http://www.policymagazine.ca/pdf/21/PolicyMagazineSeptemberOctober-2016-Finnie.pdf [retrieved 9 January 2019].

Finnie, Ross Marc Frenette, Richard E. Mueller, and Arthur Sweetman, eds. 2010 *Pursuing Higher Education in Canada: Economic, Social and Policy Dimensions.* Montreal: McGill-Queen's University Press.

——— **2018** "Information and Communication Technology Talent: The Skills We Need—Framing the Issues." *Canadian Public Policy* 44(S1): Siii–Six.

Finnigan, Ryan, and Jo Mhairi Hale 2018 "Working 9 to 5? Union Membership and Work Hours and Schedules." *Social Forces* 96(4): 1541–68.

Firebaugh, Glenn, and Brian Harley 1995 "Trends in Job Satisfaction in the United States by Race, Gender, and Type of Occupation." *Research in Sociology of Work* 5: 87–104.

Fisher, Cynthia D. 2003 "Why Do Lay People Believe That Satisfaction and Performance Are Correlated? Possible Sources of a Commonsense Theory." *Journal of Organizational Behavior* 24(6): 753–77.

Fisher, Susan R., and Margaret A. White 2000 "Downsizing in a Learning Organization: Are There Hidden Costs?" *Academy of Management Review* 25(1): 244–51.

Flecha, Ramon, and Pun Ngai 2014 "The Challenge for Mondragon: Searching for the Cooperative Values in Times of Internationalization." *Organization* 21(5): 666–82.

Fleming, Peter, and Andrew Sturdy 2011 "'Being Yourself' in the Electronic Sweatshop: New Forms of Normative Control." *Human Relations* 64(2): 177–200.

Fleury, Dominique 2008 "Low-Income Children." *Perspectives on Labour and Income* 20(Summer): 51–60.

Florida, Richard 2002 *The Rise of the Creative Class: And How It's Transforming Work, Leisure, Community and Everyday Life.* New York: Basic Books.

——— **2005** *The Flight of the Creative Class: The New Global Competition for Talent.* New York: HarperCollins.

Foot, David K., and Daniel Stoffman 2001 *Boom, Bust & Echo 2000: Profiting from the Demographic Shift in the 21st Century.* Toronto: Stoddart Publishing.

Foot, David, Keith Ambachtsheer, Don Drummond, and Louise Theriault 2015 "Four Experts on Where Aging in Canada Is Headed." *Globe and Mail*, November 13.

***Forbes* Magazine 2013** "The World's Billionaires." http://www.forbes.com/billionaires/.

Forcadell, Francisco Javier 2005 "Democracy, Cooperation and Business Success: The Case of Mondragon Corporacion Cooperativa." *Journal of Business Ethics* 56(3): 255–74.

Forget, Evelyn L. 2011 "The Town with No Poverty: The Health Effects of a Canadian Guaranteed Annual Income Field Experiment." *Canadian Public Policy* 37(3): 283–305.

Forrest, Anne 2000 "Pay Equity: The State of the Debate." In Yonatan Reshef, Colette Bernier, Denis Harrison, and Terry H. Wagar, eds., *Industrial Relations in a New Millennium.* Selected Papers from the 37th Annual Canadian Industrial Relations Association Conference, May 25–27, 2000, Edmonton, Alberta.

Forsberg, Aaron 2000 *America and the Japanese Miracle: The Cold War Context of Japan's Postwar Economic Revival, 1950–1960.* Chapel Hill: University of North Carolina Press.

Fortin, Pierre 1996 "The Unbearable Lightness of Zero-Inflation Optimism." In Brian K. MacLean and Lars Osberg, eds., *The Unemployment Crisis: All for Nought?* Montreal: McGill–Queen's University Press.

Foster, Jason 2012 "Making Temporary Permanent: The Silent Transformation of the Temporary Foreign Worker Program." *Just Labour* 19(Fall): 22–46.

———— **2014** "From 'Canadians First' to 'Workers Unite': Evolving Union Narratives of Migrant Workers." *Relations Industrielles/Industrial Relations* 69(2): 241–65.

Foster, Jason, and Bob Barnetson 2012 "Justice for Janitors in Alberta: The Impact of Temporary Foreign Workers on an Organizing Campaign." *Journal of Workplace Rights* 16(1): 3–29.

———— **2016** *Health and Safety in Canadian Workplaces.* Edmonton: Athabasca University Press.

Foster, Jason, Alison Taylor, and Candy Khan 2015 "The Dynamics of Union Responses to Migrant Workers in Canada." *Work, Employment and Society* 29(3): 409–26.

Foucault, Michel 1977 *Discipline and Punish: The Birth of the Prison.* Harmondsworth, England: Penguin.

Fox, Bonnie 1997 "Reproducing Differences: Changes in the Lives of Partners Becoming Parents." In Meg Luxton, ed., *Feminism and Families.* Halifax: Fernwood Publishing.

Fox, Bonnie, and Pamela Sugiman 1999 "Flexible Work, Flexible Workers: The Restructuring of Clerical Work in a Large Telecommunications Company." *Studies in Political Economy* 60(Autumn): 59–84.

Fox, Dan, and Melissa Moyser 2018 "The Economic Well-Being of Women in Canada" in *Women in Canada: A Gender-Based Statistical Report.* Ottawa: Statistics Canada. Cat. no. 89-503-X.

Fox, Elizabeth R., Gillian Pascall, and T. Warren 2009 "Work–Family Policies, Participation and Practices: Fathers and Childcare in Europe." *Community, Work & Family* 12(3): 313–26.

Frager, Ruth A. 1992 *Sweatshop Strife: Class, Ethnicity, and Gender in the Jewish Labour Movement of Toronto 1900–1939.* Toronto: University of Toronto Press.

Franco, Lucas A. 2019 "Organizing the Precariat: The Fight to Building and Sustain Fast Food Worker Power" *Critical Sociology* 45(4–5): 517–31.

Frangi, Lorenzo, and Marc-Antonin Hennebert 2015 "Expressing Confidence in Unions in Quebec and the Other Canadian Provinces: Similarities and Contrasts in Findings." *Relations Industrielles/Industrial Relations* 70(1): 131–56.

Frankopan, Peter 2019 *The New Silk Roads: The Present and Future of the World.* New York: Alfred A. Knopf.

Fraser, Nancy 1997 "After the Family Wage: A Post-Industrial Thought Experiment." In Nancy Fraser, *Justice Interruptus: Critical Reflections on the "Postsocialist" Condition.* New York: Routledge.

Frazier, Latoya Ruby, and Daniel Kaufman 2019 "The End of the Line." *New York Times Magazine.* https://www.nytimes.com/interactive/2019/05/01/magazine/

lordstown-general-motors-plant.html [retrieved May 4, 2019].

Freeman 2018 "Ben Barres: Neuroscience Pioneer, Gender Champion." *Nature* 562: 492.

Freeman, Richard B. 1995 "The Future for Unions in Decentralized Collective Bargaining Systems: U.S. and U.K. Unionism in an Era of Crisis." *British Journal of Industrial Relations* 33: 519–36.

Freeman, Richard B., and J. L. Medoff 1984 *What Do Unions Do?* New York: Basic Books.

Frege, Carola 2005 "The Discourse of Industrial Democracy: Germany and the U.S. Revisited." *Economic and Industrial Democracy* 26(1): 151–75.

Frenette, Marc 2001 "Overqualified? Recent Graduates, Employer Needs." *Perspectives on Labour and Income* 13(Spring): 45–53.

——— **2007a** *Why Are Youth from Lower-Income Families Less Likely to Attend University?* Analytical Studies Branch Research Paper No. 295. Ottawa: Statistics Canada.

——— **2007b** "Life after High Tech." *Perspectives on Labour and Income* 19(3): 21–29.

——— **2017** "Postsecondary Enrolment by Parental Income: Recent National and Provincial Trends." *Economic Insights.* Ottawa: Statistics Canada. Catalogue no. 11-626-X-No. 070.

Frenkel, Stephen J., Marek Korczynski, Karen A. Shire, and May Tam 1999 *On the Front Line: Organization of Work in the Information Economy.* Ithaca, NY: ILR Press.

Frey, Carl Benedikt 2019 *The Technology Trap: Capital, Labor, and Power in the Age of Automation.* Princeton, NJ: Princeton University Press.

Frey, Carl Benedict, and Michael A. Osborne 2017 "The Future of Employment: How Susceptible are Jobs to Computerization." *Technological Forecasting & Social Change* 114: 254–80.

Friedman, Andrew L. 1977 *Industry and Labour: Class Struggle at Work and Monopoly Capitalism.* London: Macmillan.

Friedman, Thomas L. 2000 *The Lexus and the Olive Tree.* New York: Anchor Books.

——— **2005** *The World Is Flat: A Brief History of the 21st Century.* New York: Farrar, Strauss, Giroux.

Friendly, Martha, and Jane Beach 2005 *Early Childhood Education and Care in Canada 2004.* Toronto: Childcare Resource and Research Unit, University of Toronto.

Friendly, Martha, Shani Halfon, Jane Beach, and Barry Forer 2013 *Early Childhood Education and Care in Canada 2012.* Toronto: Childcare Research and Resource Unit.

Fudge, Judy 2017 "The Future of the Standard Employment Relationship: Labour Law, New Institutional Economics and Old Power Resource Theory." *Journal of Industrial Relations* 59(3): 374–92.

Fudge, Judy, and Fiona MacPhail 2009 "The Temporary Foreign Worker Program in Canada: Low-Skilled Workers as an Extreme Form of Flexible Labour." *Comparative Labor Law and Policy Journal* 31: 101–39.

Fudge, Judy, and Rosemary Owens, eds. 2006 *Precarious Work, Women and the New Economy: The Challenge to Legal Norms.* Oxford, England: Hart Publishing.

Fudge, Judy, and Kenda Strauss, eds. 2014 *Temporary Work, Agencies and Unfree Labour: Insecurity in the New World of Work.* London: Routledge.

Fuller, Linda, and Vicki, Smith 1991 "Consumers' Reports: Management by Customers in a Changing Economy." *Work, Employment and Society* 5: 1–16.

Fuller, Sylvia 2008 "Job Mobility and Wage Trajectories for Men and Women in the United States." *American Sociological Review* 73: 158–83.

——— **2011** Up and On or Down and Out? Gender, Immigration and the Consequences of Temporary Employment in Canada. *Research in Social Stratification and Mobility* 29(2): 155–80.

Fuller, Sylvia, and Todd F. Martin 2012 "Predicting Immigrant Employment Sequences in the First Years of Settlement." *International Migration Review* 46(1): 138–90.

Fuller, Sylvia, and Natasha Stecy-Hildebrandt 2014 "Lasting Disadvantage? Comparing Career Trajectories of Matched Temporary and Permanent Workers in Canada." *Canadian Review of Sociology* 51(4): 293–324.

——— **2015** "Career Pathways for Temporary Workers: Exploring Heterogeneous Mobility Dynamics with Sequence Analysis." *Social Science Research* 50: 76–99.

Fuller, Sylvia, and Leah F. Vosko 2008
"Temporary Employment and Social Inequality in Canada: Exploring Intersections of Gender, Race and Immigration Status." *Social Indicators Research* 88: 31–50.

Gabriel, Yiannis, David E. Gray, and Harshita Goregaokar 2013 "Job Loss and Its Aftermath among Managers and Professionals: Wounded, Fragmented and Flexible." *Work, Employment and Society* 27(1): 56–72.

Galarneau, Diane 2005 "Earnings of Temporary versus Permanent Employees." *Perspectives on Labour and Income* 17(Spring): 40–53.

———— **2010** "Temporary Employment in the Downturn." *Perspectives on Labour and Income* (November): 5–17.

Galarneau, Diane, and René Morissette 2009 "Immigrants' Education and Required Job Skills." *Perspectives on Labour and Income* 21(1): 5–18.

Galarneau, Diane, and Marian Radulescu 2009. "Employment among the Disabled." *Perspectives on Labour and Income* 21(2): 31–41.

Galarneau, Diane, and Thao Sohn 2013 "Long Term Trends in Unionization." *Insights on Canadian Society*. Ottawa: Statistics Canada. Cat. no. 75-006-X.

Gallie, Duncan 1978 *In Search of the New Working Class: Automation and Social Integration within the Capitalist Enterprise.* Cambridge: Cambridge University Press.

———— **2013** "Direct Participation and the Quality of Work." *Human Relations* 66(4): 453–73.

Gallie, Duncan, Alan Felstead, and Francis Green 2012 "Job Preferences and the Intrinsic Quality of Work: The Changing Attitudes of British Employees 1992–2006." *Work, Employment and Society* 26(5): 806–21.

Gallie, Duncan, Alan Felstead, Francis Green, and Hande Inanc 2017 "The Hidden Face of Job Insecurity." *Work, Employment and Society*, 31(1): 36–53.

Gandolfi, Franco 2009 "Executing Downsizing: The Experiences of Executioners." *Contemporary Management Research* 5(2): 185–200.

Gannagé, Charlene 1995 "Union Women in the Garment Industry Respond to New Managerial Strategies." *Canadian Journal of Sociology* 20(4): 469–95.

Ganster, Daniel C., Christa E. Kiersch, Rachel E. Marsh, and Angela Bowen 2011 "Performance-Based Rewards and Work Stress." *Journal of Occupational Behavior and Management* 31: 221–35.

Gardell, B. 1977 "Autonomy and Participation at Work." *Human Relations* 30: 515–33.

Garver, Paul, Kirill Buketov, Hyewon Chong, and Beatriz Sosa Martinez 2007 "Global Labor Organizing in Theory and Practice." *Labor Studies Journal* 32(3): 237–56.

Garvin, David A. 2000 *Learning in Action: A Guide to Putting the Learning Organization to Work.* Boston: Harvard Business School Press.

Gazso, Amber 2007 "Balancing Expectations for Employability and Family Responsibilities While on Social Assistance: Low-Income Mothers' Experiences in Three Canadian Provinces." *Family Relations* 56(5): 454–66.

———— **2012** "Moral Codes of Mothering and the Introduction of Welfare-to-Work in Ontario." *Canadian Review of Sociology* 49(1): 26–49.

Gazso, Amber, and Harvey Krahn 2008 "Out of Step or Leading the Parade? Public Opinion about Income Support Policy in Alberta, 1995 and 2004." *Journal of Canadian Studies* 42(1): 154–78.

Gephart, Martha A., Victoria J. Marsick, Mark E. Van Buren, and Michelle S. Spiro 1996 "Learning Organizations Come Alive." *Training & Development* (December): 35–45.

Gera, Surendra, ed. 1991 *Canadian Unemployment: Lessons from the 80s and Challenges for the 90s.* Ottawa: Economic Council of Canada.

Gerber, Theodore P., and Michael Hout 1998 "More Shock Than Therapy: Market Transition, Employment, and Income in Russia, 1991–1995." *American Journal of Sociology* 104(1): 1–50.

Gherardi, Silvia 1999 "Learning as Problem-Driven or Learning in the Face of Mystery?" *Organization Studies* 20(1): 101–23.

Gilks, Jaclyn, and Ron Logan 2010 *Occupational Injuries and Diseases in Canada, 1996–2008: Injury Rates and Cost to the Economy.* Ottawa: Human Resources and Skill Development Canada. http://publications.gc.ca/collections/collection_2011/rhdcc-hrsdc/HS21-4-2008-eng.pdf [retrieved 29 March 2019].

Gillespie, Richard 1991 *Manufacturing Knowledge: A History of the Hawthorne Experiments.* New York: Cambridge University Press.

Gindin, Sam 1995 *The Canadian Auto Workers: The Birth and Transformation of a Union.* Toronto: James Lorimer.

Gioia, Ted 2006 *Work Songs.* Durham and London: Duke University Press.

Gjerustad, Cay, and Tilmann von Soest 2012 "Socio-Economic Status and Mental Health—The Importance of Achieving Occupational Aspirations." *Journal of Youth Studies* 15: 890–908.

Glauber, Rebecca 2012 "Women's Work and Working Conditions: Are Mothers Compensated for Lost Wages?" *Work and Occupations* 39(2): 115–38.

Globe and Mail 2018 "How Much Are Canada's Top CEOs Paid?" *Globe and Mail,* June 21.

———— 2019 "What Can Canada Accomplish in the Next Century?" *Globe and Mail,* March 5.

Godard, John 1994 *Industrial Relations: The Economy and Society.* Toronto: McGraw-Hill Ryerson.

———— 1997 "Managerial Strategies, Labour and Employment Relations and the State: The Canadian Case and Beyond." *British Journal of Industrial Relations* 35(3): 399–426.

———— 2001 "Beyond the High Performance Paradigm? An Analysis of Variation in Canadian Managerial Perceptions of Reform Programme Effectiveness." *British Journal of Industrial Relations* 39(1): 25–52.

———— 2004 "A Critical Assessment of the High-Performance Paradigm." *British Journal of Industrial Relations* 42(2): 349–78.

Gold, Michael 2018 "The ABCs of LGBTQIA+." *The New York Times,* June 21.

Goldfield, Michael, and Amy Bromsen 2013 "The Changing Landscape of U.S. Unions in Historical and Theoretical Perspective." *Annual Review of Political Science* 16: 231–57.

Goldin, Claudia 2014 "AEA President Address: A Grand Gender Convergence: Its Last Chapter." *American Economic Review* 104 (March): 1–30.

Goldin, Claudia, and Cecilia Rouse 2000 "Orchestrating Impartiality: The Impact of 'Blind' Auditions on Female Musicians." *American Economic Review* (September): 715–41.

Goldrick-Rab, Sara 2006 "Following Their Every Move: An Investigation of Social Class Differences in College Pathways." *Sociology of Education* 79(1): 61–79.

Goldstein, Adam 2012 "Revenge of the Managers: Labor Cost-Cutting and the Paradoxical Resurgence of Managerialism in the Shareholder Value Era, 1984 to 2001." *American Sociological Review* 77(2): 268–94.

Gomez, Rafael, and David Foot 2013 "The Destiny of Demographic Change." *Policy Options* (April–May): 55–7.

Gordon, Brett R. 1994 "Employee Involvement in the Enforcement of the Occupational Safety and Health Laws of Canada and the United States." *Comparative Labor Law and Policy Journal* 15: 527–60.

Gordon, Catherine E. 2014 "Flexible Workplace Practices: Employees' Experiences in Small IT Firms." Relations Industrielles 69(4): 766–84.

Gordon, David M., R. Edwards, and M. Reich 1982 *Segmented Work, Divided Workers: The Historical Transformation of Labor in the United States.* New York: Cambridge University Press.

Gorman, Elizabeth, and Julie A. Kmec 2009 "Hierarchical Rank and Women's Organizational Mobility: Glass Ceilings in Corporate Law Firms." *American Journal of Sociology* 114(5): 1428–74.

Gorz, Andre 1982 *Farewell to the Working Class: An Essay on Post-industrial Socialism.* London, England: Pluto Press.

———— 1999 *Reclaiming Work: Beyond the Wage-Based Society.* Malden, MA: Polity Press.

Gottfried, Heidi, and Nagia Hayashi-Kato 1998 "Gendering Work: Deconstructing the Narrative of the Japanese Economic Miracle." *Work, Employment and Society* 12(1): 25–46.

Goutor, D. 2011 *Guarding the Gates: The Canadian Labour Movement and Immigration, 1887–1934.* Vancouver: UBC Press.

Goyder, John, and Kristyn Frank 2007 "A Scale of Occupational Prestige in Canada, Based on NOC Major Groups." *Canadian Journal of Sociology* 32(1): 63–83.

Grabb, Edward G. 2002 *Theories of Social Inequality.* 4th ed. Toronto: Harcourt Canada.

———— 2009 "Corporate Concentration, Foreign Ownership, and State Involvement in the Canadian Economy." In Edward Grabb and Neil Guppy, eds., *Social Inequality in Canada: Patterns, Problems, and Policies.* 5th ed. Toronto: Pearson/Prentice Hall.

Grabb, Edward, Jeffrey G. Reitz, and Monica Hwang 2017 *Social Inequality in Canada: Dimensions of Disadvantage.* 6th ed. Don Mills, ON: Oxford University Press.

Graham, Hilary 1991 "The Concept of Caring in Feminist Research: The Case of Domestic Service." *Sociology* 25(1): 25–61.

Graham, Laurie 1995 *On the Line at Subaru–Isuzu: The Japanese Model and the American Worker.* Ithaca, NY: ILR Press.

Grandey, Alicia, James Diefendorff, and Deborah Rupp 2013 *Emotional Labor in the 21st Century: Diverse Perspectives on the Psychology of Emotion Regulation at Work.* New York: Routledge.

Graney, Emma 2019 "UCP Labour Bill Cuts Minimum Wage for Minors, Brings Back Union Secret Ballots." *Edmonton Journal,* May 27. https://edmontonjournal.com/news/politics/ucp-to-unveil-labour-law-changes-Monday [retrieved 5 June 2019].

Green, David Alan, William Craig Riddell, and France St-Hilaire 2016 *Income Inequality: The Canadian Story.* Ottawa: Institute for Research on Public Policy.

Green, Archie, ed. 1993 *Songs about Work: Essays in Occupational Culture for Richard A. Reuss.* Bloomington IN: Folklore Institute, Indiana University.

Green, David, Thomas Lemieux, Kevin Milligan, Craig Riddell, and Nicole Fortin 2011 "The Forces That Are Driving Income Inequality." *Vancouver Sun,* December 16, A15.

Green, Francis 2001 "It's Been a Hard Day's Night: The Concentration and Intensification of Work in Late Twentieth-Century Britain." *British Journal of Industrial Relations* 39(1): 53–80.

——— 2006 *Demanding Work: The Paradox of Job Quality in the Affluent Economy.* Princeton, NJ: Princeton University Press.

Green, Francis, and David Ashton 1992 "Skill Shortages and Skill Deficiency: A Critique." *Work, Employment and Society* 6: 287–301.

Green, Francis, and Yu Zhu 2010 "Overqualification, Job Dissatisfaction, and Increasing Dispersion in the Returns to Graduate Education." *Oxford Economic Papers* 62(4): 740–63.

Green, William C., and Ernest J. Yanarella, eds. 1996 *North American Auto Unions in Crisis: Lean Production as Contested Terrain.* Albany, NY: State University of New York Press.

Greenhaus, Jeffrey H., and Nicholas J. Beutell 1985 "Sources of Conflict between Work and Family Roles." *Academy of Management Review* 10(1): 76–88.

Greenhaus, Jeffrey H., and Gary Powell 2006 "When Work and Family Are Allies: A Theory of Work–Family Enrichment." *Academy of Management Review* 31: 72–92.

Greenhouse, Steven 2015 "How Walmart Persuades Its Workers Not to Unionize." *Atlantic,* 8 June. https://www.theatlantic.com/business/archive/2015/06/how-walmart-convinces-its-employees-not-to-unionize/395051/ [retrieved 25 June 2019].

Greenwald, Richard 2015 *The Triangle Fire, The Protocols of Peace, and Industrial Democracy in Progressive Era New York.* Philadelphia: Temple University Press.

Grekou, Douwere, and Huju Liu 2018 *The Entry into and out of Self-Employment and Business Ownership in Canada.* Ottawa: Statistics Canada, Analytical Studies Branch. Catalogue no. 11F0019M-407.

Grenier, S., S. Jones, J. Strucker, T. S. Murray, G. Gervais, and S. Brink 2008 *Learning Literacy in Canada: Evidence from the International Survey of Reading Skills.* Ottawa: Statistics Canada. Cat. no. 89-552-MIE-No. 19.

Grint, K., and D. Nixon 2015 *The Sociology of Work.* 4th ed. Cambridge: Polity Press.

Gross, Dominique M., and Nicolas Schmitt 2012 "Temporary Foreign Workers and Regional Labour Market Disparities in Canada." *Canadian Public Policy* 38(2): 233–63.

Grundy, John, and Debbie Laliberte Rudman 2018 "Deciphering Deservedness: Canadian Employment Insurance Reforms in Historical Perspective." *Social Policy & Administration* 52(3): 809–25.

Gunderson, Morley 1994 *Comparable Worth and Gender Discrimination: An International Perspective.* Geneva: International Labour Office.

——— 1998 "Harmonization of Labour Policies under Trade Liberalization." *Relations Industrielles/Industrial Relations* 53(1): 24–52.

——— 2002. "The Evolution and Mechanics of Pay Equity in Ontario." *Canadian Public Policy/Analyse de Politiques* 28(s1): 117–31.

Gunderson, Morley, and Douglas Hyatt 2009 "Union Impact on Compensation, Productivity, and Management of the Organization." In Morley Gunderson and Daphne Taras, eds., *Canadian Labour and Employment Relations.* Toronto: Pearson Addison Wesley.

Gunderson, Morley, Douglas Hyatt, and Allen Ponak 1995 "Strikes and Dispute Resolution." In Morley Gunderson and Allen Ponak, eds., *Union–Management Relations in Canada.* 3rd ed. Don Mills, ON: Addison-Wesley Publishers.

Gunderson, Morley, Jeffrey Sack, James McCartney, David Wakely, and Jonathan Eaton 1995 "Employee Buyouts in Canada." *British Journal of Industrial Relations* 33: 417–42.

Guppy, Neil, and Nicole Luongo 2015 "The Rise and Stall of Canada's Gender-Equity Revolution." *Canadian Review of Sociology* 52(3): 241–65.

Guppy, Neil, Larissa Sakumoto, and Rima Wilkes 2019 "Social Change and the Gender Division of Labour in Canada." *Canadian Review of Sociology* 56(2): 178–203.

Gupta, Sanjiv 2006 "The Consequences of Maternal Employment during Men's Childhood for Their Adult Housework Performance." *Gender & Society* 20(1): 60–86.

Gupta, Tania Das, Carl E. James, Chris Andersen, Grace-Edward Galabuzi, and Roger C. A. Maaka, eds. 2018 *Race and Racialization: Essential Readings.* Toronto: Canadian Scholars.

Gupta, Tania Das, Guida Man, Kiran Mirchandani, and Roxana Ng 2014 "Class Borders: Chinese and South Asian Canadian Professional Women Navigating the Labor Market." *Asian and Pacific Migration Journal* 23(1): 55–83.

Guthrie, Doug 2006 *China and Globalization: The Social, Economic, and Political Transformation of Chinese Society.* New York: Routledge.

Guzda, Henry P. 1993 "Workplace Partnerships in the United States and Europe." *Monthly Labor Review* (October): 67–72.

Hagan, John, and Fiona Kay 1995 *Gender in Practice: A Study of Lawyers' Lives.* New York: Oxford University Press.

Hakanen, Jari J., Wilmar B. Schaufeli, and Kirsi Ahola 2008 "The Job Demands-Resources Model: A Three-Year Cross-Lagged Study of Burnout, Depression, Commitment, and Work Engagement." *Work & Stress* 22(3): 224–41.

Hakim, Catherine 2000 *Work-Life Choices in the 21st Century: Preference Theory.* Oxford: Oxford University Press.

Hamel, Gary 2007 *The Future of Management.* Boston: Harvard Business School Press.

Hammer, Tove Helland, and Ariel Avgar 2005 "The Impact of Unions on Job Satisfaction, Organizational Commitment, and Turnover." *Journal of Labor Research* 26(2): 241–66.

Hamper, Ben 1986 *Rivethead: Tales from the Assembly Line.* New York: Warner Books.

Hancock, Philip 2009 "Introduction." In Philip Hancock and Melissa Tyler, *The Management of Everyday Life.* Basingstoke, England: Palgrave Macmillan.

Handel, Michael J. 2003 "Skills Mismatch in the Labor Market." *Annual Review of Sociology* 29: 135–65.

Hansen, Jacqueline 2018 "Online Gig Economy is Growing but No One Knows by How Much." *CBC News.* https://www .cbc.ca/news/business/canada-s-digital -workers-1.4889691 [retrieved May 4, 2019].

Hansen, Jonathan P., and James S. Bowman 2016 "Electronic Surveillance at Work: An Ethical Analysis." *Administration & Society* 48(5): 628–51.

Hansen, Ken 2018 "The Problem at the Root of the RCMP's Dysfunctional Culture." *Maclean's,* January 19. https://www.macleans .ca/opinion/the-problem-at-the-root-of- the-rcmps-dysfunctional-culture/ [retrieved 27 January 2019].

Hansen, Susan 2004 "From 'Common Observation' to Behavioural Risk Management: Workplace Surveillance and Employee Assistance 1914–2003." *International Sociology* 19(2): 151–71.

Harley, Bill, Belinda C. Allen, and Leisa D. Sargent 2007 "High Performance Work Systems and Employee Experience of Work in the Service Sector: The Case of Aged Care." *British Journal of Industrial Relations* 45(3): 607–33.

Harmac Pacific 2008 "Employees." https://www.harmacpacific.com/employees.php.

Harrison, Trevor 2005 *The Return of the Trojan Horse: Alberta and the New World (Dis)Order.* Montreal: Black Rose Books.

Hartmann, Heidi 1976 "Capitalism, Patriarchy, and Job Segregation by Sex." *Signs* 1: 137–69.

Hartshorn, Ian M., and Rudra Sil 2019 "The Fate of Labor After Regime Change: Lessons from Post-Communist Poland and Post-Apartheid South Africa for Tunisia's Nobel-Prize Winning Unions." *Economic and Industrial Democracy* 40(1): 20–41.

Harvey, Geraint, Carl Rhodes, Sheena J. Vachhani, and Karen Williams 2017 "Neo-villeiny and the Service Sector: The Case of Hyper Flexible and Precarious Work in Fitness Centres." *Work, Employment and Society* 31(1): 19–35.

Hauser, Robert M., John Robert Warren, Min-Hsiung Huang, and Wendy C. Carter 2000 "Occupational Status, Education, and Social Mobility in the Meritocracy." In Kenneth Arrow, Samuel Bowles, and Steven Durlauf, eds., *Meritocracy and Economic Inequality.* Princeton, NJ: Princeton University Press.

Hausknecht, John P., Nathan J. Hiller, and Robert J. Vance 2008 "Work-Unit Absenteeism: Effects of Satisfaction, Commitment, Labor Market Conditions, and Time." *Academy of Management Journal* 51(6): 1223–45.

Hays, Sharon 1996 *The Cultural Contradictions of Motherhood.* New Haven, CT: Yale University Press.

Hazel, Myrian 2018 "Reasons for Working at 60 and Beyond." *Labour Statistics at a Glance.* Ottawa: Statistics Canada. Cat. no. 71-222-X.

Hearn, Jeff, Deborah L. Sheppard, Peta Tancred-Sheriff, and Gibson Burrell, eds. 1989 *The Sexuality of Organization.* London, England: Sage.

Heinzl, John 1997 "Nike's Hockey Plans Put Bauer on Thin Ice." *Globe and Mail,* July 2, B2.

Heisig, Ulrich 2009 "The Deskilling and Upskilling Debate." In Rupert Maclean and David N. Wilson, eds., *International Handbook of Education for the Changing World of Work.* Dordrecht, Netherlands: Springer.

Heisz, Andrew 2005 "The Evolution of Job Stability in Canada: Trends and Comparisons with U.S. Results." *Canadian Journal of Economics* 38(1): 105–27.

Held, Virginia 2006 *The Ethics of Care: Personal, Political, and Global.* Oxford and New York: Oxford University Press.

Helfen, Markus, and Michael Fichter 2013 "Building Transnational Union Networks across Global Production Networks: Conceptualizing a New Arena of Labour–Management Relations." *British Journal of Industrial Relations* 51(3): 553–76.

Hennebry, J. L., and J. McLaughlin 2012 "'The Exception That Proves the Rule': Structural Vulnerability, Health Risks, and Consequences for Temporary Migrant Farm Workers in Canada." In Patti T. Lenard and Christine Straehle, eds., *Legislated Inequality: Temporary Labour Migration in Canada.* Montreal: McGill-Queen's University Press.

Heron, Craig 2012 *The Canadian Labour Movement: A Short History.* 3rd ed. Toronto: James Lorimer and Company Ltd.

Heron, Craig, and Bryan Palmer 1977 "Through the Prism of the Strike: Industrial Conflict in Southern Ontario, 1910–14." *Canadian Historical Review* 58: 423–58.

Herzberg, Frederick 1966 *Work and the Nature of Man.* New York: World Publishing Co.

Heslin, Peter, Myrtle Bell, and Pinar Fletcher 2012 "The Devil Without and Within: A Conceptual Model of Social Cognitive Processes Whereby Discrimination Leads Stigmatized Minorities to Become Discouraged Workers." *Journal of Organizational Behavior* 33(6): 840–62.

Hessing, Melody 1991 "Talking Shop(ping): Office Conversations and Women's Dual Labour." *Canadian Journal of Sociology* 16: 23–50.

Heyes, Jason, Mark Tomlinson, and Adam Whitworth 2017 "Underemployment and Well-being in the UK Before and After the Great Recession." *Work, Employment and Society* 31(1): 71–89.

High, Steven 1996 "Native Wage Labour and Independent Production During the 'Era of Irrelevance.'" *Labour/Le Travail* 37: 243–64.

———— **2018** *One Job Town: Work, Belonging and Betrayal in Northern Ontario.* Toronto: University of Toronto Press.

Hilbrecht, Margo, Susan Shaw, Laura Johnson, and Jean Andrey 2013 "Remixing Work, Family and Leisure: Teleworkers' Experiences of Everyday Life." *New Technology, Work, and Employment* 28(2): 130–44.

Hilgart, Jeffrey 2013 *Hazard or Hardship: Crafting Global Norms on the Right to Refuse Unsafe Work.* Ithaca, NY: ILR Press.

Hill, Stephen 1988 "Technology and Organizational Culture: The Human Imperative in Integrating New Technology into Organization Design." *Technology in Society* 10: 233–53.

———— **2015** *Raw Deal: How the "Uber" Economy and Runaway Capitalism are Screwing American Workers.* New York: St Martin's Press.

Hilton, Rodney, ed. 1976 *The Transition from Feudalism to Capitalism.* London, England: New Left Books.

Hironimus-Wendt, Robert 2008 "The Human Costs of Worker Displacement." *Humanity and Society* 32(1): 71–93.

Hirschman, A. O. 1970 *Exit, Voice, and Loyalty.* Cambridge, MA: Harvard University Press.

Hirst, Paul, Grahame Thompson, and Simon Bromley 2009 *Globalization in Question.* 3rd ed. Cambridge: Polity Press.

Hjalmarsson, Marie 2009 "New Technology in Home Help Services—A Tool for Support or an Instrument of Subordination?" *Gender, Work & Organization* 16(3): 368–84.

Hochschild, Arlie 1983 *The Managed Heart: The Commercialization of Human Feeling.* Berkeley: University of California Press.

———— **1989** *The Second Shift: Working Parents and the Revolution at Home.* New York: Viking Penguin.

———— **1997** *The Time Bind: When Work Becomes Home and Home Becomes Work.* New York: Henry Holt and Company.

———— **2009** "Through the Crack in the Time Bind: From Market Management to Family Management." In Philip Hancock and Melissa Tyler, eds., *The Management of Everyday Life.* Basingstoke, Hampshire: Palgrave Macmillan.

———— **2012** *The Outsourced Self: Intimate Life in Market Times.* New York: Metropolitan Books.

Hodson, Randy 1996 "Dignity in the Workplace under Participative Management: Alienation and Freedom Revisited." *American Sociological Review* 61: 719–38.

———— **2001** *Dignity at Work.* Cambridge: Cambridge University Press.

———— **2004** "Work Life and Social Fulfillment: Does Social Affiliation at Work Reflect a Carrot or a Stick?" *Social Science Quarterly* 85(2): 221–39.

Hodson, Randy, and Robert L. Kaufman 1982 "Economic Dualism: A Critical Review." *American Sociological Review* 47: 727–39.

Hollister, Matissa 2011 "Employment Stability in the U.S. Labor Market: Rhetoric versus Reality." *Annual Review of Sociology* 37: 305–24.

Holzer, Boris 2000 "Miracles with a System: The Economic Rise of East Asia and the Role of Sociocultural Patterns." *International Sociology* 15(3): 455–78.

Hood, Christopher 2007 "What Happens When Transparency Meets Blame-Avoidance?" *Public Management Review* 9(2): 191–210.

Hook, Jennifer 2006 "Care in Context: Men's Unpaid Work in 20 Countries, 1965–2003." *American Sociological Review* 71(4): 639–60.

Hopkins, Benjamin 2017 "Occupational Health and Safety of Temporary and Agency Workers." *Economic and Industrial Democracy* 38(4): 609–28.

Horne, Rebbeca M., and Rhonda S. Breitkreuz 2018 "The Motherhood Sacrifice: Maternal Experiences of Child Care in the Canadian Context." *Journal of Family Studies* 24(2): 126–45.

Houle, Patricia, Roger Turcotte, and Michael Wendt 2017 *Changes in Parent's Participation in Domestic Tasks and Care for Children, 1986 to 2015.* Ottawa: Statistics Canada. Cat. no. 89-652-X2017001.

House, J. D. 1980 *The Last of the Free Enterprisers: The Oilmen of Calgary.* Toronto: Macmillan.

HRSDC [Human Resources and Skills Development Canada] 2007 *Compassionate Care Leave Provisions in Employment Standards Legislation.* Ottawa: HRSDC. http://www.hrsdc.gc.ca/eng/lp/spila/clli/eslc/Compass.pdf.

———— **2009** *Employment Equity Report 2008.* Ottawa: HRSDC. Cat. no. HS21-1/2008.

———— **2012** *Indicators of Well-Being in Canada: Financial Security—Low Income Incidence.* Ottawa: HRSDC. http://www4.hrsdc.gc.ca/.3ndic.1t.4r@-eng.jsp?iid=23#M_8.

——— 2013 *Aboriginal Labour Market Bulletin.* (Spring). http://www.esdc.gc.ca/eng/jobs/aboriginal/bulletins/spring2013.shtml.

Hsiung, Ping-Chun 1996 *Living Rooms as Factories: Class, Gender, and the Satellite Factory System in Taiwan.* Philadelphia: Temple University Press.

Hu, Min, Angela Daley, and Casey Warman 2019 "Literacy, Numeracy, Technology Skill, and Labour Market Outcomes among Indigenous Peoples in Canada." *Canadian Public Policy* 45(1): 48–73.

Hudson, Kenneth 2007 "The New Labor Market Segmentation: Labor Market Dualism in the New Economy." *Social Science Research* 36(1): 286–312.

Hughes, Karen D. 1995 "Women in Non-traditional Occupations." *Perspectives on Labour and Income* (Autumn): 14–19.

——— **1996** "Transformed by Technology? The Changing Nature of Women's 'Traditional' and 'Non-traditional' White-Collar Work." *Work, Employment and Society* 10: 227–50.

——— **2001** "Restructuring Work, Restructuring Gender: The Movement of Women into Non-traditional Occupations in Canada." In Victor W. Marshall, Walter R. Heinz, Helga Krüger, and Anil Verma, eds., *Restructuring Work and the Life Course.* Toronto: University of Toronto Press.

——— **2005** *Female Enterprise in the New Economy.* Toronto: University of Toronto Press.

——— **2010** "Canadian Women Entrepreneurs." In Sandra Fielden and Marilyn Davidson, eds., *International Research Handbook on Successful Women Entrepreneurs.* Cheltenham, England: Edward Elgar.

——— **2017** *Global Entrepreneurship Monitor (GEM) 2015/16 Canada Report on Women's Entrepreneurship.* University of Calgary: The Centre for Innovation Studies (THECIS).

Hughes, Karen D., and Graham S. Lowe 2000 "Surveying the 'Post-industrial' Landscape: Information Technologies and Labour Market Polarization in Canada." *Canadian Review of Sociology and Anthropology* 37(1): 29–53.

Hughes, Karen D., and J. E. Jennings, eds. 2012 *Global Women's Entrepreneurship: Diverse Settings, Questions, Approaches.* Cheltenham, England: Edward Elgar.

Hughes, Karen D., and Vela Tadic 1998 "'Something to Deal With': Customer Sexual Harassment and Women's Retail Work in Canada." *Gender, Work & Organization* 5(4): 207–19.

Human Resources Development Canada 2000a *Statistical Analysis: Occupational Injuries and Fatalities Canada.* Hull, QC: HRDC.

Humphrey, James H. 1998 *Job Stress.* Boston: Allyn and Bacon.

Hurst, Matt 2008 "Work-Related Training." *Perspectives on Labour and Income* (Summer): 25–31.

Huxley, Christopher 1979 "The State, Collective Bargaining and the Shape of Strikes in Canada." *Canadian Journal of Sociology* 4: 223–39.

Hyman, Richard 1978 *Strikes.* 2nd ed. Glasgow: Fontana.

Iaffaldano, Michelle T., and Paul M. Muchinsky 1985 "Job Satisfaction and Job Performance: A Meta-analysis." *Psychological Bulletin* 97: 251–73.

Ilg, Randy E. 1995 "The Changing Face of Farm Employment." *Monthly Labor Review* (April): 3–12.

Ilies, Remus, Kelly Schwind Wilson, and David T. Wagner 2009 "The Spillover of Daily Job Satisfaction onto Employees' Family Lives: The Facilitating Role of Work–Family Integration." *Academy of Management Journal* 52(1): 87–102.

Ikeler, Peter 2015 "Deskilling Emotional Labour: Evidence from Department Store Retail." *Work, Employment and Society* 30(6): 966–83.

Immen, Wallace 2013 "Students Seek More Fulfilling Jobs in Green Fields." *Globe and Mail*, April 22. http://www.theglobeandmail.com/report-on-business/careers/students-seek-more-fulfilling-jobs-in-green-fields/article11449129/.

Immigration, Refugees and Citizenship Canada (IRCC) 2018 *Annual Report to Parliament on Immigration.* https://www.canada.ca/content/dam/ircc/migration/ircc/english/pdf/pub/annual-report-2018.pdf [retrieved 10 July 2019].

Inanc, Hande 2018 "Unemployment, Temporary Work, and Subjective Well-Being: The Gendered Effect of Spousal Labor Market Insecurity." *American Sociological Review* 83(3): 536–66.

Industry Canada 2012 *Key Small Business Statistics July 2012*. Ottawa: Industry Canada, Small Business Branch. https://www.ic.gc.ca/eic/site/061.nsf/vwapj/KSBS-PSRPE_July-Juillet2012_eng.pdf/$FILE/KSBS-PSRPE_July-Juillet2012_eng.pdf [retrieved 15 December 2018].

Innovation, Science and Economic Development Canada 2018 "Co-operatives in Canada in 2015." https://www.ic.gc.ca/eic/site/106.nsf/eng/h_00151.html.

International Centre for Human Rights and Democratic Development 1997 *Commerce with Conscience? Human Rights and Corporate Codes of Conduct.* Montreal: ICHRDD.

International Labour Office (ILO) 1997 *World Employment Report 1997–98: Industrial Relations, Democracy and Stability.* Geneva: ILO.

Isaksen, Lise Widding, Sambasivan Uma Devi, and Arlie Hochschild 2008 "Global Care Crisis: A Problem of Capital, Care Chain, or Commons?" *American Behavioral Scientist* 52(3): 405–25.

Jackson, Andrew 2005 *Work and Labour in Canada: Critical Issues.* Toronto: Canadian Scholars' Press.

Jackson, Andrew, David Robinson, Bob Baldwin, and Cindy Wiggins 2000 *Falling Behind: The State of Working Canada, 2000.* Ottawa: Canadian Centre for Policy Alternatives.

Jackson, Andrew, and Mark P. Thomas 2017 *Work and Labour in Canada: Critical Issues.* 3rd ed. Toronto: Canadian Scholars.

Jackson, Hanna 2016 "The Census is Back and This Time It's Mandatory." *CBC News.* https://www.cbc.ca/news/politics/mandatory-census-mail-out-1.3557511 [retrieved 9 July 2019].

Jacobs, Jerry, and Kathleen Gerson 2004 *The Time Divide: Work, Family and Gender Inequality.* Cambridge, MA: Harvard University Press.

Jacoby, Sanford M. 1997 *Modern Manors: Welfare Capitalism since the New Deal.* Princeton, NJ: Princeton University Press.

———— **2005** *The Embedded Corporation: Corporate Governance and Employment Relations in Japan and the United States.* Princeton, NJ: Princeton University Press.

Jahoda, M. 1982 *Employment and Unemployment: A Social–Psychological Approach.* Cambridge: Cambridge University Press.

Jain, Hem C. 1990 "Worker Participation in Canada: Current Developments and Challenges." *Economic and Industrial Democracy* 11: 279–90.

Jansen, Giedo, Agnes Akkerman, and Kurt Vandaele 2017 "Undermining Mobilization? The Effect of Job Flexibility and Job Instability on the Willingness to Strike." *Economic and Industrial Democracy* 38(1): 99–117.

Jarman, Jennifer, Robert M. Blackburn, and Girts Racko 2012 "The Dimensions of Occupational Gender Segregation in Industrial Countries." *Sociology* 46(6): 1003–19.

Jenness, Diamond 1977 *Indians of Canada.* 7th ed. Toronto: University of Toronto Press.

Jermier, John M. 1998 "Introduction: Critical Perspectives on Organizational Control." *Administrative Science Quarterly* 43(2): 235–56.

Jha, Prem Shankar 2002 *The Perilous Road to the Market: The Political Economy of Reform in Russia, India and China.* London: Pluto Press.

Jiang, Shanhe, Richard H. Hall, Karyn L. Loscocco, and John Allen 1995 "Job Satisfaction Theories and Job Satisfaction: A China and U.S. Comparison." *Research in the Sociology of Work* 5: 161–78.

Jin, Jane 2008 "Trends in Employment and Wages, 2002 to 2007." *Perspectives on Labour and Income* 20(Winter): 5–15.

Johnson, Holly 1994 "Work-Related Sexual Harassment." *Perspectives on Labour and Income* (Winter): 9–12.

Johnson, Monica K., and Jeylan T. Mortimer 2011 "Origins and Outcomes of Judgments about Work." *Social Forces* 89(4): 1239–60.

Johnson, Monica K., Rayna A. Sage, and Jeylan T. Mortimer 2012 "Work Values, Early Career Difficulties, and the U.S. Economic Recession." *Social Psychology Quarterly* 75: 242–67.

Johnston, David W., and Wang-Sheng Lee 2013 "Extra Status and Extra Stress: Are Promotions Good for Us?" *Industrial and Labor Relations Review* 66(1): 32–64.

Johnston, Matthew S., Matthew D. Sanscartier, and Genevieve Johnston 2018 "Dirty Work, Dirty Resistance: Digital Warfare in the Era of Precarious Work." *Canadian Review of Sociology* 55(2): 278–97.

Jokinen, Tom 2019 "The Art of the Strike." *The Walrus* 16(5): 42–45.

Jones, Bryn 1996 "The Social Constitution of Labour Markets: Why Skills Cannot Be Commodities." In Rosemary Crompton, Duncan Gallie, and Kate Purcell, eds., *Changing Forms of Employment: Organisations, Skills, and Gender*. London and New York: Routledge.

Jones, Melanie, and Victoria Wass 2013 "Understanding Changing Disability-Related Employment Gaps in Britain 1998–2011." *Work, Employment and Society* 27(6): 982–1003.

Jones, Oswald 2000 "Scientific Management, Culture and Control: A First-Hand Account of Taylorism in Practice." *Human Relations* 53(5): 631–53.

Jones, Stephen R. G. 1990 "Worker Interdependence and Output: The Hawthorne Studies Reevaluated." *American Sociological Review* 55: 176–90.

Jones, Stephen R. G., and W. Craig Riddell 2019 "Unemployment, Marginal Attachment, and Labor Force Participation in Canada and the United States." *Journal of Labor Economics* 37(S2): S399–S441.

Judge, Timothy A., Joyce E. Bono, Carl J. Thoresen, and Gregory K. Patton 2001 "The Job Satisfaction–Job Performance Relationship: A Qualitative and Quantitative Review." *Psychological Bulletin* 127(3): 376–407.

Jütting, Johannes P., and Juan R. de Laiglesia, eds. 2009 *Is Informal Normal? Towards More and Better Jobs in Developing Countries*. Paris: OECD.

Kalleberg, Arne L. 1977 "Work Values and Job Rewards: A Theory of Job Satisfaction." *American Sociological Review* 42: 124–43.

———— **2008** "The Mismatched Worker: When People Don't Fit Their Jobs." *Academy of Management Perspectives* 22(1): 24–40.

———— **2009** "Precarious Work, Insecure Workers: Employment Relations in Transition." *American Sociological Review* 74(1): 1–22.

———— **2011** *Good Jobs, Bad Jobs: The Rise of Polarized and Precarious Employment Systems in the United States, 1970s to 2000s*. New York: Russell Sage Publications.

———— **2018** *Precarious Lives: Job Insecurity and Well-Being in Rich Democracies*. Cambridge: Polity Press.

Kalleberg, Arne L., and Karyn A. Loscocco 1983 "Aging, Values and Rewards: Explaining Age Differences in Job Satisfaction." *American Sociological Review* 48: 78–90.

Kalleberg, Arne L., Peter V. Marsden, Jeremy Reynolds, and David Knoke 2006 "Beyond Profit? Sectoral Differences in High-Performance Work Practices." *Work and Occupations* 33(3): 271–302.

Kalleberg, Arne L., and Steven Vallas, eds. 2018 *Precarious Work*. Vol. 31, *Research in the Sociology of Work*. Bingley, England: Emerald Publishing.

Kalleberg, Arne L., and Mark E. Van Buren 1996 "Is Bigger Better? Explaining the Relationship between Organization Size and Job Rewards." *American Sociological Review* 61: 47–66.

Kamata, Satoshi 1983 *Japan in the Passing Lane: An Insider's Account of Life in a Japanese Factory*. New York: Pantheon.

Kan, Man Yee, Oriel Sullivan, and Jonathan Gershuny 2011 "Gender Convergence in Domestic Work: Discerning the Effects of Interactional and Institutional Barriers from Large-Scale Data." *Sociology* 45: 234–51.

Kang, Sonia, Katherine DeCelles, András Tilcsik, and Sora Jun 2016 "Whitened Resumes: Race and Self-Presentation in the Labor Market." *Administrative Science Quarterly* 61(3): 469–502.

Kanter, Rosabeth M. 1977 *Men and Women of the Corporation*. New York: Basic Books.

———— **1989** *When Giants Learn to Dance: Mastering the Challenges of Strategy, Management, and Careers in the 1990s*. New York: Simon & Schuster.

Kapstein, Ethan B. 1996 "Workers and the World Economy." *Foreign Affairs* 75: 16–37.

Karasek, Robert 1979 "Job Demands, Job Decision Latitude and Mental Health Implications for Job Redesign." *Administrative Science Quarterly* 24: 285–308.

Karmel, Jonathan 2017 *Dying to Work: Death and Injury in the American Workplace*. Ithaca, NY: ILR Press.

Kashefi, Max 2011 "High Performance Work Organizations and Job Rewards in Manufacturing and Service Economies." *International Sociology* 26(4): 547–70.

———— **2012** "Social Capital in High Performance Work Organizations."

International Review of Modern Sociology 38(1): 65–91.

Kay, Fiona, Stacey L. Alarie, and Jones K. Adjei 2016 "Undermining Gender Equality: Female Attrition From Private Law Practice." *Law & Society Review* 50(3): 766–801.

Kay, Fiona M., and Elizabeth H. Gorman 2012 "Developmental Practices, Organizational Culture, and Minority Representation in Organizational Leadership: The Case of Partners in Large U.S. Law Firms." *The Annals of the American Academy of Political and Social Science* 639: 91–113.

Kay, Tamara 2011 *NAFTA and the Politics of Labor Transnationalism.* Cambridge, NY: Cambridge University Press.

Kaya, Y., and N. D. Martin 2016 "Managers in the Global Economy: A Multilevel Analysis." *The Sociological Quarterly* 57(2): 232–55.

Kazemipur, Abdolmohammad, and Shiva S. Halli 2001 "The Changing Colour of Poverty in Canada." *Canadian Review of Sociology and Anthropology* 38(2): 217–38.

Kealey, Gregory S. 1981 "The Bonds of Unity: The Knights of Labour in Ontario, 1880–1900." *Histoire Sociale/Social History* 14: 369–411.

——— **1986** "Work Control, the Labour Process, and Nineteenth-Century Canadian Printers." In Craig Heron and Robert Storey, eds., *On the Job: Confronting the Labour Process in Canada.* Montreal: McGill–Queen's University Press.

——— **1995** *Workers and Canadian History.* Montreal: McGill–Queen's University Press.

Keister, Lisa A. 2007 "Upward Wealth Mobility: Exploring the Roman Catholic Advantage." *Social Forces* 85(3): 1195–1225.

Kelan, Elisabeth K. 2008 "Emotions in a Rational Profession: The Gendering of Skills in ICT Work." *Gender, Work & Organization* 15(1): 49–71.

Kelly, Erin L., Ellen Ernst Kossek, Leslie B. Hammer, Mary Durham, Jeremy Bray, Kelly Chermack, Lauren A. Murphy, and Dan Kaskubar 2008 "Getting There from Here: Research on the Effects of Work–Family Initiatives on Work–Family Conflict and Business Outcomes." *The Academy of Management Annals* 2(1): 305–49.

Keller, Berndt, and Frank Werner 2010 "Industrial Democracy from a European Perspective: The Example of SEs." *Economic and Industrial Democracy* 31(4S): 40–54.

Keller, James 2019 "Alberta Slashes Minimum Wage for Teen Students." *Globe and Mail,* May 27.

Kerr, Clark, J. T. Dunlop, F. H. Harbison, and C. A. Myers 1973 *Industrialization and Industrial Man.* London, England: Penguin.

Kettler, David, James Struthers, and Christopher Huxley 1990 "Unionization and Labour Regimes in Canada and the United States." *Labour/Le Travail* 25: 161–87.

Kim, Hansung, and Madeleine Stoner 2008 "Burnout and Turnover Intention among Social Workers: Effects of Role Stress, Job Autonomy, and Social Support." *Administration in Social Work* 32(3): 5–25.

Kim, Marlene 2015 "Pay Secrecy and the Gender Wage Gap in the United States." *Industrial Relations* 54(4): 648–67.

Kim, Young-Mi 2013 "Diverging Top and Converging Bottom: Labour Flexibilization and Changes in Career Mobility in the USA." *Work, Employment and Society* 27(5): 860–79.

Kienlen, Alexis 2018 "Beyond Bill 6: Can Farmers and Government Find Common Ground?" *Alberta Views* (1 June 2018); https://albertaviews.ca/beyond-bill-6/ [retrieved 15 April 2019].

King, W. L. Mackenzie 1918 *Industry and Humanity: A Study in the Principles Underlying Industrial Reconstruction.* Toronto: Thomas Allen.

Kinnie, Nick, Sue Hutchinson, and John Purcell 2000 "'Fun and Surveillance': The Paradox of High Commitment Management in Call Centres." *The International Journal of Human Resource Management* 11(5): 967–85.

Kirton, Gill 2015 "Progress Towards Gender Democracy in UK Unions, 1987–2012." *British Journal of Industrial Relations* 53(3): 484–507.

Knight, Rolf 1978 *Indians at Work: An Informal History of Native Indian Labour in British Columbia, 1858–1930.* Vancouver: New Star Books.

Knighton, Tamara, Filsan Hujaleh, Joe Iacampo, and Gugsa Werkneh 2009 *Lifelong Learning among Canadians Aged 18 to 64 Years Old: First Results from the 2008 Access and Support to Education and Training Survey*

(*ASETS*). Ottawa: Statistics Canada. http://www.statcan.gc.ca/pub/81-595-m/81-595-m2009079-eng.pdf.

Knights, David, Hugh Willmott, and David Collison, eds. 1985 *Job Redesign: Critical Perspectives on the Labour Process*. Aldershot, England: Gower.

Kochan, Thomas A. 2013 "The American Jobs Crisis and Its Implications for the Future of Employment Policy: A Call for a New Jobs Compact." *ILR Review* 66(2): 291–314.

Kochan, Thomas A., Russell Lansbury, and John Paul MacDuffie, eds. 1997 *After Lean Production: Evolving Practices in the World Auto Industry*. Ithaca, NY: ILR Press.

Kochan, Thomas A., and Paul Osterman 1994 *The Mutual Gains Enterprise: Forging a Winning Partnership among Labor, Management, and Government*. Boston: Harvard Business School Press.

Kohn, Melvin L., and Carmi Schooler 1983 *Work and Personality: An Inquiry into the Impact of Social Stratification*. Norwood, NJ: Ablex.

Kopinak, Kathryn 1996 *Desert Capitalism: Maquiladoras in North America's Western Industrial Corridor*. Tucson: University of Arizona Press.

Korabik, Karen, Donna S. Lero, and Denise L. Whitehead 2008 *Handbook of Work–Family Integration: Research, Theory and Best Practices*. London: Academic Press (Elsevier).

Korczynski, Marek 2013 "The Customer in the Sociology of Work: Different Ways of Going beyond the Management–Worker Dyad." *Work Employment and Society* 27(6), NP1–NP7.

Korczynski, Marek, Randy Hodson, and Paul Edwards, eds. 2006 *Social Theory at Work*. Oxford: Oxford University Press.

Korczynski, Marek, and Cameron Lynne Macdonald 2009 *Service Work: Critical Perspectives*. London: Routledge.

Korczynski, Marek, Michael Pickering, and Emma Robertson 2013 *Rhythms of Labour, Music at Work in Britain*. Cambridge: Cambridge University Press.

Koski, Pasi, and Anu Järvensivu 2010 "The Innovation Diffusion Paradox in the Light of 'Shop Floor Games' and Micro-Politics." *Economic and Industrial Democracy* 31(3): 345–63.

Kosny, Agnieszka, and Ellen MacEachan 2010 "Gendered, Invisible Work in Non-profit Social Service Organizations: Implications for Worker Health and Safety." *Gender, Work & Organization* 17(4): 359–80.

Kossek, Ellen E., and Cynthia Ozeki 1998 "Work–Family Conflict, Policies and the Job-Life Satisfaction Relationship: A Review and Directions for Organizational Behavior–Human Resources Research." *Journal of Applied Psychology* 83(2): 139–49.

Krahn, Harvey 1995 "Non-standard Work on the Rise." *Perspectives on Labour and Income* (Winter): 35–42.

——— 1997 "On the Permanence of Human Capital: Use It or Lose It." *Policy Options* 18(6): 17–21.

——— 2017 "Choose Your Parents Carefully: Social Class, Post-secondary Education, and Occupational Outcomes." In Edward Grabb, Jeffrey G. Reitz and Monica Hwang, eds., *Social Inequality in Canada: Dimensions of Disadvantage*. 6th ed. Don Mills, Ontario: Oxford University Press.

Krahn, Harvey, Cher-Ann Chai, Shichen Fang, Nancy L. Galambos, and Matthew D. Johnson 2018 "Quick, Uncertain, and Delayed Adults: Timing, Sequencing and Duration of Youth-Adult Transitions in Canada." *Journal of Youth Studies* 21(7): 905–21.

Krahn, Harvey, and Angela Chow 2016 "Youth Unemployment and Career Scarring: Social-Psychological Mediating Effects?" *Canadian Journal of Sociology* 41(2): 117–38.

Krahn, Harvey, Tracey Derwing, Marlene Mulder, and Lori Wilkinson 2000 "Educated and Underemployed: Refugee Integration into the Canadian Labour Market." *Journal of International Migration and Integration* 1(Winter): 59–84.

Krahn, Harvey, and Nancy Galambos 2014 "Work Values and Beliefs of 'Generation X' and 'Generation Y.'" *Journal of Youth Studies* 17(1): 92–112.

Krahn, Harvey, Andrea Howard, and Nancy Galambos 2012 "Exploring or Floundering? The Meaning of Employment and Educational Fluctuations in Emerging Adulthood." *Youth & Society* 47(2): 245–66.

Krahn, Harvey, and Julie Hudson 2006 *Pathways of Alberta Youth through the Post-secondary System into the Labour Market*,

1996–2003. Pathways to the Labour Market Series, Report No. 2. Ottawa: Canadian Policy Research Networks.

Krahn, Harvey, and Graham S. Lowe 1999 "Literacy in the Workplace." *Perspectives on Labour and Income* (Summer): 38–44.

Kramer, Brent 2010 "Employee Ownership and Participation Effects on Outcomes in Firms Majority Employee-Owned Through Employee Stock Ownership Plans in the US." *Economic and Industrial Democracy* 31(4): 449–76.

Krause-Jensen, Jacob 2010 "Values at Work: Ambivalent Situations and Human Resource Embarrassment." *Social Analysis* 54(3): 126–38.

Krinsky, John, and Ellen Reese 2006 "Forging and Sustaining Labor–Community Coalitions: The Workfare Justice Movement in Three Cities." *Sociological Forum* 21(4): 623–58.

Kristal, Tali 2013 "The Capitalist Machine: Computerization, Workers' Power, and the Decline in Labor's Share within U.S. Industries." *American Sociological Review* 78(3): 361–89.

Krogman, Naomi, and Tom Beckley 2002 "Corporate 'Bail-Outs' and Local 'Buyouts': Pathways to Community Forestry." *Society and Natural Resources* 15(2): 109–27.

Kruse, Kevin 2016 "The Big Company That Has No Rules." *Forbes* (29 August): https://www.forbes.com/sites/kevinkruse/2016/08/29/the-big-company-that-has-no-rules/#72a508e056ad [retrieved 18 April 2019].

Krzywdzinski, Martin 2017 "Automation, Skill Requirements and Labor Use Strategies: High-Wage and Low-Wage Approaches to High-Tech Manufacturing in the Automotive Industry." *New Technology, Work and Employment* 32(3): 247–67.

Ku, Manwai D. 2011 "When Does Gender Matter? Gender Differences in Speciality Choice among Physicians." *Work and Occupations* 38(2): 221–62.

Kumar, Krishnan 1995 *From Post-industrial to Post-modern Society: New Theories of the Contemporary World.* Oxford, England: Blackwell.

Kumar, Pradeep 1995 *Unions and Workplace Change in Canada.* Kingston, ON: IRC Press.

Kunda, Gideon, and Galit Ailon-Souday 2005 "Managers, Markets, and Ideologies: Design and Devotion Revisited." In Stephen Ackroyd, R. Batt, P. Thompson, and P. S. Tolbert, eds., *The Oxford Handbook of Work and Organization.* Oxford, England: Oxford University Press.

Kunze, Florian, Stephan A. Boehm, and Heike Bruch 2011 "Age Diversity, Age Discrimination Climate and Performance Consequences—A Cross Organizational Study." *Journal of Organizational Behavior* 32: 264–90.

Labour Canada 1986 *Women in the Labour Force, 1985–86 Edition.* Ottawa: Labour Canada, Women's Bureau.

Labour Market Ministers 2000 *Profile of Canadian Youth in the Labour Market: Second Annual Report to the Forum of Labour Market Ministers.* Hull, QC: HRDC. Cat. no. RH61-1/2000E.

Lair, Craig, and George Ritzer 2009 "Metamanagement and the Outsourcing of Domestic Life." In Philip Hancock and Melissa Tyler, eds. *The Management of Everyday Life.* New York: Palgrave Macmillan.

Laliberte, Ron, and Vic Satzewich 1999 "Native Migrant Labour in the Southern Alberta Sugar-Beet Industry: Coercion and Paternalism in the Recruitment of Labour." *Canadian Review of Sociology and Anthropology* 36(1): 65–85.

Lam, Helen, and Yonatan Reshef 1999 "Are Quality Improvement and Downsizing Compatible? A Human Resources Perspective." *Relations Industrielles/Industrial Relations* 54(4): 727–47.

Lamb, Craig 2016 *The Talented Mr. Robot: The Impact of Automation on Canada's Workforce.* Toronto: Ryerson University (Brookfield Institute for Innovation + Entrepreneurship).

Lamba, Navjot 2003 "The Employment Experiences of Canadian Refugees: Measuring the Impact of Human and Social Capital on Employment Outcomes." *Canadian Review of Sociology and Anthropology* 40(1): 45–64.

Land, Hillary 1980 "The Family Wage." *Feminist Review* 6: 55–77.

Landsbergis, Paul A., Janet Cahill, and Peter Schnall 1999 "The Impact of Lean Production and Related New Systems of Work Organization on Worker Health." *Journal of Occupational Health Psychology* 4(2): 108–30.

Langford, Tom 1996 "Effects of Strike Participation on the Political Consciousness of Canadian Postal Workers." *Relations Industrielles/Industrial Relations* 51(3): 651–82.

Langford, Rachel, Patricia Albanese, and Susan Prentice, eds. 2017 *Caring for Children: Social Movements and Public Policy in Canada.* Vancouver: UBC Press.

Largacha-Martinez, Carlos 2011 "What Is Your Calling? SEMCO's Invitation to Participatory Management." In Ernst von Kimakowitz, Michael Pirson, Heiko Spitzeck, Claus Dierksmeier, and Wolfgang Amann, eds., *Humanistic Management in Practice.* New York: Palgrave Macmillan.

LaRochelle-Côté, Sébastien 2013 *Employment Instability among Younger Workers.* Ottawa: Statistics Canada. Cat. No. 75-004-M-No. 002.

LaRochelle-Côté, S., and J. Gilmore 2009 "Canada's Employment Downturn." *Perspectives on Labour and Income* (December): 5–12.

LaRochelle-Côté, Sébastien, and Claude Dionne 2009 "International Differences in Low-Paid Work." *Perspectives on Labour and Income* 21(June): 5–13.

Lash, Scott, and John Urry 1987 *The End of Organized Capitalism.* Cambridge: Polity Press.

——— **2013** "Book Review Symposium: Response to Reviewers of *The End of Organized Capitalism.*" *Work, Employment and Society* 27: 542–46.

Laslett, Barbara, and Johanna Brenner 1989 "Gender and Social Reproduction: Historical Perspectives." *Annual Review of Sociology* 15: 381–404.

Latif, Ehsan 2010 "Crisis, Unemployment and Psychological Well-being in Canada." *Journal of Policy Modeling* 32(4): 520–30.

Laurison, Daniel, and Sam Friedman 2016 "The Class Pay Gap in Higher Professional and Managerial Occupations. *American Sociological Review* 81(4): 668–95.

Law Commission of Ontario 2012 *Vulnerable Workers and Precarious Work—Final Report.* Toronto: Law Commission of Ontario.

Lawler, Edward E., III, and Susan Albers Mohrman 2003 *Creating a Strategic Human Resources Organization: An Assessment of Trends and New Directions.* Stanford, CA: Stanford University Press.

Laxer, Gordon 1989 *Open for Business: The Roots of Foreign Ownership in Canada.* Don Mills, ON: Oxford University Press.

——— **1995** "Social Solidarity, Democracy and Global Capitalism." *Canadian Review of Sociology and Anthropology* 32: 287–313.

Leaderman, Marsha 2019 "Ottawa Announces More than $2.7 Million for Project to Improve Process of Reporting Sexual Harassment." *Globe and Mail,* July 8 2019.

Leck, Joanne 2002 "Making Employment Equity Programs Work for Women." *Canadian Public Policy* 28: S85–S100.

Leckie, Norm, André Léonard, Julie Turcotte, and David Wallace 2001 *Employer and Employee Perspectives on Human Resource Practices.* The Evolving Workplace Series. Ottawa: Statistics Canada and Human Resources Development Canada. Cat. no. 71-584-MPE-No. 1.

Lee, Cheol Sung 2007 "Labor Unions and Good Governance: A Cross-National, Comparative Analysis." *American Sociological Review* 72(4): 585–609.

Lehmann, Wolfgang 2012 "Extra-Credential Experiences and Social Closure: Working-Class Students at University." *British Educational Research Journal* 38(2): 203–18.

Lehmann, Wolfgang, and Tracey L. Adams 2017 "Labour Markets, Inequality, and the Future of Work." In Edward Grabb, Jeffrey G. Reitz and Monica Hwang, eds., *Social Inequality in Canada: Dimensions of Disadvantage.* 6th ed. Toronto, ON: Oxford University Press.

Lehmann, Wolfgang, and Holly Trower 2018 "Forms of Capital and Habitus in the Decision to Go on Academic Exchange." *Canadian Review of Sociology* 55(1): 136–48.

Leicht, Kevin T., and Mary L. Fennell 2001 *Professional Work: A Sociological Approach.* Oxford, England: Blackwell.

Leidner, Robin 1993 *Fast Food, Fast Talk: Interactive Service Work and the Routinization of Everyday Life.* Berkeley, CA: University of California Press.

Lemieux, P. 2018. "Is NAFTA 2.0 Better than Nothing?" *Regulation* 41: 12–15.

Lenard, P. T., and C. Straehle, eds. 2012. *Legislated Inequality: Temporary Labour Migration in Canada.* Montreal: McGill-Queen's University Press.

Leontaridi, Marianthi 1998 "Segmented Labour Markets: Theory and Evidence." *Journal of Economic Surveys* 12(1): 103–9.

Levanon, Asaf, and David B. Grusky 2016 "The Persistence of Extreme Gender Segregation in the Twenty-First Century." *American Journal of Sociology* 122(2): 573–619.

Lévesque, Christian, and Gregor Murray 2010 "Trade Union Cross-Border Alliances within MNCs: Disentangling Union Dynamics at the Local, National and International Levels." *Industrial Relations Journal* 41(4): 312–32.

Levi, Margaret, David Olson, Jon Agnone, and Devin Kelly 2009 "Union Democracy Reexamined." *Politics & Society* 37(2): 203–28.

Levine, David I. 1995 *Reinventing the Workplace: How Business and Employees Can Both Win.* Washington, DC: Brookings Institution.

Levinson, Klas 2000 "Codetermination in Sweden: Myth and Reality." *Economic and Industrial Democracy* 21(4): 457–73.

Levitt, Howard 2014 "Why Internships Are Facing a Growing Backlash." *Financial Post*, March 11. http://business.financialpost.com/2014/03/11/why-unpaid-internships-are-facing-a-growing-backlash/.

Levitt, Kari Polanyi 2013 *From the Great Transformation to the Great Financialization: On Karl Polanyi and Other Essays.* Halifax: Fernwood Publishing.

Lewchuk, Wayne, and Marlea Clarke 2011 *Working Without Commitments: Precarious Employment and Health.* Montreal: McGill-Queen's University Press.

Lewchuk, Wayne, Marlea Clarke, and Alice de Wolff 2009 "Precarious Employment and the Internal Responsibility System: Some Canadian Experiences." In David Walters and Theo Nichols, eds., *Workplace Health and Safety: International Perspectives on Worker Representation.* London: Palgrave Macmillan.

Lewchuk, Wayne, A. Leslie Robb, and Vivienne Walters 1996 "The Effectiveness of Bill 70 and Joint Health and Safety Committees in Reducing Injuries in the Workplace: The Case of Ontario." *Canadian Public Policy* 22: 225–43.

Lewis, Patricia, and Ruth Simpson 2017 "Hakim Revisited: Preference, Choice and the Postfeminist Gender Regime." *Gender, Work & Organization* 24(2): 115–33.

Li, Peter S. 1982 "Chinese Immigrants on the Canadian Prairie, 1919–47." *Canadian Review of Sociology and Anthropology* 19: 527–40.

———— **2001** "The Market Worth of Immigrants' Educational Credentials." *Canadian Public Policy* 27(1): 23–38.

Liker, Jeffrey K. 2004 *The Toyota Way: 14 Management Principles from the World's Greatest Manufacturer.* New York: McGraw-Hill.

Lillie, Nathan 2005 "Union Networks and Global Unionism in Maritime Shipping." *Relations Industrielles/Industrial Relations* 60(1): 88–111.

Lin, Liang-Hung, Yu-Ling Ho, and Wei-Hsin Eugenia Lin 2013 "Confucian and Taoist Work Values: An Exploratory Study of the Chinese Transformational Leadership Behavior." *Journal of Business Ethics* 113: 91–103.

Lincoln, James R. 1990 "Japanese Organization and Organization Theory." *Research in Organizational Behavior* 12: 255–94.

Lincoln, James R., and Arne L. Kalleberg 1990 *Culture, Control, and Commitment: A Study of Work Organization and Work Attitudes in the United States and Japan.* Cambridge: Cambridge University Press.

Lincoln, James R., and Kerry McBride 1987 "Japanese Industrial Organization in Comparative Perspective." *Annual Review of Sociology* 13: 289–312.

Lindenfeld, Fran, and Pamela Wynn 1997 "Success and Failure of Worker Co-ops: The Role of Internal and External Environmental Factors." *Humanity and Society* 21(2): 148–61.

Lindsay, Sally 2007 "Gendering Work: The Masculinization of Nurse Anesthesia." *Canadian Journal of Sociology* 32(4): 429–48.

Lindsay, Sally, Tracey Adams, Robyn Sanford, Carolyn McDougall, Shauna Kingsnorth, and Dolly Menna-Dack 2014 "Employers' and Employment Counselors' Perceptions of Desirable Skills for Entry-Level Positions for Adolescents: How Does It Differ for Youth with Disabilities?" *Disability & Society* 29(6): 953–67.

Lippmann, Stephen 2008 "Rethinking Risk in the New Economy: Age and Cohort Effects on Unemployment and Re-Employment." *Human Relations* 61(9): 1259–92.

Lipsig-Mummé, Carla 2009 "Trade Unions and Labour Relations Regimes: International Perspectives in a Globalizing World." In Morley Gunderson and Daphne Taras, eds., *Canadian Labour and Employment Relations.* Toronto: Pearson Addison Wesley.

Littler, Craig R., and Peter Innes 2003 "Downsizing and Deknowledging the Firm." *Work, Employment and Society* 17(1): 73–100.

Livingstone, David W. 1999 *The Education–Jobs Gap: Underemployment or Economic Democracy.* Toronto: Garamond Press.

——— **2005** *Basic Findings of the 2004 Canadian Learning and Work Survey.* http://lifelong.oise.utoronto.ca/papers/WALLBasicSummJune05.pdf.

——— ed. **2009** *Education & Jobs: Exploring the Gaps.* Toronto: University of Toronto Press.

——— **2017** "Skills Underutilization." In Chris Warhurst, Key Mayhew, David Finegold and John Buchanan, eds., *The Oxford Handbook on Skills and Training.* Oxford: Oxford University Press.

Livingstone, David W., and David Guile 2012 *The Knowledge Economy and Lifelong Learning: A Critical Reader.* Rotterdam, The Netherlands: Sense Publishers.

Livingstone, David W., and Meg Luxton 1996 "Gender Consciousness at Work: Modification of the Male Breadwinner Norm." In David W. Livingstone and J. Marshall Mangan, eds., *Recast Dreams: Class and Gender Consciousness in Steeltown.* Toronto: Garamond Press.

Livingstone, David W., and Antonie Scholtz 2007 "Contradictions of Labour Processes and Workers' Use of Skills in Advanced Capitalist Economies." In Vivian Shalla and Wallace Clement, eds., *Work in Tumultuous Times: Critical Perspectives.* Montreal: McGill–Queen's University Press.

Lizardo, Omar 2012 "The Three Phases of Bourdieu's U.S. Reception: Comment on Lamont." *Sociological Forum* 27: 238–44.

Locke, Edwin A. 1982 "The Ideas of Frederick W. Taylor: An Evaluation." *The Academy of Management Review* 7(1): 14–24.

Lockwood, David 1966 "Sources of Variation in Working Class Images of Society." *Sociological Review* 14: 249–67.

Logan, John 2006 "The Union Avoidance Industry in the United States." *British Journal of Industrial Relations* 44(4): 651–75.

Logue, John 1981 "Saab/Trollhattan: Reforming Work Life on the Shop Floor." *Working Life in Sweden* 23(June).

Logue, John, and Jacquelyn S. Yates 1999 "Worker Ownership American Style: Pluralism, Participation and Performance." *Economic and Industrial Democracy* 20(2): 225–52.

Long, Richard J. 1995 "Employee Buyouts: The Canadian Experience." *Canadian Business Economics* (Summer): 28–41.

Looker, Dianne 2010 "Can I Get There from Here? Canadian Rural-Urban Participation Rates in Post-Secondary Education." In Ross Finnie, Marc Frenette, Richard E. Mueller, and Arthur Sweetman, eds., *Pursuing Higher Education in Canada: Economic, Social and Policy Dimensions.* Montreal: McGill-Queen's University Press.

Lopez, Steve 2006 "Emotional Labor and Organized Emotional Care: Conceptualizing Nursing Home Care Work." *Work and Occupations* 33(2): 133–60.

——— **2010** "Workers, Managers, and Customers: Triangles of Power in Work Communities." *Work and Occupations* 37(3): 251–71.

Lopez-Pacheco, Alexandra 2014 "A Little-Used Model." *Edmonton Journal*, January 2, B3.

Lowe, Graham S. 1981 "Causes of Unionization in Canadian Banks." *Relations Industrielles/Industrial Relations* 36: 865–92.

——— **1987** *Women in the Administrative Revolution: The Feminization of Clerical Work.* Toronto: University of Toronto Press.

——— **1998** "The Future of Work: Implications for Unions." *Relations Industrielles/Industrial Relations* 53(2): 235–57.

——— **2001** *Employer of Choice? Workplace Innovation in Government: A Synthesis Report.* Ottawa: Canadian Policy Research Networks.

Lowe, Graham S., and Frank Graves 2016 *Redesigning Work: A Blueprint for Canada's Future Well-being.* Toronto: University of Toronto Press.

Lowe, Graham S., and Harvey Krahn 1999
"Reconceptualizing Youth Unemployment."
In Julian Barling and E. Kevin Kelloway,
eds., *Young Workers: Varieties of Experience.*
Washington, DC: American Psychological
Association.
———— **2000** "Work Aspirations and Attitudes
in an Era of Labour Market Restructuring:
A Comparison of Two Canadian Youth
Cohorts." *Work, Employment and Society*
14(1): 1–22.
**Lowe, Graham S., Harvey Krahn, and Jeff
Bowlby 1997** *1996 Alberta High School
Graduate Survey: Report of Research Findings.*
Edmonton: Population Research Laboratory,
University of Alberta.
**Lowe, Graham S., and Grant Schellenberg
2001** *What's a Good Job? The Importance
of Employment Relationships.* CPRN Study
W-05. Ottawa: Canadian Policy Research
Networks.
Lowen, Aaron, and Paul Sicilian 2009
"Family-Friendly Fringe Benefits and the
Gender Wage Gap." *Journal of Labor Research*
30: 101–19.
Lucas, Rex A. 1971 *Minetown, Milltown,
Railtown.* Toronto: University of Toronto
Press.
Luce, Stephanie 2004 *Fighting for a Living
Wage.* Ithaca, NY: Cornell University Press.
Luffman, Jacqueline 2003 "Taking Stock of
Equity Compensation." *Perspectives on Labour
and Income* 15(Summer): 26–33.
**Luffman, Jacqueline, and Deborah Sussman
2007** "The Aboriginal Labour Force in
Western Canada." *Perspectives on Labour and
Income* 19(1): 30–44.
Luong, May 2010 "The Financial Impact of
Student Loans." *Perspectives on Labour and
Income* (January): 5–18.
Lupton, Ben 2006 "Explaining Men's Entry
into Female-Concentrated Occupations: Issues
of Masculinity and Social Class." *Gender, Work
& Organization* 13(2): 103–28.
Luxton, Meg 1980 *More Than a Labour of
Love.* Toronto: Women's Press.
**Lynd, Robert S., and Helen Merrell Lynd
1929** *Middletown: A Study of Modern
American Culture.* New York: Harcourt and
Brace.
**Lyness, K. S., J. C. Gornick, P. Stone, and
A. R. Grotto 2012** "It's All about Control:
Worker Control over Schedule and Hours

in Cross-National Context." *American
Sociological Review* 77(6): 1023–49.
**Macey, William H., and Benjamin
Schneider 2008** "The Meaning of Employee
Engagement." *Industrial and Organizational
Psychology* 1(1): 3–30.
Macdonald, David 2018 *Climbing Up and
Kicking Down: Executive Pay in Canada.*
Ottawa: Canadian Centre for Policy
Alternatives.
———— **2019** *The Double-Pane Glass Ceiling:
The Gender Pay Gap at the Top of Corporate
Canada.* Ottawa: Canadian Centre for Policy
Alternatives.
MacDonald, I. T. 2014. Towards Neoliberal
Trade Unionism: Decline, Renewal and
Transformation in North American Labour
Movements. *British Journal of Industrial
Relations,* 52(4): 725–52.
**McDonald, J. A., and R. Thornton
2016** "Have Pay Equity Laws in Canada
Helped Women? A Synthetic-Control
Approach." *American Review of Canadian
Studies* 46(4): 452–73.
Macdonald, Keith M. 1995 *The Sociology of
the Professions.* Thousand Oaks, CA: Sage
Publications.
MacEwen, A. 2018 "Welcome Movement on
Progressive Trade Agenda in USMCA." *Policy
Options.* https://policyoptions.irpp.org/maga-
zines/october-2018/welcome-movement-on-
progressive-trade-agenda-in-usmca/ [retrieved
May 4, 2019].
Mackenzie, Hugh 2016 *Staying Power: CEO
Pay in Canada.* Ottawa: Canadian Centre for
Policy Alternatives.
**MacLean, Brian K., and Lars Osberg, eds.
1996** *The Unemployment Crisis: All for
Nought?* Montreal: McGill–Queen's University
Press.
Macleod, Gus 1997 *From Mondragon to
America: Experiments in Community Economic
Development.* Sydney, NS: University College
of Cape Breton Press.
MacPhail, Fiona, and Paul Bowles 2009
"Corporate Social Responsibility as Support
for Employee Volunteers: Impacts, Gender
Puzzles and Policy Implications in Canada."
Journal of Business Ethics 84(3): 405–16.
MacPherson, Alex 2019 "Saskatoon Co-op
Employees Vote for Deal to End Strike."
Saskatoon StarPhoenix, April 17. https://
thestarphoenix.com/news/local-news/

saskatoon-co-op-employees-vote-for-deal-to-end-strike [retrieved 29 April 2019].

Mahon, Rianne 1984 *The Politics of Industrial Restructuring: Canadian Textiles.* Toronto: University of Toronto Press.

Mahon, Rianne, with Sonya Michel 2002 *Child Care Policy at the Crossroads: Gender and Welfare State Restructuring.* London, England: Routledge.

Mahutga, Matthew C. 2014 "Global Models of Networked Organization, the Positional Power of Nations and Economic Development." *Review of International Political Economy* 21(1): 157–94.

Mainiero, Lisa, and Kevin Jones 2013 "Sexual Harassment versus Workplace Romance: Social Media Spillover and Textual Harassment in the Workplace." *Academy of Management Perspectives* 27(3): 187–203.

Mandel, Hadas 2013 "Up the Down Staircase: Women's Upward Mobility and the Wage Penalty for Occupational Feminization, 1970–2007." *Social Forces* 91(4): 1183–207.

Mann, Sandi, and Lynn Holdsworth 2003 "The Psychological Impact of Teleworking: Stress, Emotions and Health." *New Technology, Work and Employment* 18(3): 196–211.

Manser, Marilyn E., and Garnett Picot 1999 "Self-Employment in Canada and the United States." *Perspectives on Labour and Income* (Autumn): 37–44.

Marchak, M. Patricia 1981 *Ideological Perspectives on Canada.* 2nd ed. Toronto: McGraw-Hill Ryerson.

Marin, Alexandra 2012 "Don't Mention It: Why People Don't Share Job Information, When They Do, and Why It Matters." *Social Networks* 34: 181–92.

Maroto, Michelle, David Pettinicchio, and Andrew C. Patterson 2019 "Hierarchies of Categorical Disadvantage: Economic Insecurity at the Intersection of Disability, Gender, and Race." *Gender & Society* 33(1): 64–93.

Marquardt, Richard 1998 *Enter at Your Own Risk: Canadian Youth and the Labour Market.* Toronto: Between the Lines.

Marshall, Katherine 1993 "Dual Earners: Who's Responsible for Housework?" *Canadian Social Trends* (Winter): 11–14.

——— **1996** "A Job to Die For." *Perspectives on Labour and Income* (Summer): 26–31.

——— **1997** "Job Sharing." *Perspectives on Labour and Income* (Summer): 6–10.

——— **2000** "Incomes of Young Retired Women: The Past 30 Years." *Perspectives on Labour and Income* 12(Winter): 9–17.

——— **2003** "Benefits of the Job." *Perspectives on Labour and Income* 15(Summer): 7–14.

——— **2006** "Converging Gender Roles." *Perspectives on Labour and Income* (July): 5–17.

——— **2011** "Generational Change in Paid and Unpaid Work." *Canadian Social Trends* (July): 13–24. Statistics Canada Cat. no. 11-008-X.

Marshall, Victor W., and Margaret M. Mueller 2002 *Rethinking Social Policy for an Aging Society: Insights from the Life Course Perspective.* Ottawa: Canadian Policy Research Networks.

Martin, Gary 2000 "Employment and Unemployment in Mexico in the 1990s." *Monthly Labor Review* (November): 3–18.

Martin, Jack K., and Paul M. Roman 1996 "Job Satisfaction, Job Reward Characteristics, and Employees' Problem Drinking Behaviors." *Work and Occupations* 23: 4–25.

Martin, Jack K., and Constance L. Shehan 1989 "Education and Job Satisfaction: The Influences of Gender, Wage-Earning Status, and Job Values." *Work and Occupations* 16: 184–99.

Martin, Joanne 2002 *Organizational Culture: Mapping the Terrain.* Thousand Oaks, CA: Sage Publications.

Marquis, Susan L. 2017 *I Am Not a Tractor: How Florida Farmworkers Took on the Fast Food Giants and Won.* Ithaca, NY: ILR Press.

Massoni, Kelly 2004 "Modeling Work: Occupational Messages in *Seventeen* Magazine." *Gender & Society* 18(1): 47–65.

Matthews, Roy A. 1985 *Structural Change and Industrial Policy: The Redeployment of Canadian Manufacturing, 1960–80.* Ottawa: Supply and Services Canada.

Maximova, Katerina, and Harvey Krahn 2005 "Does Race Matter? Earnings of Visible Minority Graduates from Alberta Universities." *Canadian Journal of Higher Education* 35(1): 85–110.

Mayer-Ahuja, Nicole, and Harald Wolf 2007 "Beyond the Hype: Working in the German Internet Industry." *Critical Sociology* 33(1–2): 73–99.

Mayo, Elton 1945 *The Social Problems of an Industrial Civilization.* Cambridge, MA: Harvard University Press.

McCabe, Darren 1999 "Total Quality Management: Anti-union Trojan Horse or Management Albatross?" *Work, Employment and Society* 13(4): 665–91.

McCormack, A. Ross 1978 *Reformers, Rebels and Revolutionaries: The Western Canadian Radical Movement, 1899–1919.* Toronto: University of Toronto Press.

McCormick, Chris, ed. 1998 *The Westray Chronicles: A Case Study of an Occupational Disaster.* Halifax: Fernwood Publishing.

McDaniel, Susan, Lloyd Wong, and Bonnie Watt 2015 "An Aging Workforce and the Future Labour Market in Canada." *Canadian Public Policy* 41(2): 97–108.

McDowell, Linda 2009 *Working Bodies: Interactive Service Employment and Workplace Identities.* Chichester, England: Wiley Blackwell.

McFarlane, Seth, Roderic Beaujot, and Tony Haddad 2000 "Time Constraints and Relative Resources as Determinants of the Sexual Division of Domestic Work." *Canadian Journal of Sociology* 25(1): 61–82.

McGowan, Rosemary A., and Eddy S. Ng 2016 "Employment Equity in Canada: Making Sense of Employee Discourses of Misunderstanding, Resistance, and Support." *Canadian Public Administration* 59(2): 310–29.

McGregor, Douglas 1960 *The Human Side of Enterprise.* New York: McGraw-Hill.

McIntyre, Lynn, Cynthia Kwok, J. C. Herbert Emery, and Daniel J. Dutton 2016 "Impact of a Guaranteed Annual Income Program on Canadian Seniors' Physical, Mental and Functional Health." *Canadian Journal of Public Health* 107(2): 176–82.

McKay, Lindsey, Sophie Mathieu, and Andrea Doucet 2016 "Parental-Leave Rich and Parental-Leave Poor: Inequality in Canadian Labour Market Based Leave Policies." *Journal of Industrial Relations* 58(4): 543–62.

McKay, Shona 1996 "You're (Still) Hired." *Report on Business* magazine, December, 54–60.

McKinsey 2019 *The Present and Future of Women and Work in Canada.* https://www.mckinsey.com/featured-insights/gender-equality/the-present-and-future-of-women-at-work-in-canada [retrieved June 1, 2019].

McLaughlin, Heather, Christopher Uggen, and Amy Blackstone 2017 "The Economic and Career Effects of Sexual Harassment on Working Women." *Gender & Society* 31(3): 333–58.

McLuhan, Marshall 1964 *Understanding Media: The Extensions of Man.* New York: McGraw-Hill.

McMahon, Martha 2005 *Engendering Motherhood: Identity and Self-Transformation in Women's Lives.* New York: Guilford Press.

McRae, Susan 2003 "Constraints and Choices in Mothers' Employment Careers: A Consideration of Hakim's Preference Theory." *British Journal of Sociology* 54(3): 317–38.

Meissner, Martin 1971 "The Long Arm of the Job: A Study of Work and Leisure." *Industrial Relations* 10: 239–60.

Meissner, Martin, E. W. Humphreys, S. M. Meis, and W. J. Scheu 1975 "No Exit for Wives: Sexual Division of Labour and the Cumulation of Household Demands." *Canadian Review of Sociology and Anthropology* 12: 424–39.

Mendelsohn, Matthew 2012 "Changes to EI Leave the Job Unfinished." *Globe and Mail,* June 4.

Mendenhall, Ruby, Ariel Kalil, Laurel J. Spindel, and Cassandra M. D. Hart 2008 "Job Loss at Mid-Life: Managers and Executives Face the 'New Risk Economy'" *Social Forces* 87(1): 185–209.

Menzies, Heather 1996 *Whose Brave New World? The Information Highway and the New Economy.* Toronto: Between the Lines.

Merton, Robert K. 1952 "Bureaucratic Structure and Personality." In Robert K. Merton, A. P. Gray, B. Hockey, and H. C. Selvin, eds., *Reader in Bureaucracy.* New York: Free Press.

Messerschmidt, James W., Martin Messner, Raewyn Connell, and Patricia Yancey Martin, eds. 2018 *Gender Reckonings: New Social Theory and Research.* New York: NYU Press.

Meyer, Stephen 1981 *The Five Dollar Day: Labor Management and Social Control in the Ford Motor Company, 1908–1921.* Albany, NY: State University of New York Press.

Michels, Robert 1959 *Political Parties: A Sociological Study of the Oligarchical Tendencies* *of Modern Democracy.* New York: Dover Publications. (Orig. pub. 1915.)

Micklethwait, John, and Adrian Wooldridge 1996 *The Witch Doctors: Making Sense of the Management Gurus.* New York: Times Books.

Middleton, Chris 1988 "The Familiar Fate of the *Famulae:* Gender Divisions in the History of Wage Labour." In R. E. Pahl, ed., *On Work: Historical, Comparative and Theoretical Approaches.* Oxford, England: Basil Blackwell.

Milan, Anne 2015 "Family and Living Arrangements." In *Women in Canada: A Gender-Based Statistical Report.* Ottawa: Statistics Canada. Catalogue no. 80-503-X.

Milan, Anne, Leslie-Anne Keown, and Covadogna Robies Urquijo 2011 "Families, Living Arrangements, and Unpaid Work." In *Women in Canada: A Gender-Based Statistical Report.* Ottawa: Statistics Canada. Catalogue no. 89-503-X.

Milan, Anne, and Kelly Tran 2004 "Blacks in Canada: A Long History." *Canadian Social Trends* (Spring): 2–7.

Milanovic, Branko 2016 *Global Inequality: A New Approach for the Age of Globalization.* Cambridge, MA: Harvard University Press.

Milkman, Ruth 1991 *Japan's California Factories: Labor Relations and Economic Globalization.* Los Angeles: Institute of Industrial Relations, University of California at Los Angeles.

———— **1997** *Farewell to the Factory: Auto Workers in the Late Twentieth Century.* Berkeley: University of California Press.

Miller, Danny, and Jon Hartwick 2002 "Spotting Management Fads." *Harvard Business Review,* October, 26–27.

Miller, Gloria 2004 "Frontier Masculinity in the Oil Industry: The Experience of Women Engineers." *Gender, Work & Organization* 11(1): 47–73.

Miller, Karen A., Melvin L. Kohn, and Carmi Schooler 1985 "Educational Self-Determination and the Cognitive Functioning of Students." *Social Forces* 63(4): 923–44.

Mills, C. Wright 1948 *The New Men of Power.* New York: Harcourt-Brace.

———— **1956** *White Collar: The American Middle Classes.* New York: Oxford University Press.

Mills, Melinda 2004 "Demand for Flexibility or Generation of Insecurity: The Individualization of Risk, Irregular Work

Shifts and Canadian Youth." *Journal of Youth Studies* 7(2): 115–39.

Milner, Henry 1989 *Sweden: Social Democracy in Practice.* Oxford: Oxford University Press.

Mintzberg, Henry 1989 *Mintzberg on Management: Inside Our Strange World of Organizations.* New York: Free Press.

Mishel, Lawrence, and Jared Bernstein 2003 "Wage Inequality and the New Economy in the US: Does IT-Led Growth Generate Wage Inequality?" *Canadian Public Policy* 29(S1): S203–S221.

Mishra, Aneil K., and Gretchen M. Spreitzer 1998 "Explaining How Survivors Respond to Downsizing: The Roles of Trust, Empowerment, Justice, and Work Redesign." *Academy of Management Review* 23(3): 567–88.

Moen, Phyllis, Erin L. Kelly, and Kelly Chermack 2008 "Learning from a Natural Experiment: Studying a Corporate Work-Time Policy Initiative." In A. C. Crouter and A. Booth, eds., *Work-Life Policies That Make a Real Difference for Individuals, Families, and Organizations.* Washington, DC: Urban Institute Press.

Moen, Phyllis, Erin L. Kelly, Wen Fan, Shi-Rong Lee, David Almeida, Ellen Ernst Kossek, and Orfeu M. Buxton 2016 "Does a Flexibility/Support Organizational Initiative Improve High-Tech Employees' Well-Being? Evidence from the Work, Family, and Health Network." *American Sociological Review* 81(1): 134–64.

Moen, Phyllis, Jack Lam, Samantha Ammons, and Erin Kelly 2013 "Time Worked by Overworked Professionals: Strategies in Response to the Stress of Higher Status." *Work and Occupations* 40(2): 79–114.

Mohamed, Norshidah, Nor Shahriza Abdul Karim, and Ramiah Hussein 2010 "Linking Islamic Work Ethic to Computer Use Ethics, Job Satisfaction and Organisational Commitment in Malaysia." *Journal of Business Systems, Governance and Ethics* 5(1): 13–22.

Mohr, Robert D., and Cindy Zoghi 2008 "High-Involvement Work Design and Job Satisfaction." *Industrial and Labor Relations Review* 61(3): 275–96.

Mondragon Corporation 2019 "About Us." https://www.mondragon-corporation.com/en/about-us/ [retrieved 20 April 2019].

Moore, Thomas 2018 "Occupational Career Change and Gender Wage Inequality." *Work and Occupations* 45(1): 82–121.

Morgan, Gareth 1997 *Images of Organization.* Thousand Oaks, CA: Sage Publications.

Morissette, René 1997 "Declining Earnings of Young Men." *Canadian Social Trends* (Autumn): 8–12.

Morissette, René, and Yuri Ostrovky 2007 *Income Instability of Lone Parents, Singles and Two-Parent Families in Canada, 1984 to 2004.* Analytical Studies Branch Research Paper No. 297. Ottawa: Statistics Canada. Cat. no. 11F0019MIE-No. 297.

Morissette, René, Grant Schellenberg, and Cynthia Silver 2004 "Retaining Older Workers." *Perspectives on Labour and Income* 16(Winter): 33–38.

Morissette, René, and Rizwan Sultan 2013 "Twenty Years in the Careers of Immigrant and Native-Born Workers." *Economic Insights*, Issue 32 (November): 1–4. Statistics Canada Cat. no. 11-626-X.

Morissette, René, and Xuelin Zhang 2005 "Escaping Low Earnings." *Perspectives on Labour and Income* 17(Summer): 37–44.

——— 2007 "Revisiting Wealth Inequality." *Perspectives on Labour and Income* 19(1): 6–17.

Morris, Stuart, Gail Fawcett, Laurent Brisebois, and Jeffrey Hughes 2018 *A Demographic, Employment and Income Profile of Canadians with Disabilities, 2017.* Ottawa: Statistics Canada. Cat. no. 89-654-X2018002.

Morita, Masaya 2001 "Have the Seeds of Japanese Teamworking Taken Root Abroad?" *New Technology, Work and Employment* 16(3): 178–90.

Morris, Stuart, Gail Fawcett, Laurent Brisebois, and Jeffrey Hughes 2018 *A Demographic, Employment and Income Profile of Canadians with Disabilities, 2017.* Ottawa: Statistics Canada. Cat. no. 89-654-X2018002.

Morton, Desmond 2007 *Working People: An Illustrated History of the Canadian Labour Movement.* 5th ed. Montreal: McGill-Queen's University Press.

Moss-Racusin, Corinne A., John F. Dovidio, Victoria L. Brescoll, Mark J. Graham, and Jo Handelsman 2012 "Science Faculty's Subtle Gender Biases Favor Male Students." *Proceedings of the National Academy of Sciences* 109(41): 16474–79.

Mousteri, Victoria, Michael Daly, and Liam Delaney 2018 "The Scarring Effect of Unemployment on Psychological Well-being Across Europe." *Social Science Research* 72: 146–69.

Moyser, Melissa 2017 "Women and Paid Work" in *Women in Canada: A Gender-Based Statistical Report.* Ottawa: Statistics Canada. Cat. no. 89-503-X.

Moyser, Melissa, and Amanda Burlock 2018 "Time Use: Total Work Burden, Unpaid Work and Leisure." In *Women in Canada: A Gender-Based Statistical Report.* Ottawa: Statistics Canada. Cat. no. 80-503-X.

Mueller, Frank, Raffaella Valsecchi, Chris Smith, Jonathan Gabe, and Mary Ann Elston 2008 "'We Are Nurses, We Are Supposed to Care for People': Professional Values among Nurses in NHS Direct Call Centres." *New Technology, Work and Employment* 23(1–2): 2–16.

Mueller, Steffen 2012 "Works Councils and Establishment Productivity." *Industrial and Labor Relations Review* 65(4): 880–98.

Müller-Jentsch, Walther 2008 "Industrial Democracy: Historical Development and Current Challenges." *Management Revue* 19(4): 260–73.

Mumford, Enid 2006 "The Story of Socio-technical Design: Reflections on its Successes, Failures and Potential." *Information Systems Journal* 16(4): 317–42.

Munro, Daniel 2019 *Skills, Training, and Lifelong Learning.* Ottawa: Public Policy Forum.

Munro, Daniel, Cameron MacLaine, and James Stucky 2014 *Skills—Where Are We Today?* Ottawa: Conference Board of Canada.

Munsch, Christin 2016 "Flexible Work, Flexible Penalties: The Effect of Gender, Childcare, and Type of Request on the Flexibility Bias." *Social Forces* 94(4): 1567–91.

Murphy, Brian, Paul Roberts, and Michael Wolfson 2007 "High-Income Canadians." *Perspectives on Labour and Income* 19(4): 7–19.

Murphy, Brian, Xuelin Zhang, and Claude Dionne 2012 *Low Income in Canada: A Multi-line and Multi-index Perspective.* Ottawa: Statistics Canada Cat. no. 75F0002M-No. 001.

Mustard, Cam, John N. Lavis, and Aleck Ostry 2005 "Work and Health: New Evidence and Enhanced Understandings." In

Jody Heymann, C. Hertzman, M. Barer, and R. Evans, eds., *Creating Healthier Societies: From Analysis to Action*. Oxford: Oxford University Press.

Muszynski, Alicja 1996 *Cheap Wage Labour: Race and Gender in the Fisheries of British Columbia*. Montreal: McGill–Queen's University Press.

Myles, John 2000 "Incomes of Seniors." *Perspectives on Labour and Income* 12(Winter): 23–32.

Myles, John, and Jill Quadagno, eds. 2005 *States, Labour Markets and the Future of Old Age Policy*. Philadelphia: Temple University Press.

Mythen, Gabe 2005 "Employment, Individualization and Insecurity: Rethinking the Risk Society Perspective." *The Sociological Review* 53(1): 129–49.

National Union of Public and General Employees 2019 "Extending Protections for Wildfire Fighters: BCGEU." https://nupge.ca/content/extending-protections-wildfire-fighters-bcgeu [retrieved 29 April 2019].

Naylor, James 2019 "Standing Together." *Canadian History Magazine* (April–May): 20–30.

Neckerman, Kathryn M., and Florencia Torche 2007 "Inequality: Causes and Consequences." *Annual Review of Sociology* 33: 335–57.

Nelson, Daniel 1980 *Frederick W. Taylor and the Rise of Scientific Management*. Madison, WI: University of Wisconsin Press.

Nelson, Fiona 1996 *Lesbian Motherhood: An Exploration of Canadian Lesbian Families*. Toronto: University of Toronto Press.

Nelson, Joel I. 1995 *Post-industrial Capitalism: Exploring Economic Inequality in America*. Thousand Oaks, CA: Sage Publications

Neumark, David, Ian Burn, and Patrick Button 2016 "Experimental Age Discrimination Evidence and the Heckman Critique." *American Economic Review* 106(5): 303–8.

Ng, Eddy, and Nick Rumens 2017 "Diversity and Inclusion for LGBT Workers: Current Issues and New Horizons for Research." *Canadian Journal of Administrative Sciences* 34(2): 109–20.

Nickel, Rod, and Nia Williams 2019 "Indigenous-Led Offer Could End Trudeau's Trans Mountain Nightmare." *Globe and Mail*, July 2.

Niezen, Ronald 1993 "Power and Dignity: The Social Consequences of HydroElectric Development for the James Bay Cree." *Canadian Review of Sociology and Anthropology* 30: 510–29.

Nilsson, Tommy 1996 "Lean Production and White Collar Work: The Case of Sweden." *Economic and Industrial Democracy* 17: 447–72.

Nishman, Robert F. 1995 *Worker Ownership and the Restructuring of Algoma Steel in the 1990s*. Kingston, ON: IRC Press.

Nixon, Ashley E., Joseph J. Mazzola, Jeremy Bauer, Jeremy R. Krueger, and Paul E. Spector 2011 "Can Work Make You Sick?: A Meta-analysis of the Relationships between Job Stressors and Physical Symptoms." *Work and Stress* 25(1): 1–22.

Noonan, Mary C., and Jennifer L. Glass 2012 "The Hard Truth about Telecommuting." *Monthly Labor Review* (June): 38–45.

Nyberg, Daniel, and Graham Newell 2014 "Collaboration, Co-operation, or Collusion? Contrasting Employee Responses to Managerial Control in Three Call Centres." *British Journal of Industrial Relations* 52(2): 308–32.

Oakes, Leslie S., Barbara Townley, and David J. Cooper 1998 "Business Planning as Pedagogy: Language and Control in a Changing Institutional Field." *Administrative Science Quarterly* 43: 257–92.

O' Donahue Wayne, and Lindsay Nelson 2014 "Alienation: An Old Concept with Contemporary Relevance for Human Resource Management." *International Journal of Organizational Analysis* 22(3): 301–16.

OECD [Organisation for Economic Co-operation and Development] 2004 *OECD Employment Outlook 2004*. Paris: OECD. IXBN 92-64-01045-9.

———— **2012** *OECD Factbook 2011–12*. Paris: OECD.

———— **2018a** *Multinational Enterprises in the Global Economy*. Paris: OECD.

———— **2018b** *Indigenous Employment and Skills Strategies in Canada*. Paris: OECD.

———— **2019** *The Future of Work: OECD Employment Outlook*. Paris: OECD.

OECD and Statistics Canada 2011 *Literacy for Life: Further Results from the Adult Literacy*

and *Life Skills Survey Second International ALL
Report*. Ottawa: Statistics Canada. Cat. no.
89-604-XWE-2011001.

**O'Faircheallaigh, Ciaran, and Tony
Corbett 2005** "Indigenous Participation
in Environmental Management of Mining
Projects: The Role of Negotiated Agreements."
Environmental Politics 14(5): 629–47.

**Oldham, Greg R., and J. Richard Hackman
2010** "Not What It Was and Not What
It Will Be: The Future of Job Redesign
Research." *Journal of Organizational Behavior*
31: 463–79.

Ollivier, Michèle 2000 "'Too Much Money off
Other People's Backs': Status in Late Modern
Societies." *Canadian Journal of Sociology* 25(4):
441–70.

Olsen, Gregg 2008 "Labour Market Policy
in the United States, Canada and Sweden:
Addressing the Issue of Convergence." *Social
Policy & Administration* 42(4): 323–41.

O'Neill, Jeff 1991 "Changing Occupational
Structure." *Canadian Social Trends* (Winter):
8–12.

O'Neill, Jim 2018 "These 11 Countries Could
be the Future of The Global Economy." *World
Economic Forum*. https://www.weforum.org/
agenda/2018/04/these-11-countries-could-be-
the-future-of-the-global-economy/.

Ontario 2014 *Report and Final
Recommendations of the Ontario Minimum
Wage Advisory Panel*. Toronto: Ontario
Ministry of Labour.

Ontario Equal Pay Coalition 2017 "History
of Pay Equity Advocacy in Ontario." http://
equalpaycoalition.org/history-of-pay-equity-
advocacy-in-ontario/ [retrieved June 19, 2019].

**Orbach, Maya, Maegan Demko, Jeremy
Doyle, Benjamin N. Waber, and Alex
Pentland 2015** "Sensing Informal Networks
in Organizations." *American Behavioral
Scientist* 59(4): 508–24.

Orme, W. A., Jr. 1996 *Understanding NAFTA:
Mexico, Free Trade, and the New North
America*. Austin: University of Texas Press.

Ortiz, Luis 2010 "Not the Right Job, But a
Secure One: Over-education and Temporary
Employment in France, Italy and Spain."
Work, Employment and Society 24(1): 47–64.

Osberg, Lars, Fred Wein, and Jan Grude 1995
Vanishing Jobs: Canada's Changing Workplace.
Toronto: Lorimer.

Ospina, Sonia 1996 *Illusions of Opportunity:
Employee Expectations and Workplace
Inequality*. Ithaca: Cornell University Press.

Osterman, Paul 2000 "Work Reorganization in
an Era of Restructuring: Trends in Diffusion
and Effects on Employee Welfare." *Industrial
and Labor Relations Review* 53(2): 179–96.

———— **2010** "Job Design in the Context of
the Job Market." *Journal of Organizational
Behavior* 31: 401–11.

**Osterman, Paul, and M. Diane Burton
2005** "Ports and Ladders: The Nature and
Relevance of Internal Labor Markets in a
Changing World." In Stephen Ackroyd, R.
Batt, P. Thompson, and P. S. Tolbert, eds., *The
Oxford Handbook of Work and Organization*.
Oxford: Oxford University Press.

Osterman, Paul, and Beth Shulman 2011
*Good Jobs America: Making Work Better for
Everyone*. New York: Russell Sage Foundation.

Ostroff, Frank 1999 *The Horizontal
Organization: What the Organization of
the Future Actually Looks Like and How It
Delivers Value to Customers*. New York: Oxford
University Press.

Ostry, Sylvia 1968 *The Female Worker in
Canada*. Ottawa: Queen's Printer.

O'Toole, James, ed. 1977 *Work, Learning
and the American Future*. San Francisco:
Jossey-Bass.

Ott, Brian 2016 "The Limits of Control
in Service Work: Interactive Routines and
Interactional Competence." *Research in the
Sociology of Work* 29: 155–83.

Owram, Doug 1996 *Born at the Right Time: A
History of the Baby Boom Generation*. Toronto:
University of Toronto Press.

Palameta, Boris 2004 "Low Income among
Immigrants and Visible Minorities."
Perspectives on Labour and Income
16(Summer): 32–37.

Palmer, Bryan 1975 "Class, Conception
and Conflict: The Thrust for Efficiency,
Managerial Views of Labor and the Working
Class Rebellion, 1902–22." *Radical Review of
Political Economics* 7: 31–49.

———— **1979** *A Culture in Conflict: Skilled
Workers and Industrial Capitalism in Hamilton,
Ontario, 1860–1914*. Montreal: McGill–
Queen's University Press.

———— **1992** *Working Class Experience:
Rethinking the History of Canadian Labour,*

1800–1991. 2nd ed. Toronto: McClelland & Stewart.

Palmer, Craig, and Peter Sinclair 1997 *When the Fish Are Gone: Ecological Disaster and Fishers in Northwestern Newfoundland.* Halifax: Fernwood Publishing.

Panitch, Leo, and Donald Swartz 1993 *The Assault on Trade Union Freedoms: From Wage Controls to Social Contract.* Toronto: Garamond.

Park, Jungwee 2012 "Job-Related Training of Older Workers." *Perspectives on Labour and Income* (Summer): 27–36.

Parker, Jane, and Janice Foley 2010 "Progress on Women's Equality with U.K. and Canadian Trade Unions: Do Women's Structures Make a Difference?" *Relations Industrielles/Industrial Relations* 65(2): 281–303.

Parr, Joy 1990 *The Gender of Breadwinners: Women, Men and Change in Two Industrial Towns 1880–1950.* Toronto: University of Toronto Press.

Parreñas, Rhacel Salazar 2001 *Servants of Globalization: Women, Migration and Domestic Work.* Stanford, CA: Stanford University Press.

Parthasarathy, Balaji 2004 "India's Silicon Valley or Silicon Valley's India? Socially Embedding the Computer Software Industry in Bangalore." *International Journal of Urban and Regional Research* 28(3): 664–85.

Patrias Carmela 2016 "More Menial Than Housemaids? Racialized and Gendered Labour in the Fruit and Vegetable Industry of Canada's Niagara Region, 1880–1945." *Labour/Le Travail*: 69–104.

Patterson, E. Palmer, II 1972 *The Canadian Indian: A History since 1500.* Don Mills, ON: Collier-Macmillan.

Patterson, Martha 2018 "Who Works Part-Time and Why?" *Labour Statistics at a Glance.* Ottawa: Statistics Canada. Cat. no. 71-222-X.

Patterson, Martha, Myriam Hazel, and Dylan Saunders 2018 *Annual Review of the Labour Market, 2018.* Ottawa: Statistics Canada. Cat. no. 75-004-M-2019002.

Payne, Jonathan 2009 "Emotional Labour and Skill: A Reappraisal." *Gender, Work & Organization* 16(3): 348–67.

Pedulla, David 2013 "The Hidden Costs of Contingency: Employers' Use of Contingent Workers and Standard Employees' Outcomes." *Social Forces* 92(2): 691–722.

———— **2016** "Penalized or Protected? Gender and the Consequences of Nonstandard and Mismatched Employment Histories." *American Sociological Review* 81(2): 262–89.

Pedulla, David, and Sarah Thébaud 2015 "Can We Finish the Revolution? Gender, Work-Family Ideals, and Institutional Constraint." *American Sociological Review* 80(1): 116–39.

Pendleton, Andrew, and Andrew Robinson 2010 "Employee Stock Ownership, Involvement, and Productivity: an Interaction-Based Approach." *Industrial and Labor Relations Review* 64(1): 3–29.

Pentland, H. Claire 1981 *Labour and Capital in Canada, 1650–1860.* Toronto: James Lorimer.

Perales, Francisco 2013 "Occupational Sex-Segregation, Specialized Human Capital and Wages: Evidence from Britain." *Work Employment and Society* 27(4): 600–20.

Perlow, Leslie 2012 *Sleeping with Your Smartphone: How to Break the 24/7 Habit and Change the Way You Work.* Boston: Harvard Business School Publishing.

Pérotin, Virginie 2016 *What Do We Really Know About Worker Co-operatives?* Co-operatives UK: https://www.uk.coop/sites/default/files/uploads/attachments/worker_co-op_report.pdf [retrieved 20 April 2019].

Peters, Thomas J., and Robert H. Waterman Jr. 1982 *In Search of Excellence.* New York: Warner.

Peters, Tom 1987 *Thriving on Chaos: Handbook for a Management Revolution.* New York: Alfred A. Knopf.

Petersen, Trond, Ishak Saporta, and Marc-David L. Seidel 2000 "Offering a Job: Meritocracy and Social Networks." *American Journal of Sociology* 106: 763–816.

Petter, Olivia 2019 "National Go Home on Time Day." *The Independent.* https://www.independent.co.uk/life-style/national-go-home-on-time-day-2019-what-why-working-families-a8968636.html [retrieved June 28 2019].

PEW Research Center 2013 *A Survey of LGBT Americans.* https://www.pewsocialtrends.org/2013/06/13/a-survey-of-lgbt-americans/.

Pfeffer, Carla 2017 *Queering Families: The Postmodern Partnerships of Cisgender Women* and *Transgender Men.* New York: Oxford University.

Pfeffer, Jeffrey 1994 *Competitive Advantage through People: Unleashing the Power of the Workforce.* Boston: Harvard University Press.

Pfeffer, Jeffrey, and Robert I. Sutton 2000 *The Knowing–Doing Gap: How Smart Companies Turn Knowledge into Action.* Boston: Harvard Business School Press.

Phelan, Jo 1994 "The Paradox of the Contented Female Worker: An Assessment of Alternative Explanations." *Social Psychology Quarterly* 57: 95–107.

Pichler, Shaun, and Enrica Ruggs 2018 "LGBT Workers." In Adrienne J. Colella and Eden B. King, eds., *The Oxford Handbook of Workplace Discrimination.* Oxford: Oxford University Press.

Picot, Garnett 1987 "The Changing Industrial Mix of Employment, 1951–1985." *Canadian Social Trends* (Spring): 8–11.

———— **1998** "What Is Happening to Earnings Inequality and Youth Wages in the 1990s?" *Canadian Economic Observer* (September): 3.1–3.18.

———— **2008** *Immigrant Economic and Social Outcomes in Canada: Research and Data Development at Statistics Canada.* Ottawa: Statistics Canada. Cat. no. 11F0019M-No. 319.

Pierce, Jennifer 1995 *Gender Trials: Emotional Lives in Contemporary Law Firms.* Berkeley and Los Angeles: University of California Press.

Pierson, Ruth Roach 1986 *They're Still Women After All: The Second World War and Canadian Womanhood.* Toronto: McClelland and Stewart.

Piketty, Thomas 2014 *Capital in the Twenty-first Century.* Boston: Harvard University Press.

Piore, Michael J., and Charles F. Sabel 1984 *The Second Industrial Divide: Possibilities for Prosperity.* New York: Basic Books.

Piotrowski, Martin, Arne Kalleberg, and Ronald R. Rindfuss 2015 "Contingent Work Rising: Implications for the Timing of Marriage in Japan." *Journal of Marriage and Family* 77(5): 1039–56.

Pirson, Michael A., and Paul R. Lawrence 2010 "Humanism in Business—Towards a Paradigm Shift?" *Journal of Business Ethics* 93(4): 553–65.

Piva, Michael J. 1979 *The Condition of the Working Class in Toronto, 1900–1921.* Ottawa: University of Ottawa Press.

Podolny, Joel M., and Karen L. Page 1998 "Network Forms of Organization." *Annual Review of Sociology* 24: 57–64.

Pohler, Dionne, and Andrew Luchak 2015 "Are Unions Good or Bad for Organizations? The Moderating Role of Management's Response." *British Journal of Industrial Relations* 53(3): 423–59.

Polanyi, Karl 1957 *The Great Transformation.* Boston: Beacon Press.

Pollert, Anna 1988 "The Flexible Firm: Fixation or Fact?" *Work, Employment and Society* 2: 281–316.

Ponak, Allen, and Daphne Taras 1995 *Right-to-Work.* Submission to Alberta Economic Development Authority Joint Review Committee.

Pope Francis 2013 "General Audience Saint Peter's Square" [transcript]. May 1, 2013. http://w2.vatican.va/content/francesco/en/audiences/2013/documents/papa-francesco_20130501_udienza-generale.html.

Popper, Micha, and Raanan Lipshitz 2000 "Organizational Learning: Mechanisms, Culture, and Feasibility." *Management Learning* 31(2): 181–96.

Poutsma, Erik, John Hendrickx, and Fred Huijgen 2003 "Employee Participation in Europe: In Search of the Participative Workplace." *Economic and Industrial Democracy* 24(1): 45–76.

Powell, Gary 2019 *Women and Men in Management.* 5th ed. Thousand Oaks: Sage Publications.

Pratt, Courtney 2007 "'New Big Thing' Could Put Brakes on CEO Pay." *Globe and Mail,* June 11, B2.

Premji, S., Y. Shakya, M. Spasevski, J. Merolli, S. Athar, and Precarious Employment Core Research Group 2014 "Precarious Work Experiences of Racialized Immigrant Woman in Toronto: A Community-Based Study." *Just Labour* 22: 122–43.

Press, Jordan 2018 "Liberals Eye Closer Look at 'Right to Disconnect' in Labour Rule Revamp." *Globe and Mail,* August 30.

Presser, Harriet 2003 *Working in the 24/7 Economy: Challenges for American Families.* New York: Russell Sage Foundation.

Pringle, Rosemary 1989 "Bureaucracy, Rationality and Sexuality: The Case of Secretaries." In Jeff Hearn, Deborah L. Sheppard, Peta Tancred-Sheriff, and Gibson Burrell, eds., *The Sexuality of Organization*. London: Sage.

Prince, Michael J. 2009 *Absent Citizens: Disability Politics and Policy in Canada*. Toronto: University of Toronto Press.

Prokopenko, Elena, and Feng Hou 2018 *How Temporary Were Canada's Temporary Foreign Workers?* Ottawa: Statistics Canada. Analytic Studies Branch. Cat. no. 11F0019M.

Pruijt, Hans 2003 "Teams between Neo-Taylorism and Anti-Taylorism." *Economic and Industrial Democracy* 24(1): 77–101.

Pullman, Ashley, and Lesley Andres 2018. "General and Work-based Extrinsic Educational Beliefs across Time: From Late Youth to Middle Adulthood." *Journal of Youth Studies* (published online 10 July 2019).

Pupo, Norene 1997 "Always Working, Never Done: The Expansion of the Double Day." In Ann Duffy, Daniel Glenday, and Norene Pupo, eds., *Good Jobs, Bad Jobs, No Jobs: The Transformation of Work in the 21st Century*. Toronto: Harcourt-Brace Canada.

Pupo, Norene J., and Andrea Noack 2010 "Dialling for Service: Transforming the Public-Sector Workplace in Canada." In Norene J. Pupo and Mark P. Thomas, eds., *Interrogating the New Economy: Restructuring Work in the 21st Century*. Toronto: University of Toronto Press.

Pupo, Norene, and Andrea M. Noack 2014 "Organizing Local Messengers: Working Conditions and Barriers to Unionization." *Canadian Journal of Sociology* 39(3): 331–56.

Pupo, Norene J., and Mark P. Thomas, eds., 2010 *Interrogating the New Economy: Restructuring Work in the 21st Century*. Toronto: University of Toronto Press.

Pyle, Kenneth 1996 *The Making of Modern Japan*. 2nd ed. Lexington: D.C. Heath and Company.

Quinn, Robert 2015 *The Positive Organization: Breaking Free from Conventional Cultures, Constraints and Beliefs*. Oakland CA: Berrett-Koehler.

Racette, Sherry Farrell 2012 "Nimble Fingers and Strong Backs: First Nations and Metis Women in Fur Trade." In Carol Williams, ed., *Indigenous Women and Work: From Labor to Activism*. Urbana: University of Illinois Press.

Radl, Jonas 2012 "Too Old to Work, or Too Young to Retire? The Pervasiveness of Age Norms in Western Europe." *Work, Employment and Society* 26(5): 775–71.

Raff, Daniel M. G. 1988 "Wage Determination Theory and the Five-Dollar Day at Ford." *The Journal of Economic History* 48(2): 387–99.

Randle, Keith 1996 "The White-Coated Worker: Professional Autonomy in a Period of Change." *Work, Employment and Society* 10: 737–53.

Rankin, Tom 1990 *New Forms of Work Organization: The Challenge for North American Unions*. Toronto: University of Toronto Press.

Ranson, Gillian 1998 "Education, Work and Family Decision-Making: Finding the 'Right Time' to Have a Baby." *Canadian Review of Sociology and Anthropology* 35(4): 517–33.

——— 2010 *Against the Grain: Couples, Gender, and the Reframing of Parenting*. Toronto: University of Toronto Press.

Rayman, Paula M. 2001 *Beyond the Bottom Line: The Search for Dignity at Work*. New York: Palgrave.

Rege, Mari, Kjetil Telle, and Mark Votruba 2009 "The Effect of Plant Downsizing on Disability Pension Utilization." *Journal of the European Economic Association* 7(4): 754–85.

Reich, Robert B. 1991 *The Work of Nations: Preparing Ourselves for 21st-Century Capitalism*. New York: Alfred A. Knopf.

——— 2000 *The Future of Success*. New York: Alfred A. Knopf.

——— 2015 *Saving Capitalism: For the Many, Not the Few*. New York: Alfred Knopf.

Reid, Frank 1982 "Wage-and-Price Controls in Canada." In John Anderson and Morley Gunderson, eds., *Union–Management Relations in Canada*. Don Mills, ON: Addison-Wesley.

Reitz, Jeffrey G. 2007a "Immigrant Employment Success in Canada, Part I: Individual and Contextual Causes." *Journal of International Migration and Integration* 8: 11–36.

——— 2007b "Immigrant Employment Success in Canada, Part II: Understanding the Decline." *Journal of International Migration and Integration* 8: 37–62.

Reitz, Jeffrey G., and Anil Verma 2004 "Immigration, Race, and Labor: Unionization and Wages in the Canadian Labor Market." *Industrial Relations* 43(4): 835–54.

Reshef, Yonatan, and Charles Keim 2014 *Bad Time Stories: Government-Union Conflicts and the Rhetoric of Legitimation Strategies.* Toronto: University of Toronto Press.

Reshef, Yonatan, and Sandra Rastin 2003 *Unions in the Time of Revolution: Government Restructuring in Alberta and Ontario.* Toronto: University of Toronto Press.

Reskin, Barbara 1998 *The Realities of Affirmative Action in Employment.* Washington, DC: American Sociological Association.

Reskin, Barbara F., and Debra B. McBrier 2000 "Why Not Ascription? Organizations' Employment of Male and Female Managers." *American Sociological Review* 65: 210–33.

Reskin, Barbara, and Irene Padavic 2002 *Men and Women at Work.* 2nd ed. Thousand Oaks, CA: Pine Forge Press.

Richardson, Charley 1996 "Computers Don't Kill Jobs, People Do: Technology and Power in the Workplace." *Annals of the American Academy of Political and Social Science* (March): 167–79.

Riddell, W. Craig 1985 "Work and Pay: The Canadian Labour Market: An Overview." In W. Craig Riddell, ed., *Work and Pay: The Canadian Labour Market.* Toronto: University of Toronto Press.

——— **2005** "Why Is Canada's Unemployment Rate Persistently Higher Than In The United States." *Canadian Public Policy* 31(1): 93–100.

Ridgeway, Cecilia 2011 *Framed by Gender: How Gender Inequality Persists in the Modern World.* Oxford and New York: Oxford University Press.

——— **2014** "Why Status Matters for Inequality." *American Sociological Review* 79(1): 1–16.

Ridley-Duff, Rory 2010 "Communitarian Governance in Social Enterprises: Case Evidence from the Mondragon Cooperative Corporation and School Trends Ltd." *Social Enterprise Journal* 6(2): 125–45.

Rieger, Sarah 2018 "Postal Workers, Union Allies Protest Strike-Breaking Legislation." *CBC News*, December 2. https://www.cbc.ca/news/canada/calgary/postal-protests-calgary-edmonton-1.4929407 [retrieved 29 April 2019].

Rifkin, Jeremy 1995 *The End of Work: The Decline of the Global Labor Force and the Dawn of the Post-market Era.* New York: Putnam.

Rinehart, James 1978 "Contradictions of Work-Related Attitudes and Behaviour: An Interpretation." *Canadian Review of Sociology and Anthropology* 15: 1–15.

——— **1984** "Appropriating Workers' Knowledge: Quality Control Circles at a General Motors Plant." *Studies in Political Economy* 14: 75–97.

——— **2006** *The Tyranny of Work: Alienation and the Labour Process.* 5th ed. Toronto: Thomson Nelson.

Rinehart, James, Christopher Huxley, and David Robertson 1997 *Just Another Car Factory: Lean Production and Its Discontents.* Ithaca, NY: ILR Press.

Rivera, Lauren A. 2012 "Hiring as Cultural Matching: The Case of Elite Professional Firms." *American Sociological Review* 77(6): 999–1022.

——— **2016** *Pedigree: How Elite Students Get Elite Jobs.* Princeton, NJ: Princeton University Press.

Roberts, Karen, Doug Hyatt, and Peter Dorman 1996 "The Effect of Free Trade on Contingent Work in Michigan." In Karen Roberts and Mark I. Wilson, eds., *Policy Choices: Free Trade among NAFTA Nations.* East Lansing, MI: Michigan State University Press.

Roberts, Wayne 1990 *Cracking the Canadian Formula: The Making of the Energy and Chemical Workers Union.* Toronto: Between the Lines.

Robertson, David, James Rinehart, Christopher Huxley, and the CAW Research Group on CAMI 1992 "Team Concept and Kaizen: Japanese Production Management in a Unionized Canadian Auto Plant." *Studies in Political Economy* 39(Autumn): 77–107.

Robertson, David, and Jeff Wareham 1987 *Technological Change in the Auto Industry.* Willowdale, ON: Canadian Auto Workers.

Rodrik, Dani 2007 *One Economics, Many Recipes.* Princeton and Oxford: Princeton University Press.

Rodriquez, Jason 2017 "Doing More With Less: Intensive Care and the Logic of Flexible Teamwork." *Research in the Sociology of Work* 39: 117–40.

Roethlisberger, F. J., and W. J. Dickson 1939 *Management and the Worker*. Cambridge, MA: Harvard University Press.

Rollings-Magnusson, Sandra 2000 "Canada's Most Wanted: Pioneer Women on the Western Prairies." *Canadian Review of Sociology and Anthropology* 37(2): 223–38.

Rónas-Tas, Ákos 1994 "The First Shall Be Last? Entrepreneurship and Communist Cadres in the Transition from Socialism." *American Journal of Sociology* 100: 40–69.

Roscigno, Vincent J., Sherry Mong, Reginald Byron, and Griff Tester 2007 "Age Discrimination, Social Closure and Employment." *Social Forces* 86(1): 313–34.

Roscigno, Vincent J., Carsten Sauer, and Peter Valet 2018 "Rules, Relations, and Work." *American Journal of Sociology* 123(6): 1784–825.

Rosenblat, Alex 2018 *Uberland: How Algorithms are Rewriting the Rules of Work*. Oakland, CA: University of California Press.

Rosenfeld, Jake 2014 *What Unions No Longer Do*. Cambridge, MA: Harvard University Press.

Rosenthal, Patrice, Stephen Hill, and Riccardo Peccei 1997 "Checking Out Service: Evaluating Excellence, HRM and TQM in Retailing." *Work, Employment and Society* 11(3): 481–503.

Ross, Peter, Greg J. Bamber, and Gillian Whitehouse 1998 "Employment, Economics and Industrial Relations: Comparative Statistics." In Greg J. Bamber and Russell D. Lansbury, eds., *International and Comparative Employment Relations*. 3rd ed. Thousand Oaks, CA: Sage Publications.

Ross, Stephanie, and Jason Russell 2018 "'Caterpillar Hates Unions More Than It Loves Profits': The Electro-Motive Closure and the Dilemma of Union Strategy." *Labour/Le Travail* 81(Spring): 53–85.

Ross-Smith, Anne, and Kate Huppatz 2010 "Management, Women, and Gender Capital." *Gender, Work & Organization* 17(5): 547–66.

Rothstein, Jeffrey 2005 "Selective Participation: Controlling Workers' Input at General Motors." *Research in the Sociology of Work* 16: 151–75.

Rowe, Reba, and William E. Snizek 1995 "Gender Differences in Work Values: Perpetuating the Myth." *Work and Occupations* 22: 215–29.

Roy, Donald 1952 "Quota Restriction and Goldbricking in a Machine Shop." *American Journal of Sociology* 57: 427–42.

——— 1959–60 "'Banana time': Job Satisfaction and Informal Interaction." *Human Organization* 18: 158–68.

Rubery, Jill 1996 "The Labour Market Outlook and the Outlook for Labour Market Analysis." In Rosemary Crompton, Duncan Gallie, and Kate Purcell, eds., *Changing Forms of Employment: Organisations, Skills and Gender*. London: Routledge.

Rubery, Jill, and Damian Grimshaw 2001 "ICTs and Employment: The Problem of Job Quality." *International Labour Review* 140(2): 165–92.

Ruddick, Sara 1995 *Maternal Thinking: Towards a Politics of Peace*. Boston: Beacon Press.

Russell, Bob 1990 *Back to Work? Labour, State, and Industrial Relations in Canada*. Scarborough, ON: Nelson.

——— 1997 "Rival Paradigms at Work: Work Reorganization and Labour Force Impacts in a Staple Industry." *Canadian Review of Sociology and Anthropology* 34: 25–52.

——— 1999 *More with Less: Work Reorganization in the Canadian Mining Industry*. Toronto: University of Toronto Press.

Ryerson, Stanley B. 1968 *Unequal Union: Confederation and the Roots of Conflict in the Canadas, 1815–1873*. Toronto: Progress Books.

Sainato, Michael 2019 "We are not Robots: Amazon Warehouse Employees Push to Unionize." *The Guardian* (1 January 2019). https://www.theguardian.com/technology/2019/jan/01/amazon-fulfillment-center-warehouse-employees-union-new-york-minnesota [retrieved 9 April 2019].

Sallaz, Jeffrey J. 2004 "Manufacturing Concessions: Attritionary Outsourcing at GM's Lordstown, USA Assembly Plant." *Work, Employment and Society* 18(4): 687–708.

Samra, Joti 2017 *The Evolution of Workplace Mental Health in Canada: Research Report (2007–2017)*. https://www.hrpa.ca/Documents/Public/Thought-Leadership/The-Evolution-of-Workplace-Mental-Health-in-Canada.pdf [retrieved 1 April 2019].

Sanchez, Laura, and Elizabeth Thomson 1997 "Becoming Mothers and Fathers: Parenthood, Gender and the Division of Labor." *Gender & Society* 11(6): 747–72.

Sandberg, Ake 1994 " 'Volvoism' at the End of the Road?" *Studies in Political Economy* 45: 170–82.

Sangster, Joan 1978 "The 1907 Bell Telephone Strike: Organizing Women Workers." *Labour/Le Travail* 3: 109–30.

————— **1995** "Doing Two Jobs: The Wage-Earning Mother, 1945–70." In Joy Parr, ed., *A Diversity of Women: Ontario, 1945–1980.* Toronto: University of Toronto Press.

————— **2010** *Transforming Labour: Women and Work in Postwar Canada.* Toronto: University of Toronto Press.

————— **2011** *Through Feminist Eyes: Essays on Canadian Women's History.* Edmonton: Athabasca University Press.

Sargent, Timothy C. 2000 "Structural Unemployment and Technological Change in Canada, 1990–1999." *Canadian Public Policy* 26(S1): 109–23.

Sass, Robert 1986 "Workplace Health and Safety: Report from Canada." *International Journal of Health Services* 16: 565–82.

————— **1995** "A Conversation about the Work Environment." *International Journal of Health Services* 25: 117–28.

Sassen, Saskia 2002 "Global Cities and Survival Circuits." In Barbara Ehrenreich and Arlie Russell Hochschild, eds., *Global Woman: Nannies, Maids, and Sex Workers in the New Economy.* New York: Metropolitan Books.

Satzewich, Vic, ed. 1998 *Racism and Social Inequality in Canada: Concepts, Controversies and Strategies of Resistance.* Toronto: Thompson Educational Publishing.

Saul, John R. 1995 *The Unconscious Civilization.* Toronto: Anansi.

Savage, Mike 2015 *Social Class in in the 21st century.* London: Penguin.

Savage, Mike, Fiona Devine, Niall Cunningham, Mark Taylor, Yaojun Li, Johs Hjellbrekke, Brigitte Le Roux, Sam Friedman, and Andrew Miles 2013 "A New Model of Social Class? Findings from the BBC's Great British Class Survey Experiment." *Sociology* 47(2): 219–50.

Schalk, René, and Adriënne van Rijckevorsel 2007 "Factors Influencing Absenteeism and Intention to Leave in a Call Centre." *New Technology, Work and Employment* 22(3): 260–74.

Schantz, Amanda, Kerstin Alfes, Catherine Bailey, and Emma Soane 2015 "Drivers and Outcomes of Work Alienation: Reviving a Concept." *Journal of Management Inquiry* 24(4): 382–93.

Schecter, Stephen, and Bernard Paquet 1999 "Contested Approaches in the Study of Poverty: The Canadian Case and the Argument for Inclusion." *Current Sociology* 47(3): 43–64.

Schein, Edgar H. 2004 *Organizational Culture and Leadership.* 3rd ed. San Francisco: Jossey-Bass.

Schellenberg, Grant, and Hélène Maheux 2007 "Immigrants' Perspectives on Their First Four Years in Canada: Highlights from Three Waves of the Longitudinal Survey of Immigrants to Canada." *Canadian Social Trends* (Special Edition): 2–17.

Schellenberg, Grant, and Yuri Ostrovsky 2008 "The Retirement Plans and Expectations of Older Workers." *Canadian Social Trends* (Winter): 11–34.

Schellenberg, Grant, and Cynthia Silver 2004 "You Can't Always Get What You Want: Retirement Preferences and Experiences." *Canadian Social Trends* (Winter): 2–7.

Schieman, Scott, and Paul Glavin 2016 "The Pressure-Status Nexus and Blurred Work-Family Boundaries." *Work and Occupations* 43(1): 3–37.

Schirle, Tammy 2015 "The Gender Wage Gap in the Canadian Provinces, 1997–2014." *Canadian Public Policy* 41(4): 309–19.

Schissel, Bernard, and Terry Wotherspoon 2003 *The Legacy of School for Aboriginal People: Education, Oppression, and Emancipation.* Don Mills, ON: Oxford University Press.

Schneider, Benjamin, Mark G. Ehrhart, and William H. Macey 2013 "Organizational Climate and Culture." *Annual Review of Psychology* 64: 361–88.

Schooler, Carmi 1984 "Psychological Effects of Complex Environments during the Life Span: A Review and Theory." *Intelligence* 8: 259–81.

————— **1996** "Cultural and Social-Structural Explanations of Cross-National Psychological Differences." *Annual Review of Sociology* 22: 323–49.

Schor, Juliet 1991 *The Overworked American: The Unexpected Decline of Leisure*. New York: Basic Books.

———— 1998 *The Overspent American*. New York: Basic Books.

Schörpf, Philip, Jörg Flecker, Annika Schönauer, and Hubert Eichmann 2017 "Triangular Love-hate: Management and Control in Creative Crowdworking." *New Technology, Work and Employment* 32(1): 43–58.

Schott, Jeffrey, and Gary Hufbauer 2007 "NAFTA Revisited." *Policy Options* (October): 83–88.

Schouteten, Roel, and Jos Benders 2004 "Lean Production Assessed by Karasek's Job Demand–Job Control Model." *Economic and Industrial Democracy* 25(3): 347–73.

Schuetze, Hans 2012 "Large Archipelago, Small Bridges, and Infrequent Ferries: Lifelong Learning and Canadian Higher Education." In Maria Slowey and Hans Schuetze, eds., *Global Perspectives on Higher Education and Lifelong Learners*. New York: Routledge.

Schur, Lisa, Adrienne Colella, and Meera Adya 2016 "Introduction to Special Issue on People with Disabilities in the Workplace." *International Journal of Human Resource Management* 24(14): 1471–76.

Schwartz, Nelson D., and Michael Corkery 2018 "In Its Heyday, Sears Spread the Wealth. Companies Today Don't." *New York Times*, October 23, A1.

Scott, Robert E., Carlos Salas, and Bruce Campbell 2006 *Revisiting NAFTA: Still Not Working for North America's Workers*. Economic Policy Institute Briefing Paper no. 173. http://epi.3cdn.net/6def605657a958c3d a_85m6ibu0h.pdf.

Seeman, Melvin 1975 "Alienation Studies." *Annual Review of Sociology* 1: 91–125.

Segal, David 2012 "Apple's Retail Army, Long on Loyalty but Short on Pay." *New York Times*, June 23.

Seligman, Martin 2013 *Flourish: A Visionary New Understanding of Happiness and Well-being*. New York: Atria.

Selmi, Michael, and Sonia Weil 2013 "Can All Women Be Pharmacists? A Critique of Hanna Rosin's *The End of Men*." *Boston University Law Review* 93(3): 851–70.

Semler, Ricardo 2007 "Out of This World: Doing Things the Semco Way." *Global Business and Organizational Excellence* 26(5): 13–21.

Semuels, Alana 2015 "Getting Rid of Bosses: Can a Company Succeed If No One Is In Charge?" *Atlantic Monthly*, July 8. https://www.theatlantic.com/business/archive/2015/07/no-bosses-worker-owned-cooperatives/397007/ [retrieved 19 April 2019].

Senge, Peter M. 1990 *The Fifth Discipline: The Art and Practice of the Learning Organization*. New York: Doubleday.

Sennett, Richard 1998 *The Corrosion of Character: The Personal Consequences of Work in the New Capitalism*. New York: W.W. Norton.

Sennett, Richard, and Jonathan Cobb 1972 *The Hidden Injuries of Class*. New York: Knopf.

Seok-Woo, Kwon, and Paul S. Adler 2014 "Social Capital: Maturation of a Field of Research." *Academy of Management Review* 39(4): 412–22.

Seron, C., S. Silbey, E. Cech, and B. Rubineau 2018 "'I am Not a Feminist, but …': Hegemony of a Meritocratic Ideology and the Limits of Critique amongst Women in Engineering." *Work and Occupations* 45(2): 131–67.

Sev'er, Aysan 1999 "Sexual Harassment." Special Issue. *Canadian Review of Sociology and Anthropology* 36(4).

Sewell, Graham 1998 "The Discipline of Teams: The Control of Team-Based Industrial Work through Electronic and Peer Surveillance." *Administrative Science Quarterly* 43: 397–428.

Sewell, Graham, and Barry Wilkinson 1992 "Someone to Watch Over Me: Surveillance, Discipline and Just-in-Time Labour Process." *Sociology* 26(2): 271–89.

Shaker, Erika, and David MacDonald 2015 *What's the Difference? Taking Stock of Provincial Tuition Fee Policies*. Ottawa: Canadian Centre for Policy Alternatives.

Shalla, Vivian 2002 "Jettisoned by Design? The Truncated Employment Relationship of Customer Sales and Service Agents under Airline Restructuring." *Canadian Journal of Sociology* 27(1): 1–32.

———— 2004 "Time Warped: The Flexibilization and Maximization of Flight Attendant Working Time." *The Canadian*

Review of Sociology and Anthropology 41(3): 345–68.

———— **2007a** "Theoretical Reflections on Work: A Quarter-Century of Critical Thinking." In Vivian Shalla and Wallace Clement, eds., *Work in Tumultuous Times: Critical Perspectives*. Montreal: McGill–Queen's University Press.

———— **2007b** "Shifting Temporalities: Economic Restructuring and the Politics of Working Time." In Vivian Shalla and Wallace Clement, eds., *Work in Tumultuous Times: Critical Perspectives*. Montreal: McGill–Queen's University Press.

Shalla, Vivian, and Wallace Clement, eds. 2007 *Work in Tumultuous Times: Critical Perspectives*. Montreal: McGill–Queen's University Press.

Shanahan, Michael J. 2000 "Pathways to Adulthood in Changing Societies: Variability and Mechanisms in Life Course Perspective." *Annual Review of Sociology* 26: 667–92.

Shapiro, Sidney A. 2014 "Dying at Work: Political Discourse and Occupational Health and Safety." *Wake Forest Law Review* 49(3): 831–47.

Sharman, Shalendra D. 2009 *China and India in the Age of Globalization*. Cambridge: Cambridge University Press.

Sharp, Isadore 2009 *Four Seasons: The Story of a Business Philosophy*. Toronto: Viking Canada.

Sharpe, Andrew, and Jill Hardt 2006 *Five Deaths a Day: Workplace Fatalities 1993–2005*. Ottawa: Centre for the Study of Living Standards.

Sheikh, Munir 2013 "Good Government and Statistics Canada: The Need for True Independence." *Academic Matters: The Journal of Higher Education* (May).

Shewell, Hugh 2004 *"Enough to Keep Them Alive": Indian Welfare in Canada, 1873–1965*. Toronto: University of Toronto Press.

Shields, Margot 2000 "Long Working Hours and Health." *Perspectives on Labour and Income* 12(Spring): 49–56.

Shildrick, Tracy, Robert MacDonald, Colin Webster, and Kayleigh Garthwaite 2013 *Poverty and Insecurity: Life in Low-Pay, No-Pay Britain*. Cambridge: Polity Press.

Shin, Taekjin 2017 "Workforce Downsizing and Shareholder Value Orientations Among Executive Managers at Large U.S. Firms." *Research in the Sociology of Work* 30: 185–217.

Shuey, Kim, Andrea Willson, and Katherine Bouchard 2017 "Disability and Social Inequality in Canada." In Edward Grabb, Jeffrey G. Reitz, and Monica Hwang, eds., *Social Inequality in Canada: Dimensions of Disadvantage*. 6th ed. Toronto: Oxford University Press.

Shorter, Edward, and Charles Tilly 1974 *Strikes in France, 1830–1968*. Cambridge, MA: Cambridge University Press.

Siciliano, Michael L. 2016 "Control From on High: Cloud-computing, Skill and Acute Frustration Among Analytics Workers in the Digital Publishing Industry." *Research in the Sociology of Work* 29: 125–53.

Sidani, Yusuf, and Dima Jamali 2010 "The Egyptian Worker: Work Beliefs and Attitudes." *Journal of Business Ethics* 92: 433–50.

Sidani, Yusuf, and Jon Thornberry 2009 "The Current Arab Work Ethic: Antecedents, Implications, and Potential Remedies." *Journal of Business Ethics* 91: 35–49.

Siltanen, Janet 1994 *Locating Gender: Occupational Segregation, Wages and Domestic Responsibilities*. London, England: UCL Press.

Siltanen, Janet, Alette Willis, and Willow Scobie 2009 "Flows, Eddies, Swamps and Whirlpools: Inequality and the Experience of Work Change." *Canadian Journal of Sociology* 34(4): 1003–32.

Simon, Jesse, Kevin Burton, Emily Lockhart, and Susan O'Donnell 2014 "Post-Secondary Distance Education in a Contemporary Colonial Context: Experiences of Students in a Rural First Nation in Canada." *The International Review of Research in Open and Distributed Learning* 15(1): 1–19.

Simon, Melanie, Kelly O'Ferrall, Allison Di Cesare 2018 "Back to 2017: New Ontario Government Revokes Pre-election Employment Law Changes." Osler, November 27. https://www.osler.com/en/resources/regulations/2018/back-to-2017-new-ontario-government-revokes-pre-election-employ-ment-law-changes [retrieved 5 June 2019].

Simms, Melanie, and Deborah Dean 2015 "Mobilizing Contingent Workers: An Analysis of Two Successful Cases." *Economic and Industrial Democracy* 36(1): 173–90.

Simms, Melanie, Dennis Eversberg, Camille Dupuy, and Lena Hipp 2018 "Organizing Young Workers Under Precarious Conditions:

What Hinders or Facilitates Union Success."
Work and Occupations 45(4): 420–50.

Singh, Dianna, and Paul Glavin 2017 "An
Occupational Portrait of Emotional Labor
Requirements and Their Health Consequences
for Workers." *Work and Occupations* 44(4):
424–66.

**Singh, Parbudyal, and Natasha Loncar
2010** "Pay Satisfaction, Job Satisfaction,
and Turnover Intent." *Relations Industrielles/
Industrial Relations* 65(3): 470–90.

Sinha, M. 2013 *Portrait of Caregivers, 2012.*
Ottawa: Minister of Industry.

Skof, Karl 2010 "Trends in the Trades:
Registered Apprenticeship Total Registrations,
Completions and Certification, 1991
to 2007." *Education Matters: Insights on
Education, Learning and Training in Canada*
6(6). Statistics Canada Cat. no. 81-004-X.

Slowey, Maria, and Hans Schuetze, eds. 2012
*Global Perspectives on Higher Education and
Lifelong Learners.* New York: Routledge.

Smith, Adam 1976 *The Wealth of Nations.*
Chicago: University of Chicago Press. (Orig.
pub. 1776.)

Smith, Michael R. 1999 "The Production
of Flexible Attitudes in the Canadian Pulp
and Paper Industry." *Relations Industrielles/
Industrial Relations* 54(3): 581–608.

———— **2001** "Technological Change, the
Demand for Skills, and the Adequacy of
Their Supply." *Canadian Public Policy* 27(1):
1–22.

Smith, Vicki 1994 "Braverman's Legacy: The
Labour Process Tradition at 20." *Work and
Occupations* 21: 403–21.

———— **1997** "New Forms of Work
Organization." *Annual Review of Sociology*
23: 315–39.

———— **2002** *Crossing The Great Divide: Worker
Risk and Opportunity in the New Economy.*
Cornell University Press.

———— **2006** "'It's the End of Work as We
Know It … But Maybe Not'." *Work and
Occupations* 33(3): 303–6.

Smith, Vicki, and Esther Neuwirth 2008 *The
Good Temp.* Ithaca, NY: ILR Press.

**Smucker, Joseph, Axel van den Berg, Michael
R. Smith, and Anthony C. Masi 1998**
"Labour Deployment in Plants in Canada
and Sweden: A Three-Industry Comparison."
Relations Industrielles/Industrial Relations
53(3): 430–56.

Sosteric, Mike 1996 "Subjectivity and
the Labour Process: A Case Study in the
Restaurant Industry." *Work, Employment and
Society* 10: 297–318.

Spalding, Derek 2010 "The New Face of
Business." *Nanaimo Daily News*, January 29,
A1.

Spencer, Dale, and Niki Carlan 2008 "The
Complexities of the Automotive Industry:
Positive and Negative Feedbacks in Production
Systems." *Canadian Journal of Sociology* 33(2):
265–90.

Spilerman, Seymour 2000 "Wealth and
Stratification Processes." *Annual Review of
Sociology* 26: 497–524.

**Spitzer, Denise, Anne Neufeld, Margaret
Harrison, Karen D. Hughes, and Miriam
Stewart 2003** "My Wings Have Been Cut,
Where Can I Fly? Gender, Migration and
Caregiving—Chinese and South Asian
Canadian Perspectives." *Gender & Society*
17(2): 267–86.

Staber, Udo 1993 "Worker Cooperatives
and the Business Cycle: Are Cooperatives
the Answer to Unemployment?" *The
American Journal of Economics and Sociology*
52: 129–43.

**Stabler, Jack C., and Eric C. Howe
1990** "Native Participation in Northern
Development: The Impending Crisis in the
NWT." *Canadian Public Policy* 16: 262–83.

Stall, Nathan 2019 "We Should Care More
about Caregivers." *Canadian Medical
Association Journal* 191(9): E245–E246.

Stanford, Jim 2005 "Revisiting the 'Flexibility
Hypothesis.'" *Canadian Public Policy* 31(1):
109–16.

———— **2017** "The Resurgence of Gig Work:
Historical and Theoretical Perspectives." *The
Economy and Labour Relations Review* 28(3):
382–401.

**Stansfeld, Stephen, and Bridget Candy
2006** "Psychosocial Work Environment and
Mental Health—A Meta-analytic Review."
*Scandinavian Journal of Work Environment &
Health* 32(6): 443–62.

Stasiulis, Daiva, and Abigail B. Bakan 2003
*Negotiating Citizenship: Migrant Women in
Canada and the Global System.* New York:
Palgrave MacMillan.

Statistics Canada 1998 "1996 Census: Labour
Force Activity, Occupation and Industry,
Place of Work, Mode of Transportation to

Work, Unpaid Work." *The Daily,* March 17. https://www150.statcan.gc.ca/n1/daily-quotidien/980317/dq980317-eng.htm.

Statistics Canada 2000 *Women in Canada 2000: A Gender-Based Statistical Report.* Ottawa: Statistics Canada. Cat. no. 89-503-XPE.

———— **2003** *Canada's Ethnocultural Portrait: The Changing Mosaic.* 2001 Census Analysis Series. http://www.statcan.gc.ca.

———— **2004** "The Near-Retirement Rate." *Perspectives on Labour and Income* 16(Spring): 68–72.

———— **2005** *Women in Canada: A Gender-Based Statistical Report.* Ottawa: Statistics Canada. Cat. no. 89-503-XIE. http://www.statcan.gc.ca/bsolc/olc-cel/olc-cel?catno=89-503-x&lang=eng.

———— **2006** *Income and Earnings, 2006 Census.* Ottawa: Statistics Canada. Cat. no. 97-563-XWE2006062. http://www.statcan.gc.ca/bsolc/olc-cel/olc-cel?catno=97-563-X2006062&lang=eng.

———— **2007a** *The Canadian Labour Market at a Glance.* Ottawa: Statistics Canada. Cat. no. 71-222-X.

———— **2007b** *Participation and Activity Limitation Survey 2006: Analytical Report.* Ottawa: Statistics Canada. Cat. no. 89-628-XIE-No. 002. http://www.statcan.gc.ca/pub/89-628-x/89-628-x2007002-eng.pdf.

———— **2008c** *Canada's Ethnocultural Mosaic, 2006 Census.* Ottawa: Statistics Canada. Cat. no. 97-562-X. http://www12.statcan.ca/census-recensement/2006/as-sa/97-562/pdf/97-562-XIE2006001.pdf.

———— **2008d** *Education, 2006 Census.* Ottawa: Statistics Canada. Cat. no. 97-560-XIE.

———— **2008e** *Workplace and Employee Survey Compendium 2005.* Cat. no. 71-585-X.

———— **2008f** *2006 Census: Aboriginal Peoples in Canada in 2006: Inuit, Métis, and First Nations, 2006 Census: Findings.* Ottawa: Statistics Canada. Cat. no. 97-558-XIE2006001. http://www12.statcan.ca/census-recensement/2006/as-sa/97-558/index-eng.cfm?CFID=348861&CFTOKEN=58769179.

———— **2009** *Lifelong Learning among Canadians Aged 18 to 64 Years: First Results from the 2008 Access and Support to Education and Training Survey.* Ottawa: Statistics Canada. Cat. no. 81-595-M2009079.

———— **2010** *Projections of the Diversity of the Canadian Population 2006 to 2031.* Ottawa: Statistics Canada. Cat. no. 91-551-X. http://www.statcan.gc.ca/pub/91-551-x/91-551-x2010001-eng.pdf.

———— **2011** *Guide to the Labour Force Survey.* Ottawa: Statistics Canada. Cat. no. 71-543-G.

———— **2013a** *Immigration and Ethnocultural Diversity in Canada.* Ottawa: Statistics Canada. Cat. no. 99-010-X2011001. http://www12.statcan.gc.ca/nhs-enm/2011/as-sa/99-010-x/99-010-x2011001-eng.pdf.

———— **2013b** *Aboriginal Peoples in Canada: First Nations People, Métis and Inuit.* Ottawa: Statistics Canada. Cat. no. 99-011-X2011001. http://www12.statcan.gc.ca/nhs-enm/2011/as-sa/99-011-x/99-011-x2011001-eng.pdf.

———— **2013c** *The Educational Attainment of Aboriginal Peoples in Canada: National Household Survey (NHS).* Ottawa: Statistics Canada. Cat. no. 99-012-X2011003. http://www12.statcan.gc.ca/nhs-enm/2011/as-sa/99-012-x/99-012-x2011003_3-eng.pdf.

———— **2013d** *Low Income Lines 2011–12.* Ottawa: Statistics Canada. Cat. no. 75F0002M-No. 002.

———— **2013e** *Commuting to Work: National Household Survey (NHS) 2011 Brief.* Ottawa: Statistics Canada. Cat. no. 99-012-X2011003.

———— **2013f** *2011 National Household Survey. Data Tables: Employment Income Statistics in 2010 by National Occupational Classification.* Cat. no. 99-014-X2011042. https://www12.statcan.gc.ca/nhs-enm/2011/dp-pd/dt-td/Index-eng.cfm.

———— **2014** *Graduating in Canada: Profile, Labour Market Outcomes and Student Debt of the Class of 2009–2010, Revised.* Ottawa: Culture, Tourism and the Centre for Education Statistics. https://www150.statcan.gc.ca/n1/pub/81-595-m/2014101/section04-eng.htm.

———— **2015** *Population Projections for Canada (2013 to 2063), Provinces and Territories (2013 to 2038).* Ottawa: Statistics Canada. Cat. no. 91-520-X.

———— **2016** *Data Tables, 2016 Census, National Occupational Classification by Class of Worker.* Cat. no: 98-400-X2016368.

———— **2017a** *Working Seniors in Canada.* Ottawa: Statistics Canada. Catalogue no. 98-200-X2016027. https://www12.statcan. gc.ca/census-recensement/2016/as-sa/98-200-x/2016027/98-200-x2016027-eng.pdf [retrieved 9 July 2019].

———— **2017b** "Immigrant and Ethnocultural Diversity: Key Results from the 2016 Census." *The Daily*, October 25.

———— **2017c** "Aboriginal Peoples in Canada: Key Results from the 2016 Census." *The Daily*, October 25.

———— **2017d** "Aboriginal People and the Labour Market." *The Daily*, March 16.

———— **2017e** "Education in Canada—Key Results from the 2016 Census." *The Daily*, November 29.

———— **2017f** *Canadian Post-secondary Enrolments and Graduates, 2015/16.* https://www150.statcan.gc.ca/n1/daily-quotidien/171207/dq171207c-eng.htm [retrieved May 20 2019].

———— **2017g** "Life in the Fast Lane: How are Canadians Managing." *The Daily*, November 14.

———— **2018a** *Guide to the Labour Force Survey.* Ottawa. Cat. no. 71-543-G.

———— **2018b** National Occupation Classification 2016. Ottawa: Statistics Canada. Cat. no. 12-583-X.

———— **2018c** "Canadian Survey on Disability, 2017." *The Daily*, November 28.

———— **2019a** "Pension Plans in Canada, as of January 1, 2018." *The Daily.* https://www150. statcan.gc.ca/n1/en/daily-quotidien/190619/dq190619f-eng.pdf?st=4joAgdJm [retrieved 9 July 2019].

———— **2019b** *Labour Market Experiences of First Nations People Living Off-Reserve: Key Findings from the 2017 Aboriginal Peoples Survey.* Ottawa: Statistics Canada. Cat. no. 89-653-X2018003.

———— **2019c** "Work Absence Statistics of Full-Time Employees by Sex and Public and Private Sector." CANSIM Table 279-0035. https://www150.statcan.gc.ca/t1/tbl1/en/tv.action?pid=1410019601 [retrieved 1 April 2019].

Stecy-Hildebrandt, Natasha, Sylvia Fuller, and Alisyn Burns 2019 "'Bad' Jobs in a 'Good' Sector: Examining the Employment Outcomes of Temporary Work in the Canadian Public Sector." *Work, Employment and Society* 33(4): 560–79.

Steptoe, Andrew, and Mika Kivikmäki 2013 "Stress and Cardiovascular Disease: An Update on Current Knowledge." *Annual Review of Public Health* 34: 337–54.

Stergiou-Kita, Mary, and 12 Others 2015 "Danger Zone: Men, Masculinity and Occupational Health and Safety in High Risk Occupations." *Safety Science* 80: 213–20.

Steinberg, Ronnie J. 1990 "Social Construction of Skill: Gender, Power, and Comparable Worth." *Work and Occupations* 17: 449–82.

Sterling, J. S., and N. Reichman 2016 Overlooked and Undervalued: Women in Private Law Practice. *Annual Review of Law and Social Science* 12: 373–93.

Stern, Robert N. 1976 "Intermetropolitan Pattern of Strike Frequency." *Industrial and Labor Relations Review* 29: 218–35.

Stiglitz, Joseph 2002 *Globalization and its Discontents.* New York: W.W. Norton.

———— **2017** *Globalization and Its Discontents Revisited: Anti-Globalization in the Age of Trump.* New York: W.W. Norton.

Stinson, Jane 2010 "Labour Casualization in the Public Sector." In Norene J. Pupo and Mark P. Thomas, eds., *Interrogating the New Economy: Restructuring Work in the 21st Century.* Toronto: University of Toronto Press.

Stirpe, Luigi, Jaime Bonache, and Antonio Revilla 2014 "Differentiating the Workforce: The Performance Effects of Using Contingent Labor in a Context of High-Performance Work Systems." *Journal of Business Research* 67: 1334–41.

Stone, Pamela 2007 *Opting Out? Why Women Really Quit Careers and Head Home.* Berkeley, CA: University of California Press.

Stonebridge, C. 2013 *Future Care for Canadians—Why It Matters.* Ottawa: Conference Board of Canada.

Storey, Robert 2009 "'They Have All Been Faithful Workers': Injured Workers, Truth, and Workers' Compensation in Ontario, 1970–2008." *Journal of Canadian Studies* 43(1): 154–85.

Storey, Robert, and Wayne Lewchuk 2000 "From Dust to DUST to Dust: Asbestos and the Struggle for Worker Health and Safety at Bendix Automotive." *Labour/Le Travail* 45(Spring): 103–40.

Strong-Boag, Veronica 1988 *The New Day Recalled: Lives of Girls and Women in English Canada, 1919–1939.* Markham, ON: Penguin Books.

Stubblefield, Al 2005 *The Baptist Health Care Journey to Excellence: Creating a Culture That WOWs!* Hoboken, NJ: John Wiley & Sons.

Sugiman, Pamela 1992 "'That Wall's Comin' Down': Gendered Strategies of Worker Resistance in the UAW Canadian Region (1963–1970)." *Canadian Journal of Sociology* 17: 24–27.

Sullivan, Maureen 1996 "Rozzie and Harriet? Gender and Family Patterns of Lesbian Coparents." *Gender & Society* 10(6): 747–67.

Sullivan, Teresa 2016 "Work, Overwork, and the Work of Randy Hodson." *A Gedenkschrift to Randy Hodson: Working with Dignity (Research in the Sociology of Work),* 28: 57–77.

Sunter, Deborah, and Geoff Bowlby 1998 "Labour Force Participation in the 1990s." *Perspectives on Labour and Income* (Autumn): 15–21.

Super, Donald E., and Branimir Šverko, eds. 1995 *Life Roles, Values, and Careers: International Findings of the Work Importance Study.* San Francisco: Jossey-Bass.

Sussman, Deborah 1998 "Moonlighting: A Growing Way of Life." *Perspectives on Labour and Income* (Summer): 24–31.

———— **2000** "Unemployment Kaleidoscope." *Perspectives on Labour and Income* 12(Autumn): 9–15.

Swanson, Jean 2001 *Poor-Bashing: The Politics of Exclusion.* Toronto: Between the Lines.

Swift, Jamie 1995 *Wheel of Fortune: Work and Life in the Age of Falling Expectations.* Toronto: Between the Lines.

Synder, Karrie Ann, and Adam Isaiah Green 2008 "Revisiting the Glass Escalator: The Case of Gender Segregation in a Female Dominated Occupation." *Social Problems* 55(2): 271–99.

Szelényi, Iván, and Eric Kostello 1996 "The Market Transition Debate: Toward a Synthesis?" *American Journal of Sociology* 10: 1082–96.

Tanner, Julian, Rhonda Cockerill, Jan Barnsley, and A. P. Williams 1999 "Flight Paths and Revolving Doors: A Case Study of Gender Desegregation in Pharmacy." *Work, Employment and Society* 13(2): 275–93.

Tapia, Maite, and Lowell Turner 2018 "Renewed Activism for the Labor Movement: The Urgency of Young Worker Engagement." *Work and Occupations* 45(4): 391–419.

Taras, Daphne G. 2002 "Alternative Forms of Employee Representation and Labour Policy." *Canadian Public Policy* 28(1): 105–16.

Taylor, Alison, Jason Foster, and Carolina Cambre 2012 "Training 'Expendable' Workers: Temporary Foreign Workers in Nursing." *Globalization, Societies and Education* 10(1): 95–117.

Taylor, Alison, and Harvey Krahn 2013 "Living Through our Children: Exploring the Education and Career 'Choices' of Racialized Immigrant Youth in Canada." *Journal of Youth Studies* 16(8): 1000–21.

Taylor, Frederick Winslow 1911 *The Principles of Scientific Management.* New York: Norton.

Taylor, Frederick Winslow 1913 "What Is Scientific Management?" *Industrial Canada.* April: 1224–26.

Taylor, Peter Shawn 2019 "The Retirement Age in Canada Is Too Low—And That's a Growing Problem." *Maclean's,* 1 February. https://www.macleans.ca/opinion/the-retire-ment-age-in-canada-is-too-low-and-thats-a-growing-problem/ [retrieved 9 July 2019].

Teasdale, Nina 2013 "Fragmented Sisters: The Implications of Flexible Employment Policies for Professional Women's Workplace Relationships." *Gender, Work & Organization* 20(4): 397–412.

Teeple, Gary 1972 "Land, Labour and Capital in Pre-Confederation Canada." In Gary Teeple, ed., *Capitalism and the National Question in Canada.* Toronto: University of Toronto Press.

Tehrani, Noreen 2004 "Bullying: A Source of Chronic Traumatic Stress?" *British Journal of Guidance & Counselling* 32(3): 357–66.

Terkel, Studs 1971 *Working.* New York: Pantheon.

Thébaud, Sarah 2015 "Business as Plan B: Institutional Foundations of Gender Inequality in Entrepreneurship Across 24 Industrialized Countries." *Administrative Science Quarterly* 60(4): 671–711.

Therrien, Pierre, and André Léonard 2003 *Empowering Employees: A Route to Innovation.* The Evolving Workplace Series. Ottawa:

Statistics Canada and Human Resources Development Canada. Cat. no. 71-584-MEI-No. 8.

Thiede, Brian C., Daniel T. Lichter, and Scott R. Sanders 2015 "America's Working Poor: Conceptualization, Measurement, and New Estimates." *Work and Occupations* 42(3): 267–312.

Thomas, Derrick 2009 "The Impact of Working in a Non-official Language on the Occupations and Earnings of Immigrants in Canada." *Canadian Social Trends* (Summer): 12–20.

Thomas, Derrick 2010 "Foreign Nationals Working Temporarily in Canada." *Canadian Social Trends* (June).

Thomas, Mark 2010 "Labour Migration and Temporary Work: Canada's Foreign-Worker Programs in the 'New Economy.'" In Norene J. Pupo and Mark P. Thomas, eds., *Interrogating the New Economy: Restructuring Work in the 21st Century*. Toronto: University of Toronto Press.

Thompson, Paul 2016 "Dissent at Work and the Resistance Debate: Departures, Directions, and Dead Ends." *Studies in Political Economy* 97(2): 106–23.

Tilly, Charles 1979 *From Mobilization to Revolution*. Reading, MA: Addison-Wesley.

Tippett, Elizabeth C. 2019 "The Legal Implications of the MeToo Movement." *Minnesota. Law Review* 103: 229–302.

Todeschini, Maya Morioka 2011 "'Webs of Engagement': Managerial Responsibility in a Japanese Company." *Journal of Business Ethics* 101: 45–59.

Toffler, Alvin 1980 *The Third Wave*. New York: Bantam.

Tomlinson, Michael 2007 "Graduate Employability and Student Attitudes and Orientations to the Labour Market." *Journal of Education and Work* 20(4): 285–304.

Toneguzzi, Mario 2015 "'A Worrisome Trend' for Canada's Workforce as Work Ethic, Quality of New Hires Deteriorate." *Financial Post*, September 3. https://business.financialpost.com/executive/c-suite/a-worrisome-trend-for-canadas-workforce-as-work-ethic-quality-of-new-hires-deteriorate [retrieved 14 December 2018].

Torres, Sara, Denise L. Spitzer, Karen D. Hughes, Jacqueline Oxman-Martinez, and Jill Hanley 2012 "From Temporary Worker to Resident: The Live-in Caregiver Program (LCP) and Its Impact through an Intersectional Lens." In Patti Lenard and Christine Straehle, eds., *Temporary Foreign Work in Canada*. Montreal: McGill–Queen's University Press.

Towers, I., L. E. Duxbury, C. Higgins, and J. Thomas 2006 "Time Thieves and Space Invaders: Technology, Work and Organization." *Journal of Organizational Change Management* 19(5): 593–618.

Townley, Barbara 1993 "Foucault, Power/Knowledge and Its Relevance for Human Resource Management." *Academy of Management Review* 18(3): 518–45.

———— **1994** *Reframing Human Resource Management: Power, Ethics and the Subject at Work*. London, England: Sage Publications.

Tran, Kelly 2004 "Visible Minorities in the Labour Force: 20 Years of Change." *Canadian Social Trends* (Summer): 7–11.

Treathaway, Natasha 2000 *Domestic Work: Poems*. Minneapolis, MN: Graywolf Publishing.

Tronto, Joan 1993 *Moral Boundaries: A Political Argument for an Ethic of Care*. New York and London: Routledge.

Trusson, Clive, Donald Hislop, and Neil F. Doherty 2018 "The Role of ICTs in the Servitisation and Degradation of IT Professional Work." *New Technology, Work and Employment* 33(2): 149–70.

Truth and Reconciliation Commission of Canada (TRCC) 2015 *What We Have Learned: Principles of Truth and Reconciliation*. Montreal: McGill-Queen's University Press.

Tucker, Eric 1992 "Worker Participation in Health and Safety Regulation: Lessons from Sweden." *Studies in Political Economy* 37: 95–127.

———— **2003** "Diverging Trends in Worker Health and Safety Protection and Participation in Canada, 1985–2000." *Relations Industrielles/Industrial Relations* 58(3): 395–424.

———— **2018** "Uber and the Unmaking and Remaking of Taxi Capitalisms: Technology, Law and Resistance in Historical Perspective." In Derek McKee, Finn Makela, and Teresa Scassa, eds., *Law and the Sharing Economy: Regulating Online Market Platforms*. Ottawa: University of Ottawa Press.

Tufts, Steven, and John Holmes 2010
"Student Workers and the 'New Economy' of Mid-Sized Cities: The Cases of Peterborough and Kingston, Ontario." In Norene J. Pupo and Mark P. Thomas, eds., *Interrogating the New Economy: Restructuring Work in the 21st Century*. Toronto: University of Toronto Press.

Turcotte, Martin 2010 "Working at Home: An Update." *Canadian Social Trends* (December): 3–11.

———— **2013** *Family Caregiving: What Are the Consequences?* Ottawa: Minister of Industry.

Turcotte, Roger 2014 "Persons with Disabilities and Employment." *Insights on Canadian Society*. Ottawa: Statistics Canada. Catalogue no. 75-006-X.

———— **2015** *Volunteering and Charitable Giving in Canada*. Ottawa: Statistics Canada. Catalogue no. 89-652-X2015001.

Twenge, Jean M. 2006 *Generation Me: Why Today's Young Americans are More Confident, Assertive, Entitled – and More Miserable than Ever Before*. New York: Free Press.

———— **2016** "Do Millennials Have a Lesser Work Ethic? The Actual Science from National Survey Data." *Psychology Today Canada*. https://www.psychologytoday.com/ca/blog/our-changing-culture/201602/do-millennials-have-lesser-work-ethic [retrieved 14 December 2018].

Twenge, Jean M., Gabrielle N. Martin, and Brian H. Spitzberg 2018 "Trends in US Adolescents' Media Use, 1976–2016: The Rise of Digital Media, The Decline of TV, and the (Near) Demise of Print". *Psychology of Popular Media Culture* 8(4): 329-45.

Underhill, Cathy 2006 "Training through the Ages." *Perspectives on Labour and Income* 18(4): 26–36.

"Union at Mine Dealing with Automated Trucks" 2019 *The Herald*, April 10. https://www.merrittherald.com/union-at-mine-dealing-with-automated-trucks/ [retrieved 29 April 2019].

"Unions on Decline in Private Sector" 2012 *CBC News*, September 2. https://www.cbc.ca/news/canada/unions-on-decline-in-private-sector-1.1150562 [retrieved 29 April 2019].

United Nations 2018 *World Trade Report 2018*. New York and Geneva: United Nations.

United Nations Economic Commission for Europe 2010 *Measuring Quality Employment: Country Pilot Reports*. Geneva: United Nations. http://www.unece.org/fileadmin/DAM/publications/oes/STATS_Measuring QualityEmploment.E.pdf.

Uppal, Sharanjit 2017 "Young Men and Women Without a High School Diploma." *Insights on Canadian Society*. Ottawa: Statistics Canada. Cat. no. 75-006-X.

Uppal, Sharanjit, and Sebastien LaRochelle-Côté 2014 "Overqualifications Amongst Recent University Graduates." *Insights on Canadian Society*. Catalogue no. 75-006-X.

Urry, John 2007 *Mobilities*. Cambridge: Polity Press.

Usalcas, Jeannine 2008 "Hours Polarization Revisited." *Perspectives on Labour and Income* (March): 5–15.

U.S. Bureau of Labor Statistics 2012 *Charting International Labor Comparisons*. http://www.bls.gov.

U.S. Bureau of Labor Statistics 2013 *International Comparisons of Annual Labor Force Statistics, 1970–2012*. Full Series by Indicator and Underlying Levels. http://www.bls.gov/fls/#laborforce.

Uttal, Lynet 2009 "(Re)Visioning Family Ties to Communities and Contexts." In Sally A. Lloyd, April L. Few, and Katherine R. Allen, eds., *Handbook of Feminist Family Studies*. Thousand Oaks, CA: Sage Publications.

Vahtera, Jussi, Mika Kivimäki, Jaana Pentti, Anne Linna, Marianna Virtanen, Pekka Virtanen, and Jane E. Ferrie 2004 "Organisational Downsizing, Sickness Absence, and Mortality: 10-Town Prospective Cohort Study." *British Medical Journal* 328(7439): 555.

Vaisey, Stephen 2006 "Education and Its Discontents: Overqualification in America, 1972–2002." *Social Forces* 85(2): 835–64.

Valdés, Gonzalo, and Stephen R. Barley 2016 "Be Careful What You Wish for: The Learning Imperative in Postindustrial Work." *Work and Occupations* 43(4): 466–501.

Vallas, Steven Peter 2003 "Why Teamwork Fails: Obstacles to Workplace Change in Four Manufacturing Plants." *American Sociological Review* 68: 223–50.

Van Bavel, Jan, Christine R. Schwartz, and Albert Esteve 2018 "The Reversal of the Gender Gap in Education and Its Consequences for Family Life." *Annual Review of Sociology* 44(1): 341–60.

Vance, J. P. 2016 *Hillbilly Elegy: A Memoir of a Family and Culture in Crisis.* New York: Harper.

van den Berg, Annette, Yolanda Grift, and Arjen van Witteloostuijn 2011 "Works Councils and Organizational Performance: The Role of Top Managers' and Works Councils' Attitudes in Bad vis-à-vis Good Times." *Journal of Labor Research* 32: 136–56.

van den Berg, Axel, and Joseph Smucker, eds. 1997 *The Sociology of Labour Markets: Efficiency, Equity, Security.* Scarborough, ON: Prentice-Hall.

vanden Heuvel, Katrina 2019 "The Fight for $15 Has Created A Road Map for Change." *Washington Post* July 23. https://www.washingtonpost.com/opinions/2019/07/23/fight-has-created-road-map-change/

Van Houten, Donald R. 1990 "The Political Economy and Technical Control of Work Humanization in Sweden during the 1970s and 1980s." *Work and Occupations* 14: 483–513.

Van Kirk, Sylvia 1980 *Many Tender Ties: Women in Fur-Trade Society, 1670–1870.* Winnipeg: Watson and Dwyer.

Varghese, Jeji, Naomi T. Krogman, Thomas M. Beckley, and Solange Nadeau 2006 "Critical Analysis of the Relationship between Local Ownership and Community Resiliency." *Rural Sociology* 71(3): 505–27.

Vaughan, Diane 1999 "The Dark Side of Organizations: Mistake, Misconduct, and Disaster." *Annual Review of Sociology* 25: 271–305.

Veltmeyer, Henry 1983 "The Development of Capitalism and the Capitalist World System." In J. Paul Grayson, ed., *Introduction to Sociology: An Alternative Approach.* Toronto: Gage.

Vidal, Matt 2007 "Lean Production, Worker Empowerment, and Job Satisfaction: A Qualitative Analysis and Critique." *Critical Sociology* 33: 247–78.

Vogel, David 2005 *The Market for Virtue: The Potential and Limits of Corporate Social Responsibility.* New York: The Brookings Institute.

Vosko, Leah F. 1998 "Regulating Precariousness? The Temporary Employment Relationship under the NAFTA and the EC Treaty." *Relations Industrielles/Industrial Relations* 53(1): 123–53.

——— 2000 *Temporary Work: The Gendered Rise of a Precarious Employment Relationship.* Toronto: University of Toronto Press.

——— 2002 "The Pasts (and Futures) of Feminist Political Economy in Canada: Reviving the Debate." *Studies in Political Economy* 68: 55–83.

——— 2010 *Managing the Margins: Gender, Citizenship, and the International Regulation of Precarious Employment.* Oxford, England: Oxford University Press.

——— ed. 2005 *Precarious Employment: Understanding Labour Market Insecurity in Canada.* Montreal: McGill–Queen's University Press.

Vosko, Leah, John Grundy, Eric Tucker, Mark P. Thomas, Andrea M. Noack, Rebecca Casey, Mary Gellatly, and Jennifer Mussell 2017 "The Compliance Model of Employment Standards Enforcement: An Evidence-Based Assessment of Its Efficacy in Instances of Wage Theft." *Industrial Relations Journal* 48(3): 256–73.

Vosko, Leah, Nancy Zukewich, and Cynthia Cranford 2003 "Precarious Jobs: Towards a New Typology." *Perspectives on Labour and Income* 15(Winter): 39–49.

Vrankulj, Sam 2012 *Finding Their Way: Second Round Report on the CAW Worker Adjustment Tracking Project.* http://www.caw.ca/assets/images/phase-Two-Tracking-study.pdf.

Waite, Sean, and Nicole Denier 2015 "Gay Pay for Straight Work: Mechanisms Generating Disadvantage." *Gender & Society* 29(4): 561–88.

——— 2019 "A Research Note on Canada's LGBT Data Landscape: Where We Are and What the Future Holds." *Canadian Review of Sociology* 56(1): 93–117.

Wajcman, Judy 2015 *Pressed for Time: The Acceleration of Life in Digital Capitalism.* University of Chicago Press, 2015.

Walby, Sylvia 1990 *Theorizing Patriarchy.* Oxford, England: Basil Blackwell.

Waldie, Paul 2005 "How Health Costs Hurt the Big Three." *Globe and Mail,* March 22, B1.

Wall, Sarah 2015 "Dimensions of Precariousness in an Emerging Sector of Self-Employment: A Study of Self-Employed Nurses. *Gender, Work & Organization*, 22(3): 221–36.

Wallace, Jean 2014 "Gender and Supportive Co-Worker Relations in the Medical Profession." *Gender, Work & Organization* 21(1): 1–17.

Wallace, Jean, and Fiona Kay 2012 "Tokenism, Organizational Segregation, and Coworker Relations in Law Firms." *Social Problems* 59(3): 389–410.

Walmsley, Ann 1992 "Trading Places." *Report on Business Magazine*, March 17–27.

Walsworth, Scott, and Richard J. Long 2012 "Is the Union Employment Suppression Effect Diminishing? Further Evidence from Canada." *Relations Industrielles/Industrial Relations* 67(4): 654–80.

Walters, David 2006 "One Step Forward, Two Steps Back: Worker Representation and Health and Safety in the United Kingdom." *International Journal of Health Services* 36(1): 87–111.

Wanner, Richard A. 1999 "Expansion and Ascription: Trends in Educational Opportunity in Canada, 1920–1994." *Canadian Review of Sociology and Anthropology* 36(3): 409–42.

——— **2009** "Social Mobility in Canada: Concepts, Patterns, and Trends." In Edward Grabb and Neil Guppy, eds., *Social Inequality in Canada: Patterns, Problems, and Policies*. 5th ed. Toronto: Pearson/Prentice Hall.

Warhurst, Chris, Françoise Carré, Patricia Findlay, and Chris Tilly, eds. 2012 *Are Bad Jobs Inevitable? Trends, Determinants and Responses to Job Quality in the Twenty-First Century*. Basingstoke, England: Palgrave Macmillan.

Warhurst, Chris, Key Mayhew, David Finegold, and John Buchanan, eds. 2019 *The Oxford Handbook on Skills and Training*. Oxford: Oxford University Press.

Warhurst, Chris, and Dennis Nickson 2007 "Employee Experience of Aesthetic Labour in Retail and Hospitality." *Work, Employment and Society* 21(1): 103–120.

Warner, J. 2013 "The Opt-Out Generation Wants Back In." *New York Times Magazine*. https://www.nytimes.com/2013/08/11/magazine/the-opt-out-generation-wants-back-in.html.

Warr, Peter, and Ilke Inceoglu 2018 "Work Orientations, Well-Being and Job Content of Self-employed and Employed Professionals." *Work, Employment and Society* 32(2): 291–311.

Warren, Tracey 2007 "Conceptualizing Breadwinning Work." *Work, Employment and Society* 21(2): 317–36.

——— **2011** "Researching the Gender Division of Unpaid Domestic Work: Practices, Relationships, Negotiation, and Meaning." *The Sociological Review* 59(1): 129–48.

Watkins, Mel 1991 "A Staples Theory of Economic Growth." In Gordon Laxer, ed., *Perspectives on Canadian Economic Development*. Toronto: Oxford University Press.

Weaver, Robert D., Nazim Habibov, and Lida Fan 2010 "Devolution and the Poverty Reduction Effectiveness of Canada's Provincial Social Welfare Programs: Results from a Time-Series Investigation of a Canadian National Survey." *Journal of Policy Practice* 9(2): 80–95.

Weber, Max 1946 "Bureaucracy." In H. H. Gerth and C. Wright Mills, eds., *From Max Weber*. New York: Oxford University Press.

——— **1958** *The Protestant Ethic and the Spirit of Capitalism*. New York: Scribner.

Weiss, Donald D. 1976 "Marx versus Smith on the Division of Labour." *Monthly Review* 28: 104–18.

Weller, Sally A. 2012 "Financial Stress and the Long-Term Outcomes of Job Loss." *Work, Employment and Society* 26(1): 10–25.

Welter, Friederike, Ted Baker, David B. Audretsch, and William B. Gartner 2017 "Everyday Entrepreneurship—A Call for Entrepreneurship Research to Embrace Entrepreneurial Diversity." *Entrepreneurship Theory and Practice* 41(3): 311–21.

Wente, Margaret 2019 "What's So Scary About Hauwei?" *Globe and Mail*, January 11.

West, Darrell 2015 "*What Happens if the Robots Take All the Jobs?*" Brookings Centre for Technological Innovation. https://www.brookings.edu/blog/techtank/2018/04/18/will-robots-and-ai-take-your-job-the-economic-and-political-consequences-of-automation/.

————— 2018 *The Future of Work: Robotics, AI, and Automation*. Washington, DC: Brookings Institution Press.

Weyzig, Francis 2009 "Political and Economic Arguments for Corporate Social Responsibility: Analysis and a Proposition Regarding the CSR Agenda." *Journal of Business Ethics* 86(4): 417–28.

Wharton, Amy 1993 "The Affective Consequences of Service Work: Managing Emotions on the Job." *Work and Occupations* 20(2): 205–32.

————— 2009 "The Sociology of Emotional Labor." *Annual Review of Sociology* 35: 147–65.

Wheatley, Daniel 2017 "Employee Satisfaction and Use of Flexible Working Arrangements." *Work, Employment and Society* 31(4): 567–85.

Wheeler, Hoyt N. 2008 "A New Frontier for Labor: Collective Action by Worker Owners." *Labor Studies Journal* 33(2): 163–78.

White, Jerry P. 1990 *Hospital Strike: Women, Unions, and Public Sector Conflict.* Toronto: Thompson Educational Publishing.

White, Julie 1990 *Mail and Female: Women and the Canadian Union of Postal Workers.* Toronto: Thompson Educational Publishing.

White, Lynn, Jr. 1962 *Medieval Technology and Social Change.* Oxford, England: Oxford University Press.

White, Michael, Stephen Hill, Patrick McGovern, Colin Mills, and Deborah Smeaton 2003 "'High-Performance' Management Practices, Working Hours and Work–Life Balance." *British Journal of Industrial Relations* 41(2): 175–95.

Whitehead, T. N. 1936 *Leadership in a Free Society.* Cambridge, MA: Harvard University Press.

Whittaker, D. H. 1990 "The End of Japanese-Style Employment?" *Work, Employment and Society* 4: 21–47.

Whittal, Michael, Herman Knudson, and Herman Huijgen, eds. 2007 *Towards a European Labour Identity: The Case of the European Work Council.* New York: Routledge.

Whyman, Philip 2004 "An Analysis of Wage-Earner Funds in Sweden: Distinguishing Myth from Reality." *Economic and Industrial Democracy* 25(3): 411–45.

Whyte, Martin King 2009 "Paradoxes of China's Economic Boom." *Annual Review of Sociology* 35: 371–92.

Wilensky, Jeanne L., and Harold L. Wilensky 1951 "Personnel Counseling: The Hawthorne Case." *American Journal of Sociology* 57: 265–80.

Wilkinson, K., J. Tomlinson, and J. Gardiner 2017 "Exploring the Work–Life Challenges and Dilemmas Faced by Managers and Professionals Who Live Alone. *Work, Employment and Society* 31(4): 640–56.

Wilkinson, Richard, and Kate Pickett 2009 *The Spirit Level: Why Greater Equality Makes Societies Stronger.* London: Penguin Books.

Wilke, Richard, and Bruce Stokes 2018 *In Advanced and Emerging Economies Alike, Worries about Job Automation.* PEW Research Centre.

Williams, Cara 2008 "Work–Life Balance of Shift Workers." *Perspectives on Labour and Income* 9(August): 5–16.

————— 2010 "Economic Well-Being." In *Women in Canada: A Gender-Based Statistical Report.* Ottawa: Statistics Canada. Cat. no. 89-503-X.

Williams, Carol, ed. 2012 *Indigenous Women and Work: From Labor to Activism.* Urbana: University of Illinois Press.

Williams, Christine L. 1989 *Gender Differences at Work: Women and Men in Nontraditional Occupations.* Berkeley, CA: University of California Press.

————— 1992 "The Glass Escalator: Hidden Advantages for Men in the 'Female Professions.'" *Social Problems* 39(3): 253–67.

————— 1995 *Still a Man's World: Men Who Do "Women's Work."* Berkeley, CA: University of California Press.

————— 2011 "The Glass Escalator Revisited: Gender Inequality in Neoliberal Times." *Gender & Society* 27(5): 609–29.

————— 2018 "Sexual Harassment in Organizations: A Critique of Current Research and Policy." In *Sexual Harassment and Sexual Consent.* London: Routledge.

Williams, Christine, and Patti Guiffre 2011 "From Organizational Sexuality to Queer Organizations: Research on Homosexuality and the Workplace." *Sociological Compass* 5(7): 551–63.

Williams, Joan C. 2010 *Reshaping the Work–Family Debate.* Cambridge, MA: Harvard University Press.

Williams, Joan C., Jennifer L. Berdahl, and Joseph A. Vandello 2016 "Beyond Work-Life 'Integration.'" *Annual Review of Psychology* 67: 515–39.

Williams, Joan C., Mary Blair-Loy, and Jennifer L. Berdahl 2013 "Cultural Schemas, Social Class, and the Flexibility Stigma." *Journal of Social Issues* 69(2): 209–34.

Williams, Joan C., and Amy Cuddy 2012 "Will Working Mothers Take Your Company to Court?" *Harvard Business Review* 90(9): 94–100.

Williams, Joan C., and Rachel Dempsey 2014 *What Works for Women at Work*. New York: New York University Press.

Wilmers, Nathan 2017 "Labor Unions as Activist Organizations: A Union Power Approach to Estimating Union Wage Effects." *Social Forces* 95(4): 1451–77.

Wilson, John 2000 "Volunteering." *Annual Review of Sociology* 26(1): 215–40.

Wingrove, Josh, and Dawn Walton 2013 "Alberta Jail Guard Wildcat Strike Leaves Main Courthouses in Gridlock." *Globe and Mail*, April 29.

WinSETT 2016 *Increasing Women in Science, Engineering, Trades and Technology: The Business Case*. https://www.winsett.ca/publications/BusinessCaseResearchPaper2017.pdf [retrieved June 12, 2019].

Winson, Anthony, and Belinda Leach 2002 *Contingent Work, Disrupted Lives: Labour and Community in the New Rural Economy*. Toronto: University of Toronto Press.

Winters, L. Alan, and Shahid Yusuf, eds. 2007 *Dancing with Giants: China, India and the Global Economy*. Washington, DC: World Bank.

Witz, Ann 1992 *Professions and Patriarchy*. London, England: Routledge.

Wolfe, R. 2018 "Is the USMCA Just a Lesser NAFTA?" *Policy Options*. https://policyoptions.irpp.org/magazines/november-2018/usmca-just-lesser-nafta/ [retrieved May 4, 2019].

Womack, James P., Daniel T. Jones, and Daniel Roos 1990 *The Machine That Changed the World*. New York: Harper Perennial.

Wood, Linda Solomon 2013 "Hard Work, High Pay in the Tar Sands 'Hell.'" *Vancouver Observer*, July 9.

Wood, Stephen 1989a "The Japanese Management Model." *Work and Occupations* 16: 446–60.

———, ed. 1989b *The Transformation of Work? Skill, Flexibility and the Labour Process*. London: Unwin Hyman.

Wood, Stephen, David Holman, and Christopher Stride 2006 "Human Resource Management and Performance in U.K. Call Centres." *British Journal of Industrial Relations* 44(1): 99–124.

Wood, Stephen, Karen Niven, and Johan Braeken 2016 "Managerial Abuse and the Process of Absence among Mental Health Staff." *Work, Employment and Society* 30(5): 783–801.

Woodcock, Jamie 2017 *Working the Phones: Control and Resistance in Call Centres*. London: Pluto Press.

World Bank 1991 *World Development Report 1991: The Challenge of Development*. Oxford: World Bank and Oxford University Press. http://wdronline.worldbank.org/worldbank/a/c.html/world_development_report_1991/chapter_1_world_economy_transition.

World Bank 1993 *The East Asian Miracle: Economic Growth and Public Policy*. New York: Oxford University Press.

——— 2001 *Rethinking the East Asian Miracle*. New York: Oxford University Press and the World Bank.

——— 2005 *East Asia Update*, April 2005. http://siteresources.worldbank.org/INTEAPHALFYEARLYUPDATE/Resources/eapupdate.pdf.

——— 2018 Open Data Indicators. https://data.worldbank.org/ [retrieved 19 July 2019].

World Commission on Environment and Development 1987 *Our Common Future*. Oxford, England: Oxford University Press.

World Economic Forum 2017 *The Inclusive Growth and Development Report*. Geneva: World Economic Forum.

World Trade Organization (WTO) 2013 *International Trade Statistics, 2012*. http://www.wto.org/english/res_e/statis_e/its2012_e/its2012_e.pdf.

World Trade Organization (WTO) 2018 *Highlights of World Trade 2017*. https://www.wto.org/english/res_e/statis_e/wts2018_e/wts2018chapter02_e.pdf [retrieved April 20 2019].

Worth, Nancy 2016 "Feeling Precarious: Millennial Women and Work." *Environment and Planning D: Society and Space* 34(4): 601–16.

Worth, Sean 2005 "Beating the 'Churning' Trap in the Youth Labour Market." *Work, Employment and Society* 19(2): 403–14.

Wray-Lake, Laura, A. K. Syvertson, L. Briddell, D. W. Osgoode, and C. A. Flanagan 2011 "Exploring the Changing Meaning of Work for American High School Seniors from 1976 to 2005." *Youth & Society* 43: 1110–35.

Wrege, Charles D., and Richard M. Hodgetts 2000 "Frederick W. Taylor's 1899 Pig Iron Observations: Examining Fact, Fiction, and Lessons for the New Millennium." *Academy of Management Journal* 43(6): 1283–91.

Wright, Erik Olin 2009 "Understanding Class: Toward an Integrated Analytic Approach." *New Left Review* 60: 101–16.

Wright, Erik Olin, C. Costello, D. Hachen, and J. Sprague 1982 "The American Class Structure." *American Sociological Review* 47: 709–26.

Wu, Qingjun, Zhaoyang Sun 2014 "Collective Consultation Under Quota Management: China's Government-led Model of Labour Relations Regulation." *International Labour Review* 153(4): 609–33.

Wu, Xiaogang, and Yu Xie 2002 "Does the Market Pay Off? Earnings Returns to Education in Urban China." *American Sociological Review* 68: 425–42.

Wylie, William N. T. 1983 "Poverty, Distress, and Disease: Labour and the Construction of the Rideau Canal, 1826–1832." *Labour/Le Travail* 11: 7–30.

Yassad, Lahouaria, and Vincent Ferrao 2019 "Self-Employed Canadians: Who and Why?" *Labour Statistics at a Glance.* Ottawa: Statistics Canada. Catalogue no. 71-222-X.

Yates, Charlotte 2000 "Staying the Decline in Union Membership: Union Organizing in Ontario, 1985–1999." *Relations Industrielles/Industrial Relations* 55(4): 640–71.

———— **2006** "Challenging Misconceptions about Organizing Women into Unions." *Gender, Work & Organization* 13(6): 565–84.

Yates, Charlotte, Wayne Lewchuk, and Paul Stewart 2001 "Empowerment as a Trojan Horse: New Systems of Work Organization in the North American Automobile Industry." *Economic and Industrial Democracy* 22(4): 517–41.

Yeates, Nicola 2009 *Globalizing Care Economies and Migrant Workers: Explorations in Global Care Chains.* Basingstoke, England: Palgrave Macmillan.

Yoder, Janice D. 1991 "Rethinking Tokenism: Looking Beyond Numbers." *Gender & Society* 5(2): 178–92.

Young, Emily 2014 "Davos 2014: Google's Schmidt Warning on Jobs." *BBC News*, January 23. http://www.bbc.co.uk/news/business-25872006 (retrieved 25 March 2019).

Young, Marisa C. 2010 "Gender Differences in Precarious Work Settings." *Relations Industrielles/Industrial Relations* 65(1): 74–97.

Youngdahl, Jay 2008 "Mapping the Future: Cross-Border Unionizing Strategies." *New Labor Forum* 17(2): 71–81.

Yuen, Jennifer 2010 "Job-Education Match and Mismatch: Wage Differentials." *Perspectives on Labour and Income* 11(4): 16–26.

Yuill, Chris 2011 "Forgetting and Remembering Alienation Theory." *History of the Human Sciences* 24(2): 103–19.

Zatzick, Christopher D., and Roderick D. Iverson 2011 "Putting Employee Involvement in Context: A Cross-level Model Examining Job Satisfaction and Absenteeism in High-involvement Work Systems." *The International Journal of Human Resource Management* 22(17): 3462–76.

Zbaracki, Mark J. 1998 "The Rhetoric and Reality of Total Quality Management." *Administrative Science Quarterly* 43(3): 602–36.

Zeitlin, Irving M. 1968 *Ideology and the Development of Sociological Theory.* Englewood Cliffs, NJ: Prentice-Hall.

Zeitlin, M. 1974 "Corporate Ownership and Control." *American Journal of Sociology* 79: 1073–119.

Zeytinoglu, Isik U., and Gordon B. Cooke 2005 "Non-standard Work and Benefits: Has Anything Changed since the Wallace Report?" *Relations Industrielles/Industrial Relations* 60(1): 29–63.

Zeytinoglu, Isik U., Gordon B. Cooke, Karlene Harry, and James Chowhan 2008 "Low-Paid Workers and On-the-Job Training in Canada." *Relations Industrielles/Industrial Relations* 63(1): 5–29.

Zeytinoglu, Isik U., Margaret Denton, Sharon Davies, Andrea Baumann, Jennifer Blythe, and Linda Boos 2007 "Associations between Work Intensification, Stress and Job Satisfaction: The Case of Nurses in Ontario." *Relations Industrielles/Industrial Relations* 62(2): 201–25.

Zeytinoglu, Isik U., and Jacinta K. Muteshi 2000 "Gender, Race and Class Dimensions of Nonstandard Work." *Relations Industrielles/Industrial Relations* 55(1): 133–65.

Zhang, W., I. Alon, and C. Lattemann, eds. 2018 *China's Belt and Road Initiative: Changing the Rules of Globalization.* New York: Springer.

Zhang, Wei, Christopher McLeod, and Mieke Koehoorn 2016 "The Relationship Between Chronic Conditions and Absenteeism and Associated Costs in Canada." *Scandinavian Journal of Work, Environment & Health* 42(5): 413–22.

Zimmerman, Mary K., Jacquelyn S. Litt, and Christine E. Bose 2006 *Global Dimensions of Gender and Carework.* Stanford, CA: Stanford University Press.

Zou, Min 2015 "Gender, Work Orientations and Job Satisfaction." *Work, Employment and Society* 29(1): 3–22.

Zuberi, Dan 2013 *Cleaning Up: How Hospital Outsourcing Is Hurting Workers and Endangering Patients.* Ithaca, NY: Cornell University Press.

Zuboff, Shoshana 1988 *In the Age of the Smart Machine: The Future of Work and Power.* New York: Basic Books.

collective voice face, unions, 333

Collins, Randall, 147

colonialization, 7

Communications, Energy and Paperworkers Union of Canada (CEP), 297, 340, 343

community work, 228, 238–239

company union, 354

comparable worth, 217

comparative industrial relations, 347

Compassionate Care benefits, 237

compensation, 98

compensatory leisure hypothesis, 438

Competing Devotions, 234

competition, 12–13

compliance, employee, 266

computer numerical control (CNC) machines, 316

concession bargaining, 349, 362–363

conciliation, 338

Condition of the Working Class in England, The, 14

Confederation of National Trade Unions (CNTU), 337

conflict
    class, worker exploitation and, 13–15
    human capital theory, 136
    in human relations theory, 268
    institutionalized, 338, 356
    organized v. unorganized, 356
    related to globalization, 29
    in union–management relations, 330–331
    work–family, 239–247
    working class and, 11

conflict perspective, 15, 299, 303–305

Confucian work ethic, 400

consensus approach, 16, 136, 299

contingent work, 33. *See also* nonstandard work arrangements

continuous bargaining, 297

contracts, employment, 17

contract work, 109–111

co-operatives, producer, 385–387

core housework, 231

core sector, 143, 144

corporate health promotion, 376

corporate social responsibility (CSR), 288, 289

corporate welfare, 266

corporations, multinational, 30

cost accounting techniques, 261

Coupland, Douglas, 411

CPRN (Canadian Policy Research Networks), 428

C/QPP (Canada/Quebec Pension Plan), 63

craft unionism, 335, 336

craftwork, 10–11

creative economies, 25–26

creative professionals, 26

Creese, Gillian, 351

Cuddy, Amy, 246

Culbert, Samuel, 260

cultural capital concept, 51, 141–142, 163

cultural stereotypes, 214

CUPE (Canadian Union of Public Employees), 332, 342, 351

CUPW (Canadian Union of Postal Workers), 355–356

customer service agents, 312

D

Dalton, Melville, 259

Daniels, Arlene Kaplan, 227

deaths, work-related, 368–369

decentralization of authority, 274

decision-making autonomy, 313

Deepwater Horizon oil spill, 259

deferential workers, 406

deindustrialization, 9, 27

"demand–control" model, 436–437

demographers, 60

demographic shifts, 60

designated groups, 216

deskilling, 307–309, 313–314

despotic organization of work, 310

di Leonardo, Micaela, 238

direct control, 309

disabled people, 72

Discipline and Punish, 49

discouraged workers, 116